Story

Lustige und spannende Texte über die fünf Lehrwerkskinder aus Greenwich und Decorah erwarten dich auf den **Story**-Seiten.

Check-out

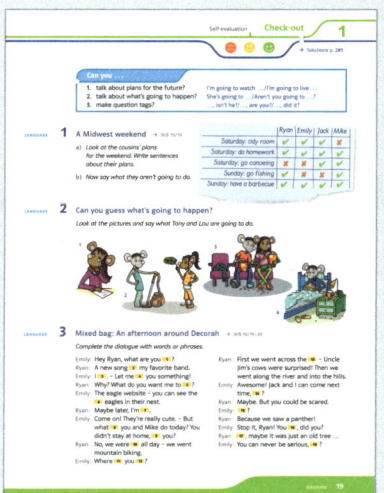

Mit diesen Übungen am Ende der *Unit* kannst du deinen Lernfortschritt selbst überprüfen. Die Lösungen stehen dir im Anhang zur Verfügung.

Across cultures, Revision und Focus

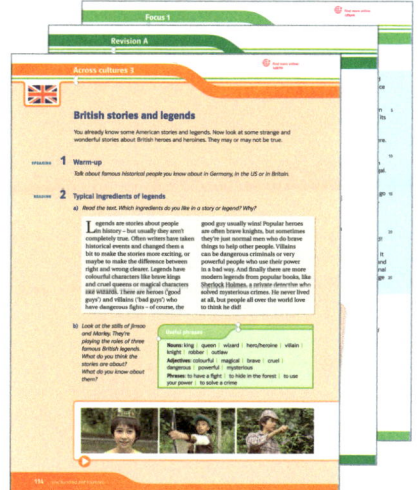

Zwischen den *Units* findest du **Across cultures** zum Kennenlernen der britischen/amerikanischen Alltagskultur, **Revision** für die Wiederholung des Lernstoffs und **Focus** mit spannenden Sachthemen.

Hi. I'm Tony.

🌐 Find more online:
rj68s7

Auf einigen Seiten im Buch findest du Green-Line-Codes. Diese führen dich zu weiteren Übungsmaterialien. Gib den Code einfach in das Suchfeld auf www.klett.de ein.

Symbole

→ △ 130/1	zusätzliche / leichtere Aufgabe im Practice pool
→ ▲ 130/2	anspruchsvollere Aufgabe im Practice pool
→ WB 7/4	Übung im Workbook
→ G2	Grammatik im Anhang
→ S3	Arbeitsmethode *(Skill)* im Anhang
🧑‍🤝‍🧑	Partnerarbeit
🧑‍🤝‍🧑🧑	Gruppenarbeit
📄	Produkt für dein Portfolio
S1/23 ◉	Schüler-CDs (Audio)
L1/35 ◉	Lehrer-CDs (Audio)
🎬	Lehrer-DVD (Film)

→ Practice pool

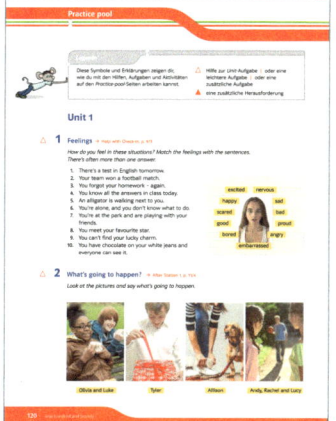

Die roten Dreiecke zeigen dir, dass du hinten im **Practice pool** weitere Übungsmöglichkeiten findest.

Grammar

Im Anhang **Grammar** findest du viele Beispiele, Regeln, Tipps und Übungen zum grammatischen Lernstoff aus den *Stations*.

Und im Anhang findest du auch das Vokabular, eine alphabetische Wortliste (E→D/D→E) und vieles mehr …

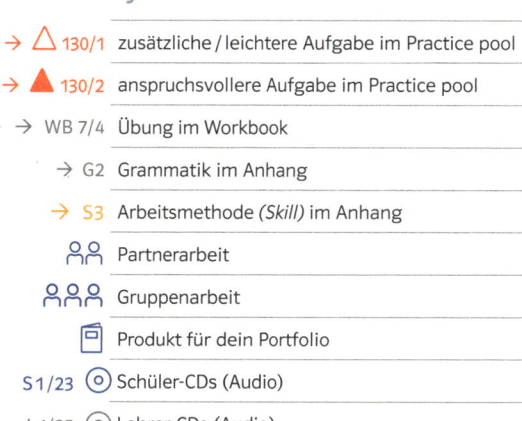

Green Line 2
Lehrerfassung
für Klasse 6 an Gymnasien in Bayern

Autorinnen und Autoren: Louise Carleton-Gertsch, München; Jennifer Baer-Engel, Göppingen; Marion Horner, Ipswich; Carolyn Jones, Beckenham; Jon Marks, Ventnor; Alison Wooder, Ventnor; sowie Paul Dennis, Lahnstein; Barbara Greive, Dortmund; Cornelia Kaminski, Fulda; unter Mitwirkung von Michael Mattison, Anette Mohamud, Manuela Moll und Melissa Braun-Keller, Stuttgart

Beratung: Dr. Thomas Becker, Nürnberg; Christel Beck-Zangenberg, Erlangen; Elmar Beyersdörfer, Gräfelfing; Wolfgang Funk, Bamberg; Michael Kleis, Geltendorf; Berit Möckel, Nürnberg; Uli Nürnberger, München; Wolfram Scharrer, Laaber; Prof. Harald Weisshaar, Bisingen

Für besondere Unterstützung danken wir herzlich Ms Susan Bolton von der **Thomas Tallis School**, London.

Zusatzmaterial für Schülerinnen und Schüler zu diesem Band:

Workbook + Audio-CDs + Übungssoftware
978-3-12-803026-5

Workbook + Audio-CDs
978-3-12-803025-8

Trainingsbuch Schulaufgaben mit Lösungsheft und CD-ROM
978-3-12-803021-0

Vokabellernheft
978-3-12-803077-7

sowie eine Reihe von abgestimmten
English Readers

Zusätzliche Informationen in der Lehrerfassung

Produktiver Lernwortschatz

Rezeptiver Wortschatz

Neue Grammatik

△→ ▲→ **Help with/Instead of/After . . .:** Verweis auf unterstützende/alternative/weiterführende Aufgaben im *Practice pool* des Schülerbuchs für leistungsschwächere bzw. -stärkere Schüler/innen.

HA: Vorschlag zur Hausaufgabe.

Folie 1: Hier können Sie Folie 1 des Folienordners einsetzen.

KV 1: Hier können Sie Kopiervorlage 1 des Lehrerbuchs einsetzen.

Voc.: Hier sind Verweise auf Wortschatzhilfen im Schülerbuch und Workbook (WB) angegeben.

Lösung: Hier finden Sie Lösungen bzw. Erwartungshorizonte (EH) zu den geschlossenen und halboffenen Aufgaben.

1. Auflage

1 | 5 4 3 2 1 | 2022 21 20 19 18

Alle Drucke dieser Auflage sind unverändert und können im Unterricht nebeneinander verwendet werden. Die letzte Zahl bezeichnet das Jahr des Druckes.

Redaktion: Monique Kunhar, Rebecca Keller; Gaby Bauer-Negenborn, Weßling; Lektorat editoria: Cornelia Schaller, Fellbach; Anja Treinies, Düsseldorf
Herstellung: Marietta Heymann

Gestaltung: Petra Michel, Essen
Umschlaggestaltung: know idea, Freiburg; Koma Amok, Stuttgart
Illustrationen: Peer Kramer, Düsseldorf; jani lunablau, Barcelona *(Muskottchen und Extra line)* sowie Christian Dekelver, Weinstadt *(Karten)*
Satz: Satzkiste GmbH, Stuttgart
Reproduktion: Schwaben-Repro, Stuttgart
Druck: DBM Druckhaus Berlin-Mitte GmbH, Berlin

Printed in Germany
ISBN 978-3-12-803022-7

Green Line 2

Lehrerfassung

von
Louise Carleton-Gertsch
Jennifer Baer-Engel
Marion Horner
Carolyn Jones
Jon Marks
Alison Wooder
Paul Dennis
Barbara Greive
Cornelia Kaminski

Ernst Klett Verlag
Stuttgart · Leipzig

Legende

VOC Vocabulary	Kompetenzaufgabe	Across cultures	**‹ ›** Fakultativ

Legende

VOC Vocabulary   Kompetenzaufgabe   Across cultures   ❮❯ Fakultativ

Inhalt

Lektionsteil/Thema	Kompetenzen/Medien/Inhalte	Sprachliche Mittel

Legende

VOC Vocabulary   Kompetenzaufgabe   Across cultures   ‹ › Fakultativ

Find more online:
zc49tn

(handwritten notes at top of page)
likes | dislikes
- riding | - bananas
- playing darts | - playing indoors
Sailing | - going to the city
- hanging out with friends in Decorah

Unit 1

L 1/1 ◉
My friends and I

A

Holly

Luke

Olivia

Dave

Jay

Jay, don't you know that embarrassing outfits always end up in the yearbook? LOL! ☺

B

Jay

Luke says Jay is a real show-off, but we can't write that in the yearbook!

C

Jay

Luke

A fun day in the country, ha ha!

SPEAKING **1** **Talk about the yearbook photos** → Folie 1

What can you see? Where are the girls and boys? What do you think they're doing or saying?

LISTENING **2** **Living in Decorah, Iowa**

→ Wants to write about Decorah in the yearbook

L 1/2 ◉
a) *What does Holly want to know and why?*

→ S21–23
b) *What do you learn about Emily, her home town Decorah and the city of Minneapolis? Make notes in a grid with these headings:*

likes | dislikes | Minneapolis | Decorah

Useful phrases

My favourite activity is riding … | I love the huge fields/the green hills … | to stay outdoors/indoors | to hang out with friends/at the mall | to watch eagles

(handwritten notes)
Minneapolis *Decorah*
- city near Decorah
- big mall with many shops and cafés
- new art museum
- too loud and hot
- isn't very big
- lots of tourists visit
- watch Decorah Eagles

In Unit 1 you learn
- words about feelings
- the language of plans (going-to future)
- how to say what's going to happen
- how to make good conversation (question tags, questions with prepositions, feedback)

These things can help you to discuss plans and keep up a conversation.

D

An awesome trip to the Milwaukee Art Museum – and we learned a lot too.

What a cool day – our team won!

F

Emily

(handwritten note) by a river

E

Emily

My friends love to do crazy things!

SPEAKING **3** **Feelings** → WB 3/1–2   happy   embarrassed   excited   nervous   proud   bored

→ △ 120/1
△ → Help with . . .

Voc.: Describing people and animals, WB (Word bank), pp. 2–3

→ S1–4

a) *Take turns to act out different feelings. Can the others guess your word?*

b) *Look at the photos. How do you think the characters feel? Say why.*

Example: Photo B: I think Jay feels happy because he's having fun in London.

c) *Make a mind map for 'feelings'. Add new words when you read through this unit.*

Across cultures

Yearbooks are an American tradition, but now they are popular in British schools too. Students on a yearbook team work together to make a fun book for their class, with photos of students and reports about activities during the school year. How do you collect the highlights in the school year?

L1/3 ⊚

I don't even know if she's nice

Emily

"What are you going to do this weekend?"
Dave asks Emily.

She answers, "Actually I wanted to
practice for the barrel race next month, but
5 Mom's friends from Minneapolis are going
to visit with their daughter Madison. She's in
a wheelchair, but she wants to learn how to
ride. Aunt Amy is going to teach her."

"You *aren't* going to spend your time on
10 your aunt's farm with your horses again?"

Dave teases Emily. "You really are a country
girl. *I'm* going to watch the latest action
movie this weekend, and I love all the
exciting events in London!"

Emily smiles. "You know what I think   15
about big cities, Dave. We have a movie
theater too, and to me there's nothing more
exciting than our Decorah barrel race! We
have fields and birds and trees, but you just
have cars and buildings and a lot of bad air." 20

"And does Madison like the country too?"
Dave wants to know.

Emily sounds a bit worried. "You know,
they're going to move to Decorah next
month and Madison is going to be in my   25
class. Our parents want us to be friends, but
I don't even know if she's nice."

Dave laughs, "Don't worry – she likes
horses. I'm sure she's a nice girl!"

READING

Voc.: American
English, p. 196;
Numbers, p. 197

1 Talk about the text → WB 4/3

1. What is Emily going to do at the weekend?
2. Say what other plans there are in the text.
3. Say what Dave and Emily think about life
   in the city and life in the country.

Across cultures 🇺🇸

In the US, a 'city' doesn't have to be
big: Decorah is a city with about 8,000
people. What makes a city a city?
Make a mind map and talk about it.

LANGUAGE

2 Find the rule for *going to* → WB 4/4 → G1

a) *Find phrases with **going to** in the text.
   Which part of the time line are they
   about?*

b) *How do you make **going to** forms?
   Write the rule and put it in your folder.*

Tony

← yesterday ← today → tomorrow →

SPEAKING

3 Plans for the weekend → G1

a) *Look at the list and take turns to talk about
   Dave's plans for the weekend.*

b) *Your turn: Now tell your partner about your
   plans for the weekend.*

✔ play computer games
✘ go shopping with Jay
✔ watch a film with Luke
✘ go to a museum with Olivia
✔ work on the yearbook

Lösung: a) Dave is going to play computer games. He isn't going to go shopping with Jay. Dave is going to watch
a film with Luke. He isn't going to go to a museum with Olivia. Dave is going to work on the yearbook.

LANGUAGE

→ △ 120/2

△ → After . . .

4 **What's going to happen?** → G1   → **Folie 2, HA**

Write about the people in the picture. Find your own verbs.

Start: 1. The old man and woman **are going to sit down.**
          2. The man in the wheelchair **is going to . . .**

How can you tell? **You can see** that the old man and woman are pointing at the bench and walking there.

Lösung: EH: 2. The man in the wheelchair is going to open the door. 3. A boy is going to help the man in the wheelchair. 4. A woman and a girl are going to buy some ice cream. 5. A boy and a girl are going to watch a movie at the city cinema. 6. A girl is going to play her saxophone. 7. The man and the woman in the back are going to get on the bus. 8. The woman in the front is going to . . .

SPEAKING

→ ▲ 121/3

→ S28

▲ → After . . .

5 **Play a game: Guess our plans** → WB 5/5 → G1

A friend is going to visit you. Think of something interesting to do with him/her. Don't tell your partner. Your partner must then ask yes/no questions and find out what it is. Take turns.

Example: A: Are you going to do something with animals?   B: No, we aren't.
          A: Are you going to do sports?   B: Yes, we are.
          A: Are you going to play basketball?   B: Yes, we are. You guessed right!

LISTENING

L1/5 ◉

→ ▲ 122/4

▲ → After . . .

Voc.: City and country, p. 197

6 **City or country?** → WB 6/6–7 → **KV 1**

Listen to Emily and Madison. They are talking about living in the country and living in the city. What do they like about where they live? What don't they like? Take notes.

Madison   Emily

WRITING

→ △ 123/5

→ S13–14

△ → Help with . . .

7 **Your turn: When I grow up, . . .** → **Folie 3, KV 89, HA**

What are you going to do when you grow up? Are you going to live in the city or in the country? Write a short text and explain why.

L 1/6

Come on, Em! → Folie 4

Ryan and his cousin Mike are watching Emily and Mike's brother Jack in the youth barrel race.

Ryan: Jack's next, isn't he?

Mike: Yeah, then Emily. Isn't she nervous because she's riding Scarlet?

5 Ryan: Well, she is a bit. Scarlet is very young and it's their first race together, you know. Emily was always so good with Rusty, wasn't she? But now Jack's riding him.

10 Mike: Look, here come Jack and Rusty.

Ryan: Wow, they're fast!

Mike: Yeah! COME ON, JACK! What are you waiting for?

Ryan: He's riding very close to the barrels!

15 Mike: And that last barrel almost fell over!

Ryan: But it didn't, did it? Lucky Jack!

Judge: Jack Ness, nineteen point five two seconds!

Mike: Cool, Jack's now in first place!

Ryan: And here comes Em! COME ON, EM! 20

Mike: Look at her – she and Scarlet are a great team, aren't they?

Ryan: Careful, not too close!

Mike: That was an awesome turn!

Ryan: Now she's going around the last 25 barrel! GO, GO … OH NO! Her hat!!!

Judge: Emily Andersen, twenty-one point three four seconds!

Ryan: Poor Em! Her horse got scared when her hat fell off. And that cost her 30 almost three seconds!

Mike: She looks really mad, doesn't she?

Ryan: Sure – she practiced so much! What a shame! – But who is she talking to now? Can you see who it is? 35

Mike: I think she's talking to Mom. – Here she is. And now she's smiling again!

Ryan: Hey Em, you aren't too disappointed, are you?

Emily: Well, Aunt Amy says I can still be 40 proud because I trained Rusty for three years, and he won. And there's a barrel race in Cedar Rapids next month. She's going to take Jack and me. Isn't that great? 45

Ryan: Cool, but first I'm going to fix your hat!

READING **8** The barrel race

Describe what happened in the race and say why Emily wasn't sad in the end.

LANGUAGE **9** Question tags: You can find the rule, can't you? → G2

→ △ 123/6
△ → After …

a) *Find question tags in the text.*

b) *What can you say about positive and negative forms?*

Lou

SPEAKING 10 **Are you sure?** → WB 6/8 → G2

a) *Make the correct question tags.*

1. Mike is Emily's cousin, …?
2. Emily loves horses, …?
3. Her uncle Jim has more than two horses, …?
4. Emily didn't win the race, …?

L 1/7 ◎
→ ▲ 123/7
▲ → After …

b) *Listen to the sentences from a). Are the people sure about their answers or not? Listen again and repeat the sentences.*

> **Across cultures**
>
> – In English, question tags are a good way to **start a conversation** and to **get feedback**. Here's an example from an American football match: "Hey, this is a great game, isn't it?" – "Yeah, it is. Are the Minnesota Vikings your favorite team too?"
>
> – Also, it's important **to know this difference** with question tags: When it's a *real* question, your voice goes up. When it *isn't*, your voice goes down. Just listen to the examples in **Ex. 10b).**

LANGUAGE 11 **What are Tony and Lou doing?** → WB 7/9 → G3

→ △ 123/8
→ S3
△ → After …

*Ask what Tony and Lou are doing. Use the verbs below. Then answer the questions. Don't forget the **prepositions**!*

Example: What is Lou *waiting for*? Lou is *waiting for* the bus.

1 wait – bus **2** write – Alex **3** look – watch **4** think – problem **5** talk – party

LISTENING 12 **Keeping up a conversation** → WB 7/10–11

L 1/8 ◎

People use questions, question tags, feedback words and fillers (they don't mean much) to keep up a conversation and show that they are interested. Copy the grid and complete it with more feedback words and phrases from Emily and Dave's dialogue.

Asking for feedback	Giving feedback	Fillers
…, isn't it? Did you really …? …	I see. I love … too. …	oh I mean …

SPEAKING 13 **Your turn: What did you do last weekend?** → KV 2, Diktat- und Transfertext

👥
→ S16, S27

*Talk with your partner about what you **both** did last weekend. Use questions, question tags, words and phrases from your grid in exercise 12 and remember to be polite.*

The new boy → S24–25

→ S24–25

VIEWING

1   Film scenes → KV 3, KV 4

1 📽

a) *Watch (00:00–03:01). Look at the headings for Scene A and B and at the phrases on the right. Match the phrases with the right scene.*

Scene A: After school   **Scene B:** The new boy

sneaking around   a bad day?

friends again   why lemons?

trouble (between friends)

Lösung: a) After school: a bad day?, trouble (between friends), friends again;
The new boy: sneaking around, why lemons?
b) EH: I think he .../ Maybe he ... is shopping for his mum./... is buying things for school./ ... is helping his dad.

b) *Jinsoo and Marley want to know why Nick is buying all those things. What do **you** think Nick is up to? What happens next? Talk about your ideas and then watch the last part of the film (03:02–04:45).*

c) *Do you like the film's ending? Explain why/why not. Write two or three sentences.*

Example: I think the ending is nice/funny/surprising/boring/... because ...

VIEWING

2   Film and music

Lösung: a) EH:
01:58–02:50 The music asks a question: What is Nick doing? It's slow and a bit scary – even aggressive.
03:13–03:20 The music is happy. The boys have the answer! Nick is buying things for his experiment.
03:54–04:03/04:06–04:46 During the experiment the music is cool because it's a cool experiment. At the end of the film the music is loud and fast because Nick is excited about his time machine.
b) Mood/Feelings: sad, angry, unfriendly, hurt
Music: slow, sad, (perhaps) loud, aggressive (a fight/an argument)

a) *Before you read the box on the right, watch (01:58–04:45) again and listen to the music in the different scenes. What can you say about the music? Why do you think the filmmakers use music that way?*

b) *Now read the box. Then look at the photo. Which adjectives describe the mood and the feelings in the scene? What kind of music would **you** use for the scene?*

Film skills

Films don't work the same way as texts. A film tells a story with words – *and* with **pictures**, **sounds** and **music** too. So you have the story in a film, and you have different ways to tell that story. These are called the audio-visual effects of a film.

Examples: If you want to show that a person is sad, you can use slow and sad music. For an action scene, you can use loud and fast music.

Mood/Feelings:

excited   sad   tired   happy

angry   unfriendly   hurt   silly

...

Music:

funny   slow   loud   aggressive

sad   fast   sweet   happy   cool

scary   ...

How to use a dictionary → S5

> Think! Do you really need a dictionary? What do you do first when you see a new English word? What do you do if you don't know how to translate a German word into English?

1 Talk about different kinds of dictionaries

a) *Match A–E to the right kind of dictionary. (Some sentences are correct for more than one kind.)*

Online … In a book … In an electronic dictionary …

A the words are in a list in alphabetical order.
B you write in the search box to look up a word.
C you can see the different meanings of the word.
D you can hear the word's pronunciation.
E there are two parts: first there are words in one language and then there are words in the other language.

b) *What other information do the different dictionaries give?*

c) *Which kind of dictionary do **you** like to use? Explain why.*

2 Practise with the alphabet → WB 8/12–13

a) *Revision: Take turns to say the alphabet in English.*

b) *Work with the first two lines of the story ("I don't even know if she's nice") in Station 1. Write all the words in alphabetical order. (Be careful: Don't only look at the first letters – look at the next letters too.) Then check with your partner. Is the order correct?*

3 Find the correct meaning → WB 8/14–15 → KV 5, KV 6

a) *English → German: When you find more than one meaning for a word, choose the right meaning for the sentence. Look up the words in blue and translate them into German.*

1. Take the second street on the right. That's the right way to the station.
2. I haven't got time to sit and chat today. We can chat when I come next time.
3. This is a very small room. There's room for only one bed.

b) *German → English: Sometimes you need different English words for the same German word. Look up the German words and complete the sentences.*

1. **tragen**: a) The students … a blue uniform.
   b) They … their books to school in a bag.
2. **treffen**: a) I often … my friends in the park.
   b) Try to … that tree with your ball.
3. **Karte**: a) Can you find Wales on the …?
   b) Look at the … for our special lunch.

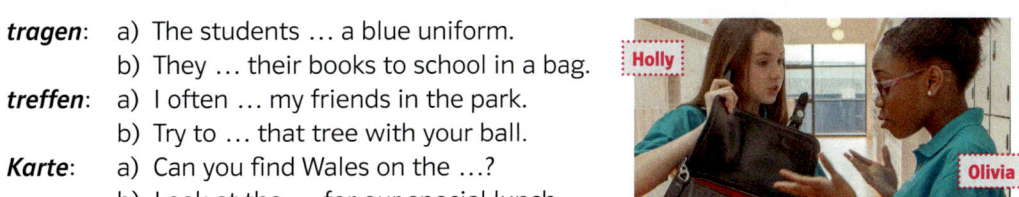

Holly

Olivia

What a **wonderful** world → Folie 5, KV 7

S 1/3–8
L 1/10–15

Beginning

A "Big news today!" Holly said as she walked home from school with Luke and Jay. "Friends of the Earth are having a poster competition, and the prize is a
5 day out in London at the Natural History Museum!"

"Cool!" Luke said. "What do you have to do?"

"Make a poster with the title 'What a
10 Wonderful World' – just listen to the song for ideas," Holly answered.

Luke was excited. "Why don't we do a poster together, Jay?" he asked.

"Maybe …" Jay said, but he was
15 unsure. 'I know that song,' he thought, 'and we can make a great poster!' But something felt wrong … He really didn't want to share his ideas with anyone.

When he came home, he called Luke.
20 "I want to enter the competition," he said, "but not together. I'm going to try alone." He wanted to be the winner.

Luke was very surprised, but he didn't want to show it. "Cool," he said. "Me too!
25 And I'm sure I can win!" Then, after the phone call, he thought to himself: 'Just you wait, Jay Azad!'

main part (body)

B That evening Jay started to write and draw his first ideas. He talked to himself.
30 "OK, so on the left, there's a dirty street with lots of cars and rubbish everywhere, and on the right we can see the 'wonderful world' with no cars, birds in the trees, flowers everywhere …"
35 He stopped. It was a bit boring. 'I need a big idea to make it more fun,' he thought. Suddenly, he noticed a manga magazine on his bedroom floor.

"Mangas!" he shouted. "That's it!"
40 He was very good at art and started to do some cool manga drawings. But how could he use them on his poster?

C That same evening Luke was at home too. He thought about his own ideas and felt very confident. 'OK, Jay,' he thought. 45 'If you don't want to work with me, fine – because I know I can win!'

"Hey, Irina!" he shouted. "Imagine this … My poster is a manga world. Each character has a different job and they all 50 work together to make the world a better place. They all have special costumes and their names all start with the same letters as the activities – Rokuro does recycling, Tomoko looks after the trees, Satoshi 55 cleans the streets … What do you think?"

Irina was quiet for a moment. "It's great!" she said at last. "You're going to win!"

D The next day Luke and Jay sat together 60 in their Maths class, but their heads were full of pictures instead of numbers. Luke smiled to himself – he was proud of his brilliant idea! But Jay was really unhappy.

When it was time for break, Luke got 65 up and went to get a drink. He left his bag on the table with his exercise book on top. Jay looked at it quickly – and he couldn't believe his eyes! There were little pictures all over it … Mangas! 70

Jay looked again and laughed – Luke's drawings were really bad! But then he noticed some words too …

Bunko – bees, Fumio – flowers … 'That's
75 so clever!' he thought. 'I can use that idea
for my poster. I'm going to redo it – and
I'm much better at drawing than Luke!'

E After school the friends walked home
together. Luke decided to make Jay feel
80 nervous.

"My poster is amazing!" he said. "I
can't wait to get home and do some more
work on it. Is your poster finished?"

"Almost," said Jay. "I just need a bit
85 more time to think of some cool names
for my mang…" He stopped. Luke was
shocked.

"No! Not mangas! That's my idea – you
can't steal it!" he shouted.

90 "Calm down!" said Olivia. "It's only a
competition."

"Yes, but Jay wanted to enter alone!"
Luke shouted. He was very angry now.
"That's unfair! When he didn't have good
95 ideas, he stole my ideas!"

"I didn't – I had my own ideas!"

"Did you look in my bag at break
time?" Luke asked as he pushed Jay.

Jay turned round and hit Luke's arm.
100 "Stop!" Dave shouted. He stood
between the boys and tried to stop the
fight. "Are you crazy?! I thought you were
friends!"

"But Jay can't just steal my ideas!"

105 Jay was upset now. "I can't talk to you
for another minute," he said. "You idiot!"

Stop and think:
Is Luke right to be angry with Jay?
What should Jay do now?

Ending /solution

F Dave tried again. "Stop, Jay! Listen, Luke –
why don't you help each other?"

"I wanted to work together, but he 110
didn't," Luke answered.

Jay was still angry. "You can't draw!"

"So what? You think you're special
just because you're good at art!" Luke
answered. "But where's your big idea? You 115
haven't got one!"

Jay didn't answer. Nobody spoke for a
long time. Then at last Jay opened his bag
and took out some papers. "I'm sorry!"
he said. "Look, I always planned to use 120
mangas. And I drew these at break time,
after I saw your pictures. I just didn't have
any good ideas, and your idea with the
names was so cool. – Come on, let's do a
poster together, like you said yesterday." 125

"I'm not sure," Luke said. He really
wasn't ready to be friends again, and he
wanted Jay to know how it felt when your
friend didn't want to work with you!

Jay stood next to Luke and gave him 130
his papers. Luke looked at them and saw
Tomoko in the trees and Fumio with the
flowers – his ideas. But the drawings were
just brilliant!

"OK," Luke said at last, "let's try and 135
work together."

"Cool!" Jay answered. "Let's show
everyone what a real manga story is!"

SPEAKING **1** **Friends?** → WB 9/16 → **KV 7**

a) *Talk about what Jay did and what you think of it. Do you know situations like that?*

b) *Do you like the ending? Say why/why not.*

c) *Say what is good or bad about working together with somebody.*

READING **2** **Looking at the story** → WB 9/17

→ S8–9

a) *Usually a story has three* main parts*:* beginning*, middle and end. Match the parts (A–F) of the story with the three main parts. Which main part says what the story is about? Which part is about a problem? Which part is about the solution?*

Lösung: a)/b)
Beginning: what the story is about – A;
Middle: the problem – B–E;
End: the solution – F

b) *Make a grid with these headings:* **Main part** *(beginning, middle, end)* | **Letters** | **What happens?** *Use it to* sum up *what happens in each main part.*

VOCABULARY **3** **Word families**

→ S4

a) *Use words from the same family to* rewrite *these sentences from the text. The examples of* related *words can help you.*

Word families can help you to guess the meaning of new words.

Examples: *unlucky – lucky; speaker – to speak; to* retell *– to tell*

wasn't sure

1.   *… but he was unsure (lines 14/15).*
2.   *He wanted to be the winner (line 22).*
3.   *But Jay was really unhappy (line 64).*
4.   *'I'm going to redo it …' (line 76).*
5.   *"That's unfair!" (line 94)*

Lösung: a) 1. … but he wasn't sure, 2. He wanted to win, 3. But Jay wasn't happy, 4. 'I'm going to do it again', 5. "That's not fair!"
b) 1. player, 2. dancer, 3. singer, 4. cleaner, unclean, 5. listener, 6. unclear, 7. writer, to rewrite, 8. to reenter

b) *Now add words from the same family to these words:*

1.   to play – …
2.   to dance – …
3.   to sing – …
4.   to clean – …
5.   to listen – …
6.   clear – …
7.   to write – …
8.   to enter – …

VOCABULARY **4** **Inside – outside** → **Diktat- und Transfertext**

Voc.: Feelings and reactions, p. 201

a) *In this story we don't only learn what the characters say to other characters, but also what they think, or what they say when they are alone. Go through the story and look for examples. Where and how did you find them?*

b) *Find language for* strong *feelings in the story and collect different words/phrases in a mind map. Then make little dialogues.*

→ S3–4

Vocabulary skills

To **show strong feelings**, use special words and phrases like 'really' or 'amazing'. (You can also show strong feelings when you say things in a **loud voice**).

Example: A: What's your favourite club?
B: Drama Club. I **love** acting.

A: Do you like school?
B: I **like** Maths, but I **really hate** PE.

amazing
very
language for strong feelings
really
awesome
so
That's it!

Can you . . .

1. talk about plans for the future? _ _ _ _   I'm going to watch …/I'm going to live …
2. talk about what's going to happen? _   She's going to …/Aren't you going to …?
3. make question tags? _ _ _ _ _ _ _ _ _   …, isn't he?/…, are you?/…, did it?

LANGUAGE **1** **A Midwest weekend** → WB 10/18 → **HA**

a) *Look at the cousins' plans for the weekend. Write sentences about their plans.*

b) *Now say what they aren't going to do.*

	Ryan	Emily	Jack	Mike
Saturday: tidy room	✔	✔	✔	✘
Saturday: do homework	✔	✔	✔	✔
Saturday: go canoeing	✘	✘	✔	✔
Sunday: go fishing	✔	✘	✘	✔
Sunday: have a barbecue	✔	✔	✔	✔

LANGUAGE **2** **Can you guess what's going to happen?** → **KV 8**

Look at the pictures and say what Tony and Lou are going to do.

LANGUAGE **3** **Mixed bag: An afternoon around Decorah** → WB 10/19–20   → **KV 9, HA**

Complete the dialogue with words or phrases.

Emily: Hey Ryan, what are you 1 ?
Ryan: A new song 2 my favorite band.
Emily: I 3 . – Let me 4 you something!
Ryan: Why? What do you want me to 5 ?
Emily: The eagle website – you can see the 6 eagles in their nest.
Ryan: Maybe later, I'm 7 .
Emily: Come on! They're really cute. – But what 8 you and Mike do today? You didn't stay at home, 9 you?
Ryan: No, we were 10 all day – we went mountain biking.
Emily: Where 11 you 12 ?

Ryan: First we went across the 13 – Uncle Jim's cows were surprised! Then we went along the river and into the hills.
Emily: Awesome! Jack and I can come next time, 14 ?
Ryan: Maybe. But you could be scared.
Emily: 15 ?
Ryan: Because we saw a panther!
Emily: Stop it, Ryan! You 16 , did you?
Ryan: 17 , maybe it was just an old tree …
Emily: You can never be serious, 18 ?

Find more online:
cd9p4k

S1/9–13
L1/16–20

Regions of the US

US history began in the **Northeast**. Part of it is named New England because the first white settlers there were from England. Many place names in the Northeast come from England, e.g. New York, New Hampshire, Essex or Oxford.

The Northeast has a lot of coast, but also hills and farms. It often has winter blizzards, summer and fall hurricanes and is famous for its colorful trees in the fall. [5]

In New York City, America's largest city, you can hear about 800 different languages because people from all over the world live there.

The farmers in the **South** produced a lot of cotton from the 18th to the 20th century. They used slaves from Africa to work in the cotton fields until 1865, when the Civil War ended and slavery became illegal. [10] A lot of African-Americans still live in the South. Today the farmers there grow a lot of other things too, like corn, wheat and fruit.

But when 98 million tourists go to Florida every year, they don't go to see the farms. They spend millions of dollars at the theme parks. [15] There are almost 20 in and around Orlando alone! You can visit this sunny state with its beautiful beaches all year because of the hot summers and short winters. A lot of retired people move to Florida because they don't like the cold winters in the Northeast and the [20] Midwest. But actually it rains more in the South, and it's very humid!

Arizona, New Mexico and western Texas are part of the **Southwest**. It is a very dry region with a lot of deserts. Texas is famous for its oil and cattle. You can see something wonderful in Carlsbad Caverns National Park, New Mexico. In the evening about 750,000 bats fly out of a huge [25] cave. It takes three hours until all the bats are out of the cave!

SPEAKING

1 Five regions → WB 11/1, 12/2 → **Folie 6**

→ S18–19

Voc.: Measurements and currencies, p. 202; Animals in the US, WB (Word bank), pp. 6–7

a) *Describe the pictures and talk about what you can do in the different regions. Where would you like to go and what would you like to do there?*

b) *Find a title for each region to describe what is special about it.*

WRITING

2 Your turn: German regions → WB 12/3 → **KV 10, KV 89, HA**

a) *Choose one of these regions in Germany: Black Forest, North Sea coast, Bavarian Alps. Find a picture for it and write about it. Use the texts on these pages as a model.*

b) *Read and correct each other's texts. Say what you like about your partner's text.*

Death Valley in California, a state in the **West**, is also a very dry and hot place. Temperatures there can be 122 °F (50 °C) or more! While it doesn't rain enough in some states in the
30 West, there is snow all year in the Rocky Mountains. The Winter Olympics took place in the West more than once, e.g. in Salt Lake City in 2002, but the mountains are also great for summer hiking. California has some of the largest trees in the world: Some are more than 100 meters tall!
35 There is a huge difference between the country and the big cities in the US. People love the feeling of freedom in large states like Wyoming. It has only 577,000 people on an area three and a half times the size of Bavaria, but 1,615,000 sheep and cattle. Cities on the West Coast are
40 very busy. In Hollywood people make millions of dollars with movies.
Alaska and Hawaii are part of the West too.

People call the **Midwest** America's 'breadbasket' because it produces most of the food for the US. There is good
45 farmland in the middle of the country, so European settlers came to live there, a lot of Germans too. You can find huge fields and lots of cattle in the Midwest, but the area around the Great Lakes is also an important industrial region. Chicago is the largest city there. It has a very busy
50 airport. By the way: The US is so big, it takes about six hours to fly from the East Coast to the West Coast, while it takes only one hour and fifteen minutes to fly from Munich to Hamburg.

4

5

6

LISTENING

3 **Young people at the summer camp** → KV 11, Diktat- und Transfertext

L 1/22 ⊚
→ S21–23

Lösung: a) Lynn: West, Josh: Northeast/New England, Sal: Midwest, Jude: Southwest, Becca: South

Voc.: Weather words, p. 203; Weather, WB (Word bank), p. 10

a) *Listen to the five children. They come from five different cities. Look for the cities on the map at the back and say which region they're in.*

b) *What information about their region do Lynn, Josh, Sal, Jude and Becca give? Fill in a grid with these headings:*

city | state | history | weather | other information

c) *Who would you like to visit? Explain why. Write a short text message to the person. Introduce yourself and where you live. Say why you want to visit him/her.*

Useful phrases

… is famous for … | a big bridge | it gets cold/hot | English/German/French settlers | work in the film/computer industry | lots of open space | … is a … fan

Find more online:
2hs9zv

Unit 2

L1/23–24

The Sunshine State

June 12

Almost to G-ma and G-pa's house – 5 more hours. This is the Capitol building in Tallahassee.　　1:16 PM ✓✓

1

June 14

We rode a boat like this on our boat tour of the Everglades – before we saw the alligators!　　2:24 PM ✓✓

2

June 17

On our way to the beach in Florida.　　9:20 AM ✓✓

June 15

The whole street is dancing to Latin rhythms.　6:03 PM ✓✓

3

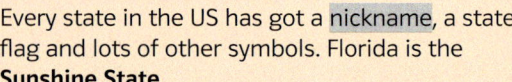

Emily　　　　　Ryan

SPEAKING

1　What you can see and do in Florida → Folie 7

→ ▲ 124/1
▲ → After …

Lösung: a) A4, B7, C5, D3, E1, F6, G2

Voc.: Describing people and animals, Describing things, WB (Word bank), pp. 2–4

→ S27–28

a) *Look at Emily's messages. Match the sentences A–G to the photos.*

b) *Talk about the photos. Think of another sentence about each photo.*

c) *What did you do in your last holidays? Which of the activities in the photos would you like to do? Say why.*

Across cultures

Every state in the US has got a nickname, a state flag and lots of other symbols. Florida is the **Sunshine State**.

State flower: orange blossom
Animal: panther
Tree: palm
Fruit: orange
Choose symbols for your state.

In Unit 2 you learn
- words to describe the culture and history of a place
- ways to give extra information in a sentence
- ways to compare people or things
- useful phrases for a presentation

These things can help you to give a short talk.

June 17

What a beautiful beach!
9:35 AM ✓✓

5

June 22

This is for you, dad! I bet you'd like to be here with us. 😊   3:25 PM ✓✓

June 19

At the theme park. Thanks G-ma and G-pa! I ♥ roller coasters!   11:49 AM ✓✓

6

7

A We're going to stay here until we don't look like we're from Iowa anymore!

B 3-2-1 take-off at Kennedy Space Center!

C That's what I call the perfect place for a summer vacation.

D Ryan would love to play with the Cuban musicians!

E It's a long long way from Iowa to Florida.

F What a ride! G-pa even rode with us! Isn't he cool?

G They look friendly and slow, but they can kill you.

LISTENING **2** **We're taking it easy, Mom!** → WB 13/1–2

L 1/25 ◉
→ S21–23

a) *Emily is talking to her mother on the phone and telling her about the last few days in Florida with her grandparents. Which of the places in the photos does she talk about? What does she say about them?*

Lösung: b) 24: It took them 24 hours to drive to Florida. 2: They stayed at a hotel overnight two times. 70: Emily's grandad is almost 70 years old.

b) *What numbers can you hear in the text? Explain what they mean.*

c) *Which parts of the phone call are typical of a conversation between parents and children?*

d) *Bring your own holiday photo and act a phone conversation between yourself and your mum/dad. Take turns.*

→ S16

Voc.: Adjectives from numbers and nouns, p. 205

Useful phrases

a long/five-hour drive | to stay overnight | That's fine with me/us. | to take somebody somewhere | to take it easy | I have to go = I gotta go | to say hi/hello to somebody

L 1/26 ◎

The most awesome music!

After his vacation in Florida, Ryan talks to his music teacher, Mr. Gibson.

"Mr. Gibson, they played the most awesome music at this Cuban street festival in Florida. And the drums! They were faster
5 than anything!"

"So you liked the Latin rhythms?" Mr. Gibson asked him.

"I did! They're great! But the singers were cool too. Everyone was so happy," Ryan
10 replied. "Mr. Gibson, I've got an idea. We can make our next school concert even more exciting with a Cuban music group with lots of percussion instruments! We could even start a new club. I can make a cajón alone,
15 I mean it's really just a wooden box, and then it's less expensive than a new one." Ryan got really excited now. "My dad's got the best video program at home, so we can make a music video to find members for the
20 new club! We don't want fewer than five people in the group. And we should practice three times a week so we can get better – fast. After one month we can play our first school concert. The coolest thing would
25 be a street festival or the State Fair. That's even bigger! And maybe I can invite one of the …"

Mr. Gibson stopped Ryan and said: "Great ideas, but Ryan, this is Iowa. Not Florida. I don't think the cattle show at the State
30 Fair is ready for Latin rhythms. Let's make a flyer for the new club first and see what happens."

At first Ryan was a little disappointed, but the next day he came back to Mr. Gibson
35 and showed him some pictures.

"For the flyer we can use one of these pictures from the festival. And when I give people the flyers, I can play the maracas. One of the musicians gave them to me.
40 He was the nicest of them all and he says there's nothing more important than percussion," Ryan explained.

"Wait, Ryan," Mr. Gibson said. "What was that picture?"
45

"Oh yeah, well, that was a little embarrassing. I fell into the drums," Ryan said.

"I hope it wasn't as bad as it looks!" Mr. Gibson laughed.
50

"Actually it was worse than it looks! But there are some even funnier pictures of me, look here!"

READING **1** ## Big ideas → WB 14/3

Answer these questions on the text.

Voc.: Music, p. 205;
Musical instruments,
WB (Word bank), p. 5

1. Why did Ryan tell Mr. Gibson about the festival?
2. What's special about Cuban music groups?
3. What can you say about the two Cuban percussion instruments in the text?
4. Ryan and Mr. Gibson have different ideas about how to get people to join the new group. What are they?
5. What do you think about these ideas? Which is the best? Say why.

Ryan

Find Cuba on the map. Over one million people in Florida are of Cuban origin. About 80% of **Cuban-Americans** speak Spanish at home and it is the second most common language in the US. Cuban food, music and traditions are also part of their culture.

Are there people from other places in your home town? What do you know about their culture?

LANGUAGE **2** **Find the rule: More about adjectives** → WB 14/4 → G4

a) *Copy the grid and use the text to complete it with the missing forms.*

Basic form	Comparative form	Superlative form
awesome	more awesome	…
exciting	…	most exciting
fast	…	the fastest
big	…	the biggest
nice	nicer	…
funny	…	the funniest
good	…	…
bad	…	the worst

Lösung: a) most awesome, more exciting, faster, bigger, the nicest, funnier, better, the best, worse

b) *Which two regular ways are there to make the comparative and superlative forms of adjectives? Which adjectives are irregular?*

c) *Find more adjectives in the text and add them to your grid.*

You must learn the spelling rules and the irregular forms by heart.

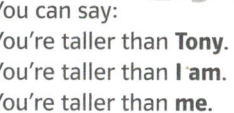

SPEAKING **3** **Good, better, the best!** → G5 → **Folie 8**

→ △ 124/2
△ → After …

Work in small groups to make sentences with comparisons. Partner A chooses an adjective and uses it in a sentence. Take turns and use the adjective in different forms.

You can say:
You're taller than **Tony**.
You're taller than **I am**.
You're taller than **me**.

Example:
A: History is **a good** subject.
B: But Maths is **better than** History.
C: History is **as good as** Geography.
D: But not **as good as** Biology.
E: And English is **the best** subject!

Useful phrases

= as … as … | ≠ not as … as … | > -er/
more … than … | < -er/less … than …

LANGUAGE
→ 124/3
 → After …

4 Life in a different country → WB 15/5–6, 16/7 → G5 → HA

Here is what Amrita from Cuba says about life in Miami.
Put in the correct adjective forms. Careful: You may need to add 'as' or 'the'.

Lösung: 1. bigger,
2. better, 3. as hot,
4. fewer, 5. newer,
6. the prettiest,
7. the tallest, 8. the
best, 9. closer,
10. as expensive

"The US is much (**1** big) than Cuba – Cuba is only an island! People often ask me if the weather in Miami is (**2** good) than in Havana. Well, in Miami it's almost (**3** hot) as it is in Cuba, but there are (**4** few) rainy days in Havana. Lots of things in the US are (**5** new) than in my country, and I really

like that. I know that Miami isn't (**6** pretty) city in America and it doesn't have (**7** tall) buildings, but I think it's one of (**8** good) places to live. There's a lot to do here. The ocean is (**9** close) than I thought and the theme parks aren't (**10** expensive) as I thought! I love Miami!"

SPEAKING
→ 125/4
→ 125/5
△ → After …
▲ → After …

5 Emily in Iowa and Amrita in Florida → G5

Compare Emily and Amrita.
Use these forms: more/less/fewer than, (not) as … as and … than.

Example: *Amrita has got more brothers and sisters than Emily.*
Her hair is longer …

Lösung: Her hair is longer than Emily's. Emily is as old as Amrita. She is taller than Amrita. Amrita speaks more languages than Emily and she is better at swimming than her.

Voc.: Comparing things, p. 206

Emily
1 brother
12 years old
long hair
tall
speaks English
good at swimming

Amrita
2 brothers, 3 sisters
12 years old
very long hair
short
speaks English and Spanish
very good at swimming

WRITING
→ S11–14

6 How to: Write a flyer → WB 16/8 → Folie 9, KV 12

a) *Look at Ryan and Mr. Gibson's flyer for the Latin Rhythms Club.*
Would you like to join the club? Say why or why not.

b) *Now read the skills box. Choose **one** of the clubs on the right. With a partner, make a flyer for it.*

Maths Club   Computer Club

Singing Club   History Club   Science Club

c) *Exchange your flyers with another pair of students and check each other's work.*

Writing skills

When you write a flyer, make sure
- it's easy to read
- it has all the important information about your club: its **name**, **what** you do, **when** and **where** you meet (day and time), **why** people should join
- you welcome people with a special welcome message and a slogan!

The Decorah High School
LATIN RHYTHMS CLUB

When?   Mondays at 3:15
Where?   The band room
What?   Learn about a new
    style of music and
    some new instruments

Why? We want to
• start a Latin Rhythms band
• play on stage and on the street
• have a good time!

Everyone can dance to the rhythm!

L 1/29 ◎ # The people who made Florida

Emily and Ryan are discussing Emily's
presentation about Florida history.

Ryan: Don't start 14,000 years ago!
Emily: I know how to do a presentation,
5   Ryan! I only mention the first Native
        Americans who lived there then.
        Then I jump to the 1500s, when the
        first Europeans tried to colonize
        Florida. The Native Americans say
10   that the white men grew from foam
        that came out of the ocean. The sun
        melted away the foam on the beach,
        and then the white men were there.
        Florida was under Spanish rule from
15   1513 to 1763, under British rule until
        1783, then it went to the Spanish
        again. It wasn't a state until 1845.
Ryan: Whoa! That's a lot of dates, Em. Do
        you really think that's interesting for
20   your classmates?
Emily: Well, maybe not, but they should
        know about all the different people
        who made Florida. Like the settlers
        who built all the Spanish-style
25   buildings. And the Native Americans
        that helped runaway slaves who
        came to Florida in the 1700s and 1800s
        because slavery was illegal there. Isn't
        that cool?
30 Ryan: Hey, you know what G-pa told me?
        The first city Europeans founded, a
        city which is still there today, is St.
        Augustine. And that's where the first

baby whose parents were Europeans
was born in 1566.   35
Emily: You're going back in time again.
        I want to talk more about the new
        immigrants and the traditions they
        started. Remember all the great
        Cubans we met at the music festival? 40
Ryan: How could I forget? Should I get my
        maracas?
Emily: No thanks! The Cubans whose parents
        immigrated in the 1960s brought
        other things I want to show too. Our   45
        teacher says we should make our
        presentations attractive to as many
Voc.   senses as possible.
Ryan: Like the sense of hearing? Maracas!
Emily: RYAN! Like the sense of taste. I made 50
        this specialty the Cubans sold at the
        festival, *arroz con pollo*. Try it.
Ryan: Aaargh! Help! Em! Water! How much
        chili did you put in there?
Emily: Maybe a little too much?   55

READING **7** ## Correct the sentences → WB 17/9

Example: The people who lived in Florida first were the Spanish.
        → The people who lived in Florida first were the Native Americans.

Voc.: History, p. 208

1. The first Europeans who got to Florida didn't want to stay there.
2. The first city they founded doesn't exist any more.
3. Ryan forgot about the Cubans who they met.
4. Emily made a specialty that she tried at a supermarket.

Lösung: 1. The first Europeans who got to Florida tried to colonize it. 2. The first city they founded is still there today.
3. Ryan remembers all the great Cubans who they met. 4. Emily made a specialty that the Cubans sold at the festival.

LANGUAGE **8**   **Find the rule** → G6

a) *Look at the text again. Collect the nouns in front of the relative pronouns* **who, which, that,** *and* **whose.**

b) *Check if the nouns are people or things. When do you use which relative pronoun?*

LANGUAGE **9**   **Facts about Florida** → WB 17/10 → G6

→ △ 125/6
△ → After . . .

Match the sentence parts.

Example: The Spanish man who/that …

Lösung: 1. f) who/that, 2. a) whose, 3. d) which/that, 4. e) which/that, 5. b) who/that, 6. c) which/that

1. The Spanish man		a) parents came from Cuba speak Spanish at home.
2. People in Florida	who/that	b) love nice weather move to Florida today.
3. Miami is a name	which/that	c) has more than 300 skyscrapers.
4. Hurricanes		d) comes from the Native American word Mayaimi.
5. Lots of people	whose	e) hit Florida can be very dangerous.
6. Miami is a city		f) first landed in Florida was Juan Ponce de León.

LANGUAGE **10**   **Contact clauses** → G6   → **Folie 10, KV 13**

a) *Contact clauses are relative clauses without relative pronouns. Translate the sentences to understand the difference between 1. and 2. and say why you can make a contact clause in 2.*

1. **Ryan** is a boy. **He** likes music.
   Ryan is a boy **who** likes music.

2. **Ryan** is a boy. **Everybody** likes **him.**
   Ryan is a boy **(who) everybody** likes.

→ △ 125/7
△ → After . . .

Lösung: b) You don't need the relative pronoun in sentences 2 and 4.

b) *Check the sentences. Say where you don't need the relative pronoun.*

1. Children that are interested in history must go to the museum in Tallahassee.
2. There are many things that you can do in that museum.
3. People who like ships can see models.
4. The programs for children which they have on Saturdays are really cool.
5. And sometimes you can cook specialties which are of Cuban origin.

LANGUAGE **11**   **Make one sentence from two** → WB 18/11–12, 19/13 → G6

→ △ 126/8
→ ▲ 126/9
△ → After . . .
▲ → After

Example: History is a **school subject**. I really like **it**.
→   History is a **school subject (which)** I really like.

1. In our history class we talked about a famous place in Florida. We all know it.
2. First we looked at a picture. We found it on the state's website.
3. Then we watched a movie. It was from 1969.
4. Finally we made a poster. We called it 'Kennedy Space Center: Taking America to the moon!'

Lösung: 1. . . . (which/that) we all know. **2.** . . . (which/that) we found on the state's website. **3.** . . . which/that was from 1969. **4.** . . . (which/that) we called 'Kennedy Space Center: Taking America to the moon!'

WRITING **12**

→ ▲ 126/10
→ S12
▲ → After …

How to: Write prompt cards → WB 20/14 → **Folie 11, KV 14**

Read the skills box. Then look at the text on page 27 again. Add more key words to the prompt card about Native Americans. Then make prompt cards about the Europeans and the Cubans in Florida.

Who: Native Americans
What: lived in FL first, …
Where: Florida
When: 14,000 years ago, …

Writing skills

In a presentation, don't read whole sentences from the page. Use **prompt cards**. On these cards, you write **key words** to help you to remember the main ideas in your presentation. Write important people, events, places, and dates under the headings: **Who** | **What** | **Where** | **When**

MEDIATION **13**

→ ▲ 127/11
▲ → After …

Keep away from alligators! → **Diktat- und Transfertext**

Dein englischer Austauschpartner Bob mailt dir einen deutschen Internet-Artikel, den er nicht ganz versteht, und bittet dich um Hilfe. Schreibe ihm eine Mail. Fasse darin zunächst in einem Satz für Bob zusammen, was passiert ist. Dann suche alle Informationen über Alligatoren aus dem Text heraus und gib sie auf Englisch für ihn wieder.

Lösung: EH: Dear Bob, Of course I can help you with the German article. It's about a very big alligator in Florida that walked across a field where people play golf, so the people there felt very scared. The article gives a lot of facts about alligators in Florida: They can be up to six metres long. They live in and near the water. Sometimes they go into areas where people live. Most of the time they aren't dangerous, but they can kill people because they're very good at swimming and they're very strong so they can pull you under water like the animals they usually eat. So you should be careful when you find an alligator in your garden! If you have any more questions, please let me know. Bye for now, (name)

Riesen-Alligator spaziert über Golfplatz in Florida

Ein außergewöhnlich großer Alligator hat Golfern in Florida einen mächtigen Schrecken eingejagt. Aufnahmen im Internet zeigen den gemütlichen Spaziergang des riesigen Tieres quer über den Platz.
Charles Helms wollte eigentlich nur einen entspannten Nachmittag auf dem Golfplatz verbringen. Doch dann wurde er Zeuge eines beeindruckenden Auftritts. "Ich war fassungslos und still", sagte der Mann gegenüber *ABC Action News*.

5

Ein riesiger Alligator stolzierte quer über den Golfplatz Buffalo Creek in Palmetto, Florida. Solche Tiere sind in dem US-Bundesstaat zwar nicht ungewöhnlich. Ein derart gigantisches Exemplar hatte nach eigener Aussage aber auch Helms noch nie zuvor gesehen. Zunächst glaubte der Hobby-Golfer, der mit einem Freund auf dem Platz unterwegs war, an einen Scherz.

10

Helms und sein Begleiter schätzten die Länge des Alligators auf mindestens 14 bis 15 Fuß, also deutlich über vier Meter.

15

Wendy Schofield, eine Angestellte des Buffalo Creek, ließ der Zwischenfall kalt: „Er stört niemanden – und niemand stört ihn. Er ist wie ein Maskottchen für den Platz", erzählte Schofield *News 3 Las Vegas*.

Angeblich patrouilliert der Alligator seit mehreren Jahren über die Fairways und Greens der Anlage. „Er ist hier schon seit sehr, sehr langer Zeit", so Schofield weiter.

20

Alligatoren sind im US- Bundesstaat Florida Alltag. Die bis zu sechs Meter langen Echsen leben in Sümpfen und tummeln sich in Seen und großen Flüssen. Immer wieder verirren sich einzelne Exemplare in bewohnte Gebiete.

Meist gehen solche Begegnungen glimpflich aus, im Wasser kann aber selbst eine Begegnung mit einem relativ kleinen Vertreter dieser Spezies tödlich enden. Die Tiere sind perfekte Schwimmer, haben enorm viel Kraft und sind darauf spezialisiert, ihre Beute unter Wasser zu ziehen.

25

The film star → S24–25

SPEAKING

1 Your turn: One day I want to be a/an …

a) What is your 'dream job'? Why is it so great?

b) Talk about the pros and cons of the jobs on the right.

actor   dancer   pilot
police officer   vet

VIEWING

2 Laura's problem → KV 15

2 📽 Watch the film. What is Laura's dream job? But what is her problem?
Lösung: Laura wants to be a great actor like Polly McCane, but she forgets her lines when she is in a room full of people.

VIEWING

3 Good advice? → KV 16

a) Watch (01:38–04:00) again. What advice do people give Laura? Take notes.

b) Talk about the advice for Laura. Here are some ideas:

A: Polly is a star, so she knows best!
B: Well, Marley isn't a star and *his* advice is great too: "Believe in yourself".

c) Look at the still on the right (04:35). What is Laura thinking at this moment in the film? Look at the phrases.

d) Now watch the rest of the film. Why does Laura thank Polly?

> **Useful phrases**
>
> Don't panic! | Don't be nervous! |
> Just relax! | I'm sure you're good at … |
> You're always so confident. | Try again. |
> Take a deep breath. | Believe in yourself!

SPEAKING

4 What a great film!

In groups of three to four, talk about something **you** saw at the cinema – or want to see. These phrases from the film can give you ideas.

> **Useful phrases**
>
> That was such a great film!
> I'm/I was really impressed with …
> I just love … He's/She's my favourite actor.
> I can't wait for … | I really want to …

How to give a good presentation → S15–17

1 What makes a presentation good? → **KV 17**

Copy the grid and collect your ideas about a good presentation.

What you talk about	How you present it	How you organise things
Give facts.	Make eye contact with your audience.	Be on time.
...	Speak clearly.	...
	...	

2 Two presentations

3–4 **a)** *Watch two presentations. What are they about? Which presentation do you like better?*

b) *Work in groups of three. Each of you chooses one of the headings in Ex. 1. Then watch the presentations again. Focus on your heading and take notes for each film. Add things from each presentation and note down what is missing.*

c) *Talk about your notes. Discuss what makes the presentations good/not so good.*

3 Make a good presentation → WB 20/15–16

Improve Lou's presentation text below. The phrases in the box can help you. You can think of facts that aren't in the text. Then practise your presentation and read it out loud several times.

Lösung: EH: Hello and welcome to the Drama Club's presentation! Do you enjoy role plays and acting? Then you should join our Drama Club. It's really so much fun because you can act different roles. Let me tell you a personal story. When I started, at first I was very shy, but the teacher and the others were so nice and now I feel very confident. Let's take a look at the flyer with all the information. We meet every Thursday at 3 p.m. in room B32. We'd love to see you there!

> Hello and welcome to the Drama Club's presentation! Do you enjoy ...?

> Er – OK, I'm from Drama Club. We meet every week. I wanted to give you a flyer, but – sorry, I forgot it at home. Oh, and what else did I want to tell you? I can't remember ...

> **Useful phrases**
>
> Hello and welcome to ... | My name is ... | Today I'd like to ... | Let's take a look at ... | Let me tell you a personal story ... It's connected to the topic because ... | First ..., second ..., third ... | It's fantastic/really interesting/so much fun because ...

Join our club!

In this task, work in groups of four. Each group is a school club. At a 'club market', each group prepares a short talk (two to three minutes) about its club. Why is it special? Why is it the best club? You want as many classmates as possible to join **your** club! Each person in your group has a different job to make your presentation great.

Step 1

Which club? → **Folie 9**

a) *First decide together which club your group wants to be. Here are some ideas; maybe you've got ideas of your own.*

Drama
Mangas
Tae kwon do
Juggling
Singing
Foreign languages
Fanzines

b) *Now choose a time slot for your presentation on the club market's timetable. Your teacher will check that everyone chooses a different time.*

1:15   1:20   1:25   1:30   1:35   1:40

Step 2

Think of ideas for your club

a) *What's important to know about your club? What do you do when you meet? Collect information and facts that can interest new members. Answer these questions:*
What | When | Where | Why | Who | ...

b) *Now talk about what makes your club special and what makes it better than the other clubs. Remember, you want new members!*

What makes the Cheese Club special? Well, there's always free cheese at the cheese shop! Mmm …

Step 3

Make your club sound great → HA

a) *Collect words and phrases which can make your club sound great. Write sentences with them.*

b) *Now think of a slogan for your club.*

Example:

Drama Club: "Once a week you need some drama in your life!"

> Look back at the **Skills page** for phrases to make your club sound interesting.

> Look back at the **Skills page** for help with presentation skills. **Station 2** is the place to look for help with prompt cards.

Step 4

Pair A: Write your flyer

One pair in your group writes the flyer for your club. Give important information on it, and make it easy to read.

Pair B: Write your prompt cards

The other pair decides what needs to go on the prompt cards for the presentation. Write your prompt cards.

> For help with a flyer, look at **Station 1** again.

Step 5

Check each other's work → KV 12

The pair that wrote the prompt cards now checks the flyer; the pair that wrote the flyer checks the prompt cards. Talk about changes in your group.

Step 6

You're on! → KV 18

a) *Decide together who in your group gives the talk, and then practise together. Give him/her tips!*

b) *Now give your short presentation. Don't forget the flyer!*

Step 7

Which club do YOU want to join?

a) *As a class, talk about the different presentations.*

b) *Decide for yourself which club **you** want to join.*

c) *Class activity: Put a flyer for each club on a different table. Then each student goes to the table of the club he/she wants to join. Which club has the most new members?*

S 1/18–20
L 1/31–33

A perfect day for treasure hunting → **Folie 12, KV 19**

Antonio

A It was July 23, 1715 – Antonio's last day on
land in Havana, Cuba before he left with
Admiral Juan Esteban de Ubilla and his
silver fleet. The 15-year-old Spanish cabin
5 boy was more excited than nervous before
the long voyage back to Europe.

What could go wrong? His captain
was a confident sailor. His ships were full
of silver, gold and other treasures from
10 Mexico. It was time for Antonio and the
others to start their voyage on the twelve
'treasure ships'. Antonio wanted to be a
sailor and now he could show the captain
that he was as good as the older men
15 aboard the San Pedro.

"The storm from yesterday means
today is a perfect day for treasure hunting,"
Emily and Ryan's grandpa told them at
breakfast.
20 "Sometimes the storms and waves
uncover gold or silver coins, or other
valuable objects," he explained. Emily
and Ryan's grandparents belonged to a
treasure-hunting club. The grandchildren
25 often made jokes about it, but only when
their grandparents couldn't hear them.
Nobody believed in treasures anymore
and they were too old to play pirates.

Antonio didn't see any of the treasure, but
30 the ships were heavier now than when they
first got to Mexico. There was also enough
fresh water and food for a six-week voyage.

But Antonio didn't want to stay in Spain
although his family was still there. His
plans were sailing, sailing, sailing. Some   35
day he was going to have his own ship,
bigger than this one, and he wanted to
bring treasures back to Spain.

At the beach in Fort Pierce they got the
metal detector out of the car trunk. Ryan   40
gave Emily a look that said, "This is almost
as embarrassing as Mom when she's
singing in the car."

"Let me show you how it works,"
Grandpa said. "You hold the detector   45
with two hands. Like this. Move it slowly
from left to right in front of you. When it
beeps, stop right away and then we dig!"
Grandma decided that the children should
watch first.   50

It was a beautiful day for sailing – blue
skies and no clouds – and they were ready
early. But Antonio didn't have time for the
weather because he was too busy. He and
the other men fired the cannon that gave   55
the signal "Time to sail!" With a good wind,
they could make it to the coast of Florida
in one week.

Emily

Ryan

grandparents

B They were walking very slowly on the
beach. There were fewer people than   60
usual, but that was because of the storm
yesterday when it was even windier than
tornado season in Iowa. Suddenly the
metal detector beeped and Grandpa got
his shovel.   65

"Can I dig, Grandpa?" Ryan asked. But Grandpa didn't even hear him because he was so busy with his shovel. He dug very slowly and carefully and at the bottom of
70 the hole there was … a soda can.

Antonio took out his food for the day and drank some water. The wine was for his evening meal. He ate three ounces of dried fish but was still hungry. He had to save the
75 rest for the evening. He wanted to forget that he was hungry so he looked for work on deck. There was always work on a ship and although he was tired, on deck was always better than below deck where the
80 cabin was only as tall as he was.

After two hours Grandma said, "It's time for a break." So they stopped and took out their picnic lunch.
"Grandma," Emily asked, "is it often like
85 this? That you don't find anything?"
"That's why it's called a treasure. Because it's something special," she answered. "But isn't it fun?" Then she and Grandpa lay down on the sand for a nap.

90 After almost one week of good sailing weather, the 12 ships were near Florida. But July 29 was very quiet. There was no wind, only slow, rolling waves. There were fewer sea birds around the ships. The men
95 tied things down because everything was rolling and moving. The older sailors knew that something was going to happen.
The next morning was dark and it stayed like that all day. The older sailors
100 were as horrified as Antonio. All of the ships stayed close together and then the wind came back. Next the waves started. They crashed onto the deck and pulled things back into the ocean. The water hurt
105 the sailors' faces, arms and legs.

C After five minutes Grandma and Grandpa fell asleep. Emily and Ryan looked at each other and their eyes spoke a secret language. They didn't make a sound as

they stood up and Ryan took the metal 110 detector. At first they took slow, careful steps and then they ran. Soon they were half a mile away and Ryan turned on the metal detector. They didn't notice as the water got closer and closer and the waves 115 higher and higher. Suddenly the detector beeped once. Then a wave crashed over it and it was silent.

Antonio helped to untie a lifeboat and all the men prayed. At 2:30 in the morning 120 on July 31 there was a horrible sound. The hurricane threw the first of the Spanish ships into a coral reef on the coast of Florida. The ship hit the reef again and again. And soon the other ships did the 125 same.

Emily looked at Ryan with big eyes. She was more afraid than Ryan was. Before the next big wave came, Ryan gave the detector to Em. Then he quickly scooped 130 up sand. They ran away from the high waves and sat down in the sand. Ryan felt something in his hands. It was round – like a coin – but there were algae all over it.

When Antonio woke up, he was on the 135 sand with the hot sun in his eyes. Eleven of the twelve ships got smashed to pieces. More than 1,000 men died, Admiral Ubilla too, and about 1,500 survived. Most of the ships – with the treasure and the cannons – 140 were already at the bottom of the ocean.

VOCABULARY **1** **Guessing new words** → WB 21/17

→ S10, S4

There are some new words in the text that you don't have to look up. Look at the words in blue print and use a grid like this to say what they mean and how you can tell.

These tips can help you:
– I know a similar word in German/another language.
– I know a related word in English.
– In this context it can only have one meaning.
– I have an idea what kind of word it is.
– I can tell if it is a positive or a negative word.

English word	Meaning	How can you tell?
silver	Silber	similar in German
voyage	Reise	similar in French
valuable	wertvoll	an adjective that describes gold, silver, treasure

WRITING **2** **Working with the stories** → WB 21/18

a) *Work in groups of three. In your group, each of you (A, B and C) writes about the main ideas of the two stories in different ways:*

A: Find 6–8 key words/phrases from each story. Write down why they're important.
B: Tell the main ideas of each story in 6–8 sentences.
C: In 6–8 sentences, talk about your reaction to the stories.

Then tell each other your ideas and compare them.

→ △ 127/12
△ → Help with …

b) *Choose one of these writing tasks: Compare Antonio's story to Emily and Ryan's.*
Or: Find a possible ending for Emily and Ryan's or Antonio's story. → HA

SPEAKING **3** **Make a dialogue** → WB 21/19

→ S16–17

Choose one of the scenes, make a dialogue and act it out.

1. Emily and Ryan before they go to the Treasure Coast with their grandparents.
2. The grandparents wake up on the beach and find that Emily and Ryan aren't there.
3. Grandpa is telling them about treasure ships that crashed near his home.
4. Emily and Ryan are making plans about the money from their treasure.

WRITING **4** **What's the story behind it?** → HA, Diktat- und Transfertext

→ S11–14

Choose one object from the treasure-hunting club and create a little story about its history.

Useful phrases

… belonged to | She lived in … | It was for … | They travelled … | The voyage was … | They used it for …

> **Can you . . .**
>
> 1. make comparisons with adjectives? ___ It's bigger than/as big as … | It's the most exciting/…
> 2. give more information about people/ things? ___ The people who/that … | The city which/that … | The girl whose parents came from Cuba …
> 3. talk about interesting facts? ___ It's really interesting that … | The first settlers who came to … were …

LANGUAGE **1** **Manatees[1] in Florida** → WB 22/20 → **Folie 11**

Put in relative pronouns where you need them.

1. Manatees are water animals … bodies are grey and about ten feet long.
2. The plants … they eat are usually on the bottom.
3. The places … they live in during the winter must be warm.
4. Tourists … want to be close to them can swim with the manatees … live in the Crystal River.

1 **manatee** ['mænəti:] Seekuh

LANGUAGE **2** **Comparing theme parks** → KV 20, HA

Write sentences to compare these three theme parks. Which of them do you like best?

	Dinosaur Park	**Water Adventure**	**Sky High**
Opened	1984	2003	2015
Visitors/year	750,000	1.2 million	1.8 million
Roller coasters	3	6	18
Fastest (miles/hour)	65	50	95
Tickets	$36	$36	$52

LANGUAGE **3** **Mixed bag: What Amrita thinks …** → WB 22/21 → **KV 21, HA**

'Sunshine ⬛1⬛ is the best ⬛2⬛ for Florida. It has ⬛3⬛ almost all around it and so of course lots of ⬛4⬛ too. And that is the ⬛5⬛ exciting thing about Florida for me. I love water sports, and the rolling ⬛6⬛ and the hot sand make me ⬛7⬛ it easy. The islands ⬛8⬛ belong to Florida are ⬛9⬛ Florida Keys. Forty Keys ⬛10⬛ connected by the Overseas Highway with ⬛11⬛ very long bridges. Florida has interesting ⬛12⬛ too, like manatees and ⬛13⬛. But the ⬛14⬛ are ⬛15⬛ dangerous and faster ⬛16⬛ they look! People ⬛17⬛ aren't careful can get hurt. Florida has a very colorful ⬛18⬛ because lots of people ⬛19⬛ other countries ⬛20⬛ to live here and brought their food, music, etc. There were Native ⬛21⬛, black ⬛22⬛, Spanish and French people and people from ⬛23⬛ like me, and lots more!

Find more online:
b6i8qp

American stories and traditions

Every country has famous people and important events, and we like to hear interesting or exciting stories about them. Some of them explain why things became what they are like today. Sometimes it's easy to know when a story isn't true, but not always!

READING

S1/21–22
L2/1–2 ⊚

1 The history of Halloween → Folie 13

a) *Long ago, when people in Ireland saw strange lights over dangerous bogs[1] at night, they told a story to explain what the lights were. Read the jack-o'-lantern story and say what you think: Why did Irish people tell their children this scary story?*

Jack was a bad man who played a trick on the devil to make him climb up a tree. Jack only let the devil come down from the tree when he promised never to take Jack's soul to hell. But then, when he was old, Jack couldn't die and go to heaven because he was bad, but he also couldn't go to hell because of the devil's promise, so he couldn't die at all! The devil gave Jack a light from the fires of hell, but he didn't help Jack again.

So bad Jack's scary ghost still walks over the bogs at night with the devil's light in a turnip[2] with holes in it. That's why he's called 'Jack of the lantern', 'Jack-o'-lantern' for short.

b) *Now read about Halloween and answer the questions.*

1. What do Americans do for Halloween today?
2. How is that different to the old traditions in Ireland?

Long ago, the Irish people believed that ghosts like Jack, or dead people's souls, walked around in the nights at the end of autumn, around the time of Halloween (31st October). So they made big fires or put turnip lanterns outside their houses to keep the ghosts away. When a lot of Irish people went to live in America around 1840, they took the stories and the tradition with them. They made 'jack-o'-lantern' faces in pumpkins to decorate their houses. Americans still like to read scary stories, put on scary party costumes or watch scary movies for Halloween.

LISTENING

L2/3 ⊚

L2/4 ⊚

2 Trick-or-treating and souling → WB 23/1

a) *Listen to part 1. What are Dale and Macy going to do this year?*

b) *Listen to part 2. Make notes on:*

1. souling
2. different tricks and treats

c) *Talk about what you do for Halloween.*

1 bog [bɒg] Sumpf, Moorgebiet | **2 turnip** ['tɜːnɪp] Steckrübe

READING **3** **Paul Bunyan and Babe the Big Blue Ox¹**

S1/23
L2/5 **a)** *Read this legend. Then look at the US map at the back of the book.*
Find the places in the story. What happened at each place?

Many years ago, Paul Bunyan was born in Maine. For just one day his parents needed ten cows for his milk. One day, Paul decided to go west with his pet Babe, an ox. On the way, Babe needed a drink, so Paul quickly dug five great lakes for Babe. When they got to Minnesota, Paul and Babe ran around and played. Their big feet made the 10,000 lakes there. Then Paul began his job as a lumberjack². He cut down a whole forest when he used his axe. Soon he moved west again, but he cried when he left his lumberjack friends in the Midwest. His tears ran down to the Gulf of Mexico and made the Mississippi River. Paul wanted to take the quickest path to the West, so he tied the beginning of the road to Babe and the ox pulled the road. That's why there are long, straight roads in America. Out in the West, Paul got tired, and he dragged³ his axe behind him. That's how he made the Grand Canyon.

b) *Find more special places on the map. What do you think: How did Paul make those?*

c) *Find legends about landscapes in Germany. Tell one to the class.*

LISTENING **4** **My favourite legend** → WB 23/2

L2/6–8 **a)** *Emily is doing a project on American legends. Look at the introductions. Then listen to Emily's interviews. Compare the characters. What did they do? Is the story real or invented?*

feather

cherry

cannon

Voc.: Stories, p. 213

A The Sky Girl, from the Sky Country, and Algon the Hunter, from the Earth, found a way to live together.

B George Washington was the first US president and a great leader. But when he was a child, he did something bad.

C Molly Pitcher fought in the Revolutionary War with her husband and other soldiers.

b) *Why do you think people tell the legends on this page?*

c) *Which is your favourite legend on these two pages? Explain why.*

> **Useful phrases**
>
> It's true/exaggerated/invented. | It explains/shows … | X is a hero/heroine because …/uses magic/a trick to …/changes into …/is strong/honest/brave.

SPEAKING **5** **Invent your own story that could become a legend** → KV 22

Voc.: Describing people and animals, WB (Word bank), pp. 2–3

'Hot seat': Invent a character for a good story that could become a legend. Where did he or she live? What did he or she look like and do? Then let the class interview you. Answer their questions.

1 ox [ɒks] Ochse | **2 lumberjack** ['lʌmbəˌdʒæk] Holzfäller | **3 to drag** [dræg] schleifen, schleppen

〈Revision A〉 ist fakultativ und dient der Festigung/Wiederholung. Es werden keine neuen Sprachmittel eingeführt.

LISTENING

1 Don't worry! → WB 24/1

L 2/9 ⊙ *Listen to a phone call between Emily's mum (Debbie) and Madison's mum (Gina). Madison's family is going to move to Decorah and Gina is a bit worried about some things. Debbie tries to help her. Copy the grid and make notes.*

What Gina is worried about	Debbie's ideas for help
…	…

LANGUAGE

2 Question tags

Make sentences with question tags and read them out loud.

1. You're not sure what the American English word for 'autumn' is.
2. You think your friend likes Mangas too, but you aren't sure.
3. Your friend sneezes[1]. You aren't sure if it is because your guinea pig is in the room.
4. You can't really remember the new timetable, but you think you've got PE after break.
5. You don't remember if Jack won the barrel race.
6. It was cold this morning, but now you can see the sun. You're not sure if you need gloves.

Lösung: 1. The American English word for 'autumn' is 'fall', isn't it? 2. You like Mangas too, don't you? 3. You sneezed because my guinea pig is in the room, didn't you? 4. We have PE after break, don't we? 5. Jack won the barrel race, didn't he? 6. I don't need gloves, do I?

SPEAKING

3 Decorah and Minneapolis → WB 24/2 → Folie 3

Look at the pictures and the information about Decorah and Minneapolis. Talk to your partner and compare the two cities.

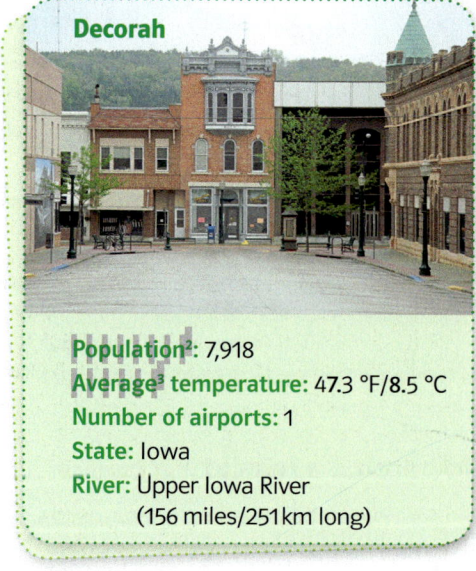

Decorah

Population[2]: 7,918
Average[3] **temperature:** 47.3 °F/8.5 °C
Number of airports: 1
State: Iowa
River: Upper Iowa River (156 miles/251 km long)

Minneapolis

Population: 413,651
Average temperature: 46.1 °F/7.9 °C
Number of airports: 3
State: Minnesota
River: Mississippi (2,320 miles/3,734 km long)

1 **to sneeze** [sniːz] niesen | 2 **population** [ˌpɒpjuˈleɪʃn] Einwohner | 3 **average** [ˈævrɪdʒ] Durchschnitts-

LANGUAGE

4 Walt Disney World → WB 24/3

Read the text about Walt Disney World in Florida. Find ten mistakes and write the correct sentences in your exercise book. Then mark the words you corrected.

Lösung: 1. the happiest place (l. 3), 2. as big as San Francisco! (l. 4), 3. many other places which/that are (l. 6), 4. the Disney stories (l. 9), 5. go inside Cinderella's castle (l. 9), 6. go there (l. 11), 7. by car (l. 11), 8. It picks you up (l. 12), 9. doesn't it (l. 13), 10. it's going to be great fun (l. 14)

Come and visit Florida's most famous place for tourists: Walt Disney World.

People say it's the most happiest place in the world. The park is huge – about as big like San Francisco! There are theme parks, water parks and many other places who are very popular. Take a ride on the crazy roller coasters, have fun in the water park, meet the animals from the Disney storys or go inside Cinderellas[1] castle and feel like a king or queen. You can go here with car or use Disney's Magical Express. It pick you up[2] at the airport and takes you to the park. This sounds great, does it? Plan your next trip and visit us – it's to be great fun.

5

10

LANGUAGE

5 Mixed bag: A flyer for the Drama Club at TTS → WB 25/4–5 → **KV 23, KV 24**

Lösung: a) 1. who/that, 2. join, 3. don't you, 4. famous/important, 5. for, 6. who/that, 7. have to/must, 8. 're going, 9. which/that/–, 10. is going, 11. fun, 12. than, 13. information, 14. who/that

b) EH: The brochure isn't a good example because it's too long, there's too much information, it's difficult to read etc.
Five ways to make the text better: think of a heading, give only the important information, add more pictures, design it more clearly, think of an interesting slogan etc.

a) *Put in the missing words. Sometimes there's more than one possible answer.*

b) *Do you think the flyer is a good example of this kind of project? Why/Why not? Find five ways to make the text better.*

TTS Drama Club

We invite all students **1** love theatre to **2** the TTS Drama Club! Our next play[3] is William Shakespeare's 'Romeo and Juliet'. You all know Shakespeare, **3** ? He is Britain's most **4** writer[4]. But this isn't just a play: This is a musical of 'R&J', so we are looking **5** LOTS of boys and girls **6** can act. But don't forget: in a musical actors[5] **7** act, sing and dance! And this isn't a historical 'R&J'! No, we **8** to show the London of TODAY! So forget about the costumes **9** they had in Shakespeare's days.
This year's play **10** to be much more **11** **12** the play last year. For more **13** ,just ask one of the teachers **14** teach Drama in Years 7 and 9.

1 **Cinderella** [ˌsɪndrˈelə] Aschenputtel | 2 **to pick up** [ˌpɪkˈʌp] abholen | 3 **play** [pleɪ] Theaterstück |
4 **writer** ['raɪtə] Schriftsteller | 5 **actor** ['æktə] Schauspieler, Darsteller

Find more online:
9g86yv

Unit 3

L2/10–11

Off to the Rockies!

| Green Moose Camp | In the Rockies | Activities | Outdoor rules |

Why come to the Rocky Mountains?

Because they're awesome! They're the longest line of mountain ranges in America – it's over 3,000 miles long (that's 4,800 km). They go from the south of the US right up to Canada in the north. And Green Moose Camp is right in the middle of them, in Colorado, the state with all 30 of the highest peaks in the Rocky Mountains!

Native Americans climbed these peaks to get their eagle feathers. Explorers came to the Rockies to look for gold and silver. It's still real wilderness here. The forests and lakes are huge, and you can hike for miles and not see anyone else all day.

The wild animals are amazing! You can see bighorn sheep every day around GMC, and with luck you can see a moose, a black bear or even a cougar. Come and explore the great outdoors! It's huge here, it's wild, it's dangerous and exciting: a real adventure.

"I love it here – I don't want to go home!"

SPEAKING

1 The Rockies are awesome! → Folie 14, KV 25

→ ▲128/1
▲→ After …

a) *Guess the meanings of these words from the context before you look them up: 'range', 'peak', 'explorer', 'wilderness', 'to hike', 'adventure'. Most of them are similar to French words.*

Voc.: Animals in the US, WB (Word bank), pp. 6–7

b) *Look at these two website pages and describe what visitors to the Rockies can see and do.*

c) *Find the Rocky Mountains on the map of the US. Note down the states they go through.*

Lösung: a) range: French ranger = *aufstellen*; *Kette, Reihe*; peak: French pic = *Gipfel*, mountain top; explorer: to explore, noun ending in -er (word family); wilderness: German *Wildnis*; to hike: hiking (word family); adventure: French aventure = *Abenteuer*

SPEAKING

2 Your turn: Find out more about the Rockies

→ S17

→ △128/2
△→ Help with …

Choose one of these topics, make notes and give a one-minute talk to the class.

the highest mountains   wild animals   winter sports

national parks, e.g. Rocky Mountain NP, Yellowstone NP or Glacier NP

In Unit 3 you learn
- words to describe outdoor activities
- the past progressive
- how to plan and write a travel report
- more ways to connect sentences,
  e.g. *while, so that*

These things can help you to write a travel report.

| Green Moose Camp | In the Rockies | Activities | Outdoor rules |

Here at GMC, there's something for everyone.
Maybe you think you know all about rafting, riding, climbing and swimming – but here it's faster, higher, bigger, and a real challenge for your team!

Would you like to sleep under the stars?
Teens can go with their group leaders on a three-day backpacking trip, follow the old Native American trails and camp outdoors under the stars. Look out for wild animals there. Feel the lonely wilderness around you. Be an explorer!

Do you want to climb one of the highest peaks?
Do some real climbing on Longs Peak. Tell your friends back home that it's nearly as high as Mount Elbert, the tallest peak in the Rockies at 14,440 feet (4,401 m) high!

Do you want to try something different?
Mountainboarding is great for everyone. Jump on your board and get started! Or try our zipline – it's wild, it's cool, it's fun!

And before you go to bed …
Don't forget the traditional evenings around the campfire. We eat together, sing silly songs and talk about our day.

"Now I have great friends from all over the US!"

LISTENING

L 2/12 ◉

→ S21–23

Voc.: Outdoor activities, p. 215

3 **What's camp like, Ryan?** → WB 26/1–2

a) *Listen and make notes.*

1. What are Emily and Ryan talking about? Explain the situation.
2. What is Ryan looking forward to? Compare Ryan's activities at camp in Iowa last year with the activities at Green Moose Camp.
3. What is Emily worried about? How does Ryan help?

b) *Would you like to do these things? Why/Why not?*

| sleep under the stars | go on a zipline |

| see wild animals | sit around a campfire |

Across cultures 🇺🇸

Every year, 14 million kids go to **summer camp** in the US. Some are special camps like science, music or sports camps like baseball, but most camps have team challenge or competition activities like swimming, climbing and hiking. Kids also get points for their team when they help at camp and tidy their log cabins. You can't take cell phones to most camps. Are there summer camps like these in Germany?

L 2/13 ◉ # The Rockies are full of surprises! → Folie 15

Emily wanted to know more about Green Moose Summer Camp, so she talked to her cousin Mike.

"Can you tell me a little more about what
5 you did there last year, Mike?" Emily asked. "Sure," he replied. "It was awesome! I'd love to go back again. But hang on – I can show you my picture, Em. I drew it as part of my report for school about summer camp."

10 "Hey, you're so good at drawing, Mike," Emily said when she saw the picture. "It's really great!"

Mike was a bit embarrassed, "Thanks, Em! It took ages to draw, but it was fun." He
15 added, "I didn't have much time to write the real report. My teacher wasn't happy …"

While Mike was talking, Emily was looking at the picture. "What was going on here?" she asked. "That's the blob – it's
20 like a huge trampoline." Mike was grinning. "Todd was sitting on one end and Maya was standing on the platform. When Maya jumped onto the blob, Todd flew into the water. The blob is one of the best things at camp!"
25

Emily pointed at something in the picture. "What's that long thing in the middle of the lake?" She sounded surprised.

Mike laughed. "That was my canoe!" he answered. "While I was turning to watch 30 Todd and Maya, the canoe turned over and I fell into the water. I got so wet! I'm under the canoe in my picture. It was difficult to climb in again."

"What were these girls looking at?" Emily 35 wanted to know. "Guess!" Mike said. Emily thought for a moment. "I don't know – maybe a bird?" Mike laughed, "No – it was a porcupine. Grace and Ava were watching Jessie on the zipline when they heard a 40 noise in the tree. When they looked up, they got a real shock. The porcupine was sitting in the tree and was watching them. The Rockies are full of surprises!"

READING **1** ## What did Mike like? → WB 27/3

Say what you think Mike liked and what he didn't like about his day on the lake. Explain why.

Lösung: EH: Mike liked the many activities on the lake, for example the huge trampoline and the zipline. You can have lots of fun there. He didn't like it when he fell into the water because it was really difficult for him to climb into the canoe again.

SPEAKING **2** **What were they doing when Mike fell into the water?** → WB 28/4 → G7

Look at the picture and say what the other children were doing when Mike fell into the water.

Start like this: Maya **was waiting** to jump onto the blob.
Grace and Ava **were** …

Do you remember how to make the progressive form of a verb?
For the past progressive, look at G7 in the Grammar.

LANGUAGE **3** **Find the rule: The simple past and the past progressive** → WB 28/5 → G7

a) *Find examples of the past progressive. How do you make the forms?*

b) *When you want to say that two things happened at the same time in the past, you can do this in three ways. Which of the rules A–C goes with which sentence? Find another example for each one in the text.*

1. When Maya jumped onto the blob, Todd flew into the water.
2. Grace and Ava were watching Jessie on the zipline when they heard a noise in the tree.
3. While Mike was talking, Emily was looking at the picture.

Lösung: b) 1B, 2A, 3C
c) 1. d) Scott and Juan were shouting while they were playing ball. **2. c)** Grace and Ava were shocked when they saw the porcupine in the tree. **3. a)** Jada took a photo while Jessie was ziplining across the lake. **4. b)** Mike was turning round when his canoe turned over.

Time ⟶

A Something happened in the middle of something else.

B Two things happened at the same time, or one thing happened directly after the other.

C Two longer actions were happening at the same time.

→ △128/3
→ ▲129/4
△ → After …
▲ → After …

c) *Look at Mike's picture again. Match the parts. What happened at the lake that afternoon?*

1. Scott and Juan were shouting		a) Jessie was ziplining across the lake.
2. Grace and Ava were shocked	**when**	b) his canoe turned over.
3. Jada took a photo	**while**	c) they saw the porcupine in the tree.
4. Mike was turning round		d) they were playing ball.

We mice were having a picnic **when** a dog **came** round the corner.
We ran into the house **while** the dog **was eating** our picnic.

SPEAKING **4** **Your turn: What were you doing?** → WB 29/6–7 → **KV 26**

Talk with your partner about what you were doing at different times, and what happened/was happening at the same time. Then write down what your partner was doing.

→ ▲129/5
▲ → After …

Example: Partner A: What were you doing this time last Saturday?
Partner B: I was playing tennis while my dad was making a cake.
Partner A writes: My partner was playing tennis while his dad was making a cake.

1. this time last Saturday
2. at eight o'clock last night
3. ten minutes ago
4. when the teacher came in

READING **5** Mike's travel report

a) *Emily wants to know more about Green Moose Camp, so Mike shows Emily his report too.
"The second half isn't very good because I spent a long time on the picture and the first part,
but then I only had ten minutes to write the rest," he says. Read Mike's report and the skills
box. Then look at the second part again (ll. 18–37) and explain what isn't so good about it.*

Lösung: a) EH:
The second part isn't
so good because . . .
– it doesn't follow a
chronological order,
– Mike doesn't describe
people's feelings,
– he doesn't make the
text exciting or even
interesting: there are
no comparative or
superlative forms of
adjectives,
– the sentences sound
the same and start in a
similar way,
– he doesn't link the
sentences with
connectives.
b) EH: In his first
paragraph Mike writes
about an exciting event
and how the people
felt and reacted. He
uses many adjectives
and connectives to link
his sentences. You can
imagine the scene very
well. The paragraph has
got a clear structure.
c) Mike didn't write
about Tuesday.

My week at summer camp by Mike Ness

It was great at GMC. Every night we sat
around the campfire and sang songs. I liked
that time best. And I loved the bear song!

My favourite day was Monday. Everyone
was more excited than normal because
we were going on a hike – to Longs Peak,
one of the highest mountains in Colorado!
It was a perfect day – the sun was shining
and it wasn't too hot. We were telling jokes
and singing while we were walking. But
suddenly the group leader said, "Shhh!" and
pointed to the other side of the canyon. A
big, golden cougar was sleeping on a rock
in the sun. Nobody moved or said anything.
When it opened its eyes, we all held our
breath. But it just got up and walked away.
Awesome!

Monday wasn't the only exciting day, of
course! Every day there was something
new. On Sunday, like most other days, we 20
had breakfast at 7:30 a.m. We always
got up at 7 a.m. Then we tidied our log
cabins. (On Saturday I got to camp.
I said goodbye to Mom and met the other
people in my group.) Our team didn't get 25
the most points, so we didn't win the prize
for tidiest cabin at the end of the week.
On Thursday we went rafting in a canyon.
We did that on Wednesday afternoon too.
On Friday night we had a talent show and 30
I sang a song. Friday was hot so we spent
the day at the lake, played on the blob and
had canoe races. The picture shows what
else we did. On Wednesday morning we
went hiking along a mountain trail and 35
saw a coyote. On Saturday we went home
again. Camp was cool.

b) *Use the skills box to
explain why Mike's first
paragraph about Monday
(lines 4–17) is good.*

c) *Find a better structure for
Mike's report. Plan one
part for each day. Which
day didn't Mike write
about? Think of an activity
for that day too.*

Writing skills

Plan your report:
– Plan the different **parts/paragraphs** of the text
in chronological order.
– Note the **main ideas** for each part:
What happened **when**?

When you write a report,
– write **what** happened,
– explain **when**, **where** and **why** it happened,
– say **who** was there,
– describe the people's **feelings**,
– use **comparative** and **superlative** forms of adjectives
to make the report exciting,
– link sentences with **connectives** (although, while,
because, so that, …),
– and try not to begin every sentence in the same way.

WRITING **6 Make Mike's report more interesting** → WB 29/8

a) *Read the second part of Mike's report. Choose three sentences from the text. Write three questions about each sentence and give them to your partner. Then think of interesting answers to your partner's questions.*

Example: On Friday evening we had a talent show and I sang a song.
Questions: What song did Mike sing? How did he **feel**? **Who** liked the song?
Answers: Mike sang the bear song. He was a bit nervous, but everybody liked it.

b) *Use the tips to write a better paragraph (6–8 sentences) for Mike about one of his days at Green Moose Camp. Use what you know about the camp! Discuss with a partner what is better than in Mike's report and why.* → **HA**

WRITING **7 Your turn: A short report about the holidays** → **KV 27, HA**

→ S11–14 *Write a report about something special that you did in the holidays. Write 6–8 sentences:*

Voc.: Wild animals, p. 216; Describing people and animals, Describing things, WB (Word bank), pp. 2–4

Example: In August my family and I went for a boat ride on a lake …

Useful phrases

When? Two months ago/In July/Last summer

Where? We went to Australia/Berlin/ a holiday camp/…

Who? My friends and I/My brother/ My dog

What? We went on a trip/We visited …/ played …/helped …

Why? We wanted to visit my grandma/ see the castle/go to the beach/…

Feelings? I felt happy/nervous/scared./ It was fun/cool …

WRITING **8 A game: What was happening when …?** → WB 30/9 → **KV 28**

a) *Work with a partner. Imagine you went to summer camp last summer. Think of something funny that happened to you when you were there. Make a grid with the questions from the useful phrases box and write a word or short phrase for each question about what happened.*

b) *Exchange grids with another pair. Write a story that includes all of the words/phrases in their grid. Then exchange your stories and tell the other pair if you like their story or not and why.*

L 2/15 ◉ **Rules for campers at Green Moose Camp** → Folie 16

| Green Moose Camp | In the Rockies | Activities | Outdoor rules |

Rules for hiking   Wear hiking boots, long pants and shirts with long sleeves so that insects can't bite you. Remember to take lots of water because it can get hot in the mountains. Always carry a bottle or two with you. Put on sunscreen before you go, but don't forget your rain jacket either! Always stay on the trail and wait for the other hikers in your group.

Pick up trash   It's uncool to throw trash into lakes and rivers or leave it somewhere on the ground! When you see trash outside the camp, pick it up and take it back to camp – you never know, maybe you can reuse some things!

Look out for wild animals   Never throw food away outside! Animals come if they smell food – so make sure that they can't find any food near the camp! Although it's unusual to see animals inside the camp area, it sometimes happens. But never touch wild animals. They often bite if they're scared!

Stay safe   You can only leave the camp in your group and when you're with a group leader. Never leave the camp alone!

Are you still unsure? Reread these rules so that you know what you need to do.

VOCABULARY
→ ▲129/6
→ S10
▲ → After ...

9 **Word building**

a) *Look at the blue words in the text.*
Use the tip box to explain what they mean.

> *un-* **+ adjective:**
> you get the opposite
> → **un**happy = sad
>
> *re-* **+ verb:**
> it means 'again'
> → **re**play = play again
>
> **verb +** *-er*:
> a person who does sth
> → sing**er** = a person who sings

b) *Find the odd ones out. Make a grid (a person who.../not a person) for these words.*

| teacher | burger | buyer | monster | answer | camper |

| under | swimmer | summer | rider | winner | colder |

Lösung: a) hikers: people who go hiking; uncool: not really cool or nice; to reuse: to use sth again; unusual: the opposite of usual; leader: a person who leads a group of people, for example; unsure: not sure about sth; to reread: to read sth again

READING
→ △130/7
△ → After ...

10 **They often bite if they are scared** → WB 31/10–11, 32/12 → G8

a) *Match the sentence parts. Use the linking words* **because, although, if** *or* **so that**.

Lösung: a)
1. d) so that,
2. c) because,
3. a) although,
4. b) if

1. Wait for the other hikers in your group
2. Pick up trash when you see it
3. Animals sometimes come into the camp
4. You're always safer

a) they don't do this very often.
b) the group leader is with you.
c) maybe you can reuse things.
d) you all stay together.

b) *Use linking words and complete these sentences.* → HA

1. I always pick up trash ...
2. I'm scared of wild animals ...
3. Our cabin isn't very tidy ...

4. We have to stay inside at night ...
5. We go swimming ...
6. I love summer camp ...

MEDIATION **11**

→ △130/8
→ △130/9
→ S20
△ → Help with ...
△ → After ...

Tips and rules for hiking in the Alps → KV 29, HA

Du machst gerade Urlaub mit deinen Eltern in Oberstdorf. Ein amerikanischer Tourist schaut sich einen Flyer an, der wichtige Informationen für Wandertouren enthält. Er versteht den Text nicht, also hilfst du ihm. Erkläre ihm die wichtigsten Regeln und Tipps auf Englisch.

Die Allgäuer Berge sind wunderschön, aber auch gefährlich. Bereiten Sie sich gut darauf vor, unterwegs zu sein. Die Bergrettung, die Alpenverbände und alle Bergführer bitten Sie, diese Tipps sorgfältig zu lesen und bei jeder Bergwanderung zu beherzigen!

1. Planung: Bedenken Sie, dass die geplante Wanderung zu den Fähigkeiten aller Wanderer in der Gruppe passen muss, besonders wenn Kinder dabei sind. Planen Sie viel Zeit ein, um locker vor Anbruch der Dunkelheit am Ziel anzukommen. Ohne den Wetterbericht zu kennen, sollte keiner loslaufen. Die Sonne mag am Anfang strahlen, das Wetter kann aber schnell umschlagen. Nehmen Sie immer Kleidung für jedes Wetter mit. Vernünftige Bergschuhe, eine Wanderkarte, ausreichend Proviant, Sonnenschutz und Wasser sind Pflicht! Ein Erste-Hilfe-Set muss auch dabei sein. Zum Schluss bitte nicht vergessen: Informieren Sie jemanden, z. B. Gastgeber, Hüttenwirte oder Ihre Familie, über Ihr Ziel und wann Sie dort ankommen wollen.

2. Wanderung: Starten Sie so früh wie möglich. Dann sind die Wege eher frei und Sie haben genügend Zeit, wichtige Pausen zu machen. Denken Sie daran: Wer vom markierten Weg abweicht, wird nicht so schnell gefunden, wenn etwas Unvorhergesehenes passiert! Bleiben Sie da, wo es sicher ist.

3. Notfälle: Ganz wichtig: Für die Alpen gilt folgendes Notfallsignal: Alle 10 Sekunden ein Signal geben. Das kann Licht, Pfeifen oder Rufen sein. Achtung: In den Bergen gibt es nicht überall Handyempfang – verlassen Sie sich also nicht auf Ihr Handy!

LISTENING **12**

L 2/17 ⊚

→ △131/10
△ → After ...

Lösung: a) Emily and her mother are in a shop. They're looking for boots and clothes which Emily needs for summer camp.

Can you help me, please?

a) *Listen and say what Emily is doing.*

b) *Make notes to answer these questions:*

1. What does Emily need?
2. What does she like?
3. What does/doesn't she get and why?
4. How much do the things cost?

> **Useful phrases**
>
> to try sth on in the fitting room | to fit perfectly | to have a look at sth | I need a size 4. | I need a bigger/smaller size.

SPEAKING **13**

👥

→ △131/11
→ S16–17
△ → Instead of ...

Voc.: Phrasal verbs, p. 218

Your turn: Buying clothes for camp → WB 32/13–14 → Diktat- und Transfertext

Read the role cards and act out your dialogue. Then swap roles.

> **Things you can buy/sell:**
> long pants | hiking boots | a rain jacket | socks | a hat | a T-shirt with long sleeves

Partner A: Buyer
You need clothes for camp and have $60. Choose two things to buy. Try things on. One thing doesn't fit, so ask for a different size. Do you like the colour? Ask the assistant for help. Check the price and buy at least one thing.

Partner B: Shop assistant
Think of prices for the clothes you sell. Help the buyer and be polite. There's one thing you haven't got in the right size. You have a special offer for one thing.

A shopping trip to London → S24–25

SPEAKING **1** ## Warm-up → Folie 17

What do you remember about London? Write down famous sights there. Then tell the class.

VIEWING **2** ## Out and about in London → KV 30

5 *Watch the film. Which part do* **you** *really like? Why?*

VIEWING **3** ## A closer look → KV 30

Watch again and answer the questions. These ideas can help.

1. Why do you think Jinsoo's sister, Mina, is with the boys?
2. Where did Jinsoo want to go? Why didn't they go there?
3. What was the problem with Mina at Camden Market?

> Jinsoo and Mina's dad
>
> adult/child ticket
>
> sightseeing/normal bus
>
> look after   expensive

VIEWING **4** ## Setting and atmosphere in film scenes → KV 31

a) *First read the skills box. Then watch scenes* **A** *(01:15 – 01:50) and* **B** *(01:57 – 02:06) again. Say why you think they're important or interesting for the film.*

b) *In Ex. 2 you named a favourite scene. Now talk about its setting and atmosphere. These words can help:*

> cool   crazy   famous   funny
>
> interesting   international   multi-ethnic
>
> lots to see/discover   people everywhere

c) *Write a short description of what Jinsoo, Marley, Nick and Mina could do in a* **different** *location in London. Look at your lists from Ex. 1 for ideas.*

> ### Film skills
>
> In a film, the viewer needs to know what the film's **setting** is, so the choice of **locations** in a film is important. A famous place like London really needs to *look* like London!
>
> **Atmosphere** is important too: crowds, places, views, water, things to look at or buy, cool shops … These things can create a special atmosphere for the viewer.

How to find information on the internet → S6, S10

1 Start with the **homepage** of a famous **attraction's** website

Most homepages give basic information and also useful links to other pages. Try to answer these questions with the help of the homepage for a visitor centre in Rocky Mountain National Park. If the answer is not on the page, which 'quick link' do you think can help?

1. Where is the visitor centre?
2. How do I get there?
3. Is it open every day?
4. Are there any special displays at the moment?
5. Must I pay to go into the visitor centre?

Lösung: 1. The visitor centre is in Green Moose Lake, Colorado (789 Long Moose Road). **2.** The answer isn't on the homepage, but you can use the quick link 'Getting here'. **3.** It's open every day (Monday through Saturday, 8 am – 8 pm; Sunday from 8 am – 6 pm), except for Christmas (December 25). **4.** There's no answer on this webpage, but you can use the quick link 'What's new'. **5.** No, you needn't pay. Entry to the visitor centre is free.

G GREEN MOOSE LAKE VISITOR CENTER

| Home | Events | Weather | Webcams | Contact us |

Location: 789 Long Moose Road, Green Moose Lake, Colorado 80537
Entry to the visitor center is free. Ranger tours from $10 per person!
Open: Monday through Saturday, 8 am – 8 pm; Sunday 8 am – 6 pm, except Dec 25. Call us at 1-800-443-7837. Call center hours: 9 am – 6 pm.

Quick links:
- Visitor center
- Maps & Info
- Getting here
- Photo gallery
- What's new
- Group information

2 Skim and scan internet texts → WB 33/15

a) *Skim the text on the right for the **gist**. What is it about? How can the information help visitors?*

b) *Now scan the text for **details** about animals. Make notes.*

Try to guess new words. Don't worry about words that aren't important.

Lösung: b) Details about animals:
– Visitors can watch wild animals like squirrels or different kinds of birds near the visitor centre.
– Visitors can also see the symbol of Rocky Mountain National Park, the bighorn sheep, which is America's largest wild sheep: it can weigh over 300 pounds and grow up to three feet tall. Entry to the visitor centre is free.

| Home | **Activities** | Weather | Webcams | Contact us |

The visitor services team is always here to help you with advice on activities, restaurants and hotels. Come here for information about wildlife and maps of all the trails in the park. You can watch wild animals near the visitor center during the day, like squirrels or different kinds of birds. The center is handicap accessible, with free wireless internet and public restrooms. Outside we have picnic areas and free parking. There are guided tours for people of all ages. If you're here with kids, don't miss our Junior Ranger Program! Look out for bighorn sheep, the symbol of Rocky Mountain National Park. North America's largest wild sheep can weigh over 300 pounds and grow up to three feet tall. Watch them climb the mountains at breathtaking speed!

3 Practise with different websites → WB 34/16

Choose a sight in the US or the UK (an idea from this unit or your own idea). Find useful or interesting information about it on the internet and tell your partner what you found out. Use an online dictionary to look up new words.

Our travel report

For your yearbook, work in groups of four and write a short travel report about a class trip. It can be a real trip – or a fantasy trip! It needn't be long, but it's important to make it interesting for your readers.

Step 1

Choose an idea for your trip

a) *What kind of class trip can your group write about? Do you want to use one of these photos? Or have you got your own great idea? Discuss different ideas and then choose **one** idea for your travel report.*

1
2
3

1. rafting | to paddle | current | to capsize
2. science fiction | aliens | planet | spaceship
3. to go sightseeing | youth hostel | party | trouble

b) *Work with a placemat to collect ideas for your report. You each think about one of the four topics below. Write down ideas in your part of the placemat.*

1. The place: How did you get there?
2. The people: Who is in the report?
3. Typical activities: What did you do or see during the first part of your trip?
4. A special adventure (e.g. problem, surprise): What happened? What did you do?

> For help with new words, look at the **Skills page** in Unit 1.
>
> For help with placemats, look at **S26** in the **Skills section**.

c) *Choose which ideas you want to use and write them down in the middle of the placemat.*

Step 2

Plan your travel report

a) *Your report has got four parts.*
Together write a plan that shows the key ideas in each part.

Part 1: The beginning: Here you describe how you got to the place.
Part 2: The first day(s): Here you describe typical activities for this kind of trip.
Part 3: The special adventure: Say what happened, but don't tell the whole story. This part of the report finishes with a problem or an exciting situation.
Part 4: The ending: Explain how the adventure finished; find a good ending.

b) *Decide who writes which part of the report.*

For help with how to write a plan, look at the skills box in **Station 1** again.

Step 3 → HA

Write your part of the travel report

The skills box in **Station 1** helps you to write your part of the travel report.

For help with simple past and past progressive, look at **Station 1** again.

Station 1 in **Unit 2** helps you with adjectives.

a) *Work with the plan from Step 2 and make notes about the information in your part. Don't write sentences – just important words and phrases.*

b) *Read through your notes. Have you got interesting ideas and words?*

c) *Now write your part of the report. Don't forget to use the simple past.*

Step 4

Improve your part of the report

Look at **S13** and **S14** in the **Skills section** for tips on how to check texts.

Work with a partner from your group. Check each other's texts. Help each other to improve the texts.

Step 5

Finish your travel report → KV 27

a) *Put the four parts together and read the whole report. Are you happy with it? If not, discuss it and improve it.*

b) *Now think of the best way to present your report. Use photos or pictures too.*

S 1/26–28
L 2/18–20 ◉

You wanted an outdoor adventure! → Folie 18

It was the last day of the summer vacation and Ryan was thinking about the most exciting thing that happened to him at camp …

5 It all happened when I was on a three-day hiking trip in the Colorado wilderness with a group from Green Moose Summer Camp. On our last night we were sitting around the campfire and talking about all 10 our outdoor adventures. Poor Jeff didn't have much to talk about because he lives in San Francisco and doesn't go to the countryside very much. I told my group about the time when I saw bear tracks in 15 the hills near Decorah when I was on a camping trip with Uncle Jim and Mike. Jeff was really interested and asked lots of questions. After some time, everyone started to yawn, so our group leader told 20 us to go to our tents.

When I was getting ready to go to bed, Jeff whispered, "Hey, Ryan, why don't we go for a walk down the trail? Let's go and have some fun!" I knew it was against the 25 rules, but I thought it was kind of cool. And I didn't want to let Jeff, the city kid, go out alone and then get into trouble in the wilderness. So I grabbed my flashlight and we went outside.

Although the moon was shining, it was 30 still pretty dark outside. We tiptoed past the other tents and went towards the trail through the trees. It got darker and darker as we walked along the trail and then the moon went behind a cloud. Everything 35 went black – even our flashlights didn't help much. After that we started to hear all kinds of sounds – like things or animals that were moving in the trees. Jeff was nervous and started to look around. "Let's 40 go back," he said. I pretended to be brave and said, "Come on, Jeff – you wanted an outdoor adventure. Now you're having one! Welcome to the great outdoors!"

Suddenly we heard a different kind of 45 noise. A loud noise. And *scary*.

Something was grunting. Jeff's eyes opened really wide and he grabbed my arm, "What was that?" "Shh!" I put my finger in front of my mouth. Jeff looked 50 around. He was very nervous, and I was feeling scared too. But one of us had to stay calm and think! Then we heard it again. But this time it sounded much nearer. "It's coming from over there!" I said and 55 pointed to the lake.

Stop and think:
How does the story go on?
What are your ideas?

These are two possible endings to Ryan's story:

A And then we saw it. Something huge and black was splashing through the water. "It's a bear. RUN!" shouted Jeff. He started to
60 run backwards when the black bear looked up. It looked right at us.

Jeff didn't know that it's wrong to run away from a bear, but of course I knew what to do. I grabbed Jeff's arm. "Stand
65 still!" I said. "Remember the rules: Don't run! Bears attack people who run. Start to shout and clap your hands." Jeff didn't do anything – he was standing as still as a statue. So we were lucky that I stayed cool
70 and shouted and clapped for both of us!

Then two things happened at the same time. The moon came back out, so we could see much better, and the bear lifted its head. Only it wasn't a bear, because
75 bears don't have antlers[1]! It stared at us. "What is it?" Jeff asked. His face was all white. I was almost laughing. "Don't worry! It's a moose!" I said. "But when it starts to come nearer, then we need to run away.
80 Moose are only dangerous if you get too close to them." But nothing happened. The moose drank some water from the lake and then it just walked back into the trees.

Jeff and I ran back along the trail. We
85 didn't stop until we could see the tents again. "Hey, it's a good thing I was with you, isn't it, city kid?" I said. "But your idea was great and it was an awesome adventure, Jeff!"
90 Jeff's face was still white, but he started to smile. "Yeah Ryan, thanks for everything. But I'm not going to say it was just a moose and I was so scared! Let's tell everyone it was really a bear."

B There was something huge and black in 95 the water. It was standing very still and was watching us. It didn't make any more sounds. We stood very still too, and waited for a long, long time.

Suddenly the moon came out from 100 behind the cloud and we saw what it was. It wasn't an animal at all – it was a big stone at the side of the lake. No wonder it wasn't moving! Jeff looked at me and then we both started to laugh. How silly! 105

But suddenly we heard the grunting again – on our left. We stopped laughing and looked at each other – we didn't know what to do. We turned slowly and saw a huge black bear which was standing on the 110 trail behind us. And it was staring directly at us.

Jeff was really scared. "What now?" he whispered. "Don't run!" I said. "Start to shout and clap your hands. We have 115 to make it go away!" Although I was really scared too, I added, "Remember, bears don't usually like people." Jeff and I shouted and clapped our hands like crazy, and we were watching the bear all 120 the time. At last, the bear ran away. Soon we couldn't see it anymore – we were safe!

I grabbed Jeff's arm and we turned and went back along the trail. We were very careful and often looked back towards 125 the trees, but the bear didn't come back. Soon we could see the tents again and Jeff stopped. He looked at me and said, "I don't want to have any more adventures like that! That was terrible." "Yeah, it was a bit 130 scary, wasn't it?" I said. "But hey – we saw a real bear!"

1 antlers [ˈæntləz] Geweih

READING **1** **Questions about Ryan's adventure** → WB 34/17

→ ▲131/12
→ S6–8
▲ → After …

a) *You want to sum up Ryan's story. With your partner, choose one ending. Think of five or six questions about the whole story whose answers sum up its main ideas. Write down your questions and answers.*

b) *Compare your questions and answers with another pair. Whose answers sum up the story better?*

c) *Which of the two endings do you like best? Say why. The phrases can help you.*

> **Useful phrases**
>
> Ending A/B is better because … | It's more realistic/more fun/ more exciting/more interesting than … | It isn't so … | I like Ryan/ Jeff in A/B because …

Ryan

READING **2** **Is Ryan a hero?** → KV 32

a) *Make a freeze frame to show Ryan's typical character in each ending. Partner A shows Ryan in ending A, and Partner B shows Ryan in ending B.*

b) *Look at ending A. Which sentences show that Ryan thinks that he's a hero? Note the line numbers.*

→ ▲131/13
▲ → After …

c) *Here is a diagram for the exciting points in ending B. Say what happens at points 1–5.*

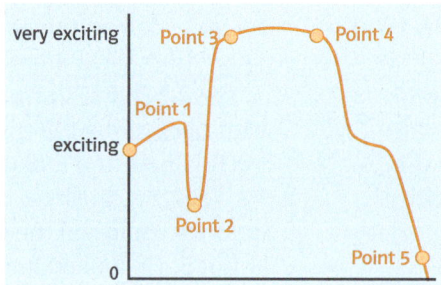

Example:
Point 1: Ryan and Jeff hear noises and see something big and black in the water.

Point 2: …

WRITING **3** **Back at camp** → WB 34/18 → **Diktat- und Transfertext**

Choose one of these tasks.

a) *Write what happened when they got back to camp. Did they tell the group leader about their adventure? Did they tell the other boys?*
Or:

b) *What happened when they got back to camp? What did the group leader say? Work in groups and write a short scene. Act it out.*

> **Can you . . .**
>
> 1. say what was happening in the past?
> They were eating … when a cat jumped …
> He was laughing … while he was walking …
> 2. link ideas?
> I went swimming although/because/so that …
> If it rains, the mountains are dangerous.

LANGUAGE

1 Simple past or past progressive? → HA

Talk about Sunny's day.

Example: Sunny was sleeping when Ryan and Emily got home from camp.

1. sleep | when | Ryan and Emily | get home from camp
2. jump up | when | Emily | walk through the door
3. wait in the kitchen | while | the children | put their things away
4. stand next to the door | when | Emily | come down to the kitchen
5. get excited | when | Emily | take the ball out of the cupboard
6. watch Emily | while | family | have dinner

LANGUAGE

2 What Madison did at summer camp → KV 33, HA

Use linking words to make this text better. Write it in your exercise book.

Madison's summer camp was perfect for her. They had great activities for people in wheelchairs. Madison called Emily. She could tell Emily all about camp. They went riding there every day. Most people at camp were in wheelchairs. They had special teachers. They taught them how to ride the horses. Madison liked the last night best. They had a party with fireworks.

Madison

LANGUAGE

3 Mixed bag: What Emily did at camp → WB 35/19–20 → KV 34, HA

Complete the dialogue with words or phrases.

Mike: So how was the great ⬛1 ?
Emily: It was awesome! I met a really fun
girl – Sia. We were in the same team
and slept in the same log ⬛2 .
Our team won a lot of swimming
races ⬛3 Sia is a really good ⬛4 .
Mike: Sounds good! Did you see any ⬛5
animals?
Emily: Sure! One day we saw a ⬛6 when we
were near the lake. It had really big
antlers! We didn't see a bear, but the
group ⬛7 showed us some cougar ⬛8
near the camp.

Mike: Were you scared?
Emily: No, I really wanted to see one ⬛9
I could tell Ryan all about it. It's so
⬛10 – you saw one and we didn't!
Mike: What else did you do?
Emily: I went ⬛11 boarding – it's so cool ⬛12
you go really fast! We also spent a lot
of time at the lake ⬛13 the water was
really cold! The last evening we had a
⬛14 – Sia and I sang a silly song. It was
so much fun – I hope I can go to ⬛15
again next year!

Find more online:
bh2v4p

Living together

SPEAKING **1** **Warm-up: Different abilities**

Voc.: What I'm good/
bad at, p. 220

a) *Write down in green, on one piece of paper, one thing you're really good at. On another, write down in red what you can't do very well. (Look in the box on p. 220 for help.) Fold the pieces of paper, put them in a box and mix them. In class, take all the statements from the box and put them into groups. Talk about them. What advice can you think of for people's red statements?*

b) *Talk about what it feels like when you know that there are other people who are bad at the same things as you or bad at other things. Explain why.*

SPEAKING **2** **People with or without disabilities, or just people?** → **Folie 19, KV 35**

→ S26

a) *Talk about the people in the pictures. What can/can't they do?*
Some of them have physical or intellectual disabilities.

A teacher and a student are communicating in sign language

A group of American friends at the bowling alley

A happy family with two kids (The boy goes to a special school because he learns more slowly than his sister.)

Young people with guide dogs at a golf event in California

b) *The idea of inclusion at school is that it helps to teach children with and without disabilities together at the same schools. In the US inclusive schooling started in the 1970s, in the UK in the 1990s. The German school system is changing now because Germany signed the Convention on the Rights of Persons with Disabilities (CRPD) in 2009. Are there inclusive classes or activities at your school? What can help to make inclusion a success?*

MEDIATION

3 Sports for everyone → KV 36

→ S20

Dein britischer Gastschüler, der sich sehr für Sport interessiert, versteht diesen deutschen Artikel nicht ganz. Er bittet dich, ihm einige Punkte zu erklären:

the reason why this article is in the paper | cactus shoes | the Special Olympics organisation | examples of sports in Special Olympics competitions

Lösung: EH:
- Tim Kollberg was faster than taller runners and was first in the race. Together with another three members of his team he won another race too. He is only twelve years old and has got Down's syndrome.
- Tim calls the shoes he wears in the competition "cactus shoes" because they have got little sticks that look like those of a cactus.
- In the Special Olympics people with an intellectual disability or with more than one disability take part.
- There are 18 different sports, like golf, horseback riding, track and field, soccer, swimming and bowling.

Der Junge mit den Kaktusschuhen

Tim Kollberg hatte sich die faustdicke Überraschung für den letzten Tag der deutschen Ausgabe der Special Olympics aufgehoben. Der zwölf Jahre alte Fellbacher lief am Freitag mit seinen Kaktusschuhen, wie Tim seine Spikes nennt, im 75-Meter-Sprintfinale seinen ihn an Körpergröße weit überragenden Konkurrenten davon. Es ist nicht die einzige Goldmedaille, die der Junge mit Down-Syndrom aus Hannover mitgebracht hat. Mit Reka Schatz, Timo Stockhause und Jakob Sproll siegte Tim Kollberg im 4x100-Meter-Staffel-Wettbewerb. Der Erfolg im Hopp-Lauf, wie Tim sagt, weil „hopp" das Kommando für die Stabübergabe ist, die in Hannover perfekt klappte, war unerwartet, und zudem hat Tim mit 2,18 Metern Platz sechs im Weitsprung belegt.

Special Olympics heißt die weltweit größte Sportbewegung für Menschen mit geistiger oder mehrfacher Behinderung, anders als die Paralympics, an denen Menschen mit Körperbehinderung teilnehmen. Die Special Olympics sind vom Internationalen Olympischen Komitee anerkannt und dürfen als einzige Organisation den Ausdruck „Olympics" weltweit nutzen. Mit Special Olympics soll die Akzeptanz von Menschen mit geistiger Behinderung in der Gesellschaft verbessert werden. Die Special-Olympics-Bewegung wurde 1968 von Eunice Shriver gegründet, deren ältere Schwester Rosemary Kennedy behindert war. Bei der diesjährigen deutschen Auflage in Hannover gingen rund 4.800 Sportler aus ganz Deutschland in 18 Disziplinen – darunter außer Leichtathletik auch Golf, Reiten, Fußball, Schwimmen oder Bowling – an den Start.

LISTENING

4 Special needs → WB 36/1–2 → KV 37

a) *Write about what can be useful for these five people. Use your own ideas too.*

1. Gwen from Greenwich: partially sighted
2. Leo from Washington: deaf
3. Madison from Minneapolis: can't walk
4. Jack from Decorah: can't concentrate
5. Lisa from New York: slow learner

wheelchair | hearing aid | special computer | special teacher | stand up and walk for a while | use/learn sign language | read out loud | wear special glasses

L2/21

b) *Gwen is a new girl at TTS. Listen to her conversation with Holly and Olivia. Explain why Gwen needs their help. What else do we learn about her? What activities are there at TTS for students with special needs?*

Find more online:
q3y5iy

Unit 4

Sport is good for you!

A   Camel racing

B   Marathon

C   BMX

D   Rugby

LISTENING

1 **On the radio** → **KV 38**

L 2/22

→ S21–23

Gwen is preparing for the TTS sports and health project week. She's listening to sports programmes on the radio. Which sports? Three of them are in the photos. Which ones?

Lösung: Sports: marathon (running), tennis, football, wheelchair basketball, rugby. Sports in the photos: running (marathon) (B), rugby (D), wheelchair basketball (E)

SPEAKING

2 **Talk about sports** → **Folie 20**

→ S4
→ ▲132/1
▲→ After …

Use the word cloud from Ex. 1 to describe the sports in the photos. Where and why are these sports popular?

Vocabulary skills

You can use **word clouds** to show how often a word is in a text. The more often a word is in the text, the bigger it is. You can make word clouds on your computer.

In Unit 4 you learn
- words for sports
- words for health and accidents
- the language of news reports
- the present perfect

These things can help you to talk or write about sports, experiences in the past, and things which have just happened and are still important now.

E Wheelchair basketball

LISTENING **3** TTS sport and health projects

L 2/23

Lösung a) Gwen: skiing. She likes winter sports. Olivia: rugby. She likes team sports. Other sports: football, netball, swimming, running, cycling, skating.

a) *Olivia is talking to Gwen. Say which sports they're going to use for their projects and why. Which other sports do they talk about?*

b) *Why is sport good for your health?*

Across cultures

The **number one sport** in Britain is football, rugby is number two. Other popular team sports in Britain are cricket and hockey. What about Germany?

VOCABULARY **4** Sports words → WB 37/1–2 → **KV 39**

→ S17, S5

Voc.: Sports, p. 222

Make a grid with words and phrases for the sports you're interested in and give a two-minute talk. Be careful: In English there are a lot of special words for each sport, e.g. 'Feld' or 'Schläger'. Look up the different translations in a dictionary. Use these four headings:

Sport | Place | Equipment | Team/Individual sport

Use a dictionary.

L 2/24

Have you ever run in a marathon?

Jay

Holly

Luke

Gwen

Dave

Olivia

"Have you ever seen the London Marathon?" Gwen asked.

"Of course we have!" Holly said. "It starts right here in Greenwich Park."

5 "I want to run in it," Luke said. "But I've checked: You can't until you're 18."

"But haven't you heard of the *mini* marathon?" Gwen asked.

"No, I haven't," Jay said. "What's that?"

10 "It's for 11- to 17-year-olds," Gwen explained. "It's just the last part of the race, and it's before the *real* marathon."

"Are you going to run in it?" Olivia asked Gwen. "I know you like running."

"It isn't that easy," Gwen said. "There are 15 teams for different parts of London, and there are trials to find the fastest runners."

"Where are the trials?" Dave asked.

"For the Greenwich team, here in the park, next Saturday," Gwen said. 20

"Let's do it!" Olivia said. "Who's in?"

"Me," said Gwen. "It was my idea, remember?"

"I'm in too!" Luke said.

Nobody said a word. Then Jay said, "No 25 thanks, I'm out. I've never enjoyed running much. It isn't cool. And Dave has never run in a race. Right, Dave?"

"I've run in races before, but not in a big one like that," Dave said. 30

Holly said, "I've only ever run in short races too, and I'm not very good at running. But I've got an idea: Why don't you run for charity? People often do charity runs to raise money." 35

"That's great," Olivia said. "We can ask our parents, teachers and friends to give money. So it's Gwen, Luke and me."

"Er … just one thing," Gwen said. "Can we run together? You know, my eyes …" 40

"Of course," Olivia said.

"Yeah," Luke said, "we'll be Team Thomas Tallis! The fastest, coolest team in Greenwich. No, in *London*! Look out, here we come!" 45

READING **1** Are you going to run in it?

a) *Would you like* to run in a marathon? Why/Why not?

b) *Answer these questions:*

1. Say who likes/doesn't like running.
2. What's Holly's idea?
3. Who isn't going to run in the trials for the mini marathon?

Across cultures

The **London Marathon** is one of the world's biggest races, with over 35,000 runners. It starts in Greenwich Park and finishes at Buckingham Palace. Have you ever watched a marathon? What running events are there in your area?

LANGUAGE

2 Find the rule → WB 38/3–4 → G9 → Folie 21

Lösung: a) Irregular verbs: see, seen; hear, heard; run, run; Regular verbs (infinitive + ed): check, checked; enjoy, enjoyed.
c) Questions (question word +) have/has + subject (+ adverb) + past participle + rest of the sentence. Answers: Yes, subject + have/has. No, subject + haven't/hasn't.

a) *There are examples of a new tense in the text, the present perfect. Look at these sentences and the verb forms in the box. What is different between verbs like* **see** *and verbs like* **check**?

I have run in a race before.
Have you ever watched a marathon?

Infinitive –	Past participle
see	– **seen**
check	– **checked**
hear	– **heard**
enjoy	– **enjoyed**
run	– **run**

There's a list of irregular verbs on page 295.

b) *Now make two sentences like this about Dave.*

He … … . | … he ever … ?

c) *Write down how you make and answer questions in the present perfect.*

LANGUAGE

3 Say who has done what → G9 → HA

Lösung:
1. Have … been;
2. haven't, has been;
3. Have … heard;
4. have, 've/have watched;
5. Have … run;
6. haven't, has played;
7. Has … prepared, has;
8. Has … given, hasn't

… you ever **1** (be) to London? – No, I …, but my sister **2** (be) there.
… you **3** (hear) of the London Marathon? – Yes, I …, I **4** (watch) it three times.
… your parents ever **5** (run) in a marathon? – No, they …, but my dad **6** (play) in an international tennis match.
… your little brother ever **7** (prepare) a meal? – Yes, he … He always helps in the kitchen.
… your grandma ever **8** (give) you extra pocket money? – No, she …

SPEAKING

4 Your turn: Find somebody who … → WB 39/5–6, 40/7

→ S27

a) *Write at least three questions for your classmates with* **Have you ever …?** *The words on the right can help.*

Voc.: For, p. 223

Examples:
Have you ever seen …?
Have you ever been to …?
Have you ever eaten …?

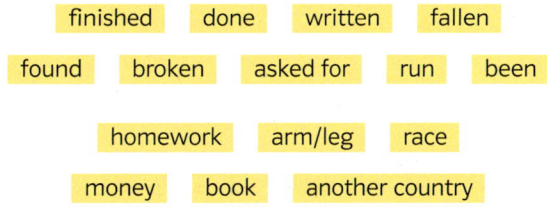

finished	done	written	fallen
found	broken	asked for	run	been

homework	arm/leg	race
money	book	another country

b) *Ask some of your classmates the questions you wrote.*

c) *Write down what you've found out and tell the class.*

Example: Nicolas and Maria have been to Austria, but Tom and Lara haven't.

Have you ever been to Austria?

No, I haven't.

L 2/27 ◉

Have you been to the doctor's yet? → KV 40

Gwen

Olivia

Gwen: Hi Olivia. Are you still at home?

Olivia: Hi Gwen. Yes, I'm at home. I haven't left for school yet.

Gwen: Good. I've just had an idea. Let's train for the marathon trials. Do you want to go for a run in the park after school today?

5

Olivia: Great idea, but I've hurt my foot! I think I've twisted my ankle.

Gwen: Oh no! Have you been to the doctor's yet?
10

Olivia: No, I haven't. I hope it isn't serious. But it hurts when I walk, and I can't run on Saturday with pain like this.

Gwen: But you've already prepared for the trials!
15

Olivia: I know, it's so unfair! I've done everything I can! I've bought new running shoes, I've stopped eating chocolate, I've found information on the internet about the *best* way to run, I've –
20

Gwen: Listen, don't worry. I can train with Luke today, and maybe you can join us tomorrow.
25

Olivia: OK. Have you already asked Luke?

Gwen: No, not yet. I can ask him at school today. See you there.

Olivia: Yeah, see you later. Bye!

READING **5** Questions on the text

1. Why does Gwen call Olivia?
2. What's Olivia's problem?
3. What has Olivia done to prepare for the marathon trials?

Lösung: 1. Gwen calls Olivia because she wants to train with her for the marathon trials. 2. Olivia's problem is her foot. It hurts when she walks. 3. Olivia has done a lot: She's bought new running shoes, she's stopped eating chocolate, and she's found information on the internet about the best way to run.

LANGUAGE **6** The checklist → G9

👥

→ △ 132/2

△ → After ...

Ask and answer questions about what the friends have done or haven't done.

Example: Has Gwen **called** Olivia **yet?** – Yes, she **has.**

Lösung: 2. Has Holly made a poster for the charity run yet? – No, she hasn't. 3. Has Luke run three miles yet? – Yes, he has. 4. Has Olivia read a book about running yet? – Yes, she has. 5. Has Jay written a chant to cheer the runners yet? – No, he hasn't. Etc.

Things to do	Who?	Done?
1. call Olivia	Gwen	✔
2. make a poster for the charity run	Holly	✘
3. run three miles	Luke	✔
4. read a book about running	Olivia	✔
5. write a chant to cheer the runners	Jay	✘
6. find a good place to watch the marathon	Dave	✘
7. tell their parents about the marathon	Gwen, Luke, Olivia	✔

LANGUAGE **7** **What has just happened?** → G9 → **Folie 22, KV 41**

→ △ 132/3
△ → After …

Example: Mrs Elliot has just cleaned the windows.

Lösung: 2. Mr Azad has just finished preparing dinner. **3.** Luke has just come back from a walk with Sherlock. **4.** Jamie has just fallen off his bike. **5.** Amber has just bought a new dress. **6.** Olivia has just tidied her desk. **7.** Shahid has just written a text message. **8.** Lucy has just gone to bed.

Mrs Elliot – clean ✓

Mr Azad – finish

Luke – come back

Jamie – fall off

Amber – buy

Olivia – tidy

Shahid – write

Lucy – go to

VOCABULARY **8** **At the doctor's** → WB 40/8–9, 41/10-11 → **Diktat- und Tranfertext**

→ S10

Voc.: Health, p. 224

Read Olivia's dialogue. Make and act out your own dialogues with the ideas in the box.

Doctor: Hello Olivia!
Olivia: Hello Doctor Barnett.
Doctor: So, what's the problem today?
Olivia: I've had an accident and hurt my
5   foot.
Doctor: Can you walk on it?
Olivia: No, I can't.
Doctor: Let me have a look. – Oh yes, you've twisted your ankle.
10 Olivia: Is it serious, Doctor?
Doctor: No, it isn't. But you need to stay in bed for a day and then walk very slowly for a couple of days.
Olivia: Oh no, so I can't run in the
15   marathon trials on Saturday …
Doctor: No, you really shouldn't.

> **Useful phrases**
>
> I've hurt my hand/foot/arm/head/ shoulder. | I've got a headache/ backache/stomachache. | I feel bad/ sick and I can't … | I've got a cold/a cough/a fever. | You need to … | You shouldn't … | You can take pills /…

Olivia: Can I go to school again after a day at home?
Doctor: Yes, you can go to school then, but maybe someone can take you to   20 school in the car.
Olivia: Yes, my mum can take me in her car.
Doctor: That's good. Here's a prescription for an ointment. You can put it on your ankle to stop the pain.   25
Olivia: Great, thank you.
Doctor: Look after your foot, Olivia, and get well soon!
Olivia: Oh thank you, Doctor Barnett. Bye!

L3/1 ⊙ **An interview with Ayla**

Dave and Holly have interviewed Ayla
Bayram, a Year 12 student at TTS and the
school's best runner.

Ayla

Dave: Hi Ayla. How are you?
5 Ayla: I'm fine, thanks.
Holly: Thanks for your time.
Ayla: No problem!
Dave: Er, you had the fastest time in the
   mini marathon last year. But have
10   you ever run in a *real* marathon?
Ayla: I've never run in a real marathon, no.
   But two months ago I ran in a half
   marathon. It was great!
Holly: Are you going to run in this year's
15   mini marathon?
Ayla: I haven't decided yet. But I'm still 17
   this year, so maybe I should run! –
   Are *you* going to run?
Holly: Us? Er, no, we aren't. But our friends
20   Luke and Gwen are! Do you have any
   tips for them?
Ayla: Yes: Always wear *real* running shoes
   – but never *new* shoes.
Holly: Is there anything else?
25 Ayla: Oh, and don't run too fast too early;
   you don't want a cramp!
Dave: Have you ever won any awards?

Ayla: Yes, I have. I won the 'Best Maths
   Student' award two years ago. But
   no sports awards – sorry!   30
Holly: Have you ever had an accident?
Ayla: Oh, I've had *lots* of accidents! Two
   years ago I had one at the mini
   marathon: I fell and broke my arm!
Dave: Can you describe how you felt?   35
Ayla: Well, it was strange: While I was
   running, I felt fine, but *after* the race
   it really, really hurt.
Dave: Oh, I've never broken anything.
Holly: I have! I fell off a chair and broke my 40
   arm when I was a little girl.
Ayla: So you know what it's like. Ouch!

READING   **9** **Match the parts**

Lösung: 1. c), 2. d), 3. e),
4. b), 5. f), 6. a)

1. Ayla has never run
2. She finished
3. Ayla broke her arm
4. Holly broke her arm
5. Ayla ran
6. Dave has been

a) lucky; he hasn't broken anything yet!
b) when she was just a little girl.
c) in a real marathon before.
d) with the fastest time last year.
e) when she fell two years ago.
f) in a half marathon two months ago.

LANGUAGE   **10** **Signal words** → G9–10

Find these signal words in the text.
Which tenses do they go with?

when I was …   last …   never

ever   after   yet   ago

Lösung: signal words with the present perfect: never, yet, ever (already, just, before); **signal words with the**
simple past: last year, two months / years ago, after the race, when I was a little girl (yesterday, in 1997)

LANGUAGE **11**   **Questions and answers** → WB 42/12 → G9–10 → **KV 42, HA**

→ △ 133/4
→ ▲ 133/5
△ → Help with …
▲ → After …

Make questions and answers like the examples. Use the present perfect and simple past.

Examples: **Have** you ever **been** to England? – Yes, I have. I **was** in London last …
Have you ever **seen** a ghost? – No, but I **saw** a strange light when I …

LANGUAGE **12**   **Simple past or present perfect?** → WB 42/13, 43/14 → G9–10 → **KV 43, HA**

→ △ 134/6
→ ▲ 134/7
△ → After …
▲ → After …

Lösung: 1. 've/have never seen, 2. saw, 3. was, 4. felt, 5. went, 6. has never happened, 7. said, 8. got, 9. told, 10. 've/have never given, 11. was, 12. lost, 13. pulled, 14. 've/have seen, 15. ran

Luke wrote his cousin Jan in Cracow an e-mail about a funny basketball game.
Put the verbs in the simple past or the present perfect. First look for signal words.

… I **1** (never see) a basketball game like the one I **2** (see) yesterday. It **3** (be) so embarrassing! First, one reporter suddenly **4** (feel) sick in front of the camera and **5** (go) to find the toilet! "Er, er, we're so sorry: This **6** (never happen) before!" the other reporter **7** (say). After that it **8** (get) worse. Before the game the star player **9** (tell) a reporter: "I **10** (never give) the crowd a bad show, so I think I can give them a good show in this game too!" He **11** (be) right: Ten minutes later, he **12** (lose) his shorts when a player from the other team **13** (pull) at them! And then, just when I thought, "I **14** (see) too many embarrassing things today," a strange man **15** (run) onto the court with no clothes on!

MEDIATION **13**   **An interview with James Lockhart** → WB 43/15–16, 44/17 → **HA**

→ S20

*An deiner Schule findet die Aktion „Fit und gesund"
statt. Hierfür möchtest du einen kurzen Artikel für die
Schülerzeitung schreiben, der folgende Fragen beantwortet:
„Wie wird man fit und gesund? Welche Rolle spielt die
Ernährung dabei? Wie behält man die Motivation?" Du bist
auf einen Auszug aus einem Interview mit dem ehemaligen
Rugbyspieler James Lockhart gestoßen, den du für deinen
Artikel nutzen möchtest. Denke an eine passende Überschrift.*

James, what has been the best moment in your career?
Well, there have been so many highlights, it's impossible to name just one.

What is your advice to people who want to get fit and healthy?
The most important thing is that YOU must want to get fit and improve your health. Always remember that you are only doing it for yourself. When you have made that decision, start with small goals.

How important is food to your fitness?
Food is as important as regular training. It helps you to get fit and also to stay fit. When I was a professional athlete, I had a strict nutrition programme. During a normal training day I usually had eggs and toast for breakfast and a protein drink with milk and banana in the mid-morning. For lunch and dinner I had pasta with vegetables and chicken. I didn't usually eat after 7 pm.

Have you got any tips on how to stay motivated?
Experience has taught me that you can only be motivated if you know why you are doing something. Sometimes it helps to write down your goal and your motivation. It is also a good idea to have a training partner …

A picnic in the park → S24–25

VIEWING

1 Understanding the first part of the story → KV 44

6 *Watch (00:00–03:55). Then match the sentences/the sentence parts below.*

1. Marley's ankle hurts.
2. Laura is going to stay with her grandad in Kent
3. Marley wants to watch the football match,
4. Marley thinks it's unfair
5. Jinsoo's mum has made 'kimbap'[1].
6. At first, Jinsoo doesn't like the idea

a) but his dad needs his help in the attic.
b) that everyone is going to watch football and he can't.
c) that Alicia is going to come to Kent too.
d) It's typical Korean snack food.
e) and invites her friends to visit her.
f) He thinks he has twisted it.

SPEAKING

2 How's your ankle? → KV 44

a) *Watch the rest of the film. What does Marley do? The phrases can help you.*

b) *What does Marley's father say at the end? Do you think he's right? Say why/why not. Think about it from Marley's point of view and from Mr Thompson's too. Look at the box again.*

> **Useful phrases**
>
> to fake an injury/a headache/…
> to teach somebody a lesson
> It's fair/unfair because …
> I think/don't think his father is right …
> Marley deserves it/doesn't deserve it …

c) *Your turn: Have you ever faked anything? Did you get away with it? Tell the class.*

VOCABULARY

3 The picnic → KV 45

a) *The friends are having different food for their picnic. Look at the photo and the food words and say what looks good.*

b) *Your turn: In class, talk about **your** 'perfect picnic'. What food from your country/your area/other countries could you have?*

kimbap   sandwiches (egg & cress[2]/cheese & tomato)

Scotch eggs[3]   quiche[4]   pasta salad[5] with tuna[6]

---

1 **kimbap** ['kɪmbæp] *koreanischer Snack aus Seegras, Reis, Rindfleisch, Käse und Ei* | 2 **cress** [krɛs] *Kresse* | 3 **Scotch egg** [skɒtʃˌ'eg] *hart gekochtes Ei in Wurstbrät* | 4 **quiche** [kiːʃ] *Quiche* | 5 **pasta salad** [ˌpæstə 'sæləd] *Nudelsalat* | 6 **tuna** ['tjuːnə] *Thunfisch*

How to understand news reports and take notes → S21–23

For the Unit task, you need to know what the parts of a radio report are and what language is typical for a radio report. This page can help you.

1 A mountain rescue

L 3/3 ◉

Lösung: Time: earlier this morning. Place: nearby Scafell Pike, area of the Lake District National Park. People: group of teenage hikers from Bristol; Sharon (girl with broken leg); Danny Sampson, friend of Sharon; mountain rescue people; Annie Price, rescue service; Sean Abbott, reporter; Sandy, newsreader. Event: teenage hikers walking along mountain path; path fell away under the feet of 17-year-old girl; fell 50 metres, broke leg; friends called mountain rescue service; hospital.

Scafell Pike, Lake District, UK

> **Useful phrases**
>
> to get hurt | to have an injury | to take sb to hospital in a helicopter | to get in close enough

Listen to a radio report and take notes in a grid with these headings:
time | place | people | event. *Then use your notes to answer the questions:*

1. What was the accident?
2. Why did it happen?
3. What did the mountain rescue team do?
4. Why was the rescue difficult?
5. How serious was the accident?
6. How is the way the news presenter and the reporter speak different to the way the witnesses speak?

2 The language of a radio report → WB 45/18–19 → KV 46, KV 47

Read the boxes. Then listen to the report again. Note down which phrases from the bigger box you can hear in the report.

*Also, note down **other** interesting or typical phrases for the news presenter, the reporter, the witness. Why do you think they are typical?*

Lösung: News presenter at radio station: Good morning, everyone (to all our listeners)./We've just received news of …/Now we're going to hear from our reporter at the scene: Can you describe the … Reporter at the scene: What where you doing when …?/What else can you tell us? Eyewitness: I couldn't believe my eyes!/ This is (It's) strange.

> **Vocabulary skills**
>
> The situations are different, but the **language** of radio reports is often the same:
>
> – **News presenters** and **reporters** stay more formal and use a language of facts.
> – An **eyewitness** has just seen something dramatic, strange or maybe scary; the language he/she uses often shows more feelings.

> **Useful phrases**
>
> **News presenter at radio station:**
> Hello/Good morning to all our listeners out there. | We've just received news of … | Now we're going to hear from our reporter at the scene: Can you describe the …/Can you tell us about the … | Stay with us for more …
>
> **Reporter at the scene:**
> What were you doing when …? | Where were you when …? | What have you seen? | Has anyone else …? | What else can you tell us?
>
> **Eyewitness at the scene:**
> I couldn't believe my eyes! | This is strange/dramatic/exciting/…: I've never seen anything like it! | I didn't know what was happening. | I was watching TV when suddenly I heard/saw …

The aliens have landed! → Folie 23

Imagine that aliens have landed on Earth – in Greenwich Park! In this Unit task, you and your group write your own radio report about this strange event. For the report, there are five roles: **three witnesses**; a **reporter** who interviews the witnesses; the **radio news presenter**. Your job is to write – and record – a fun report. Your report should be 3–4 minutes long. Be as creative as possible!

News presenter at radio station

Assistant at sweet shop

Greenwich man in garden

Doctor at hospital

Reporter in Greenwich Park

Step 1

The situation

In groups of five, look at the scenes above. Talk about what you think is happening/ has happened in each scene. Take a close look at the words in the box. You need them to talk about the pictures.

Martian[1] | Mars | space | spaceship | UFO | light | sky | star | customer[2] | stomachache | human[3] | to land | to invade[4] | to come in peace[5] | to make friends | to get sick on (too much) chocolate[6] | strange-looking[7] | bright[8] | friendly

Examples:

A: In this scene, you can see that the aliens have landed.

B: What's happening at the hospital? Have the aliens eaten too much chocolate?

C: Look at the park scene: Do you think the aliens want to make friends?

---

1 **Martian** ['mɑːʃn] Marsmensch | 2 **customer** ['kʌstəmə] Kunde/Kundin | 3 **human** ['hjuːmən] Mensch | 4 **to invade** [ɪn'veɪd] eindringen | 5 **in peace** [ɪn 'piːs] in Frieden | 6 **to get sick on sth** [get 'sɪk ɒn] sich an etw. den Magen verderben | 7 **strange-looking** ['streɪndʒ ˌlʊkɪŋ] seltsam aussehend | 8 **bright** [braɪt] hell

Step 2

Choose roles and form expert groups

a) *In your group, each of you chooses one of the five roles.*

b) *Form expert groups with all the students who have **the same role as you**. In your new group, talk about what kind of things **your character** should/ could say in a radio report. Make notes – and be creative!*

Examples:

A: *(doctor group)* As a doctor, I want to tell the reporter how the aliens are feeling. The people should know that they got sick on chocolate. They don't speak English, but we know they're feeling better; they're smiling now!

B: *(reporter group)* A reporter should ask how the man in his garden felt when he first saw the UFOs. I'm sure it was a big shock! – Oh, and a reporter should ask how the aliens *paid* for their chocolate at the shop!

> For typical phrases for reporters and witnesses, have another look at the **Skills page** you've just done.

Step 3

Plan and write your report

a) *Go back to your home group. Each of you is now an expert for one of the roles. Talk about how you all want to put the report together. Think about these points first:*

How should it start? | How should it end: Does the news presenter tell the listeners to listen for more information later? Is the Martians' visit to Earth over? | Which order are the interviews in? | How serious (or silly) should the presenter and the reporter be? | Remember that the presenter needs to say something after every reporter interview.

b) *Now write your report, interview by interview. Each person writes some of it.* → HA

c) *Peer-editing: Give your part to somebody else and check each other's texts.*

d) *One of you now reads it to the rest of the group. Does it sound like a radio report? Does it sound interesting enough? Make changes to improve the text if necessary.*

Step 4

Practise and record your report → HA

a) *Practise your report a few times, and record yourselves with a smartphone. Does it sound right? Remember: Don't read from the page!*

b) *Now record your final report.*

c) *Play it for the class. Tell the groups what you liked about **their** reports.*

> Lou, do you think there are mice on Mars?

> Maybe we can go back to Mars with the aliens and find out!

S1/33–37
L3/4–8 ◉ **Hey, don't call *me* silly!** → Folie 24

A In Greenwich, it's almost time for the mini marathon to start …

Gwen: It's too bad Olivia can't join us.
Luke: But she can cheer us on with the others and help us to do well today.
Gwen: Yes, for us *and* for 'See with your Heart'. It means a lot to me, as a partially sighted person.
Luke: Your charity means something to *all* of us, Gwen. – But anyway, remember: You mustn't let go of my hand!

Gwen: Luke, that's *my* line: *I'm* the one who can't see well, remember?
Luke: Oh, sorry. I'm just nervous. Do you think I've trained enough?
Gwen: Well, I have! I did lots of extra training. But I can't speak for *you*.
Luke: Great, that really helps.
Gwen: Don't think so much, silly. Just run. And not too fast too soon!
Luke: Hey, don't call *me* silly – look at *them* in their crazy animal costumes. Can you see them?
Gwen: Er, not very well. But there are always people in fancy dress at events like these. They're running for charity too.
Luke: Oh yes: a pet charity, I'm sure; they've got cat and dog costumes. But how can they *run* in them?!
Gwen: No idea. – But hey, look! There are Holly and Olivia! But hm, where are Dave and Jay?

B A few minutes into the race …

Gwen:
This feels GREAT! My big day, after all that training … Now is the moment – MY moment! I can show them how good I am. Just breathe … run … enjoy it! … But what about Luke? Can he keep up? He didn't do any extra training like me. And *he's* worried about *me*? … Oh, those silly runners in the animal costumes in front of us – they aren't really taking this seriously. … What are they doing? Jumping from right to left and getting in the way. Clowns! … I hope they don't get in *our* way.

C Ten minutes later …

Gwen:
Ouch! What's that?! Oh, my stomach; it *really* hurts. … Oh no, I mustn't stop! I'm running for the charity – *and* for Luke! … I don't want to be the new girl with the funny glasses; I want to be the new girl with fast legs! Oh, but my stomach… Come on, just run! … RUN!

D Not far from the finish line …

Gwen:
I think that stupid cramp is gone. YES! And
Luke is still doing fine too. … We're still
55 running fast: I think our time is going to
be *really* good. … I want to see our photos
on the ITS website! "Gwen Parker, the new
running star". Sounds great! – OH NO!!!!!!!!!
What's happening?!?! Oh no, I don't want to
60 fall!

E Just after the race …

Luke: Gwen, we did it, WE DID IT!

Gwen: Yes, we did! And it feels GREAT!

Luke: Well, *now* it feels great. But during
65 the race I had a bad cramp. You
started too fast for me!

Gwen: *You* had a cramp? Oh, now I feel
better.

Luke: I had a cramp and now *you* feel
70 better? I don't understand.

Gwen: Well, I had a cramp too – but I
didn't want to tell you; I didn't
want to stop the race.

Luke: And I didn't want to tell *you* and
75 hear, "You didn't train enough!"

Gwen: Well, we *both* finished, yippee! And
'See with your Heart' gets some
money too!

Luke: Well, they almost *didn't*: That
80 stupid dog and that stupid cat
almost ruined everything for us! I
couldn't believe my eyes when they
pulled out a smartphone and took
a selfie. That one boy fell because
85 of them, and we almost fell too!

Gwen: They took a *selfie*? In the middle
of the race? Oh, I knew those two
were trouble!

Olivia: *(suddenly)* Yes, that's what the race
90 officials thought too so they finally
took the dog and the cat out of the
race. – Look who I've found!

Luke: Dave and Jay?!?!

Gwen: YOU were the dog and the cat?!?!
Aaaargh!!! 95

Dave: Don't be angry, please! We're really
sorry. We only wanted to surprise
you.

Jay: Yes, we trained in secret and ran
for the pets' charity! 100

Gwen: But somebody *fell* because of you
two. Luke and I almost fell! I'm
sure that boy trained hard. Have
you ever thought of that?

Jay: Well, er … 105

Dave: We said sorry, Gwen.

Gwen: Well, don't tell *me*. Have you told
the boy yet?

Dave: Er, no.

Gwen: Well, *tell* him. *(smiling now)* So we 110
can finally forgive you.

Luke: But I'm not sure 'sorry' is enough.
How about a present for

Olivia: That sounds good. I'
have nice present 115

Gwen: Yes boys, you
nice for hi
someth
too.
P

Luke:

READING

1 **Working with the text** → WB 46/20

a) *Think of the tips on page 36. How can you guess the meanings of these words in the text: 'stomach' (l. 45), 'finish line' (l. 51), 'stupid' (l. 80), 'to ruin' (l. 81), 'to surprise' (l. 97), 'in secret' (l. 99)?*

b) *Find answers to these questions in the text.*

1. What different kinds of texts are there in parts A–E?
2. What reasons do the characters have to run in a marathon?
3. What can cause problems in a marathon race?
4. What do we learn about Gwen and Luke's hopes and fears?
5. What can you say about their relationship?

→ △ 135/8
△ → Instead of ...

c) *Use the text and the pictures to retell what happened.*

READING

2 **What do you think?**

a) *Find adjectives to describe Gwen, Luke, Jay and Dave and their actions.*

→ △ 135/9
→ S9
△ → Help with ...

Voc.: Positive and negative words, p. 226

b) *Find positive and negative things in the story that they did. Use words from a) to discuss what you think about their actions.*

Here are some ideas: On the one hand it was **good** that … On the other hand it was really stupid … | I think Gwen was **brave** … But it was also **dangerous** …

VOCABULARY

3 **Looking at spoken language** → KV 48

→ △ 135/10
→ ▲ 135/11
△ → Help with ...
▲ → After ...

Read the dialogues and Gwen's thoughts out loud. How do Gwen and Luke talk to each other? What language do they use to express their feelings? Collect words and phrases you would like to use again in a mind map.

WRITING

4 **Another story** → WB 46/21 → **KV 89, Diktat- und Transfertext**

→ S11–14

a) *Write about what **isn't** in the story. Choose one of these two topics. You can write a story, a dialogue or a comic. Use your vocabulary from Ex. 2.*

- The race from Jay and Dave's point of view.
- "Can you forgive us?": Jay and Dave talk to the boy who fell because of them.

b) *Peer-edit each other's work and give feedback.*

Can you . . .

1. talk about experiences in your life/in somebody else's life? .... Have you ever played rugby?
2. talk about things which have (just) happened? .... I've hurt my foot!
3. use *just*, *already* and *yet*? .... I haven't had my dinner yet.

LANGUAGE

1 What do Luke and Dave talk about? → WB 47/22 → HA

Complete the dialogues.

Example: Dave: write | your report? → Have you already written your report?
Luke: no | have | no time yet → No, I haven't. I haven't had time yet.

1. Luke: find | interesting information on the internet yet?
   Dave: yes | find | yesterday after school.
2. Luke: Jay | draw | new mangas for his report yet?
   Dave: yes | draw | cool new characters at lunch.

3. Dave: see | two new manga comics yet?
   Luke: yes | already finish | one of them.
4. Luke: see | Olivia today?
   Dave: no | but send | text an hour ago.
5. Dave: Holly | write | about guinea pigs?
   Luke: hope not! | write | about guinea pigs last year.

LANGUAGE

2 BMX: Popular but a bit dirty! → KV 49, HA

Dave wrote a text for the health project about the history of BMX. Complete his text with the correct verb forms: simple past or present perfect.

The full name of BMX is 'bicycle motocross'. It is a sport that **1** (become) very popular with young people. It **2** (start) with children in the USA in about 1970. At first, the children **3** (use) normal bikes on mud roads; there **4** (be) no special BMX bikes. But then a few bicycle companies **5** (discover) the sport, and the world **6** (have) its first BMX bikes. It's a fast, dangerous sport, and there **7** (be) many serious accidents. That's why many parents are *not* big fans. In one survey with parents last year, BMX **8** (not be) at the top of the list of 'favourite sports'. One mother said: "I **9** (see) dirty football and rugby uniforms, but my children's BMX clothes after a race? They're the worst!"

LANGUAGE

3 Mixed bag: A dangerous sport → WB 47/23 → KV 50, HA

Megan: What's the problem with your leg?
Lilly: I've had a riding **1** and **2** my ankle.
Megan: Oh no, **3** ?
Lilly: Well, I was riding too fast, so I fell **4** the horse. I don't go riding very often, so I don't have much **5** .

I went to the hospital and the doctor gave me a **6** for an ointment.
Megan: I am so sorry! **7** ?
Lilly: Yes, I still have a headache and my leg **8** . On the one hand riding is really fun, but **9** it's a dangerous sport.

S1/38
L3/9 ⊙

Getting around

The Bauer family arrives at London Heathrow Airport from Germany and goes to the information desk to find out how to get to central London.

Mrs B: Hello! Can you help us, please? We'd like to get to our hotel. It's near Russell Square in Bloomsbury.

Man: Ah, yes – Holborn Tube station is the nearest one. That's very easy. You can take the Piccadilly Line from here – it stops at Holborn.

Mrs B: That sounds good. How long does it take?

Man: About fifty minutes, and you don't have to change trains.

Mr B: What about the Heathrow Express? It's faster, isn't it?

Man: It's a little faster, but not much. You can take the Heathrow Express to Paddington, then change to the Bakerloo Line to Oxford Circus, then change to the Circle Line. It's only two stops to Holborn. But it's easier to take the Piccadilly Line because you don't have to change. And it's cheaper.

Mrs B: Then let's take the Tube. What kind of ticket do we need? We're here for three days, but we're going to walk a lot.

Man: Well, then it's probably best to buy three singles – not return tickets – to London. You need two adult singles and one child. You can buy them at the machine over there. The machines take cash or credit cards.

Mr B: Thanks for your help! One last question – when does the next train leave?

Man: Don't worry, the trains leave every ten minutes. The next one leaves at 9:30. And there's a lift down to the platforms – it's easier with your luggage. Enjoy your stay in London!

VOCABULARY

1 Travel words

→ S1–3

Find travel words in the text. Write down phrases with each one.

Voc.: Travel words, p. 228

Example: to arrive at the airport, to change trains, …

SPEAKING

2 How do we get there? → G11 → **KV 51, Diktat- und Transfertext**

You want to travel from London to Bath. Talk about the alternatives. Say what it costs and how long it takes.

Voc.: Transport, WB (Word bank), p. 8

Start like this: The first coach leaves at …

Coach from London Victoria to Bath

16:30 ↓ 19:30	17:30 ↓ 20:40	18:30 ↓ 21:05
		Fastest
3h 0m	3h 10m	2h 35m
0 changes	0 changes	0 changes
£ 23.80	£ 23.80	£ 23.80

Train from London Paddington to Bath

16:00 ↓ 17:24	16:30 ↓ 17:59	17:00 ↓ 18:27	17:30 ↓ 18:58
1h 24m	1h 29m	1h 27m	1h 28m
0 changes	0 changes	0 changes	0 changes
Cheapest			
£ 43.40	£ 43.40	£ 92.50	£ 92.50

LISTENING

3 Travel **announcements** → WB 48/1–3 → **KV 52**

L 3/10 ⊚
→ S21–23

Lösung: a)
1. airport,
2. airport,
3. train station,
4. train station,
5. airport

a) *Listen to the travel announcements. Note down where you can hear each one (airport or train station) and what it is about.*

b) *Add the new phrases to your list from exercise 1.*

> **Useful phrases**
>
> Flight XY21/The plane/train/is delayed/late/ready for boarding.
> to arrive at …/to depart from …
> Passengers/People need to/mustn't
> … go to Gate X/Platform Y.
> … leave their luggage unattended.
> … bring/show their boarding passes.

SPEAKING

4 Can you tell me the way to …? → WB 49/4 → **Folie 25**

Voc.: Telling the way, WB (Word bank), p. 8

a) *Look at the map of London at the back. You're at Victoria Station. Make dialogues with your partner.*

Example:

> Excuse me. Can you tell me the way to the Houses of Parliament, please?

> Yes, of course! Go down Victoria Street, past Westminster Abbey, to Parliament Square at the end of the road. Turn right into Abingdon Street. The Houses of Parliament are on the left.

> **Useful phrases**
>
> **Asking the way:** Excuse me, please. How do I get to …? | Can you tell me the way to …, please?
>
> **Telling the way:** Go down/past … | Go straight on. | Cross over the road/river. | Turn right/left into … | It's opposite …/on the right/on the left.

Ask the way to:
1. Buckingham Palace   2. Marble Arch   3. The London Eye   4. Covent Garden

b) *Your partner is at Marble Arch. He/She doesn't know where you are. Choose a place on the map and tell your partner how to get there. Can he/she find you?*

MEDIATION

5 Our hotel → WB 49/5

→ S20

Dein Cousin, der schlecht sieht, sucht ein Hotel in London. Er zählt seine Wünsche auf. Lies die Beschreibung und erkläre ihm, ob dieses Hotel für ihn geeignet ist und warum/warum nicht.

> nicht zu groß | gut erreichbar | zentrumsnah | modern eingerichtet | Frühstück um 7 Uhr | Schwimmbad | mit kostenlosem WLAN

Our attractive four star hotel is in the heart of the theatre district, close to the British Museum. You can walk to most of the London shows in less than five minutes. It's 150 m away from Holborn Tube station, and Covent Garden is just one stop away. Children are very welcome. The hotel has 15 double, 10 single and two family rooms. All rooms are newly decorated and en suite (shower/bath), with complimentary tea and coffee and free Wifi internet access. There are quiet rooms at the back, while the front rooms have great views. No pets please!

- Breakfast buffet 6–10 am, £9 per person
- Sauna, small pool and sports facilities
- Underground car park, £10 per night

⟨Revision B⟩ ist fakultativ und dient der Festigung/Wiederholung. Es werden keine neuen Sprachmittel eingeführt.

LISTENING

1 Uncle Jim's scary story

L 3/14

When Uncle Jim reads Ryan's travel report about summer camp, he remembers his own trip to the Rockies a long time ago. Listen to the story about Longs Peak, Adams Falls and ghosts and answer these questions:

1. When did Uncle Jim see the ghosts?
2. Who were they?

3. What didn't the ghosts do?
4. What does Ryan think about the story?

LANGUAGE

2 Emily's dream[1]

Lösung: 1. had, 2. are you listening, 3. asks, 4. was thinking, 5. started, 6. am listening, 7. answers, 8. says, 9. read, 10. were writing/ wrote, 11. do you remember, 12. came, 13. were walking, 14. saw, 15. only looked, 16. started, 17. wanted, 18. was, 19. started, 20. woke, 21. was still shouting, 22. don't know, 23. was, 24. want

Emily tells Mike about her dream. Put in the correct verb form: present or past tense? Simple or progressive?

"Mike, I **1** (have) the strangest dream last night!" Emily says. "Mike? **2** (you, listen) to me?" she **3** (ask). "Oh sorry, Emily, I **4** (think) of something else when you **5** (start) to talk to me. But I **6** (listen) to you now!" Mike **7** (answer). "Good", Emily **8** (say), "I **9** (read) your travel report yesterday. You **10** (write) about a cougar, **11** (you, remember)? Well, in my dream that cougar **12** (come) to Decorah! Ryan and I **13** (walk) home from school when we suddenly **14** (see) it. First it **15** (only, look) at us, but then it **16** (start) to chase us. Of course we **17** (want) to run away, but the cougar **18** (be) faster. I **19** (start) to shout and when I **20** (wake) up, I **21** (still, shout). I really **22** (not, know) why I **23** (be) so afraid of that beautiful animal in my dream. I **24** (want) to see a real cougar at camp now!"

LANGUAGE

3 An e-mail for Emily → WB 50/1–2

Lösung: 1. have just come, 2. have never heard, 3. was, 4. found, 5. was, 6. worked, 7. was, 8. had, 9. took, 10. did not see, 11. were climbing, 12. showed, 13. stood, 14. saw, 15. were sitting, 16. heard, 17. was, 18. found out, 19. were making, 20. wanted

Dave writes an e-mail to Emily to tell her about camp in the Shropshire Hills. Complete the e-mail with the correct verb forms: simple past, past progressive or present perfect.

Hi Emily,

Thanks for your e-mail and photos from summer camp in the Rocky Mountains. I **1** (just, come) back from camp in the Shropshire Hills. I guess you **2** (never, hear) of this area, it's near the Welsh border[2]. It **3** (be) my first time at camp because there aren't as many summer camps in Britain as in the US. But my mum **4** (find) the perfect camp for me: There **5** (be) a video games workshop every morning! We **6** (work) on our own 3D game, that **7** (be) really cool! They **8** (have) some great software and we **9** (take) our own game home with us at the end of the week. We **10** (not, see) any dangerous animals, but while we **11** (climb), our group leader **12** (show) us a red fox[3]. It **13** (stand) very close to us when we **14** (see) it. One evening we **15** (sit) around the campfire when we suddenly **16** (hear) a loud grunting noise. That **17** (be) really scary! In the end we **18** (find out) that two boys **19** (make) the noise. They **20** (want) to play a trick on us.

Hope to hear from you soon 😊, Dave

1 **dream** [driːm] Traum | 2 **Welsh border** [ˌwelʃ ˈbɔːdə] Grenze zu Wales | 3 **fox** [fɒks] Fuchs

VOCABULARY

4 False friends

a) *Complete these statements with the right words. Be careful, some of them are false friends: They look like German words, but their meanings are different.*

Lösung: a) 1. give,
2. spend, 3. become,
4. get, 5. have to,
6. mustn't, 7. fast,
8. nearly/almost

1. Olivia: "Let's run for charity and ask our parents and friends to **1** money. It's a better way to **2** money than to buy things you don't need!"

2. Gwen: "I'm glad that charity runs have **3** more popular. Running is healthy, and charities **4** some money too!"

3. Jay: "Dave, we don't **5** to wear costumes, if you don't like it, but I think it's a great idea. And we **6** tell Luke and the girls about it – it's going to be a surprise."

4. Luke: "Gwen is a **7** runner, so I soon got a cramp. And then we **8** fell because the dog and cat stopped to take selfies."

b) *Together with a partner, think of more false friends and make sentences.*

READING

5 Are they crazy? → WB 51/3

a) *Skim the text for the gist. Say what it is about in 2–3 sentences.*

Lösung: a) The text is about the Ben Nevis race. Every year in early September runners run up Ben Nevis and back down again.

b) Numbers: 1,344 metres: height of Ben Nevis; 125,000: number of people that climb Ben Nevis every year; 9.9 miles: distance to the top and back down again; 1,340 metres: height difference the runners have to overcome; 1984: year in which Kenny Stewart broke the record; 1 hour, 25 minutes and 34 seconds: the time in which Kenny Stuart ran the race; September 27, 1895: date when William Swan was the first person to run up and down the mountain; 2 hours and 41 minutes: the time in which William Swan ran up and down the mountain;

BEN NEVIS

You've probably heard of Ben Nevis in Scotland. With its 1,344 metres it's the highest mountain in Great Britain. Each year 125,000 people climb this mountain and enjoy the great view from the top. It usually takes a few hours to get to the peak. But if you go up on the first Saturday in September, you can see people who run up or down the mountain. You think they're crazy? Well, they probably are … They run in the Ben Nevis Race, which takes place every year in early September. The race starts and finishes in Fort William. The runners don't just run up the mountain, but also back down again – that's a distance of 9.9 miles with a height[1] difference of 1,340 metres. In 1984 Kenny Stuart ran up and down the mountain in 1 hour, 25 minutes and 34 seconds – that's still the record[2] today. To run up and down the mountain, you must be really fit. Only runners with a lot of experience are allowed to take part in the race. The weather can change quickly in the mountains, so the runners must take a hat and a whistle[3] with them. But who had this crazy idea anyway? The first person who ran up and down the mountain was William Swan. On 27th September, 1895 he ran from Fort William to the top of the mountain and back in 2 hours and 41 minutes. He probably didn't know what he started …

b) *Scan the text. What numbers are there in the text and what do they mean? What does it tell you about rules for runners and the history of the race? Take notes.*

Rules for runners: Runners must have a lot of experience; they must take a hat and a whistle with them. The history of the race: On September 27, 1895, William Swan was the first person to run up and down Ben Nevis. He started at Fort William.

SPEAKING

6 Telling the way → Folie 25, KV 53, KV 54

Voc.: Telling the way, WB (Word bank), p. 8

Work with the map of London at the back. Take turns to tell the way from Buckingham Palace to the London Eye, from there to the National Gallery, from there to Big Ben and back.

1 height [haɪt] Höhe | **2** record ['rekɔːd] Rekord | **3** whistle ['wɪsl] Trillerpfeife

7 **Dictionary work**

Read this newspaper article and do exercises a) to c).

Life as a wunderkind

14-year-old violinist Louisa Lee from Littletown has received a sensational invitation: A world-famous orchestra has asked her to join them on their European
5 tour next month and perform some great pieces of classical music.

Surprised at first by this invitation, she's now very excited and proud of it. Some of the world's best musicians as well
10 as her violin teachers say that Louisa's talent is extraordinary, and she has been one of the youngest students ever to receive a full scholarship for the College of Classical Music.
15 She started playing the violin at the age of five and her parents soon recognised her talent. The teenager practises a couple of hours every day and has won several competitions. She loves
20 playing and her goal is to become a professional musician. Her parents don't know where her musical talent came from as neither of them has ever played an instrument. At first it was difficult for the
25 family because they had to save every penny to fund Louisa's training. Her

parents think there's too little support for young people with talents in arts and music compared to sports. They say that most schools provide better chances for 30 athletes than for musicians. It was often a problem for Louisa to take part in competitions because she missed lessons and tests at school. But this is no longer a problem because her mother has started 35 to teach her at home.

"I want to take up a career in music. Although it's hard work, it's lots of fun too," the teenager says. "Now I'm really looking forward to the big tour. And I'm very 40 grateful to my parents for their support, especially to my mum because she gave up her job to teach me and go on tour with me."

a) *Try to understand the new words in the text. Collect all the new words in a grid like the one below. Use a dictionary if you can't guess their meanings.*

Word or phrase	Translation	How I found out
wunderkind	Wunderkind	German
violinist	Violinistin	German: Violinistin
world-famous	…	word family: world + famous
extraordinary	…	French: extraordinaire
scholarship	…	Latin: scholaris
to recognise	…	French: reconnaître

b) *Explain who Louisa is and how her talent has changed her parents' lives. Would you like to have a special talent like the one she has? What are the pros and cons?*

c) *Read this text and use a dictionary to find out which of the* blue *words or phrases* **don't** *fit the context. Look up the right words and correct the text. Eight of the words look almost like German words but have different meanings. Write down these pairs of false friends together with their correct translations like this:*

Example: *to become – werden; bekommen – to get, to receive.*

Lösung: c)
Blue words or phrases that don't fit:
1. Dear Sir or Madam,
2. invite, 3. grandson,
4. asked, 5. letter,
6. imagination,
7. modern/new,
8. committed,
9. almost/nearly,
11. perform,
12. sensitive,
14. couldn't bear it,
17. earn, 18. pension
Blue words or phrases that are OK:
10., 13., 15., 16., 19.

(1) Very honoured ladies and gentlemen, I'm writing to you today because I want you to (2) load in my (3) ankle for the singing contest in your talent show. He has (4) pleased me to write this (5) brief. Karl is only twelve years old, but he writes his own songs. He has a lot of (6) fantasy and loves (7) actual music. He's very (8) engaged and practises (9) fast every day. (10) For this reason I'd like you to let him (11) occur in your show. Please don't say no because he's a very (12) sensible child and it's his (13) heart's desire so he (14) wouldn't hold it out if he couldn't (15) take part. I know that he would be (16) overjoyed to sing in your show. Maybe he can (17) deserve a lot of money as a singer, and that would be great because my (18) rent is very small so I can't support his career. (19) Yours sincerely,
Hans Müller

LANGUAGE **8** **Mixed bag: A trip to Silverwood** → WB 51/4

Lösung: 1. Have you ever been, **2.** park, **3.** biggest, **4.** rides, **5.** went, **6.** present, **7.** forward, **8.** drive, **9.** half, **10.** went/drove, **11.** became, **12.** looked, **13.** sky, **14.** side, **15.** arrived, **16.** got/received/bought, **17.** discussed/talked about, **18.** coaster, **19.** watch/see, **20.** wait, **21.** slide, **22.** going to be, **23.** was talking, **24.** went/became, **25.** came, **26.** Welcome, **27.** help, **28.** decide, **29.** what, **30.** cat, **31.** should/must, **32.** restaurant, **33.** try, **34.** happy

[1] to Silverwood? If not, you should go!

It's a great theme [2], one of the [3] in the Northwest with more than 65 attractions, like amazing [4], slides and shows. Last weekend I [5] there with my family. It was my birthday [6] from my parents, and I was really looking [7] to the trip. The [8] was about five and a [9] hours, and it was really boring in the car at first. But then we [10] through a forest up into the mountains and the landscape [11] more interesting. When we [12] out of the car windows, we saw eagles up in the blue [13] and even a young moose by the [14] of the road. We finally [15] at Silverwood and paid to get in. We [16] a map of the park and [17] what we wanted to do first. Mom was hungry, Dad was tired, my brother wanted to look at a model of the scariest roller [18] in the park, my sister wanted to [19] a stunt show, and I couldn't [20] to get on the big water [21]. 'Oh dear,' I thought, 'this is [22] difficult.' Everyone [23] at the same time. But suddenly we all

[24] quiet: A huge orange cat on two legs [25] out of a building and shouted: "[26] to Silverwood! I'm Garfield. Can I [27] you?" My dad said, "We can't [28] where to go first. So can you tell us [29] to do?" The [30] answered: "Of course you [31] go to the Italian [32] first and [33] my favorite lasagna." We all started to laugh and Mom was [34].

Find more online:
jg2j4t

Unit 5

L 3/16 ⊙

Stay in touch

A

Luke

Dave

Jay

Dave: Social networks are cool. But nasty comments and cyber bullies *aren't* so cool.

Luke: Yes, but there are special networks for kids with more protection. Look, I've created a new profile with my parents!

I see you've got a new friend on Mousebook. Who's Jon?

He's just a friend, Tony. Don't be jealous!

SPEAKING **1** **Media and TTS students: A survey** → **Folie 26**

Read what TTS students say about different media in A–E. Which of the activities have you done this week?

VOCABULARY **2** **Media collocations**

→ △ 136/1

△ → Instead of ...
→ 53

Voc.: Media collocations, p. 230; Media, WB (Word bank), p. 9

Lösung: siehe S. 230 (Voc.)

Match these verbs and nouns to make phrases to talk about media.

Example: I like to text friends and post new photos. What about you?

change	post	receive	send	read
talk to	reply to	play	join	check
chat	take part in	write	text	have

profile	photo	text message	forum
social network	video game	video chat
magazine	discussion	each other	friend

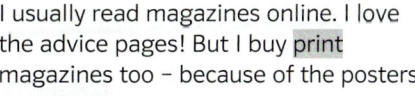

In Unit 5 you learn
- media vocabulary and phrases
- the language of giving and getting advice
- modals and their substitute forms
- writing skills for letters and replies

These things can help you to talk or write about communication in your life.

> I can't live without my smartphone – I check my messages all the time!

> I usually read magazines online. I love the advice pages! But I buy print magazines too – because of the posters.

B

C

Olivia

Holly

> Special interest forums are a great way to find interesting information online. I found 'Pet Paradise', and now Olivia and I know almost everything about guinea pigs.

> This is my favourite video game. My cousin and I always compare our scores on video chat!

D

E

LISTENING

3 **More about the survey** → **KV 55**
→ WB 52/1–2

L 3/17–21 ⊙

→ S21–23

Lösung a)
smartphone/
mobile; special
interest forums;
online magazines/
print magazines;
video games; social
networks

a) *Listen and make a list of the media the TTS students use.*

b) *Listen again and take notes. What do the students say about the media?*

Useful phrases

Smartphones/Social networks/… are great because they're fun/practical/easy to use/…

… are great for meeting …/for staying in touch with …/for sharing information about …

Which media?	What's positive?	What's not so positive?
smartphone/mobile	texts/easy to stay in touch	texts from parents!
special interest forums	…	…

c) *Your turn: Talk about how you use different media.*

L 3/22 ⊙

Dear Ruby

Holly and Olivia have found an interesting problem in the 'agony aunt' pages of their favourite magazine.

Dear Ruby,

I'm writing to you because I don't know what to do. Last week I had a big fight with my mum and I feel really bad about it. She hates the rap music I listen to and says it's too loud. The worst thing is she talked to my dad about it and the two of them say that I mustn't listen to loud music in my room while they're at home. But that's nearly all the time! Whenever I come home from school, my mum is there, and she always asks me why I don't practise the piano more. She could play the piano really well when she was young, and she gave concerts at the age of ten. Now she wants me to do the same. I like the piano, but I don't want to be a musician like her. She doesn't understand that I need a little time for myself and that my music makes me feel so much better when I'm sad. Can you please help? I would really like to hear your advice.
Lauren

Dear Lauren,

I'm sorry you're feeling so upset. I know how hard it is to feel that your parents don't understand you at all; it was the same with me when I was young. It doesn't mean you're not OK the way you are! As a first step, my advice is to be self-critical: Are you overreacting? Maybe the situation isn't as serious as you think. The next step is to talk to your parents in a friendly way and tell them how you feel. Things usually get better as soon as you talk. Why don't you explain to them that you work hard at school and your favourite music helps you to relax? Your parents also need to understand that you like the piano, but only for fun, so tell them that. Another tip: Although it isn't the same thing, it may also be a good idea to use headphones. When your parents are tired from work, they probably need some quiet time to relax. I hope you and your parents can find a way to understand each other's needs and to stop fighting.
Ruby

READING   **1**   **Understanding the problem**

→ ▲ 136/2
▲ → After …

a) *Words or phrases which are made up of parts you already know are often easy to guess. Explain what 'the two of them', 'self-critical', 'to overreact', 'as soon as' or 'headphones' mean.*

b) *Answer these questions about Lauren's letter and Ruby's reply.*

1. Why is Lauren writing to Ruby?
2. What is her mother's problem?
3. What advice does Ruby give?
4. Give your opinion: Do you think Ruby's advice is good? Say why/why not.

Lösung: a) 1. the two of them: both of them **2. be self-critical:** think about what you could do yourself **3. you overreact:** your reaction is too strong **4. as soon as:** right away **5. headphones:** sth you use to listen to music so that only you can hear it

VOCABULARY

2 The right vocabulary for advice → WB 53/3 → HA

Lösung: a) 1. My advice is to see it from your parents' side. 2. Why don't you try to talk to them? 3. As a first step, try to be self-critical. 4. The next step is to explain how you feel. 5. I'm sorry you're having trouble with your parents. 6. I know what it's like to be in your situation. 7. Another tip: Try to think of each other's needs.

a) *Here are some important advice phrases. Find them in the text. You can use them to give advice. Write a sentence with each phrase. You can write about the same problem as in the text or about something different.*

Useful phrases

My advice is to be self-critical/to see it from the other side/to find a compromise.
Why don't you try/think/ask …?
As a first step …
The next step is to talk to/write to/…
I'm sorry you're feeling sad/**you're** having trouble with …
I know how hard it is to …/what it's like to …
Another tip: …

b) *Look at the situations in the pictures. What's the situation? What's your advice?*

hurt leg

show bad test

spend money

LANGUAGE

3 Using linking words → WB 53/4 → G12 → HA

→ ▲ 136/3
→ S14
▲→ After …

Read what different teens say about how they use different social media websites. Put these words in the gaps. There's sometimes more than one correct answer.

after | before | as soon as | until | whenever | because

Lösung: 1. until/before, 2. Whenever/As soon as, 3. Before/Whenever; as soon as/after, 4. because/after, 5. because

1. I'm careful. I never give out my phone number ___ I've met a new friend face-to-face.
2. ___ somebody starts asking too many personal questions, I just block them.
3. ___ you post photos of yourself online, remember: ___ you post them, they're probably on the internet forever!
4. I was angry with my cousin ___ she posted that awful photo of me at the lake.
5. I don't get much attention online ___ I don't post pictures very often!

WRITING

4 Your turn: Media in your life → WB 54/5

Voc.: Media, WB (Word bank), p. 9

Write 5–6 sentences about yourself like the ones you see in Ex. 3. Think about these ideas:

- How much information about yourself do you share online? Why? How often?
- Do you and your friends use media in different ways? How?

You can give your text to a partner and peer-edit each other's work.

L 3/24 ⊙

Forum? What forum? → Folie 27

Luke: Dad, I wasn't allowed to go over to Jay's house yesterday. But can I … er, what on earth are you doing? There's water everywhere!

5 Dad: Really? Where?

Luke: Very funny. What's happened?

Dad: There's a problem with one of the pipes. I must fix it before your mum comes home and goes crazy!

10 Luke: Dad, do you know what you're doing?

Dad: Of course! It's just taking longer than I thought. I had to have a good look at everything first.

Luke: You could look at a forum for help.

15 Dad: Forum? What forum? You mean on the internet? So I can't fix my own washing machine – is that what you think? I don't need the internet.

Luke: But you're wasting so much time!
20 I *cannot* believe you don't just look online – there's step-by-step advice for everything!

Dad: Well, when I was young, I wasn't able to look everything up on the internet.
25 But I still learned to do things my way, step-by-step.

Luke: Your way? Hm …

Dad: I've done this a million times before. You should watch me and learn! – Er,
30 what are you doing with *my* tablet?

Luke: Well, I can use it, can't I? Anyway, let's see … hm … Oh yes, look: I've found a great website. Hey, over 1,000 people have given it five stars!

Dad: You shouldn't believe everything you 35 read online, Luke!

Luke: OK, just listen. You see that knob on the right?

Dad: Yes, I think I can reach it.

Luke: You must turn it off, then you … 40

15 minutes later …

Luke: Yes! It's working! These forums are great! No, please, you needn't say "thanks". Advice is free!

Dad: Fantastic! I fixed it. I told you, didn't I? 45

Luke: Only because I'm a genius!

Dad: With a *very* big head. Now, may I have my tablet back, please?

READING **5** Luke knows best? → HA

a) *Mr Elliot and his son have different ideas about how to solve the problem. What are they?*

b) *Have you ever had conversations like this one with family or friends? Tell the class.*

SPEAKING **6** The day I fixed my …

Tell your partner about a time when you fixed something. How did you do it?

→ △ 137/4
△ → Help with …   **Voc.:** Fixing things, p. 232

LANGUAGE   **7**   Are you able to do it yourself?

a) *Read the dialogue and find all the forms of* **be able to, be allowed to** *and* **have to**.

Luke: When I went to ask Dad if I was allowed to go over to Jay's house, I found him in front of the washing machine. He had to fix it before
5   Mum came home. Was he able to do it himself? It didn't look good. Everything was wet.

Dave: Oh dear! Were you able to help him?

Luke: Yes, I was. Usually I'm not allowed to
10   use his tablet, but I needed to look online for a way to fix the machine, so I was allowed to. Dad wasn't able to do it himself, so he was ready to try it out when I said: "Dad, today everyone
15   looks for instructions on the internet! People explain how to do things step by step with photos and videos. It's really helpful."

Dave: Yeah, you're right. I'm always able to find information by experts on all   20 kinds of subjects very quickly. Today people don't have to go to a library for everything any more. So we're able to save a lot of time.

Luke: Yeah, but you have to be careful! If   25 you aren't able to check if the person who has written the article really is an expert, you shouldn't believe everything you read. It often helps if you're allowed to read and comment   30 on other people's comments.

Dave: So your dad was able to fix the washing machine with your help and you were allowed to go over to Jay's house in the end?   35

Luke: Yes, and later I even got an ice cream!

b) *Make a grid with all the forms (1st, 2nd and 3rd person singular and plural) of* **be able to** *for the past tense (positive and negative statements and questions).*

LANGUAGE   **8**   Find the rule: *Can and its substitute forms*   → WB 54/6–7   → G13

a) *In which sentences from the text on p. 86 does* **can** *mean the same as the words in sentences A or B on the right?*

b) *Make more sentences for the two meanings of* **can**.

A: I'm good at Maths, so **I'm able to** help my little brother with his homework.
B: My little brother **isn't allowed to** use social networks.

LANGUAGE   **9**   Substitute forms: *Be able to, be allowed to* and *have to*   → WB 55/8–9   → G13

a) *Find one good example of each of the three substitute forms in the two texts and write it down in a grid like the one on the right.*

	Present	Past
können		
dürfen		
müssen		

b) *What were you (not) able/allowed to do in the past? What did you (not) have to do in the past? What's it like now? Tell your partner.*

→ △ 137/5
→ ▲ 137/6

△ → Help with …
▲ → After …

Examples: When I was four, I **wasn't able to** swim. Now I can.
When I was ten, I **wasn't allowed to** have my own phone. Now I have one.
When I was five, I **didn't have to** do homework. Now I have to do it.

LANGUAGE **10**   *Should, shouldn't* and *could* for advice   → WB 56/10, 57/11–12   → G14   → **KV 56**

→ △ 138/7
△ → After . . .

*Tony is having a very bad day. Look at his problems, then write sentences with advice for him. Use **should**, **shouldn't** or **could**. The ideas on the right can help.*

Example: Lou hasn't got time for me today! – You **shouldn't** be too disappointed.

1. I forgot Lou's birthday yesterday!
2. I've got a new neighbour.
3. I've left my money at home.
4. I want to do something nice for Dad.
5. I want to buy a new phone but haven't got enough money.
6. Someone has stolen my bike!

ask a friend   buy flowers

go to the police

be too disappointed ✔   say hello

take him to a football game

help your parents at home for pocket money

**Lösung: 1. You should/could buy her some flowers today.
2. You should say hello to him/her. 3. You could ask a friend. 4. Well, you could take him to a football game then.
5. You should help your parents at home for pocket money. 6. You should go to the police.**

MEDIATION **11**   **Young people and smartphones**   → KV 57

L 3/27 ◉
→ △ 138/8
△ → After . . .

Dein englischer Austauschpartner ist zu Besuch. Im Radio hört ihr eine Reportage.
Dein Austauschpartner versteht nicht alles und hat folgende Fragen: "What does the younger student like about the group chat with the class? What negative points are there about group chats? What are 'digitale Helden' and why are they important?"

MEDIATION **12**   **Pet Paradise**

→ S20

Daves Freund möchte verreisen und bittet ihn auf seine beiden Meerschweinchen aufzupassen. Dave fragt sich, ob man Katzen und Meerschweinchen zusammen halten kann und was er dabei beachten sollte, um Konflikte zu vermeiden. Im Forum „Pet Paradise" sucht er mit Olivia nach Antworten. Sie finden zwei Einträge auf Deutsch, die sie nicht ganz verstehen, und bitten Pia um Hilfe. Schreibe Pias Antwort an Dave als englische E-Mail und beantworte seine Fragen.

Verstehen sich Katzen und Meerschweinchen?

 von Pauline – Dienstag, 18:29   Man kann Katzen und Meerschweinchen problemlos zusammen halten, jedoch sind verschiedene Räume empfehlenswert. Wenn die Tiere zusammen in einem Raum sind, würde ich sie nie unbeaufsichtigt lassen – manchmal werden die Katzen plötzlich aggressiv. Außerdem sollte man den Tieren genügend Zeit geben, sich kennen zu lernen. Bei uns zu Hause klappt das problemlos. Wir möchten uns nun noch zwei Hasen anschaffen. Hat hiermit jemand Erfahrungen gemacht?

 von Schweinchenfan – Samstag, 13:12   Im Tierheim sagte man mir, dass Meerschweinchen in der Regel nicht von Katzen als Beutetiere betrachtet werden. Daher können beide Tiere zusammen leben, bei vielen entwickelt sich sogar eine Freundschaft. Aber auch wenn die Tiere sich gut verstehen, ist es ratsam, sie immer im Blick zu haben. Man sollte außerdem darauf achten, dass die Katzen die Meerschweinchen beim Spielen nicht unbeabsichtigt verletzen oder verängstigen. Bei mir leben unsere zwei Katzen und drei Meerschweinchen schon seit drei Jahren friedlich zusammen. Wer hat ähnliche Erfahrungen gesammelt?

READING **13** **Are you media mad?**   → **Diktat- und Transfertext**
                                           → WB 57/13

→ △ 139/9
→ ▲ 139/10
△ → After . . .
▲ → After . . .

Take the test and find out how media mad you are!
Do you agree with your results? Why/why not?

Voc.: Permission,
p. 232

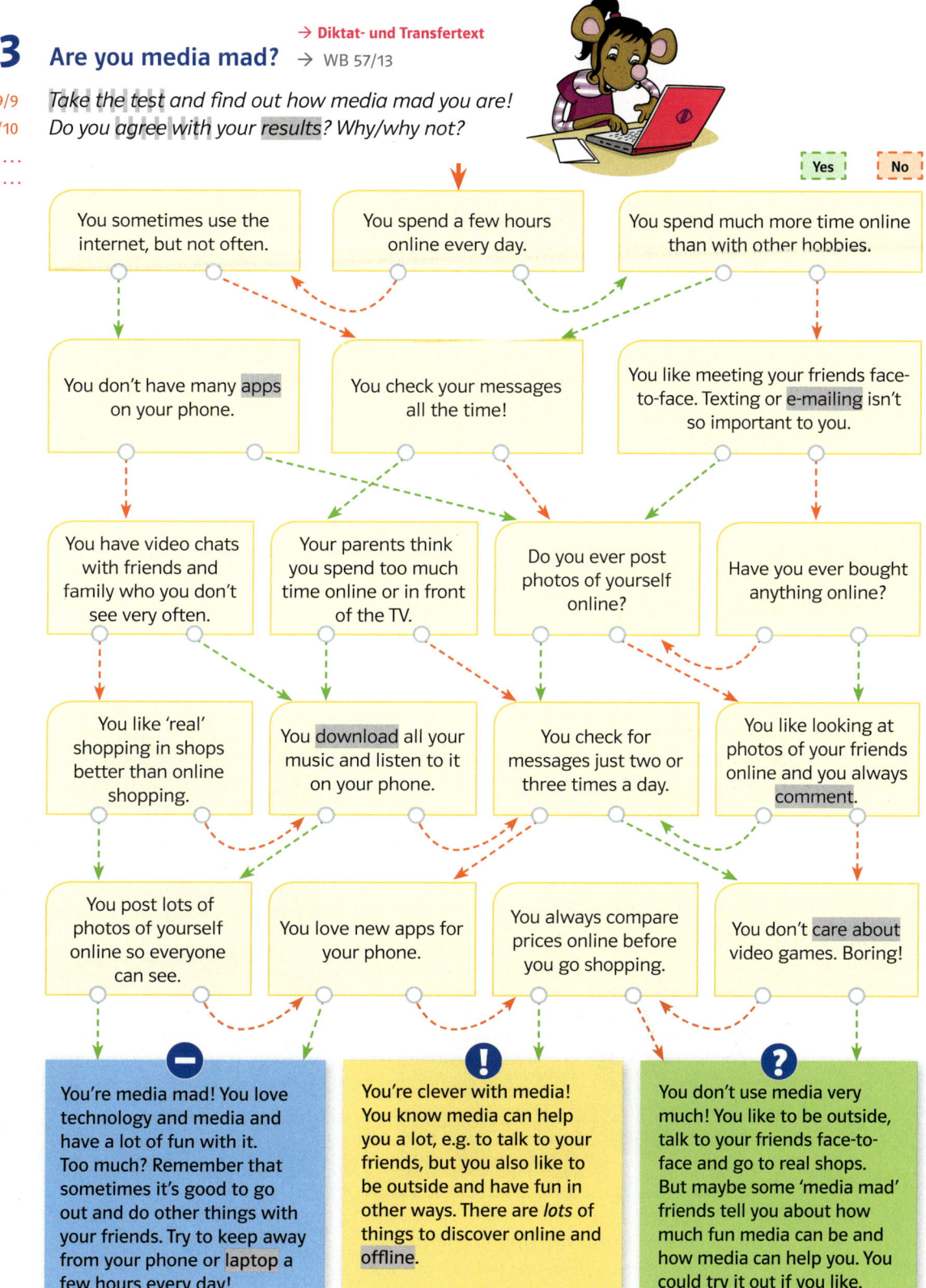

| Yes | No |

You sometimes use the internet, but not often.

You spend a few hours online every day.

You spend much more time online than with other hobbies.

You don't have many apps on your phone.

You check your messages all the time!

You like meeting your friends face-to-face. Texting or e-mailing isn't so important to you.

You have video chats with friends and family who you don't see very often.

Your parents think you spend too much time online or in front of the TV.

Do you ever post photos of yourself online?

Have you ever bought anything online?

You like 'real' shopping in shops better than online shopping.

You download all your music and listen to it on your phone.

You check for messages just two or three times a day.

You like looking at photos of your friends online and you always comment.

You post lots of photos of yourself online so everyone can see.

You love new apps for your phone.

You always compare prices online before you go shopping.

You don't care about video games. Boring!

➖ You're media mad! You love technology and media and have a lot of fun with it. Too much? Remember that sometimes it's good to go out and do other things with your friends. Try to keep away from your phone or laptop a few hours every day!

❗ You're clever with media! You know media can help you a lot, e.g. to talk to your friends, but you also like to be outside and have fun in other ways. There are *lots* of things to discover online and offline.

❓ You don't use media very much! You like to be outside, talk to your friends face-to-face and go to real shops. But maybe some 'media mad' friends tell you about how much fun media can be and how media can help you. You could try it out if you like.

Where's Maisie? → S24–25

VIEWING

1 Little dog, big trouble

a) *Have you ever lost a pet? How did you feel? Tell the class about it.*

7 **b)** *Watch the film and then talk about the roles of Laura, Nathan and Polly in the story.*

Examples: A: I think Nathan is awful. He's too busy with girls and then …
B: Laura has great friends! They all help …

c) *Now imagine you are Laura. She wants to tell Alicia about what happened with Maisie.*

Start like this: Alicia, I can't believe what Nathan did! He lost Maisie! He was …

SPEAKING

2 Media in the film scenes → KV 58

Watch the film again. How many different kinds of media can you see in the film?
Say how they helped the friends to find Maisie.
Lösung: mobile telephone calls, text messages, messages on online social networks,
video chat on a smartphone, print media ('missing' posters), online news

SPEAKING

3 Close-ups → KV 59

a) *Read the skills box.*

Lösung: b) EH: Laura:
Laura can't believe it.
She's got her Maisie back
again./Laura is so happy
because Polly found
Maisie in the park./Laura
really loves her dog – and
she likes Polly too./ …
Nathan: Nathan is
Laura's big brother and
he wants to look cool for
Polly./Nathan thinks he's
so cool and he offers to
buy Polly a drink./Nathan
likes himself a lot, and
he thinks Polly likes him
too./ …

> ### Film skills
>
> In Unit 1 you learned how music can
> help to show/describe feelings or
> atmosphere. Another way to do this in
> films is with **close-ups**: very close shots
> of a character's face. In this example, the
> girl isn't sure: Should she give Nathan
> her phone number, or not?
>
> With the camera so close, you can 'read'
> the question in her face!

b) *Look at scenes A and B from the film.*
What do the two close-ups tell us?
The ideas on the right can help you.

can't believe it | is happy again | loves her
dog | wants to look cute/cool for Polly |
thinks he's so cool | likes himself a lot | …

How to write a letter and a reply → S11–14

When you write a letter – to an agony aunt, for example – your letter should have different parts. This page shows you how to put a letter and a reply together.

1 The parts of a letter → KV 60

a) *Read this letter to an agony aunt, and then read the reply. The box on the right shows you which parts of the letters there are. You need to know this for Ex. 2.*

Dear Ruby,

I'm writing to you because I just don't know what to do.
I'm 13, and a new friend has invited me to go on holiday with his family this summer, to Spain. They always go to really cool places, and we just go camping. We never have much money. Before I met my friend, camping was fun. But it doesn't sound fun now. My parents say: "No, you can't go." That isn't fair, is it? I feel like I'm missing a lot of fun. I'm angry with my parents. What do you think, Ruby?
Thanks for your help!

Yours, Ben

> Begin with a greeting.
>
> The main idea(s): In an advice letter, the main idea is the problem.
>
> Ask for advice.
>
> Say 'Thank you'.
>
> Your name (often with 'Yours')

Dear Ben,

Yes, I understand that a cool holiday in Spain sounds like fun. But my advice is to ask yourself this: Is your friend really a good friend? Do you care about each other? Why don't you ask him to come with your family on a camping trip. If he's a good friend, you can have fun together anywhere, can't you? It needn't be on a beach in Spain.
I hope this advice helps!

Ruby

> Begin with a greeting.
>
> The main idea(s): A reply should show understanding/feelings.
>
> Give advice.
>
> Finish your letter.
>
> Name

Look back at the phrases box in Station 1 for the language of advice.

b) *Say what you think about Ben's problem and Ruby's advice.*

2 Write your own letter and reply → WB 58/14–16 → KV 61, HA

a) *Your partner writes a short letter to an agony aunt, and you write another short letter about a **different** problem. Choose one of the ideas below or an idea of your own:*

- "My friends say I'm weird because I don't like their music."
- "My two best friends are good at everything and I'm not."

b) *When you're both finished, exchange letters and write a reply to each other with advice.*

S 2/7–12
L 3/29–34

It's a disaster! → Folie 28

Frank Preston

Gwen   Olivia   Holly

A Dave's dad, Frank, stopped his car in front
of his house. It was raining very hard – he
wasn't able to see the house from his car,
but he was able to see that all the lights
5 were on. The storm was getting worse
every minute, with lots of thunder and
lightning. He waited for a while and then
quickly got out of the car, ran for the house
and opened the front door. As he went
10 inside, he nearly fell over all the bags and
shoes. 'I see Dave's friends are here again!'
he thought. He shouted, "Hello everyone!"
But there wasn't a sound. "Hello-o-o?!" he
called again. Nothing. "That's strange," he
15 thought.

> **Stop and think:**
> Why do you think the
> house is so quiet?

He looked in the kitchen – nobody was
there. Next, he looked in the living room
and saw Gwen, Holly and Olivia. "Hi girls!"
he said, but they didn't notice him because
20 they were watching a *loud* music video
on Olivia's laptop. Then he saw Jay in the
corner.

"How are you, Jay?" he asked, but Jay
was busy with text messages and music on
his tablet PC. Frank went upstairs. As soon 25
as he opened the door to Dave's bedroom,
he saw Dave and Luke. They were sitting
on the bed wearing headphones and
playing a video game – they didn't notice
Frank. "Well, they all look *very* happy to see 30
me, I must say!" he said to himself, as he
went back downstairs.

B Jay took off his headphones and tapped
the girls' shoulders. "I was thinking," he
said. "We should talk about that party we 35
want to have soon."

"Yeah, I was thinking about that too,"
Olivia answered. "We can have it at my
house. My dad and Claire say it's OK. Look,
I've already written the invitation." 40

"Great! Let's post a message with the
invitation and tell everyone to go to Olivia's
house on –"

"No!" Olivia shouted. "We can't just post
the invitation like *that*! A lot of people we 45
don't know could see it and come to my
house. No, we can only invite people face-
to-face. People we *know*."

"Olivia, it's much quicker by internet,"
Jay said. "Come on, let's just do it! It's fun! 50
He then grabbed Olivia's laptop.

"Jay, what are you doing?!" Olivia cried.

"I'm going to post it, what do you
think?" They all started fighting for the
laptop. At first they were laughing and 55
joking, but then the girls saw that Jay was
serious! They were horrified and tried to
push him away from the laptop, but Jay
was quicker. "Party on Friday 22nd at my
house, 52 Begbie Road. Come and have 60
fun!" it said in the invitation text. But just
as Jay was pressing 'post', there was a very
loud "BANG!" and everything went black.

C Suddenly, the house became very loud
and all the friends started shouting at the
same time: "What's happened?" – "I can't
see!" – "My computer has crashed!" – "Oh
no, we're offline too!" – "I can't find my
phone!" – "Help! I don't like the dark!"

Frank shouted, "Calm down, it's only
a power cut! Wait a moment while I find
some candles."

"Did you really send that message?"
whispered Holly. "I don't know, I think so!"
Jay said.

"To Olivia's friends?" Holly asked.

"No. To *everyone*! But I'm not sure …"
He was really starting to worry now, but he
didn't want to tell the girls. Five minutes
later, they were all sitting round the
kitchen table in candlelight.

"Dad, what do we need candles for?"
asked Dave. "Look, our phones have all got
torches!"

"Sometimes, the old ways are better!"
smiled Frank. "The only problem we have
right now," Frank went on, "is that we can't
cook – and I'm *really* hungry!"

"How is that a problem?" asked Luke.

"Who needs to cook when there are pizza
apps?" Dave and Luke started to show
Mr Preston fantastic apps for his phone.
Mr Preston was impressed! But nobody
noticed that Jay wasn't speaking. 'What
have I done?' he thought to himself.

"I was just showing off and I went a bit
crazy for a moment. Please tell me the
power cut stopped the message." Then he
said, "Luke, Dave: Can I borrow a phone?
I need to check something and I left mine
in the other room." But they were busy
with Mr Preston and his new pizza app.

D Frank was still talking about the old days.
"When I was young, we *talked* to each
other, we didn't text all the time."

"Oh no, he *loves* this topic!" Dave
said and, as he spoke, there was a loud
CLICK, and all the lights were back on.

The girls ran to the living room and waited
nervously to get back online.

"Come on, come on!" Holly said. And
suddenly they were online again. They
went on to their social network site and …
"Fantastic!" shouted Olivia. "The power cut
stopped the message! But let's teach Jay
a lesson." Gwen and Holly smiled at each
other.

E Jay walked slowly back into the living
room.

"You're in *big* trouble now!" Olivia said.

"How many messages are there?" he
whispered. His face was white. He felt sick.
"More than 50!" Holly said. "Listen to
these: 'You don't know us but we *love*
parties – see you there!', or 'Party? Cool! I
love meeting new people!'"

Now Jay felt *really* sick. "It's a disaster!"
he said. Holly and Olivia were trying very
hard not to laugh.

"What's so funny?" Jay asked.

"Don't worry. The power cut stopped
your message. Nobody got it," Olivia said.

"But you're lucky, Jay Azad!" Holly
added. "And you *really* should leave the
party invitations to us next time!"

"That," said Jay, "is no problem at all!"

READING **1** **Understanding the story** → WB 59/17–18 → **KV 62**

a) *Do you think 'It's a disaster!' is a good title for the story? Say why or why not. What ideas for a different story title do you have?*

b) *There are two main characters in this story: One is Frank, and the other is Jay. Find sentences in the text that show how they both* feel left out *at some point in the story.*

   Example: He shouted, "Hello everyone!" But there wasn't a sound. (Frank, lines 12–13)

→ △ 139/11
→ S17
△ → Help with …

c) *Do a role play for one of these situations. Use ideas from the text.*
   – *One of you is Frank, the other is Dave's mum. She asks him what happened.*
     Or:
   – *One of you is Jay, the other is Olivia. They talk about what happened and what they were feeling.*

WRITING **2** **Writing about** pros and cons → **HA, Diktat- und Transfertext**

→ S9 a) *Make a grid with examples of things people can do today with* modern *technology and examples of things people did or used when Frank was very young. There are a lot of examples in the text, but you can find more and add them to your grid.*

New world	Old world
– watch a video	– use candles
– send text messages …	…

→ S14 b) *What are the pros and cons of modern technology? First read the skills box. Then write about the two worlds. The phrases box can help you too.*

Lösung: a) New world: watch a video, send text messages, post messages, use the internet, use apps, …;
Old world: use candles, write notes or letters, write invitation cards, invite people face-to-face, use a normal phone, read brochures or books, etc.

Writing skills

Use these words/phrases to link ideas and give information:

When things happen (time):
When my parents were young…, then …, now …, today …, before …, after …, as …, when …

Where things happen (place):
in the house, on my phone/PC, everywhere

Why things happen (reasons):
… because …

What else happens:
and …, or …, but …

Useful phrases

Today we've got … | We can … | It's great that … because … | We weren't able to… before we had … | (Not) everything was …, I think … is better than … | But … can be dangerous. We should …

Unsocial Networking

Can you ...

1. talk about media in your life? ____ I use ... to send/receive/post/chat/play/read/look up/ take part in ...
2. link ideas? ____ I do it when/after/before/because ...
3. give advice to somebody? ____ Why don't you ...? | You should ... | You could ...
4. use substitute forms for modals? He wasn't allowed/able to come with us. He had to do his History homework.

VOCABULARY

1 Activities on Mousebook → WB 60/19

Read the text and choose the correct verb.

Every morning Tony **asks | watches | checks** his messages on the social network Mousebook because he wants to **stay in touch | send e-mails | text** with his friends. His favourite profile is Lou's profile. She often **checks | changes | blocks** her profile picture, and Tony always likes the new ones!

SPEAKING

2 What can you say to give these people advice? → KV 63, HA

1. Your brother has hurt his foot.
2. Your friend missed his favourite TV show.
3. Your friend's parents are angry with her: She isn't allowed to use her smartphone for a week.

LANGUAGE

→ KV 64, HA

3 **Fill in** the right forms: *can, be able to, be allowed to, must, have to* → WB 60/20

When I was young, we **1** make phone calls from everywhere because there were no mobile phones. Now you **2** use your smartphones nearly everywhere. But you **3** use them at school, are you? There **4** be rules for using them, right? 30 years ago you **5** look for information in books. Today you **6** look things up on the internet. When we were young, we **7** watch videos sometimes, but today you **8** watch videos online all day.

LANGUAGE

4 Mixed bag: Your picture or mine? → HA

Last week my friend Ava **1** some photos on her **2** network **3** she wanted to **4** with her friends. **5** I **6** the message that there were new photos on her **7**, I checked it and **8** that there was one **9** showed me and her **10** the beach. I **11** her to block it for other people **12** I don't **13** anyone else to **14** me in my bikini. In her **15** it wasn't a problem. She likes the picture **16**, **17** it's her favourite **18**, and she thinks we **19** look really good in it. But I have a **20** to decide who **21** see photos of me **22** the internet, and **23** we found a **24**: She used a computer programme and **25** out the part of the photo **26** showed her **27** she **28** post it without my picture.

Find more online:
i8v3s5

S 2/13
L 3/35

The Celts and the Romans in Britain → Folie 29, Folie 30

→ Folie 29, Folie 30

BC (before Christ)

450

The Celts in Britain

350

250

150

55
54

*Christ 0

43

60/61

150

The Romans in Britain

250

350

410

440

AD (Anno Domini)

A Celtic warrior tells his story:
"It's all over! Boudicca, our warrior queen, is dead! She was so strong and brave. But let me start at the beginning. My name is
5 Drustan and I'm going to tell you about my people and the Romans …

Over a hundred years ago, the powerful Roman leader Julius Caesar tried to invade our country. He wanted to land near Dubris,
10 but our warriors fought to keep him away. Then a bad storm made Caesar's ships leave.

Caesar wanted Britain to be part of the Roman Empire.

A year later, he came back with a bigger army. After many battles, some of our tribes made peace with him. But Caesar soon left
15 again. I think he had more important things to do. Thank the gods!

Around one hundred years later, the Romans came back again. Their new leader, Emperor Claudius, brought thousands of
20 soldiers with him and they also had huge grey animals with long noses. When our tribes saw them, they were horrified.

Claudius and his army fought more battles against our tribes. We tried so hard to stop them, but they won in the end, in a 25 battle near the river Tamesis. And this time, they stayed here.

Our people lived in peace with the Romans for the next seventeen years. The Romans built bigger towns and long, 30 straight stone roads, and we traded with them and learned about their gods. But then our king died and everything changed. The Romans decided that they didn't want to share the land with our queen and her 35 children. Instead, they took all of our land and were very cruel to us. Queen Boudicca was so angry that she attacked the Romans with her army.

Boudicca was a Celtic leader and Queen of the Iceni tribe.

Our warriors fought well and we burned 40 down three big Roman towns – one of them was Londinium. We were so proud! But soon all was lost! There was a terrible battle and the Romans won. Then our queen took her own life because she did not want to be 45 their prisoner. What's going to happen to us all now?"

READING

1 The Celtic warrior's story – what happened? → WB 61/1 → KV 65

a) *Who does Drustan talk about? Write down the names and make notes.*

→ S18 b) *Describe the pictures above. Which part of the story do they show?*

c) *Copy the time line and match the events in the story to the dates. Write a sentence to explain what happened for each date.*

SPEAKING

2 **Celtic culture and Roman buildings** → **Folie 29**

S 2/14
L 3/36 ⊙

Explain in English to a French friend what these short texts say about the Celts and the Romans.

Lösung: EH:
The Celts lived in the British Isles from 500 BC. They were brave and clever. They were also good at art. They decorated their shields with circles and special shapes and made beautiful jewellery.
The Romans thought the Celts were barbarians. They built forts and walls to protect their empire against them. One wall was very long and high. It was called Hadrian's Wall. The emperor Hadrian started to build it in the northwest around 117 AD, but it took at least six years until it was finished.

The Celts arrived in the British Isles around 500 BC. The Romans called them 'barbarians', but they were brave and clever. This is the Battersea Shield from Boudicca's time. You often see circles and shapes like these in Celtic art. You can still buy Celtic jewellery today, and some people still speak Celtic languages, like Welsh and Gaelic.

Around 117 AD, the Roman emperor Hadrian decided to build a great wall across England with several large and many small forts to protect the Roman Empire in the northwest. Hadrian's Wall was 73 miles long and about five metres high. Around 15,000 soldiers needed at least six years to build it!

LISTENING

→ **Folie 30, KV 66, Diktat- und Transfertext**
→ WB 62/2–3

3 **What did the Celts and Romans leave behind?**

→ S21–23

a) *Look at the map of Britain at the back of your book. Find towns and rivers that are also on the map of Roman Britain. Note their Roman names and their names today.*

L 3/37 ⊙

Lösung: a) Cities:
Londinium – London; Dubris – Dover; Aquae Sulis – Bath; Deva – Chester; Mamucium – Manchester; Eboracum – York; Vindolanda – Vindolanda;
Rivers: Tamesis – Thames; Sabrina – Severn; Abus – Humber

b) *A family is visiting the museum at the old Roman fort Vindolanda, near Hadrian's Wall. Copy the headings and write down what you learn about them.*

The fort   The village   Roman baths

Roman food   The Vindolanda tablets

c) *Talk about what the Romans and Celts left behind. Use the photos, the map and the texts, and listen to the Vindolanda tour again to find information. Add the new dates to your time line.*

ROMAN BRITAIN

SPEAKING

4 **Your turn: Be a history detective!**

Find out about something that happened in Roman times near where you live. Give a one-minute talk to the class.

Find more online:
3vw7a5

Unit 6

Goodbye Greenwich

A | A beach in Cornwall, in the southwest of England

B | A medieval 'living history' show at Caerphilly Castle in Wales

SPEAKING

→ △ 140/1
△ → After ...

1 Parts of the British Isles → Folie 31

Look at the pictures and find the places on the map at the back of your book. Which part of the British Isles do they belong to? Which part of them looks most interesting to you and why?
Lösung: A: England, B: Wales, C: Ireland, D: Scotland

LISTENING

L 4/1 ⊙
→ S21–23

Voc.: Parts of the British
Isles, p. 236

2 Come on Dave, don't be so negative!

a) *Dave is talking about his parents' plans and his mum's vet surgery. What is the problem from Dave's point of view? Listen and take notes.*

b) *Now talk about the different places that Dave and his friends discuss. Make a grid for your answers with these headings:*

Place | **Landscape** | **Things to do** | **Other information**

In Unit 6 you learn
• to describe places
• to talk about plans for a journey
• to talk about the future with *will*
• to make conditional sentences with *will*
These things can help you to talk or write about places in the British Isles.

C   Pony trekking in Ireland

D   The Edinburgh Festival in the Scottish capital

VOCABULARY

3   Places → WB 63/1–2

a) *Collect vocabulary in different categories like landscapes, sights and activities.*

b) *Each of you does the following: Take four cards and write **one** of your words/ phrases from a) on each card. Shuffle all the cards and pick four. Choose a place in the British Isles and take turns to talk about it with the words on your cards.*

→ S17   c) *Your turn: Find information about a German region (e.g. the North Sea) and give a two-minute talk.* → HA

Lösung: a) Landscapes: seaside, beach, island, river, lake, forest, fields, mountain; Sights: city, village, harbour, castle

Useful phrases

to spend your holidays at the seaside | to visit a castle/village by the sea | to watch the ships/boats in the harbour | to do water sports/to go surfing/windsurfing/ sailing

Across cultures

Did you know that palm trees grow in the southwest of England? Some call it the **English Riviera**. Are there any surprising facts about the region where you live?

L 4/2 ⊚   # Moving to the middle of nowhere → **Folie 32**

Dave's parents have found a beautiful house near St Agnes, in the Cornish countryside.
Dave is very sad to leave.

Dave: Oh no, why do we have to move to the middle of nowhere? London is just fine. And I'll miss you so much!

Olivia: But the house looks fantastic! And your mum never wanted to live in the city. She'll be happy there with her new surgery and all the farm animals and pets to work with, won't she?

Dave: Yes, but will I be happy? Has anyone ever asked *me*? If I want to see farm animals, I can go to Mudchute Farm.

Luke: What about your dad? Will he find work there?

Dave: Well, he travels a lot anyway. He'll stay in London with Aunt Frances when he has to work there. I think it'll be OK for *him*. But me?

Holly: Oh Dave, I'll miss you too! I'm so sorry you won't be able to go to the park with us any longer.

Jay: And we won't be able to play video games together.

Gwen: Come on now, it's not the end of the world. There are games you can play online. Oh, and we'll text you and have lots of video chats together.

Olivia: And we'll come to visit you! Cornwall is a great place. Most British people go there for a holiday. I've been there with my mum.

Dave: That's nice for people on holiday – but *I'll* be in a new school, and there'll be nobody I know. It'll be horrible. And I'm sure Sid will hate it too.

Jay: Don't worry, you'll make lots of new friends. But what about Olivia's idea? We could go to Cornwall to visit you.

Holly: All of us together, in Cornwall? Wow! I'll ask my mum.

Luke: Well, maybe. I'll think about it. But we'll have to find the money first, won't we?

Gwen: I'm sure we'll find a way to get there.

Olivia: Will it be OK for us to stay with Dave?

Luke: I'm sure it will. His parents are cool.

Dave: That's a wonderful idea. It'll be great to see you all there.

READING   **1**   **Questions about the future** → WB 64/3

1. What does Dave say about the Prestons' future in Cornwall?
2. What do his friends say to make him feel better?
3. What will the friends need to do before they go to Cornwall? Think about these things: parents, dates, transport, money.

Examples:

1. He'll miss his friends. His mum will be happy …
2. They'll miss him too. They'll text him …
3. They'll have to ask their parents …

LANGUAGE   **2**   ## Rules for the *will* future   → WB 64/4   → G15

*Find 4–5 sentences with **will** or **won't** in the text. Say if they're* predictions *about the future or* spontaneous reactions/decisions *and write them down in a grid.*

Prediction	Spontaneous reaction/decision
…	…

LANGUAGE   **3**   ## How will we get there?   → KV 67

→ ▲ 140/2
→ △ 141/3
▲ → After …
△ → After …

Luke goes to a travel agent's to ask about the journey to St Agnes.

a) *Complete dialogue A with forms of the **will future** and read it with a partner.*

b) *Now do the same with dialogue B.*

Train + bus: London Paddington to St Agnes
Time: 6 – 7 hours
Prices: £50 – £70
Children under 12 must travel with an adult.

Coach + bus: London Victoria to St Agnes
Time: 8 hours
Prices: £65 – £75
Children under 14 must travel with an adult.

A

Luke: My friends and I want to go to Cornwall, but we're worried that tickets (be) expensive.
Assistant: Don't worry. It (not be) too expensive. But it depends on the date. Give me your dates and I (check) for you.
    (a few minutes later)
    Yes, on those dates, train tickets per person are £5 cheaper than by coach. – Oh, but now I see better prices for the next day. Between £10 and £15 cheaper by train.
Luke: £15 cheaper per person? Cool! My friends (like) that.

Assistant: Well, I can't promise £15, but it (be) a better price than a day earlier. – Oh, and children under 12 need to travel with a person who is 16 or older.
Luke: Oh, that (not be) a problem. – Anyway, I (talk) to my friends and come back to book the tickets.

B

Olivia: (we go) by train or by coach?
Luke: I think we (go) by train. It (be) cheaper and (not take) so long.
Gwen: And we (not have) to find an adult to go with us.
Holly: There's just one problem: Where (I get) the money?

Lösung: a) will be – won't be – I'll/I will check – will like – it'll/it will be – won't be – I'll/I will talk
b) Will we – we'll/we will go – It'll/It will be – won't take – won't have – will I get

LISTENING   **4**   ## Preparing for the trip   → WB 64/5, 65/6

L 4/5 ⊙

Listen to the dialogue and answer the questions.

a) *What's Holly's problem? What can she do and who can help her?*

b) *What will these people do? Say one sentence about each person: Dave, Granny Rose, Luke, the girls, the boys, Luke's grandparents, Holly and Amber.*

Lösung: a) Holly wants to visit Dave together with her friends, but she hasn't got enough money for the tickets. She could ask her father, sell some of her things or take on a small job. In the end, Amber can help her.

Sally Richardson
Holly
Amber

LANGUAGE   **5**   **Dave's farewell party**[1]   → WB 65/7, 66/8–10   → G16   → **Folie 32**

→ ▲ 141/4
▲ → After …

Read part A. Find all the sentences about the future and say when you use which tense. Then use the same rules to complete the dialogue (part B) with future forms.

Lösung: Part B:
1. 'm going to wear (plan), 2. 'll be (prediction), 3. 'll be (think, hope, be sure), 4. 're going to have (plan), 5. leaves (timetable), 6. 'll take (prediction), 7. 'll be (prediction), 8. 'll be (think, hope, be sure), 9. will be really surprised (prediction)/ is really going to be surprised (first signs already showing)

A   Dave is going to move to Cornwall soon. Luke and Jay are talking about their plans.

    "I'm so sad that Dave is going to move to Cornwall. I'm going to miss him so much!"
5   Luke says.

    "Me too," Jay adds. "I hope he'll find a lot of new friends there …" Then he has an idea: "But we should try to have some fun while we're still here together. Let's organise
10   a farewell party!"

    "That's a good idea!" Luke shouts. "But I haven't got much time now because football training is at 4 p.m. I don't think I'll be able to come to your house until 5.30."
15   Jay replies: "OK, so let's meet later at my house. I'll tell Olivia and Holly."

B   It's 5.35 at Jay's house. Holly can't come, and Olivia isn't there yet.

Luke: Hey Jay, I **1** my costume from your
20   birthday party again.

Jay: Luke, we had a costume party last year! How about a picnic with lots of cake? The weather forecast says it **2** sunny this week.

Luke: Oh yes, you can all come to my house, 25 we have a small garden. I'm sure it **3** OK for my parents – Oh, there's Olivia, let's tell her about our plan!

Jay: Hi Olivia! We **4** a farewell party for Dave at Luke's house. Can you come 30 on Saturday at 3 p.m.?

Olivia: Great! But I've got a netball game in Blackheath in the morning. Just let me check, I think I can get to your house by bus … Oh yes, the bus **5**   35 at 2:44 p.m. It **6** about 15 minutes to get to your house, so I **7** there at about 3 p.m., great! I'm sure it **8** a lot of fun!

Jay: Dave **9** (really be surprised) on 40 Saturday!

MEDIATION   **6**   **The weather forecast**   → **Folie 33**

→ △ 141/5
→ S20
△ → Help with …

Du verbringst den Urlaub im Oberallgäu. Ein Tourist aus Schottland möchte morgen eine fünfstündige Wandertour machen. Er zeigt dir die folgende Wettervorhersage.
Erkläre ihm, wie das Wetter morgen werden wird und was das für seine Pläne bedeutet.

Voc.: Weather, WB (Word bank), p. 10

Wettervorhersage Oberallgäu: Während es heute bei Höchsttemperaturen über 30°C und bis zu acht Sonnenstunden noch sehr heiß ist, zieht morgen eine Schlechtwetterfront von Südwesten herein. Am Morgen wird es bei viel Sonnenschein noch trocken und warm bleiben. Jedoch ist vor allem am Nachmittag und Abend mit starken Unwettern zu rechnen, örtlich können sich heftige Gewitter bilden. Besonders im Bergland besteht Gefahr durch orkanartige Windböen mit Geschwindigkeiten bis zu 105 km/h und Blitzschlag. Durch starke Niederschläge kann es zu Überflutungen kommen. Dabei wird sich die Luft deutlich abkühlen und es werden nur noch Temperaturen um die 20°C erreicht werden. Die Kaltfront wird sich aber nicht lange halten können und so wird es übermorgen schon wieder aufklaren und freundlicher werden. Zum Wochenende erwarten wir dann wieder mehr Sonnenschein bei mäßiger Bewölkung und Höchsttemperaturen um die 25°C, die Niederschlagswahrscheinlichkeit sinkt dabei auf unter 10%.

---

1 farewell party [feəˈwel ˌpɑːti] Abschiedsfeier

How to get information → S11–14

For the Unit task you'll need information about different parts of the British Isles: England (e.g. Cornwall, or maybe London), Scotland, Wales and Ireland (Northern Ireland or the Republic of Ireland).

1 Where to get information

If you want to collect pictures and facts about interesting places, you can write to a tourist board and ask for free material. What else can you do?

2 Asking for information → WB 67/11–13

Make four groups, one for each of the regions you learned about on the Check-in pages. Find out e-mail addresses of organisations that have interesting material. Then write a polite e-mail to ask for the material. Some of them don't give you their e-mail addresses but ask you to fill in an internet contact form. Make sure you don't write to the same organisation about the same material more than once!

> **Writing skills**
>
> Before you send off your e-mail or contact form, **remember**:
> – Don't forget your greetings.
> – Who are you?
> – What do you want to do?
> – What do you need?
> – How do you ask in a polite way?
> – What information about yourselves do you need to give?

Dear Sir or Madam,

We are students of a German grammar school. We would like to do a project about the British Isles and need information about Scotland for it.
Could you please send us some free material about interesting places in Scotland, Scottish history and things to do in Scotland?
Here is our address:
...-Gymnasium
Class ...
...straße (XX)
D-(XXXXX) ...

Thank you very much for your help.

Best wishes,
The students of Class (...)

3 Working with the material

*When you have enough material, go through it together in your group.
Make notes of interesting ideas for a presentation, and look for the best photos.*

L 4/6 ⊙ # Visit Cornwall – you'll love it! → KV 68, KV 69, Folie 34

Where is Cornwall?

If you look at a map of Great Britain, you'll find Cornwall in the far west. Look north, west or south of Cornwall and you'll find the same 'neighbour': the Atlantic Ocean. Cornwall's coastline is almost 300 miles long and gets more sun than any other part of the UK.

Why do more than 3 million tourists visit Cornwall every year?

If you like dramatic landscapes, beautiful fishing harbours and wonderful beaches and if you're into water sports, you'll find that Cornwall is just the right place for your holiday.
But Cornwall has more to offer than its coastline and water sports. There are lots of other outdoor activities, like adventure sports, pony trekking or golf. And if you aren't into sports at all, you can visit a lot of very interesting sights.
If you go to Bodmin Moor, you'll get to know a wild landscape with prehistoric monuments that you can explore on great walking trails. And if you visit the Eden Project near St Austell, you can look at beautiful and useful plants from around the world and learn about the environment. It's the most popular tourist attraction in Cornwall.
If you visit one of the museums, you'll learn a lot about Cornwall's Celtic past or its mining history. You can still see Celtic culture in Bronze Age monuments, Celtic crosses and Cornish place names. Like Irish, Scottish Gaelic or Welsh, Cornish is a Celtic language and a few people in Cornwall still speak it besides English – but you'll be very lucky if you hear it.
If you want to eat real Cornish food, you should try pasties[1]. (And if you're still hungry, try cream tea[2] with scones[3], clotted cream[4] and jam!)
When you're here, don't forget to come in and say 'hello' at one of our many visitor centres!

Voc.: Holiday accommodation, WB (Word bank), p. 10

8 🎬
Mehr zum Thema Cornwall

READING **7** ## Tourist information about Cornwall → WB 68/14 → Folie 34

Voc.: Places and what you can do there, p. 238

Olivia has found this text about Cornwall on the internet. Say what information there is about the geography, tourism, things to do, sights, history and food.

LANGUAGE **8** ## What will happen if …? → WB 68/15 → G17 → KV 70

*Collect all the sentences with **if** from the text. They have two parts: an **if clause** and a **main clause**. There are three basic patterns, but in one example the order is different:*

If …, … will …	If …, … can …	If …, … should … If …, try …
…	…	…

---

1 **pasty** ['pæsti] Pastete | 2 **cream tea** [ˌkriːm 'tiː] Nachmittagstee | 3 **scone** [skɒn] brötchenartiges Buttergebäck |
4 **clotted cream** [ˌklɒtɪd 'kriːm] Sahne *(aus erhitzter Milch)*

LANGUAGE **9** **Find the rule** → WB 69/16 → G17

→ ▲ 142/6
▲ → After . . .

Lösung: a) 1. B, 2. C, 3. A

a) *Match the three patterns with the meanings. Then write the rule and put it in your folder.*

1. If you go to Cornwall, you'll see a lot of beautiful beaches.
2. If you go to Cornwall, you can do water sports.
3. If you go to Cornwall, you should try cream tea.

A Advice
B Prediction
C Possibility

→ △ 142/7
△ → After . . .

b) *In German, there's only one word for **if** and **when**. Can you explain the difference between sentences 1. and 2. with the information in brackets?*

1. If I go to Cornwall, I'll go surfing. (I don't know if we'll go to Cornwall or to Italy.)
2. When Dave goes to Cornwall, he'll miss his friends. (We know he'll go there, but we don't know when.)

Lösung: b) In sentence 1, the speaker is not sure if he'll go to Cornwall.
In sentence 2, the speaker knows that Dave is going to go to Cornwall.

LANGUAGE **10** **Go on with the story** → WB 69/17

👥👤

→ △ 142/8
△ → After . . .

Play a game in class: One student starts with an if-sentence.
The next student uses the main clause as an if-clause and makes
a new sentence, and so on.

Example: If I go on holiday, I'll take my dog. → If I take my dog,
he'll be happy. → If my dog is happy, he'll … → …

SPEAKING **11** **Languages in the British Isles** → **Folie 34**

→ △ 143/9
△ → Help with . . .

Explain the blue words. Most of them are of Latin/French origin. Then check with a dictionary.

Lösung: 1. Something that developed wasn't there before, but it exists now.
2. extinct = dead, no longer there
3. literature = books, texts you can read
4. frequently = often
5. Polish = from Poland

Celtic languages have existed for a long time in the British Isles. The progressive form in English probably developed because of this long contact with Celtic languages. Manx and Cornish are almost extinct, but some people still speak Irish, Scottish Gaelic or Welsh, and you can watch TV and read literature in these languages. But there are also newer immigrant languages in the British Isles. The ones you hear most frequently are Polish and several different languages from India.

> **Across cultures**
>
> Everybody in the British Isles speaks English. But some parts still have their own **Celtic languages:**
> Ireland → Irish;
> Scotland → Scottish Gaelic;
> Wales → Welsh; Cornwall → Cornish;
> Isle of Man → Manx.
> What languages do people in your class speak besides German?

LISTENING **12** **Announcements** → WB 70/18–20 → **KV 71**

L 4/8–11 ⊙
→ S23

Lösung: b) dialogues 1–3: station/train; dialogue 4: airport

a) *Mr Preston travels a lot. Listen to four little dialogues and find out this information for each scene. Take notes:*

1. where he is
2. where he wants to go
3. what sight they talk about
4. what the announcement is about.

b) *Say in what way the fourth dialogue is different from the other three.*

LANGUAGE **13**　*May, might* and *can/could* for possibilities → G18

→ △ 143/10

△ → After …

a) *Read the text below. Use **let's** and **maybe** to rewrite Luke's and Olivia's answers.*

Jay:　"What could we do in Cornwall? Any ideas?"

Luke:　"We could go surfing!"

Olivia:　"Well, outdoor activities may not be a good idea. I checked the weather forecast. It may rain next week and it might even be stormy …"

b) *The friends are preparing Dave's farewell party. Complete the dialogue with the modals **may**, **might** and **can/could**.*

Olivia:　"What `1` we bring for the picnic?

Holly:　"I `2` make a cake."

Jay:　"And I `3` bring crackers!"

Luke:　"Oh, Dave would love them, but Sherlock `4` be scared, because they `5` be too loud for him. He `6` even run away."

Olivia:　"Right! And it `7` rain on Saturday. That `8` be a problem. "

Luke:　"No, we `9` go inside then. Please be on time, Dave will be here at 3 p.m."

Holly:　"I `10` be a bit late because I have to be at the doctor's at 2:30 p.m. I'm looking forward to the party!"

READING **14**　British history: A poem about the Romans　→ KV 72, Diktat- und Transfertext

S 2/19
L 4/12

→ ▲ 143/11

▲ → After …

a) *Explain what the poem says about the Romans and what they did in Britain.*

The Romans in Britain
(A history in 40 words)

by Judith Nicholls

The Romans gave us aqueducts[1]
fine buildings and straight roads,
where all those Roman legionaries[2]
marched with heavy loads[3].

They gave us central heating[4],
good laws[5], a peaceful home …
Then after just four centuries
they shuffled[6] back to Rome.

Useful phrases

to build (a bridge, a road, a town) |
to supply somebody (with water, food) |
to rule (a country)

b) *Think of how you could complete this little poem about Britain.*

Great Britain is an island.
It is in the North …
It's got green fields and mountains.
It's where I'd like to …

The biggest city is …
It's got a lot to show.
There's always something happening
It's where I'd like to…

1 **aqueduct** [ˈækwɪdʌkt] Aquädukt (Wasserleitung) | 2 **legionary** [ˈliːdʒənəri] Legionär | 3 **heavy load** [ˌhevi ˈləʊd] schwere Last | 4 **central heating** [ˌsentrl ˈhiːtɪŋ] Zentralheizung | 5 **law** [lɔː] Gesetz | 6 **to shuffle** [ˈʃʌfl] schlurfen

▶ The caves → S24–25

SPEAKING

1   Things to do in the country

Talk about which of these activities you find interesting.

1. feeding animals
2. milking cows
3. exploring a cave
4. swimming in a lake
5. playing in an adventure playground
6. reading ghost stories
7. walking
8. geocaching

VIEWING

2   Themes → KV 73

9 🎬   *Watch the film. Then say which themes below play a role in the film. Explain why/why not. Which of them are more important/the most important?*

1. food
2. city and country life
3. school
4. children and adults
5. stories
6. sports
7. love
8. ghosts

VIEWING

3   Suspense: What's going to happen? → KV 74

Watch the film again, find examples of the ideas below and take notes. They can help you to talk about elements that create suspense in a story.

Story: What about …
– Laura's grandpa?
– ghosts?
– getting lost?
– phones, maps and torches?

Acting: What about …
– people's faces?

Audiovisual effects: What about …
– darkness?
– strange sounds, a voice in the caves?
– dramatic music?

Film skills

Elements that create suspense:
– clues in the story about what could happen
– acting
– music
– light
– sounds

WRITING

4   Laura and her grandpa

→ S16   *Write a scene that comes after the last scene in the film:
Laura and her grandpa talk about what has really happened and why.
Act it out and film it.*

Our big British Isles quiz

You're going to work in four groups. You're going to make question cards for a quiz about the British Isles (Wales, England, etc.). You can use information in this book and from other sources. When you're finished, you'll be able to play a quiz game.

Step 1

Get organised

Make four groups of 4–6, one for a different part of the British Isles. In your group, agree on 16 interesting sights or places in your region. Each of you makes 2–4 question cards so you have one for each sight in the end.

For ideas, look at **this unit** and **the other units** in the book. Use the information material you got from **books**, the **internet** and **tourist boards**.

Step 2

Prepare your cards

Make cards that look like this on the front and back. But don't finish them until you've done Step 3.

Tower of London

(A question about the sight/place/thing)
Which of these animals never lived at the Tower?

(Three answers, two of which are wrong)
a) a polar bear that loved to fish
b) a raven that was able to talk
c) a zebra that liked beer

(The right answer)

Step 3

Test your cards

a) *Show a picture of the sight/place/
thing you want to use for the front of
your card. Read the question and the
three answers. The others guess which
answer is right. Correct them if they're
wrong. You can give tips to help them.*

b) *Are the questions, answers and tips
OK? If a quiz question is too difficult,
make changes or give more tips.*

c) *Now make your cards.*

Useful phrases

Ideas for tips:
In this place you can …
It's famous for …
One of the attractions here is …
If you want to …, you will … here.
If you're interested in history, you
   should …
It's in the north/east/south/west.
… built it.

Step 4

Play the quiz game in your groups

– *Shuffle the 16 cards for your group and place them on a table face down.*
– *Each group draws four cards from each group.*
– *In each group, shuffle all the cards again.*
– *Every player draws the same number of cards. One player starts and
  reads out the card to the person next to him/her. If the person gets the
  answer right, he/she can keep the card.*
– *When you've used all the cards once, the person with the most cards wins!*

Step 5

Your 'British Isles Top 5'

a) *Copy an outline of the map of Britain at the
back of this book.*

b) *Mark your 'Top 5' sights/places on the map.
Write information about them next to each one.*

c) *Gallery walk: Look at the other posters and try
to guess the sights/places.*

For help with
gallery walks,
look at **S30** in the
Skills section.

I think that's the capital of Scotland.
Do you know its name?

Edinburgh?

S 2/20–24
L 4/13–17

Things will get better → Folie 35

A "Come in, come in!" Mrs Preston said from the hall of the big old house by the sea. "I'll make some tea."

"We can't have tea, Mum," Dave said.
5 "There's no electricity, remember?"

"Oh, yes," she answered. "Well, a glass of water then?"

"Er … OK, yes please, Mrs Preston," Olivia said.

10 "Hi," Dave said to his friends and his granny. "Thanks for coming. Good journey?"

"Yeah, the journey was fine, thanks," Luke answered. "But *you* don't look fine.
15 What's the matter? Is everything OK?"

"No, not really," Dave said. "We've been here a week, and there's no electricity yet. Dad is in London, the cat has run away, I haven't got any friends and I'm really
20 missing my old life in Greenwich. It's awful here. I hate it."

"Oh, Dave!" Granny Rose said. "Don't be sad. You've only been here a week. Things will get better. You know they will."

B "Here are your glasses of water," Mrs Preston said. Then she looked at one of the glasses. "Oh dear," she said. "Why is this water brown? I think we've got a problem with the water now too."

"Let's go out," Dave said to his friends. 30 "We'll go up to the coastal path, to the old mine. Is that OK, Mum?"

"Yes, that's fine," Dave's mum answered. "See you later. I'll call a plumber."

"But it's Sunday," Granny Rose said. 35 "If you call a plumber on a Sunday, it'll be *really* expensive."

C The friends were standing on a hill by an old building. It had a tall chimney, but no roof. There was a strong wind from the sea, 40 and it brought lots of big black clouds.

"This old building looks a bit scary," Holly whispered.

"Don't be silly. It's just one of many old mine buildings in this area. Tin was really 45 important here," Olivia said. "Going right back to Celtic times. Tin from Cornwall went all over the world. But now there's almost no tin left."

"Looks like a great place for 50 geocaching!" Luke said excitedly as he grabbed his smartphone. "Let's see if there's a cache somewhere near here. – Yes, there must be a difficult puzzle cache."

"Really?" Dave asked, "Let's solve the 55 puzzle and get to that cache!"

Suddenly a deep voice behind them boomed, "Hey you, what are you doing here?! Keep away from MY treasure!"

The friends were scared. They turned 60 around and saw a big man with a serious face. He was wearing a kind of skirt and trousers. He had wild hair and looked dangerous, not only because of the long spear in his hand. 65

"I'm sorry, we – we didn't want to steal anything from you. We didn't know the cache was yours," Dave said. He was really scared.

Suddenly the sun came out again and 70 the man's face went from scary to much friendlier.

"Hello!" he said to Dave. "I was only joking. Have you just moved into number 7?"

75 "Er, yes," Dave said. "And you are a Celtic warrior?"

"I'm Bob," the man said. "Your new neighbour."

"Ah," Dave said. "So you're on your way 80 to a fancy dress party, aren't you?"

The others just looked at Bob's strange clothes and said nothing.

"Oh, don't worry!" Bob laughed. "I don't always wear these clothes. I'm in the local 85 history society. We do shows about the history of Cornwall. These are clothes from Celtic times."

"Right," Dave said. "Nice to meet you."

"I just came up to say hello," Bob said. 90 "Tea at my house anyone?"

D "This is my wife, Helen," Bob said. The friends were standing in the kitchen of Bob's house. "And these are my children, Jago and Tamara." The boy and girl were 95 both about 13. "Good old Cornish names."

"Hello Dave. I'm Jago," the boy said.

"We're twins," the girl said. "Do you like computers, Dave?"

"Not now, Tamara," Bob said. "I'm sure 100 Dave doesn't want to hear about your new computer games."

Then Olivia saw a big bag of tools on the kitchen floor.

"What do you do, Mr … er …?

105 "Call me Bob. I'm a plumber. And Helen here's an electrician. We do the plumbing and electrics for half the village. Well, the *whole* village, really."

Then Bob's bag of tools moved. A cat came out of it. 110

"That's the cat that moved in here last week," Bob said.

"Sid!" Dave shouted. "There you are!"

E An hour later, there were thirteen people and a cat in Dave's garden. The friends, Bob 115 and his family, Granny Rose and Dave's parents were all sitting around a big garden table. There was tea and a cake.

"We were on the train before you," Granny Rose said to Dave's dad. "I didn't 120 know you were coming today."

"Change of plan at work," Dave's dad said. "I can be here all this week."

"Thanks again for fixing the water," Dave's mum said to Bob. "Are you sure I 125 can't pay you for …"

"No, no," Bob said. "It was a five-minute job, and we're neighbours. But I'll have another piece of Rose's cake, if that's OK."

"And I'll have a look at your electrics 130 tomorrow morning," Helen added.

Dave turned to Luke. "I think it'll be OK here after all," he said.

READING

→ S6-8

1 Understanding the text → WB 71/21

a) *Find headings for parts A–E of the story.*

b) *Answer these questions:*

1. What problems do the Prestons have in their new home?
2. What do the friends think of Bob at first? What do we get to know about him?
3. Think of what Granny Rose said at the end of part A. At the end of the story, was she right? Explain.

Lösung: a)
A: Cornwall is awful,
B: Problems with the water, C: The stormy coast and a scary man, D: Dave's new neighbours,
E: Cornwall is OK

SPEAKING

2 Help for Dave → Diktat- und Transfertext

Talk about what everyone can do to make Dave happier in his new home.

Example: Tamara and Jago can play computer games with him.

WRITING

→ S11-14

Voc.: Difficult prepositions, p. 240; Describing people and animals, Describing things, WB (Word bank), pp. 2–4

3 Creative writing → WB 71/22 → KV 75, HA

a) *Write a diary entry for one of the characters about what happened on their first day in Cornwall and what he/she felt. Read your partner's text and give feedback. Think about what the character is like, what he/she knows and what he/she probably thinks.*

b) *Write a postcard from one of Dave's friends to his/her parents at home.*

> ### Writing skills
>
> A **diary entry** is a very personal text. Usually nobody else reads it. It's like writing to a close friend. Put the date at the top and start writing about what happened, what was important and how you feel about it. You can also write about your hopes and plans for the future.

EH: b) Holly:
Dear Mum and Amber,
We've arrived in St Agnes. Our journey was good. The Prestons still have a few problems with their house, but their neighbours Bob and Helen are very nice and they'll help them. They have got two children too. That's great for Dave! We had tea and a cake in the garden.
Love, Holly

Greetings from St Agnes

Dear Mum and Dad,

How are you? We arrived in St Agnes yesterday. There is a beautiful harbour with nice sailboats, and we're camping really close to the sea. The weather is great, and we've spent a lot of time at the beach.

See you soon,

Megan

> **Can you ...**
>
> 1. say what will happen in the future? __   Tomorrow there will be ...
> 2. talk about the future with 'if'? _ _ _ _   If you ..., you can/will/should ...
> 3. talk about places and regions? _ _ _ _   It's in ... | It has got ... | There are ... | You can ... there.
> 4. use modals to talk about possibilities? _ _ _ _ _ _ _ _ _ _ _ _   It could ... | He might ... | I may ...

LANGUAGE

1 Tomorrow's weather forecast → HA

Complete the weather forecast with the correct forms of the verbs in the box.

Tomorrow ⬛1 a nice day. There ⬛2 a lot of sun. There ⬛3 too many clouds. In the morning, it ⬛4 cool, but it ⬛5 nicer in the afternoon. It ⬛6 a fine day for outdoor activities. You can be sure it ⬛7 . But in the evening there ⬛8 more wind, and at night the weather ⬛9 . Clouds ⬛10 and at about 12 o'clock it ⬛11 to rain.

be (5x)

not be

change

get

move in

not rain

start

LANGUAGE

2 Mixed bag: Holiday plans → WB 72/23 → KV 76, HA

Put in the missing words or phrases.

A: ⬛1 I ⬛2 you that we ⬛3 go to Cornwall in the summer? I'm really ⬛4 to this holiday!
B: We ⬛5 there last year. The beaches there are ⬛6 ! ⬛7 you like surfing, you ⬛8 Cornwall.
A: Yes, I'm sure I ⬛9 like it. I hope the weather ⬛10 nice ⬛11 we ⬛12 spend a lot of ⬛13 on the beach.
B: Oh yes, that ⬛14 be great! We still ⬛15 found a place to go on holiday. There's ⬛16

we can agree on. Everyone in ⬛17 family ⬛18 to go to a ⬛19 place.
A: I ⬛20 . Oh dear! But ⬛21 you have no ⬛22 where to go, you ⬛23 go to the ⬛24 . They ⬛25 give you ⬛26 and help you to ⬛27 a hotel and ⬛28 the tickets.
B: Mum says we ⬛29 go camping, and Dad ⬛30 to go ⬛31 car, but yes, we ⬛32 get some ideas there.

LANGUAGE

3 *If* or *when*? → WB 72/24–25 → KV 77, HA

1. ... I get up, I'll make breakfast. – ... I get up before you, I'll make breakfast. | 2. I won't do my homework today ... my teacher doesn't want it tomorrow. – I'll do my homework ... I'm at home after school. | 3. ... I can find the time, I'll write my friends a postcard from Cornwall – My friends will be happy ... they get my postcard from Cornwall. | 4. The friends will call Dave ... they arrive at the station. – The friends will call Dave ... they arrive late.

Find more online:
hd87f9

British stories and legends

You already know some American stories and legends. Now look at some strange and wonderful stories about British heroes and heroines. They may or may not be true.

SPEAKING

1 Warm-up

Talk about famous historical people you know about in Germany, in the US or in Britain.

READING

2 Typical ingredients of legends → **Folie 36, KV 78, KV 22**

a) *Read the text. Which ingredients do you like in a story or legend? Why?*

Lösung: a) Typical ingredients of legends: stories about people in history; usually not completely true; often show the difference between right and wrong; colourful characters, e.g. kings, queens, wizards; good and bad characters: heroes and villains; heroes usually win fights; heroes: brave knights or normal people who do brave things; villains: criminals or powerful people; more modern legends from popular books, e.g. Sherlock Holmes

Legends are stories about people in history – but usually they aren't completely true. Often writers have taken historical events and changed them a bit to make the stories more exciting, or maybe to make the difference between right and wrong clearer. Legends have colourful characters like brave kings and cruel queens or magical characters like wizards. There are heroes ('good guys') and villains ('bad guys') who have dangerous fights – of course, the good guy usually wins! Popular heroes are often brave knights, but sometimes they're just normal men who do brave things to help other people. Villains can be dangerous criminals or very powerful people who use their power in a bad way. And finally there are more modern legends from popular books, like Sherlock Holmes, a private detective who solved mysterious crimes. He never lived at all, but people all over the world love to think he did!

b) *Look at the stills of Jinsoo and Marley. They're playing the roles of three famous British legends. What do you think the stories are about? What do you know about them?*

Useful phrases

Nouns: king | queen | wizard | hero/heroine | villain | knight | robber | outlaw

Adjectives: colourful | magical | brave | cruel | dangerous | powerful | mysterious

Phrases: to have a fight | to hide in the forest | to use your power | to solve a crime

VIEWING

3 Stories and legends (1) → Folie 36

10 **a)** *Watch the film and take notes about the three legends.*

Lösung: b) 1. a), d), g); 2. c), f), h); 3. b), e)

b) *Find the correct information for each character. Then talk about them. Use relative clauses.*

1. Sherlock Holmes was a private detective.
2. Robin Hood was a famous outlaw.
3. King Arthur was a powerful king.

a) Dr Watson was his assistant.
b) Many people think Tintagel was his castle.
c) He lived in Sherwood Forest near Nottingham.
d) He lived in Baker Street in London.
e) His knights sat at the Round Table.
f) He loved Maid Marian.
g) He solved many mysterious crimes.
h) He stole from the rich and gave to the poor.

VIEWING

4 Stories and legends (2)

→ KV 79, KV 80
→ WB 73/1–2

Lösung a) Sherlock Holmes: typical outfit: cape and cap, magnifying glass; Robin Hood: green hat with a feather, green top, bow and arrow; King Arthur: crown

a) *Watch the film again. Which characters have which props?*

b) *Your turn: Read the skills box. Then find out about another character from a legend or story, maybe a woman (like Boudicca, the Celtic queen who fought against the Romans; Vivien, the Lady⁶ of the Lake, who gave King Arthur his sword⁷ Excalibur; or Miss Marple, a detective in Agatha Christie's crime stories.) Which costume, props or set could you give that character in a film? Why?*

c) *Role play: In groups of three, each of you chooses to be one of the characters. Your characters meet. Talk to each other about*

1. where you live
2. what you do
3. what you wear and carry
4. what's good and bad about your life.

Example:
A: Hi there. I'm Robin, I help the poor.
B: And I'm Miss Marple. I love to solve mysterious crimes.
C: …

bell	castle	bow and arrow¹
gloves	cape²	crown³
lucky charm	magnifying glass⁴	cap⁵

Film skills

A film uses more than pictures, sounds and words to tell a story. It also uses **costumes**, **props** and a **set**. The characters wear **costumes** and they carry or use **props**. We can also see where they live – this is called the **set**.

Example:
If you want to show that a woman is a queen, she can wear a crown and beautiful clothes and live in a castle.

Robin, you don't think you're the *only* hero in this forest, do you?

Of course not, Marian.

1 **bow and arrow** [ˌbəʊ ən ˈærəʊ] Pfeil und Bogen | 2 **cape** [keɪp] Umhang |
3 **crown** [kraʊn] Krone | 4 **magnifying glass** [ˈmæɡnɪfaɪŋ ˌɡlɑːs] Lupe |
5 **cap** [kæp] Kappe; Mütze | 6 **lady** [ˈleɪdi] Herrin; Dame | 7 **sword** [sɔːd] Schwert

⟨Revision C⟩ ist fakultativ und dient der Festigung/Wiederholung. Es werden keine neuen Sprachmittel eingeführt.

SPEAKING

1 An interview with a Celtic warrior → WB 74/1–2

*Imagine you are living in the year 2231. People have invented a time machine and you go back in time to interview the Celtic warrior Drustan. Act out dialogues with a partner. One of you is the interviewer, the other is Drustan. Use **modals** to ask questions and give answers. The ideas below will help you. Remember to be polite.*

ask you some questions?   live in peace with the Romans?

carry a shield in the battles?   defeat¹ the Romans?

make Boudicca their prisoner?   invite you to use the time machine?

LANGUAGE

2 But I don't know anybody in Cornwall! → WB 75/3 → HA

*Put in the right forms of **be able to, be allowed to** or **have to**. Sometimes you will need negative forms. Be careful with the tenses!*

Lösung: 1. have to,
2. won't be able,
3./4. am (I) not allowed/
won't I be allowed,
5. will be able,
6. will have to,
7./8. am (I) not allowed,
9. will be able to,
10. are not allowed,
11. am not allowed,
12. will have to,
13. will have to

Dave: Mum, do we really **1** move to Cornwall? If we move there, I to see my friends every day. Why **3** I **4** to stay in London with Aunt Frances?

Mrs Preston: Because we want to have you with us. You know that I **5** to work with a lot more animals in Cornwall.

Dave: And who cares about me? I don't know anybody in Cornwall and I **6** find new friends there. Why **7** I **8** to do what I want?

Mrs Preston: I am sure you **9** find a lot of new friends.

Dave: But I don't want new friends. I will go to London every weekend to meet my friends there.

Mrs Preston: Don't be silly. You know you **10** to travel on your own.

Dave: I **11** to do anything at all!

Mrs Preston: Dave, let's move to Cornwall and see how it is. If you really don't like it there, we **12** think about what to do.

Dave: I guess I **13** make the best of it … But I am looking forward to my friends' visit!

SPEAKING

3 Sounds and spelling

L 4/18 ◉
Lösung: b) Schöpfung/
Erschaffung, saisonal/
jahreszeitlich, Harmonie

a) *Some English words look almost like German words, but the sounds are different. You already know the words in black. Say them and then check with the CD.*

L 4/19 ◉

b) *Now say the **new words**. Can you tell what they mean in German? Check the pronunciation with the CD.*

attraction	industrial	colony
information	national	gallery
protection	personal	geography
organisation	traditional	industry
creation	seasonal	harmony

1 **to defeat** [dɪˈfiːt] besiegen

MEDIATION **4** ## A holiday activity pass → WB 75/4 → **HA**

Eure Nachbarn sind vor Kurzem aus Schweden nach München gezogen und sprechen noch nicht
so gut Deutsch, aber dafür Englisch. Sie haben zwei Kinder im Alter von 12 und 15 Jahren und
haben folgende Fragen an dich zu einem Infoflyer:
"When can you use the activity pass, and who can use it? What can you do with it?"
Beantworte die Fragen mit den Informationen aus dem Flyer.

Lösung: EH: This
activity pass is for all
children and teenagers
between six and 17
who are living in or
around Munich. You
can use it during
Bavarian holidays from
fall to summer. With
this pass, you can go to
swimming pools, use
public transport and
take part in the holiday
programme during the
summer holidays. So
it's perfect for you!

Informationen zum Ferienpass

Wie lange gilt der Münchner Ferienpass?

Er gilt von den Herbstferien bis zum Ende der Sommerferien und beinhaltet viele Tipps für aufregende Unterneh-
mungen.

Wer kann ihn nutzen? Der Münchner Ferienpass gilt
für Kinder und Jugendliche von sechs bis 17 Jahren. Alle
können ihn kaufen, egal wo sie wohnen, ob in München oder umliegenden Landkreisen. Auch Kinder
und Jugendliche, die nicht in München und Umgebung leben, können diesen Pass erwerben. Er gilt
nur in den bayerischen Schulferien.

Was kostet der Münchner Ferienpass? 14 Euro für Kinder und Jugendliche bis zu
14 Jahren. Er beinhaltet die Bäder[1]-Nutzung, die MVV[2]-Nutzung in den Sommerferien und das
Ferienpassprogramm.

10 Euro für Jugendliche von 15 bis 17 Jahren. Er beinhaltet die Bäder-Nutzung und das
Ferienpassprogramm, aber nicht die MVV-Nutzung.

Bitte für den Kauf des Ferienpasses unbedingt ein aktuelles Foto des Kindes zur Verkaufsstelle
mitbringen und dort abstempeln lassen.

Wann und wo wird der Münchner Ferienpass verkauft? Ab Mitte Oktober wird der
Münchner Ferienpass an verschiedenen Verkaufsstellen in München und Umgebung verkauft.

WRITING **5** ## The world 50 years from now[3] → KV 81, KV 82

In a short text, make predictions about the future. What will life be like 50 (or 100, 200) years from
*now? Use the **will** future in your text, and think of these ideas:*

Voc.: Describing
people and animals,
Describing things,
WB (Word bank),
pp. 2–4

how people will
live/travel |
what people will
eat/drink | what
school/nature/
technology will be
like | how people
will communicate
with each other

forest skyscrapers to live in

robots for cleaning the house

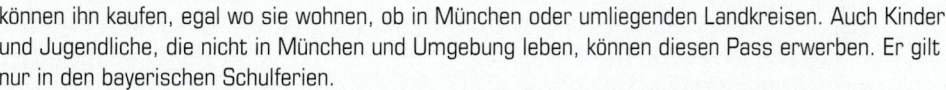

1 **Bäder** swimming pools | 2 **MVV** public transport (buses, trains etc.) in and around Munich |
3 **50 years from now** in fünfzig Jahren

6   A legend: How Arthur became king

Read the text and do the exercises.

Sir Ector looked at his son.

"There is something very special about the tournament here in London tomorrow. The Archbishop has organised it – because
5   we have to find a new king. When King Uther died thirteen years ago, there was nobody to follow him. Then the knights and lords began to fight against each other. The fighting has been terrible!"

10   Kay listened as his father went on. "Well, when many of the greatest knights and lords were in London for Christmas church service, they saw something very strange. Outside the cathedral, in the
15   middle of the square, there was a very big stone. And in the middle of the stone was the handle of a great sword. When they went nearer, they could see these words on the stone – in beautiful gold letters:
20   THE ONE WHO PULLS THIS SWORD OUT OF THIS STONE IS THE TRUE KING OF BRITAIN. Well, you can imagine what happened then! The knights and lords went crazy! They pushed each other out of
25   the way to get to the stone. Everyone tried to pull the sword out. One after the other. But not one of them could move it."

"And then?" Kay said.

"Then suddenly Merlin, the old wizard
30   from Wales, appeared and said, 'Our true king is not here yet. But he will come! And then something wonderful will happen.' And he asked the Archbishop to organise a big tournament for the beginning of
35   February – so all the knights of Britain could be there for it!"

"So will I have the chance to try too, father? To pull the sword out? Now that I'm a knight too?"

40   "Yes, I think so," said his father. "After the tournament everyone will be able to try."

When Sir Ector, Kay and his squire Arthur were on their way to the great tournament outside the walls of London
45   town, Kay suddenly stopped his horse.

"Father! I've forgotten my sword!" he cried. "We'll have to go back."

"But we'll miss the beginning of the tournament if we go back now," Sir Ector
50   said.

"I'll ride back to the inn and get it for you, Kay," said young Arthur. "I'm your squire, so it's my fault really." So Arthur turned his horse round and rode
55   back to the town. But the door of the inn was closed and everybody was at the tournament, of course.

'What on earth can I do?' thought Arthur. 'People will laugh at Kay and he'll
60   be angry with me if I go back without it.'

He rode through the streets for a while and tried to think of a plan. And then, suddenly, there he was in the big square in front of the cathedral. When he saw
65   the great sword in the stone, he couldn't believe his luck. The gold letters shone in the sun, but Arthur didn't even notice them.

"Just what I was looking for!" he cried
70   as he jumped off his horse and ran over to the stone. Nobody saw Arthur as he took the handle of the sword in his hands and pulled. The sword came out of the stone right away.
75

a) *Are these statements true or false? Correct the false ones in your exercise book.*

1. King Uther tells Sir Ector about the sword in the stone.
2. Merlin says that the person who pulls out the sword will be king.
3. It was the Archbishop's idea to organise a big tournament.
4. Sir Ector doesn't want Kay to go back and get his sword.
5. Arthur remembers the sword in the stone and wants to get it for Kay.
6. Arthur will become king because he pulls the sword out of the stone.

b) *Find the words with the following meanings in the text:*

1. a competition for knights
2. a part of a tool to put your hands on
3. to be there suddenly
4. a young man who works for a knight and looks after his sword and shield
5. a place to stay for travelling people
6. It was my mistake.

c) *Which of these things doesn't play a role in the text?*

LISTENING **7** A science-fiction story

L 4/20 ◉

Listen to the story and do the following exercises:

a) *What is the main theme of the story?*

A science and technology
B Christmas
C a meeting with aliens
D similar traditions
E religious questions
F an accident in space

b) *What do you learn about the four astronauts? Match the pieces of information.*

1. Rajiv is
2. Thomas is
3. Laila is
4. Susanne is

a) the captain of the space ship.
b) from Britain.
d) a German.
c) from India.

c) *Put the sentences into the correct order.*

A The countdown stops.
B The space ship takes off.
C One astronaut is running to Mission Control.
D The astronauts talk about festivals in different cultures.
E Laila asks about the shopping bag.

d) *Make a grid with these headings and complete it with information from the story:*

Name of astronaut | Country | Festival | Festival activities

Tony

Legende

Diese Symbole und Erklärungen zeigen dir, wie du mit den Hilfen, Aufgaben und Aktivitäten auf den *Practice-pool*-Seiten arbeiten kannst.

△ Hilfe zur *Unit*-Aufgabe | oder eine leichtere Aufgabe | oder eine zusätzliche Aufgabe

▲ eine zusätzliche Herausforderung

Unit 1

△ **1 Feelings** → Help with Check-in, p. 9/3

How do you feel in these situations? Match the feelings with the sentences. There's often more than one answer.

1. There's a test in English tomorrow.
2. Your team won a football match.
3. You forgot your homework – again.
4. You know all the answers in class today.
5. An alligator is walking next to you.
6. You're alone, and you don't know what to do.
7. You're at the park and are playing with your friends.
8. You meet your favourite star.
9. You can't find your lucky charm.
10. You have chocolate on your white jeans and everyone can see it.

excited   nervous
happy   sad
scared   bad
good   proud
bored   angry
embarrassed

Lösung: EH:
1. I feel nervous because there's a test in English tomorrow.
2. I feel proud because my team won a football match.
3. I feel bad because I forgot my homework again.
4. I feel good because I know all the answers in class today.
5. I feel scared because an alligator is walking next to me.
6. I feel bored because I'm alone and I don't know what to do. Etc.

△ **2 What's going to happen?** → After Station 1, p. 11/4

Look at the pictures and say what's going to happen.

Lösung: 1. Olivia and Luke are going to drink some tea.
2. Tyler is going to get a great (birthday) present.
3. Allison is going to walk her dog.
4. Andy, Rachel and Lucy are going to play basketball.

Olivia and Luke

Tyler

Allison

Andy, Rachel and Lucy

▲ **3** **My plans for a trip to the Midwest** → After Station 1, p. 11/5

You're going to go on a trip to the Midwest[1] with your family. This website tells you some of the things you can do there. Choose two or three activities you find interesting. Write an e-mail to an English friend and tell him/her what you're going to do and why.

Mount Rushmore National Memorial, South Dakota
Here you can see the faces of four American presidents cut into the mountain. They are huge – about 18 m tall! About three million visitors come here every year to see this famous symbol of freedom and American culture and to visit the museum. Discover more here about the many faces of American history, the Black Hills and the story of Mount Rushmore.

Chicago, Illinois
Chicago is a city of opposites in the heart of the US – skyscrapers and busy city life right next to great parks and water sports on Lake Michigan. Fans watch their basketball heroes, the Chicago Bulls, or the two world-famous baseball teams, the White Sox and Chicago Cubs. Shopping malls, big events, the Lincoln Park Zoo – there's something for everyone here.

Henry Ford Museum, Michigan
If you like technology, this is the perfect place for you! See historic trains, America's first cars, the Mark IV race car, airplanes, machines and computers in interactive displays and learn about Henry Ford's famous car factory system, stories of inventions and the people behind them. New technology also made lives easier for people in their homes. See household devices like lamps, fridges or telephones from the past.

Albert the Bull, Iowa
Albert isn't just a big bull, he's huge! He is 10 m high and 11 m long and he looks after the people in the small town of Audubon. But don't worry, Albert isn't dangerous. You can find this friendly Hereford bull next to Highway 71. Albert has his own park and invites you to stay on his campground near Audubon's swimming pool. About 20,000 people visit him every year and listen to his story in the information kiosk next to him. Come and say hello.

Buffalo in Theodore Roosevelt National Park, North Dakota
Would you like to see a real wild buffalo? We have hundreds here. The American president Roosevelt made this part of North Dakota into an awesome national park to keep them safe. Or maybe you want to sleep under the stars? Bring the kids and go riding, hiking or fishing.

1 Midwest [ˌmɪdˈwest] Mittlerer Westen

▲ 4 Mediation: A trip to the Midwest → After Station 1, p. 11/6

Zusammen mit deinen Eltern und deinem kleinen Bruder wirst du in den Sommerferien deine Tante in den USA besuchen. Sie möchte mit euch einen zweitägigen Ausflug unternehmen und schickt drei Flyer mit Ausflugszielen. Deine Eltern können nicht gut Englisch und bitten dich, die Flyer anzusehen und ihnen zu sagen, welcher Ausflug für die Familie am besten geeignet ist und warum. Deine Eltern möchten ein Angebot mit Übernachtung, Essen und Eintritten, das für euch fünf unter 400 $ kostet. Außerdem sollte es für deinen Bruder und dich zusätzliche Freizeitangebote geben, da deine Eltern etwas Zeit mit deiner Tante alleine verbringen möchten. Für dich ist es wichtig, dass Internet verfügbar ist.

Explore Chicago

With attractions around every corner you'll find fun every day of the year. Not sure what to see first? Take a tour! We offer all-inclusive vacation package deals every weekend.

Bike Tour: See Chicago in a whole new way!

Top sights: The Chicago Lake Front, Navy Pier, North Avenue Beach, Lincoln Park Zoo, night time water and light festival.
– All sights are free for everyone to enjoy.
– Taste foods from restaurants along the way.
– Please note that the group must stay together at all times!

How to get here: The tour starts at Navy Pier at 10pm. Make sure you're there on time!

Price: Adults $100, Under 16s $49 (including one night at a biker's hostel¹, meals, bike rental). Free public wireless internet available throughout the city.

Indiana Dunes

15 miles of sandy beach along the southern shore of Lake Michigan offer a wide variety of activities – from swimming in the summer to skiing and snowshoeing in the winter. We offer free activities for children and teenagers (outdoor adventure program, fishing school and hiking tours). Be prepared, be safe and have fun!

Transportation:
– Go by train and take the free shuttle from Miller Train Station to the beach
– parking fee: $6 per car, $30 per bus

Camping: (only during summer months):
– camping fee (for groups): $30 per night
– full board camping: enjoy breakfast, lunch and dinner at the beach bar: $30 per person per day
– high speed internet access: $5 per day

Great Galena Balloon Race in Galena, IL

Eagle Ridge Resort hosts balloon races, 'Night Glow' evening shows and rides for the public. The balloon rides, great food, kids' activities (8–14 years) and live music mean there's something for everyone. Just relax and watch the balloons with friends or family.

Saturday:
5–10pm: Live Music: The Swingin' Doors
12am–9pm: All-you-can-eat buffet
8–10 pm: Classic Car Show
5–9pm: Tethered balloon rides
Sunday: Hot Air Balloons — Balloon Race
Enjoy balloons, live music, etc. Bring a blanket and grab a spot on the lawn to watch the balloons.
11am–9pm: All-you-can-eat buffet

When? First weekend in August
Price (Saturday and Sunday)? Admission¹: $10; All-you-can-eat buffet: $50
Parking? Follow the signs, park at the East Course and take the free shuttle.
Where to stay? Galena Bed and Breakfast, only $70 for a double room and $50 for a one-bed room. Free Wi-Fi.

---

1 **admission** [ədˈmɪʃn] Eintritt

△ **5** **City or country?** → Help with Station 1, p. 11/7

Copy the table and add your own ideas. These words and phrases can help you to write your text.

What are you going to do?	Country or city?	Why?
work with animals/people/ computers/in an office … | be a vet/doctor …	live in the country because … | … so I want to live in …	busy streets/lots of people/ things to do/exciting events … | fresh air/explore nature …

△ **6** **A game: Question tags** → After Station 2, p. 12/9

1. *Write short positive and negative sentences on little pieces of paper.*
   Example: This is a cool T-shirt.
2. *Your teacher then collects the papers.*
3. *Now stand up in two lines. Your teacher reads out a sentence from your list to the first two students in the lines.*
4. *You must complete the sentence with the right question tag.*
   Example: This is a cool T-shirt, **isn't it**?

The student who gives the right answer first can sit down; the other student has to go to the back of the queue again.

▲ **7** **You can hear the difference, can't you?** → After Station 2, p. 13/10b)

ஃ *You and your partner write six sentences with question tags – three of them must be **real** questions. Take turns to read your sentences to each other. Your partner has to listen and then answer. Remember: A real question needs a real answer, not just a short answer!*

△ **8** **Matching verbs and prepositions** → After Station 2, p. 13/11

Lösung: a) count on, point at, hang out with, be interested in, trip over, worry about

a) *Match each verb on the left with one preposition on the right. Use each verb and each preposition only once.*

| count \| point \| hang out \| be interested \| trip \| worry | ➕ | about \| on \| in \| with \| over \| at |

ஃ b) *Now work with a partner. Take turns to ask and answer questions. Use your verbs and prepositions from a).*

Unit 2

▲ 1 Kennedy Space Center → After Check-in, p. 22/1

*Make a poster about the Kennedy Space Center. Use facts from the text to show what people can do there. Don't forget to add pictures! **Or:** Make a poster for another cool place in Florida.*

Visit a place out of this world! Your 'journey[1] into space' starts at Kennedy Space Center on Merrit Island, Florida. Meet and talk to real astronauts, come nose-to-nose with a space shuttle and take a look at our blue planet in the 3D theater. Do you want to know what it feels like to be an astronaut? In our Shuttle Launch[2] Experience you can find out! The countdown starts: 3 – 2 – 1 … and your space shuttle takes off! It feels like you are going 17,500 miles per hour into space. Check our calendar when you plan your trip – maybe you can even watch a real take-off. What are you waiting for? Come and start your journey into space!

△ 2 Who's the best? → After Station 1, p. 25/3

Tony and Lou are having a fight! What do they say?

Lösung: 1. bigger, 2. big, 3. nicer, 4. more popular, 5. funnier, 6. funny, 7. worse, 8. faster, 9. taller, 10. more intelligent, 11. faster

Tony: I'm **1** (big) than you, Lou!
Lou: OK, I'm not as **2** (big) as you, but I am **3** (nice).
Tony: Maybe. But I'm **4** (popular) than you!
Lou: Oh no, you aren't. That's because I'm **5** (funny) than you.
Tony: You aren't as **6** (funny) as I am. Your jokes are **7** (bad) than my jokes! And I'm **8** (fast) than you.
Lou: That's because you're **9** (tall). But I'm **10** (intelligent). I can use my skates – and then I'm **11** (fast) than you!

▲ 3 Compare! → After Station 1, p. 26/4

| Carrie (8/135cm) | Craig (32/180cm) | Helen (60/160cm) | John (67/168cm) | Liz (41/174cm) |
| Joe (4/116cm) | Matt (42/175cm) | Jack (12/180cm) | Louise (32/177cm) | |

a) *Compare the members of the Bradley family (age/size).*

b) *Who is who in the Bradley family? The Bradleys are going on a trip. Find out who is going by car, riding a motorbike or walking. Then draw the Bradleys' family tree.*

The oldest member of the family is going by car, together with his son[3] and grandson[4]. The old man's son is as tall as his grandson. Craig is Jack's uncle. The boy's father is one year older than the boy's mother. She is the only daughter of the two oldest members of the family. She is walking with her husband[5], mother and her brother's children. They are the two smallest members of the family. Their mother is the tallest woman in the family and she is riding her motorbike.

1 journey ['dʒɜːni] Reise | **2 launch** [lɔːntʃ] Start | **3 son** [sʌn] Sohn | **4 grandson** ['grænsʌn] Enkel | **5 husband** ['hʌzbənd] Ehemann

△ **4** **Who's the tallest?** → After Station 1, p. 26/5

Find out about your classmates! Choose one of the ideas in the box, find two partners and stand next to each other. Who is taller than you? Who has got the most interesting hobby? When you have got a group, shout "Stop!" and present your group to the class. Then find the next group.

| tall/short | young/old | boring/interesting hobby | big/small family |

| long/short way to school | young/old parents | silly/nice brother/sister |

▲ **5** **The very best thing** → After Station 1, p. 26/5

*Choose two of these things and write a short text about them. Use **than** and **as … as** too. You can start like this: The tastiest meal[1] I had in my whole life was … It was tastier than …*

| tasty meal [1] | good film | nice teacher | funny book | exciting holiday | bad joke |

△ **6** **A school trip which was really cool** → After Station 2, p. 28/9

Do you need who/that, which/that or whose? Read what Amrita tells Emily and put in the right relative pronoun.

Lösung: 1. whose, 2. which/that, 3. whose, 4. who/that, 5. whose, 6. who/that, 7. which/that

The teacher ⬚1 lessons we like the most is Mrs Jordan. Last year, she took us on a class trip and the coolest place ⬚2 we visited was the Pirate[2] and Treasure Museum in St. Augustine. The men ⬚3 costumes were black and red were very funny – they looked like pirates! They're the men ⬚4 show the museum to all the visitors. They told us about the ghosts[3] ⬚5 voices you can hear if you're quiet enough. They're the ghosts of all the sailors ⬚6 died[4] when the pirates attacked them many, many years ago! The 'pirates' told us lots of stories about events ⬚7 took place in Florida – very close to our home town!

△ **7** **More contact clauses** → After Station 2, p. 28/10b)

*Read the sentence pairs. Which sentence in each pair **doesn't** need a relative pronoun?*

Lösung: 1. b), 2. a), 3. b), 4. a), 5. a), 6. b)

1. a) Lots of children that are interested in nature go to Florida.
   b) Lots of children that I know go to Florida.
2. a) Most of the animals which you can see in Florida don't hurt you.
   b) Most of the animals which are in Florida don't hurt you.
3. a) I'm friends with lots of the kids who live near Grandma's house.
   b) I'm friends with lots of the kids who I see near Grandma's house.
4. a) This is a website which I use a lot for information about Florida.
   b) This is a website which helps me a lot with information about Florida.
5. a) I think the places that we visit with our grandparents are fun.
   b) I think the places that don't cost a lot are usually the best.
6. a) Grandparents who move to Florida often do lots of fun things!
   b) Grandparents who I know in Florida often do lots of fun things!

1 tasty meal [ˈteɪsti ˈmiːl] leckeres Essen | **2 pirate** [ˈpaɪrət] Pirat | **3 ghost** [ɡəʊst] Geist | **4 to die** [daɪ] sterben

△ 8 Make one sentence from two → After Station 2, p. 28/11

Replace[1] the words in blue with a relative pronoun and make a new sentence.

Examples: Last lesson we talked about a famous person. We all know him.
→ Last lesson we talked about a famous person who/that we all know.
The Treasure Club organises competitions. They are really exciting.
→ The Treasure Club organises competitions which/that are really exciting.

1. In Florida there are lots of activities. You can do them outside.
2. I'm learning the cajón with a new friend. He can play really fast!
3. I can show you a cool song. We played it yesterday.
4. Yesterday we went to a waterpark. It was awesome.
5. At Cape Canaveral I met an astronaut. I liked him very much.
6. Do you know the people? They are talking to Grandma.

▲ 9 Puzzles → After Station 2, p. 28/11

a) *Complete the sentences with* **who/that, which/that** *or* **whose**.

Lösung: a)
1. which/that,
2. which/that,
3. who/that,
4. which/that,
5. whose,
6. which/that

1.	It's something	has four legs[2], but can't walk.
2.	It's something	you must break before you can eat it!
3.	I'm someone	is always cold and must never feel warm!
4.	It's something	is yours, but your friends use it more than you do!
5.	I'm a person	chair is a throne[3].
6.	It's something	is tall when it's new and not so tall when it's old.

b) *Can you guess the answers?*

Answers: a table/a chair | an egg | a snowman[4] | your name | a king/a queen | a candle

▲ 10 The Florida Keys → After Station 2, p. 29/12

Read the article. Find the important information and put it on prompt cards.

The Florida Keys are a small group of tropical islands south of Florida. The Keys are actually more than 1,700 islands, but you can only get to 43 of them over bridges. There are many islands where nobody lives, and you can only get there by boat. The first bridges people built[5], in 1912, were for trains. But in 1935 a huge hurricane hit the Keys and broke parts of the bridges. Just a few years later, they built a modern bridge for cars – the Seven Mile Bridge. It runs across almost seven miles of open water and is one of the most beautiful places in Florida. The bridge is so long, you can't see the other end, just the blue water around you. Today tourists love the Keys because they can go swimming, sail and see beautiful plants and fascinating animals.

1 Replace … [rɪˈpleɪs] ersetze … | **2 leg** [leg] Bein | **3 throne** [θrəʊn] Thron | **4 snowman** [ˈsnəʊmæn] Schneemann | **5 °to build** [bɪld] (er)bauen

▲ **11** **Mediation: Florida history** → After Station 2, p. 29/13

Emily hat dir von ihrer Präsentation über die Geschichte Floridas erzählt. Du hast gestern einen interessanten Artikel über Florida im Internet gefunden und möchtest Emily nun bei ihrer Präsentation helfen. Beantworte Emilys E-Mail mit den Informationen aus dem Artikel.

Hi,
Thanks for helping me with my presentation! Ryan isn't a big help. :-/ I'd like to talk more about the first Europeans who came to Florida: where they arrived[1] (I guess it was in St. Augustine), why they came here and how Florida got its name. Is there any information about that in your article?
Thanks, Emily

ST. AUGUSTINE

Einen Ort mit größerer Symbolkraft hatte Antón de Alaminos, damals der beste Navigator der spanischen Armada, sich nicht aussuchen können. Es war der 27. März 1513, „Pascua Florida", wie Ostern auf Spanisch auch heißt. Die nahe Küste, die er ansteuerte, erschien von den drei Karavellen-Seglern aus gesehen unproblematisch. Man befand sich etwa vor Cape Canaveral, von wo aus [knapp 500 Jahre später] die Mondraketen des US-amerikanischen Apollo-Programms gestartet wurden. Juan Ponce de León, Kommandant der drei Schiffe, meinte bei der Ankunft, er habe eben eine sehr große Insel entdeckt. Florida nannte er sie, eben weil man Ostern, am Tag der Auferstehung, angekommen war. Nicht unbeeindruckt freilich war man auch von den Indianern, auf die man in Florida traf. Dabei hatten er und seine Leute eigentlich etwas ganz anderes gesucht. Den Spaniern [waren] auf der Insel Hispaniola Erzählungen der Taino-Indianer zu Ohren gekommen über einen Quell auf einer sagenhaften Insel, aus dem derjenige, der ihn betritt, um Jahrzehnte verjüngt wieder hinaustritt. Sollte gerade ihm das Glück zuteilwerden, jenen Jungbrunnen zu finden? In St. Augustin, einem Ort etwas nördlich von Cape Canaveral, behauptet man nicht nur, dass der Spanier damals dort angelandet sei, sondern verkauft dort ein Wässerchen, für das die Kundschaft viel Geld ausgibt, mancher wohl tatsächlich im Glauben, er blicke morgen im Spiegel einer jugendlichen Person in die Augen. St. Augustin gilt heute als älteste Siedlung von Europäern auf US-amerikanischem Boden, gegründet 1565, lange nach Ponce de León.

△ **12** **How does the story end?** → Help with Story, p. 36/2b)

Use these ideas to find endings for the stories.

Ending	Antonio	Ryan
happy, sad, funny, a surprise, disappointed, (un)lucky, strange	Who helped Antonio? | What did he eat? | Did he find some treasure? | Did he sail again?	Did Ryan find a real treasure? | Were his grandparents angry? | Was his picture in the newspaper[2]?

1 to arrive [ə ˈraɪv] ankommen | **2 newspaper** [ˈnjuːzˌpeɪpə] Zeitung

Unit 3

▲ **1** **Why come to the Alps?** → After Check-in, p. 42/1

Use the information in the mind map and write a text for a tourist information flyer about the Alps.
*Use adjectives like **awesome – great – amazing – exciting** to make your text sound interesting.*

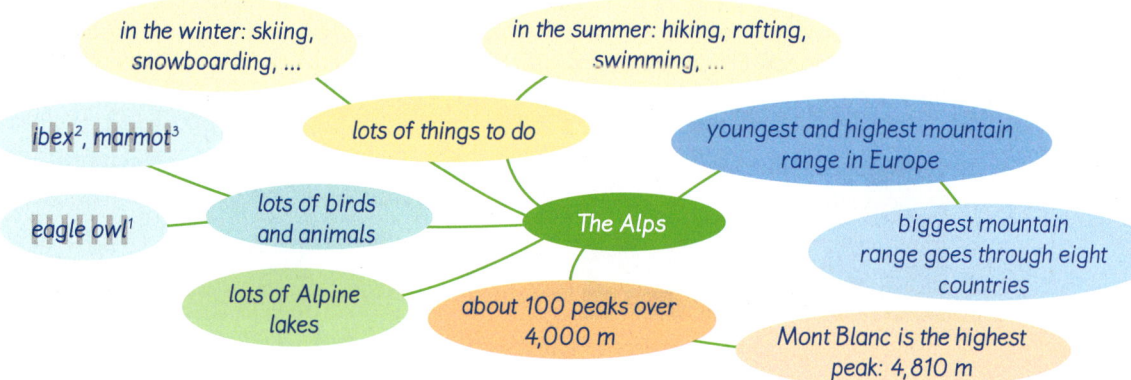

in the winter: skiing, snowboarding, ...

in the summer: hiking, rafting, swimming, ...

ibex², marmot³

lots of things to do

youngest and highest mountain range in Europe

eagle owl¹

lots of birds and animals

The Alps

biggest mountain range goes through eight countries

lots of Alpine lakes

about 100 peaks over 4,000 m

Mont Blanc is the highest peak: 4,810 m

△ **2** **Find out more** → Help with Check-in, p. 42/2

Prompt cards help you to structure your talk. These questions help you to find information for your prompt cards.

What?
- What are the names of these mountains/ animals?
- What sports can you do?
- What can you do in the national park?

Where?
- Where are these mountains/ national parks?
- Where do these animals live?
- Where can you do these sports?

Describe?
- How high are the mountains?
- How big are the animals?
- How popular are the sports?
- How popular are the parks?

Fun fact?
- Can you find a fun fact about one of the mountains/ animals/sports/ parks?

△ **3** **When or while?** → After Station 1, p. 45/3c)

*Decide if you need **when** or **while**.*

Lösung:
1. when,
2. When,
3. while,
4. While,
5. when

1. We were watching a film 🟨 Mum came home.
2. 🟨 I saw my brother, he was buying lots of sweets.
3. I read a whole magazine 🟨 I was waiting for the bus.
4. 🟨 my dog was sleeping, my cat stole his dinner!
5. Amber was preparing a presentation 🟨 her phone rang.

1 eagle owl [ˈiːɡlˌaʊl] Uhu | **2 ibex** [ˈaɪbeks] Steinbock | **3 marmot** [ˈmɑːmət] Murmeltier

▲ **4** **A crazy day at home** → After Station 1, p. 45/3c)

Use these photos and write a short story about a crazy day at home. Think of your own crazy ideas too. Use the simple past and the past progressive.

You can start like this: First, breakfast was crazy. While Mum was …, our dog … her breakfast! Then, while Mum and Dad were …, we … in the kitchen. But when …

▲ **5** **Act it out and guess** → After Station 1, p. 45/4

One student leaves the classroom. 3–4 other students act out an activity without words. When the teacher shouts "Stop!", everyone stops. Now the student comes back in and sees the 'frozen'[1] student. With yes/no questions, he/she must guess what the others were doing.

Were you eating something?

No, we weren't. Try again!

▲ **6** **Guessing and explaining words** → After Station 2, p. 48/9

a) *Find the odd ones out. Make a grid for words with 're-' = again and 'un-' = not.*

Lösung: a) odd words out: understand, relax, record

| unsure | redo | retell | untie | uncool | understand | relax | rewrite |
| reread | replay | record | reuse | unfriendly | reorganise | unattractive |

👥 **b)** *Write definitions for five of the words below. Swap definitions with a partner and guess each other's words.*

Example: A person who is not happy is… → unhappy

swimmer	unlucky	reread	unfair	buyer	(football) player
learner	unnecessary	renew	unimportant	settler	reopen
seller	rethink	speaker

1 frozen ['frəʊzn] hier: erstarrt

△ 7 Make one sentence from two → After Station 2, p. 48/10

*Use **so that**, **because**, **although**, **while** or **if**. Decide where you need commas!*

1. Of course you need a map. Then you can find the way.
2. You are hiking in the Rockies. You must not forget to drink lots of water.
3. It gets hot in the Rockies in the summer. Some of the lakes are really cold.
4. Don't forget to take a camera with you. You can sometimes see wild animals.
5. It's easy to go the wrong way. You leave the trail.

△ 8 Mediation: Tips and rules for hiking in the Alps → Help with Station 2, p. 49/11

Read the text and find English words to explain these ideas:

1. zu den Fähigkeiten passen
2. vor Anbruch der Dunkelheit
3. loslaufen
4. vernünftige Bergschuhe
5. ausreichend Proviant
6. es gibt nicht überall Handyempfang

△ 9 Mediation: Abenteuerzeltlager → After Station 2, p. 49/11

In den letzten Ferien war dein englischer Austauschpartner Jacob zu Besuch. Ihr möchtet nun in den Sommerferien zusammen auf ein Zeltlager gehen. In deiner Schule lag folgender Flyer aus und du hast Jacob gleich davon erzählt. Lies seine E-Mail und beantworte seine Fragen in deiner E-Mail mit den Informationen aus dem Flyer.

> Hi,
> The camp sounds interesting! My parents and I would like to know a few more things.
> How much does it cost? Which activities can we do there? What do I have to bring with me (I hope not too much)? And can I bring my mobile phone? Can't wait to hear from you!
> Jacob

Abenteuerzeltlager in der fränkischen Schweiz

Unser Abenteuerzeltlager inmitten der einzigartigen Natur der fränkischen Schweiz findet dieses Jahr wieder an drei Terminen statt. Teilnehmen können Jugendliche im Alter von 10–14 Jahren. Euch erwarten ereignisreiche Tage auf dem Naturcampingplatz.

Preis: 260€ pro Person inklusive Busfahrt zum Bahnhof;
250€ pro Person bei individueller An- und Abreise

Freizeitangebote und Betreuung: Zu unserem abwechslungsreichen Programm gehören der Besuch der Burg Pottenstein, eine Kanufahrt auf dem Schöngrundsee, Klettern im einzigartigen Naturpark, Schwimmen im Höhenwaldbad, eine Nachtwanderung mit Lagerfeuer und natürlich eine Abschlussparty – hier bleiben keine Wünsche offen! Die Betreuer werden euch bei allen Aktivitäten begleiten und auch mit euch im Zeltlager übernachten.

Termine: Jeweils die zweite Woche (Montag–Freitag) in den Oster-, Pfingst- und Sommerferien.

Was du mitbringen solltest: Besonders wichtig ist angemessene Kleidung (das Camp findet bei jedem Wetter statt!), Sonnencreme, festes Schuhwerk, etwas Taschengeld und gute Laune! Eure Handys lasst ihr bitte zu Hause – unser Naturpark befindet sich sowieso in einem Funkloch.

△ 10 Ryan goes shopping → After Station 2, p. 49/12

Lösung: 1. boots, 2. camp, 3. buy, 4. online, 5. him, 6. on, 7. some, 8. goes, 9. cousin, 10. assistant, 11. some, 12. colour, 13. would/'d, 14. ones/ boots, 15. size, 16. because, 17. good, 18. perfectly, 19. look, 20. special, 21. price, 22. buys/takes, 23. one, 24. anything, 25. too, 26. left

Complete the text.

Ryan needs new hiking `1` for the summer `2`. He wanted to `3` them `4`, but his mother wants `5` to try them `6` first and gives him `7` money. So he `8` shopping with his `9` Mike. An `10` shows them `11` green boots, but Ryan doesn't like the `12`. He `13` like blue `14`, but he needs a bigger `15`, so in the end he chooses black ones `16` they are `17` quality and fit `18`. Then he has a `19` at some T-shirts. There's a `20` offer: two for the `21` of one. So he `22` a blue T-shirt with a moose and a black `23` with a wolf. The assistant asks him if he needs `24` else. He remembers that he needs new socks to wear in the boots `25`. Finally, there's no money `26`, but he's ready for camp!

△ 11 Going shopping → Instead of Station 2, p. 49/13

👥 *Before you do the role play, complete the dialogue using the phrases on the right. Partner A is the buyer and partner B is the assistant.*

Lösung: 1. g), 2. b), 3. d), 4. f), 5. c), 6. a), 7. h), 8. e)

Buyer: Hi! `1`? I need a new shirt with long sleeves for camp.
Assistant: Sure. The shirts are over here. `2`?
Buyer: I don't really know. I think I need small.
Assistant: OK. Let's have a look. `3`?
Buyer: Cool! Oh dear, it's too big! `4`?
Assistant: `5`. Yes, here you go.
Buyer: This one's perfect! `6`?
Assistant: It costs fifteen dollars. `7`. You can get two for twenty-five dollars.
Buyer: That sounds good! I think I'll take this one too. `8`.

a) How much does it cost?
b) What size do you need?
c) Let me check.
d) What about this one?
e) Blue's my favourite colour.
f) Do you have a smaller size?
g) Can you help me, please?
h) But we have a special offer this week.

▲ 12 Group activity: Your most exciting outdoor adventure → After Story, p. 56/1

👥👥 *Imagine an exciting adventure story. Write three sentences to begin the story and then pass it on to a group member who goes on with the story and writes three more sentences. The last group member finishes the story.*

You can start like this: Together with a friend …

▲ 13 What a wonderful world → After Story, p. 56/2c

👥 *Reread the story 'What a wonderful world' in Unit 1. Then draw a diagram with the exciting points. Compare your line with your partner's line. What happens at each point?*

Unit 4

▲ **1** **A sports quiz** → After Check-in, p. 60/2

a) *You and your partner each make notes about one sport that you both like: where people play, what equipment they need, how many players there are in a team, etc. For new words, use a dictionary. Don't show your notes to your partner.*

b) *Write 5–6 quiz questions with the information in your notes.*

Example: How many players are in a basketball team? **A.** 7 **B.** 6 **C.** 5

c) *Test your partner with your quiz! Who knows the most about the same sport?*

△ **2** **Have you done it yet?** → After Station 2, p. 64/6

a) *First check the past participle forms of the verbs. Then make dialogues with your partner.*

Example: **1.** "There's a new 3D movie. Have you watched it yet?" – "…"

1. There's a new 3D movie. (watch)
2. I've bought new running shoes. (see)
3. There's a charity run next week. (hear)
4. Your parents and teachers could give money for the charity run. (ask)
5. Wow, you've bought a new racquet. (try)

b) *Now ask your partner what he or she has done today.*

△ **3** **Great runners** → After Station 2, p. 65/7

Lisa and Mark help to organise the London Marathon. Complete the sentences and put the verbs into the present perfect.

Lösung:
1. have you already written,
2. have just written,
3. haven't got,
4. have found,
5. Have they won,
6. have never heard,
7. have run,
8. has won,
9. hasn't won,
10. Have you checked,
11. have just copied,
12. haven't had,
13. have looked

Lisa: We need some great runners this year. Mark, **1** (you already write) an e-mail to last year's winners?

Mark: Yes, I **2** (just write) it. But I **3** (not get) answers from everyone yet. What about the German twins[1], Klara and Lena – I **4** (find) some information about them on the internet.

Lisa: **5** (they win) anything yet? I **6** (never hear) of them.

Mark: They **7** (run) in a few important races. Klara **8** (win) one big marathon once. Lena **9** (not win) yet, but she was 'Best European' in the Hamburg Marathon.

Lisa: **10** (you check) if they have a website?

Mark: Of course I have. Here, I **11** (just copy) the contact details for you. Let's write them an e-mail. We **12** (not have) famous twins in the Marathon yet, have we?

Lisa: No, it's a good idea to ask them. But wait till I **13** (look) at their website first!

1 twins [twɪnz] Zwillinge

△ **4**   **Ask interview questions** → After Station 3, p. 67/11

a) *For her health project, Olivia is going to interview Nick Ashton, a member of the Greenwich Rugby Football Club (RFC). Read the internet profile about Nick that Olivia found.*

NICK ASHTON: Nick is 21 and joined Greenwich RFC in 2014. Read about him!

Goals: – to play for England one day, of course!
– to get through the next season with no broken arms, legs or anything else!

Nick likes ... 😊
– getting the ball and sprinting (→ see photo!).
– fast action sports like rugby!

Nick doesn't like... 😟
– all the attention[1] football gets.
– going to the weight room[2] every day. ("But I always go; rugby players need their muscles!")

b) *Write questions that Olivia could ask Nick. The phrases can help you.*

👥 **c)** *Act out the dialogues in small groups. One of you is Nick, the others ask interview questions.*

> **Useful phrases**
>
> Have you ever …? | Did you …? | Are you going to …? | What do you do every day/before big games/… | How often do you …? | Describe what you/how you … | Can you please tell me about … | What happened after you …? | Do you have any tips for …?

▲ **5**   **Writing an article** → After Station 2, p. 67/11

Prepare 5–6 questions and do an interview with a person at your school or in your home town who has done something interesting. Ask him/her if you can record the interview.
Use the German information and a dictionary to write an article for an English school magazine. Here are some ideas:

1. A person who raises money for charity.
2. A person who helps other people, e.g. children, older people, refugees[3].
3. A person who works for the volunteer fire brigade[4] or as a paramedic[5].
4. A person who does environmental[6] activities.
5. A person who has set up his/her own company.
6. A person who has an interesting job.

1 attention [əˈtenʃn] Aufmerksamkeit | **2 weight room** [ˈweɪt rʊm] Kraftraum | **3 refugee** [ˌrefjʊˈdʒiː] Flüchtling | **4 volunteer fire brigade** [vɒlənˈtɪə ˈfaɪə brɪˌgeɪd] freiwillige Feuerwehr | **5 paramedic** [pærəˈmedɪk] Sanitäter | **6 environmental** [ɪnˌvaɪrənˈmentl] Umwelt-

6 Boys' day! → After Station 2 p. 67/12

Dave and Jay are on the phone. Complete their phone call with the right verb forms in the simple past or present perfect. Sometimes you just need a short answer.

Jay

Dave

Lösung:
1. haven't told,
2. wanted,
3. didn't see,
4. has bought,
5. thought,
6. have you already told,
7. have,
8. did Luke say,
9. told,
10. has ('s) already asked,
11. has just given,
12. did,
13. Have you asked,
14. haven't,
15. didn't ask

Dave: So what's the plan for Saturday, Jay? You **1** (tell) us yet!

Jay: I **2** (want) to tell you yesterday, but I **3** (not see) you after school. – Listen, I I have tickets for the rugby match between Greenwich and Sidcup! My dad **4** (buy) them as a present for me and two friends!

Dave: Hey, you've got a cool dad. I love rugby! – So when are we going to meet?

Jay: Well, I **5** (think) it would be a good idea to have a picnic in the park first.

Dave: Cool. **6** (you already tell) Luke?

Jay: Yes, I **7** .

Dave: And what **8** (Luke say) when you **9** (tell) him?

Jay: He thinks it sounds great too. He **10** (already ask) his dad for help with the food. Can you buy some drinks, Dave?

Dave: No problem. My mum **11** (just give) me some extra pocket money because I **12** (do) well in the Maths test last week. So what drinks do we want?

Jay: Just lemonade and water?

Dave: OK. **13** (you ask) the girls if they want to come, Jay?

Jay: The girls?! No, I **14** . It's a *boys'* day! And they **15** (not ask) *us* to come to their sleepover party last weekend, did they?

Dave: No, but who would *want* to be at their sleepover?!

7 A game: Who is it? → After Station 2, p. 67/12

1. *Choose a famous star, a person in the class or somebody else **everybody** knows.*
2. *On a card, write five activities this person has already/never done, or did at some time. But don't write his/her name!*
3. *Then collect and shuffle¹ all the cards.*
4. *Take turns to read out the information. The others must guess who it is.*

Example:

- started to play football when he was five
- has played for Schalke and Bayern
- started to play for the German national football team in 2009
- has been the "world's best goalkeeper²"
- won the World Cup in 2014

Answer: Manuel Neuer

1 to shuffle [ˈʃʌfl] mischen | **2** goalkeeper [ˈɡəʊlˌkiːpə] Torwart

△ **8** **The London Mini Marathon** → Instead of Story, p. 74/1c

These words and phrases for the three pictures can help you to retell the story.

Olivia wasn't there, so … | Luke was a bit worried … | Gwen told Luke, "Don't …" | Luke saw two people in …

Ten minutes later, Gwen suddenly felt … | She didn't want to stop because … | The two runners in the funny costumes …

Suddenly, … pulled out a phone and … | The race officials … | But Gwen and Luke finished … | Olivia found out …

△ **9** **Adjectives** → Help with Story, p. 74/2

Lösung: 1. interesting ↔ boring, 2. friendly, nice ↔ nasty, 3. happy ↔ unhappy, sad, 4. funny ↔ serious, 5. clever, confident ↔ stupid, nervous/unsure, 6. fair ↔ unfair, awful

Find the right adjectives. Then write them down together with their opposites.

1. Something which everyone wants to know about is …
2. A person who always talks in a nice and friendly way to other people is …
3. A person who feels good is …
4. Something that makes you laugh is …
5. A person who understands things well and knows how to act is …
6. A person who uses the same rules for everyone is …

△ **10** **Useful phrases from the story** → Help with Story, p. 74/3

You can start your mind map like this:

▲ **11** **A game: Freeze frame!** → After Story, p. 74/3

Get together in groups of four or five. Choose a scene from the story and practise a freeze frame of that scene. (Practise in another room so your classmates can't see you.) Back in the classroom, the others then shout "One … two … freeze[1]!" and your group does its freeze frame. Your classmates must guess the scene and explain how they guessed.

1 to freeze [friːz] erstarren

Unit 5

△ 1 Media collocations → Instead of Check-in, p. 82/2

Lösung: a) vgl. Übersicht
S. 230 (Voc.)

a) *Write down all the media collocations in the text.*

Tony loves the world of media! He checks his text messages all the time. He loves texting his friends. He sends and receives text messages during lessons too. (Bad boy!) And Tony has joined a popular social network: He's on Mousebook, of course. He often posts photos and changes his profile. It's important for Tony to stay in touch with his friends, so he often talks to them on video chat. At weekends, he often plays video games or takes part in discussions. It's easy to forget the time when you're online! But one thing is more important than any kind of media for Tony. Guess who? It's Lou, of course! It's much nicer to be with her than just to chat with her on Mousebook!

b) *You can use some of the verbs with more than one noun, e.g., you can **change** your **profile** and you can **check** your **profile** too. How many different media collocations of nouns and verbs can you find?*

▲ 2 Ruby's answer → After Station 1, p. 84/1

*Work with a partner. On little pieces of paper, write down the different pieces of advice that Ruby has for Lauren. Then put the pieces of paper face down[1] on the table. Take turns to pick one up and talk about it. Do you think it's good advice? Why/Why not? What other pieces of advice do **you** have for Lauren? Talk about them.*

▲ 3 Using linking words: Tony and his phone → After Station 1, p. 85/3

Read what Tony's friend Robby says about Tony. Use these words to make one sentence out of the two. There's sometimes more than one way!

| after | before | as soon as | whenever | because | when |

Example: Tony plays video games too often. He doesn't call me.
→ **Whenever** Tony plays video games, he doesn't call me.

1. He got a new smartphone for his birthday. We often saw each other before that.
2. Tony can't leave his phone alone for one minute. He's really into texting.
3. I wanted to go to the cinema with him yesterday. He said yes.
4. At the cinema, someone said, "You must switch off[2] your phone. The film is starting."
5. Tony heard that. He was shocked.
6. Sometimes a phone rings at the cinema. It always makes the other people angry.

1 face down [ˌfeɪs ˈdaʊn] mit der Schriftseite nach unten | **2 to switch off** [ˌswɪtʃ ˈɒf] ausschalten

△ **4** **The day I fixed my...** → Help with Station 2, p. 86/6

Ask yourself these questions before you talk to your partner:

What did you fix? | Did it belong to you or to someone else? |
Why did you fix it and not buy a new one? | Where did you look
for help/advice? | Did you ask anybody for help? | Was it easy to
fix? | How long did it take you? | Does it still work?

△ **5** **The older you are, the more you can do...** → Help with Station 2, p. 87/9 b)

*These ideas help you to think about things you **weren't able** or **not allowed to** or **had to**
do in the past or **aren't able to** or **allowed to** or **have to** do now.*

- go cycling	- help your parents in the kitchen
- read a book	- watch TV in the evening
- go shopping	- make models
- go to school	- join a social network
- do homework	- have a sleepover

▲ **6** **'Fun' in Scotland ...** → After Station 2, p. 87/9 b)

Complete Holly and Dave's dialogue with the right forms.

Lösung: 1. wasn't allowed to, 2. were able, 3. were allowed/ were able, 4. weren't allowed, 5. had, 6. weren't allowed, 7. had, 8. weren't able

Dave: Hi Holly! Back from Scotland?
Did you enjoy your holiday?

Holly: Well, not really. You know I wanted
to visit the castle in Edinburgh,
but I ▮1▮ . My mum said it was too
expensive.

Dave: Oh, that's too bad. But you ▮2▮ to
take some photos of the castle,
weren't you?

Holly: Yes, of course. That doesn't cost anything. Amber and I ▮3▮ to go shopping on the
Royal Mile, so that was good. We went all the way down to Holyrood Palace, where
the members of the Royal Family stay when they're in Edinburgh, but we ▮4▮ to go
inside: "Too expensive", mum said. *Again.*

Dave: When I was in Edinburgh last summer, I didn't want to visit any old castles, but I ▮5▮ to
visit *lots* of them! My parents *always* take me to museums and castles.

Holly: Well, Scotland has lots of beautiful lakes. I'm sure you went swimming, right?

Dave: Wrong! My mum always says, "Forget it, the water is too cold. No swimming!" So no,
we ▮6▮ to go swimming. We ▮7▮ to visit all the different sights.

Holly: Hm, it sounds like you and I ▮8▮ to have the best time there. Maybe next time!

7 You could do that, but I think you should... → After Station 2, p. 88/10

*Read these situations and decide what advice you want to give. Do you need **could** or **should**?*
(Remember, there's a difference! Check G14 for help.)

1. Oh no. I left my phone at home!
2. This phone doesn't work at all.
3. Do you like this photo? I want to post it.
4. My computer has been so slow!
5. Hmm, 'World of Heroes' or 'Super Talents' – which game is better?
6. Susan is still angry because I sent her that text message.

Lösung: 1. You could use mine. 2. You should buy a new one. 3. You shouldn't post private photos. 4. I could check it. 5. You should/could try both. 6. You could/should tell her you're sorry.

Oh, I've got the worst headache!

I could make some tea, Tony. That always helps you.

8 Mediation: Digital detox[1] → After Station 2, p. 88/11

Du hast dich im Internet über das Thema „Digitale Auszeit" informiert und bist auf folgenden Blogartikel gestoßen. Der Blogbesucher Jannik hat Verständnisprobleme. Schreibe einen Kommentar, um seine Fragen zu beantworten.

Digital detox week   **Friday, 6:27 p.m.**

Last month my school took part in a "digital detox week". During this time students switched off[2] their mobile phones and other digital devices like laptops, tablets, game consoles and television.

At the beginning of the week it was really difficult for me to live without my mobile phone and game console. I often watched videos on the internet or played a game after school. But during the "digital detox week" I wasn't allowed to do so. I soon got bored because I suddenly had plenty of time and didn't know what to do. About 25% of the students who started the "digital detox week" gave up – I didn't, because I wanted to show everyone that I'm strong enough. It was hard at first, but after a few days I started to enjoy that I didn't have to check my phone all the time. I suddenly had enough time to do other activities. I read a book, went cycling and went for long walks with our dog. I also spent more time with my friends instead of just texting them. But it was hard to organise when to meet my friends. I had to call all of them on the phone – at home, of course, or we had to plan everything at school. That's a lot easier in a chat. The "digital detox week" is over now. My friends and I use all different kinds of media again, but I think in a different way. I try not to be online just because I don't know what else to do. I also try to contact people only if it's necessary and don't tell them about things that aren't important. It was a great experience and I think everyone should try it!

Jannik wrote: **Friday, 7:48 p.m.**

Hallo zusammen! Abbys Artikel klingt interessant, nur leider verstehe ich nicht alles :-/ Vielleicht kann mir jemand helfen und meine Fragen beantworten: Wie ging es Abby während der digitalen Auszeit? Würde sie eine digitale Auszeit weiterempfehlen? Vielen Dank!

1 detox [ˈdiːtɒks] Entgiftung | **2 to switch off** [ˌswɪtʃ ˈɒf] ausschalten

△ **9** **Media mad** → After Station 2, p. 89/13

Work with a partner. Choose a statement or question from the test and read it out loud to your partner. He/She has to comment on it. Then it's his/her turn.

Example: A: "You check your messages all the time!"
B: When I'm bored, I often check them. But when I'm with my friends, I don't do that. What about you?

▲ **10** **A survey** → After Station 2, p. 89/13

Use some of the questions/statements from the test to make a survey. First ask the students in your class, then ask your parents and some other adults and note down for each group and each question how many people answered yes and how many answered no. Turn the numbers into percentages[1]. Present your results to the class and compare the differences you have found between students and adults. Use diagrams to show what you have found out.

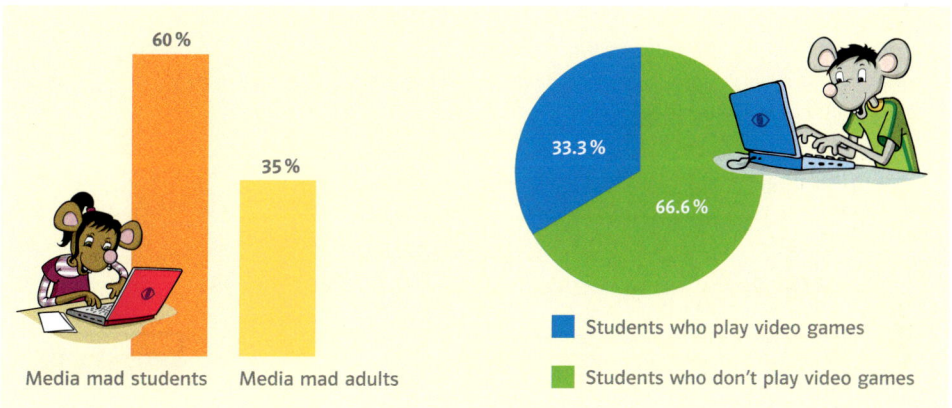

60 %

35 %

Media mad students   Media mad adults

33.3 %

66.6 %

■ Students who play video games
■ Students who don't play video games

△ **11** **Writing a dialogue** → Help with Story, p. 94/1c)

These ideas could help you with your role play. Write down your dialogue before or after you act it out.

Mrs Preston	Mr Preston	Jay	Olivia
Didn't you ask them what …? | What happened when …? | That sounds like a lot of fun, but …?	When I got home, I wasn't able to … | I was angry because … | The kids used their smartphones to …	I was thinking about the party and … | It takes so long to write … | I'm sorry, I wasn't thinking when … | I was so worried when …	Don't you know how dangerous it is to …? | We were really lucky that … | I think next time you should …

1 percentage [pəˈsentɪdʒ] Prozentsatz, Anteil

Unit 6

Lou

△ 1 Talking about places → After Check-in, p. 98/1

Where should these people go on holiday?

Start like this: Lou should go to Wales. She can visit …

1. Lou likes stories about the past and she likes to visit old places.
2. Sandy loves animals and she likes to be outside every day.
3. Andrew is interested in music and traditions.
   He loves watching shows and listening to traditional songs.
4. Ellen is a good swimmer and loves the sea.

▲ 2 Mediation: A trip to Frankfurt → After Station 1, p. 101/3

Eine spanische Familie (zwei Erwachsene, zwei Kinder) ist bei deiner Familie zu Besuch. Nachdem sie Bayern kennengelernt haben, möchten sie kommende Woche von Würzburg aus einen eintägigen Ausflug nach Frankfurt unternehmen. Du hast ihnen hierfür zwei Angebote herausgesucht. Da die Familie kein Deutsch spricht, bittet sie dich zu folgenden Punkten auf Englisch Auskunft zu geben:

| how long? | how expensive? | dogs allowed | open return |

Ihre Reiseverbindung mit dem Zug

Würzburg Hbf ↔ Frankfurt Hbf

Fahrzeit: 1h 51min (einfache Fahrt)
Umstieg: 1
Preis: 44 € für eine Person.
Jede weitere mitreisende Person kostet zusätzlich 8 €. Bitte vor Reiseantritt die Namen aller Reisenden auf dem Ticket eintragen.
Gültigkeit: ab 9 Uhr für beliebig viele Hin- und Rückfahrten am Geltungstag. Ohne Zugbindung.
Haustiere können kostenlos mitgeführt werden. Hunde und Katzen müssen jedoch in einer Box transportiert werden. Bitte achten Sie auf die Ansagen am Gleis und im Zug.

Bequem reisen mit dem Bus

Würzburg Hbf ↔ Frankfurt Hbf

Hinfahrt: Ab: 7:55 Uhr / An: 9:35 Uhr
Rückfahrt: Ab: 17:45 Uhr/An: 19:25 Uhr
Gesamtpreis: 46 €
(2 Erwachsene, 2 Kinder)
Umstieg: kein
Unsere Busse sind alle mit einer Toilette, gratis WLAN und Steckdosen ausgestattet. Die Mitnahme von Tieren ist aus Sicherheitsgründen nicht gestattet. Bis zu drei Gepäckstücke können pro Person kostenfrei mitgeführt werden. Das Ticket gilt nur für die in ihrer Reiseverbindung angegebenen Busse an dem eingetragenen Termin.

3 Will or won't? → After Station 1, p. 101/3

*Make sentences with **will** or **won't**.*

1. Luke | hope | tickets | not be | too expensive.
2. Be | cheaper | go by train?
3. Friends | have to travel | with an adult.
4. Trip | take | about seven hours.
5. Dave | pick up | friends | at the station.
6. Friends | find enough money | the trip?
7. Dave | be happy | see his friends.
8. Dave | not think | Sid | like | new home.

4 Future tenses → After Station 1, p. 102/5

Translate the sentences in blue into English. Which future tenses do you need?
Compare the German tenses and the English tenses.

1. „Vorsicht! Die Bücher fallen gleich herunter!"
2. „Unser Zug fährt um 15:37 Uhr ab. Die Fahrt dauert ungefähr drei Stunden. Ich hoffe, wir werden uns nicht langweilen."
3. „Schau die Wolken an – Es fängt gleich an zu regnen."
4. „Alle meine Freunde kommen heute Abend zur Party. Wir werden viel Spaß haben!"
5. „Du musst noch schnell einkaufen gehen? Warte, ich komme mit!"
6. „… Morgen wird es regnen. Die Sonne wird nur selten zum Vorschein kommen."

5 What will the weather be like? → Help with Station 1, p. 102/6

Here are weather pictures and words to help you.

Start like this: Today the weather is still … | But tomorrow it'll be… |
Temperatures will … | There will be …

Lösung: Today the weather is still sunny. The temperatures are over 30 degrees and there isn't any wind or rain. But tomorrow it'll only be sun in the morning and then it'll be cloudy. It'll still be warm. Temperatures will be 25 degrees and there won't be too much wind. The next day there will be a storm with thunder and lots of wind and rain. The temperatures will fall to 20 degrees.

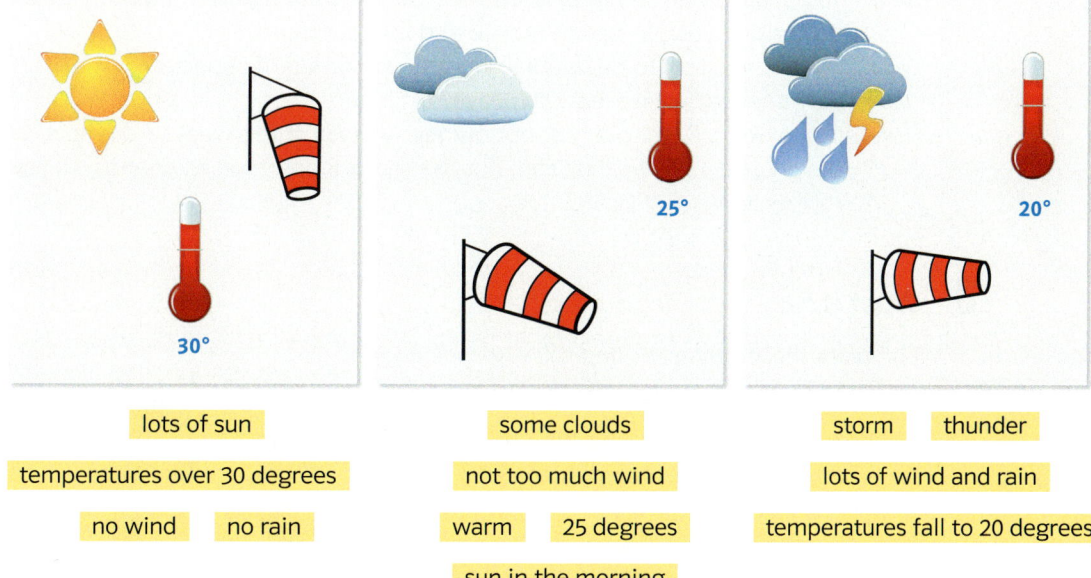

lots of sun

temperatures over 30 degrees

no wind   no rain

some clouds

not too much wind

warm   25 degrees

sun in the morning

storm   thunder

lots of wind and rain

temperatures fall to 20 degrees

▲ **6** **German tourist attractions** → After Station 2, p. 105/9a)

*Match the tourist attractions with the places or regions in Germany. Write tips for tourists using **if + will/can/should** or the **imperative**. Add more information if you like. Remember: When you write your sentences, you can start with the **if-clause** or with the **main clause**!*

Example: If you want to see lots of Roman buildings, you should visit Trier./You should visit Trier if you want to see lots of Roman buildings.

lots of Roman buildings			Berlin
fish market in the harbour			the Black Forest
a famous cake	go		Zugspitze
Germany's capital	see		Cologne
a very big cathedral (church)	➕ visit ➕		Hamburg
Germany's biggest island	like		Loreley
a boat trip to a famous rock	enjoy		Neuschwanstein
Germany's highest peak			Rügen
a beautiful castle			Trier

△ **7** **Do we really need to leave Greenwich?** → After Station 2, p. 105/9b)

*Read Dave and Mr Preston's dialogue and decide if you need **if** or **when**.*

Lösung:
1. when,
2. when,
3. when,
4. if,
5. If,
6. when,
7. if

Dad: Dave, your mum just doesn't feel at home in Greenwich any more. You'll understand **1** you're older.

Dave: But I'm *not* older, Dad. It's *now*, I'm young, and I know that **2** we leave Greenwich, I'll be really sad.

Dad: Yes, you may be sad at first. But **3** you try to change your point of view, things will get better. Can you please try, for me and for your mum?

Dave: Well, … **4** I try to be happier, will you do something special for me?

Dad: **5** I say yes, will it cost a lot, Dave?

Dave: No, it won't. Don't worry about money. Anyway, three weeks from now, **6** we're in our new house, I know I'll be sad. But **7** I have a party for my friends, I'll feel *much* better, I know it! May I? PLEASE …?

△ **8** **What if?** → After Station 2, p. 105/10

Complete these sentences and say what you will do.

1. If I need help with my homework, …
2. If my team wins the game tonight, …
3. If I don't like my new computer game, …
4. If I feel sick tomorrow, …
5. If it's sunny this afternoon, …
6. If we go to the cinema this weekend, …
7. If I make a cake, …

△ **9 Languages in the British Isles** → Help with Station 2, p. 105/11

Match the parts of the statements about languages that people speak in the British Isles.
Then use some of the phrases to talk about languages people speak in your class.

Lösung:
1. c),
2. d),
3. a),
4. b)

1. English is the most important

2. Cornish isn't the only Celtic

3. Polish is the biggest immigrant

4. Welsh is the only official

a) language. Urdu and Punjabi are the
   second biggest immigrant languages.

b) language in the UK besides English.
   People speak it in Wales.

c) language in the UK. There are about
   60 million speakers there.

d) language in the British Isles. People
   speak Irish, Scottish Gaelic and Manx too.

Turkish Italian Greek

Russian Bavarian Franconian

△ **10 Getting ready for Cornwall** → After Station 2, p. 106/13

Luke is getting ready for the trip to Cornwall. Complete the dialogue with the correct words or
*phrases. Use **could, may, might** or **will**. Sometimes there is more than one correct answer.*

Lösung:
1. could/may/might be,
2. might even need,
3. 'll get,
4. could make,
5. will be,
6. could/may/might be,
7. could/may/might be,
8. 'll look for,
9. 'll be.

Mum: I hope you haven't forgotten
anything. What about sunscreen?
You never know, it **1** (be) sunny
in Cornwall. You **2** (even need)
sunglasses or a hat.

Luke: Hm, I guess you're right, Mum.

Mum: And what about a snack? I know
you **3** (get) hungry on the train.
I **4** (make) you a sandwich if you
want one.

Luke: Oh, thanks, but I've already made
sandwiches for all of us. I'm sure
the others **5** (be) hungry too.

I can't find Sherlock, do you know
where he **6** (be)?

Mum: Oh Sherlock … he **7** (be) in the
garden …

Luke: OK, then I **8** (look for) him in the
garden.

Mum: Well, actually, now I remember,
your dad went for a walk with him.
I don't know where they went, but
I'm sure they **9** (be) back soon.

Sherlock: Woof, woof!

Luke: Sounds like they're back!

▲ **11 A poem about your home town** → After Station 2, 106/14

Write a poem about your town or area. The word groups below rhyme[1]; they can help you to write
your poem. Maybe you can think of more words in English that rhyme.

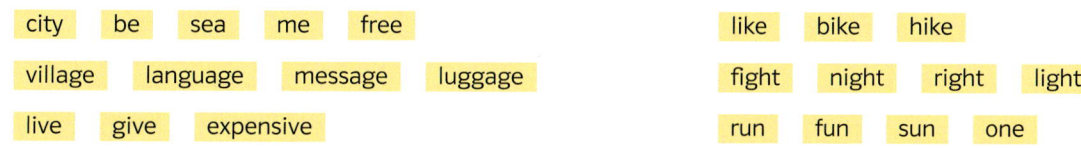

city be sea me free

village language message luggage

live give expensive

like bike hike

fight night right light

run fun sun one

1 to rhyme [raɪm] sich reimen

Dies ist ein fakultativer Auszug aus einem Jugendbuch. Für das Textverständnis zentrale Wörter sind unter dem Text annotiert.

→ **Folie 37, KV 83, KV 84**

S 2/25–29
L 4/21–25

Middle school: How I got lost[1] in London

Rafe Khatchadorian is not very popular with his classmates, and his best friend Leo only exists in Rafe's head. A lot of things go wrong for Rafe, like on his school trip to London to study Living History (when you visit special museums where they show how people lived in the past). When they go to see a famous
5 London wax museum, he makes some silly mistakes, and his popularity score – a number to show how much the others like him – falls and falls.

The big event of the day was a tour around Madame Fifi's House of Wax. Now, of course we were excited about seeing the
10 main attractions – Will and Kate! David Beckham! Rihanna! – but we were *really* excited about the basement[2]. Because in the basement was Madame Fifi's Temple of Terrors, where you could see beheadings[3],
15 people on spikes[4] and other horrible things. In other words, all the blood[5].

Yeah, yeah, we saw all the famous people. But do you *really* want to stand eye to eye with Tom Cruise? *You do?*

20 Not me. I wanted stuff from *my* world. So I stayed longest at Henry VIII (he had six wives[6] and beheaded two of them!), Winston Churchill (he said "We shall never surrender"[7] to Adolf Hitler!), Charles

Darwin (it's thanks to him we know that 25
we come from monkeys[8]!), Guy Fawkes (he tried to blow up[9] Parliament … Wait: should we like him or not?)

I was sad to leave the upper floors. And also … 30

"Scared …?" Leo whispered.
"No, of course I'm not scared," I said.
"Frightened?"
"Frightened is the same as scared," I told him. "And no, I'm not frightened." 35

But, let me tell you a secret[10]: I *was* nervous.

"Is everyone ready?" Gordon, our tour guide, asked.
"Yeah," we all replied. 40

I remembered my popularity score today (-11) and decided to be brave, so my "Yeah" was the loudest. "YEAH!"

"Right, then, let's go," Gordon said. He opened the door but then stopped. "Does 45
anybody in the group have a weak heart[11]?" he asked.

"No," we replied.
"NO!" came my voice, the loudest.
"And everyone knows about the 50
haunting[12]?"

"YEAH!" I shouted, really enjoying myself.

Everyone looked at me – Gordon too.
"What is your name, young man?" he 55
asked.

---

1 **to get lost** [ɡet ˈlɒst] verschwinden; verloren gehen | 2 **basement** [ˈbeɪsmənt] Keller | 3 **beheading** [bɪˈhedɪŋ] Enthauptung | 4 **on spikes** [ɒn ˈspaɪks] aufgespießt | 5 **blood** [blʌd] Blut | 6 **wives** [waɪvz] Ehefrauen | 7 **we shall never surrender** [wi ʃæl ˌnevə srˈendə] wir werden uns nie ergeben | 8 **monkey** [ˈmʌŋki] Affe | 9 **to blow up** [bləʊ ˈʌp] in die Luft sprengen | 10 **secret** [ˈsiːkrət] Geheimnis | 11 **weak heart** [ˌwiːk ˈhɑːt] schwaches Herz | 12 **haunting** [ˈhɔːntɪŋ] Spuk

"Rafe," I said in a very small voice.

"And you know about the haunting, do you, Rafe?"

60 "Yes," I said in an even smaller voice.

"You read about it on the Madame Fifi's website?" he asked, with a strange smile.

"Yes, sir," I replied.

Everyone looked at me. They all 65 really wanted to hear the story about the haunting but thanks to me, they didn't get the chance. Gordon just said: "Excellent. Let's go!" – and my popularity score went down again, to -22.

70 He opened the door and we saw the stone steps that went down into the dark[13]. Down and down we went. At the bottom we heard a loud noise. One of the girls cried out[14], but Gordon told her it was just 75 a passing[15] London Underground train. (OK, it wasn't "one of the girls" who cried out, it was me. Like I say, it was dark …)

Slowly, we started to see the wax figures.

80 "Cool," we said when we saw the heads on spikes, the murderers[16], the blood … Really scary stuff. Stuff that had *actually happened*[17].

"Now, Rafe …" Gordon said. "I'm sure 85 you can tell us about the famous Temple of Terrors story?"

NO WAY. I shook my head "no". Gordon smiled. "Well, let me tell you then …"

"Over a hundred years ago, two gentlemen 90 are taking a tour around the famous Madame Fifi's House of Wax. With them is a lady and they both want to impress[18] her.

"Do you know this Temple of Terrors?" the first one says. "They say it's very scary."

95 "Oh yes, very scary," the second man says.

Eleanor (the lady) says: "Oh, Cedric, it sounds terrible[19]."

Both men see their chance to impress their lady friend. 100

"But I don't believe it," William says.

"Well, William," Cedric says, "let's go down and find out just how scary it is."

And the two men take the stone steps down into the Temple of Terrors. 105

"Well," William says. He looks around in the dark at the scary wax figures and feels very nervous. "I'm not frightened at all!"

"Frightened? Not me!" Cedric says, when he suddenly needs to use the bathroom. 110

"So, let's spend[20] the night here!" William says.

"Good idea!" Cedric says.

And so, because the men badly[21] want to impress Eleanor, they both agree[22] to spend 115 the night …

"They couldn't stay the whole night," Gordon continued. "They soon ran out screaming[23], their eyes wide with terror. And the next day, someone found both 120 men at their homes …"

We looked at Gordon in complete silence. "Dead[24]."

From: *Middle School: How I Got Lost in London* by James Patterson

---

13 dark [dɑːk] Dunkelheit | **14 to cry out** [ˌkraɪ ˈaʊt] aufschreien | **15 passing** [ˈpɑːsɪŋ] vorbeifahrend | **16 murderer** [ˈmɜːdrə] Mörder | **17 stuff that had actually happened** [stʌf ðæt həd ˌæktʃuəli ˈhæpnd] Dinge, die tatsächlich passiert waren | **18 to impress sb** [ɪmˈpres] jmdn. beeindrucken | **19 terrible** [ˈterəbl] schrecklich | **20 to spend** [spend] verbringen | **21 badly** [ˈbædli] unbedingt | **22 to agree** [əˈgriː] einwilligen | **23 screaming** [ˈskriːmɪŋ] schreiend | **24 dead** [ded] tot

Dies ist ein fakultativer Auszug aus einem Jugendbuch. Für das Textverständnis zentrale Wörter sind unter dem Text annotiert.

→ **Folie 38, KV 85**

S 2/30–34
L 4/26–30

Horrid[1] Henry's Christmas play[2]

Henry is about ten years old. He is not a very nice child, so people call him Horrid Henry. Henry doesn't like school, but he wants to be really famous one day. When his teacher tells the class about her plans for a new Christmas play, Henry sees his chance to play the lead[3] – Joseph.

5 But the teacher knows Henry really well and already has other plans …

Horrid Henry sat low down in his chair and watched the clock – it was moving *so* slowly! 'Please go faster!' he thought. Only five more minutes until he could go home!
10 Already Henry could taste the crisps that were waiting for him in his bag outside.

Miss Battle-Axe[4] talked on and on about school dinners (yuck[5]), the new drinking fountain blah blah blah, Maths homework
15 blah blah blah, the school Christmas play blah blah … what? Did Miss Battle-Axe say … Christmas play? Horrid Henry sat up.

"This is a new play with singing and
20 dancing," Miss Battle-Axe continued[6]. "And both the older and the younger children are taking part[7] this year."

Singing! Dancing! Showing off[8] in front of the whole school! Years ago, when Henry was still at primary school[9], he played 25 eighth sheep in the Christmas play and he took the baby from the manger[10] and didn't want to give him back. Henry hoped Miss Battle-Axe didn't remember. Because Henry needed to play the lead this time. 30 Who else could be an all-singing, all-dancing Joseph?

"I want to be Mary!" all the girls shouted.

"I want to be a wise man[11]!" Rude Ralph 35 shouted.

"I want to be a sheep!" Anxious Andrew shouted.

"I want to be Joseph!" Horrid Henry shouted. 40

"No, me!" Jazzy Jim shouted.

"Me!" Brainy Brian shouted.

"Quiet!" Miss Battle-Axe shouted. "*I'm* the director[12], and *I* decide about who can act each part. Margaret. You are Mary." She 45 gave her a thick[13] script.

Moody Margaret shouted: "I'm so happy! I'm so happy!" All the other girls looked at her angrily.

"Susan, Linda – you're the donkey[14]; 50 cows, Fiona and Clare. Blades of grass[15] …" Miss Battle-Axe continued through her list.

"Choose me for Joseph, choose me for Joseph," Horrid Henry prayed. Of course, 55

---

1 **horrid** ['hɒrɪd] gemein | 2 **Christmas play** ['krɪsməs ˌpleɪ] Krippenspiel | 3 **the lead** [liːd] Hauptrolle |
4 **Miss Battle-Axe** [ˌmɪs 'bætlæks] Fräulein Streitaxt | 5 **yuck** [jʌk] igitt | 6 **to continue** [kən'tɪnjuː] fortfahren |
7 **to take part** [ˌteɪk 'pɑːt] teilnehmen | 8 **to show off** [ˌʃəʊ 'ɒf] angeben | 9 **primary school** ['praɪmri ˌskuːl]
Grundschule | 10 **manger** ['meɪndʒə] Krippe | 11 **wise man** ['waɪz ˌmæn] einer der Heiligen Drei Könige | 12 **director**
[dɪ'rektə] Regisseur | 13 **thick** [θɪk] dick | 14 **donkey** ['dɒŋki] Esel | 15 **blade of grass** [ˌbleɪd əv 'grɑːs] Grashalm

the best actor in the school always gets the star part. And the best actor was Henry, wasn't he?

"I'm a sheep, I'm a sheep, I'm a
60 beautiful sheep!" Singing Soraya sang.

"I'm a shepherd[16]!" Jolly Josh smiled.

"I'm an angel[17]," Magic Martha whispered.

"I'm a blade of grass," Weepy William
65 cried[18].

"And Joseph is …"

"Me!" Henry shouted.

"Me!" New Nick, Greedy Graham, Dizzy Dave and Aerobic Al shouted.

70 "… Peter," Miss Battle-Axe said. "From Miss Lovely's class."

Horrid Henry felt sick[19]. Perfect Peter? His *younger* brother? Perfect Peter gets the star part?

75 "It's not fair!" Horrid Henry cried.

Miss Battle-Axe looked at him angrily. "Henry, you're …" Miss Battle-Axe looked at her list.

"Please not a blade of grass, please not a blade of grass," Horrid Henry prayed.
80 Miss Battle-Axe always knew how to make him feel *really* silly and small.

"… the innkeeper[20]."

The innkeeper! Horrid Henry sat up and smiled. How silly he was! Of course,
85 the innkeeper was the star part! He already imagined the scene: Henry the innkeeper is washing glasses and pouring out big drinks to all his happy customers[21] and singing a song. He has a nice long
90 argument[22] about why there is no room at the inn, and finally, he has the chance to close the door in Moody Margaret's face. Wow! Maybe he can even sing a second song like 'Ten Green Bottles'. He can sing
95 and dance and his less talented classmates can play the bottles who he can knock off[23] the wall, one by one. What fun!

Miss Battle-Axe gave a page to Henry. "Your script," she said.
100

From: *Horrid Henry Rules the World*
by Francesca Simon

16 **shepherd** [ˈʃepəd] Hirte | 17 **angel** [ˈeɪndʒl] Engel | 18 **to cry** [kraɪ] weinen | 19 **He felt sick.** [ˌfelt ˈsɪk] Ihm war schlecht. | 20 **innkeeper** [ˈɪnkiːpə] Herbergswirt | 21 **customer** [ˈkʌstəmə] Kunde/ Kundin | 22 **argument** [ˈɑːgjəmənt] Streit | 23 **to knock off** [ˌnɒk ˈɒf] herunterstoßen

Extra line

Diese Doppelseite ist fakultativ. Für das Textverständnis zentrale Wörter sind unten annotiert.

Poetry corner

1 Man, I look cool!

a) *Read the poem and explain:*

1. Who is telling the story?   2. What is different today?   3. What is funny?

b) *Think about actions or feelings for each line. Perform the poem in front of the class: Partner A reads the poem aloud. Partner B mimes the actions and feelings.*

S 2/35
L 4/31

Halloween party

We're having a Halloween party at school.
I'm dressed up like Dracula. Man, I look cool!
I dyed[1] my hair black and I cut off my bangs[2].
I'm wearing a cape and some fake plastic fangs[3].

I put on some makeup to paint my face white
like creatures that only come out in the night.
My fingernails, too, are all pointed and red.
There's no doubt I look like the evil undead[4].

My mom drops me off and I run into school
and suddenly feel like the world's biggest fool[5].
The other kids stare like I'm some kind of freak.
The Halloween party is not till next week.

Kenn Nesbitt

2 Write your own haiku

S 2/36
L 4/32

a) *A haiku is a Japanese poem which always has 17 syllables[6] in three lines: 5 – 7 – 5. It doesn't need to rhyme or have a special rhythm. It is often about something in nature, like a season, or something small that you can see. Read these haiku poems aloud and explain why they are typical haiku poems. How are they different to the poem in exercise 1?*

Lösung: a) The poems are much shorter than the poem in number 1 because there are only three lines and 17 syllables. The poem "Halloween party" is telling a longer story. All three poems in number 2 are about nature.

b) *Write your own haiku poem. Draw a picture or choose a photo for it. Make a class display.*

Autumn
Early September
Red fruit on the golden trees
Apples taste so good.

Rebecca Keller

The frog
An old silent pond[7] …
A frog jumps into the pond,
splash! Silence again.

Matsuo Basho

Looking out of the back bedroom window without my glasses

What's that amazing
new lemon-yellow flower?
Oh yes, a football.

Wendy Cope

1 **to dye** [daɪ] färben | 2 **to cut off bangs** [kʌt ˌɒf ˈbæŋs] Ponyfransen abschneiden | 3 **fang** [fæŋ] Reißzahn |
4 **evil undead** [ˈiːvl ʌnˈded] böse Untote | 5 **fool** [fuːl] Narr | 6 **syllable** [ˈsɪləbl] Silbe | 7 **pond** [pɒnd] Teich

3 On a light¹ night like tonight …

S 2/37
L 4/33

a) *First listen. Then practise this tongue twister².*

b) *Stand in a circle. One person starts to read the poem. When he/she makes a mistake, the next person goes on. Repeat the poem around the circle until everyone can say it without any mistakes. Who's the fastest?*

Night lights

There's no need to light³ a night-light
On a light night like tonight;
For a night-light's light's a slight⁴ light
When the moonlight's white and bright⁵.

4 Concrete poetry

S 2/38–39
L 4/34–35

a) *Concrete poetry is when the shape of the poem shows what it is about. Guess what these poems are about before you read them. Then find important words in each poem and explain why they are where they are in the shape.*

Lösung: EH: a) The first poem is about rain and an umbrella. The most important word is umbrella because the speaker needs it against the rain. The second poem is about a dog and a woman. They're going for a walk. The most important words here are: lady, walking, purple hair, in the air, string, and ring. When we read them, we already learn a lot about the story.

It's raining!

pitter plip rain from falls the sky
patter plop! and I stay dry
I open my umbrella⁶ up

Heidi B. Roemer

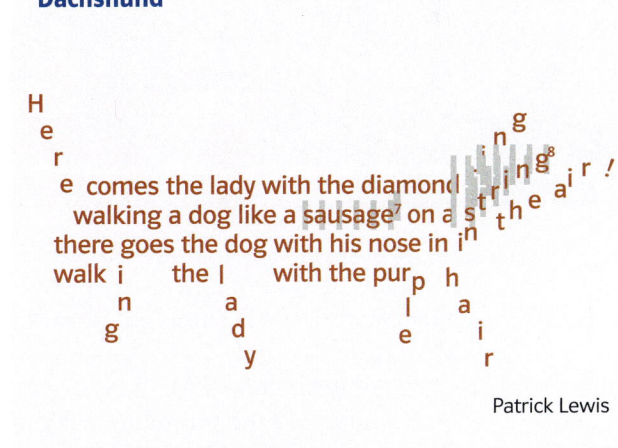

Dachshund

Here comes the lady with the diamond string⁸ in the air!
walking a dog like a sausage⁷ on a
there goes the dog with his nose in
walk in the lady with the purple hair
ring

Patrick Lewis

b) *Pitter, patter, plip and plop are sound words for rain. Match the pictures with these sounds.*

Lösung b)
rustle – leaves (picture 2); meow – cat (picture 5); woof – dog (picture 3); zoom – fast/sports car (picture 6); tick tock – clock (picture 1); splash – water (picture 4)

rustle   meow   woof   zoom   tick tock   splash

c) *Write your own shape poem. You can use sound words or words in different sizes or shapes.*

1 light [laɪt] hell | **2 tongue twister** [ˈtʌŋ ˌtwɪstə] Zungenbrecher | **3 to light** [laɪt] anzünden | **4 slight** [slaɪt] schwach, gering | **5 bright** [braɪt] strahlend, glänzend | **6 umbrella** [ʌmˈbrelə] Regenschirm | **7 sausage** [ˈsɒsɪdʒ] Wurst | **8 string** [strɪŋ] Schnur

Dies ist ein fakultativer Auszug aus einem Jugendbuch. Für das Textverständnis zentrale Wörter sind unter dem Text annotiert.

→ Folie 39, KV 86, KV 87

S 2/40–44
L4/36–40

Ten-tonne truck

Zoe finds a rat in her room. She wants to train it like she trained her pet hamster (who could break-dance), but she knows she isn't allowed to keep any pets. Raj, a shopkeeper[1] who is the 'agony aunt' of the town, tells her to set Armitage the rat free[2] in the park.

5 "What am I going to do with him, Raj? I'm not allowed to keep him at home; he's the reason why I was suspended[3] from school. My stepmother hated my hamster, she is *never* going to let me keep a rat."

10 Raj thought for a moment. "Maybe you should set him free," he finally said.
"Free?" Zoe said, with a tear in her eye.
"Yes. Rats shouldn't be pets …"
"But this little one is so cute …"
15 "Maybe, but he's going to grow. He can't spend his whole life in your pocket."
"But I love him, Raj, I really do."
"I'm sure you do, Miss Zoe," Raj said. "And if you love him, you should set him
20 free."
So this was goodbye. Zoe knew deep down she would never be able to keep

Armitage for long. There were a hundred reasons, but the most important one was: HE WAS A RAT. 25

Children don't have rats as pets. They have cats and dogs and hamsters and mice and rabbits and tortoises. Some kids even have ponies, but never rats. Rats live underground, not in little girls' bedrooms. 30

Zoe walked sadly out of Raj's shop. It was true that sometimes he tried to sell his customers[4] a half-eaten chocolate bar, but all the kids in town knew that when they needed advice, he was the best. 35

And so she had to say goodbye to Armitage. Zoe took the long way back to her flat, through the park. She thought this was the perfect place to set little Armitage free. There were always bits of bread for 40 the ducks – Armitage could eat these. He could drink from the pond[5] and take a bath in it. And maybe there was a squirrel or two he could make friends with.

The little girl carried the little rat in her 45 hand. It was the middle of the afternoon and there were just a few old ladies and their dogs in the park. Armitage wrapped his tail around her thumb – maybe he knew that something was wrong … 50

Zoe walked as slowly as possible. Finally, she reached the middle of the park. She was looking for a nice quiet place. Then she bent down[6] to the ground slowly and opened her hand. But Armitage didn't 55 move. He just stayed in her hand. It was breaking Zoe's heart …

1 shopkeeper ['ʃɒpˌkiːpə] Ladenbesitzer | **2** to set sb/sth free [ˌset 'friː] jmdn./etw. freilassen | **3** to be suspended [bi səˈspendɪd] (vorübergehend) der Schule verwiesen werden | **4** customer ['kʌstəmə] Kunde | **5** pond [pɒnd] Teich | **6** to bend down [ˌbend 'daʊn] sich bücken

Zoe shook[7] her hand a little, but Armitage only held on tighter[8] to her
60 fingers. She was fighting back tears when she picked the rat up gently[9] and put him carefully on the grass. Once again Armitage didn't move. He just looked up at her sadly. Zoe kissed him gently on his
65 little pink nose.

"Goodbye, little friend," she whispered. "I'm going to miss[10] you."

A tear dropped from her eye.

The little rat turned his little head to
70 one side, like a friend who was trying to understand her. This just made it harder for Zoe.

Finally, Zoe took a big breath and stood up. "Don't look back!" she told herself.
75 But after a few steps she had to look one last time at the place she left him. To Zoe's surprise, Armitage wasn't there.

"He has already run away to the safety[11] of the bushes," she thought. She looked at
80 the grass, but it was long and he was short, and the grass didn't move. Zoe turned

round and sadly started to walk home.

She left the park and crossed the road. For a moment, there was no noise of cars, and in the silence, Zoe heard a small 'eek'. 85 She turned round quickly, and in the middle of the road was Armitage.

He was following her!

"Armitage!" she shouted excitedly. He didn't want to be free; he wanted to be with 90 her! She was so happy. Now she didn't have to imagine all kinds of terrible scenes any more: A hungry swan[12] couldn't eat him for dinner, and a ten-tonne truck couldn't run him over[13]. 95

At that moment, she heard a loud thundering noise. Something came along the road towards Armitage, who was still moving slowly to get to Zoe. It was a ten-tonne truck! 100

Zoe wasn't able to move, she just watched the truck which was speeding[14] closer and closer towards Armitage. How could the driver see a baby rat in the road?

From: *Ratburger* by David Walliams

---

7 **to shake** [ʃeɪk] schütteln | **8** **tight** [taɪt] fest | **9** **gently** [ˈdʒentli] sanft |
10 **to miss sb/sth** [mɪs] jmdn./etw. vermissen | **11** **safety** [ˈseɪfti] Sicherheit | **12** **swan** [swɒn] Schwan |
13 **to run sth over** [ˌrʌnˈəʊvə] etw. überfahren | **14** **to speed** [spiːd] rasen

Dies ist ein fakultativer Auszug aus einem Jugendbuch. Für das Textverständnis zentrale Wörter sind unter dem Text annotiert.

→ Folie 40, KV 88

S 2/45–48
L 4/41–44

A harp[1] on the water – a Welsh legend

Most countries have their legends – stories told from generation to generation. These stories talk of kings and queens, of fights between good and bad, rich and poor. Maybe you know the legend of Robin Hood, or of King Arthur? This one from Wales is about what happened to a very cruel[2] king.

5 Long long ago, at the beginning of time on this island, there was a very cruel king who lived in a stone palace where the lake of Bala is now. People said about him: "He kills who he can," and it was true – he 10 killed many.

One day, not long after he became king, and while he was still a young man, he was walking in his garden and thinking about cruelty when he suddenly heard a 15 voice. It sounded like something between a silver bell and a bird's cry and it said: "Vengeance[3] will come. Vengeance will come." Then he heard a second voice, farther away than the first. It asked: "When 20 will it come? When will it come?" Then the first voice replied: "In the third generation.

The third generation." At this he laughed loudly and shouted through the garden: "If it doesn't come before that, why should I care?" 25

And he planned to be crueller than ever.

Years later, the king's three sons[4] were born and they were even crueller than he was. One day he was again walking 30 in the garden when he heard the same voices. They were crying the same words: "Vengeance will come. When will it come? In the third generation, the third generation." Again he laughed loudly. 35 "I laugh in the face of vengeance," he shouted. And he hurried back into the palace to teach his sons more cruelty.

Years passed[5], until the day when the whole palace was celebrating the birth of 40 a son to the king's son and heir[6]. The king sent his guards[7] out into the country. They had to tell everyone who loved the king (and their own lives too) to hurry to the palace to celebrate. One guard had to find 45 a harp player with white hair who lived high up in the hills; he should play music for all the people who came to eat and dance in the palace that night.

The harp player didn't want to come, 50 but he had to. When he saw the silver candlesticks, the golden cups[8] and the beautiful dresses of the ladies, it felt like a strange dream and he couldn't say a word. He wasn't in the mood[9] to play as he 55 watched the faces of the king and his sons

---

1 harp [hɑːp] Harfe | **2 cruel** [ˈkruːəl] grausam | **3 vengeance** [ˈvendʒns] Rache | **4 son** [sʌn] Sohn |
5 to pass [pɑːs] vorübergehen | **6 heir** [eə] Thronfolger | **7 guard** [gɑːd] Wächter | **8 cup** [kʌp] Tasse, Becher |
9 in the mood [ɪn ðə ˈmuːd] in der Laune

The moon moved behind a black cloud. In the dark the harp player couldn't see his hand in front of him and the noise of water below told him that it was dangerous to move. 85

He suddenly thought that he was crazy to follow the voice of a bird, and he remembered sadly that his harp was back at the palace. "I must go back before the 90 dancing starts!" he shouted. But when he thought of those cruel faces he was so horrified that he couldn't move. He was so tired and it was so dark … He fell asleep quickly. 95

In the morning, he got up and rubbed[11] the sleep from his eyes. Then he rubbed them again and again because when he looked towards the palace, there was no palace there! He saw only a huge, calm lake 100 where before there were walls and towers[12]. And his harp was swimming on the water towards him.

with their hard smiles and ice-cold eyes. But the king said: "Play!", and so he had to play.

60 At midnight there was a break between the eating and dancing. The harp player was left alone, with nothing to eat and drink, in a quiet corner. Suddenly he heard a clear voice which said: "Vengeance will 65 come. Vengeance will come." He turned to the window, and in the light of the moon he could see a small brown bird which was flying around in the garden. It seemed[10] to invite him to follow!

70 He was very tired, but he stood up and left the palace. The bird flew in front of him and showed him the path he should take. At the palace wall he stopped for a moment, but "Vengeance, vengeance!" the 75 brown bird cried. Now it seemed as easy to go on as to go back. So they went on and on until the harp player could see the hill in front of them.

When they reached the top of the hill 80 at last, he was so tired that he had to sit down. For the first time the bird was silent.

'A Harp on the Water' from *Welsh Legends and Folktales* by Gwyn Jones

---

10 to seem [si:m] scheinen | **11 to rub** [rʌb] reiben | **12 tower** [taʊə] Turm

Vocabulary skills

S1 Vokabelheft

Führe ein dreispaltiges Vokabelheft, in dem du auch neue
Vokabeln notieren kannst, die nicht in der Wortliste stehen.
Die erste Spalte ist für die englische Vokabel bestimmt, die
zweite für die Übersetzung und die dritte für Beispielsätze
oder alles, was dir hilft, dir die Bedeutung zu merken, z.B.
Bilder, *mind maps*, Beziehungen zu anderen Wörtern, auch
in anderen Sprachen.

S2 Vokabelkartei

Es lohnt sich, eine Vokabelkartei anzulegen, um Vokabeln
zu lernen. Sie besteht aus Karteikarten für die Vokabeln und
einem Karton mit fünf Fächern für die Karten.
Schreibe das englische Wort auf die Vorderseite der
Karteikarte und die deutsche Bedeutung auf die Rückseite.
Zusätzlich kannst du weitere Merkhilfen notieren. Stelle
zunächst alle Karten ins erste Fach.
Übe jeden Tag fünf bis zehn Minuten, und zwar so: Nimm
eine Karte nach der anderen heraus und überprüfe, ob du
die Übersetzung weißt (deutsch – englisch, englisch –
deutsch). Wenn ja, stellst du die Karte ins zweite Fach.
Mache weiter, bis das erste Fach leer ist. Das zweite Fach
bearbeitest du dann genauso, allerdings nicht jeden Tag,
sondern nur einmal in der Woche, das dritte Fach alle zwei
Wochen usw.

S3 Wörter im Zusammenhang

Wörter sind die Bausteine der Sprache. Du musst sie
natürlich lernen und jedes für sich verstehen. Zur
Beherrschung einer Sprache gehört aber auch zu wissen,
welche Kombinationen dieser Bausteine möglich sind.
Deshalb ist es wichtig, mit den Wörtern schon die richtigen
Kombinationen mitzulernen. Schreibe Wörter möglichst
immer in typischen Zusammenhängen auf.

Mit Verben kannst du passende Ergänzungen mitlernen, z.B.:

*to **read** a book, a magazine, a comic, a manga*
*to **write** a letter, an e-mail, an invitation, a blog*
*to **go** swimming, shopping, home, away, to the cinema*

Du solltest auch wissen, wann bestimmte grammatische Formen auf bestimmte Wörter folgen. Schreibe dir passende Beispiele zusammen mit der Vokabel auf, z. B.:

I would like to swim, to read, to go shopping
I like swimming, reading, going shopping

Welche die richtigen Präpositionen sind, muss man in jeder Sprache auswendig lernen. Notiere auch dafür Beispiele und lerne sie, z. B.:

The party is on Friday, at seven, at the weekend.
My house is in Dover Street. We're on the road to London.
London is on the Thames.

S4 Methoden

Du hast schon mehrere Methoden gelernt, wie du dir Vokabeln besser einprägen kannst:

– Klebezettel mit englischen Wörtern an die entsprechenden Gegenstände in deinem Zimmer kleben

– Wörter als Bildwörter oder mit passenden Bildern aufmalen

– Wörter zusammen mit anderen, die zu einem Thema gehören, in *mind maps* anordnen

– Wörter pantomimisch darstellen und gegenseitig erraten lassen

– Wörter aussprechen, zusammen mit ihrer Übersetzung und vielleicht einem Beispielsatz aufnehmen und immer wieder anhören

– Wörter mit ähnlichen Wörtern in anderen Sprachen notieren

– Wörter, die miteinander in Beziehung stehen, zusammen notieren, z. B. verwandte Wörter, Gegensatzpaare, zusammengehörige Paare

S5 Umgang mit dem zweisprachigen Wörterbuch

Es gibt verschiedene Arten von Wörterbüchern: ein- oder zweisprachige, gedruckte oder digitale. Das *Dictionary* in deinem Schülerbuch ist eine Art vereinfachtes zweisprachiges Wörterbuch, in dem alle neuen Wörter aufgeführt und erklärt sind, die du in den Texten im Buch kennengelernt hast. Um die richtige Aussprache einer Vokabel in einem gedruckten Wörterbuch nachzuschlagen, musst du die Lautschrift beherrschen. Bei digitalen Wörterbüchern kannst du dir die Wörter richtig ausgesprochen anhören. Du musst nicht blättern, sondern nur das gesuchte Stichwort richtig eingeben.

Bei einem vom Lehrwerk unabhängigen Wörterbuch musst du lernen, aus den vielen zusätzlichen Informationen genau diejenigen herauszufiltern, die gerade wichtig sind.

Englisch – Deutsch

Stichwort
Unterscheidung mehrerer gleich geschriebener Einträge

Nummerierung
verschiedene Bedeutungen eines Stichwortes

Zusätze zur Übersetzung

Lautschrift
Aussprache

mean¹ [miːn] *adj* ❶ *esp* Brit (*miserly*) geizig, knauserig ❷ (*unkind*) gemein, fies *fam* ❸ Am (*vicious*) aggressiv; (*dangerous*) gefährlich; *dog* bissig ❹ (*bad*) schlecht; **no ~ feat** eine Meisterleistung
mean² <meant, meant> [miːn] *vt* ❶ (*signify*) *word, symbol* bedeuten; **no ~s no** nein heißt nein ❷ (*intend to convey*) *person* meinen; **what do you ~ by that?** was willst du damit sagen? ❸ (*be sincere*) **I ~ what I say** ich meine es ernst, was ich sage ❹ (*intend*) wollen; **he didn't ~ any harm** er wollte nichts Böses; **I've been ~ing to phone you for weeks** ich will dich schon seit Wochen anrufen; **it was ~t to be a surprise** das sollte eine Überraschung sein; **to ~ business** es ernst meinen; **to ~ well** es gut meinen; **to be ~t for each other** füreinander bestimmt sein ❺ (*result in*) bedeuten, heißen *fam*
mean³ [miːn] **I.** *n* (*average*) Mittel *nt*; (*average value*) Mittelwert *m*; (*fig*) Mittelweg *m* **II.** *adj* durchschnittlich

Übersetzung

Flexionsformen
z. B. Hinweis auf Pluralformen oder unregelmäßige Verbformen

Wortklasse
Prüfung, welcher Eintrag im gegebenen Satz passt

Deutsch – Englisch

Zusätze zur Grammatik

Zusätze zur Verwendung

Regionale Varianten

bis [bɪs] **I.** (*präp +akk*) ❶ *zeitlich* till, until; (*nicht später als*) by; **~ jetzt** up to now; **~ morgen!** see you tomorrow!; **~ bald!** see you soon!; **~ anhin** schweiz (*bis jetzt*) up to now ❷ *räumlich* as far as; **~ dort/dorthin/dahin** to, up to; **~ hierher** up to this point; **~ wo/wohin …?** where … to? ❸ (*erreichend*) up to; **ich zähle ~ drei** I'll count [up] to three; **die Tagestemperaturen steigen ~ [zu] 30°C** daytime temperatures rise to 30°C; **Kinder ~ sechs Jahre** children up to the age of six ❹ (*mit Ausnahme von*) ▪ **~ auf** [*o* schweiz ~ **an**] except [for] **II.** *konj* ❶ (*ungefähre Angabe*) to; **400 ~ 500 Gramm Schinken** 400 to 500 grams of ham ❷ *zeitlich* **~ es dunkel wird, möchte ich zu Hause sein** I want to be home by the time it gets dark; **ich warte noch, ~ es dunkel wird** I'll wait until it gets dark
Bisamratte *f* muskrat
Biscaya *f s.* **Biskaya**
Bischof, Bischöfin <-s, Bischöfe> [ˈbɪʃɔf,

Kollokationen/ Verwendungsmuster
In welchen Verbindungen kommt das Wort vor?

Reading skills

S6 Schnelllesetechniken

Normalerweise denkst du während des Lesens nicht darüber nach, wie du dabei vorgehst. Wenn du aber eine Aufgabe zu einem Text bekommst oder eine bestimmte Information suchst, liest du bewusster und gezielter. Diese Techniken helfen dir, wenn die Zeit begrenzt ist.

Skimming („den Rahm abschöpfen")	Scanning („maschinell durchsuchen")
Wenn du danach gefragt wirst, worum es in einem Text geht, sollst du ihn nicht einfach nacherzählen, sondern nur das Wichtigste *(gist)* zusammenfassen. Dazu kannst du den ganzen Text überfliegen und darauf achten, ob bestimmte Wörter *(key words)* oder Personen häufiger vorkommen. Auch die Überschrift oder Bilder können dir helfen einzuschätzen, was wichtig ist und was nicht. Diese Art des Schnelllesens nennt man *skimming*.	Wenn du nach bestimmten Einzelheiten *(details)* in einem Text gefragt wirst, musst du ihn überfliegen und die Stellen mit der wichtigen Information finden. Dazu suchst du gezielt nach passenden Stichwörtern *(key words)*. Sie zeigen an, welche Teile du genauer lesen solltest, um die gesuchte Information zu bekommen. Diese Art des Überfliegens nennt man auch *scanning*.

S7 Wichtige Inhalte von Texten herausfinden

Wenn du einen Text liest, solltest du danach immer folgende Fragen beantworten können:

Who ...?	*What ...?*	*When ...?*	*Where ...?*
Wer ist beteiligt?	*Was geschieht?*	*Wann?*	*Wo?*

Dazu kannst du Schnelllesetechniken anwenden, Markierungen im Text machen und dir Fragen und Anmerkungen notieren (**S9**). Wenn du den Text noch genauer liest, kannst du weitere Fragen beantworten, z. B. Warum geschieht etwas? Wenn es eine Geschichte ist, wer erzählt sie? Für wen wurde der Text geschrieben (Adressat)?

S8 Gliederung als Hilfe

Um einen Text besser zu verstehen, kann es dir helfen, ihn in mehrere Abschnitte zu gliedern. Orientiere dich dabei z. B. an Absätzen und inhaltlichen Punkten, die du dir markiert hast. Überlege anschließend, was in den einzelnen Teilen jeweils das Wichtigste ist, und formuliere passende Überschriften. Dies erleichtert es dir, Zusammenfassungen von Texten zu geben oder *Mediation*-Aufgaben zu lösen.

A Henry hopes to play the lead

B Henry is disappointed

C Henry sees the positive side of things

S9 Textbearbeitung mit Markierungen und Notizen

Im geliehenen Buch darfst du das zwar nicht, aber auf Kopien oder in Arbeitsheften solltest du dir angewöhnen, wichtige Stellen in Texten zu markieren und Randnotizen zu machen (z. B. Fragen oder Anmerkungen). Verwende am besten verschiedene Farben: Markiere z. B. wichtige inhaltliche Punkte grün und Informationen zu den Personen blau. Wörter, die du nachschlagen musst, solltest du auch hervorheben. Unterstreiche sie beispielsweise und notiere die richtige Übersetzung am Rand. So fällt dir das erneute Lesen leichter.

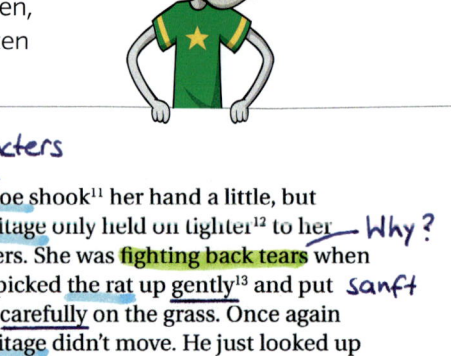

characters

Zoe shook[11] her hand a little, but Armitage only held on tighter[12] to her — Why? fingers. She was fighting back tears when she picked the rat up gently[13] and put *sanft* him carefully on the grass. Once again — *vorsichtig* Armitage didn't move. He just looked up at her sadly. Zoe kissed him gently on his little pink nose. — friends! — emotions "Goodbye, little friend," she whispered. "I'm going to miss[14] you."

S10 Umgang mit neuen Wörtern

Viele Wörter kannst du schon verstehen, obwohl du sie noch nicht gelernt hast.

1. Ähnlichkeit mit Wörtern, die du schon kennst

Oft haben verwandte Wörter den gleichen Stamm, aber andere Vorsilben oder Endungen. Wenn du z. B. *happy* schon kennst, wirst du *unhappy* sicher auch verstehen. Englische Wörter haben oft keine Endungen, aber es gibt sie in verschiedenen Wortarten. Wenn du also das Wort *guide* als Nomen kennst, kannst du dir bestimmt denken, was das Verb *to guide* oder die Zusammensetzung *travel guide* bedeutet.

2. Ähnlichkeit mit Wörtern, die du aus einer anderen Sprache kennst

Viele englische Wörter gibt es genauso oder ähnlich auch im Deutschen, z. B. *computer*, *hobby* oder *pony*. Manchmal hilft dir auch ein Wort, das du aus einer anderen Sprache kennst (Französisch, Latein, …) ein englisches Wort zu verstehen, z. B. weil es ähnlich geschrieben wird oder ähnlich klingt.

3. Verstehen der Wörter im Zusammenhang

Manchmal kannst du dir anhand eines Bildes oder einer Überschrift denken, was ein Wort in einem Text bedeutet. Und wenn du alle Wörter in einem Satz verstehst außer einem, kann dieses oft nur eine bestimmte Bedeutung haben. Was bedeutet z. B. *return* in diesem Satz?
*My dog ran away, and I was really happy when he **returned** after three days.*

Und wenn du doch im Wörterbuch nachschlagen musst, helfen dir die Tipps in **S5**.

Writing skills

S11 Planung deines Textes

Überlege, für wen dein Text bestimmt ist (Adressat) und welchen Zweck er erfüllen soll. Vor dem Schreiben machst du dir am besten einen Plan: Notiere in Stichwörtern, was in der Einleitung, dem Hauptteil und dem Schluss deines Textes stehen soll. So vergisst du nichts Wichtiges und findest auch leichter eine schöne Einleitung und einen guten Schluss.

S12 Textsorten und ihre Besonderheiten

Du kennst schon einige wichtige Textsorten und ihre Merkmale:

E-mail, letter, postcard, invitation	Achte auf die richtige Anrede für den Adressaten, z. B. *Dear …*, Grußformeln am Schluss, z. B. *Yours/Love/Best wishes*, und beachte die Höflichkeitsregeln. Denke bei einem Brief an die Angabe der Empfänger- und Absenderadresse und an das Datum.
Story	Wenn du eine Geschichte vervollständigen sollst, muss dein Teil zum vorgegebenen Text passen. Vermeide also inhaltliche Widersprüche. Außerdem sollten die Erzählperspektive (wer erzählt?) und die Erzählzeit nicht wechseln. Meistens sind Geschichten im *past tense* geschrieben. Gestalte deine Geschichten sprachlich abwechslungsreich und schmücke sie aus.
Dialogue	Wenn du einen Dialog, z. B. für eine Filmszene, schreibst, denke daran, dass du echte mündliche Sprache verwendest, also z. B. *short forms*, *question tags*, verstärkende Ausdrücke usw.
Report	Bei einem Bericht ist die Vollständigkeit und Verständlichkeit der sachlichen Informationen das Wichtigste. Er wird im *past tense* geschrieben.
Prompt cards	Wenn du dich auf eine Präsentation vorbereitest, notiere auf Karteikarten nur Stichwörter, die dich an die einzelnen Punkte des Vortrags erinnern. Schreibe z. B. wichtige Namen, Ereignisse, Orte und Daten unter die Überschriften *Who, What, When, Where*.
Flyer	Ein Flyer sollte gut lesbar sein (Schriftart und -größe) und alle wichtigen Informationen enthalten: *Who?, What?, When?, Where?, Why?* Formuliere außerdem einen ansprechenden Slogan.
Diary entry	Ein Tagebucheintrag erzählt und kommentiert vergangene und erwartete Ereignisse aus der ganz persönlichen Sicht einer Person und ist normalerweise nicht für andere Leser bestimmt.

S13 Überarbeitung deines Textes

Wenn du einen Entwurf erstellt hast, liest du ihn am besten noch einmal gründlich durch. Meistens entdeckst du so noch einige Fehler und kannst holprige Formulierungen verbessern. Nimm dabei eine Checkliste zu Hilfe (siehe rechts), damit du nichts Wichtiges vergisst. Es ist auch eine gute Übung, die Texte mit einem Partner zu tauschen und gegenseitig Korrektur zu lesen.

Checkliste

Rechtschreibung:
– Wörter richtig geschrieben?
– Am Satzanfang groß?
– Getrennt oder zusammen?

Grammatik:
– Richtige Zeitform, Satzbau, Pluralbildung usw.?

Inhalt:
– Alle wesentlichen Punkte enthalten?
– Keine inhaltlichen Fehler?
– Zusammenhänge erkennbar und logisch?

S14 Sprachliche Verbesserungen

Je größer dein Wortschatz wird, desto mehr Möglichkeiten eröffnen sich dir beim Schreiben von Texten.
Einzelne Sätze kannst du genauer und interessanter gestalten, indem du z. B. Nomen durch Adjektive oder durch weitere Nomen näher beschreibst. Verben kannst du durch adverbiale Bestimmungen ergänzen. Vergleiche die unterschiedliche Information in den beiden folgenden Sätzen:

A *I went to the shop.*

B *I went to the* big pet *shop* in Greenwich with my sister last Saturday*.*

Deinen gesamten Text kannst du flüssiger gestalten, indem du die Sätze miteinander verknüpfst. So werden logische Zusammenhänge klarer und der Text liest sich leichter. Vergleiche die beiden folgenden Textausschnitte. Der erste wirkt durch die unverbundenen Hauptsätze abgehackt. Der zweite enthält auch Satzgefüge aus Haupt- und Nebensätzen, die mit Hilfe von Verbindungswörtern *(linking words)* logische Zusammenhänge herstellen. Außerdem geben die Adjektive und Adverbien genauere Informationen und machen den Text interessanter.

A *I went to the shop. I wanted a guinea pig. We looked at all the guinea pigs. I didn't like them. We wanted to leave.*
A girl came in with a box. She brought back a guinea pig.
It was cute! I bought it. I'm happy.

B *I went to the big pet shop in Greenwich with my sister last Saturday* **because** *I wanted to buy a nice guinea pig.*
We looked at all the guinea pigs, **but** *I didn't like them.*
Just when *I wanted to leave, a girl came in with a box.*
She brought back a guinea pig **which** *was really cute.*
So *I bought it* **and** *I'm very happy now.*

Speaking skills

S15 Sprechen üben

Sprechen lernt man nur durch Sprechen. Du solltest dir angewöhnen, im Englischunterricht immer englisch zu sprechen, ob mit deiner Lehrerin/deinem Lehrer oder in der Partner- und Gruppenarbeit. Um Sprechen zu üben, solltest du allerdings viel mehr sprechen als nur im Unterricht. Vielleicht üben deine Freunde, Eltern oder Geschwister mit dir?

Eine Voraussetzung für das richtige Sprechen ist natürlich, dass du übst, die englischen Wörter richtig auszusprechen. Beim Lernen mit dem Buch kann dir die Lautschrift dabei helfen. Sage sie dir immer wieder laut vor. Einfacher und einprägsamer ist es natürlich, die Vokabeln richtig ausgesprochen anzuhören und nachzusprechen. Hilfsmittel dafür sind Audio-CDs mit den Schülerbuchtexten, Lernsoftware oder Online-Wörterbücher, in denen du jedes Wort anklicken und anhören kannst.

> **Th**ey **th**ought of **the th**ree **th**ousand **th**ankful **th**ieves.

Übe schwierig auszusprechende Laute, die anders sind als im Deutschen, z. B. das stimmhafte oder stimmlose *th* oder das *w* im Kontrast zum *v* oder ein stimmhaftes *d* oder *g* am Wortende. Dazu kannst du (lustige) Sätze erfinden, sie dir immer wieder vorsprechen und dabei das Tempo steigern, bis die Aussprache zuverlässig klappt.

> **W**hy **w**ork **w**ith **v**ocabulary **w**hen you can **v**isit a **w**onderful **v**illage **w**orld?

Wenn du ganze Texte hörst, bekommst du ein Gefühl dafür, wie die Wörter im Textzusammenhang ausgesprochen werden. Die Aussprache unterscheidet sich manchmal stark von der Aussprache der Einzelwörter. Aufeinander treffende Laute werden z. B. häufig miteinander verbunden.

> She wante**d** her ba**g** back and sai**d** what a nice hat she ha**d**.

Du hast auch schon gehört, wie die Betonung die Aussprache beeinflussen kann, wenn jemand besonders starke Gefühle ausdrücken will. Das kannst du auch üben.

> This is th**e** **e**nd **o**f **t**he story. They know ove**r** **a** hundred different stories.

> It's **so** unfair! Why doesn't anyone **ever** ask **me** what I'm feeling?

S16 Gesprochene Sprache

Auch beim Sprechen kommt es auf die Situation und deinen Gesprächspartner an, wie du dich ausdrückst. Denke z. B. auch an Höflichkeitsregeln.
In der gesprochenen Sprache ist es normal, dass Pausen, unvollständige Sätze, Wiederholungen oder Füllwörter vorkommen:

- Während bei Gleichaltrigen ein *Hi!* als Begrüßung ausreicht, ist Lehrpersonen oder fremden Erwachsenen gegenüber ein *Good morning!/ Good morning Mr/Mrs …* eher angemessen.
- Statt *I want …* sagst du höflicher *I would like …* oder *Could I please have …?*
- Entscheidungsfragen beantwortest du mit Kurzantworten, nicht einfach mit *Yes* oder *No: Yes, I do./No, I'm not.*

Well, I – I really don't know. It's – **er**, maybe you want to …?

Es ist wichtig, einem Dialogpartner immer das Gefühl zu geben, dass er einbezogen wird. Dazu dienen *feedback phrases*, Nachfragen und *question tags*.

Then we went to the city farm, Mudchute, **you know**. *And there was this cute little pig –* **you saw it too, didn't you? Guess what Linda did when she saw it!**

S17 Mündliche Aufgaben und ihre Besonderheiten

Es ist viel wichtiger, dass du regelmäßig länger zusammenhängend sprichst, als dass jedes Wort perfekt ausgesprochen und die Grammatik absolut korrekt ist. Wie wäre es, wenn jeder in deiner Klasse in einer Englischstunde eine Minute lang Englisch über ein selbst gewähltes Thema spricht? Hier findest du ein paar Tipps für bestimmte mündliche Aufgaben:

Interview	Sei höflich, aber scheue dich nicht nachzufragen, wenn du etwas nicht sofort verstehst. Achte bei der Fragestellung auf die richtige Zeitform und das richtige Hilfsverb. Antworte auch in der passenden Zeitform.
Asking/ Showing the way	Auch hier ist Höflichkeit wichtig und ganz bestimmte Vokabeln wie *go down X Street, go straight on, go past/turn left/right into Y Lane, it's on the left/right/opposite Z.*
Role play	Versetze dich in deine Rolle und versuche nachzufühlen, was die Person weiß und was sie denkt und fühlt. Verwende typische Merkmale der gesprochenen Sprache und unterstütze deine Worte mit Mimik und Gestik.
Presentation	Bereite deine Präsentation gut vor. Recherchiere die Fakten gründlich. Überlege, was dir wichtig ist und was du sagen möchtest. Besorge Material, das du zeigen willst, und bereite es so auf, dass es gut aussieht und verständlich ist. Mache dir einen Ablaufplan. Schreibe dir Notizen auf *prompt cards*. Versuche frei zu sprechen und nicht abzulesen. Übe deine Präsentation vorher und stoppe die Zeit, die du brauchst.

S18 Bildbeschreibung

Wenn du aufgefordert wirst, ein Bild zu beschreiben, solltest du Folgendes beachten:

1. Benenne, um welche Art Bild es sich handelt, und, falls bekannt, wer es wann wozu angefertigt hat.
2. Beschreibe zuerst das Thema des Bildes (*there is/are/you can see … in the photo/ picture,/it shows …*), und dann, wo sich was genau befindet und wie es aussieht.
3. Beschreibe ablaufende Vorgänge oder Handlungen stets im *present progressive*.
4. Wenn es gefragt ist, sage etwas über die Wirkung des Bildes und äußere ggf. Vermutungen darüber, was es ausdrücken soll und zu welchem Zweck es angefertigt wurde.
5. Nutze den Wortschatz und die Anregungen im unten stehenden Kasten.

Where?	**Who/What?**	**What's happening?**
in the foreground/background *on the right/left* *in the middle/centre* *at the bottom/top* *in the right-hand/left-hand corner* *in front of/behind/between* *next to* *along* *across* *outside/inside* *country/region?* *landscape?* *room?*	*a person/man/* *woman/girl/boy/* *group of people* *an animal/* *a plant/an object* *how many?* *size?* *age?* *colour?* *shape?* *Use adjectives* *and comparisons.*	*… is/are …ing* *feelings/* *atmosphere?* *Use adverbs.*

top right-hand corner

in the centre

background

bottom left-hand corner

foreground

S19 Präsentation eines Bildes

Für die Präsentation eines Bildes gelten alle unter **S18** beschriebenen Hinweise. Du solltest aber auf jeden Fall ausführlich auf die Punkte **1.** und **4.** eingehen und auch die allgemeinen Tipps zur mündlichen Präsentation unter **S17** berücksichtigen.

Mediation skills

S20 Bearbeitung von *Mediation*-Aufgaben

Mediation ist die Übertragung wichtiger Informationen aus einem gesprochenen oder geschriebenen Text in eine andere Sprache, z. B. aus dem Englischen ins Deutsche oder umgekehrt. Das machst du, wenn du bestimmte Aspekte aus einem Text für jemanden wiedergeben sollst, der die Sprache des Ausgangstexts nicht versteht. Gelegentlich kann es auch sein, dass du dolmetschen musst, also zwischen Gesprächspartnern vermittelst, die nicht dieselbe Sprache sprechen. Ganz wichtig: Es geht bei der *Mediation* niemals um eine wörtliche Übersetzung *(translation)*!

Lies dir die *Mediation*-Aufgabe gut durch und beachte besonders folgende Dinge:

Ausgangstext

Adressat:
Für wen ist die Information bestimmt?
- - -► Je nachdem, wer die Person ist und wie viel
  sie schon weiß, sprichst du sie unterschiedlich an.

Zweck:
Wozu benötigt die Person die Information?
- - -► Du musst nur die Informationen wiedergeben, die für
  den Adressaten in der jeweiligen Situation wichtig sind.
  Alles andere kannst du weglassen. Es kann aber auch
  vorkommen, dass du Dinge zusätzlich erklären musst.

wichtige Info

Beispiel: Dein Ausgangstext ist die Infobroschüre eines Museums, die alle Öffnungszeiten und Eintrittspreise enthält. Wenn dein Gegenüber dich fragt, ob das Museum heute geöffnet ist, musst du nicht unbedingt sagen, wann es sonst noch geöffnet oder geschlossen ist. Will die Person den Eintrittspreis wissen, kommt es auf ihr Alter an und darauf, ob sie allein oder mit einer Gruppe unterwegs ist.

Einen schriftlichen Ausgangstext kannst du in Ruhe durchlesen und die wichtigen Informationen auswählen. Dabei helfen dir alle Techniken, die auf S. 157/158 unter *Reading* beschrieben sind. Formuliere die entsprechenden Inhalte so, dass der Adressat sie gut verstehen kann.
Bei einer Dolmetschaufgabe wird eine echte mündliche Gesprächssituation simuliert. Deshalb musst du schneller reagieren, um möglichst viel von dem sinngemäß wiederzugeben, was die Gesprächspartner zueinander sagen.

Wenn dir ein Wort in der Zielsprache nicht einfällt, umschreibe es mit anderen Worten *(paraphrasing)*. Beachte bei der schriftlichen und mündlichen Bearbeitung von *Mediation*-Aufgaben außerdem die Tipps unter *Writing* und *Speaking* (siehe S. 159–163).

Listening skills

S21 Hörverstehen üben

Grundsätzlich ist es zur Übung immer sinnvoll, viele echte englische
Texte anzuhören, z. B. Nachrichten oder Kindersendungen in Radio
und Fernsehen oder Hörbücher. Dabei ist es nicht schlimm,
wenn du nicht jedes Wort verstehst. Dir wird außerdem auffallen,
wie unterschiedlich die Aussprache des Englischen je nach
Herkunft des Sprechers sein kann.

S22 Techniken des Hörverstehens

Analog zum Lesen gibt es auch beim Hörverstehen unterschiedliche Techniken. Beim *Listening
for gist* geht es darum, das Wichtigste in einem Hörtext zu erkennen und zusammenzufassen.
Beim *Listening for detail* hingegen sollst du einem Hörtext bestimmte Einzelheiten
entnehmen.

Listening for gist	Listening for detail
Welche Wörter und Themen kommen mehrmals vor und spielen deshalb vermutlich eine wichtige Rolle? Höre besonders auf diese und fasse die wichtigsten Inhalte des Textes zusammen.	Nach welchen bestimmten Einzelheiten im Text wirst du gefragt? Höre besonders auf Wörter, die du in der Antwort erwartest, und die Informationen dazu.

Auch beim Hörverstehen hilft eine Tabelle wie beim Leseverstehen. Du kannst darin während
des Hörens deine Notizen machen.

Who ...?	What ...?	When ...?	Where ...?

S23 Typische Hörverstehenssituationen

Manchmal hilft dir beim Hörverstehen auch die Kenntnis von typischen Textsorten
und Situationen. Wenn du die Textsorte des Hörtextes kennst, überlege dir, worauf es
beim Telefonieren, beim Dolmetschen, bei Präsentationen, Durchsagen, Radio- oder
Fernsehsendungen ankommt und welche Themen jeweils zu erwarten sind. Gelegentlich
geben dir auch Bilder Hinweise zur entsprechenden Situation: Wenn z. B. bestimmte Personen
oder Orte dargestellt sind, kannst du leichter einschätzen, worum es in dem Hörtext geht.
Achte beim Hören auf Geräusche sowie Stimme und Tonfall des Sprechers. In echten
Gesprächssituationen oder Filmen können dir auch Gestik und Mimik das Verständnis
erleichtern.

Film/Viewing skills

S24 Inhalt und Gliederung

Ein Film ist auch eine Art Text. Deshalb lassen sich viele ähnliche Fragen dazu stellen:

– Worum geht es?
– Wird eine Geschichte erzählt?
– Welche Personen spielen mit?
– Welche sind die Hauptpersonen?
– Was passiert in welcher Reihenfolge?
– Wann und wo passiert es?

– Welche Gliederung und welche Themen sind zu erkennen?
– Aus wessen Sicht wird die Geschichte erzählt?
– Wer hat den Film gemacht, für welches Publikum und wozu?

Das Anschauen und Verstehen eines Films verlangt dir jedoch nicht nur das Verständnis der Sprache ab, sondern du musst auch auf viele weitere Dinge achten.

S25 Wichtige filmische Aspekte

Wie stellen die Schauspieler den Charakter der Personen dar, die sie verkörpern? Wie drücken sie Gefühle aus?

- - ➤ Achte vor allem auf Sprache, Mimik und Gestik. Aber auch Kleidung oder Frisuren können eine Rolle spielen.

Wie werden Handlungsort und -zeit dargestellt *(setting)*?
- - ➤ Achte auf Landschaften, Gebäude und Innenräume, Kleidung und Gegenstände.

Wie wird eine bestimmte Atmosphäre geschaffen *(atmosphere)*?
- - ➤ Achte auf Licht, Farben, Musik, Geräusche.

Wie unterstützt die Musik den Inhalt des Films?
- - ➤ Beachte, wann welche Musik ertönt und wann sie wechselt.

Wie helfen bestimmte Kameraeinstellungen den Inhalt deutlicher darzustellen *(shot)*?
- - ➤ Achte z. B. auf Nahaufnahmen *(close-ups)*.

Wie wird Spannung erzeugt *(suspense)*?
- - ➤ Achte auf Vorandeutungen, Musik, Licht, Geräusche und natürlich die Gestik und Mimik der Schauspieler.

Mit der Zeit wirst du weitere filmische Mittel kennenlernen, die bestimmte Wirkungen auf den Zuschauer erzeugen.

Kooperative Lernformen

Hier findest du die Erklärung für einige ausgewählte Methoden der kooperativen Arbeit.

S26 Think – Pair – Share

1. *Think:* Du sammelst still mögliche Lösungen zu der Aufgabe. Du kannst deine Ideen in Stichpunkten notieren.
2. *Pair:* Zusammen mit deinem Partner besprichst du leise deine gesammelten Ideen.
3. *Share:* Im Klassengespräch meldet ihr euch und teilt euren Mitschülern die Ergebnisse eurer Partnergespräche mit.

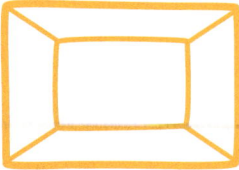

Variante: *Placemat* in Vierergruppen

S27 Milling around (Marktplatz)

Du gehst durch das Klassenzimmer, erfragst von deinen Mitschülern bestimmte Informationen und gibst auch selbst Auskunft. Versuche mit möglichst vielen Mitschülern zu sprechen und verschiedene Informationen zu sammeln. Ihr könnt auch ein Signal vereinbaren, zu dem ihr eure Gesprächspartner wechselt.

S28 Inside outside circle (Kugellager)

1. Bildet zwei Stuhlkreise, einen inneren und einen äußeren.
2. Setzt euch in den Stuhlkreisen so hin, dass immer ein Schüler des äußeren und des inneren Stuhlkreises sich gegenüber sitzen.
3. Stellt euch gegenseitig eure Fragen und beantwortet diese.
4. Rutscht im inneren oder äußeren Kreis nach dem Ende der Gesprächsrunde einen Platz weiter und beginnt ein Gespräch mit einem neuen Mitschüler.

S29 Bus stop (Lerntempoduett)

Sobald du deine Aufgabe fertig bearbeitet hast, gehst du zu einem vereinbarten Treffpunkt, dem *bus stop*. Dort wartest du auf den nächsten Mitschüler, der fertig ist, und zusammen besprecht und vergleicht ihr eure Lösungen. Anschließend verlasst ihr den *bus stop* und bearbeitet die nächste Aufgabe.

S30 Gallery walk (Museumsgang)

1. *Group work:* In der Gruppe erarbeitet ihr ein Thema und haltet euer Ergebnis, z. B. auf einem Poster, fest. Die Ergebnisse werden dann ausgestellt, wie in einer Galerie.
2. *Gallery walk:* Es werden neue Gruppen gebildet. In jeder Gruppe ist ein Schüler jeder Ausgangsgruppe. Jede Gruppe betrachtet die verschiedenen Ergebnisse der Gruppenarbeiten. Jeder präsentiert nun in der neuen Gruppe das Ergebnis seiner Ausgangsgruppe.

Grammar

Liebe Schülerin, lieber Schüler,
jede Sprache besteht aus bestimmten Bausteinen und funktioniert nach bestimmten Regeln. Die Bausteine sind z. B. einzelne Wörter (Vokabeln). Die Regeln für ihre Zusammensetzung nennt man Grammatik. Diese musst du außer den Vokabeln lernen, damit du dich verständigen kannst und damit es nicht zu Missverständnissen kommt.

Jedes Grammatikkapitel (**G**) behandelt Themen, die auf bestimmten Seiten vorne in den *Units* vorkommen (z. B. Seiten 10–11). Erklärungen, Bilder und Tabellen helfen dir, die Grammatik zu verstehen, einzelne Punkte nachzuholen, wenn du ein paar Stunden gefehlt hast, oder bestimmte Regeln für Hausaufgaben und die Vorbereitung auf Tests und Klassenarbeiten nachzuschlagen.

Ein Ausrufezeichen (❗) bedeutet: Hier musst du ganz besonders aufpassen. Mit kleinen **Aufgaben** kannst du überprüfen, ob du alles verstanden hast. Die Lösungen findest du ab Seite 291.

Grammatical terms

English term	Example	Deutsche Bezeichnung
adjective **G4**, **G5** – comparison of adjectives **G4** – comparisons with adjectives **G5**	exciting, easy, young After the hiking trip I was **more confident**. Wales is**n't as big as** England or Scotland, but it's **bigger than** Northern Ireland.	*Adjektiv* *– Steigerung der Adjektive* *– Vergleiche mit Adjektiven*
adverb of frequency	I **never** write.	*Häufigkeitsadverb*
adverbial clauses **G8**, **G12** – of time – of reason – of purpose – of concession	We read the flyer with the rules **before** we went on the hiking trip. Our group leader was happy **because** we won the prize for tidiest cabin. We put on shirts with long sleeves **so that** the insects couldn't bite us. The boys left the camp **although** they weren't allowed to go out at night.	*Adverbialsätze* *– der Zeit (Temporalsätze)* *– des Grundes (Kausalsätze)* *– des Zwecks (Finalsätze)* *– der Einräumung (Konzessivsätze)*
clause (main/subordinate)	I like him./I like him because he's nice.	*Satz (Haupt-/Neben-)*
conditional sentences – type 0 **G8** – type 1 **G17**	If it **rains**, the streets **get** wet. If you **go** to Cornwall, – you **will like** the beaches, – you **can go** surfing, – you **should visit** the Eden Project.	*Bedingungssätze* *(Konditionalsätze)*
defining relative clause **G6** – contact clause **G6b**	My presentation is about the people **who made Florida**. Ry Cooder is **a musician we talked about** in our Music lesson.	*notwendiger Relativsatz* *– notwendiger Relativsatz ohne Relativpronomen*

English term	Example	Deutsche Bezeichnung
future – going-to future **G1**, **G16** – timetable future **G11**, **G16** – will future **G15**, **G16**	Emily and Jack **are going to ride** in a barrel race. Our train **leaves** at 6.45 a.m. I**'ll miss** you so much!	*Futur* *– Futur mit* going to *– einfaches Präsens mit* *futurischer Bedeutung* *– Futur mit* will
imperative	**Be** polite. **Don't bring** your phone to school.	*Imperativ*
infinitive	be, go, play	*Infinitiv*
modal auxiliary – **G13** – **G14** – **G18** – substitute form **G13**	can, can't, must, needn't, mustn't should(n't), could may, might When I was ten, I **wasn't allowed to** have my own smartphone.	*Modalverb, modales Hilfsverb* *– Ersatzform*
noun	boy, dog, family, street	*Nomen, Substantiv*
object	Dave plays **computer games** after school.	*Objekt*
past participle **G9**	Gwen and Luke have already **prepared** for the trials. Olivia has **hurt** her foot.	*Partizip Perfekt*

past tense
– simple past **G7**, **G10**
 	
– past progressive **G7**
	Ryan and Jeff **left** the camp while we were sleeping.
	Ryan and Jeff left the camp while we **were sleeping**.
		Vergangenheit
		– einfache Form der
		  Vergangenheit
		– Verlaufsform der
		  Vergangenheit

possessive form – with *of* – s-genitive – possessive determiner	I live at the end **of** the street. This is Luke**'s** house. **my**, **your**, **his**, **her**, **its** etc.	*Besitzform* *– mit* of *– s-Genitiv* *– Possessivbegleiter*
present perfect simple **G9**, **G10**	I**'ve** never **been** to New York, but last summer we went to Florida.	*einfache Form des Perfekts*
present tense – simple present – present progressive	Olivia **plays** netball on Tuesdays. They **are sitting** at a table outside a café.	*Präsens, Gegenwart* *– einfache Form des Präsens* *– Verlaufsform des Präsens*
pronoun – demonstrative pronoun – indefinite pronoun – personal pronoun – relative pronoun **G6**	**this/that**, **these/those** **some**, **any**, **every**, **no**; **someone**, **something** etc. **I**, **you**, **he**, **she**, **it** etc. **who**, **which**, **that**, **whose**	*Pronomen* *– Demonstrativpronomen* *– Indefinitpronomen* *– Personalpronomen* *– Relativpronomen*
questions – with prepositions **G3** – question tag **G2**	What are you thinking **of**? You're a bit disappointed, **aren't you**?	*Fragen* *– mit Präpositionen* *– Bestätigungsfrage,* *Frageanhängsel*
subject	**Dave** plays computer games after school.	*Subjekt*
verb	be, go, play	*Verb*
word order	I – do – my homework – in the evenings.	*Satzstellung*

Unit 1

G1 *Das Futur mit* going to
Seiten 10–11 The going-to future

FUNKTION

Mit dem going-to future *drückst du feststehende Pläne und Absichten für die Zukunft aus. Du verwendest es auch, wenn es bereits jetzt deutliche Anzeichen dafür gibt, wie die Zukunft werden wird:*
Our visit to London **is going to be** fun.

What **are** you **going to do** tomorrow? **Are** you **going to practice** for the barrel race?

No, I'm not. Mom's friends **are going to** visit, and **I'm going to** meet their daughter.

REGEL — *Das* going-to future *bildest du aus einer* **Form von be (am/is/are) + going to + Infinitiv des Verbs***:

Aussage:	Mom's friends **are going to visit** with their daughter Madison.
Verneinung:	Emily **isn't going to practice** for the barrel race.
Ergänzungsfrage:	What **are** you **going to do** this weekend, Dave?
Entscheidungsfrage mit Kurzantwort:	**Are** you **going to go** to the movie theater? – Yes, I **am**./No, I**'m not**.

❗ *Um Zukünftiges auszudrücken, kannst du im Deutschen neben dem Futur oft auch das Präsens verwenden. Im Englischen geht das nicht. Vergleiche:*
We**'re going to visit** Minneapolis next week.
Wir **werden** *nächste Woche Minneapolis* **besuchen.**
Wir **besuchen** *nächste Woche Minneapolis.*

Wörter wie tomorrow *und* next week *können dir den Gebrauch des* going-to future *anzeigen.*

AUFGABE *What are/aren't the people going to do tomorrow? Look at the pictures and write sentences.*

Madison

Dave and Luke

Jack

Ryan

Emily and Madison

Emily

G2 *Bestätigungsfragen*

Seiten 12–13 Question tags

FUNKTION

> *Bestätigungsfragen sind kurze Fragen am Ende eines Aussagesatzes. Sie entsprechen dem deutschen „nicht wahr?", „oder?" bzw. „stimmt's?" und kommen häufig im mündlichen Sprachgebrauch vor.*

Yes, I am. I didn't win although I practiced so much.

You**'re** feeling a little disappointed, **aren't you**?

REGEL – *Du bildest Bestätigungsfragen, indem du das* **Hilfsverb** *des Hauptsatzes* **mit anderer Polung** *wiederholst – bejahte Hauptsätze verneinst du; verneinte Hauptsätze bejahst du.*

present progressive	You**'re** feeling nervous, **aren't you?**
going-to future	Emily **isn't** going to watch an action movie, **is she?**
Modalverb **can**	Emily and Madison **can** be friends, **can't they?**

– **Bestätigungsfragen** *werden immer mit dem passenden* **Personalpronomen** *gebildet, z.B.:* **Emily's parents** are watching the barrel race, aren't **they**?

– *Enthält der Hauptsatz als Vollverb nur eine* **Form von** be, *so wird diese Form zur Bildung der Bestätigungsfrage verwendet.*

Form von **be**	Madison **is** a nice girl, **isn't she?**

❗ *Beachte den folgenden Unterschied beim Verb* be *in der 1. Person Singular:*
Emily: I**'m** in your team, **aren't** I?

– *Steht im Hauptsatz kein Hilfsverb (z. B.* be, can *oder* have*), sondern nur ein* **Vollverb** *(*know, talk, …*), verwendest du wie auch sonst bei der Fragebildung eine* **Form von do**. *Die Zeitform richtet sich nach dem Hauptsatz.*

simple present	Aunt Amy **knows** a lot about horses, **doesn't** she?
simple past	We **talked** about this last week, **didn't** we?

❗ *Denke daran, die Bestätigungsfrage durch Komma vom Hauptsatz abzutrennen!*
Steigt die Intonation in der Bestätigungsfrage, handelt es sich um eine echte Frage.
Fällt die Intonation, kennt der Sprecher bereits die Antwort.

❗ *Ist* have *die einzige Verbform im Hauptsatz, handelt es sich um ein Vollverb und die Bestätigungsfrage wird mit* do *gebildet. Beim britischen Verb* have got *wird die Bestätigungsfrage genau wie die Kurzantwort mit* have *gebildet:*
We**'ve got** a good horse, **haven't** we?

simple present	We often **have** a little party after the race, **don't** we?
simple past	Ryan and Mike **had** a lot of fun, **didn't** they?

AUFGABE *Complete the dialogues. Add the correct question tags.*
Remember to look at the subjects and the verb forms carefully.

1. Ryan: Mr. Gibson played an interesting song in class today, …?
   Eddie: Its title was *I want it all*, …?
   Ryan: Yes, and it's a really cool song, …?
   Eddie: Well, yeah. I liked it.
2. Emily: We're going to work on our national park project this afternoon, …?
   Madison: Of course. Let's meet after school and go to my house.
   Emily: Good idea. Maybe we can finish the project today.
   Madison: I'm not sure. So we don't really know how long it's going to take us, …?
   Emily: That's right. But you already have some ideas, …?
   Madison: Well, erm …

G3   *Fragen mit Präpositionen*
Seite 13   Questions with prepositions

Hey, Em! What are you **worried about**?

I'm **worried about** the race.

FUNKTION   *Viele Verben werden immer mit bestimmten Prä-positionen benutzt. Darauf können Objekte oder Ortsangaben folgen. Wenn man nach diesen fra-gen will, steht die Präposition am Ende der Frage.*

REGEL — *Präpositionen stehen bei der Bildung von Fragen mit Fragewörtern am Ende der Frage. Sie bleiben immer hinter dem Verb:*

What	is she She's	waiting for waiting for	? the bus.
Where	does he He	come from comes from	? Iowa.
Where	's he He's	from from	? Decorah.

❶ *Im Deutschen kommt die Präposition bei der Fragebildung vor das Fragewort:*
Mit wem *spricht er? Er spricht* ***mit*** *seiner Tante.*
Von wo *kommt der Bus? Er kommt* ***von*** *dort hinten.*

AUFGABE *What is everyone doing? Make questions and answers with verbs and prepositions. You can work with a partner.*

1. you/think/Christmas
2. Madison/look/magazine
3. you/wait/my cousin
4. Ryan/talk/Emily's hat
5. Emily/talk/her aunt
6. Emily/write/Dave

Unit 2

G4 *Steigerung der Adjektive*
Seiten 24–25 Comparison of adjectives

FUNKTION *Du verwendest Adjektive und ihre Steigerungsformen, um Lebewesen und Sachen näher zu beschreiben und um sie miteinander zu vergleichen.*

What did you think of your first riding lesson?

I loved it. For me it was **the most exciting** event of the year.

Do you feel **more confident** now?

… and your Aunt Amy is **the best** teacher in the world!

Oh yes, it was **easier** than I thought …

REGEL — *Einsilbige Adjektive und zweisilbige Adjektive, die auf -y enden, steigerst du ähnlich wie im Deutschen, indem du -er (1. Steigerung/Komparativ) bzw. -est (2. Steigerung/Superlativ) an die Grundform (Positiv) des Adjektivs anhängst.*

— *Fast alle anderen zweisilbigen Adjektive sowie alle Adjektive mit mehr als zwei Silben steigerst du ähnlich wie in den romanischen Sprachen, indem du more (1. Steigerung/Komparativ) bzw. most (2. Steigerung/ Superlativ) vor die Grundform des Adjektivs setzt.*

	Positiv	Komparativ	Superlativ	Besonderheiten
Endungen -er, -est	*einsilbige Adjektive*			
	fast	fast**er**	the fast**est**	–
	big	bi**gg**er	the bi**gg**est	*Endkonsonant wird nach kurzem Vokal verdoppelt*
	nic**e**	nic**er**	the nic**est**	*stummes -e am Ende des Adjektivs fällt weg*
	zweisilbige Adjektive auf -y			
	eas**y**	eas**ier**	the eas**iest**	*y wird zu i, wenn das Adjektiv auf Konsonant + -y endet*
more, most	*andere zweisilbige Adjektive sowie mehrsilbige Adjektive*			
	awful	**more** awful	the **most** awful	–
	interesting	**more** interesting	the **most** interesting	–

❗ *Zweisilbige Adjektive, die auf -le, -ow oder -er enden, werden mit -er/-est gesteigert:*
simp**le** *(einfach)* – simp**ler** – the simp**lest**   *(e am Ende des Adjektivs fällt weg)*
narr**ow** *(eng, schmal)* – narrow**er** – the narrow**est**
clev**er** *(klug, schlau)* – clever**er** – the clever**est**

❗ *Einige wenige Adjektive werden unregelmäßig gesteigert. Diese musst du auswendig lernen:*
bad – worse – the worst
good – better – the best

— *Beachte auch folgende Verwendungsweisen der Steigerungsformen:*

The wave became **bigger and bigger**.	*Die Welle wurde **immer größer**.*
Which solution is **best**?	*Welche Lösung ist **am besten**?*
There's a **most beautiful** horse over there.	*Dort drüben steht ein **sehr, sehr schönes** Pferd. (Hier liegt kein Vergleich vor.)*
I think Cuban music is **the most beautiful** in the world.	*Ich finde, kubanische Musik ist **die schönste auf der Welt**.*

AUFGABE   *Write sentences and describe the pictures.*

Luke is tall. | Holly is … |
But Olivia is the … of the three.

The red car is … | The blue … |
But …

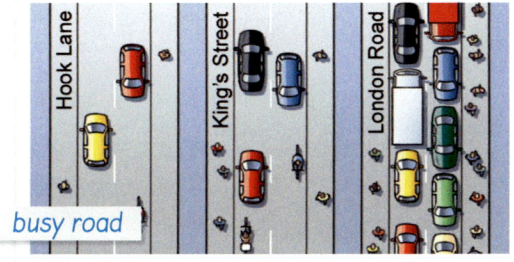

Hook Lane is … | King's Street is … |
But London Road …

Luke has got a … | Holly's idea is … |
But Dave has got …

G5   *Gleich oder verschieden: Vergleiche mit Adjektiven*

Seiten 25–26   The same or different: Making comparisons with adjectives

FUNKTION

> *Vergleiche mit Adjektiven benutzt du, um Lebewesen oder Sachen miteinander zu vergleichen.*

DID YOU KNOW …?

1. Wales is part of the UK. It is**n't as big as** England or Scotland, but it's **bigger than** Northern Ireland.
2. Mount Snowdon (1,085 m) is the highest mountain in Wales. But it is**n't higher than** Ben Nevis (1,343 m) in Scotland.
3. The River Trent (297 km) is the third longest river in the UK. It is about **as long as** the River Isar in Germany.

REGEL   — *Wenn die Lebewesen oder Sachen in Bezug auf eine Eigenschaft gleich sind, benutzt du* **as + Grundform + as**: The River Severn is **as long as** the River Neckar.
… genauso/so lang wie …

— *Wenn die Lebewesen oder Sachen in Bezug auf eine Eigenschaft* **verschieden** *sind, benutzt du entweder* **not as** + *Grundform* + **as** *oder* **1. Steigerung** + **than**:

Wales is**n't as big as** England.	*… nicht so groß wie …*
Wales is **bigger than** Northern Ireland.	*… größer als …*
Is climbing **more dangerous than** mountainboarding?	*… gefährlicher als …*
Is climbing **less dangerous than** mountainboarding?	*… weniger gefährlich als …*

🛑 *Verwechsle nicht* **than** *(als) und* **then** *(dann)!*

AUFGABE *Write sentences and compare the rivers, cities, mountains and states.*

big   small   short   high   long

Rhine: 1,233 km
Danube: 2,857 km
Inn: 522 km

Nuremberg: 517,000
Munich: 1.5 million
Cologne: 1 million

Schneeberg: 1,051 m
Zugspitze: 2,962 m
Großer Arber: 1,456 m

the Saarland: 2,570 km²
Bavaria: 70,550 km²
Saxony: 18,420 km²

G6 *Notwendige Relativsätze*

Seiten 27–28   Defining relative clauses

FUNKTION
> *Relativsätze sind Nebensätze, die ein Nomen (Bezugswort) näher beschreiben oder definieren. Notwendige Relativsätze werden deshalb so genannt, weil der Hauptsatz ohne die im Relativsatz enthaltene Information nicht eindeutig oder nicht verständlich wäre.*

My presentation is about the people.

Which people?

My presentation is about the people **who made Florida.** I want to talk about the traditions **the new immigrants started**, like Cuban food and music.

The Native Americans, the Europeans and the new immigrants.

REGEL — *Relativsätze leitest du durch ein **Relativpronomen** ein. Du verwendest:*

who *für Personen,*

which *für Sachen,*

that *für Personen oder Sachen.*

— *Das Relativpronomen* **whose** *(dt. deren, dessen) benutzt du, um Besitz oder Zugehörigkeit auszudrücken.*

— *Das* **Relativpronomen** *steht meist direkt nach dem* **Bezugswort** *und leitet den Relativsatz ein. Danach folgt die* **notwendige Information** *.*

My presentation is about **the people** . They **made Florida** .

My presentation is about **the people** **who/that** **made Florida** .

In meinem Vortrag geht es um die Menschen, die Florida zu dem gemacht haben, was es ist.

❗ *Im Gegensatz zum Deutschen trennst du solche notwendigen Relativsätze nicht durch Kommas vom Hauptsatz ab.*

— *Relativpronomen können Subjekt oder Objekt des notwendigen Relativsatzes sein:*

a) **Relativpronomen als Subjekt**

— *Die Relativpronomen* **who**, **which** *und* **that** *darfst du* **nie weglassen**, *wenn sie Subjekt im Relativsatz sind.*

Hauptsätze	Hauptsatz + Relativsatz
Compay Segundo was **a musician** . He came from Cuba.	Compay Segundo was **a musician** **who/that** came from Cuba.
Do you know **the famous film** ? It presents a Cuban music project.	Do you know **the famous film** **which/that** presents a Cuban music project?
That's the **man** . His film about the *Buena Vista Social Club* became famous.	That's the **man** **whose** film about the *Buena Vista Social Club* became famous.

b) **Relativpronomen als Objekt**

— *Die Relativpronomen* **who**, **which** *und* **that** *kannst du* **weglassen**, *wenn sie* **Objekt** *im Relativsatz sind. Das erkennst du am* **neuen Subjekt** *nach dem Relativpronomen. Solche Relativsätze nennt man* contact clauses, *weil sie ohne Relativpronomen in direktem Kontakt zum Hauptsatz stehen.*

Hauptsätze	Hauptsatz + Relativsatz
Gloria Estefan is **a singer** . We talked about her in Music class.	Gloria Estefan is **a singer** (who/that) **we** talked about in Music class.
The song was a big hit. Enrique Garcia wrote it.	**The song** (which/that) **Enrique Garcia** wrote was a big hit.
The band was *Miami Sound Machine*. People loved their songs in the 1980s.	**The band** **whose** songs **people** loved in the 1980s was *Miami Sound Machine*.

❗ *In Relativsätzen mit Präpositionen bleibt die Präposition üblicherweise am Ende hinter dem Verb. Sie kann vor das Relativpronomen* which *gezogen werden, in der Schriftsprache auch vor* who, *das dann zu* whom *wird:*
This is the song (which) we talked about. – This is the song about which we talked.
This is the musician who we talked to. – This is the musician to whom we talked.

AUFGABE **a)** *Complete the dialogues. Use the correct relative pronoun.*

1. **Ryan:** Do you have any of the Cuban-style music … people listen to in Florida?
   Emily: Yes, I do. But I'm not sure if I want to use it in my presentation. I don't like the songs … they play on TV. I want to use Cuban food.
   Ryan: Well, that isn't a bad idea either. Em, what's that under the table?
   Emily: Oh, that's the photo of St. Augustine … I wanted to show in my presentation.
2. **Jack:** Who is Ry Cooder?
   Ryan: He's one of the best guitarists in the world. He's the great musician … music projects are very famous all over the world.
   Jack: Really?
   Ryan: Yes, he was the man … wrote the soundtracks for many famous films. And he started the music project *Buena Vista Social Club*.
   Jack: OK, but I'm sorry: Those are all projects … I don't know.

b) *Which of the sentences in a) can you use without the relative pronoun?*

Unit 3

G7 Die Verlaufsform der Vergangenheit
Seiten 44–47   The past progressive

FUNKTION   *Das* **past progressive** *ist eine Zeitform der Vergangenheit. Damit beschreibst du den* **Verlauf einer Handlung zu einem bestimmten Zeitpunkt in der Vergangenheit.** *Du kennst auch schon das* present progressive, *mit dem du ausdrückst, dass eine Handlung jetzt gerade im Verlauf ist.*

Look! That's Mike. He **was turning** to watch Todd and Maya when his canoe turned over.

Mike also told me about Grace and Ava. They **were watching** Jessie on the zipline when they noticed a porcupine.

REGEL — *Mit dem* past progressive *kannst du drei verschiedene Situationen beschreiben:*

a) *Die Handlung befand sich zu einem bestimmten Zeitpunkt in der Vergangenheit noch im Verlauf, sie war also noch nicht abgeschlossen:*

9:30 10:30	At 10 o'clock yesterday Emily and Dave **were having** a video chat.
	Gestern um 10 Uhr **unterhielten sich** *Emily und Dave* **gerade** *per Videochat.*

b) *Eine Handlung befand sich noch im Verlauf, als eine neue Handlung oder ein neues Ereignis einsetzte. Diese(s) steht im* **simple past***:*

simple past	Emily **was riding** around the last barrel when her hat **fell off**.
past progressive	*Emily* **ritt gerade** *um die letzte Tonne, als ihr Hut* **herunterfiel**.

c) *Zwei Handlungen befanden sich gleichzeitig im Verlauf:*

	While Emily and Ryan **were looking at** photos, their dad **was preparing** dinner.
	Während Emily und Ryan **gerade** *Fotos anschauten,* **bereitete** *ihr Vater das Abendessen* **zu**.

— *Du bildest das* past progressive *aus der Vergangenheitsform von* **be (was/were)** *und dem* **present participle** *(= ing-Form des Verbs).*

Aussage:	Jada **was taking** photos when Mike's canoe turned over.
Verneinung:	Grace and Ava **weren't playing around** in the water.
Ergänzungsfrage:	What **was** Mike **doing** when his canoe turned over?
Entscheidungsfrage mit Kurzantwort:	**Was** Mike **ziplining** when he fell into the water? – Yes, he **was**./No, he **wasn't**.

❗ *Das* past progressive *gibt es im Deutschen nicht. Du kannst es mit „gerade dabei sein, etwas zu tun" wiedergeben. Sieh dir dazu die Übersetzungen in a) – c) noch einmal an.*

AUFGABE

What were the children doing at 4 p.m. yesterday? Work in pairs and make dialogues. Use the past progressive.

Jay   Dance class   Luke   Football Club   Holly   Sign Language Club   Olivia   Netball Club

A: Was Luke playing basketball at 4 o'clock yesterday?
B: No, he wasn't. He was playing football with his friends.

G8 *Adverbialsätze*
Seiten 48–49   **Adverbial clauses**

FUNKTION
> *Adverbialsätze sind Neben-sätze, die Beschreibungen genauerer Umstände oder logischer Zusammenhänge zu einem Hauptsatz liefern. Sie haben damit eine ähnli-che Funktion wie adverbiale Bestimmungen (z.B. Orts- oder Zeitangaben oder Häufigkeitsadverbien).*

You have to think of so many things **before** you go on a hiking trip.

Don't forget your hiking boots. **When** it rains, the trails are wet and dangerous.

REGEL — *Wie Nebensätze im Englischen grundsätzlich funktionieren und was anders ist als im Deutschen, hast du bereits gelernt: Die Satzstellung ist im Englischen in Haupt- und Nebensatz gleich. Die Kommaregeln sind anders als im Deutschen. Adverbialsätze werden nach ihrer Funktion eingeteilt und benannt (→ G12).*

🛑 *Wie im Deutschen können Nebensätze sowohl nach dem Hauptsatz als auch vor dem Hauptsatz stehen. Steht der Hauptsatz vor dem Nebensatz, setzt du kein Komma, weil die Konjunktion die Sätze klar trennt. Steht der Nebensatz vor dem Hauptsatz, trennst du beide durch ein Komma.*

— *In Satzgefügen aus Haupt- und Nebensätzen ist es wichtig, auf die richtigen Zeitformen zu achten, z.B. bei Adverbialsätzen der Zeit (→ G12), aber auch bei* **Bedingungssätzen**. *Bei diesen hängt die Zeitform von der Wahrscheinlichkeit ab, mit der ein vorausgesagtes Ereignis eintritt. Wenn man über Dinge spricht, die erfahrungsgemäß immer so sind, benutzt man im* **if-Satz und im Hauptsatz das simple present**. *Diese Variante wird auch als Typ 0 bezeichnet und die Zeitform entspricht dem Deutschen:*

Animals **come**	**if** they **smell** food.	Tiere **kommen**, **wenn** sie Futter **riechen**.
They often **bite**	**if** they **are** scared.	Sie **beißen** oft, **wenn** sie Angst **haben**.
When it **rains**,	the trails **are** wet and dangerous.	**Wenn** es **regnet**, **sind** die Wege nass und gefährlich.

Später wirst du weitere Varianten von Bedingungssätzen lernen (→ G17).

AUFGABE *Read this post by a teenager who went to summer camp. Use linking words (e.g. although, us soon as, so that) to complete the sentences, and add commas where necessary.*

I want to say thank you to my group leader Janice … she saved my life. … we went hiking, she told us to always wait for each other … we could all be safe. … I saw a porcupine in a tree, I stopped to look at it. It was fantastic! But … we had to stay together, the others didn't wait for me. … I noticed that I was alone, I started to run. Then I tripped over a rock … I was trying to get back to the others. … I fell to the ground, I couldn't move my right leg. But Janice came back to look for me … it got dark. She called for help … she and the other group leaders could take me back to the camp. You're lucky … you have a group leader like Janice!

Unit 4

G9 *Die einfache Form des Perfekts*
Seiten 62–65 **The present perfect simple**

FUNKTION *Mit dem* present perfect simple *verbindest du die Vergangenheit mit der Gegenwart.*

Have you ever **seen** the London Marathon?

Of course I **have**. It starts right here in Greenwich Park.

REGEL — *Mit dem* present perfect simple *kannst du verschiedene Situationen beschreiben:*

a) *Mit* Have you ever … *fragst du, ob jemand etwas schon ein- oder mehrmals gemacht hat. Es spielt dabei keine Rolle, wann und unter welchen Umständen es stattgefunden hat.*

Have you ever …?	**Has** Jay **ever run** in a marathon? – No, he **hasn't**. He **has never run** one mile.
In den Antworten auf die Frage findest du oft eines dieser Signalwörter: never, before, only ever, … times.	**Have** Dave and Holly **ever run** in big races? – No, Dave **hasn't run** in big races **before**. And Holly **has only ever run** in short races.
	Have the Elliots **ever watched** the London Marathon? – Yes, they **have**. They**'ve watched** it **three times**.

b) *Mit dem* present perfect simple *kannst du sagen, dass eine Handlung bereits, gerade erst oder noch nicht abgeschlossen wurde:*

already *(schon, bereits)*	Olivia **has already prepared** for the trials.
just *(gerade erst, eben)*	Gwen **has just had** an idea.
not yet *(noch nicht)*	The girls **have**n't **left** for school **yet**.

> *Die Signalwörter* never, only ever, already *und* just *stehen direkt nach dem Hilfsverb.*

c) *Außerdem kannst du ausdrücken, dass eine Handlung irgendwann in der Vergangenheit stattfand und das Ergebnis dieser Handlung bis in die Gegenwart spürbar bzw. sichtbar ist:*

I**'ve hurt** my foot. It hurts when I walk.
Olivia **has bought** new running shoes. They're still clean.

— *Du bildest das* present perfect simple *aus einer Form von* **have (have/has)** *und dem* **past participle**.

> *Das* past participle *von regelmäßigen Verben entspricht ihrer Form im* simple past. *Die Formen von unregelmäßigen Verben musst du lernen. Du findest sie in der 3. Spalte auf den Seiten 295–296.*

Aussage:	I**'ve run** in races before, but not in a big race like a marathon.
Verneinung:	Jay **hasn't run** one mile.
Ergänzungsfrage:	Who **has heard** of the mini marathon?
Entscheidungsfrage mit Kurzantwort:	**Has** Dave ever **run** in a race? – Yes, he **has**./No, he **hasn't**.

❗ *Beachte die Unterschiede zum Deutschen:*
a) *Das* present perfect simple *bildest du immer mit* **have/has + past participle**. *Vergleiche:*
I**'ve hurt** my foot. = Ich **habe** mir den Fuß **verletzt**.
I **haven't left** yet. = Ich **bin** noch nicht **losgegangen**.

b) *Auch in Sätzen, die das* present perfect simple *beinhalten, gilt im Englischen die Regel* **S – V – O**. *Das* Objekt *steht also nach der Verbform.*
Olivia **has hurt** her foot .
Olivia **hat** sich **den Fuß** verletzt.

AUFGABE   *Use the present perfect to complete the dialogues.*

A: You • ever • be • London?
B: No • you?
A: Yes • It's a great city. • You and your parents • already • make • plans for • your next holiday?
B: No • we • not make • any plans • yet • but we're going to talk about a weekend trip tomorrow.

A: You • hear • the news? Frank • break • leg. He's in hospital now.
B: Really? • I hope it's not too bad! • I• never • break • anything • in my life and • I • never • be • in hospital.
A: Lucky you! • I • be • there • three times. • – I • just • have • idea: • Let's go and visit Frank.

G10   *Das Perfekt und die einfache Vergangenheit*
Seiten 66–67   The present perfect simple and the simple past

FUNKTION

> *Das* **present perfect simple** *verwendest du, um zu sagen, dass etwas stattgefunden hat. Wenn du genau berichtest, wann und unter welchen Umständen etwas stattgefunden hat, verwendest du das* **simple past**.

Have you **seen** Aunt Amy's new horse yet?

Yes, I have. She **bought** it **last week** at the State Fair.

REGEL   — *Besonders im süddeutschen Raum wird fast ausschließlich das Perfekt verwendet, um über die Vergangenheit zu sprechen. Aufgrund der Ähnlichkeit zum* present perfect *wird man deshalb leicht verleitet, dieses falsch zu verwenden. Beachte daher: Mit genauen Zeitangaben wie* yesterday, last year, three weeks ago, when I was young *wird niemals das* present perfect *verwendet, sondern das* past tense.

I**'ve** already **run** in a marathon.

past	present	future

My dad **ran** in a marathon when he was 20.

❗ *Anders als im Deutschen sind das* simple past *und das* present perfect simple *nicht beliebig austauschbar, um Handlungen oder Ereignisse in der Vergangenheit zu beschreiben.*

AUFGABE **a)** *You and your classmates are talking about Sports Day.*
Make questions and write them in your exercise book.

Have you …	(prepare) (buy) already (start) ever (hurt) (find)	eating healthy food? a name for your team yet? your foot while you were playing sports? for Sports Day yet? new sports shoes yet?

b) *Work in small groups. Ask and answer the questions from a).*

Example: Sabrina: Have you prepared for Sports Day yet?
Martin: Yes, I have. I've already run around the park three times.
Ella: Yes, I have. I went jogging yesterday.

G11 *Einfaches Präsens mit futurischer Bedeutung*

Seiten 76–77 The timetable future

FUNKTION *Das* **simple present** *kannst du für Voraussagen verwenden, wenn durch einen festen Plan (z.B. Fahrplan, Stundenplan, Terminplan) geregelt ist, wann etwas zu geschehen hat.*

Sorry, Shahid. I'm going to be late. The next bus **leaves** in twelve minutes.

REGEL — *Nur in durch konkrete Pläne festgelegten Situationen kann das* **simple present** *für Aussagen über die Zukunft verwendet werden:*
We're going to go to London. Our train **leaves** at 9.15 a.m. from Platform 5.
The plane from New York **arrives** at 7 o'clock in the morning.
The concert **takes place** in the park. It **starts** tomorrow at 8 p.m.

AUFGABE *The Hubers are going to go to Britain tomorrow.*
Talk about their travel plans.

trip to London | plane/depart/Munich 9:20 a.m. | arrive/London Heathrow 10:25 a.m. |
the next day/train/leave London King's Cross 3 p.m. | arrive/Edinburgh 7:20 p.m.

Unit 5

G12 Adverbialsätze der Zeit, des Grundes, des Zwecks und der Einräumung

Seiten 84–86   Subordinate clauses of time, reason, purpose and concession

FUNKTION

Du kannst Adverbialsätze verwenden, wenn du deiner Hauptaussage zusätzliche Informationen hinzufügen möchtest. Mit den aus Haupt- und Nebensatz entstehenden Satzgefügen stellst du logische Verbindungen her. Sie sind stilistisch eleganter als hintereinander gereihte Hauptsätze.

Do you often go hiking?

Well, I always feel good **when** I'm outdoors. I like hiking in the Rockies **because** you can see awesome landscapes and wild animals.

REGEL   a) *Nebensätze der Zeit (= Temporalsätze):*

after *(nachdem)*	**After** I spoke to my friend, I felt much better.
as soon as *(sobald)*	Things often get better **as soon as** you talk to somebody.
before *(bevor, ehe, vor)*	**Before** they had an argument, Carol spent a lot of her free time with her friend.
until *(bis)*	Never give out your address **until** you've really met your new friend face-to-face.
when *(wenn, als)*	Ask your parents, older sister or brother **when** you need advice. **When** Carol saw the photos of her friend's new friend, it hurt her feelings.
whenever *(jedes Mal, wenn)*	**Whenever** you want to put photos of other people online, ask them first.
while *(während)*	Your friend asked for you **while** you were sleeping.

b) *Nebensätze des Grundes (= Kausalsätze):*

because *(weil)*	Carol wrote to an agony aunt **because** she had a problem.

c) *Nebensätze des Zwecks (= Finalsätze):*

so that *(sodass, damit)*	Write to Ruby **so that** she can give you advice.

d) *Nebensätze der Einräumung (= Konzessivsätze):*

although *(obwohl)*	They had a big fight **although** they were best friends.

AUFGABE *Read the posts of some* TeenLife *readers. Complete the sentences with the correct linking word. Add commas where you need them.*

Joe: I like your magazine … it's always got interesting news about my favourite stars.

Ginny: I buy *TeenLife* … I get my pocket money from my parents. I love it!

Lisa: … I read Ruby's advice, I think she really understands our problems.

Michael: I'm sure Ruby has learned a lot about teenage problems … she can help people with her advice.

Sheila: … I didn't like the make-up which came with the magazine last week, I'm going to buy *TeenLife* again. I really love the fantastic concert photos!

G13 *Modalverben und ihre Ersatzformen*

Seiten 87–88 Modals and their substitute forms

FUNKTION

Die Modalverben can, may, can't, mustn't, must *und* needn't *kannst du nur im* simple present *verwenden. Ihre Ersatzform verwendest du vor allem für alle anderen Zeitformen.*

Let's look for help on the internet.

Well, when I was young, I **wasn't able to** look everything up on the internet. But I still learned to do things my way.

	Modalverb	Ersatzform im simple present	Ersatzform im simple past
Permission Erlaubnis/Verbot be allowed to	can	Olivia **is allowed to** use her parents' computer when she likes.	She **was allowed to** play a game on it last weekend.
	can't/ mustn't	You **aren't allowed to** chat with your friends all day.	In my last school we **weren't allowed to** use computers just for fun.
	may	**Am** I **allowed to** use your tablet, Dad?	**Were** you **allowed to** use your dad's tablet when you were younger?
Ability (Un-)Fähigkeit be able to	can	Luke **is able to** help his dad with the washing machine.	He **was able to** find help on the internet.
	can't	Luke and Jamie **aren't able to** swim very fast.	When the boys were four, they **weren't able to** swim.
Necessity/Obligation Notwendigkeit/ Verpflichtung have to	must	I **have to** show Dad this advice. Mrs Elliot **has to** do the washing.	He **had to** ask somebody for help. She **had to** do the shopping yesterday.
	needn't	You **don't have to** look for the phone number. I've got it. Mr Elliot **doesn't have to** work in the evenings.	We **didn't have to** wait long until the man came to fix the pipe. He **didn't have to** pay for Luke's advice.

AUFGABE *Complete Luke's message. Use the substitute forms in the simple past.*

Hi,
Guess what? When I came home from school, there was water everywhere on the kitchen floor.
Something was wrong with the washing machine and Dad (musste) fix it before Mum came home.
Dad had no idea what he was doing … But I (durfte) use his tablet and check for advice in a forum.
I (konnte) find a helpful website quickly. All we (mussten) do was turn the knob off. So we (konnten)
solve the problem in 20 minutes and Mum (konnte) use the washing machine when she came home.
See you at school on Monday – Luke

G14 *Die Modalverben* should, shouldn't *und* could
Seiten 87–88   The modals *should, shouldn't* and *could*

FUNKTION

> *Mit den Modalverben* should, shouldn't *und* could *kannst du jemandem etwas vorschlagen oder raten.*

Have you got a problem? Well, you **could** look at a forum for help. But you **shouldn't** believe everything you read online.

REGEL — *Die Modalverben* should, shouldn't *und* could *funktionieren wie die Modalverben, die du schon kennst: Du verwendest sie im* simple present, *sie sind in allen Personen gleich und nach ihnen folgt immer ein Vollverb in der Grundform. Vergleiche:*

Mr Elliot **could look** for help on the internet.	*Herr Elliot **könnte** im Internet nach Hilfe **suchen**.*
They **should ask** their parents for advice.	*Sie **sollten** ihre Eltern um Rat **fragen**.*
You **shouldn't try** to fix everything yourself.	*Du **solltest nicht versuchen**, alles selbst zu reparieren.*

AUFGABE   *What should, could or shouldn't they do? Give advice.*

1. Olivia: In netball I pushed a girl while we were playing. She fell and hurt her hand.
2. Jay: I've ruined Dave's book.
3. Holly: Mr Fluff often explores under my bed. It's difficult to get him out when he needs to go to bed.
4. Dave: Last weekend I pulled out some flowers in Granny's garden. I thought they were weeds[1].

1 weeds [wiːdz] Unkraut

Unit 6

G15   *Das Futur mit* will
Seiten 100–102   Will future

FUNKTION   *Du verwendest das Futur mit* will *für spontane Entscheidungen, Versprechen, Hoffnungen und Vorhersagen, die die Zukunft betreffen.*

But the house looks fantastic! I'm sure your mum **will be** happy there with all the farm animals to work with.

I'll **miss** you so much!

REGEL — *Mit dem* will future …
  a) *… drückst du spontane Entscheidungen oder Versprechen aus.*

I'll **text** you.
Holly and I **will visit** you in Cornwall.

b) ... *machst du Vorhersagen über zukünftige Ereignisse.*
(Der Sprecher kann diese nicht beeinflussen. Ein typisches
Beispiel ist der Wetterbericht)

Diese Wörter können dir
den Gebrauch des will
future *anzeigen:* tomorrow,
next week/month/year, in
a year, probably, perhaps,
maybe.

Gwen:	We'**ll miss** you, Dave.
Assistant:	The trip to St Agnes **will take** about seven hours.

c) ... *sagst du, was jemand über ein zukünftiges Ereignis denkt, hofft oder vermutet.*
Diese Sätze beginnen häufig mit I hope, I think *oder* I'm sure.

Jay:	I think you'**ll make** lots of new friends quickly.
Dave:	I'm sure Sid **will hate** his new home.
Holly:	I hope everything **will be** OK.

– *Das* will future *bildest du für alle Personen aus dem Hilfsverb* **will (not) + Grundform des**
Verbs. *Die Kurzform lautet* 'll *bzw. bei verneinten Sätzen* won't.

Aussage:	Dave hopes that his friends **will visit** him in St Agnes.
Verneinung:	Aunt Frances **won't come** to Cornwall with them.
Ergänzungsfrage:	What do you think Dave's new school **will be** like?
Entscheidungsfrage mit Kurzantwort:	**Will** your dad **find** work there? – Yes, he **will**./No, he **won't**.

❗ *Um die Zukunftsform der Modalverben zu bilden, brauchst du ihre Ersatzformen (→ G13):*

can, can't → (not) be able to:	Dave hopes his friends **will be able to** find enough money to visit him in St Agnes. *... werden in der Lage sein ...*
can, can't, may, mustn't → (not) be allowed to:	The friends **won't be allowed to** go to Cornwall without an adult. *... werden nicht ... dürfen*
must, needn't → (not) have to:	Holly **will have to** ask her mum for money. *... wird ... müssen*

❗ *Verwechsle nicht „Ich will ..."* (= I want to ...) *und "I will ..."* (= Ich werde ...).

AUFGABE *What do the friends say when Dave isn't with them? Complete the sentences.*

1. Olivia: I hope Dave ... his new school. (love)
2. Holly: I'm sure the Prestons ... Granny Rose and Aunt Frances in London soon. (visit)
3. Luke: I don't think the new home ... a problem for Sid. There are lots of fields and he
   ... . He ... new cat friends quickly. He ... ! (be/be able to run around/make/not
   get bored)
4. Gwen: I hope Dave ... us. (not forget)

G16 Verschiedene Möglichkeiten, Zukünftiges auszudrücken

Seite 102   Going-to future, will future, timetable future

FUNKTION

> *Je nachdem, welche zusätzliche Bedeutung du einer Aussage über die Zukunft geben möchtest, verwendest du unterschiedliche Zeitformen.*

I'**m going to buy** a present for Dave. But I don't know what.

I'm sure you'**ll find** something at the charity shop. Let's go, the bus **leaves** in five minutes.

REGEL

– *Geht es um geplante Vorhaben oder um ein Ereignis, dessen Eintreffen sich bereits andeutet (z.B. wenn du dunkle Regenwolken am Himmel aufziehen siehst), verwendest du das* **going-to future** *(→ G1).*

– *Wenn Du dir spontan etwas vornimmst oder jemandem etwas versprichst oder wenn du eine Vermutung oder eine Vorhersage über etwas äußerst, das du nicht selbst beeinflussen kannst, verwendest du das* **will future** *(→ G15).*

– *Wenn du aufgrund eines festen Zeitplans eine Aussage über die Zukunft machst, verwendest du das* **simple present** *(→ G11).*

AUFGABE   *Choose the right verb form.*

1. Our train (leave) at 6 o'clock tomorrow morning. Don't be late! – Don't worry. I (be) on time.
2. This bag is heavy! – Wait, I (help) you.
3. Look at the sky! It (rain) very soon.
4. I've heard the weather forecast. It (not rain) this afternoon.
5. Remember to do your homework! – Sure. I (not forget) it.
6. I (take part) in a talent show. – I hope the judges (like) you!

G17 *Bedingungssätze Typ 1*

Seiten 104–105 Conditional sentences type 1

FUNKTION

> *Mit dem Bedingungssatz Typ 1 drückst du aus, was unter einer bestimmten Bedingung passieren wird. Der Sprecher hält die Bedingung für erfüllbar.*

> **If** you **like** beaches and fishing harbours, you**'ll find** that Cornwall is just the right place for you.

> Well, you **can** go fishing **if** we **go** to Cornwall. What do you think?

REGEL — *Um Vorhersagen zu machen, verwendest du im* **if-*Satz*** *das* **simple present** *und im* ***Hauptsatz*** *das* **will future***.*

if-*Satz* (simple present)	*Hauptsatz* (will future)
If you **look** at a map,	you**'ll see** that Cornwall is on the Atlantic coast.
If the friends **visit** Dave in Cornwall,	they **won't get** bored.

❗ *Wenn es nicht nur um die Zukunft geht, sondern um etwas, das immer wahr ist, benutzt du den* if-*Satz Typ 0 (→ G8). If it* **rains***, the streets* **get** *wet.*

— ***Im Hauptsatz*** *kann statt des* will future *auch ein* **Modalverb + Grundform des Verbs** *oder der* **Imperativ** *stehen.*

if-*Satz* (simple present)	*Hauptsatz* (*Modalverb + Grundform des Verbs; Imperativ*)
If you **aren't** into sports,	you **can** go to a museum. (Möglichkeit)
If you **want** to learn about the environment,	you **should** visit the Eden Project. (Ratschlag)
If you **go** to Cornwall,	**try** real Cornish food. (Ratschlag/Aufforderung)

❗ *Das deutsche Wort „wenn" hat im Englischen zwei Bedeutungen:*

a) *Mit* if *betonst du eine Bedingung (= ob etwas überhaupt passiert):*

If we go on a beach holiday, I'll try surfing.

b) *Mit* when *betonst du den zeitlichen Zusammenhang (es ist nicht die Frage, ob, sondern wann etwas passiert):*

We'll see Dave **when** he visits his granny in London.

> *Du kannst die Reihenfolge von* if*-Satz und Hauptsatz auch tauschen. Dann entfällt allerdings das Komma.*

AUFGABE *There's a teacher from Scotland at your school. In the next holidays he wants to travel around Germany. Tell him what he can and should do.*

Example: If you go to Berlin, you can visit the Brandenburg Gate.
If you go to Munich, you should try 'Weißwurst', a typical Bavarian sausage.
If you visit Frankfurt, you'll see lots of tall buildings.

G18 *Die Modalverben* can/could, may *und* might

Seite 106 The modals *can/could, may* and *might*

FUNKTION
> *Die Modalverben* can/could, may *und* might *kannst du benutzen, um über Möglichkeiten zu sprechen.*

> I don't know where my English book is.

> **Could it** be in your locker?
> It **may** be at home.
> Or it **might** even be in somebody else's bag.

REGEL — *Mit dem Modalverb* can/could *kannst du über das Vorhandensein oder die Abwesenheit einer* **Erlaubnis, Fähigkeit** *oder* **Möglichkeit** *sprechen oder auch* **Vorschläge** *machen. Dabei ist – wie im Deutschen –* could *in der Frage um Erlaubnis höflicher als* can *und drückt in der Aussage über eine Möglichkeit eine etwas geringere Wahrscheinlichkeit aus als* can.

Can I use my smartphone? – Yes, you **can**./No, you **can't**. **Could** I ask a question? – Yes, of course.	*Erlaubnis/Verbot*
She **can** speak three languages.	*Fähigkeit*
We **can/could** go outside and play with the dog.	*Möglichkeit/Vorschlag*
You **can/could** ask your teacher.	*Vorschlag/Ratschlag*

– Mit dem Modalverb **may** kannst du um Erlaubnis fragen, Erlaubnis erteilen, ein Verbot
ausdrücken oder über eine Möglichkeit sprechen.

May I borrow your pen? – Yes, you **may**./No, you **may not**.	*Erlaubnis/Verbot*
This story **may** or **may not** be true.	*Möglichkeit*

– Mit dem Modalverb **might** kannst du über eine Möglichkeit sprechen. Dabei drückt might
eine etwas geringere Wahrscheinlichkeit aus als may.

Do you think it will rain tomorrow? – It **might** not rain the whole day. The book **may** not be too boring, or it **might** even be fun.	*Möglichkeit*

AUFGABE   *Look at the situations. What could you say? Use* can, could, may *or* might.

1. You want to go to Gwen's sleepover.
   You want to know if you're allowed to go.
2. Your brother is very clever. Your friend
   has problems with his Maths homework.
   Give advice.
3. Your friend asks you if you think your
   brother will help him. Tell him/her what you
   think.
4. Someone tells you a story and you aren't
   sure if it's true.
5. You would like another piece of cake.
6. There are big black clouds in the sky. You
   want your little sister to take a rain jacket.

Vocabulary

Im **Vocabulary** findest du alle wichtigen englischen Wörter und Redewendungen aus Green Line 2 in der Reihenfolge, in der sie im Buch vorkommen. Diese musst du lernen und anwenden können. Das *Vocabulary* ist in drei Spalten aufgeteilt:

- Links stehen die englischen Wörter und Sätze. Die Lautschrift in eckigen Klammern zeigt dir, wie du die Vokabeln aussprichst (siehe unten).
- In der Mitte steht die deutsche Übersetzung.
- Rechts findest du Beispielsätze, Erklärungen, Bilder oder Hinweise auf Besonderheiten.

Die **grün** gedruckten Wörter in den Kästen im *Vocabulary* sind ein Zusatzangebot. Du kannst sie verwenden, um über bestimmte Themen zu sprechen, musst sie aber nicht lernen.

Anderen nützlichen Wortschatz für den Unterricht, den du **verstehen** musst, findest du unter **In the classroom**. Die Worterklärungen in den Fußnoten bei manchen Texten musst du nicht lernen.

Auf das *Vocabulary* folgt das **Dictionary (English – German, German – English)**. Falls du ein Wort nachschlagen musst, kannst du in diesen alphabetischen Wortlisten nachsehen. Neue Wörter aus den Filmseiten sind ebenfalls dort zu finden.

Englische Begriffe wie *e-mail*, *cool* oder *partner*, die auf Englisch und Deutsch gleich oder fast gleich geschrieben und ausgesprochen werden, stehen nicht im *Vocabulary*. Du kannst ihre Aussprache und Übersetzung aber im *Dictionary* nachschlagen.

Abkürzungen und Zeichen

5	In dieser Übung kommen die Wörter vor.	*infml*	informell	*jmd./jmds.*	jemand/-es
*	unregelmäßiges Verb (siehe Liste *Irregular verbs* im Anhang)	*pl/Pl.*	Plural	*jmdm./jmdn.*	jemandem/-en
		sg/Sg.	Singular	!	Achtung!
AE	*American English*	*ugs.*	umgangssprachlich	=	entspricht
BE	*British English*	*Fr./Lat.*	verwandte Wörter in anderen Fremdsprachen	↔	ist das Gegenteil von
sb	*somebody*	*etw.*	etwas	→	ist verwandt mit
sth	*something*				

Englische Laute

Konsonanten

[b]	**b**ed	[p]	**p**icture	
[d]	**d**ay	[r]	**r**ed	
[ð]	**th**e	[s]	**s**ix	
[f]	**f**amily	[ʃ]	**sh**e	
[g]	**g**o	[t]	**t**en	
[ŋ]	morni**ng**	[tʃ]	**ch**air	
[h]	**h**ouse	[v]	**v**ideo	
[j]	**y**ou	[w]	**w**e, **o**ne	
[k]	**c**an, mil**k**	[z]	ea**s**y	
[l]	**l**etter	[ʒ]	revi**s**ion	
[m]	**m**an	[dʒ]	**p**a**g**e	
[n]	**n**o	[θ]	**th**ank you	

Vokale

[ɑː]	c**ar**	[i]	happ**y**
[æ]	**a**pple	[iː]	t**ea**cher
[e]	p**e**n	[ɒ]	d**o**g
[ə]	**a**gain	[ɔː]	b**a**ll
[ɜː]	g**ir**l	[ʊ]	b**oo**k
[ʌ]	b**u**t	[u]	J**a**nuary
[ɪ]	**i**t	[uː]	t**oo**, tw**o**

Diphthonge

[aɪ]	**I**, m**y**
[aʊ]	n**ow**, m**ou**se
[eɪ]	n**a**me, th**ey**
[eə]	th**ere**, p**air**
[ɪə]	h**ere**, id**ea**
[əʊ]	hell**o**
[ɔɪ]	b**oy**
[ʊə]	s**ure**

Zusätzliche Zeichen

[ː]	der vorangehende Laut ist lang, z. B. *you* [juː]
[‿]	der Bindebogen zeigt, dass zwei Wörter in der Aussprache verbunden werden
[']	die folgende Silbe trägt den Hauptakzent
[ˌ]	die folgende Silbe trägt den Nebenakzent

Unit 1 My friends and I

Check-in

embarrassing [ɪmˈbærəsɪŋ]	peinlich	In the photo Jay is wearing an *embarrassing* outfit.
to **end up** [ˌendˈʌp]	enden; landen	Embarrassing photos often *end up* in the yearbook.
yearbook [ˈjɪəbʊk]	Jahrbuch	A yearbook is a book with information about events and students at the school.
LOL (= *laughing out loud*) [lɒl]	LOL	This is an embarrassing photo! *LOL*!
real [rɪəl]	echt; richtig; wirklich	Not everything you see on TV is *real*. *Fr.* réel/-le
show-off [ˈʃəʊˌɒf]	Angeber/-in	My brother is a *show-off*. He always wants to look cool.
art [ɑːt]	Kunst	Not every painting is *art*! *Fr.* art *(m)*; *Lat.* ars *(f)*
what a . . . [ˈwɒtˌə]	was für ein/-e ...; welch ein/-e ...	*What a* great idea!
2 **home town** [ˈhəʊmtaʊn]	Heimatstadt	I live in Augsburg. What's your *home town*?
likes and dislikes [ˌlaɪks ən ˈdɪslaɪks]	Vorlieben und Abneigungen	What are your *likes* and dislikes? = What do you like and what don't you like?
huge [hjuːdʒ]	riesig; riesengroß; gewaltig	Berlin is a big city. London is a *huge* city.
field [fiːld]	Feld; Wiese; Weide; Acker	I can see twelve cows in the *field* over there.
hill [hɪl]	Berg; Hügel	Our house is on a *hill* and we can look down on the river.
outdoors [ˌaʊtˈdɔːz]	draußen; im Freien	It's a nice day. Let's play *outdoors*!
indoors [ˌɪnˈdɔːz]	drinnen; im Haus	*indoors* ↔ outdoors
*to **hang out (with)** (*infml*) [ˌhæŋˈaʊt wɪð]	rumhängen (mit); sich herumtreiben (mit); sich treffen (mit)	I love to *hang out* in the park with my friends.
mall [mɔːl]	Einkaufszentrum	Let's go shopping at the *mall*.
eagle [ˈiːgl]	Adler	Look, there's an *eagle*! *Fr.* aigle *(m)*; *Lat.* aguila *(f)*
3 **feeling** [ˈfiːlɪŋ]	Gefühl	I've got a bad *feeling* about the Maths test.
embarrassed [ɪmˈbærəst]	verlegen	I'm so *embarrassed*. Don't show this photo to anyone, please. *embarrassed* → embarrassing *Fr.* embarrassé/-e
nervous [ˈnɜːvəs]	nervös; aufgeregt	I felt *nervous* before the class test. *Fr.* nerveux/nerveuse
proud (of) [ˈpraʊdˌəv]	stolz (auf)	Jay is *proud* because he won a singing contest last summer.
report [rɪˈpɔːt]	Bericht; Meldung	Who can write the *report* about the class trip? *Fr.* reportage *(f)*
during (*+ noun*) [ˈdjʊərɪŋ]	während (*+ Nomen*)	Don't eat *during* lessons.

Station 1: I don't even know if she's nice

actually [ˈæktʃuəli]	tatsächlich; wirklich; eigentlich	This isn't my father. *Actually* it's his brother.
		! *actually ≠ aktuell*
barrel [ˈbærl]	Fass; Tonne	This *barrel* is full of water. *Fr.* baril *(m)*
race [reɪs]	Wettlauf; Rennen	Can we watch the bike *race* on TV, Mum?
daughter [ˈdɔːtə]	Tochter	Sally Richardson has two *daughters*: Holly and Amber.
wheelchair [ˈwiːltʃeə]	Rollstuhl	My best friend can't walk. She's in a *wheelchair*.
*to **teach** [tiːtʃ]	unterrichten; lehren; beibringen	I want to learn English. Can you *teach* me? *to teach* → teacher
to **tease sb** [tiːz]	jmdn. aufziehen; jmdn. hänseln; jmdn. ärgern	Ryan sometimes *teases* Emily.
latest [ˈleɪtɪst]	neueste/-r/-s	What's the *latest* fantasy movie?
		! the latest news = die neuesten (nicht: spätesten) Nachrichten
movie [ˈmuːvi]	Film	Let's watch a *movie*. *movie (AE)* = film *(BE)*
movie theater *(AE)* [ˌmuːvi ˈθɪətə]	Kino *(amerik.)*	The *movie theater* is showing the latest action movie today. Let's go and watch it! *movie theater (AE)* = cinema *(BE)*
There's nothing more exciting than … [ðeəz ˌnʌθɪŋ mɔːr ɪkˈsaɪtɪŋ ðən]	Es gibt nichts Spannenderes als …	I think *there's nothing more exciting than* football.
bird [bɜːd]	Vogel	An eagle is a big *bird*.
air [eə]	Luft	Let's go for a walk and get some fresh *air*. *Fr.* air *(m)*
a bit [ə ˈbɪt]	ein bisschen; ein wenig	Before the race, she's always *a bit* nervous.
worried [ˈwʌrid]	beunruhigt; besorgt	I feel a bit *worried* about the Maths test next week.
to **move (house)** [muːv (haʊs)]	umziehen	When you *move house*, you leave your old home and go to live in a new one. *Lat.* movēre

American English

German	British English	American English
Film	film	movie
Kino	cinema	movie theater
Herbst	autumn	fall
Müll	rubbish	trash
Mathe	Maths	Math
Einkaufszentrum	shopping centre	mall

German	British English	American English
Programm; Sendung	programme	program
Dialog	dialogue	dialog
organisieren	organise	organize
üben; trainieren	practise	practice
Heimatstadt	home town	hometown
nicht mehr	not any more	not anymore
Meter	metre	meter
Herr/Frau	Mr/Mrs	Mr./Mrs.

to **worry** [ˈwʌri]	sich Sorgen machen	Don't *worry* about your friend. Everything is OK now. *to worry* → worried
1 **plan** [plæn]	Plan; Entwurf	What are your *plans* for the weekend?
life [laɪf], **lives** [laɪvz] *(pl)*	Leben	I love my *life* in the country. *life* → to live
*to **have to** [ˈhæv tə]	müssen	They *have to* make a poster for the competition.

Numbers

Numbers

1,000	one thousand	eintausend	When you write big numbers in English, use **commas** to separate the thousands!
10,000	ten thousand	zehntausend	
100,000	one hundred thousand	hunderttausend	
1,000,000	one million	eine Million	
1.5	one point five	1,5; eins Komma fünf	When there is a comma in German, use a **point** in English!

Years

1492	fourteen ninety-two	**In 1492** Columbus came to America.
the 1980s	the nineteen-eighties / the eighties	Music videos became popular **in the 1980s.**

---

4 *to **tell** [tel]	erkennen; wissen	Can you *tell* who my brother is in this picture?
to **point** [pɔɪnt]	zeigen	Olivia *pointed* at her sister and said: "This is Lucy." *Fr.* pointer
bench [benʃ]	Bank; Sitzbank	Let's sit down on this *bench* and watch the birds.
7 *to **grow up** [ˌɡrəʊˈʌp]	aufwachsen; erwachsen werden	I *grew up* in Minneapolis. It's my home town.

City and country

These words can help you to talk about life in the city or in the country.

noise	[nɔɪz]	Lärm	cheap	[tʃiːp]	billig
pollution	[pəˈluːʃn]	Verschmutzung	expensive	[ɪkˈspensɪv]	teuer
traffic jam	[ˈtræfɪk ˌdʒæm]	Stau	far away	[ˌfɑːr əˈweɪ]	weit entfernt
shopping mall	[ˈʃɒpɪŋ ˌmɔːl]	Einkaufszentrum	space	[speɪs]	Platz
event	[ɪˈvent]	Veranstaltung	pet	[pet]	Haustier
public transport	[ˌpʌblɪk ˈtrænspɔːt]	öffentlicher Nahverkehr	outdoor activity	[ˌaʊtdɔːr ækˈtɪvəti]	Freiluftaktivität

---

Station 2: Come on, Em!

youth [juːθ]	Jugend	My grandma often talks about her *youth*. *youth* → young
close [kləʊs]	nahe	Don't go too *close* to the dog.
almost [ˈɔːlməʊst]	fast; beinahe	It's *almost* 8 o'clock! You're late for school.

judge [dʒʌdʒ]	Juror/-in; Richter/-in	The *judges* at the talent show really liked my song. *Fr.* juge *(m/f)*; *Lat.* iudex *(m/f)*
point [pɔɪnt]	Punkt; Komma *(bei Zahlenangaben)*	That's right. One *point* for your team. ! Achtung: Im Englischen werden Kommazahlen mit Punkt geschrieben: one *point* five = eins Komma fünf
second ['seknd]	Sekunde	Just a *second*, I can help you! *Fr.* seconde *(f)*
turn [tɜːn]	Wendung; Drehung	My horse is famous for its *turns*.
poor [pɔː; pʊə]	arm	*Poor* people don't have much money. *Fr.* pauvre, *Lat.* pauper
*to **get** [get]	werden	I always *get* tired when I watch TV.
*to **fall off** [fɔːl ˈɒf]	herunterfallen; hinunterfallen	I *fell off* my horse last week.
mad [mæd]	verrückt; wütend	My sister always gets *mad* at me when I take her clothes.
What a shame! [ˌwɒt ə ˈʃeɪm]	Wie schade!	I can't come to your party. – Oh, *what a shame!*
to **train** [treɪn]	trainieren	Luke plays football. He *trains* every day. to train = to practise *Fr.* entraîner
to **fix** [fɪks]	reparieren; befestigen	My bike is broken. Can you *fix* it?
9 **positive** ['pɒzətɪv]	positiv	Give *positive* feedback and be friendly when your feedback isn't so *positive*. *Fr.* positif/positive
negative ['negətɪv]	negativ; verneint	I got some *negative* feedback on my last post. *negative* ↔ positive *Fr.* négatif/négative
10 **up** [ʌp]	hinauf; (nach) oben	She looked *up* and down the street. *up* ↔ down
11 **watch** [wɒtʃ]	Armbanduhr	A clock: A *watch*:
12 *to **be interested (in)** [bɪ ˈɪntrəstɪd ɪn]	interessiert sein (an); sich interessieren (für)	*Are* you *interested in* history? *to be interested (in)* → interesting
I see. [aɪ ˈsiː]	Ich verstehe.; Aha; Ach so!	Scarlet is Emily's new horse. – *I see.*
I mean [aɪ ˈmiːn]	ich meine	I'm OK. *I mean*, I'm really happy.

AE pronunciation

Remember these differences between British and American English.

	BE	AE
ask	[ɑːsk]	[æsk]
dance	[dɑːns]	[dæns]
fast	[fɑːst]	[fæst]
half	[hɑːf]	[hæf]

	BE	AE
car	[kɑː]	[kɑːr]
her	[hɜː]	[hɜːr]
other	['ʌðə]	['ʌðər]
work	[wɜːk]	[wɜːrk]

	BE	AE
better	['betə]	['bedər]
cattle	['kætl]	['kædl]
party	['pɑːti]	['pɑrdi]
bottom	['bɒtəm]	['bɒdəm]

| 13 | **both** [bəʊθ] | beide | Rusty and Scarlet are *both* good at barrel racing. *Both* horses live on Aunt Amy's farm. |
| | | | ! *both* of them = *die beiden*; *nicht:* ~~the both~~ |

Skills: How to use a dictionary

1	**electronic** [ˌelekˈtrɒnɪk]	elektronisch	Do you use an *electronic* dictionary? *Fr.* électronique
	search [sɜːtʃ]	Suche; Such-	Write the word in the *search* box.
	to **look up** [ˌlʊkˈʌp]	nachschlagen; nachschauen	You can *look up* words in a dictionary.
	meaning [ˈmiːnɪŋ]	Bedeutung; Sinn	What's the *meaning* of 'to describe'?
3	**time** [taɪm]	Mal	I listened to the song three *times*.

Story: What a wonderful world

	wonderful [ˈwʌndəfl]	wunderbar	I love this movie. It's just *wonderful*! *wonderful* = great, fantastic
	news *(sg)* [njuːz]	Nachricht(en); Neuigkeit(en)	Let me tell you the latest *news*.
			! That's good *news*. = Das ist eine gute Nachricht.
	competition [ˌkɒmpəˈtɪʃn]	Wettbewerb; Turnier	There's a painting *competition* at our school this year. *competition* = contest *Fr.* compétition *(f)*
	title [ˈtaɪtl]	Titel; Überschrift	The *title* of this story is "Problems on Springfield Farm". *Fr.* titre *(m)*; *Lat.* titulus *(m)*
	*to **feel** [fiːl]	sich anfühlen	I'm not sure if this is a good idea. It *feels* wrong.
	to **share** [ʃeə]	teilen	Jay doesn't want to *share* his ideas with Luke.
	to **enter** [ˈentə]	hineingehen; betreten; eintreten; *hier:* mitmachen	He *entered* the competition. The teacher *entered* the room. *Fr.* entrer; *Lat.* intrare
	*to **be surprised** [bi səˈpraɪzd]	überrascht sein	I *was surprised* about your picture. I didn't know you were so good at drawing. *to be surprised* → a surprise *Fr.* surprendre
	himself [hɪmˈself]	er/sich (selbst); selber	You mustn't help him. He wants to do everything *himself*.
	dirty [ˈdɜːti]	dreckig; schmutzig	I can't wear this T-shirt because it's *dirty*.
	flower [ˈflaʊə]	Blume	What a wonderful garden! Look at all the *flowers*! *Fr.* fleur *(f)*; *Lat.* flos *(m)*
	to **notice** [ˈnəʊtɪs]	bemerken; wahrnehmen	Did you *notice* this strange sound? What is it?
	drawing [ˈdrɔːɪŋ]	Zeichnung	Can I see your *drawings*? They're really good!
	could [kʊd]	konnte/-n; könnte/-n	Jay *could* use mangas for his poster. *Could* I use your rubber, please?
	confident [ˈkɒnfɪdnt]	selbstsicher; selbstbewusst	He felt *confident* because he knew his ideas were good. *Lat.* confidens
	moment [ˈməʊmənt]	Moment; Augenblick	Can you please be quiet for a *moment*? *Fr.* moment *(m)*

brilliant ['brɪliənt]	toll; prima; leuchtend	I like this game. It's *brilliant*. *Fr.* brillant/-e
*to **leave** [liːv]	lassen; verlassen; abfahren; losgehen	Don't *leave* your phone in the car.
quickly ['kwɪkli]	schnell	Jay looked at the exercise book *quickly*.
eye [aɪ]	Auge	You can see with your *eyes*.
bee [biː]	Biene	This summer there are a lot of *bees* in our garden. They love our flowers.
clever ['klevə]	schlau; klug	What a *clever* idea!
amazing [ə'meɪzɪŋ]	unglaublich; toll; erstaunlich	That's an *amazing* story! I love it.
finished ['fɪnɪʃt]	fertig	My poster is *finished*! Can you give me feedback? *Fr.* finir; *Lat.* finis (m)
shocked [ʃɒkt]	schockiert; geschockt	I was *shocked* when I heard the bad news.
*to **steal** [stiːl]	stehlen	Somebody *stole* my money! I had it here in my bag.
to **calm down** [ˌkɑːm 'daʊn]	sich beruhigen	It isn't easy for me to *calm down* before tests.
		! Das „l" in *calm* wird nicht ausgesprochen.
to **push** [pʊʃ]	stoßen; schieben; schubsen	He *pushed* me – and I fell over. That wasn't nice! *Fr.* pousser
to **turn (a)round** [ˌtɜːn (ə)'raʊnd]	(sich) umdrehen; wenden	When they heard a voice behind them, they *turned (a)round*. *to turn (a)round → a turn*
fight [faɪt]	Kampf; Streit	I'm not talking to Jay at the moment. We had a big *fight*.
upset [ʌp'set]	aufgebracht; bestürzt	Why are you so *upset*? – I can't find my phone.
idiot ['ɪdiət]	Idiot/-in	Jay called Luke an *idiot*. *Fr.* idiot/-e; *Lat.* idiota (m)
should [ʃʊd]	sollte; solltest; sollten; solltet	You *should* practise more for the barrel race.
each other [ˌiːtʃ 'ʌðə]	einander; sich; sich gegenseitig	Work with a partner and talk to *each other*.
*to **take out** [ˌteɪk 'aʊt]	herausnehmen	*Take out* your exercise book.
paper ['peɪpə]	Papier	Please take a piece of *paper*. *Fr.* papier (m)
ready ['redi]	fertig; bereit	Let's get *ready* for school now.
2 **beginning** [bɪ'gɪnɪŋ]	Anfang; Beginn	The *beginning* of the story is very exciting. *beginning ↔ end*
3 **related** [rɪ'leɪtɪd]	verwandt; bezogen	The words 'to win' and 'winner' are *related*. They are in the same word family.
		! *related to* = verwandt **mit**, bezogen **auf** *Fr.* relation (f); *Lat.* relatio (f)
4 **strong** [strɒŋ]	stark	My favourite manga character is very *strong*.
drama ['drɑːmə]	Theater; Drama	In *Drama* class, you can learn how to act scenes. *Fr.* drame (m)
to **hate** [heɪt]	hassen; nicht mögen	It's really strong language to say you *hate* somebody. *to hate ↔ to love*

Feelings and reactions

She **feels nervous/embarrassed/excited/ angry** because …	nervös/verlegen/aufgeregt/verärgert
I'm **surprised/upset/shocked**.	überrascht/bestürzt/schockiert
He's **in a good/bad mood**.	guter/schlechter Laune

Check-out

1 **fishing** [ˈfɪʃɪŋ]	Angeln; Fischen; Fischerei	My dad sometimes goes *fishing* at the weekend.

Focus 1 Regions of the US

region [ˈriːdʒən]	Region; Gegend	What *region* in Germany do you come from? *Fr.* région *(f)*; *Lat.* regio *(f)*
history [ˈhɪstri]	Geschichte	I'd like to learn more about American *history*. *Fr.* histoire *(f)*; *Lat.* historia *(f)*
to **begin [bɪˈgɪn]	beginnen; anfangen	When does the barrel race *begin*? *to begin* → a beginning
settler [ˈsetlə]	Siedler/-in	The English *settlers* started colonies in the Northeast.
fall *(AE)* [fɔːl]	Herbst	When *fall* begins, summer is over. *fall (AE)* = autumn *(BE)*
hurricane [ˈhʌrɪkən]	Hurrikan; Orkan; Wirbelsturm	In fall, there are often *hurricanes* in the Northeast.
largest [ˈlɑːdʒɪst]	der/die größte; am größten	Berlin is the *largest* city in Germany.
century [ˈsenʃri]	Jahrhundert	We live in the 21st *century*. *Lat.* centum = hundert
slave [sleɪv]	Sklave/Sklavin	In the south of the US, *slaves* worked on the cotton fields. *Fr.* esclave *(m/f)*
until [ʌnˈtɪl]	bis	You can stay at your friend's house *until* 8 o'clock. *until* = till
civil war [ˌsɪvl ˈwɔː]	Bürgerkrieg	People fought in the American *Civil War* from 1861 to 1865.
to **end** [end]	enden; beenden	The American Civil War *ended* in 1865. *to end* ↔ to begin
slavery [ˈsleɪvri]	Sklaverei	*Slavery* in the US ended after the Civil War. *slavery* ↔ freedom *slavery* → slave
illegal [ɪˈliːgl]	illegal; unrechtmäßig; rechts- widrig	Stealing is *illegal*. *Fr.* illegal/-e
African-American [ˌæfrɪkənəˈmerɪkən]	Afroamerikaner/-in; afroameri- kanisch	My family has an *African-American* background.

theme park [ˈθiːm ˌpɑːk]	Vergnügungspark *(meist mit einem bestimmten Thema)*; Themenpark	At the weekend we had lots of fun at a *theme park*.
sunny [ˈsʌni]	sonnig	It's a *sunny* day. Let's got to the park!
because of [bɪˈkɒzˌəv]	wegen	My feet really hurt *because of* my new shoes.
retired [rɪˈtaəd]	pensioniert; im Ruhestand	My granny doesn't work any more. She's *retired*.
to rain [reɪn]	regnen	It's *raining*! Let's go inside.
humid [ˈhjuːmɪd]	feucht	Our region is very *humid*. It rains a lot here. *Fr.* humide; *Lat.* umidus
dry [draɪ]	trocken	Last summer was very *dry*. There wasn't much rain. *dry* ↔ humid
desert [ˈdezət]	Wüste	There isn't much water in the *desert*. *Fr.* désert *(m)*; *Lat.* deserta *(nt pl)*
cattle *pl only* [ˈkætl]	Vieh; Rindvieh	The *cattle* are in the field.
bat [bæt]	Fledermaus	*Bats* often live in caves.
*****to fly** [flaɪ]	fliegen	Next summer we're going to *fly* to New York City.
out of [ˈaʊtˌəv]	aus … heraus	Take a pencil *out of* your pencil case, please.
cave [keɪv]	Höhle	Next weekend we're going to visit a *cave*. *Fr.* caverne *(f)*; *Lat.* caverna *(f)*
hour [aʊə]	Stunde	There are 24 *hours* in a day. *Fr.* heure *(f)*; *Lat.* hora *(f)*
temperature [ˈtemprətʃə]	Temperatur	*Temperatures* were very high this summer. *Fr.* température *(f)*
degree Fahrenheit (°F) [dɪˌgriː ˈfærnhaɪt]	Grad Fahrenheit	The temperature today is 86 *°F* = eighty-six *degrees Fahrenheit*.
degree Celsius (°C) [dɪˌgriː ˈselsiəs]	Grad Celsius	Today the temperature is 30 *°C*. ! one *degree Celsius* – thirty *degrees Celsius*
snow [snəʊ]	Schnee	Today it's cold and there's a lot of *snow*.
than [ðæn]	als *(bei Vergleichen)*	Her English is better *than* her French.
once [wʌns]	einmal; einst	Listen to the dialogue *once*.

Measurements and currencies

Length / Distance			Temperature (Fahrenheit; Celsius)		
1 **inch**	[ɪnʃ]	1 Zoll = 2,54 cm	0 °F	17,8 °C	This is the formula for TF to TC:
1 **foot**	[fʊt]	1 Fuß = 30,48 cm	32 °F	0 °C	(TF–32) x 5/9 = TC
1 **yard**	[jɑːd]	1 Yard = 91,44 cm	61 °F	16 °C	
1 **mile**	[maɪl]	1 Meile = 1,609 km	98,4 °F	37 °C	

	£	1 pound = 100 pence		$	1 dollar = 100 cents		€	1 euro [ˈjʊərəʊ] = 100 cents [sents]

meter *(AE)* ['miːtə]	Meter	This tree is 90 *meters* tall. **!** *meter (AE)* = metre *(BE)*
three and a half times [ˌθriː ənd ə 'hɑːf taɪmz]	dreieinhalbmal	Wyoming is *three and a half times* the size of Bavaria.
farmland ['fɑːmlænd]	Ackerland	We produce food on our own *farmland*.
European [ˌjʊərə'piːən]	Europäer/-in; europäisch; aus Europa	Germany is a *European* country. *Fr.* européen/-ne
industrial [ɪn'dʌstriəl]	industriell; Industrie-	In the Midwest there's farmland, but you can also find *industrial* regions. *Fr.* industriel/-e
airport ['eəpɔːt]	Flughafen	London has got five *airports*. *airport* → the air *Fr.* aéroport *(m)*
by the way [ˌbaɪ ðə 'weɪ]	übrigens	*By the way*, I like your shoes.
***to take** [teɪk]	dauern; (Zeit) brauchen	It *takes* two hours to get to London by train.
camp [kæmp]	Camp; Lager	Lots of American teenagers go to summer *camps*. *camp* → camping *Fr.* champ *(m)*; *Lat.* campus *(m)*
to introduce [ˌɪntrə'djuːs]	vorstellen; einführen; einleiten	Let me *introduce* you to my friend Peter: Peter, this is Sarah. *Fr.* introduire; *Lat.* introducere
bridge [brɪdʒ]	Brücke	A *bridge* goes over a river.
French [frenʃ]	französisch; Französisch	*French* people speak *French*.
industry ['ɪndəstri]	Industrie; Branche; Gewerbe	Hollywood is the centre of the US film *industry*. *Fr.* industrie *(f)*

3

Weather words

It's / The weather is	**cold**	kalt
	warm	warm
	hot	heiß
	cloudy	wolkig; bewölkt
	sunny	sonnig
	rainy	regnerisch
	dry	trocken
	humid	feucht
There is / are	**clouds**	Wolken
	sun	Sonne
	rain	Regen
	snow	Schnee
	wind	Wind
	a storm	ein Sturm
	a hurricane	ein Hurrikan
	a blizzard	ein Schneesturm

It's **raining**.	Es regnet.
The **sun is shining**.	Die Sonne scheint.
It's **snowing**.	Es schneit.

Unit 2 The Sunshine State

Check-in

sunshine ['sʌnʃaɪn]	Sonnenschein	Today it isn't raining. I can feel the *sunshine* on my face.
grandpa *(AE)* ['grænpɑː]	Opa	**!** *grandpa (AE) = grandad (BE)*
Latin ['lætɪn]	lateinamerikanisch; lateinamerikanisch	I love *Latin* music.
beautiful ['bjuːtɪfl]	schön; hübsch; wunderbar	Look at all the *beautiful* flowers! *beautiful* ↔ terrible *Fr.* beauté *(f)*
roller coaster ['rəʊlə ˌkəʊstə]	Achterbahn	Let's go to a theme park and ride a *roller coaster*!
*****to bet** [bet]	wetten	I *bet* you don't know how to ride a horse.
take-off ['teɪk ˌɒf]	Start; Abheben	Ready for *take-off*!
perfect ['pɜːfɪkt]	perfekt; vollkommen	There's a dance school in Greenwich. That's *perfect* for you, Jay! *Fr.* parfait/-e; *Lat.* perfectus
Cuban ['kjuːbən]	Kubaner/-in; kubanisch	I love *Cuban* rhythms.
musician [mjuːˈzɪʃn]	Musiker/-in	Who's your favourite *musician*? *musician* → music *Fr.* musicien *(m)*/musicienne *(f)*
ride [raɪd]	Fahrt; Ritt; Fahrgeschäft	The *ride* on the roller coaster was amazing! *ride* → to ride
to kill [kɪl]	töten; umbringen	Alligators *kill* small animals for food.
1 **nickname** ['nɪkneɪm]	Spitzname	My name is Peter, but my friends call me Mr. Cool. It's my *nickname*. *nickname* → name
blossom ['blɒsəm]	Blüte	These flowers have got white *blossoms*.
panther ['pænθə]	Panther; Puma	At the zoo I always look at the *panthers*.
palm tree ['pɑːm ˌtriː]	Palme	There are lots of *palm trees* on this beach. *Fr.* palmier *(m)*; *Lat.* palma *(f)*
2 *****to take it easy** [ˌteɪk ɪt ˈiːzi]	immer ruhig bleiben; auf der faulen Haut liegen	I don't have time. I'm always busy. – *Take it easy!* Take a break.
five-hour ['faɪvaʊə]	fünfstündig	We went on a *five-hour* tour around Kennedy Space Center. 'Five-hour' means 'five hours long'.
drive [draɪv]	Fahrt; Anfahrt; Autofahrt	We were dog-tired after the long *drive*.
overnight [ˌəʊvəˈnaɪt]	über Nacht	We looked for a hotel because we wanted to stay *overnight*.
That's fine with me. [ðæts ˌfaɪn wɪð ˈmiː]	Das ist in Ordnung für mich.	Your room is very small. – Don't worry. *That's fine with me.*
somewhere ['sʌmweə]	irgendwo; irgendwohin	*somewhere* → somebody → something
I gotta *(infml)* [aɪ ˈgɒtə]	ich muss	*I gotta* go = I have to go

It's a **five-hour** drive.	= The drive takes five hours.	Es ist eine Fahrt von fünf Stunden / eine **fünfstündige** Fahrt.
It's a **three-day** trip.	= The trip is three days long.	Es ist ein Ausflug für drei Tage / ein **dreitägiger** Ausflug.
Give a **two-minute** talk.	= Talk about your topic for two minutes.	Halte ein **zweiminütiges** Referat.
He's a **12-year-old** boy.	= He's 12 years old.	Er ist ein **zwölfjähriger** Junge.

Station 1: The most awesome music!

drum [drʌm]	Trommel	I've got a guitar and a *drum*. **!** a *drum* = eine Trommel the *drums* = die Trommeln/das Schlagzeug
singer [ˈsɪŋə]	Sänger/-in	Elvis Presley was a famous *singer*. *singer* → to sing
instrument [ˈɪnstrəmənt]	Instrument	I can play two *instruments*: the guitar and the sax. The guitar is an *instrument*. *Fr.* instrument *(m)*; *Lat.* instrumentum *(nt)*
cajón [kæˈhɒn]	Cajón	A *cajón* is a kind of drum.
wooden [ˈwʊdn]	hölzern; aus Holz	There are six *wooden* chairs in the living room.
less [les]	weniger	Please talk *less* and work more! *less* ↔ more
one [wʌn], **ones** [wʌnz] *(pl)*	eine/-r/-s	This sandwich is big, that *one* is bigger. **!** Wenn du im Englischen ein Nomen nicht wiederholen möchtest, kannst du es durch *one/ones* ersetzen.
member [ˈmembə]	Mitglied	Dave is a *member* of the Cooking Club. *Fr.* membre *(m)*

to play an instrument		ein Instrument spielen
to play the guitar / the piano / the trombone / the drums / the cajón / the maracas	[pɪˈænəʊ] [trɒmˈbəʊn]	Gitarre / Klavier / Posaune / Schlagzeug / Cajón / Maracas spielen
to perform live / on stage	[pəˈfɔːm laɪv] [ɒn ˈsteɪdʒ]	live / auf der Bühne auftreten
to play a gig	[gɪg]	einen Auftritt haben
to have a rehearsal	[rɪˈhɜːsl]	eine Probe abhalten
to dance to a rhythm		zu einem Rhythmus tanzen
to play music		Musik machen; Musik abspielen
to listen to music		Musik hören
to go to a concert / a musical	[ˈmjuːzɪkl]	zu einem Konzert / Musical gehen

few [fjuː]	wenige	I've got *fewer* friends than my sister.
		! He's got a *few* friends. = … ein paar Freunde. He's got *few* friends. = … wenige Freunde.
would [wʊd]	würde/-st/-n/-t	What *would* you do in this situation?
at first [ət ˈfɜːst]	zuerst; zunächst	*At first* Luke didn't like Jay very much, but then they became friends.
maracas [məˈrækəz]	Rumba-Rasseln	We need drums and *maracas* for the show.
1　to **join** [dʒɔɪn]	beitreten; sich anschließen; verbinden	Let's *join* the Computer Club! *Fr.* se joindre à
origin [ˈɒrɪdʒɪn]	Ursprung; Herkunft; Abstammung	The girl is of Cuban *origin*. *Fr.* origine *(f)*; *Lat.* origo *(f)*
Cuban-American [ˈkjuːbən ˌəˈmerɪkn]	Amerikaner/-in kubanischer Abstammung	He's *Cuban-American*. His grandparents are from Cuba.
Spanish [ˈspænɪʃ]	spanisch; Spanisch; Spanier/-in	People in Cuba speak *Spanish*.
common [ˈkɒmən]	üblich; gewöhnlich; (weit) verbreitet; gebräuchlich	The most *common* language in the US is English. The second most *common* one is Spanish. *Fr.* commun/-e
2　**missing** [ˈmɪsɪŋ]	fehlend; verschwunden	What's the *missing* word? "I really … you."
basic [ˈbeɪsɪk]	grundlegend; Grund-	In the first two years of English you learn a lot of *basic* words and phrases. *Fr.* base *(f)*; *Lat.* basis *(f)*
3　**biology** [baɪˈɒlədʒi]	Biologie	*Biology* is my favourite subject at school.
subject [ˈsʌbdʒɪkt]	Schulfach; Thema	What *subjects* do you like? English and Maths are school *subjects*. *Fr.* sujet *(m)*
4　**rainy** [ˈreɪni]	regnerisch	This summer the weather was *rainier* than last year. *rainy* ↔ sunny *rainy* → to rain
ocean [ˈəʊʃn]	Ozean	**!** The three biggest oceans are the Atlantic Ocean [ətˈlæntɪk ˌəʊʃn], the Pacific Ocean [pəˈsɪfɪk ˌəʊʃn] and the Indian Ocean [ˈɪndiən ˌəʊʃn]. *Fr.* océan *(m)*; *Lat.* oceanus *(m)*
5　**hair** [heə]	Haar; Haare	**!** Ihre Haare **sind** lang. = Her *hair* **is** long.

Comparing things

Tony:　My house is **big**.
Lou:　My sister's house is **bigger**.
Tony:　I think my house is **the biggest**.

Lou:　Your joke is **good**. But my joke is **better**.
Tony:　No, my joke is **the best**.

Lou:　Football is **exciting**, but tennis is **more exciting**, and inline skating is **the most exciting** sport.

6　to **welcome** [ˈwelkəm]	willkommen heißen	Let's go and *welcome* our new classmates.

high school [ˈhaɪ ˌskuːl]	High School *(weiterführende Schule in den USA, Oberstufe)*	A *high school* is a school in the USA for people between the ages of 15 and 18.
style [staɪl]	Stil	She always wears her own *style* of clothes. *Fr.* style *(m)*
stage [steɪdʒ]	Bühne	At a big festival, bands play on more than one *stage*.

Station 2: The people who made Florida

to **mention** [ˈmenʃn]	erwähnen	Did I *mention* that I have a cool new phone? *Fr.* mentionner
to **colonize** *(AE)* [ˈkɒlənaɪz]	kolonisieren; besiedeln	Europeans started to *colonize* North America in the 16th century. **!** *to colonize (AE)* = to colonise *(BE)* *Fr.* colonie *(f)*; *Lat.* colonia *(f)*
foam [fəʊm]	Schaum; Gischt	I love the ocean with the waves and the *foam*.
sun [sʌn]	Sonne	Today the weather is great. There's a lot of *sun*. *sun* → sunny, sunshine
to **melt** [melt]	schmelzen	Ice cream *melts* in the sun.
rule [ruːl]	Herrschaft	Cuba was under Spanish *rule* for a long time.
not ... until [ˌnɒt ʌnˈtɪl]	nicht bevor; erst wenn	He did*n't* see the car *until* it was too late.
*to **build** [bɪld]	bauen	to build → building
runaway [ˈrʌnəˌweɪ]	Ausreißer/-in; Entlaufene/-r	She's a *runaway* and lives on the street.
to **found** [faʊnd]	gründen	Europeans *founded* new cities in America. **!** Nicht verwechseln: to find, found, found (finden) *to found, founded, founded* (gründen)
*to **be born** [bi ˈbɔːn]	geboren werden	Amrita *was born* in Cuba. Now she lives in Florida.
immigrant [ˈɪmɪgrənt]	Immigrant/-in; Einwanderer/ Einwanderin	Amrita and her family are *immigrants* from Cuba. *Fr.* immigrant/-e
to **immigrate** [ˈɪmɪgreɪt]	einwandern	My family *immigrated* to the US when I was five. *to immigrate* → an immigrant
attractive [əˈtræktɪv]	attraktiv	She's an *attractive* girl. She looks really good. *Fr.* attractif/attractive
sense [sens]	Sinn	Hearing and seeing are two of our five *senses*. *Fr.* sens *(m)*; *Lat.* sensus *(m)*
hearing [ˈhɪərɪŋ]	Hören	Please say it again. I've got problems with my *hearing*.
taste [teɪst]	Geschmack	I love the *taste* of strawberries.
specialty *(AE)* [ˈspeʃlti]	Spezialität; Besonderheit	You must try the *specialty* of this restaurant. **!** *specialty (AE)* = speciality *(BE)* *Fr.* spécialité *(f)*; *Lat.* specialitas *(f)*
chili [ˈtʃɪli]	Chili	Sorry, I can't eat this food. There's too much *chili* in it. **!** *chili (AE)* = chilli *(BE)*

7	to **exist** [ɪgˈzɪst]	existieren; bestehen	Do you think aliens *exist*? *Fr.* exister
9	to **land** [lænd]	landen	After twelve hours our plane *landed* in Florida.
10	to **cook** [kʊk]	kochen	Do you know how to *cook* Cuban food?
11	**class** [klɑːs]	Unterricht	In our history *class* we talked about slavery. *Fr.* classe *(f)*; *Lat.* classis *(f)*
	finally [ˈfaɪnli]	schließlich; endlich; zum Schluss; letztlich	First … Then … *Finally* … *Lat.* finis *(m)*

History

to **conquer**	[ˈkɒŋkə]	erobern	to **rule**	[ruːl]	herrschen; regieren
to **colonise**	[ˈkɒlənaɪz]	kolonisieren	to **immigrate**	[ˈɪmɪgreɪt]	einwandern
to **found**	[faʊnd]	gründen	to **emigrate**	[ˈemɪgreɪt]	auswandern
to **settle**	[setl]	(be-)siedeln			

| 13 | *to **keep away from** [ˌkiːpˌəˈweɪ frəm] | (sich) fernhalten von; meiden | *Keep away from* too much chocolate. It isn't healthy. |
| | *to **keep** [kiːp] | halten; behalten; aufbewahren | You can *keep* the book. It's a present. |

⌛ Skills: How to give a good presentation

1	**contact** [ˈkɒntækt]	Kontakt	Don't just look at your notes. Make eye *contact*. *Fr.* contact *(m)*; *Lat.* contactus *(m)*
	audience [ˈɔːdiəns]	Publikum	The *audience* really liked the show. *Fr.* auditoire *(m)*; *Lat.* auditores *(m pl)*
	clearly [ˈklɪəli]	klar; deutlich	You need to speak *clearly* to your audience.
	on time [ɒn ˈtaɪm]	pünktlich	You're half an hour late! Why are you never *on time*? Be *on time*. = Don't be late.
3	**several** [ˈsevrl]	einige; mehrere; verschiedene	I've got *several* embarrassing photos of you. *several* = three or more, but not many
	*to **take a look at** [ˌteɪkˌə ˈlʊkˌæt]	einen Blick werfen auf	*Take a look at* the picture and tell me what you can see.
	personal [ˈpɜːsnl]	persönlich	This question is too *personal*. I don't want to answer it. *personal* → person *Fr.* personnel/-le
	*to **be connected (to/with)** [bi kəˈnektɪd]	zusammenhängen; in Zusammenhang stehen (mit)	Your question *isn't connected* to the topic.
	topic [ˈtɒpɪk]	Thema	This story is connected with the *topic* of my presentation.
	fantastic [fænˈtæstɪk]	fantastisch; großartig	Yesterday I saw a *fantastic* movie. I loved it. *Fr.* fantastique

Unit task: Join our club!

talk [tɔːk]	Vortrag; Rede	Please give a short *talk* on your home town. *talk* → to talk
juggling [ˈdʒʌglɪŋ]	Jonglieren	I'm not good at *juggling*. The balls always fall down.
foreign language [ˌfɒrɪn ˈlæŋgwɪdʒ]	Fremdsprache	A lot of British children learn French as their first *foreign language*.

Story: A perfect day for treasure hunting

treasure [ˈtreʒə]	Schatz	Just look and you can find real *treasures* in the sand on the beach. *Fr.* trésor *(m)*; *Lat.* thesaurus *(m)*
hunting [ˈhʌntɪŋ]	Jagen; Jagd	treasure *hunting* = Schatzsuche
Europe [ˈjʊərəp]	Europa	Britain is in *Europe*, but the United States is in America. *Europe* → European
to uncover [ʌnˈkʌvə]	aufdecken; frei legen	Storms and waves sometimes *uncover* treasures.
to belong (to) [bɪˈlɒŋ (tə)]	gehören (zu)	Is this your T-shirt? – No, it *belongs to* my sister.
object [ˈɒbdʒɪkt]	Gegenstand	Describe a historical *object*. *Fr.* objet *(m)*
heavy [ˈhevi]	schwer	Could you please help me with this bag? It's too *heavy* for me.
to sail [seɪl]	segeln; umsegeln	Columbus *sailed* across the ocean. *to sail* → sailor
metal [ˈmetl]	Metall	People often use *metal* detectors for treasure hunting. *Fr.* métal *(m)*; *Lat.* metallum *(nt)*
slowly [ˈsləʊli]	langsam	He *slowly* opened the door. *slowly* → slow
*to dig [dɪg]	graben	Grandpa *dug* in the sand to find treasure.
sky [skaɪ]	Himmel	You can see some eagles up there in the *sky*.
cloud [klaʊd]	Wolke	Look at the *clouds*. It's going to rain soon.
usual [ˈjuːʒl]	üblich	That's our *usual* place for treasure hunting. We go there every week. *usual* → usually *Fr.* usuel/-le
season [ˈsiːzn]	Saison; Jahreszeit	Summer is the warmest *season*. The football *season* is the time of the year when there are football matches. *Fr.* saison *(f)*
shovel [ˈʃɒvl]	Schaufel	He uncovered the treasure with his *shovel*.
carefully [ˈkeəfli]	vorsichtig; sorgfältig	He *carefully* opened the box. *carefully* → careful
hole [həʊl]	Loch	There's a big *hole* in the garden. I think Sherlock dug it!
meal [miːl]	Mahlzeit; Essen	Breakfast, lunch and dinner are *meals*.

to **save** [seɪv]	sparen; aufheben	I'm *saving* money for my trip to the US.
		! to *save* time or money = sparen
		to *save* a person's life = retten
cabin ['kæbɪn]	Kabine; Kajüte	On a ship you can stay in a *cabin* or walk around on deck.
		Fr. cabine (f)
that's why [ðæts 'waɪ]	deshalb	Luke hurt his hand. *That's why* he didn't do his homework.
*to **be called** [bi 'kɔːld]	heißen; genannt werden	What's your sister *called*?
*to **lie** [laɪ]	liegen	My phone is *lying* on the table.
		! Achte auf die Formen: to lie – lay – lying
*to **lie down** [laɪ 'daʊn]	sich hinlegen	I was tired, so I *lay down* on the sofa.
nap [næp]	Nickerchen	I'm very tired. I think it's time for an afternoon *nap*.
to **tie (to)** ['taɪ tə]	binden (an); fesseln (an)	If you *tie* a dog to something, it can't run away.
dark [dɑːk]	dunkel	It's too *dark*. I can't see anything.
to **crash** [kræʃ]	aufschlagen; zusammenstoßen	The car *crashed* into a tree.
leg [leg]	Bein	I hurt my right *leg*. I can't walk.
*to **fall asleep** [ˌfɔːl ə'sliːp]	einschlafen	Yesterday I was so tired that I *fell asleep* on the sofa.
secret ['siːkrət]	geheim	Don't tell anyone about my *secret* treasure.
		Lat. secretum (nt)
soon [suːn]	bald	I'm going to go to New York *soon*, maybe next week.
		in a short time from now; a short time later
to **turn on** [ˌtɜːn 'ɒn]	einschalten	Please *turn* the TV *on*. There's something I want to see.
to **pray** [preɪ]	beten	Some people *pray* before they go to bed.
		Fr. prier
horrible ['hɒrəbl]	schrecklich; furchtbar	Yesterday there was a *horrible* hurricane in Florida.
		horrible → horrified
		Fr. horrible; *Lat.* horribilis
*to **be afraid (of)** [bi ə'freɪd ʌv]	(sich) fürchten; Angst haben (vor)	He's *afraid of* dogs.
		! Wenn „I'm afraid" Bedauern ausdrückt und nicht Angst, kann es mit „leider" übersetzt werden: „I'm afraid I can't help you."
to **scoop** [skuːp]	schöpfen; schaufeln	*Scoop* up the sand. There could be something interesting.
*to **wake up** [weɪk 'ʌp]	aufwachen; aufwecken	I always *wake up* at 7 o'clock.
to **smash** [smæʃ]	schlagen; zerschmettern	The waves *smashed* against the boat.
to **die** [daɪ]	sterben	Robert has only got one grandma. His other grandma *died* four years ago.
		to die ↔ to be born
to **survive** [sə'vaɪv]	überleben	Our bus crashed into a tree but we all *survived*.
		Fr. survivre
1	**similar** ['sɪmɪlə]	ähnlich	My shirt is *similar* to your shirt. It has the same colours.
		Lat. similis
4	to **travel** ['trævl]	fahren; reisen	This year I'd like to *travel* to Florida.

Check-out

1	**plant** [plɑːnt]	Pflanze	Trees and flowers are *plants*. *Fr.* plante *(f)*
	warm [wɔːm]	warm	*warm* ↔ cold
3	**etc.** *(= et cetera)* [ɪtˈsetrə]	usw. *(= und so weiter)*	*etc.* is short for 'et cetera' *(Latin)*

Across cultures 1 American stories and traditions

	true [truː]	wahr	Dave is from Greenwich, isn't he? Yes, that's *true*.
1	**light** [laɪt]	Licht, Lampe	At night you need *light*.
	jack-o'-lantern [ˌdʒækəˈlæntən]	Kürbislaterne	
	Irish [ˈaɪrɪʃ]	irisch; Irisch	There are lots of nice *Irish* songs.
	scary [ˈskeəri]	unheimlich; gruselig; beängstigend	I can't fall asleep when I watch a *scary* movie. *scary* → to be scared
	devil [ˈdevl]	Teufel	Some people believe that the *devil* takes bad people with him when they die. *Fr.* diable *(m)*; *Lat.* diabolus *(m)*
	to **promise** [ˈprɒmɪs]	versprechen	Can you *promise* not to be late? *Fr.* promettre; *Lat.* promittere
	soul [səʊl]	Seele	People say everybody has got a *soul*.
	hell [hel]	Hölle	People say the devil lives in *hell*.
	heaven [ˈhevn]	Himmel	A lot of people believe that good people go to *heaven* when they die. *heaven* ↔ hell
	promise [ˈprɒmɪs]	Versprechen	Can you keep your *promise*? *promise* → to promise
	fire [faɪə]	Feuer; Kamin; Ofen	On cold days it's nice to sit by the *fire*. *fire* ↔ water
	ghost [ɡəʊst]	Geist	Sometimes there are stories of *ghosts* in old houses.
	lantern [ˈlæntən]	Laterne	It's very dark. We need a *lantern*. *Fr.* lanterne *(f)*; *Lat.* laterna *(f)*
	long ago [ˌlɒŋ əˈɡəʊ]	vor langer Zeit	*Long ago*, a lot of people believed in ghosts.
	dead [ded]	tot	My grandpa is *dead*. He died last year.
	pumpkin [ˈpʌmpkɪn]	Kürbis	At Halloween, people decorate their houses with *pumpkins*.
	*to **put on** [ˌpʊt ˈɒn]	anziehen; auftragen	We're going out now. *Put* your shoes *on*, please.
2	**trick-or-treating** [ˌtrɪk ɔːˈtriːtɪŋ]	Süßes oder Saures *(Spiel zu Halloween, bei dem Kinder von Tür zu Tür gehen und um Süßigkeiten bitten)*	At Halloween, children go from house to house and shout '*Trick or treat*!'

souling ['səʊlɪŋ]	Souling (mittelalterlicher Brauch, bei dem man durch Gabe von Broten seine Seele zu retten hoffte)	To save their souls, people gave bread or cakes to poor people who came to their doors. This was called *souling*.
treat [triːt]	besondere Freude; Belohnung	If sb gives you a *treat*, it's sth special – like sth good to eat.
3 **legend** ['ledʒənd]	Legende; Sage	*Legends* belong to the traditions of a culture. An old story – maybe true in parts. *Fr.* légende *(f)*
*to **cut** [kʌt]	schneiden; fällen	I *cut* my finger with a piece of paper.
axe [æks]	Axt	You use an *axe* to work with wood.
to **cry** [kraɪ]	weinen; schreien; rufen	She was so sad she *cried* all night. *to cry* ↔ to laugh *Fr.* crier
tear [tɪə]	Träne	I could see she was sad. There were *tears* in her eyes.
path [pɑːθ]	Pfad; Weg	This is the *path* to the beach.
road [rəʊd]	Straße	I live in King's *Road*. *road* > street > path
straight [streɪt]	gerade; direkt; geradewegs	Go *straight* to school, you're late.
landscape ['lænskeɪp]	Landschaft	I love this *landscape* with all the trees and the lakes.
4 **introduction** [ˌɪntrə'dʌkʃn]	Einführung; Einleitung; Vorstellung	The *introduction* to this text is very interesting. *introduction* → to introduce sb/sth *Fr.* introduction *(f)*; *Lat.* introductio *(f)*
invented [ɪn'ventɪd]	erfunden	Is the story real or *invented*? an *invented* character ↔ a real person
feather ['feðə]	Feder	Some Native Americans wore eagle *feathers*.
hunter ['hʌntə]	Jäger/-in	I'm a treasure *hunter*. *hunter* → to hunt
earth [ɜːθ]	die Erde; Erde; Erdboden	People and animals live on *earth*.
leader ['liːdə]	Führer/-in; Anführer/-in	Who is the *leader* of your group?
*to **fight** [faɪt]	kämpfen; (sich) streiten	My brother and I often *fight*. *to fight* → a fight
husband ['hʌzbənd]	Ehemann	My dad is my mum's *husband*.
soldier ['səʊldʒə]	Soldat/-in	A *soldier* is a person whose job is to fight, usually for his or her country.
exaggerated [ɪg'zædʒreɪtɪd]	übertrieben	I can't believe that so many people eat fast food. The numbers must be *exaggerated*.
hero ['hɪərəʊ], **heroes** ['hɪərəʊz] *(pl)*	Held	The most important character in a book or film, usually good and brave. *Fr.* héros *(m)*/héroïne *(f)*; *Lat.* heros *(m)*
heroine ['herəʊɪn]	Heldin	Who is your favourite *heroine*?
magic ['mædʒɪk]	Magie; Zauberei	How did she do it? Was it *magic* or just a trick? *Fr.* magie *(f)*; *Lat.* ars magica *(f)*

| to **change** [tʃeɪndʒ] | wechseln; (sich) ändern; (sich) verwandeln | In the legend, the hero *changes* into an eagle. *Fr.* changer |
| **honest** ['ɒnɪst] | ehrlich | Don't lie. Be *honest*! *Fr.* honnête; *Lat.* honestus |

Stories

Examples of stories		Parts of a story
legend	Legende; Sage	introduction/beginning
fairy tale ['feəri ˌteɪl]	Märchen	middle
fable [feɪbl]	Fabel	ending

What's In a story?	Is it true?	What's the story like?
hero/heroine	real	funny
character	invented	exciting
event	exaggerated	scary

| 5 | to **invent** [ɪn'vent] | erfinden | If you *invent* sth, you're the first person who thinks of it. *to invent* → invented *Fr.* inventer; *Lat.* invenire |

Unit 3 Off to the Rockies!

Check-in

off to ['ɒf tə]	auf nach	*Off to* New York! I'm so excited.
mountain range [ˌmaʊntɪn 'reɪndʒ]	Bergkette	The Rocky Mountains are a *mountain range*.
moose, moose *pl.* [muːs]	Elch	If you're lucky, you can see a *moose* in the Rockies.
kilometer (km) *(AE)* ['kɪləˌmiːtə; kɪ'lɒmɪtə]	Kilometer	The Rocky Mountains are more than 4,800 *kilometres* (3,000 miles) long. ! kilometre *(BE)* = kilometer *(AE)*
peak [piːk]	Gipfel; Spitze	Mont Blanc is the highest *peak* in Europe. *Fr.* pic *(m)*
explorer [ɪk'splɔːrə]	Entdecker/-in; Forscher/in	*Explorers* go to new places. *explorer* → to explore *Fr.* explorateur/exploratrice
wilderness ['wɪldənəs]	Wildnis	We spent a week in the *wilderness* of the Rocky Mountains.
to **hike** [haɪk]	wandern	We *hiked* all the way up to the peak. *to hike* → hiking
anyone else [ˌeniwʌn 'els]	jemand anderes	Don't tell the story to *anyone else*.

wild [waɪld]	wild	pets – farm animals – *wild* animals
		! Notice the change in pronunciation: *wild* – wilderness as in child – children. *wild* → wilderness
bighorn sheep [ˈbɪghɔːn ˌʃiːp]	Dickhornschaf	In the Rockies, you can see moose and *bighorn sheep*.
luck [lʌk]	Glück	Oh no, I can't find my keys. I haven't got any *luck* today.
cougar [ˈkuːgə]	Puma; Berglöwe	Don't move! There's a *cougar* on that tree.
the great outdoors [ðə ˌgreɪt ˌaʊtˈdɔːz]	die freie Natur	I love to enjoy *the great ourdoors*. That's why I always go camping.
adventure [ədˈventʃə]	Abenteuer	A week in the wilderness is a big *adventure*. *Fr.* aventure *(f)*
climbing [ˈklaɪmɪŋ]	Klettern; Bergsteigen	Let's go *climbing* in the mountains.
		! Achtung Aussprache: Das „b" wird nicht gesprochen. *climbing* → to climb
challenge [ˈtʃælɪndʒ]	Herausforderung	A *challenge* is sth that isn't easy and needs a lot of work and/ or skill. *Fr.* challenge *(m)*
teen [tiːn]	Teenager; Jugendliche/-r	This hiking tour is especially for *teens*. *teen* = teenager
backpacking [ˈbækpækɪŋ]	Wandern; Rucksackreisen	*Backpacking* is great. You see lots of different places.
to follow [ˈfɒləʊ]	folgen; hinterhergehen; befolgen	We *followed* our group leader to the top of the mountain.
trail [treɪl]	Weg; Pfad; Spur	On walking *trails* you can only go on foot.
to look out for [ˌlʊk ˈaʊt fə]	Ausschau halten nach; sich in Acht nehmen vor; aufpassen auf	*Look out* for bears! They can be dangerous.
nearly [ˈnɪəli]	fast; annähernd	It's *nearly* five o'clock. Let's go back! *nearly* = almost
mountainboarding [ˈmaʊntɪnˌbɔːdɪŋ]	Mountainboardfahren	I tried *mountainboarding* once, but I fell. *mountainboarding* → snowboarding → skateboarding
zipline [ˈzɪplaɪn]	Seilrutsche	I don't want to use the *zipline*. It's too high for me!
traditional [trəˈdɪʃnl]	traditionell	What's your country's *traditional* food? *traditional* → tradition *Fr.* traditionnel/-le
campfire [ˈkæmpfaɪə]	Lagerfeuer	It's fun to sit around a *campfire*, play the guitar and sing songs.

Outdoor activities

to **play** football/tennis	Fußball/Tennis spielen
to **go** skating/swimming/climbing/rafting/hiking/ziplining/mountainboarding	inlineskaten/schwimmen/klettern/schlauchbootfahren/wandern/mit der Seilrutsche fahren/mountainboardfahren gehen
to **ride** your bike/a horse	Fahrrad fahren/reiten
to **run**	laufen; rennen
to **go for a walk** in a park/in a forest/in the mountains	im Park/im Wald/in den Bergen spazieren gehen
to **climb** a mountain	einen Berg besteigen
to **do** backpacking/mountain climbing	mit dem Rucksack reisen/bergsteigen

3	to **look forward to** (+ *noun or -ing*) [ˌlʊk ˈfɔːwəd tə]	sich freuen auf	I'm *looking forward to* my grandma's visit next week. I'm *looking forward to* <u>seeing</u> her.
	kid [kɪd]	Jugendliche/-r; Kind	When I was a little *kid*, I loved playing with my toy cars. *kid* = child
	log cabin [ˈlɒɡ ˌkæbɪn]	Blockhütte	Are we going to sleep in a *log cabin*?
	cell phone (AE) [ˈsel fəʊn]	Mobiltelefon; Handy	Your *cell phone* is ringing.

Station 1: The Rockies are full of surprises!

*to **hang on** [ˌhæŋ ˈɒn]	(einen Augenblick) warten	*Hang on*. I need to ask my parents.
It took ages. [ɪt tʊk ˈeɪdʒɪz]	Es dauerte ewig.	*It took ages* to climb the mountain.
age [eɪdʒ]	Alter; Zeitalter	What's your *age*? - I'm twelve. What *age* is Scott? = How old is he? *Fr.* âge (m)
*to **go on** [ˌɡəʊ ˈɒn]	geschehen	You are too loud. What's *going on* here?
trampoline [ˈtræmpliːn]	Trampolin	I can jump very high on my *trampoline*. *Fr.* trampoline (m)
to **grin** [ɡrɪn]	grinsen	Why are you *grinning* like that? *to grin* = to smile (with a big smile)
platform [ˈplætfɔːm]	Plattform; Bahnsteig	I jumped into the water from a high *platform*.
canoe [kəˈnuː]	Kanu	Let's take a *canoe* and go down the river.
to **turn** [tɜːn]	drehen; (sich) umdrehen	I *turned* to look for my dog.
to **turn over** [ˌtɜːn ˈəʊvə]	umdrehen; umkippen	My canoe *turned over* and I fell into the water.
wet [wet]	nass	We all got really *wet* in the storm.
difficult [ˈdɪfɪklt]	schwierig	I couldn't climb the mountain. It was too *difficult* for me. *difficult* ↔ easy *Fr.* difficil/-e; *Lat.* difficilis

porcupine [ˈpɔːkjəˌpaɪn]	Baumstachler	Look, there's a *porcupine* in the tree!
noise [nɔɪz]	Lärm; Geräusch	What's all the *noise*? I can't sleep!
3 **else** [els]	andere/-r/-s; sonst noch	I don't think we need anything *else*.
directly [dɪˈrektli]	direkt; ohne Umwege	After our day in the mountains I went *directly* to bed.
to **zipline** [ˈzɪplaɪn]	mit der Seilrutsche fahren	Everyone was watching when I was *ziplining* across the river.
corner [ˈkɔːnə]	Ecke	Most rooms have four *corners*.
5 **travel** [ˈtrævl]	(das) Reisen; Reise	Tell me everything about your *travels* to India.
*to **spend** [spend]	verbringen *(Zeit)*	She *spends* all her free time with her dog.
		❗ *to spend ≠ spenden*
hike [haɪk]	Wanderung	You can go on beautiful *hikes* in the Rocky Mountains. *hike* → to hike → hiking
*to **shine** [ʃaɪn]	scheinen; glänzen	The sun *is shining*, let's go swimming.
shhh [ʃ]	psst	*Shhh*! Don't make a noise. There's a cougar on that rock.
side [saɪd]	Seite	Let's go across the bridge to get to the other *side* of the river.
canyon [ˈkænjən]	Schlucht; Canyon	This landscape has mountains and *canyons*.
golden [ˈgəʊldn]	golden; Gold-	I've got a *golden* bracelet.
*to **hold your breath** [ˌhəʊld jə ˈbreθ]	den Atem anhalten	How long can you *hold your breath*?
along [əˈlɒŋ]	entlang	I love walking *along* the river. The landscape is beautiful.
coyote [kəˈjəʊti]	Kojote; Präriewolf	On our hike, we saw a *coyote*.
so (that) [səʊ ˈðət]	damit; sodass	He saved some money *so that* he could buy a nice present.
6 **everybody** [ˈevribɒdi]	jeder; alle	*Everybody* has to tidy their log cabins. *everybody* = everyone = all the people
8 to **include** [ɪnˈkluːd]	einschließen; beinhalten	The trip is expensive, but the price *includes* all our meals. *Fr.* inclure; *Lat.* includere

---

Wild animals

alligator	cougar	hare [heə] Hase	panther
badger [ˈbædʒə] Dachs	coyote	lion [ˈlaɪən] Löwe	porcupine
bat	deer [dɪə] Hirsch	lynx [lɪŋks] Luchs	raven [ˈreɪvn] Rabe
bear	eagle	marmot [ˈmɑːmət] Murmeltier	tiger [ˈtaɪgə] Tiger
bighorn sheep	elephant [ˈelɪfnt] Elefant	marten [ˈmɑːtɪn] Marder	wolf [wʊlf] Wolf
bird	fox [fɒks] Fuchs	moose	zebra [ˈzebrə] Zebra

Station 2: Rules for campers at Green Moose Camp

boot [buːt]	Stiefel	You wear *boots* in winter because they're warmer than shoes.
pants *(pl) (AE)* [pænts]	Hosen	Should I wear long *pants* or shorts today? *Fr.* pantalon *(m)*

sleeve [sliːv]	Ärmel	In summer you wear shirts with short *sleeves*.
insect [ˈɪnsekt]	Insekt	In humid regions there are often lots of *insects*. *Fr.* insecte *(m)*
*to **bite** [baɪt]	beißen; stechen	Does your dog *bite*? It looks a bit scary!
to **carry** [ˈkæri]	tragen	Can you *carry* this box for me, please?
sunscreen [ˈsʌnskriːn]	Sonnencreme	The sun is shining. Don't forget to put on *sunscreen*.
rain [reɪn]	Regen	Today there's a lot of *rain* and no sun. *rain* → to rain → rainy
jacket [ˈdʒækɪt]	Jacke	In summer you don't need a *jacket*.
hiker [ˈhaɪkə]	Wanderer/Wanderin	There are a lot of *hikers* in the mountains.
to **pick up** [ˌpɪkˈʌp]	aufheben; abholen	There's paper on the floor. Please *pick* it *up*.
trash *(AE)* [træʃ]	Abfall; Müll	Don't throw your *trash* on the floor! **!** *trash (AE)* = rubbish *(BE)*
ground [graʊnd]	Boden; Erdboden	My phone fell onto the *ground* and broke.
*to **smell** [smel]	riechen; duften	The flowers *smell* wonderful.
to **touch** [tʌtʃ]	berühren; antippen	Don't *touch* this dog. It could bite. *Fr.* toucher
safe [seɪf]	sicher; ungefährlich	This bridge is too old. It isn't *safe* to use it. *safe* ↔ dangerous
9 **Find the odd one out!** [ˌfaɪnd ðiˌɒd wʌnˈaʊt]	Finde das Element, das nicht in die Gruppe passt!	*Find the odd one out*: cougar - canyon - bear - coyote.
opposite [ˈɒpəzɪt]	Gegenteil	What's the *opposite* of 'happy'? - 'It's 'unhappy'.
to **replay** [ˌriːˈpleɪ]	erneut spielen; erneut abspielen	I didn't understand the dialogue. Could you *replay* it, please?
10 **tidy** [ˈtaɪdi]	sauber; ordentlich	Your room is always very *tidy*.
12 to **try on** [ˌtraɪˈɒn]	anprobieren	That's a nice shirt. Why don't you *try* it *on*?
fitting room [ˈfɪtɪŋ ˌrʊm]	Umkleidekabine	Where are the *fitting rooms*? I'd like to try these pants on.
to **fit** [fɪt]	passen	These pants don't *fit*. They're too short.
perfectly [ˈpɜːfɪktli]	perfekt	This T-shirt fits *perfectly*. You look great in it.
13 **sock** [sɒk]	Socke	You can't wear these *socks* in those shoes. It looks terrible!
assistant [əˈsɪstnt]	Assistent/-in; Verkäufer/-in	I'd like to buy this jacket. Where's the shop *assistant*?

Phrasal verbs

Here are some phrasal verbs. You must learn their meanings by heart.

to **look**	schauen	to **take**	nehmen	to **turn**	drehen
to **look after**	sich kümmern um	to **take off**	abheben	to **turn on**	einschalten
to **look for**	suchen			to **turn up**	auftauchen
to **look forward to**	sich freuen auf				
to **look out for**	sich in Acht nehmen vor				
to **look up**	nachschlagen				

Skills: How to find information on the internet

1	**attraction** [əˈtrækʃn]	Attraktion; Sehenswürdigkeit	The blob is only one of Green Moose Camp's *attractions*. *Fr.* attraction (f)
	display [dɪˈspleɪ]	Vorführung; Ausstellung; Schaukasten; Anzeige	At a flower show you can see a wonderful *display* of flowers.

Unit task: Our travel report

to **paddle** [ˈpædl]	paddeln	Let's *paddle* across the lake.
current [ˈkʌrnt]	Strömung	Don't go swimming here. The *currents* are dangerous. *Fr.* courant (m)
to **capsize** [kæpˈsaɪz]	kentern	Oh no! Our boat is going to *capsize*!
planet [ˈplænɪt]	Planet	Aliens come from a different *planet*. *Fr.* planète (f)
spaceship [ˈspeɪsʃɪp]	Raumschiff	In science-fiction stories people often travel through space in *spaceships*.
*to **go sightseeing** [ˌɡəʊ ˈsaɪtsiːɪŋ]	eine Besichtigungstour machen	Let's go *sightseeing* in Chicago!
youth hostel [ˈjuːθ ˌhɒstl]	Jugendherberge	A *youth hostel* is a cheap place where young people can stay.
key [kiː]	besonders wichtig	What were the *key* points of his presentation?

Story: You wanted an outdoor adventure!

countryside [ˈkʌntrisaɪd]	Land; Landschaft	We took a trip to the *countryside*. It was beautiful. **!** in the *countryside* = auf dem Land, in der Natur
track [træk]	Spur; Fährte; Pfad; Bahn	Do you see these *tracks*? They are of a cougar.
to **yawn** [jɔːn]	gähnen	I know you're tired, but please try not to *yawn* all the time.
*to **tell sb to do sth** [ˌtel sʌmbədi tə ˈduː ˈsʌmθɪŋ]	jmdm. sagen, was er tun soll	Our teacher *told us to read* our texts again and look out for mistakes.
tent [tent]	Zelt	I don't want to sleep in a *tent*. Let's go to a youth hostel. *Fr.* tente (f); *Lat.* tentorium (nt)
*to **go for a walk** [ˌɡəʊ fər ə ˈwɔːk]	spazieren gehen	It's nice today. Let's *go for a walk*.
against [əˈɡenst]	gegen	It was *against* the rules to leave the camp at night.
to **grab** [ɡræb]	greifen; ergreifen; schnappen	Holly *grabbed* her bag and left the house.
flashlight *(AE)* [ˈflæʃlaɪt]	Taschenlampe	It's dark outside. We need *flashlights*. An electric light that you can hold in your hand.
pretty [ˈprɪti]	ziemlich; ganz schön	I think that's a *pretty* silly idea.
to **tiptoe** [ˈtɪptəʊ]	auf Zehenspitzen gehen	Shhh, you must *tiptoe*. Don't make any noise!
towards [təˈwɔːds]	in Richtung	They went out of the house and walked *towards* the river.
much [mʌtʃ]	sehr	A small flashlight doesn't help *much*.

to **pretend** [prɪˈtend]	vorgeben; vortäuschen; so tun, als ob …	Let's *pretend* we aren't scared.
to **grunt** [grʌnt]	grunzen	Shhh! I think I heard an animal *grunt*.
wide [waɪd]	weit; breit; ausgedehnt	This trail isn't *wide* enough. You need to walk behind me.
calm [kɑːm]	ruhig; friedlich	Stay *calm* and don't move! *calm* ↔ nervous *Fr.* calme
*to **go on** [ˌgəʊˈɒn]	weitergehen; weitermachen; weiterführen; fortfahren	Don't tell me how the story *goes on*. I want to read it.
to **splash** [splæʃ]	spritzen; platschen; planschen	A huge bear was *splashing* through the water.
backwards [ˈbækwədz]	rückwärts	There was no space to turn around, so we had to walk *backwards* to get out of the cave.
to **attack** [əˈtæk]	angreifen	A bear *attacked* the hikers, but a ranger saved them.
statue [ˈstætʃuː]	Statue; Standbild	Oh look, that's not a *statue*, it's a man! *Fr.* statue *(f)*; *Lat.* statua *(f)*
to **lift** [lɪft]	heben; anheben; sich heben	Could you help me to *lift* this heavy rock?
stone [stəʊn]	Stein	Look out! There are big *stones* on the trail.
no wonder [nəʊ ˈwʌndə]	kein Wunder	He only sleeps five hours a night. *No wonder* he's tired.
*to **make sb do sth** [ˌmeɪk sʌmbədi ˈduː ˈsʌmθɪŋ]	jmdn. veranlassen etw. zu tun	They *made us tidy* our cabin every day.
terrible [ˈterəbl]	schrecklich; schlimm; furchtbar	Our youth hostel was *terrible*. It was very loud and dirty. *Fr.* terrible; *Lat.* terribilis
1 **realistic** [ˌrɪəˈlɪstɪk]	realistisch	Are your plans *realistic*? *realistic* → real *Fr.* réaliste

Across cultures 2 Living together

1 **ability** [əˈbɪləti]	Fähigkeit; Begabung	He's got lots of different *abilities*. He's good at sports, Maths and singing. *Fr.* habilité *(f)*; *Lat.* habilitas *(f)*
well [wel]	gut	She loves singing but she can't sing very *well*.
statement [ˈsteɪtmənt]	Aussage; Behauptung; Erklärung	I'd like to make a *statement*. to make a *statement* = to say something
advice *(no pl)* [ədˈvaɪs]	Rat; Ratschlag	What *advice* can you give me? ! He gave me two good pieces of *advice*. Never: ~~advices~~

What I'm good/bad at

I can/can't concentrate [ˈkɒnsntreɪt]/listen for a long time/run very fast/hear/see very well/…	… mich konzentrieren …
I find it easy/difficult to learn things by heart/remember words/solve [sɒlv] puzzles/ talk in front of people/write long texts/work with a computer/ask someone for help/ explain something to other people/be polite/friendly …	… lösen …
I make/don't make a lot of mistakes when I …	
Cheering up [ˌtʃɪərɪŋ ˈʌp] sad people/Helping people in trouble/… **is easy/difficult for me.**	… Trösten …
I am very/not very good/bad at sports/Maths/English/organising things/ reading/talking/ writing/singing/dancing/playing the guitar …	
I'm scared of dogs/**spiders** [ˈspaɪdəz]/ … **when** I look down from a high building/ when I'm alone at night/…	… Spinnen …

2	**disability** [ˌdɪsəˈbɪləti]	Behinderung; Unfähigkeit	At our school there are some students with *disabilities*. *ability* ↔ *disability*
	physical [ˈfɪzɪkl]	physisch; körperlich	I'm in a wheelchair because I've got a *physical* disability.
	intellectual [ˌɪntlˈektjuəl]	intellektuell; geistig	I sometimes play *intellectual* games on my phone. *intellectual* ↔ *physical* *Fr.* intellectuel/-le
	sign [saɪn]	Zeichen; Schild	My brother can't hear. So we talk to him in *sign* language. *Fr.* signe *(m)*; *Lat.* signum *(nt)*
	guide dog [ˈgaɪd ˌdɒg]	Blindenhund	A *guide dog* is a dog that helps people who can't see.
	inclusion [ɪnˈkluːʒn]	Inklusion; Einbeziehung	At our school, we believe in the idea of *inclusion*.
	inclusive [ɪnˈkluːsɪv]	inklusiv; einschließlich; umfassend	My brother learns more slowly than me. He went to a special school, but now he is in an *inclusive* class at my school. *inclusive* → *inclusion*
	schooling [ˈskuːlɪŋ]	Schulbildung	Inclusive *schooling* is for children with and without disabilities.
	system [ˈsɪstəm]	System	What are the differences between the American and the German school *systems*?
	to sign [saɪn]	unterzeichnen; unterschreiben	Please *sign* the letter before you send it. *Fr.* signer; *Lat.* signare
	right [raɪt]	Recht	Men and women have the same *rights*.
	success [səkˈses]	Erfolg	The movie was a big *success*. *Fr.* succès *(m)*
3	**article** [ˈɑːtɪkl]	Artikel; Bericht *(in einer Zeitschrift, Zeitung)*	On the TTS website there are lots of *articles* about clubs. *Fr.* article *(m)*
	cactus, [ˈkæktəs], **cacti** *(pl)* [ˈkæktaɪ]	Kaktus	A plant that doesn't need much water, so it can even grow in the desert. *Fr.* cactus *(m)*

organisation [ˌɔːɡənaɪˈzeɪʃn]	Organisation	Betty works for an *organisation* that helps children. *organisation* → to organise
4 **need** [niːd]	Bedürfnis	People with disabilities have special *needs*.
partially sighted [ˌpɑːʃli ˈsaɪtɪd]	sehbehindert; teilsichtig	The new girl in our class is *partially sighted*.
deaf [def]	gehörlos; taub; schwerhörig	Some people are so *deaf* that they can't hear anything at all.
to **concentrate** [ˈkɒnsntreɪt]	(sich) konzentrieren	Holly *concentrated* on what her teacher said. *Fr.* se concentrer
hearing aid [ˈhɪərɪŋ ˌeɪd]	Hörgerät	Some deaf people can hear with a *hearing aid*.
glasses *(pl)* [ˈɡlɑːsɪz]	Brille	I can't read without my *glasses*.
		! *Glasses* steht immer im Plural: My *glasses* are broken. I need new ones.

Unit 4 Sport is good for you!

Check-in

camel racing [ˈkæml ˌreɪsɪŋ]	Kamelrennen	In some countries *camel racing* is more popular than horse racing.
marathon [ˈmærəθn]	Marathon	My uncle ran in a *marathon* last year.
health [helθ]	Gesundheit	Sport is good for your *health*. *health* → healthy
accident [ˈæksɪdnt]	Unfall	My sister had a bike *accident* yesterday. *Fr.* accident (m)
1 **radio** [ˈreɪdiəʊ]	Radio	In the morning, I always listen to the *radio*. *Fr.* radio (f)
programme [ˈprəʊɡræm]	Programm; Sendung	There's an interesting *programme* about camel racing on TV. *Fr.* programme (m)
runner [ˈrʌnə]	Läufer/-in	More than 30,000 *runners* run in the London Marathon.
net [net]	Netz	For tennis, you need a *net*.
racquet [ˈrækɪt]	Schläger	Oh no, I haven't got my *racquet*. – Don't worry, I've got two. *Fr.* raquette (f)
score [skɔː]	Punktestand; Spielstand	At the end of the match the *score* was 2–2.
*to **lose** [luːz]	verlieren	Our team *lost* again. What a shame! *to lose* ↔ to win
court [kɔːt]	Spielfeld	The two players are on the *court* now.
*to **catch** [kætʃ]	fangen	I threw the ball and he *caught* it. *to catch* a ball ↔ to throw a ball
to **pass** [pɑːs]	zupassen; zuspielen	The football player *passes* the ball to his team member. *Fr.* passer

to **kick** [kɪk]	schießen; treten	'Pass' means to throw or *kick* the ball to another player in the same team.
pitch [pɪtʃ]	Spielfeld; Platz	You play football on a *pitch* or field. **!** a tennis court – a football *pitch/field*
2	**the … the …** + *comparative* form [ðə … ðə]	je … desto … + *Komparativ*	*The* quicker you are with your homework, *the* earlier you can meet your friends.
4	**equipment** [ɪ'kwɪpmənt]	Ausrüstung; Ausstattung	You need lots of *equipment* to play American football. *equipment* = things you need for sports activities *Fr.* équipement
individual [ˌɪndɪ'vɪdʒuəl]	individuell; einzeln	Do you do an *individual* sport or a team sport? *Lat.* individuus

Sports

Team sport	Place	Equipment
American football	field	**ball**, **helmet** ['helmɪt], **pads** [pædz]
baseball	field	**ball**, **bat** [bæt], **glove**
basketball	court	ball
football	pitch	ball
handball	court	ball
field/ice hockey	field/rink	**stick** [stɪk], **ball/stick**, **puck** [pʌk], **helmet** ['helmɪt], **pads** [pædz]
rugby	field, pitch	ball
volleyball	court	ball

Individual sport	Place	Equipment
athletics [æθ'letɪks]	track [træk] and field	– – – –
badminton	court	**shuttlecock** ['ʃʌtlkɒk], **racquet**
golf	**course** [kɔːs]	**ball**, **club** [klʌb]
table tennis	indoor or outdoor	**ball**, **bat** [bæt]
tennis	court	ball, racquet

Verbs
to catch/hit/kick/throw/pass a ball
to score a goal/a point
to lose/to win
to win 3–0 (zu null **nil** [nɪl])
to end in a **tie** [taɪ] unentschieden ausgehen

Station 1: Have you ever run in a marathon?

ever ['evə]	jemals; überhaupt	It was our funniest project *ever*!
right here [ˌraɪt 'hɪə]	genau hier	The marathon starts *right here*.
11-year-old [ɪ'levnˌjɪərəʊld]	11-Jährige/-r	The mini marathon is for *11* to *18-year-olds*.
running ['rʌnɪŋ]	Laufen; Rennen	Gwen loves *running*. It's her favourite sport.
trial [traɪəl]	Qualifikation	There are *trials* in sports to find the best runners or players.
Who's in? [huːz 'ɪn]	Wer macht mit?; Wer ist dabei?	Let's join the football team. *Who's in?*
*to **be in** [biˌ'ɪn]	dabei sein; mitmachen	Are you going to run? Well, I'*m in*, and I hope you are too!
run [rʌn]	Rennen; Lauf	A marathon is a long *run*. *a run* → *to run* → *runner*
to **raise money** [ˌreɪz 'mʌni]	Geld sammeln	Charities *raise money* to help people.

For

for three years	drei Jahre lang	to ask **for**	bitten um
for a long time	für lange Zeit	**for** example [fər‿ɪgˈzɑːmpl]	zum Beispiel
for ages	ewig lange	**for** God's sake [fə ˌgɒdz ˈseɪk]	um Gottes willen
for miles	meilenweit	**forever** [fəˈrevə]	für immer

2	**before** [bɪˈfɔː]	schon einmal; vorher; zuvor	Have you been here *before*? Or is this your first trip?

Station 2: Have you been to the doctor's yet?

	doctor [ˈdɒktə]	Arzt/Ärztin	I've hurt my foot. I need to see a *doctor*. **!** Beachte den Unterschied: Have you seen the *doctor* yet? Have you been to the *doctor's* yet? *Doctor's* ist eine Abkürzung von *doctor's surgery*. *Fr.* docteur *(m)*
	yet [jet]	schon; noch	Have you asked your parents about the party *yet*?
	not … yet [nɒt ˈjet]	noch nicht	The friends haven*'t* left for the marathon *yet*.
	to **twist your ankle** [ˌtwɪst jɔːr ˈæŋkl]	sich den Knöchel verrenken	I've *twisted my ankle*. It hurts a lot.
	pain [peɪn]	Schmerz	I've got a really bad *pain* in my left foot.
6	**chant** [tʃɑːnt]	Sprechgesang	During a football match there are loud *chants*. *Fr.* chant *(m)*; *Lat.* cantus *(m)*
	to **cheer** [tʃɪə]	anfeuern; jubeln; zujubeln	Jay is writing a chant to *cheer* the runners in the marathon.
8	*to **have a look (at)** [ˌhæv ə ˈlʊk]	anschauen	Let me *have a look* at your ankle. Let's *have a look* at it. = Let's look at it.
	prescription [prɪˈskrɪpʃn]	Rezept *(für Arzneimittel)*	The doctor gave me a *prescription*.
	ointment [ˈɔɪntmənt]	Salbe	The doctor gave Olivia a prescription for an *ointment*.
	*to **get well** [ˌget ˈwel]	gesund werden	*Get well* soon! = Gute Besserung!
	shoulder [ˈʃəʊldə]	Schulter	I can't play tennis because my *shoulder* hurts.
	headache *(no pl)* [ˈhedeɪk]	Kopfschmerzen; Kopfweh	When I watch too much TV, I get a *headache*. **!** *Headache* steht immer im Singular: I've got a bad *headache*. headache → head
	backache [ˈbækeɪk]	Rückenschmerzen; Rückenweh	I lifted a heavy bag and now I've got terrible *backache*.
	stomachache [ˈstʌməkeɪk]	Bauchschmerzen; Bauchweh	I've got *stomachache* because I've eaten too much.
	*to **feel sick** [ˌfiːl ˈsɪk]	Übelkeit verspüren; sich schlecht fühlen	When you've got a stomachache, you often *feel sick* too. **!** I *feel sick*. = Mir ist schlecht/übel. I am sick. = Ich bin krank.
	cold [kəʊld]	Erkältung	I can't go to school today because I've got a bad *cold*.
	cough [kɒf]	Husten	Have you got a *cough*?
	fever [ˈfiːvə]	Fieber	People with a cold often have a cough and a *fever*. *Fr.* fièvre *(f)*; *Lat.* febris

pill [pɪl]   Pille; Tablette   The doctor wrote a prescription for some *pills*.

Health

to **have an accident**	einen Unfall haben
to **call the emergency service**	den Rettungsdienst rufen
to **hurt your foot/arm/leg/** …	sich den Fuß/Arm/das Bein/… verletzen
to **twist your ankle**	sich den Knöchel verrenken
to **feel a pain in** …	Schmerzen haben in/an …
to **get a prescription**	ein Rezept bekommen
to **put ointment on** …	… einsalben
to **take pills**	Tabletten nehmen
to **have a headache/backache/stomachache**	Kopfweh/Rückenweh/Bauchweh haben
to **feel bad/sick**	sich schlecht/krank fühlen
to **catch a cold/cough/fever**	eine Erkältung/Husten/Fieber bekommen

> I don't feel well today. Maybe I've caught a cold.

Station 3: An interview with Ayla

cramp [kræmp]	Krampf	I couldn't finish the race because I had a bad *cramp*. *Fr.* crampe (f)
award [ə'wɔːd]	Auszeichnung; Preis	Ayla has won a Maths *award* but no sports *award*.
what it's like [ˌwɒt ɪts … 'laɪk]	wie das ist	What is it like? Do you know *what it's like* when you break something?
12 **camera** ['kæmrə]	Fotoapparat; Kamera	When you go on a trip, don't forget your *camera*. *Fr.* caméra (f)
player ['pleɪə]	Spieler/-in; Mitspieler/-in	*player* → to play
crowd [kraʊd]	Menschenmenge	A lot of people all together in one place.

Skills: How to understand news reports and take notes

1 **rescue** ['reskjuː]	Rettung	Here is a report about a *rescue* in the mountains.
*to **get hurt** [ˌget 'hɜːt]	verletzt werden	He *got hurt* in a car accident last week.
injury ['ɪndʒəri]	Verletzung	His *injuries* were pretty bad.
hospital ['hɒspɪtl]	Hospital; Krankenhaus	After the accident, he spent two weeks in *hospital*. *Fr.* hôpital (m)
helicopter ['helɪkɒptə]	Helikopter; Hubschrauber	They took him to hospital in a *helicopter*.
presenter [prɪ'zentə]	Moderator/-in	*presenter* → to present → presentation
reporter [rɪ'pɔːtə]	Reporter/-in	My brother works as a radio *reporter*.
witness ['wɪtnəs]	Zeuge/Zeugin	The police is looking for *witnesses* of the accident.
2 **eyewitness** ['aɪwɪtnəs]	Augenzeuge/Augenzeugin	The reporter is talking to an *eyewitness*.

dramatic [drə'mætɪk]	dramatisch	The witness has seen the *dramatic* accident. *dramatic* → a drama *Fr.* dramatique
station ['steɪʃn]	Sender	What's your favourite radio *station*? *Fr.* station *(f)*
to **receive** [rɪ'si:v]	empfangen; erhalten; bekommen	Have you *received* my letter? A formal word for 'to get'. *Fr.* recevoir; *Lat.* recipere
scene [si:n]	Schauplatz	The reporter was trying to get to the *scene* of the accident.
I couldn't believe my eyes. [aɪ ˌkʊdnt bɪˌli:v maɪˌ'aɪz]	Ich traute meinen Augen nicht.	*I couldn't believe my eyes* when I saw the spaceship.

Unit task: The aliens have landed!

to **record** [rɪ'kɔ:d]	aufnehmen; aufzeichnen	Let's *record* the scene with a camera.
over ['əʊvə]	vorüber; vorbei	School is *over* at 3:15.
change [tʃeɪndʒ]	Änderung; Veränderung; Wechsel	Are there any *changes* to our plan? *change* → to change
necessary ['nesəsri]	nötig; notwendig; erforderlich	It's *necessary* to wear a hat because of the sun. *Fr.* nécessaire; *Lat.* necessarius

Story: Hey, don't call *me* silly!

silly ['sɪli]	Dummkopf	I'm angry at my little sister because she called me *silly*.
heart [hɑ:t]	Herz	I always listen to my *heart*. the *heart* of London = the centre of London
anyway ['eniweɪ]	jedenfalls; trotzdem; sowieso	She twisted her ankle, but she won the race *anyway*.
*to **let go (of)** [ˌlet 'gəʊ (əv)]	loslassen	Don't *let go of* my hand, Gwen!
fancy dress [ˌfænsi 'dres]	Verkleidung; Kostüm	I'm looking for a *fancy dress* for the party. *fancy dress* = costume
to **breathe** [bri:ð]	atmen	I've got a bad cold. I can't *breathe* well. **!** Achte auf die Aussprache: to breathe [i:] – breath [e].
*to **keep up (with)** [ˌki:p̬ˈʌp (wɪð)]	mithalten (mit); Schritt halten (mit)	Can Luke *keep up with* Gwen? = Is Luke fast enough?
*to **take sth seriously** [ˌteɪk 'sɪəriəsli]	ernst nehmen	I'm *taking* this race very *seriously*. I want to win! If a situation is serious, you must *take it seriously*. *seriously* → serious
*to **get in the way** [ˌget̬ɪn ðə 'weɪ]	stören; im Weg stehen	The people in the costumes shouldn't *get in the way* of the runners.
stomach ['stʌmək]	Magen; Bauch	I've got a strong pain in my *stomach*. *stomach* → stomachache *Fr.* estomac *(m)*
far [fɑ:]	weit	How *far* can you run?
finish line ['fɪnɪʃ ˌlaɪn]	Ziellinie	At the end of a race there's always a *finish line*.

stupid [ˈstjuːpɪd]	dumm; blöd	The *stupid* cat and dog almost made Gwen and Luke fall over. *stupid* ↔ clever **Fr.** stupide; **Lat.** stupidus
*to **be gone** [bɪ ˈɡɒn]	verschwunden sein; weg sein	Near the end of the race Gwen's cramp *was gone*.
We did it! [ˌwiː ˈdɪd ɪt]	Wir haben es geschafft!	*Luke and Gwen did it!* What a success!
to **ruin** [ˈruːɪn]	ruinieren; zerstören	Jay and Dave almost *ruined* the race for Luke and Gwen.
official [əˈfɪʃl]	Schiedsrichter/-in	In a race there are always *officials*.
to **surprise** [səˈpraɪz]	überraschen	My friends *surprised* me with a party. *to surprise* → a surprise → to be surprised **Fr.** surprendre
in secret [ɪn ˈsiːkrət]	heimlich	Jay and Dave trained *in secret*. No one knew about it.
hard [hɑːd]	hart; schwer; schwierig	German is a language that is *hard* to learn.
*to **forgive** [fəˈɡɪv]	vergeben; verzeihen	Can Gwen *forgive* them?
1 **reason** [ˈriːzn]	Grund	Why did you do it? What was the *reason*? **Fr.** raison (f)
to **cause** [kɔːz]	verursachen	What or who *caused* the accident? *to cause* → because **Fr.** cause (f); **Lat.** causa (f)

Positive and negative words

	➕	➖
What you think of something:	easy, good, great, interesting, useful; *stronger words:* amazing, fantastic, perfect	bad, boring, dangerous, difficult, hard; *stronger words:* awful, scary, terrible
What you think of a person:	beautiful, brave, clever, cute, fair, friendly, fun, funny, good, quiet, polite, popular	boring, crazy, rude, silly, stupid, unfair, unfriendly
How a person feels:	confident, good, happy, lucky	bad, embarrassed, lonely, sad, unhappy, unlucky

Which of the words are opposites? Write them down together.

hope [həʊp]	Hoffnung	I haven't got any *hope* of winning the race. *hope* → to hope
fear [fɪə]	Angst; Furcht; Befürchtung	The feeling you have when you are scared.
relationship [rɪˈleɪʃnʃɪp]	Beziehung	Is the *relationship* between you and your neighbours a good one?
2 **On the one hand …, (but) on the other hand …** [ɒn ðəˈwʌn ˌhænd … (bʌt) ɒn ðiˈʌðə ˌhænd …]	Einerseits …, (aber) andererseits …	*On the one hand* he'd like to be a better runner, *but on the other hand* he doesn't want to train very hard.
4 **point of view** [ˌpɔɪnt əv ˈvjuː]	Standpunkt; Ansicht; Perspektive	Who's right and who's wrong from your *point of view*?

Check-out

2	**bicycle motocross** [ˌbaɪsɪkl ˈməʊtəʊkrɒs]	Fahrradmotocross	On the one hand *bicycle motocross* is a dangerous sport, but on the other hand it's so much fun.
	bicycle [ˈbaɪsɪkl]	Fahrrad	I go to school by *bicycle*. ! The word 'bike' is short for '*bicycle*'. *Fr.* bicyclette *(f)*
	mud [mʌd]	Schlamm	My clothes are dirty because I fell into the *mud*.
	company [ˈkʌmpəni]	Gesellschaft; Firma; Unternehmen	My dad works for an American *company*.
	to **discover** [dɪˈskʌvə]	entdecken	When I was 11, I *discovered* that I was a good runner. *Fr.* découvrir
3	**riding** [raɪdɪŋ]	Reiten	I love *riding*, but I haven't got a horse.

Focus 2 Getting around

to **arrive** [əˈraɪv]	ankommen	We *arrived* at the airport at 6.30 a.m. *Fr.* arriver
desk [desk]	Schalter	We went to the information *desk* to ask how to get to our hotel.
central [ˈsentrl]	zentral; Zentral-	Our hotel is in *central* London. *central* → a centre *Fr.* central/-e; *Lat.* centrum *(nt)*
the Tube [tjuːb]	U-Bahn	It's too far to walk. Let's take the *Tube*. Another name for the London Underground is the *Tube*.
to **change** [tʃeɪndʒ]	umsteigen; wechseln	To get to Buckingham Palace from here, you *change onto* the Victoria line.
express [ɪkˈspres]	Eilzug	The *express* train is faster but it's more expensive. An *express* train is a fast train that doesn't stop very often.
stop [stɒp]	Haltestelle; Halt	The next *stop* is Elephant & Castle. *stop* → to stop
ticket [ˈtɪkɪt]	Fahrschein	Have you already bought our train *tickets*? *Fr.* ticket *(m)*
probably [ˈprɒbəbli]	wahrscheinlich	The next train *probably* leaves in ten minutes, but I'm not sure.
single [ˈsɪŋgl]	einfache Fahrkarte	Would you like a *single* or a return ticket?
return [rɪˈtɜːn]	Hin- und Rückfahrkarte	One ticket to Paddington, please. – Single or *return*?
adult [ˈædʌlt]	Erwachsene/-r	I need three tickets – two *adults* and one child. *adult* ↔ child *Fr.* adulte; *Lat.* adultus
cash [kæʃ]	Bargeld	I never have a lot of *cash* with me. The money that you have in your pocket.

credit card ['kredɪt ˌkɑːd]	Kreditkarte	I'd like to pay for these things with my *credit card*.
lift [lɪft]	Lift; Fahrstuhl	I don't want to walk. Is there a *lift*?
luggage *(no pl)* ['lʌgɪdʒ]	Gepäck	Can I help you with your *luggage*?
stay [steɪ]	Aufenthalt	Enjoy your *stay* in Greenwich! *stay* → to stay

Travel words

to travel	reisen		station	Bahnhof, Station
travel agent's	Reisebüro		airport	Flughafen
to book/take a journey/trip	eine Reise buchen/machen		on the road	auf der Straße; unterwegs
transport	Transport		one way; single/return	einfach/hin und zurück
by train/coach/car/Underground	mit dem Zug/Bus/Auto/mit der U-Bahn		to depart/arrive	abfahren/ankommen
			to change	umsteigen

2	**alternative** [ɔːlˈtɜːnətɪv]	Alternative	I don't want to take the train. Are there any *alternatives*? *Fr.* alternative *(f)*
	coach [kəʊtʃ]	Reisebus	We could go by train or by *coach*. A *coach* is a big bus (for holidays or long trips).
	change [tʃeɪndʒ]	Umstieg	How many *changes* are there? – Only one at Liverpool. *change* → to change
3	**announcement** [əˈnaʊnsmənt]	Ankündigung; Durchsage	I never understand the *announcements* at the station. *Fr.* annoncer; *Lat.* annuntiare
	flight [flaɪt]	Flug	I'm late for my *flight*. *flight* → to fly
	plane [pleɪn]	Flugzeug	Our *plane* leaves in two hours.
	delayed [dɪˈleɪd]	verspätet; verzögert	If there's bad weather, flights are often *delayed*.
	to board [bɔːd]	an Bord gehen; besteigen	Your plane is now ready for *boarding*. To get onto a plane, boat etc. *Fr.* monter à bord
	to depart [dɪˈpɑːt]	abfahren; abfliegen	When does the train *depart*? *to depart* = to leave *Fr.* partir, départ *(m)*
	passenger ['pæsndʒə]	Passagier/-in; Fahrgast	All *passengers* must board the plane now.
	gate [geɪt]	Gate; Flugsteig; Ausgang	Our plane leaves from *Gate* 9.
	unattended [ˌʌnəˈtendɪd]	unbeaufsichtigt	Don't leave your luggage *unattended*.
	pass [pɑːs]	Ausweis; Pass	Please show me your boarding *pass*.
4	*****to go down** [ˌgəʊ ˈdaʊn]	hinuntergehen; nach unten gehen; entlanggehen	The tourist information centre? … *Go down* Main Street. It's on the right.
	past [pɑːst]	vorbei (an); vorüber (an)	Walk *past* the tourist information centre.

straight on [streɪtˌɒn]	geradeaus	Is this Nelson Road? – No, just go *straight on* here and it's the next street on the left.
to **cross** [krɒs]	überqueren; kreuzen	You need to *cross* the street to get to the music shop.
to **turn** [tɜːn]	einbiegen; abbiegen	*Turn* right after the museum.
opposite [ˈɒpəzɪt]	gegenüber; gegenüberliegend; entgegengesetzt	Their house is on the *opposite* side of the hill.

Unit 5 Stay in touch

Check-in

	to **stay in touch (with)** [ˌsteɪ ɪn ˈtʌtʃ wɪð]	in Kontakt bleiben (mit)	E-mails are a good way to *stay in touch* with your friends.
	social network [ˌsəʊʃl ˈnetwɜːk]	soziales Netzwerk	You can chat with all kinds of people in *social networks*.
	nasty [ˈnɑːsti]	garstig; gemein	Why did you say such a *nasty* thing to me?
	comment [ˈkɒment]	Kommentar	This is serious, so I don't need your funny *comments*!
	cyber bully [ˌsaɪbə ˈbʊli]	*jemand, der andere in sozialen Netzwerken belästigt/mobbt*	*Cyber bullies* write nasty comments in social networks.
	protection [prəˈtekʃn]	Schutz	Kids on social networks need *protection* from cyber bullies. *Fr.* protection *(f)*
	profile [ˈprəʊfaɪl]	Profil; Porträt	Luke's *profile* looks cool.
	media [ˈmiːdiə]	Medien	Radio, TV and the internet are all *media*. *Fr.* médias *(f) (pl)*; *Lat.* medium *(nt)*
	letter [ˈletə]	Brief	I like *letters* better than e-mails. *Fr.* lettre *(f)*; *Lat.* litterae *(f) (pl)*
	print [prɪnt]	gedruckt; Druck-	I never buy *print* magazines. I always read them online.
	interest [ˈɪntrəst]	Interesse	Video games are one of my biggest *interests*. *interest* → interesting → be interested (in)
	paradise [ˈpærədaɪs]	Paradies	This place is so beautiful. It's like *paradise*. *Fr.* paradis *(m)*
2	to **post** [pəʊst]	online stellen; posten	Have you *posted* the photos of the class trip?
	*to **take part (in)** [ˌteɪk ˈpɑːt (ɪn)]	teilnehmen (an)	Let's *take part in* the new Drama Club at school.
	to **text** [tekst]	eine SMS schicken	Can you *text* me when we are going to meet this afternoon? *to text* → a text message
	discussion [dɪˈskʌʃn]	Diskussion	I had a *discussion* about video games with my parents. *discussion* → to discuss
3	**practical** [ˈpræktɪkl]	praktisch	Smartphones are a *practical* way to stay in touch. *Fr.* pratique

mobile [ˈməʊbaɪl]	Handy; Mobiltelefon		**!** mobile (phone) *(BE)* = cell phone *(AE)*

Media collocations

to **check**	checken, überprüfen	my **e-mails**/my **profile**/ my **friend's profile**	meine E-Mails/mein Profil/ das Profil meines Freundes
to **change**	ändern	my **profile**	mein Profil
to **post** to **share**	posten; hochladen teilen	**photos**/**information about** …	Fotos/Informationen über …
to **read**/to **write**/ to **reply to**	lesen/schreiben/ antworten auf	**texts**/**text messages**/**e-mails**	SMS-Nachrichten/E-Mails
to **send**/to **receive**	senden/empfangen	**texts**/**text messages**/ **e-mails**/**photos**/ **information**	SMS-Nachrichten/E-Mails/ Fotos/Informationen
to **chat with** to **text** to **stay in touch with**	chatten mit eine SMS schreiben in Kontakt bleiben mit	**a friend**	einem Freund
to **join** to **take part in**	beitreten teilnehmen an	**a discussion**/**a social network**/ **a forum**	einer Diskussion/einem sozialen Netzwerk/einem Forum
to **have** to **take part in**	führen teilnehmen an	**a discussion**/**a video chat**	eine Diskussion/einen Videochat einer Diskussion/einem Videochat
to **play**	spielen	**video games**	Computerspiele

Station 1: Dear Ruby

agony aunt [ˈægəniˌɑːnt]	Kummerkastentante	Lauren didn't want to talk about her problem with her friends or her family. So she wrote a letter to her favourite magazine's *agony aunt*.
… what to do. [ˈwɒt tə duː]	… was ich tun soll.	I don't know *what to do*.
the two of them [ðə ˈtuː ˌəv ðəm]	beide	My brothers sent me a photo of *the two of them*.
whenever [wenˈevə]	wann immer; jedes Mal, wenn; so oft	*Whenever* I ask my brother for something, he says "no".
self-critical [ˈselfˌkrɪtɪkl]	selbstkritisch	The agony aunt's advice is to be more *self-critical*. I think she's right.
to overreact [ˌəʊvəriˈækt]	überreagieren	I know you're angry with him, but don't *overreact* and say bad things about him, OK?
as soon as [əz ˈsuːnˌəz]	sobald	Things usually get better *as soon as* you talk to the person you're fighting with.
headphones *(pl)* [ˈhedfəʊnz]	Kopfhörer	Take my *headphones* and listen to this!
1 **opinion** [əˈpɪnjən]	Meinung	I think we should talk to her. What's your *opinion*? In my *opinion* … = I think … *Fr.* opinion *(f)*; *Lat.* opinio *(f)*
2 **compromise** [ˈkɒmprəmaɪz]	Kompromiss	It isn't always easy to find a *compromise*. *Fr.* compromis *(m)*

3	**after** [ˈɑːftə]	nachdem	**!** *after* the show = nach *after* the show finished = nachdem
	face-to-face [ˌfeɪstəˈfeɪs]	*hier:* persönlich; von Angesicht zu Angesicht	It's fun to meet people *face-to-face* and not just in social networks.
	to **block** [blɒk]	blockieren; abblocken	You can *block* messages from people you don't like.
	forever [fəˈrevə]	für immer; ewig	Photos that you post on the internet never go away. They can stay there *forever*.
	attention [əˈtenʃn]	Aufmerksamkeit; Beachtung	Now that I have your *attention*, please listen to me. *Fr.* attention *(f); Lat.* attentio *(f)*

Station 2: Forum? What forum?

*to **be allowed to (do sth)** [bɪˌəˈlaʊd tə]	dürfen	Students *aren't allowed to* use mobiles at school.
*to **go over to** [ˌgəʊ ˈəʊvə tə]	hinübergehen zu; zu jmdm. nach Hause gehen	Come on, let's *go over* to your house.
What on earth …? [ˌwɒt ˌɒn ˈɜːθ]	Was um alles in der Welt …?	*What on earth* is this?
pipe [paɪp]	Rohr; Rohrleitung	He broke a *pipe* and now there's water everywhere!
*to **go crazy** [ˌgəʊ ˈkreɪzi]	ausflippen; durchdrehen; verrückt werden	I think I'm *going crazy*: I don't understand the Maths homework at all!
washing machine [ˈwɒʃɪŋ məˌʃiːn]	Waschmaschine	Your clothes are dirty. Put them in the *washing machine*. *washing machine* → to wash
to **waste** [weɪst]	verschwenden	You're *wasting* your time, Dad!
cannot [ˈkænɒt]	kann nicht; können nicht	You *cannot* help me with this. *cannot* = can't
step-by-step [ˌstepbaɪˈstep]	Schritt-für-Schritt-	On the internet, there's *step-by-step* advice for everything.
*to **be able to (do sth)** [bɪˌeɪbl tə]	fähig sein zu; können	When my grandma lived in the next town, we *were able to* see her often. Now she lives far away.
still [stɪl]	dennoch	I don't have any money, but I'm *still* going to go to London.
I've done this a million times before. [ˌaɪv dʌn ðɪs ə ˌmɪljən taɪmz bɪˈfɔː]	Ich habe das schon eine Million Mal gemacht.	I can fix my computer. *I've done this a million times before.*
knob [nɒb]	Griff	Cupboard doors often have *knobs*.
to **reach** [riːtʃ]	erreichen; dran kommen	My mum put the chocolate on top of the cupboard so my little sister can't *reach* it.
to **turn off** [ˌtɜːn ˈɒf]	abschalten; ausschalten	Please *turn off* the TV. It's time to go to bed.
to **work** [wɜːk]	*hier:* funktionieren	Is the washing machine *working* again?
genius [ˈdʒiːniəs]	Genie	How did you do it? You're a *genius*! *Fr.* génie *(m); Lat.* ingenium *(nt)*
With a very big head! [ˌwɪð ə ˌveri bɪg ˈhed]	Und ein Angeber!	I'm a genius! – *With a very big head!*

5 **son** [sʌn] Sohn The Elliots have two *sons:* Jamie and Luke.

Fixing things

to **fix**	[fɪks]	reparieren; befestigen	to **take apart**	[ˌteɪk ə'pɑ:t]	auseinandernehmen
to **glue**	[glu:]	kleben	to **put together**	[ˌpʊt tə'geðə]	zusammensetzen
to **mend**	[mend]	flicken	**tool**	[tu:l]	Werkzeug
to **repair**	[rɪ'peə]	reparieren	**hammer**	['hæmə]	Hammer
to **sew**	[səʊ]	nähen	**scissors** *(pl)*	['sɪzəz]	Schere
to **screw sth to sth**	[skru:]	etw. anschrauben an etw.	**screwdriver**	['skru:draɪvə]	Schraubenzieher
to **unscrew**	[ʌn'skru:]	losschrauben	**spanner**	['spænə]	Schraubenschlussel

7 **by** [baɪ] von; durch This is a report *by* Mike Ness.

library ['laɪbri] Bibliothek; Bücherei You can read books in a *library* or take them home.

10 **police** [pə'li:s] Polizei There has been an accident. Let's call the *police*.

! The *police* <u>are</u> looking for a dangerous man.
Fr. police *(f)*

Permission

Question	Positive answer	Permission yes / no
Can I ask you a question?	Yes, you can.	You can ask questions during the presentation./ You can't ask questions during the presentation.
Could I have some tea, please?	Yes, of course.	You can have some tea now./You can't have any tea now.
May I go outside?	Yes, you may.	You may go outside./You may not go outside at night. You mustn't go outside at night.
Am I allowed to …?	Yes, you are.	You're allowed to …/You aren't allowed to …

13 **result** [rɪ'zʌlt] Ergebnis; Resultat Have we got the test *results* yet? Who got the most points?
Fr. résultat *(m)*

to **(e-)mail** ['i:meɪl] mailen; per E-Mail schicken Could you *e-mail* me your part of the class project?

to **download** [ˌdaʊn'ləʊd] herunterladen *(aus dem Internet)* I've *downloaded* a new video. Let's watch it.

to **comment (on)** ['kɒment (ɒn)] kommentieren Please don't *comment* on my test results!
Fr. commenter

to **care (about)** ['keər əˌbaʊt] wichtig nehmen; sich kümmern (um); sich interessieren (für) We're having this discussion because I *care about* you.
If you *care about* something, then it's important to you.

Skills: How to write a letter and a reply

for example [fər ɪg'zɑ:mpl] zum Beispiel I speak four languages, *for example* English and French.

1 to **miss** [mɪs] verpassen; versäumen Try not to *miss* the bus! You may *miss* the beginning of the concert.

Yours . . . [jɔ:z] Viele Grüße … *(am Ende von Briefen und Mails)* Please write back soon. *Yours*, Dave
! You can end a letter or e-mail like this.

anywhere ['eniweə]	irgendwo; überall (egal, wo)	Are there any souvenir shops *anywhere*?
understanding [ˌʌndə'stændɪŋ]	Verständnis	What can you say to show *understanding*?
2 weird [wɪəd]	merkwürdig; seltsam; sonderbar	That's *weird*. You say you don't know me, but I think I've seen you before. *weird* = strange

Story: It's a disaster!

disaster [dɪ'zɑːstə]	Desaster; Katastrophe; Unglück	Frank's day was a *disaster*. *Fr.* désastre *(m)*
*to **be on** [biˌ'ɒn]	an sein; laufen	The race *is on*.
thunder *(no pl)* ['θʌndə]	Donner	In a storm there's usually *thunder* and lightning.
lightning *(no pl)* ['laɪtnɪŋ]	Blitz	There was a bad storm with thunder and *lightning*.
*to **get out of** [get ˌaʊtˌəv]	aussteigen; herauskommen aus	He *got out of* the car quickly and ran to the house.
front door [ˌfrʌnt 'dɔː]	Haustür	Every house has a *front door*. Some have back doors too.
PC *(= personal computer)* [piː'siː]	PC	I need to work with the *PC* today.
upstairs [ʌp'steəz]	nach oben; im Obergeschoss; oben	Let's play *upstairs* in my room.
downstairs [ˌdaʊn'steəz]	nach unten; im Untergeschoss; unten	My mobile is ringing. I think it's coming from *downstairs*. *downstairs* ↔ upstairs
*to **take off** [ˌteɪkˌ'ɒf]	abnehmen; herunternehmen; ausziehen	*Take off* your shoes before you jump on the bed!
to **tap** [tæp]	antippen	Jay *tapped* Olivia's shoulder.
to **joke** [dʒəʊk]	scherzen	Don't worry, I'm only *joking*! *to joke* → a joke *Lat.* iocus *(m)*
to **press** [pres]	drücken; pressen	Don't *press* 'send'. The e-mail isn't finished. *Fr.* presser
*to **go black** [ˌgəʊ 'blæk]	schwarz werden	After the bang everything *went black*.
to **crash** [kræʃ]	abstürzen	Has your computer ever *crashed*?
power cut ['paʊə ˌkʌt]	Stromausfall	The city went black because of a *power cut*.
candlelight *(no pl)* ['kændlaɪt]	Kerzenlicht	When there was a power cut, we were sitting together in *candlelight*.
torch [tɔːtʃ]	Fackel; Taschenlampe	It's dark outside. We need *torches*. **!** *torch (BE)* = flashlight *(AE)* *Fr.* torche *(f)*
only ['əʊnli]	einzige/-r/-s	I'm the *only* girl in my tutor group without glasses.
right now [ˌraɪt 'naʊ]	jetzt gleich; sofort; gerade	*Right now* I don't have any problems.
impressed [ɪm'prest]	beeindruckt	The friends were *impressed* with Jay's dancing and singing. *Fr.* impressionner

*to **show off** [ʃəʊˈɒf]	angeben	My brother always *shows off* with his expensive smartphone. *to show off* → a show-off
to **borrow** [ˈbɒrəʊ]	(sich) ausleihen	Can I *borrow* this T-shirt? – OK, but please remember to give it back.
mine [maɪn]	mein/-er/-e/-es	Whose bag is this? – It's *mine*.
nervously [ˈnɜːvəsli]	nervös; aufgeregt	He was laughing *nervously* while he was talking to the girl he liked.
site [saɪt]	Website	This is my favourite guitar music *site*.
to **try hard** [ˌtraɪ ˈhɑːd]	sich anstrengen; sich Mühe geben	I *tried hard* to win the competition.
*to **leave** [liːv]	überlassen	I can't fix my mobile. – *Leave* it to me. I've done this a million times before.
1	*to **feel left out** [ˌfiːl left ˈaʊt]	sich ausgeschlossen fühlen	Did Frank *feel left out*?
2	**pros and cons** [ˌprəʊz ən ˈkɒnz]	Argumente für und gegen etw.	Discuss the *pros and cons* of social networks. *Lat.* pro, contra
	modern [ˈmɒdn]	modern	Smartphones, computers and tablets are *modern* technologies. *Fr.* moderne
	to **link** [lɪŋk]	verbinden	Try to *link* your ideas.

Focus 3 The Celts and the Romans in Britain

Celt [kelt]	Kelte/Keltin	The *Celts* were very brave.
Roman [ˈrəʊmən]	Römer/-in; römisch	London was originally a *Roman* town. *Lat.* Romanus/-a/-um
Celtic [ˈkeltɪk; ˈseltɪk]	keltisch	In this museum we can see lots of *Celtic* things. *Celtic* → a Celt *Fr.* celtique; *Lat.* Celticus
warrior [ˈwɒriə]	Krieger	The Celtic *warriors* were fighting hard.
powerful [ˈpaʊəfl]	stark; mächtig	Who's the most *powerful* person in the world?
to **invade** [ɪnˈveɪd]	einmarschieren (in); eindringen (in); überfallen	The Romans *invaded* the country. *Fr.* envahir, invasion (f); *Lat.* invadere
empire [ˈempaɪə]	Reich; Kaiserreich	the Roman *Empire*, the British *Empire* *Fr.* empire (m); *Lat.* imperium (nt)
army [ˈɑːmi]	Armee	an *army* = a big number of soldiers
battle [ˈbætl]	Schlacht; Kampf	Armies fight in *battles*.
tribe [traɪb]	Stamm; Volksstamm	There were lots of different Celtic *tribes*. *Fr.* tribu (f)
peace [piːs]	Frieden	We just want to live in *peace*.
to **thank** [θæŋk]	danken	She *thanked* her friend for her help.
god [gɒd]	Gott	The Celts believed in many *gods*.

emperor [ˈemprə]	Kaiser	Augustus was the first Roman *emperor*. *Fr.* empereur *(m)*; *Lat.* imperator *(m)*
nose [nəʊz]	Nase	The Celts were scared of the animals with the long *noses*.
to **trade** [treɪd]	Handel treiben	*to trade* = to buy, sell or exchange things
instead [ɪnˈsted]	stattdessen	It's too cold for swimming. Let's go for a walk *instead*.
cruel [ˈkruːəl]	grausam	People are sometimes *cruel* to each other. *Fr.* cruel/-le
*to **burn down** [ˌbɜːn ˈdaʊn]	abbrennen; niederbrennen	The Celts *burned down* the Roman towns.
lost [lɒst]	verloren	The battle was *lost*. *lost* → to lose
prisoner [ˈprɪznə]	Gefangene/-r	After the battle was lost, the warriors became *prisoners*.
1 **BC (= before Christ)** [ˌbiːˈsiː]	vor Christus	The Celts arrived in the British Isles around 500 *BC*.
AD (= Anno Domini) [ˌeɪˈdiː]	nach Christus	The Romans built Hadrian's Wall around 117 *AD*. *AD* ↔ BC
2 **shield** [ʃiːld]	Schild	In the museum we saw a Celtic *shield*.
circle [ˈsɜːkl]	Kreis; Ring	Please sit in a *circle*. *Fr.* cercle *(m)*; *Lat.* circulus *(m)*
Welsh [welʃ]	walisisch; Walisisch; Waliser/-in	*Welsh* people are from Wales. Some of them still speak *Welsh*.
Gaelic [ˈɡeɪlɪk]	gälisch; Gälisch	*Gaelic* is a Celtic language.
fort [fɔːt]	Fort; Festung	They built *forts* to protect the country. *Lat.* fortis
to **protect** [prəˈtekt]	beschützen; schützen	The Celtic warrior tried to *protect* his tribe. *to protect* → a protection *Fr.* protéger; *Lat.* protegere
4 **detective** [dɪˈtektɪv]	Detektiv/-in	I love *detective* stories. A *detective* is sb who tries to find out things.

Unit 6 Goodbye Greenwich

Check-in

medieval [ˌmediˈiːvl]	mittelalterlich	Is every castle *medieval*? – No, of course not. *Fr.* médiéval/-e
living history show [ˌlɪvɪŋ ˈhɪstəri ˌʃəʊ]	*Show, in der historischer Alltag nachgespielt wird*	We went to see a *living history show* with our teacher.
pony trekking [ˈpəʊni ˌtrekɪŋ]	Ponyreiten im Gelände	You go *pony trekking* in the country.
Scottish [ˈskɒtɪʃ]	schottisch	Edinburgh is the *Scottish* capital. *Scottish* → Scotland
3 **at the seaside** [ət ðə ˈsiːsaɪd]	am Meer	*at the seaside* = by the sea

harbour [ˈhɑːbə]	Hafen	The weather is bad, so the boats are staying in the *harbour*. 
*to **grow** [grəʊ]	wachsen	All kinds of flowers *grow* in our garden.

Parts of the British Isles

The British Isles — Scotland, Northern Ireland, Republic of Ireland, Wales, England

Great Britain — Scotland, Wales, England

The United Kingdom — Scotland, Northern Ireland, Wales, England

---

Station 1: Moving to the middle of nowhere

	nowhere [ˈnəʊweə]	nirgendwo; nirgendwohin	Dave doesn't want to move to the middle of *nowhere*. *nowhere* → somewhere → everywhere
	Cornish [ˈkɔːnɪʃ]	aus/in Cornwall; kornisch	Dave and his parents are going to move to a *Cornish* town. *Cornish* → Cornwall
	to **miss** [mɪs]	vermissen	I *miss* you. = Du fehlst mir.
	to **stay** [steɪ]	übernachten	We *stayed* at a really nice hotel.
	(not) any longer [nɒt ˌeni ˈlɒŋgə]	(nicht) mehr; (nicht) länger	I don't like it here; I *don't* want to stay here *any longer*.
	all of us [ˈɔːl əv ˌʌs]	wir alle	*All of us* are excited about the trip to Cornwall.
1	**transport** [ˈtrænspɔːt]	Verkehrsmittel; Transport	*Transport* can be expensive. *Fr.* transport (m); *Lat.* transportare
2	**prediction** [prɪˈdɪkʃn]	Vorhersage; Voraussage	If you say "The weather will be good tomorrow", you are making a *prediction*.
	reaction [riˈækʃn]	Reaktion	I don't understand your *reaction*. *reaction* → to overreact *Fr.* réaction (f)
3	**travel agent's** [ˈtrævl ˌeɪdʒnts]	Reisebüro	You can get travel information at the *travel agent's*.
	journey [ˈdʒɜːni]	Reise; Fahrt	On our *journey* through England we met a lot of nice people.
	to **depend (on)** [dɪˈpend (ɒn)]	abhängen von	The price of the ticket *depends on* the date. *Fr.* dépendre (de)
	to **book** [bʊk]	buchen; reservieren	You can *book* a ticket, a hotel room or a table at a restaurant.
5	**weather forecast** [ˈweðə ˌfɔːkɑːst]	Wettervorhersage	I'd like to watch the *weather forecast* on TV. It tells you what the weather will be like.

Skills: Getting information

1	**tourist board** ['tʊərɪst ˌbɔːd]	Tourismuszentrale; Tourismus-behörde	I'm going to write to the *tourist board* to get information about Cornwall. At a *tourist board* you can get information about a country or region.
	material [məˈtɪəriəl]	Material	I'm looking for *material* for my poster. *Fr.* matériel *(m)*; *Lat.* materia *(f)*
2	***to send off** [ˌsendˈɒf]	abschicken	Before you *send off* your e-mail, read it again.
	form [fɔːm]	Formular	You often have to fill in *forms* on the internet.
	in a polite way [ɪn ə pəˈlaɪt ˌweɪ]	auf höfliche Art	If you want something, ask *in a polite way*.
	yourselves [jɔːˈselvz]	ihr/euch/Sie/sich (selbst); selber	Did you enjoy *yourselves*? – Oh yes, the party was really great.
	Dear Sir or Madam [dɪə ˌsɜːr ɔː ˈmædəm]	Sehr geehrte Dame, sehr geehrter Herr	*Dear Sir or Madam,* You begin a formal letter like this.
	grammar school [ˈɡræmə ˌskuːl]	Gymnasium	Next year my brother will start *grammar school*. A school (in Britain) that is similar to the German 'Gymnasium'. *Fr.* grammaire *(f)*; *Lat.* grammatica *(f)*
	Best wishes [ˌbest ˈwɪʃɪz]	Viele Grüße; Herzliche Grüße	*Best wishes*, Karen Fisher You can finish a formal letter like this.

Station 2: Visit Cornwall – you'll love it!

	coastline [ˈkəʊstlaɪn]	Küste; Küstenverlauf	Cornwall's *coastline* is almost 300 miles long.
	to offer [ˈɒfə]	anbieten	Can I *offer* you something to drink? *Fr.* offrir; *Lat.* offerre
	***to get to know** [ˌɡet tə ˈnəʊ]	kennenlernen	I would like to *get to know* your friends.
	prehistoric [ˌpriːhɪˈstɒrɪk]	vorgeschichtlich; prähistorisch	Tomorrow we are going to visit some *prehistoric* monuments. *prehistoric* → history
	environment [ɪnˈvaɪrnmənt]	Umwelt; Umgebung	We must protect the *environment*. Our *environment* is the world (or area) we live in. *Fr.* environnement *(m)*
	mining [ˈmaɪnɪŋ]	Bergbau	Cornwall has a long *mining* history.
	Bronze Age [ˈbrɒnz ˌeɪdʒ]	Bronzezeit *(ca. 2200–800 v. Chr.)*	This monument is from the *Bronze Age*.
	cross [krɒs]	Kreuz	In Cornwall you can see lots of Celtic *crosses*. *Fr.* croix *(f)*; *Lat.* crux *(f)*
	besides [bɪˈsaɪdz]	neben	Do you speak any languages *besides* German?
	jam [dʒæm]	Marmelade; Konfitüre	I love my toast with butter and *jam*.
7	**geography** [dʒiˈɒɡrəfi]	Geografie; Erdkunde	What do you know about the *geography* of Cornwall? *Fr.* géographie *(f)*; *Lat.* geographia *(f)*

tourism [ˈtʊərɪzm]	Tourismus	*Tourism* is important for our region. *tourism* → tour, tourist

Places and what you can do there

Places		Activities	
in a city/town	in einer Stadt	to visit a museum/castle	ein Museum/Schloss besichtigen
in the fields	auf den Wiesen und Feldern	to go to a festival	ein Festival besuchen
in the forest	im Wald	to get to know the capital of …	die Hauptstadt von … kennen lernen
in the mountains	in den Bergen	to go hiking/climbing/mountain biking/pony trekking	wandern/klettern/Mountainbike fahren/wanderreiten gehen
on an island	auf einer Insel		
at the seaside, by the sea, on the coast	am Meer, an der Küste	to go for a walk	spazieren gehen
		to climb a mountain	einen Berg besteigen
on the beach, on the shore	am Strand, am Meeresufer	to go fishing	angeln gehen
on the river bank, on the shore	am Flussufer	to go swimming/surfing/ windsurfing	schwimmen/surfen/windsurfen gehen
in the sea	im Meer		
in a river	in einem Fluss		
in a lake	in einem See		

9	**possibility** [ˌpɒsəˈbɪləti]	Möglichkeit	*possibility* → possible **Fr.** possibilité (f)
13	**might** [maɪt]	könnte/n (vielleicht)	Maybe he'll play well in the match. He *might* even win it!
	stormy [ˈstɔːmi]	stürmisch	It's *stormy* today. *stormy* → a storm
14	to **supply** [səˈplaɪ]	versorgen	Shops *supply* people with the things they need.
	to **rule** [ruːl]	herrschen; regieren	A king or queen *rules* a country.

Story: Things will get better

*to **come in** [ˌkʌmˈɪn]	hereinkommen	Mrs Preston invites the friends to *come in*.
hall [hɔːl]	Flur; Diele; Korridor	We went through the front door and walked through the *hall*.
electricity [ˌelɪkˈtrɪsəti]	Elektrizität; Strom	If there's no *electricity*, you can't watch TV. **Fr.** électricité (f)
What's the matter? [ˌwɒts ðə ˈmætə]	Was ist los?; Was hast du?	You look sad. *What's the matter* with you?
Oh dear! [əʊ ˈdɪə]	Oje!	I've hurt my leg. – *Oh dear!*
*to **go out** [ˌgəʊˈaʊt]	ausgehen; hinausgehen	Let's *go out!* *to come in* ↔ *to go out*
coastal path [ˌkəʊstl ˈpɑːθ]	Küstenweg	Let's walk along the *coastal path*.

mine [maɪn]	Mine	People don't use this old *mine* anymore. *mine* → mining *Fr.* mine *(f)*
plumber ['plʌmə]	Installateur/-in; Klempner/-in	A *plumber* can fix your water pipes. *Fr.* plombier *(m)*
by [baɪ]	bei; neben; an	We've got a house *by* the sea. *by* = next to
chimney ['tʃɪmni]	Kamin; Schornstein	Our house has got a big *chimney*. *Fr.* cheminée *(f)*; *Lat.* caminus *(m)*
roof [ru:f]	Dach	a *roof* with a chimney
tin [tɪn]	Zinn	There's an old *tin* mine near Dave's house.
geocaching ['dʒi:əʊˌkæʃɪŋ]	Geocaching	*Geocoaching* is a kind of treasure hunting.
excitedly [ɪk'saɪtɪdli]	aufgeregt; begeistert	"We're going to visit Dave in Cornwall," Holly said *excitedly*. *excitedly* → excited, exciting
to **solve** [sɒlv]	lösen	Dave and his friends want to *solve* the puzzle. *Lat.* solvere
deep [di:p]	tief	You mustn't go into *deep* water if you can't swim.
to **boom** [bu:m]	dröhnen	A loud voice *booms*.
skirt [skɜ:t]	Rock	I've bought a new pink *skirt*.
trousers *(pl)* ['traʊzəz]	Hose	Would you like to wear a skirt or *trousers*? **!** *Trousers* steht immer im Plural: You've got cool *trousers*. trousers *(BE)* = pants *(AE)*
spear [spɪə]	Speer	The warrior's *spear* is broken.
local ['ləʊkl]	örtlich; lokal	The schools in your area are your *local* schools. *Fr.* local/-e; *Lat.* locus *(m)*
society [sə'saɪəti]	Verein; Gesellschaft	Bob is a member of a local history *society*. *Fr.* société *(f)*
Nice to meet you. [ˌnaɪs tə 'mi:t ju:]	Nett, dich/Sie/euch kennen zu lernen.	Hello, I'm Tom. – Hi Tom, *nice to meet you*. You can say this when you meet a person for the first time.
wife [waɪf], **wives** [waɪvz] *(pl)*	Ehefrau	Mr and Mrs Preston are husband and *wife*.
twin [twɪn]	Zwilling; Zwillings-	My birthday and my brother's birthday are on the same day. We're *twins*.
tool [tu:l]	Werkzeug; Gerät	A plumber needs special *tools*.
electrician [ˌelɪk'trɪʃn]	Elektriker/-in	An *electrician* can fix the lights in our house. *electrician* → electricity
plumbing ['plʌmɪŋ]	Sanitärarbeit	He's a plumber. He does the *plumbing* for the whole town. *plumbing* → a plumber
electrics [ɪ'lektrɪks]	Elektrik	An electrician can fix the *electrics* in your house. *electrics* → an electrician, electricity

to **turn to** [ˈtɜːn tə]	sich wenden an; sich zuwenden	I *turned to* him but he wasn't there any more.
3 **creative** [kriˈeɪtɪv]	kreativ	In *creative* writing exercises you can use your own ideas. *creative* → to create *Fr.* créatif/créative; *Lat.* creare
diary entry [ˈdaɪəriˌentri]	Tagebucheintrag	Diane writes a *diary entry* each day. A *diary entry* is a personal text in which you write about what happened and what you felt.
sailboat [ˈseɪlbəʊt]	Segelboot	We saw lots of *sailboats* in the harbour. *sailboat* → a boat

Difficult prepositions

at		on		in	
at 6 o'clock	um 6 Uhr	on Sunday	am Sonntag	in April	im April
at night	in der Nacht	on Sundays	sonntags	in 2016	2016
at the weekend	am Wochenende	on 7th July	am 7. Juli	in the afternoon	am Nachmittag
at home	zu Hause	on the right/ left	auf der rechten/ linken Seite	in pairs	paarweise; zu zweit
at school	in der Schule	on the phone	am Telefon	in the photo	auf dem Foto
at work	bei der Arbeit	on the road	auf der Straße	in the street	auf der Straße
at the doctor's	beim Arzt	on holiday	im Urlaub	in the world	auf der Welt
at the Prestons'	bei den Prestons	on the internet	im Internet	in English	auf Englisch
at last	endlich	on time	pünktlich	in the end	am Ende

Across cultures 3 British stories and legends

2 **ingredient** [ɪnˈgriːdiənt]	Zutat	Something is missing in this cake; hm, what *ingredient* did I forget? *Fr.* ingrédient *(m)*
completely [kəmˈpliːtli]	völlig	What you're saying isn't *completely* true! Some of it is wrong. *Fr.* complet/complète
writer [ˈraɪtə]	Autor/-in; Schriftsteller/-in; Verfasser/-in	William Shakespeare was a very famous *writer*. *writer* → to write
magical [ˈmædʒɪkl]	magisch; Zauber-	The world of Harry Potter is a *magical* world. *Fr.* magique; *Lat.* magicus
wizard [ˈwɪzəd]	Zauberer	Harry Potter is a *wizard*.
villain [ˈvɪlən]	Bösewicht	In legends there's often a hero and a *villain*. *villain* ↔ hero *Fr.* vilain/-e

knight [naɪt]	Ritter	The *knights* protected the castle.
criminal [ˈkrɪmɪnəl]	Kriminelle/-r; Verbrecher/-in	The police are looking for *criminals*. *criminal* = villain *Fr.* criminel/-le
power [paʊə]	Kraft; Macht; Stärke	Heroes often have special *powers*. *power* → powerful
private detective [ˌpraɪvət dɪˈtektɪv]	Privatdetektiv/-in	There are lots of books and films about Sherlock Holmes, the famous *private detective*. *Fr.* détective privée *(m/f)*
mysterious [mɪˈstɪəriəs]	mysteriös; geheimnisvoll	The story of the ghost in the castle is *mysterious*.
crime [kraɪm]	Verbrechen; Kriminalität	It's a *crime* to steal something. *crime* → a criminal *Fr.* crime *(m)*; *Lat.* crimen *(nt)*
robber [ˈrɒbə]	Räuber/-in	A *robber* is a criminal.
outlaw [ˈaʊtlɔː]	Geächtete/-r; Gesetzlose/-r	Robin Hood was a famous *outlaw*.
*to **hide** [haɪd]	(sich) verstecken	My sister sometimes *hides* my things. She thinks it's funny.
3 **the Round Table** [ðə ˌraʊnd ˈteɪbl]	die Tafelrunde	King Arthur and his knights met at the *Round Table*.
the rich [ðə rɪtʃ]	die Reichen	Robin Hood stole money from *the rich*.
the poor [ðə pʊə]	die Armen	Robin Hood wanted to help *the poor*. *the poor* ↔ the rich
4 **prop** [prɒp]	Requisite	You need lots of *props* for a film.
crime story [ˈkraɪm ˌstɒri]	Krimi; Kriminalgeschichte	I love reading *crime stories* about private detectives.
set [set]	Umgebung; Rahmen	A film's *set* shows where the people live, work, etc.

Dictionary

In dieser alphabetischen Wortliste findest du das gesamte Vokabular von *Green Line* 1 und 2.
Namen stehen in einer extra Liste am Ende des ***Dictionary***. Einträge, die aus mehreren Wörtern bestehen,
kannst du meist unter verschiedenen Stichwörtern nachschlagen. So ist z. B. *after all* unter *after* und unter *all* eingetragen.
Die Fundstellen stehen immer hinter dem jeweiligen Wort und zeigen dir an, wo es zum ersten Mal vorkommt, z. B.:
accident ['æksɪdnt] Unfall **II U4**, 61 kommt zum ersten Mal vor in Band 2, Unit 4, Seite 61
airport ['eəpɔːt] Flughafen **II F1**, 21 kommt zum ersten Mal vor in Band 2, Focus 1, Seite 21.
U = Unit, AC = Across cultures, F = Focus
Die mit * gekennzeichneten Verben sind unregelmäßig.
Die mit ° gekennzeichneten Vokabeln sind rezeptiv. Sie müssen nicht aktiv beherrscht werden.
Die Vokabeln mit **grünen** Fundstellen sind individueller Wortschatz.
Die Vokabeln, deren Fundstellen in Spitzklammern ⟨ ⟩ stehen, z. B. **aggressive** [ə'gresɪv] aggressiv ⟨**II U1**, 14⟩, gehören
nicht zum Lernwortschatz.

English-German dictionary

A

a [ə] ein/-e I
  a bit [ə 'bɪt] ein bisschen; ein wenig
  II U1, 10
  a couple of [ə 'kʌpl əv] ein paar I
  a few [ə 'fjuː] ein paar; wenige; einige I
  a hundred [ə 'hʌndrəd; wʌn 'hʌndrəd]
  einhundert; hundert I
  a little [ə 'lɪtl] ein wenig; etwas I
  a lot [ə 'lɒt] viel I
  a lot of [ə 'lɒt əv] viel/-e; eine Menge I
  a lot to learn [ə ˌlɒt tə 'lɜːn] viel zu
  lernen I
a.m. ['eɪ'em] vormittags *(Uhrzeit)* I
ability [ə'bɪləti] Fähigkeit; Begabung
  II AC2, 58
*to be **able to** (do sth) [bi ˌeɪbl tə] fähig sein
  zu; können **II U5**, 87
aboard [ə'bɔːd] an Bord I
about [ə'baʊt] ungefähr; circa; etwa I
  out and **about** [ˌaʊt ən ə'baʊt] unterwegs
  ⟨**II U3**, 50⟩
about [ə'baʊt] über; von I
  What **about** …? ['wɒt əbaʊt] Was ist
  mit …?; Wie wär's mit …? I
  What is … **about**? [wɒt ˌɪz ə'baʊt] Worum
  geht es in/im …? I
above [ə'bʌv] oben °**II U4**, 70
accessible [ək'sesəbl] zugänglich °**II U3**, 51
accident ['æksɪdnt] Unfall **II U4**, 61
across [ə'krɒs] auf der anderen Seite von;
  über; hinüber; herüber; quer durch I
  Across cultures [əˌkrɒs 'kʌltʃəz] Interkulturelles I
to **act** [ækt] spielen *(Theater)* I
  to **act** a scene [ˌækt ə 'siːn] eine Theaterszene spielen I
acting ['æktɪŋ] Schauspielen ⟨**II U6**, 107⟩
action ['ækʃn] Handlung; Action; Aktion I
activity [æk'tɪvəti] Aktivität I
  outdoor **activity** [ˌaʊtdɔːr æk'tɪvəti] Freiluftaktivität **II U1**, 11
actor ['æktə] Schauspieler ⟨**II U2**, 30⟩

actually ['æktʃuəli] tatsächlich; wirklich;
  eigentlich **II U1**, 10
AD (= Anno Domini) [eɪ'diː] nach Christus
  II F3, 96
to **add** [æd] hinzufügen; ergänzen I
address [ə'dres] Adresse I
admiral ['ædmɪrəl] Admiral °**II U2**, 34
adult ['ædʌlt] Erwachsene/-r **II F2**, 76
adventure [əd'ventʃə] Abenteuer **II U3**, 42
advice [əd'vaɪs] Rat; Ratschlag **II AC2**, 58
*to be **afraid** (of) [bɪ ə'freɪd əv] (sich)
  fürchten; Angst haben (vor) **II U2**, 35
African-American [ˌæfrɪkənə'merɪkən] Afro-
  amerikaner/-in; afroamerikanisch **II F1**, 20
after ['ɑːftə] nach *(zeitlich)* I
  after all [ˌɑːftər 'ɔːl] doch; schließlich;
  immerhin I
  after that [ˌɑːftə 'ðæt] danach I
after ['ɑːftə] nachdem **II U5**, 85
afternoon [ˌɑːftə'nuːn] Nachmittag I
again [ə'gen] wieder; noch einmal; noch
  mal I
against [ə'genst] gegen **II U3**, 54
age [eɪdʒ] Alter; Zeitalter **II U3**, 44
  Bronze **Age** ['brɒnzˌeɪdʒ] Bronzezeit *(ca.
  2200–800 v. Chr.)* **II U6**, 104
  It took **ages.** [ɪt tʊk 'eɪdʒɪz] Es dauerte
  ewig. **II U3**, 44
travel **agent's** ['trævl ˌeɪdʒnts] Reisebüro
  II U6, 101
aggressive [ə'gresɪv] aggressiv ⟨**II U1**, 14⟩
ago [ə'gəʊ] vor *(zeitlich)* I
long **ago** ['lɒŋ əˌgəʊ] vor langer Zeit
  II AC1, 38
agony aunt ['ægəniˌɑːnt] Kummerkastentante **II U5**, 84
to **agree** (on) [ə'griː] sich einigen (auf)
  °**II U6**, 108
to **agree** (with) [ə'griː] einer Meinung sein
  (mit); zustimmen °**II U5**, 89
hearing **aid** ['hɪərɪŋˌeɪd] Hörgerät **II AC2**, 59
air [eə] Luft **II U1**, 10
airport ['eəpɔːt] Flughafen **II F1**, 21

alga ['ælgə], algae ['ældʒiː] Alge °**II U2**, 35
alien ['eɪliən] Außerirdische/-r; außerirdi-
  sches Wesen I
all [ɔːl] alle/-s; ganz I
  after **all** [ˌɑːftər 'ɔːl] doch; schließlich;
  immerhin I
  all around [ˌɔːl ə'raʊnd] überall; rundherum; rings umher I
  all night [ɔːl 'naɪt] die ganze Nacht I
  all over [ˌɔːl 'əʊvə] überall (in) I
  at **all** [ət 'ɔːl] überhaupt I
  all of us ['ɔːl əvˌʌs] wir alle **II U6**, 100
bowling **alley** ['bəʊlɪŋ ˌæli] Bowlingbahn I
alligator ['ælɪgeɪtə] Alligator I
*to be **allowed** to (do sth) [bi ə'laʊd tə]
  dürfen **II U5**, 87
almost ['ɔːlməʊst] fast; beinahe **II U1**, 12
alone [ə'ləʊn] allein; ohne fremde Hilfe I
along [ə'lɒŋ] entlang **II U3**, 46
aloud [ə'laʊd] laut °**II U3**, 47
alphabet ['ælfəbet] Alphabet I
alphabetical [ˌælfə'betɪkl] alphabetisch
  °**II U1**, 15
already [ɔːl'redi] schon; bereits I
also ['ɔːlsəʊ] auch I
alternative [ɔːl'tɜːnətɪv] Alternative **II F2**, 76
although [ɔːl'ðəʊ] obwohl I
always ['ɔːlweɪz] immer; ständig I
amazing [ə'meɪzɪŋ] unglaublich; toll;
  erstaunlich **II U1**, 17
American [ə'merɪkən] amerikanisch; aus
  Amerika; Amerikaner/-in I
  Native **American** [ˌneɪtɪv ə'merɪkən]
  Ureinwohner/-in Amerikas; Indianer/-in;
  indianisch I
Cuban-**American** ['kjuːbən] Amerikaner/-in
  kubanischer Abstammung **II U2**, 25
an [ən] ein/-e I
and [ænd; ənd] und I
angry ['æŋgri] wütend; zornig; verärgert;
  böse I
animal ['ænɪməl] Tier I

ankle ['æŋkl] Fußgelenk; Fußknöchel
II U4, 64
to twist your **ankle** [ˌtwɪst jɔːr ˈæŋkl] sich
den Knöchel verrenken **II U4**, 64
announcement [əˈnaʊnsmənt] Ankündigung; Durchsage **II F2**, 77
another [əˈnʌðə] ein/-e andere/-r/-s; noch
ein/-e **I**
answer ['ɑːnsə] Antwort **I**
to **answer** ['ɑːnsə] antworten; beantworten **I**
to **answer** the phone [ˈɑːnsə ðə ˈfəʊn]
einen Anruf entgegennehmen **I**
answering machine [ˈɑːnsrɪŋ məˌʃiːn]
Anrufbeantworter **I**
any ['eni] irgendein/-e/-er; irgendwelche **I**
not … **any** [ˌnɒtˌeni] kein/-e/-en **I**
(not) **any** longer [nɒtˌeni ˈlɒŋgə] (nicht)
mehr; (nicht) länger **II U6**, 100
not **any** more [ˌnɒtˌeni ˈmɔː] nicht mehr **I**
anybody ['enibɒdi] jeder (beliebige);
irgendjemand **I**
anyone ['eniwʌn] jeder (beliebige); irgendjemand **I**
anyone else [ˌeniwʌnˈels] jemand anderes **II U3**, 42
anything ['eniθɪŋ] irgendetwas **I**
not … **anything** [ˌnɒtˈeniθɪŋ] nichts **I**
Anything else? [ˌeniθɪŋˈels] Sonst noch
etwas? **I**
anyway ['eniweɪ] jedenfalls; trotzdem;
sowieso **II U4**, 72
anywhere ['eniweə] irgendwo; überall (egal,
wo) **II U5**, 91
*to take apart [ˌteɪkəˈpɑːt] auseinanderneh-
men **II U5**, 87
app [æp] App **II U5**, 89
apple ['æpl] Apfel **I**
April ['eɪprl] April **I**
How are you? [ˌhaʊˈɑː jə] Wie geht es dir?;
Wie geht es euch?; Wie geht es Ihnen? **I**
area ['eəriə] Areal; Gebiet; Fläche **I**
arm [ɑːm] Arm **I**
army ['ɑːmi] Armee **II F3**, 96
around [əˈraʊnd] um … herum; umher **I**
all **around** [ˌɔːləˈraʊnd] überall; rundherum; rings umher **I**
to turn **around** [tɜːnˌəˈraʊnd] (sich)
umdrehen; wenden **II U1**, 17
to **arrive** [əˈraɪv] ankommen **II F2**, 76
Art [ɑːt] Kunstunterricht **I**
art [ɑːt] Kunst **II U1**, 9
article ['ɑːtɪkl] Artikel; Bericht (in einer
Zeitschrift, Zeitung) **II AC2**, 59
as [æz] wie **I**
as … **as** [əz … əz] so … wie **I**
as [æz] während; indem **I**
as soon **as** [əz ˈsuːnˌəz] sobald **II U5**, 84
to **ask** [ɑːsk] fragen; bitten **I**
to **ask** for [ˈɑːsk fə] fragen nach; bitten
um **I**
*to fall **asleep** [ˌfɔːləˈsliːp] einschlafen **I**

assistant [əˈsɪstnt] Assistent/-in; Verkäufer/
-in **II U3**, 49
at [æt; ət] in; auf; bei; an; um (bei Uhrzeitangaben) **I**
at all [ətˈɔːl] überhaupt **I**
at first [ətˈfɜːst] zuerst; zunächst **II U2**, 24
at home [ətˈhəʊm] zu Hause **I**
at last [ətˈlɑːst] endlich; schließlich **I**
at least [ətˈliːst] mindestens; wenigstens **I**
at the back of [ət ðə ˈbækˌəv] hinten; am
Ende; im hinteren Teil **I**
at the moment [ət ðə ˈməʊmənt] im Moment; gerade **I**
at the same time [ət ðə ˌseɪm ˈtaɪm] zur
selben Zeit; gleichzeitig **I**
at the seaside [ət ðə ˈsiːsaɪd] am Meer
II U6, 99
at the weekend [ət ðə ˌwiːkˈend] am
Wochenende **I**
athletics (no pl) [æθˈletɪks] Leichtathletik
II U4, 61
atmosphere ['ætməsfɪə] Atmosphäre;
Stimmung ⟨**II U3**, 50⟩; ⟨**II U5**, 90⟩
to **attack** [əˈtæk] angreifen **II U3**, 55
attention [əˈtenʃn] Aufmerksamkeit; Beachtung **II U5**, 85
attic ['ætɪk] Dachboden ⟨**II U4**, 68⟩
attraction [əˈtrækʃn] Attraktion; Sehenswürdigkeit **II U3**, 51
attractive [əˈtræktɪv] attraktiv **II U2**, 27
audience ['ɔːdiəns] Publikum **II U2**, 31
audio-visual effect [ˌɔːdiəʊˌvɪʒuəl ɪˈfekt]
audiovisueller Effekt ⟨**II U1**, 14⟩; ⟨**II U6**, 107⟩
August ['ɔːgəst] August **I**
aunt [ɑːnt] Tante **I**
agony **aunt** [ˈægəniˌɑːnt] Kummerkastentante **II U5**, 84
autumn ['ɔːtəm] Herbst **I**
award [əˈwɔːd] Auszeichnung; Preis **II U4**, 66
away [əˈweɪ] weg **I**
far **away** [ˌfɑːr əˈweɪ] weit weg **II U1**, 11
right **away** [ˌraɪt əˈweɪ] sofort; gleich **I**
*to run **away** [ˌrʌn əˈweɪ] wegrennen **I**
*to throw **away** [ˌθrəʊ əˈweɪ] wegwerfen **I**
awesome ['ɔːsəm] super; spitze; beeindruckend **I**
awful ['ɔːfl] schrecklich; furchtbar **I**
axe [æks] Axt **II AC1**, 39

B

baby ['beɪbi] Baby; Säugling **I**
back [bæk] Rückseite; Rücken °**II U6**, 108
at the **back** of [ət ðə ˈbækˌəv] hinten; am
Ende; im hinteren Teil **I**
back [bæk] zurück **I**
backache ['bækeɪk] Rückenschmerzen;
Rückenweh **II U4**, 65
background ['bækgraʊnd] Hintergrund **I**
backpacking ['bækpækɪŋ] Wandern; Rucksackreisen **II U3**, 43

backwards ['bækwədz] rückwärts **II U3**, 55
bacon ['beɪkn] Schinkenspeck; Speck **I**
bad [bæd] schlecht; böse; schlimm (ugs.) **I**
bad luck [ˌbæd ˈlʌk] Pech; Unglück **I**
Too **bad**! [ˌtuː ˈbæd] Zu dumm!; Schade! **I**
badger ['bædʒə] Dachs **II U3**, 47
badminton ['bædmɪntən] Badminton **I**
bag [bæg] Tasche; Tüte **I**
mixed **bag** [ˌmɪkst ˈbæg] buntes Allerlei;
bunte Mischung **I**
baked beans (pl) [ˌbeɪkt ˈbiːnz] weiße Bohnen in Tomatensoße **I**
ball [bɔːl] Ball **I**
banana [bəˈnɑːnə] Banane **I**
band [bænd] Band; Musikgruppe **II U2**, 26
Bang! [bæŋ] Peng! **II U5**, 92
river **bank** [ˌrɪvə ˈbæŋk] Flussufer **II U6**, 104
snack **bar** ['snæk ˌbɑː] Café; Imbissstube **I**
barbarian [bɑːˈbeəriən] Barbar °**II F3**, 97
barbecue ['bɑːbɪkjuː] Grill; Grillparty **I**
bargain ['bɑːgɪn] Schnäppchen **I**
to **bark** [bɑːk] bellen **I**
barrel ['bærl] Fass; Tonne **II U1**, 10
baseball ['beɪsbɔːl] Baseball **I**
basic ['beɪsɪk] grundlegend; Grund- **II U2**, 25
basketball ['bɑːskɪtbɔːl] Basketball **I**
bat [bæt] Fledermaus **II F1**, 20; Schläger
(Baseball, Tischtennis) **II U4**, 61
bath [bɑːθ] Bad; Badewanne **I**
bathroom ['bɑːθrʊm] Bad; Badezimmer **I**
battle ['bætl] Schlacht; Kampf **II F3**, 96
BC (= before Christ) [biːˈsiː] vor Christus
II F3, 96
*to **be** [biː] sein **I**
*to **be** able to (do sth) [biˌeɪbl tə] fähig
sein zu; können **II U5**, 87
*to **be** about [biˈbaʊt] gehen um; handeln von **I**
*to **be** afraid (of) [biˈfreɪd əv] (sich)
fürchten; Angst haben (vor) **II U2**, 35
*to **be** allowed to (do sth) [biˈlaʊd tə]
dürfen **II U5**, 87
*to **be** born [biˈbɔːn] geboren werden
II U2, 27
*to **be** called [biˈkɔːld] heißen; genannt
werden **II U2**, 35
*to **be** connected (to/with) [biˈkənektɪd]
zusammenhängen; in Zusammenhang
stehen **II U2**, 31
*to **be** gone [biˈgɒn] verschwunden sein;
weg sein **II U4**, 73
*to **be** good at [biˈgʊd ət] gut sein in **I**
*to **be** in [biˈɪn] dabei sein; mitmachen
II U4, 62
*to **be** in a good mood [biˌɪn ə ˌgʊd ˈmuːd]
guter Laune sein **II U1**, 18
*to **be** in the way [biˈɪn ðə ˈweɪ] im Weg
sein/stehen **I**
*to **be** interested (in) [biˈɪntrəstɪd ɪn]
interessiert sein (an); sich interessieren
(für) **II U1**, 13
*to **be** into [biˈɪntə] mögen; stehen auf **I**

*to **be** jealous (of) [bi 'dʒeləs] eifersüchtig sein (auf); neidisch sein (auf) I

*to **be** late [bi 'leɪt] zu spät dran sein; zu spät kommen I

*to **be** lucky [bi 'lʌki] Glück haben I

*to **be** made up of [bi ˌmeɪd ˈʌp ˌəv] bestehen aus I

*to **be** named after [bi 'neɪmd ˌɑːftə] benannt sein nach I

*to **be** on [bi 'ɒn] an sein; laufen II U5, 92

*to **be** right [bi 'raɪt] recht haben I

*to **be** scared (of) [bi 'skeəd ˌəv] Angst haben (vor) I

*to **be** sorry [bi 'sɒri] leid tun I

*to **be** surprised [bi sə'praɪzd] überrascht sein II U1, 16

*to **be** unlucky [bi ˌʌn'lʌki] Pech haben I

*to **be** up to [bi ˌʌp tə] vorhaben ⟨II U1, 14⟩

*to **be** worth [bi 'wɜːθ] wert sein I

*to **be** wrong [bi 'rɒŋ] unrecht haben; sich irren I

Be careful! [bi: 'keəfl] Vorsicht!; Pass/ Passt auf! I

Be polite. [ˌbi: pə'laɪt] Sei/Seid höflich. I

Here you **are**. [ˌhɪə ju ˈɑː] Bitte schön. I

How **are** you? [ˌhaʊ ˈɑː jə] Wie geht es dir?; Wie geht es euch?; Wie geht es Ihnen? I

How much **is/are** …? [ˌhaʊ 'mʌtʃ ɪz/ɑː] Wie viel (kostet/kosten) …? I

I'm from … [aɪm frɒm] Ich bin aus … I

beach [biːtʃ] Strand I

bean [biːn] Bohne I

baked **beans** (pl) [ˌbeɪkt 'biːnz] weiße Bohnen in Tomatensoße I

bear [beə] Bär II U3, 42

polar **bear** [ˌpəʊlə 'beə] Eisbär I

beautiful ['bjuːtɪfl] schön; hübsch; wunderbar II U2, 9

because [bɪ'kɒz] weil; da I

because of [bɪ'kɒz ˌəv] wegen II F1, 20

*to **become** [bɪ'kʌm] werden I

bed [bed] Bett I

*to go to **bed** [ˌgəʊ tə 'bed] ins Bett gehen I

bedroom ['bedrʊm] Schlafzimmer I

bee [biː] Biene II U1, 17

to **beep** piepsen °II U2, 34

beer [bɪə] Bier °II U6, 108

before [bɪ'fɔː] schon einmal; vorher; zuvor II U4, 63

before [bɪ'fɔː] vor (zeitlich); bevor I

*to **begin** [bɪ'gɪn] beginnen; anfangen II F1, 20

beginning [bɪ'gɪnɪŋ] Anfang; Beginn II U1, 18

behind [bɪ'haɪnd] hinter I

to **believe** [bɪ'liːv] glauben I

I couldn't **believe** my eyes. [aɪ ˌkʊdnt bɪˌliːv maɪ ˌaɪz] Ich traute meinen Augen nicht. II U4, 69

to **belong** (to) [bɪ'lɒŋ (tə)] gehören (zu) II U2, 34

below [bɪ'ləʊ] unterhalb; unten I

bench [benʃ] Bank; Sitzbank II U1, 11

besides [bɪ'saɪdz] neben II U6, 104

best [best] beste/-r/-s; am besten; am liebsten I

Best wishes [ˌbest 'wɪʃɪz] Viele Grüße; Herzliche Grüße II U6, 103

*to **bet** [bet] wetten II U2, 23

better ['betə] besser; lieber I

between [bɪ'twiːn] zwischen I

bicycle ['baɪsɪkl] Fahrrad II U4, 75

bicycle motocross [ˌbaɪsɪkl 'məʊtəʊkrɒs] Fahrradmotocross II U4, 75

big [bɪg] groß I

bighorn sheep ['bɪghɔːn ˌʃiːp] Dickhornschaf II U3, 42

bike [baɪk] Fahrrad I

mountain **biking** ['maʊntɪn ˌbaɪkɪŋ] Mountainbikefahren I

dollar **bill** ['dɒlə ˌbɪl] Dollarnote; Dollarschein I

biology [baɪ'ɒlədʒi] Biologie II U2, 25

bird [bɜːd] Vogel II U1, 10

birthday ['bɜːθdeɪ] Geburtstag I

Happy **Birthday**! [ˌhæpi 'bɜːθdeɪ] Alles Gute zum Geburtstag!; Herzlichen Glückwunsch zum Geburtstag! I

biscuit ['bɪskɪt] Keks I

a **bit** [ə 'bɪt] ein bisschen; ein wenig II U1, 10

*to **bite** [baɪt] beißen; stechen II U3, 48

black [blæk] schwarz I

*to go **black** [ˌgəʊ 'blæk] schwarz werden II U5, 92

blizzard ['blɪzəd] Schneesturm; Blizzard II F1, 20

blob [blɒb] Fleck °II U3, 44

to **block** [blɒk] blockieren; abblocken II U5, 85

blossom ['blɒsəm] Blüte II U2, 22

*to **blow** out [ˌbləʊ ˈaʊt] ausblasen; auspusten I

blue [bluː] blau I

BMX [ˌbiːem'eks] BMX II U4, 60

board [bɔːd] Tafel I

tourist **board** ['tʊərɪst ˌbɔːd] Tourismuszentrale; Tourismusbehörde II U6, 103

to **board** [bɔːd] an Bord gehen; besteigen II F2, 77

boat [bəʊt] Boot I

boating lake ['bəʊtɪŋ ˌleɪk] See zum Rudern I

bonfire ['bɒnfaə] Lagerfeuer; Freudenfeuer I

book [bʊk] Buch I

exercise **book** ['eksəsaɪz ˌbʊk] Übungsheft I

to **book** [bʊk] buchen; reservieren II U6, 101

to **boom** [buːm] dröhnen II U6, 110

boot [buːt] Stiefel II U3, 48

bored [bɔːd] gelangweilt I

boring ['bɔːrɪŋ] langweilig I

*to **be** **born** [bi 'bɔːn] geboren werden II U2, 27

to **borrow** ['bɒrəʊ] (sich) ausleihen II U5, 93

both [bəʊθ] beide II U1, 13

bottle ['bɒtl] Flasche I

bottom ['bɒtəm] Boden; unterer Teil; Grund I

bowl [bəʊl] Schale; Schälchen; Schüssel I

bowling alley ['bəʊlɪŋ ˌæli] Bowlingbahn I

box [bɒks] Box; Kasten; Schachtel; Kiste I

boy [bɔɪ] Junge I

cabin **boy** ['kæbɪn ˌbɔɪ] Schiffsjunge I

bracelet ['breɪslət] Armband I

bracket ['brækɪt] Klammer °II U6, 105

brave [breɪv] mutig; tapfer I

bread [bred] Brot I

breadbasket ['bred ˌbɑːskɪt] Brotkorb II F1, 21

break [breɪk] Pause I

lunch **break** ['lʌnʃbreɪk] Mittagspause I

*to **break** [breɪk] brechen; zerbrechen I

breakfast ['brekfəst] Frühstück I

*to have **breakfast** [ˌhæv 'brekfəst] frühstücken I

breath [breθ] Atem; Atemzug II U3, 46

*to hold your **breath** [ˌhəʊld jə 'breθ] den Atem anhalten II U3, 46

Take a deep **breath**. [ˌteɪk ə ˌdiːp 'breθ] Atme(t) tief ein. ⟨II U2, 30⟩

to **breathe** [briːð] atmen II U4, 72

bridge [brɪdʒ] Brücke II F1, 21

brilliant ['brɪliənt] toll; prima; leuchtend II U1, 16

*to **bring** [brɪŋ] bringen; mitbringen I

British ['brɪtɪʃ] britisch; Brite/Britin I

broken ['brəʊkn] gebrochen; kaputt I

Bronze Age ['brɒnz ˌeɪdʒ] Bronzezeit (ca. 2200–800 v. Chr.) II U6, 104

brother ['brʌðə] Bruder I

brown [braʊn] braun I

*to **build** [bɪld] bauen II U2, 27

building ['bɪldɪŋ] Gebäude I

cyber **bully** [ˌsaɪbə 'bʊli] jemand, der andere in sozialen Netzwerken belästigt/mobbt II U5, 82

*to give the **bumps** [ˌgɪv ðə 'bʌmps] hochleben lassen I

burger ['bɜːgə] Hamburger I

*to **burn** down [ˌbɜːn 'daʊn] abbrennen; niederbrennen II F3, 96

bus [bʌs] Bus I

bus station ['bʌs ˌsteɪʃn] Busbahnhof I

busy ['bɪzi] belebt; beschäftigt I

but [bʌt] aber I

butter ['bʌtə] Butter I

*to **buy** [baɪ] kaufen I

buyer ['baɪə] Käufer/-in I

by [baɪ] bei; neben; an II U6, 110

by (bike) [baɪ] mit (dem Fahrrad) I; von; durch II U5, 87

by the sea [ˌbaɪ ðə 'siː] am Meer II U6, 104

by the way [ˌbaɪ ðə 'weɪ] übrigens II F1, 21

*to go **by** … [ˈgəʊ baɪ] fahren mit … I
Bye! [baɪ] Tschüss! I

C

cabin [ˈkæbɪn] Kabine; Kajüte II U2, 35
　cabin boy [ˈkæbɪn ˌbɔɪ] Schiffsjunge I
　log **cabin** [ˈlɒg ˌkæbɪn] Blockhütte II U3, 43
cache [kæʃ] Cache II U6, 110
cactus [ˈkæktəs], **cacti** (pl) [ˈkæktaɪ] [ˈkæktəs] Kaktus II AC2, 59
café [ˈkæfeɪ] Café I
cafeteria [ˌkæfəˈtɪəriə] Cafeteria I
cajón [kæˈhɒn] Cajón II U2, 24
cake [keɪk] Kuchen; Torte I
call center [ˈkɔːl ˌsentə] Callcenter °II U3, 51
phone **call** [ˈfəʊn ˌkɔːl] Anruf; Telefonanruf I
to **call** [kɔːl] nennen; anrufen; rufen I
　*to be **called** [bi ˈkɔːld] heißen; genannt werden II U2, 35
caller [ˈkɔːlə] Anrufer/-in I
to **calm** down [ˌkɑːm ˈdaʊn] sich beruhigen II U1, 17
calm [kɑːm] ruhig; friedlich II U3, 54
camel racing [ˈkæml ˌreɪsɪŋ] Kamelrennen II U4, 60
camera [ˈkæmrə] Fotoapparat; Kamera II U4, 67
camp [kæmp] Camp; Lager II F1, 21
camper [ˈkæmpə] Camper/-in II U3, 48
campfire [ˈkæmpfaɪə] Lagerfeuer II U3, 43
camping [ˈkæmpɪŋ] Camping; Zelten I
can [kæn] Dose; Büchse I
can [kæn; kən] können; dürfen I
　can't [kɑːnt] kann nicht; können nicht I
　Can you name …? [ˌkæn jʊ ˈneɪm] Kannst du … nennen? I
candle [ˈkændl] Kerze I
candlelight (no pl) [ˈkændlaɪt] Kerzenlicht II U5, 93
candy (AE) [ˈkændi] Süßigkeiten I
cannon [ˈkænən] Kanone °II U2, 34
cannot [ˈkænɒt] kann nicht; können nicht II U5, 87
canoe [kəˈnuː] Kanu II U3, 44
canoeing [kəˈnuːɪŋ] Kanufahren I
canyon [ˈkænjən] Schlucht; Canyon II U3, 46
capital [ˈkæpɪtl] Hauptstadt I
to **capsize** [kæpˈsaɪz] kentern II U3, 52
captain [ˈkæptɪn] Kapitän/-in; Mannschaftsführer/-in I
car [kɑː] Auto I
card [kɑːd] Karte; Spielkarte I
　credit **card** [ˈkredɪt] Kreditkarte II F2, 76
　prompt **card** [ˈprɒmpt kɑːd] Stichwortkarte; Rollenkarte °II U2, 29
to **care** (about) [ˈkeər əˌbaʊt] wichtig nehmen; sich kümmern (um); sich interessieren (für) II U5, 89
Be **careful**! [ˌbi: ˈkeəfl] Vorsicht!; Pass/Passt auf! I

carefully [ˈkeəfli] vorsichtig; sorgfältig II U2, 35
carrot [ˈkærət] Karotte; Möhre I
to **carry** [ˈkæri] tragen II U3, 48
cash [kæʃ] Bargeld II F2, 76
castle [ˈkɑːsl] Schloss; Burg I
cat [kæt] Katze I
*to **catch** [kætʃ] fangen II U4, 60
category [ˈkætəgri] Kategorie; Klasse °II U6, 99
cattle pl only [ˈkætl] Vieh; Rindvieh II F1, 20
to **cause** [kɔːz] verursachen II U4, 74
cave [keɪv] Höhle II F1, 20
to **celebrate** [ˈseləbreɪt] feiern I
cell phone (AE) [ˈsel fəʊn] Mobiltelefon; Handy II U3, 43
degree **Celsius** (°C) [ˌdɪgriː ˈselsiəs] Grad Celsius II F1, 21
Celt [kelt] Kelte/Keltin II F3, 96
Celtic [ˈkeltɪk; ˈseltɪk] keltisch II F3, 96
cent [sent] Cent (Währung) I
call center [ˈkɔːl ˌsentə] Callcenter °II U3, 51
central [ˈsentrl] zentral; Zentral- II F2, 76
centre [ˈsentə] Zentrum; Center I
　community **centre** [kəˈmjuːnəti ˌsentə] Gemeindezentrum I
　leisure **centre** [ˈleʒə ˌsentə] Freizeitzentrum I
　tourist information **centre** [ˌtʊərɪst ˌɪnfəˈmeɪʃn ˌsentə] Touristeninformation I
century [ˈsenʃri] Jahrhundert II F1, 20
cereal (no pl) [ˈsɪəriəl] Frühstückszerealie; Getreideprodukt (z. B. Cornflakes oder Müsli) I
chair [tʃeə] Stuhl; Sessel I
challenge [ˈtʃælɪndʒ] Herausforderung II U3, 43
change [tʃeɪndʒ] Änderung; Veränderung; Wechsel II U4, 71; Umstieg II F2, 76
to **change** [tʃeɪndʒ] wechseln; (sich) ändern; sich verwandeln II AC1, 39; umsteigen II F2, 76
chant [tʃɑːnt] Sprechgesang II U4, 64
character [ˈkærəktə] Charakter; Figur I
charity [ˈtʃærɪti] Wohltätigkeitsverein; wohltätige Zwecke; Wohlfahrt I
　charity shop [ˈtʃærɪti ˌʃɒp] Second-Hand-Laden I
lucky **charm** [ˌlʌki ˈtʃɑːm] Glücksbringer; Talisman I
to **chase** [tʃeɪs] jagen; nachjagen I
video **chat** [ˈvɪdiəʊ ˌtʃæt] Videochat I
to **chat** [tʃæt] plaudern; chatten (sich online unterhalten) I
cheap [tʃiːp] billig; preiswert I
to **check** [tʃek] überprüfen; prüfen; kontrollieren I
Check-in [ˈtʃekɪn] Einchecken I
checklist [ˈtʃeklɪst] Checkliste °II U4, 64
Check-out [ˈtʃekaʊt] Auschecken I
to **cheer** [tʃɪə] anfeuern; jubeln; zujubeln II U4, 64

to **cheer** sb up [tʃɪər ˈʌp] jmdn. aufheitern II AC2, 58
cheese [tʃiːz] Käse I
chicken [ˈtʃɪkɪn] Huhn; Hähnchen I
child [tʃaɪld], **children** (pl) [ˈtʃɪldrən] Kind I
　only **child** [ˈəʊnli ˌtʃaɪld] Einzelkind I
chili [ˈtʃɪli] Chili II U2, 27
chimney [ˈtʃɪmni] Kamin; Schornstein II U6, 110
chips (pl) (BE) [tʃɪps] Pommes frites I
chocolate [ˈtʃɒklət] Schokolade I
choice [tʃɔɪs] Wahl; Auswahl 〈II U3, 50〉
*to **choose** [tʃuːz] auswählen; wählen II U1, 15
Christian [ˈkrɪstʃn] christlich I
chronological [ˌkrɒnəˈlɒdʒɪkl] chronologisch °II U3, 46
church [tʃɜːtʃ] Kirche I
cinema [ˈsɪnəmə] Kino I
circle [ˈsɜːkl] Kreis; Ring II F3, 97
city [ˈsɪti] Stadt; Großstadt I
civil war [ˌsɪvl ˈwɔː] Bürgerkrieg II F1, 20
to **clap** [klæp] klatschen I
　Clap your hands. [ˌklæp jɔː ˈhændz] Klatsche/Klatscht in die Hände. I
class [klɑːs] Klasse; Schulklasse I; Unterricht II U2, 28
classmate [ˈklɑːsmeɪt] Klassenkamerad/-in; Mitschüler/-in I
classroom [ˈklɑːsrʊm] Klassenzimmer I
clause [klɔːz] Satz (Teil eines Satzgefüges) °II U2, 28
　contact **clause** [ˈkɒntækt ˌklɔːz] Relativsatz ohne Relativpronomen °II U2, 28
　if-**clause** [ˈɪf ˌklɔːz] if-Satz °II U6, 104
　main **clause** [ˈmeɪn ˌklɔːz] Hauptsatz °II U6, 104
to **clean** [kliːn] säubern; reinigen I
to **clear** out [ˌklɪər ˈaʊt] ausräumen; entrümpeln I
clear [klɪə] klar; deutlich I
clearly [ˈklɪəli] klar; deutlich II U2, 31
clever [ˈklevə] schlau; klug II U1, 17
click [klɪk] Klicken; Klick II U5, 93
to **climb** [klaɪm] klettern; besteigen; steigen I
climbing [ˈklaɪmɪŋ] Klettern; Bergsteigen II U3, 43
clock [klɒk] Uhr I
　o'**clock** [əˈklɒk] Uhr (Zeitangabe bei vollen Stunden) I
to **close** [kləʊz] schließen; zumachen I
close [kləʊs] eng; knapp I; nahe II U1, 12
　That was **close**! [ˌðæt wəz ˈkləʊs] Das war knapp! I
close-up [ˈkləʊsʌp] Nahaufnahme 〈II U5, 90〉
clothes (pl) [kləʊðz] Kleider; Kleidung I
cloud [klaʊd] Wolke II U2, 34
　word **cloud** [ˈwɜːd ˌklaʊd] Wörterwolke °II U4, 60
cloudy [ˈklaʊdi] bedeckt; bewölkt II F1, 21
clown [klaʊn] Clown II U4, 72

club [klʌb] Klub; Verein; AG I; Schläger (Golf) II U4, 61

Cooking **Club** [ˈkʊkɪŋ ˌklʌb] Koch-AG I

clue [kluː] Hinweis; Spur ⟨II U6, 107⟩

coach [kəʊtʃ] Trainer/-in I; Reisebus II F2, 76

coast [kəʊst] Küste I

coastal path [ˌkəʊstl ˈpɑːθ] Küstenweg II U6, 110

roller **coaster** [ˈrəʊlə ˌkəʊstə] Achterbahn II U2, 23

coastline [ˈkəʊstlaɪn] Küste; Küstenverlauf II U6, 104

coffee [ˈkɒfi] Kaffee I

coin [kɔɪn] Münze I

coke [kəʊk] Cola I

cold [kəʊld] Erkältung II U4, 65

cold [kəʊld] kalt I

to **collect** [kəˈlekt] sammeln I

collocation [ˌkɒləˈkeɪʃn] Wortverbindung °II U5, 82

to **colonize** [ˈkɒlənaɪz] kolonisieren; besiedeln II U2, 27

colour [ˈkʌlə] Farbe I

What **colour** is …? [ˌwɒt ˈkʌlər_ɪz] Welche Farbe hat …? I

colourful [ˈkʌləfl] farbenfroh; bunt I

*to **come** [kʌm] kommen I

*to **come** down [ˌkʌm ˈdaʊn] herunterkommen I

*to **come** in [ˌkʌm_ˈɪn] hereinkommen II U6, 110

Come on! [ˌkʌm_ˈɒn] Komm schon!; Komm jetzt! I

comic [ˈkɒmɪk] Comicheft II U4, 74

comment [ˈkɒment] Kommentar II U5, 82

to **comment** (on) [ˈkɒment(_ɒn)] kommentieren II U5, 89

common [ˈkɒmən] üblich; gewöhnlich; (weit) verbreitet; gebräuchlich II U2, 25

to **communicate** [kəˈmjuːnɪkeɪt] kommunizieren; sich verständigen I

communication [kəˌmjuːnɪˈkeɪʃn] Kommunikation °II U5, 83

community centre [kəˈmjuːnəti ˌsentə] Gemeindezentrum I

company [ˈkʌmpəni] Gesellschaft; Firma; Unternehmen II U4, 75

comparative [kəmˈpærətɪv] Komparativ- °II U2, 25

to **compare** (with/to) [kəmˈpeə] vergleichen (mit) I

comparison [kəmˈpærɪsn] Vergleich °II U2, 25

competition [ˌkɒmpəˈtɪʃn] Wettbewerb; Turnier II U1, 16

to **complete** [kəmˈpliːt] vervollständigen II U1, 13

completely [kəmˈpliːtli] völlig II AC3, 114

compromise [ˈkɒmprəmaɪz] Kompromiss II U5, 85

computer [kəmˈpjuːtə] Computer I

pros and cons [ˌprəʊz_ən ˈkɒnz] Argumente für und gegen etw. II U5, 94

to **concentrate** [ˈkɒnsntreɪt] (sich) konzentrieren II AC2, 59

concert [ˈkɒnsət] Konzert I

conditional sentence [kənˌdɪʃnl ˈsentəns] Bedingungssatz °II U6, 99

confident [ˈkɒnfɪdnt] selbstsicher; selbstbewusst II U1, 16

to **connect** [kəˈnekt] verbinden; anschließen °II U3, 43

*to be **connected** (to/with) [bi kəˈnektɪd] zusammenhängen; in Zusammenhang stehen II U2, 31

connective [kəˈnektɪv] Verbindungswort °II U3, 46

to **conquer** [ˈkɒŋkə] erobern II U2, 29

contact [ˈkɒntækt] Kontakt II U2, 31

contact clause [ˈkɒntækt ˌklɔːz] Relativsatz ohne Relativpronomen °II U2, 28

to **contact** [ˈkɒntækt] sich in Verbindung setzen; kontaktieren °II U3, 51

contest [ˈkɒntest] Wettkampf; Wettbewerb I

context [ˈkɒntekst] Kontext; Zusammenhang II U2, 36

conversation [ˌkɒnvəˈseɪʃn] Konversation; Gespräch; Unterhaltung I

to **convince** [kənˈvɪns] überzeugen °II U2, 32

to **cook** [kʊk] kochen II U2, 28

cooker [ˈkʊkə] Herd I

cookie (AE) [ˈkʊki] Keks I

cooking [ˈkʊkɪŋ] Kochen I

Cooking Club [ˈkʊkɪŋ ˌklʌb] Koch-AG I

*to leave it to **cool** [ˌliːv_ɪt tə ˈkuːl] kalt stellen I

cool [kuːl] cool; super I

to **copy** [ˈkɒpi] abschreiben; kopieren I

coral reef [ˌkɒrəl ˈriːf] Korallenriff °II U2, 35

corn [kɔːn] Korn; Mais; Getreide I

corner [ˈkɔːnə] Ecke II U3, 45

Cornish [ˈkɔːnɪʃ] in Cornwall; kornisch II U6, 100

to **correct** [kəˈrekt] korrigieren; verbessern; berichtigen II U2, 27

correct [kəˈrekt] richtig; korrekt I

*to **cost** [kɒst] kosten I

costume [ˈkɒstjuːm] Kostüm I

cotton [ˈkɒtn] Baumwolle I

cougar [ˈkuːgə] Puma; Berglöwe II U3, 42

cough [kɒf] Husten II U4, 65

could [kʊd] konnte/-n; könnte/-n II U1, 16

to **count** (on) [ˈkaʊnt_ɒn] zählen (auf) I

country, **countries** (pl) [ˈkʌntri] Land I

countryside [ˈkʌntrisaɪd] Land; Landschaft II U3, 54

a **couple** of [ə ˈkʌpl_əv] ein paar I

course [kɔːs] Platz (Golf) II U4, 61

of **course** [əv ˈkɔːs] natürlich; selbstverständlich I

court [kɔːt] Spielfeld II U4, 60

cousin [ˈkʌzn] Cousin/Cousine I

cow [kaʊ] Kuh I

coyote [kəˈjəʊti] Kojote; Präriewolf II U3, 46

cramp [kræmp] Krampf II U4, 66

to **crash** [kræʃ] aufschlagen; gegen etwas krachen II U2, 35; abstürzen II U5, 93

crazy [ˈkreɪzi] verrückt I

*to go **crazy** [ˌgəʊ ˈkreɪzi] ausflippen; durchdrehen; verrückt werden II U5, 87

cream [kriːm] Creme; Sahne I

ice **cream** [ˌaɪs ˈkriːm] Eis; Eiscreme I

to **create** [kriˈeɪt] schaffen; erschaffen; erfinden II U2, 36

creative [kriˈeɪtɪv] kreativ II U6, 112

credit card [ˈkredɪt] Kreditkarte II F2, 76

cricket [ˈkrɪkɪt] Cricket II U4, 61

crime story [ˈkraɪm ˌstɒri] Krimi; Kriminalgeschichte II AC3, 115

crime [kraɪm] Verbrechen; Kriminalität II AC3, 114

criminal [ˈkrɪmɪnəl] Kriminelle/-r; Verbrecher/-in II AC3, 114

crisp (BE) [krɪsp] Kartoffelchip I

cross [krɒs] Kreuz II U6, 104

to **cross** [krɒs] überqueren; kreuzen II F2, 77

*to keep your fingers **crossed** [ˌkiːp jɔː ˌfɪŋgəz ˈkrɒst] die Daumen drücken I

crowd [kraʊd] Menschenmenge II U4, 67

cruel [ˈkruːəl] grausam II F3, 96

to **cry** [kraɪ] weinen; schreien; rufen II AC1, 39

CU (= See you) [ˈsiː juː] Bis dann!; Bis … I

Cuban [ˈkjuːbən] Kubaner/-in; kubanisch II U2, 23

Cuban-American [ˈkjuːbən] Amerikaner/-in kubanischer Abstammung II U2, 25

culture [ˈkʌltʃə] Kultur I

Across **cultures** [əˌkrɒs ˈkʌltʃəz] Interkulturelles I

cupboard [ˈkʌbəd] Küchenschrank; Schrank I

current [ˈkʌrnt] Strömung II U3, 52

curry [ˈkʌri] Curry (Gewürz oder Gericht) I

custard [ˈkʌstəd] Vanillesoße; Vanillepudding I

*to **cut** [kʌt] schneiden; fällen II AC1, 39

cute [kjuːt] niedlich; süß I

cyber bully [ˌsaɪbə ˈbʊli] jemand, der andere in sozialen Netzwerken belästigt/mobbt II U5, 82

cycling [ˈsaɪklɪŋ] Radfahren I

D

dad [dæd] Papa I

to **dance** [dɑːns] tanzen I

dancer [ˈdɑːnsə] Tänzer/-in ⟨II U2, 30⟩

dangerous [ˈdeɪndʒrəs] gefährlich I

dark [dɑːk] dunkel II U2, 35

darkness [ˈdɑːknəs] Dunkelheit ⟨II U6, 107⟩

date [deɪt] Datum I

daughter [ˈdɔːtə] Tochter II U1, 10

day [deɪ] Tag I

one **day** [wʌn ˈdeɪ] eines Tages ⟨II U2, 30⟩

dead [ded] tot II AC1, 38

deaf [def] gehörlos; taub; schwerhörig **II AC2**, 59

Oh **dear**! [əʊ 'dɪə] Oje! **II U6**, 110

Dear … [dɪə] Lieber …; Liebe … *(Anrede in Briefen)* **I**

  Dear Sir or Madam [dɪə ˌsɜːrˌɔː 'mædəm] Sehr geehrte Dame, sehr geehrter Herr **II U6**, 103

December [dɪ'sembə] Dezember **I**

to **decide** [dɪ'saɪd] (sich) entscheiden **I**

decision [dɪ'sɪʒn] Entscheidung °**II U6**, 101

deck [dek] Deck **I**

to **decorate** ['dekəreɪt] dekorieren; verzieren; schmücken **I**

decorations *(pl)* [ˌdekə'reɪʃnz] Dekoration; Schmuck **I**

deep [diːp] tief **II U6**, 110

deer, deer *(pl)* [dɪə] Hirsch **II U3**, 47

degree Celsius (°C) [ˌdɪgriː 'selsɪəs] Grad Celsius **II F1**, 21

degree Fahrenheit (°F) [ˌdɪgriː 'færnhaɪt] Grad Fahrenheit **II F1**, 21

delayed [dɪ'leɪd] verspätet; verzögert **II F2**, 77

to **depart** [dɪ'pɑːt] abfahren; abfliegen **II F2**, 77

to **depend** (on) [dɪ'pend ˌ(ɒn)] abhängen von **II U6**, 101

to **describe** [dɪ'skraɪb] beschreiben **I**

description [dɪ'skrɪpʃn] Beschreibung ⟨**II U3**, 50⟩

desert ['dezət] Wüste **II F1**, 20

to **deserve** [dɪ'zɜːv] verdienen ⟨**II U4**, 68⟩

desk [desk] Schalter **II F2**, 76

detail ['diːteɪl] Detail; Einzelheit °**II U3**, 51

detective [dɪ'tektɪv] Detektiv/-in **II F3**, 97

  private **detective** [ˌpraɪvət dɪ'tektɪv] Privatdetektiv/-in **II AC3**, 114

detector [dɪ'tektə] Detektor; Suchgerät °**II U2**, 34

devil ['devl] Teufel **II AC1**, 38

diagram ['daɪəgræm] Diagramm; Schaubild °**II U3**, 56

dialog *(AE)* ['daɪəlɒg] Dialog; Gespräch **II U1**, 10

dialogue ['daɪəlɒg] Dialog; Gespräch **I**

diary ['daɪəri] Tagebuch **II U6**, 112

  diary entry ['daɪəri entri] Tagebucheintrag **II U6**, 112

dictionary ['dɪkʃnri] Wörterbuch **I**

to **die** [daɪ] sterben **II U2**, 35

difference ['dɪfrəns] Unterschied **I**

different ['dɪfrnt] anders; unterschiedlich; verschieden **I**

difficult ['dɪfɪklt] schwierig **II U3**, 44

*to **dig** [dɪg] graben **II U2**, 34

dinner ['dɪnə] Abendessen **I**

directly [dɪ'rektli] direkt; ohne Umwege **II U3**, 45

dirty ['dɜːti] dreckig; schmutzig **II U1**, 16

disability [ˌdɪsə'bɪləti] Behinderung; Unfähigkeit **II AC2**, 58

disappointed [ˌdɪsə'pɔɪntɪd] enttäuscht **I**

disaster [dɪ'zɑːstə] Desaster; Katastrophe; Unglück **II U5**, 92

to **discover** [dɪ'skʌvə] entdecken **II U4**, 75

to **discuss** [dɪ'skʌs] diskutieren **II U2**, 27

discussion [dɪ'skʌʃn] Diskussion **II U5**, 82

likes and **dislikes** [ˌlaɪks ən ˌdɪslaɪks] Vorlieben und Abneigungen **II U1**, 8

display [dɪ'spleɪ] Vorführung; Ausstellung; Schaukasten; Anzeige **II U3**, 51

*to **do** [duː] machen; tun **I**

  *to **do** our hair [ˌduː aʊə 'heə] uns frisieren; unsere Haare machen **I**

  Don't worry! [ˌdəʊnt 'wʌri] Keine Sorge! **I**

  We **did** it! [ˌwiː 'dɪd ˌɪt] Wir haben es geschafft! **II U4**, 73

doctor ['dɒktə] Arzt/Ärztin **II U4**, 64

dog [dɒg] Hund **I**

  guide **dog** ['gaɪd ˌdɒg] Blindenhund **II AC2**, 58

  hot **dog** [ˌhɒt 'dɒg] Hot Dog *(Würstchen im Brötchen)* **I**

  to walk the **dog** [ˌwɔːk ðə 'dɒg] den Hund ausführen; mit dem Hund spazieren gehen **I**

I'm **dog-tired**. [ˌaɪm ˌdɒg'taɪəd] Ich bin hundemüde. **I**

dollar bill ['dɒlə ˌbɪl] Dollarnote; Dollarschein **I**

door [dɔː] Tür **I**

  front **door** [ˌfrʌnt 'dɔː] Haustür **II U5**, 92

down [daʊn] entlang; herunter; hinunter **I**

  *to come **down** [ˌkʌm 'daʊn] herunterkommen **I**

  *to go **down** [ˌgəʊ 'daʊn] hinuntergehen; nach unten gehen; entlanggehen **II F2**, 77

  to note **down** [ˌnəʊt 'daʊn] notieren; aufschreiben °**II U2**, 31

  to place face **down** [pʊt ˌfeɪs 'daʊn] umgedreht hinlegen °**II U6**, 109

  *to sit **down** [ˌsɪt 'daʊn] sich hinsetzen; sich setzen **I**

  *to write **down** [ˌraɪt 'daʊn] aufschreiben **I**

to **download** [ˌdaʊn'ləʊd] herunterladen *(aus dem Internet)* **II U5**, 89

downstairs [ˌdaʊn'steəz] nach unten; im Untergeschoss; unten **II U5**, 92

drama ['drɑːmə] Theater; Drama **II U1**, 18

dramatic [drə'mætɪk] dramatisch **II U4**, 69

*to **draw** [drɔː] zeichnen **I**; ziehen °**II U6**, 109

drawing ['drɔːɪŋ] Zeichnung **II U1**, 16

dream [driːm] Traum ⟨**II U2**, 30⟩

dress [dres] Kleid **I**

  fancy **dress** [ˌfænsi 'dres] Verkleidung; Kostüm **II U4**, 72

dried [draɪd] getrocknet °**II U2**, 35

drink [drɪŋk] Getränk **I**

*to **drink** [drɪŋk] trinken **I**

drive [draɪv] Fahrt; Anfahrt; Autofahrt **II U2**, 23

drum [drʌmz] Trommel **II U2**, 24

dry [draɪ] trocken **II F1**, 20

during *(+ noun)* ['djʊərɪŋ] während *(+ Nomen)* **II U1**, 9

DVD [ˌdiːviː'diː] DVD **I**

E

e. g. *(= for example)* [ˌiː'dʒiː] z. B. *(= zum Beispiel)* **I**

each [iːtʃ] jede/-r/-s **I**

  each other [ˌiːtʃ ˌʌðə] einander; sich; sich gegenseitig **II U1**, 17

each [iːtʃ] pro Person; pro Stück **I**

eagle ['iːgl] Adler **II U1**, 8

early ['ɜːli] früh **I**

to **earn** [ɜːn] verdienen **I**

earth [ɜːθ] die Erde; Erde; Erdboden **II AC1**, 39

  What on **earth** …? [ˌwɒt ˌɒn 'ɜːθ] Was um alles in der Welt …? **II U5**, 87

east [iːst] Osten; Ost- **I**

easy ['iːzi] einfach; leicht **I**

  *to take it **easy** [ˌteɪk ɪt ˌiːzi] immer ruhig bleiben; auf der faulen Haut liegen **II U2**, 23

*to **eat** [iːt] essen; fressen **I**

audio-visual **effect** [ˌɔːdiəʊvɪʒʊəl ɪ'fekt] audiovisueller Effekt ⟨**II U1**, 14⟩; ⟨**II U6**, 107⟩

egg [eg] Ei **I**

eight [eɪt] acht **I**

eighteen [ˌeɪ'tiːn] achtzehn **I**

eighty ['eɪti] achtzig **I**

not **either** [nɒt … 'aɪðə; nɒt … 'iːðə] auch nicht **I**

electrician [elɪk'trɪʃn] Elektriker/-in **II U6**, 111

electricity [elɪk'trɪsəti] Elektrizität; Strom **II U6**, 110

electrics [ɪ'lektrɪks] Elektrik **II U6**, 111

electronic [elek'trɒnɪk] elektronisch **II U1**, 15

element ['elɪmənt] Element ⟨**II U6**, 107⟩

elephant ['elɪfənt] Elefant **II U3**, 47

eleven [ɪ'levn] elf **I**

else [els] andere/-r/-s; sonst noch **II U3**, 45

Anything **else**? [ˌeniθɪŋ 'els] Sonst noch etwas? **I**

what **else** [ˌwɒt 'els] was sonst; was noch **I**

e-mail ['iːmeɪl] E-Mail **I**

to **e-mail** ['iːmeɪl] mailen; per E-Mail schicken **II U5**, 89

embarrassed [ɪm'bærəst] verlegen **II U1**, 9

embarrassing [ɪm'bærəsɪŋ] peinlich **II U1**, 8

to **emigrate** ['emɪgreɪt] emigrieren; auswandern **II U2**, 29

emperor ['emprə] Kaiser **II F3**, 96

empire ['empaɪə] Reich; Kaiserreich **II F3**, 96

end [end] Ende; Schluss **I**

  in the **end** [ɪn ði 'end] schließlich; zum Schluss **I**

to **end** [end] enden; beenden **II F1**, 20

  to **end** up [ˌend 'ʌp] enden; landen **II U1**, 8

ending ['endɪŋ] Ende; Schluss *(einer Geschichte)* **I**

English [ˈɪŋglɪʃ] englisch; Englisch; aus England; Engländer/-in I
English-speaking [ˈɪŋglɪʃˌspiːkɪŋ] englischsprachig I
I'm **English**. [aɪm ˈɪŋglɪʃ] Ich bin Engländer/-in.
to **enjoy** [ɪnˈdʒɔɪ] genießen; sich freuen an I
enough [ɪˈnʌf] genug; genügend I
to **enter** [ˈentə] hineingehen; betreten; eintreten; *hier:* mitmachen II U1, 16
entry [ˈentri] Eintritt °II U3, 51
diary **entry** [ˈdaɪəri entri] Tagebucheintrag II U6, 112
environment [ɪnˈvaɪrnmənt] Umwelt; Umgebung II U6, 104
equipment [ɪˈkwɪpmənt] Ausrüstung; Ausstattung II U4, 61
er [ɜː] äh I
escalator [ˈeskəleɪtə] Rolltreppe I
etc. (= *et cetera*) [ɪtˈsetrə] usw. (*= und so weiter*) II U2, 37
euro [ˈjʊərəʊ] Euro (*Währung*) I
European [jʊərəˈpiːən] Europäer/-in; europäisch; aus Europa II F1, 21
even [ˈiːvn] sogar; selbst I
evening [ˈiːvnɪŋ] Abend I
in the **evenings** [ɪn ðiˈiːvnɪŋz] abends I
event [ɪˈvent] Ereignis; Veranstaltung I
ever [ˈevə] jemals II U4, 62
every [ˈevri] jede/-r/-s I
everybody [ˈevribɒdi] jeder; alle II U3, 47
everyone [ˈevriwʌn] jeder; alle I
everything [ˈevriθɪŋ] alles I
everywhere [ˈevriweə] überall; überallhin I
exaggerated [ɪgˈzædʒreɪtɪd] übertrieben II AC1, 39
example [ɪgˈzɑːmpl] Beispiel I
for **example** [fər ɪgˈzɑːmpl] zum Beispiel II U5, 91
except [ɪkˈsept] außer; bis auf °II U3, 51
to **exchange** [ɪksˈtʃeɪndʒ] austauschen II U3, 47
excited [ɪkˈsaɪtɪd] aufgeregt; begeistert I
excitedly [ɪkˈsaɪtɪdli] aufgeregt; begeistert II U6, 110
exciting [ɪkˈsaɪtɪŋ] spannend; aufregend I
Excuse me … [ɪkˈskjuːz mi] Entschuldigung!; Entschuldigen Sie! I
exercise [ˈeksəsaɪz] Übung; Aufgabe I
exercise book [ˈeksəsaɪz ˌbʊk] Übungsheft I
to **exist** [ɪgˈzɪst] existieren; bestehen II U2, 27
expensive [ɪkˈspensɪv] teuer I
experience [ɪkˈspɪəriəns] Erfahrung; Erlebnis °II U4, 61
expert [ˈekspɜːt] Experte/Expertin II U4, 71
to **explain** [ɪkˈspleɪn] erklären I
to **explore** [ɪkˈsplɔː] auf Entdeckungsreise gehen; sich umschauen; erkunden; erforschen I

explorer [ɪkˈsplɔːrə] Entdecker/-in; Forscher/-in II U3, 42
express [ɪkˈspres] Eilzug II F2, 76
to **express** [ɪkˈspres] ausdrücken °II U4, 74
extra [ˈekstrə] extra; zusätzlich I
eye [aɪ] Auge II U1, 16
I couldn't believe my **eyes**. [aɪ ˌkʊdnt bɪˌliːv maɪˈaɪz] Ich traute meinen Augen nicht. II U4, 69
eyewitness [ˈaɪwɪtnəs] Augenzeuge/Augenzeugin II U4, 69

F

fable [ˈfeɪbl] Fabel II AC1, 39
face [feɪs] Gesicht I
to place **face** down [pʊt ˌfeɪs ˈdaʊn] umgedreht hinlegen °II U6, 109
face-to-face [ˌfeɪstəˈfeɪs] *hier:* persönlich; von Angesicht zu Angesicht II U5, 85
fact [fækt] Fakt; Tatsache I
degree **Fahrenheit** (°F) [dɪgriː ˈfærnhaɪt] Grad Fahrenheit II F1, 21
fair [feə] Messe; Jahrmarkt I
fair [feə] gerecht; fair I
fairy tale [ˈfeəri ˌteɪl] Märchen II AC1, 39
to **fake** [feɪk] vortäuschen; fälschen ⟨II U4, 68⟩
fall (*AE*) [fɔːl] Herbst II F1, 20
*to **fall** [fɔːl] fallen; hinfallen I
*to **fall** asleep [ˌfɔːl əˈsliːp] einschlafen I
*to **fall** off [ˌfɔːl ˈɒf] herunterfallen; hinunterfallen II U1, 12
*to **fall** over [ˌfɔːl ˈəʊvə] hinfallen; umkippen I
family [ˈfæmli] Familie I
family tree [ˈfæmli ˌtriː] Stammbaum I
famous [ˈfeɪməs] berühmt I
fan [fæn] Fan; Anhänger/-in II F1, 21
fancy dress [ˌfænsi ˈdres] Verkleidung; Kostüm II U4, 72
fantastic [fænˈtæstɪk] fantastisch; großartig II U2, 31
fantasy [ˈfæntəsi] Fantasie; Traum- I
fanzine [ˈfænziːn] Fanzeitschrift II U2, 32
far [fɑː] weit II U4, 73
far away [ˌfɑːr əˈweɪ] weit weg II U1, 11
farm [fɑːm] Farm; Bauernhof I
farmer [ˈfɑːmə] Farmer/-in; Landwirt/-in II F1, 20
farmland [ˈfɑːmlænd] Ackerland II F1, 21
fast [fɑːst] schnell I
father [ˈfɑːðə] Vater I
favourite [ˈfeɪvrɪt] Lieblings- I
My **favourite** … [maɪ ˈfeɪvrɪt] Mein/-e Lieblings… I
What's your **favourite** …? [ˈwɒts jə ˌfeɪvrɪt] Was ist dein/-e Lieblings…? I
fear [fɪə] Angst; Furcht; Befürchtung II U4, 74
feather [ˈfeðə] Feder II AC1, 39
February [ˈfebruri] Februar I

*to **feed** [fiːd] füttern; ernähren ⟨II U6, 107⟩
feedback [ˈfiːdbæk] Feedback; Rückmeldung II U1, 13
*to **feel** [fiːl] fühlen; sich fühlen I; sich anfühlen II U1, 16
*to **feel** left out [ˌfiːl left ˈaʊt] sich ausgeschlossen fühlen II U5, 94
*to **feel** sick [ˌfiːl ˈsɪk] Übelkeit verspüren; sich schlecht fühlen II U4, 65
feeling [ˈfiːlɪŋ] Gefühl II U1, 9
festival [ˈfestɪvl] Festival; Fest I
fever [ˈfiːvə] Fieber II U4, 65
few [fjuː] wenige II U2, 24
a **few** [ə ˈfjuː] ein paar; wenige; einige I
science **fiction** [ˌsaɪəns ˈfɪkʃn] Science-Fiction (*Zukunftsdichtung*) II U3, 52
field [fiːld] Feld; Wiese; Weide; Acker II U1, 8
fifteen [ˌfɪfˈtiːn] fünfzehn I
fifty [ˈfɪfti] fünfzig I
fight [faɪt] Kampf; Streit II U1, 17
*to **fight** [faɪt] kämpfen; (sich) streiten II AC1, 39
to **fill** in [fɪlˈɪn] ausfüllen II U5, 95
filler [ˈfɪlə] Füllwort °II U1, 13
film [fɪlm] Film I
to **film** [fɪlm] filmen; drehen ⟨II U6, 107⟩
filmmaker [ˈfɪlmˌmeɪkə] Filmemacher/-in ⟨II U1, 14⟩
final [ˈfaɪnl] endgültig II U4, 71
finally [ˈfaɪnli] schließlich; endlich; zum Schluss; letztlich II U2, 28
*to **find** [faɪnd] finden; herausfinden I
*to **find** out [ˌfaɪndˈaʊt] herausfinden I
Find the odd one out! [ˌfaɪnd ðiˌɒd wʌˌn ˈaʊt] Finde das Element, das nicht in die Gruppe passt! II U3, 48
fine [faɪn] gut; in Ordnung; schön I
I'm **fine**. [ˌaɪm ˈfaɪn] Mir geht's gut. I
That's **fine** with me. [ðæts ˌfaɪn wɪð ˈmiː] Das ist in Ordnung für mich. II U2, 23
finger [ˈfɪŋgə] Finger I
*to keep your **fingers** crossed [kiːp jɔː ˌfɪŋgəz ˈkrɒst] die Daumen drücken I
finish line [ˈfɪnɪʃ ˌlaɪn] Ziellinie II U4, 73
to **finish** [ˈfɪnɪʃ] beenden; enden; fertigstellen; aufhören II U3, 53
finished [ˈfɪnɪʃt] fertig II U1, 17
fire [faɪə] Feuer; Kamin; Ofen II AC1, 38
to **fire** [faɪə] abfeuern; schießen mit °II U2, 34
fireworks (*pl*) [ˈfaəwɜːks] Feuerwerk I
first [fɜːst] erste/-r/-s; zuerst; als Erstes I
at **first** [ət ˈfɜːst] zuerst; zunächst II U2, 24
first language [ˌfɜːst ˈlæŋgwɪdʒ] Muttersprache I
fish, **fish** (*pl*) [fɪʃ] Fisch I
fishing [ˈfɪʃɪŋ] Angeln; Fischen; Fischerei II U1, 19
*to **fit** [fɪt] passen II U3, 49
fitting room [ˈfɪtɪŋ ˌrʊm] Umkleidekabine II U3, 49

*to get **fit** [ˌget ˈfɪt] in Form kommen; fit werden **I**

five [faɪv] fünf **I**

five-hour [ˈfaɪvaʊə] fünfstündig **II U2**, 23

to **fix** [fɪks] reparieren; befestigen **II U1**, 12

flag [flæg] Flagge; Fahne **I**

flashlight (AE) [ˈflæʃlaɪt] Taschenlampe **II U3**, 54

flat [flæt] Wohnung **I**

flea market [ˈfliː ˌmɑːkɪt] Flohmarkt **I**

fleet [fliːt] Flotte °**II U2**, 34

flight [flaɪt] Flug **II F2**, 77

floor [flɔː] Fußboden **I**

flower [ˈflaʊə] Blume **II U1**, 16

*to **fly** [flaɪ] fliegen **II F1**, 20

flyer [ˈflaɪə] Flyer **I**

foam [fəʊm] Schaum; Gischt **II U2**, 27

to **focus** (on) [ˈfəʊkəs ɒn] sich konzentrieren (auf) °**II U2**, 31

to **fold** [fəʊld] falten; klappen °**II AC2**, 58

folder [ˈfəʊldə] Ordner; Mappe **I**

to **follow** [ˈfɒləʊ] folgen; hinterhergehen; befolgen **II U3**, 43

the **following** [ðə ˈfɒləʊɪŋ] Folgendes; das Folgende °**II U6**, 99

food [fuːd] Essen; Lebensmittel **I**

foot [fʊt], **feet** (pl) [fiːt] Fuß **I**

football [ˈfʊtbɔːl] Fußball **I**

for [fɔː; fə] für **I**

  for God's sake [fə ˈgɒdz ˌseɪk] um Gottes willen **II U4**, 62

  for example [fər ɪgˈzɑːmpl] zum Beispiel **II U5**, 91

weather **forecast** [ˈweðə ˌfɔːkɑːst] Wettervorhersage **II U6**, 102

foreign language [ˌfɒrɪn ˈlæŋgwɪdʒ] Fremdsprache **II U2**, 32

forest [ˈfɒrɪst] Wald **I**

forever [fəˈrevə] für immer; ewig **II U5**, 85

*to **forget** [fəˈget] vergessen **I**

*to **forgive** [fəˈgɪv] vergeben; verzeihen **II U4**, 73

form [fɔːm] Form **I**; Formular **II U6**, 103

to **form** [fɔːm] formen; bilden **II U4**, 71

formal [ˈfɔːml] formal; formell; förmlich °**II U4**, 69

fort [fɔːt] Fort; Festung **II F3**, 97

forty [ˈfɔːti] vierzig **I**

forum [ˈfɔːrəm] Forum **II U5**, 83

to look **forward** to [ˌlʊk ˈfɔːwəd tə] sich freuen auf **II U3**, 43

to **found** [faʊnd] gründen **II U2**, 27

four [fɔː] vier **I**

  Four and six is ten. [ˌfɔːr ənd ˌsɪks ɪz ˈten] Vier plus sechs ist zehn. **I**

fourteen [ˌfɔːˈtiːn] vierzehn **I**

fox [fɒks] Fuchs **II U3**, 47

freeze frame [ˈfriːz ˌfreɪm] Standbild °**II U3**, 56

free [friː] frei; kostenlos **I**

  free time [ˌfriː ˈtaɪm] Freizeit **I**

freedom (no pl) [ˈfriːdəm] Freiheit; Unabhängigkeit **I**

freeze frame [ˈfriːz ˌfreɪm] Standbild °**II U3**, 56

French [frenʃ] französisch; Französisch **II F1**, 21

  the **French** (pl) [ðə ˈfrenʃ] die Franzosen **I**

fresh [freʃ] frisch **I**

Friday [ˈfraɪdeɪ] Freitag **I**

fridge [frɪdʒ] Kühlschrank **I**

friend [frend] Freund/-in **I**

  *to make **friends** [ˌmeɪk ˈfrendz] Freundschaft schließen **I**

  That's what **friends** are for. [ˌðæts wɒt ˈfrendz ˌɑː ˌfɔː] Dafür sind Freunde da. **I**

friendly [ˈfrendli] freundlich; nett **II U2**, 23

fries (pl) (AE) [fraɪz] Pommes frites **I**

from [frɒm; frəm] aus; von **I**

  from … to [frəm … tə] von … bis **I**

  Where … **from**? [ˌweə … ˈfrɒm] Woher …? **I**

front [frʌnt] Vorderseite; Front-; Vorder- °**II U6**, 108

  front door [ˌfrʌnt ˈdɔː] Haustür **II U5**, 92

  in **front** of [ɪn ˈfrʌnt əv] vor **I**

fruit [fruːt] Frucht; Obst **I**

full [fʊl] voll; ganz **I**

full (of) [ˈfʊl əv] voll (von) **I**

fun [fʌn] Freude; Spaß **I**

  *to have **fun** [ˌhæv ˈfʌn] Spaß haben; sich amüsieren **I**

  It's **fun**. [ɪts ˈfʌn] Es macht Spaß. **I**

fun [fʌn] lustig; witzig; fröhlich **I**

funny [ˈfʌni] lustig; witzig **I**

future [ˈfjuːtʃə] Zukunft °**II U6**, 99

G

Gaelic [ˈgeɪlɪk] gälisch; Gälisch **II F3**, 97

gallery [ˈgælri] Kunstgalerie; Galerie °**II U3**, 51

  gallery walk [ˈgælri ˌwɔːk] Museumsrundgang; Vernissage °**II U6**, 109

game [geɪm] Spiel **I**

garage [ˈgærɑːʒ] Garage **I**

garden [ˈgɑːdn] Garten **I**

gate [geɪt] Gate; Flugsteig; Ausgang **II F2**, 77

genius [ˈdʒiːniəs] Genie **II U5**, 87

geocaching [ˈdʒiːəʊˌkæʃɪŋ] Geocaching **II U6**, 110

Geography [dʒiˈɒgrəfi] Geografie; Erdkunde **I**

geography [dʒiˈɒgrəfi] Geografie; Erdkunde **II U6**, 104

German [ˈdʒɜːmən] deutsch; Deutsch; aus Deutschland; Deutsche/-r **I**

*to **get** [get] bekommen; holen; bringen; besorgen; kaufen **I**; werden **II U1**, 12

  *to **get** away with [ˌget əˈweɪ wɪð] davonkommen mit ⟨**II U4**, 68⟩

  *to **get** fit [ˌget ˈfɪt] in Form kommen; fit werden **I**

*to **get** hurt [ˌget ˈhɜːt] verletzt werden **II U4**, 69

*to **get** in the way [ˌget ɪn ðə ˈweɪ] stören; im Weg stehen **II U4**, 72

*to **get** into [ˌget ˈɪntə] einsteigen; hineingelangen **I**

*to **get** lost [ˌget ˈlɒst] verloren gehen; sich verirren ⟨**II U6**, 107⟩

*to **get** on people's nerves [ˌget ɒn ˌpiːplz ˈnɜːvz] jemandem auf die Nerven gehen **I**

*to **get** organised [ˌget ˈɔːgənaɪzd] sich organisieren °**II U6**, 108

*to **get** out of [ˌget ˈaʊt əv] aussteigen; herauskommen aus **II U5**, 92

*to **get** right [ˌget ˈraɪt] richtig beantworten °**II U6**, 109

*to **get** there [ˈget ðeə] hinkommen **I**

*to **get** to [ˌget tə] kommen zu; kommen nach; erreichen **I**

*to **get** to know [ˌget tə ˈnəʊ] kennenlernen **II U6**, 104

*to **get** up [ˌget ˈʌp] aufstehen (aus dem Bett) **I**

*to **get** well [ˌget ˈwel] gesund werden **II U4**, 65

  Time to **get** up! [ˌtaɪm tə ˌget ˈʌp] Es ist Zeit aufzustehen! **I**

ghost [gəʊst] Geist **II AC1**, 38

gig [gɪg] Auftritt; Gig **II U2**, 24

girl [gɜːl] Mädchen **I**

  a **girl** from Germany [ə ˌgɜːl frəm ˈdʒɜːməni] ein Mädchen aus Deutschland **I**

gist [dʒɪst] das Wesentliche °**II U3**, 51

*to **give** [gɪv] geben; schenken **I**

  *to **give** the bumps [ˌgɪv ðə ˈbʌmps] hochleben lassen **I**

glass [glɑːs] Glas **I**

glasses (pl) [ˈglɑːsɪz] Brille **II AC2**, 59

glove [glʌv] Handschuh **I**

to **glue** [gluː] kleben **II U5**, 87

G-ma (infml) [ˈdʒiːmɑː] Oma **II U2**, 22

*to **go** [gəʊ] gehen; fahren **I**

  *to **go** black [ˌgəʊ ˈblæk] schwarz werden **II U5**, 92

  *to **go** by … [ˈgəʊ baɪ] fahren mit … **I**

  *to **go** crazy [ˌgəʊ ˈkreɪzi] ausflippen; durchdrehen; verrückt werden **II U5**, 87

  *to **go** down [ˌgəʊ ˈdaʊn] hinuntergehen; nach unten gehen; entlanggehen **II F2**, 77

  *to **go** for a walk [ˌgəʊ fər ə ˈwɔːk] spazieren gehen **II U3**, 54

  *to **go** on [ˌgəʊ ˈɒn] geschehen **II U3**, 44; weitergehen; weitermachen; weiterführen; fortfahren **II U3**, 54

  *to **go** out [ˌgəʊ ˈaʊt] ausgehen; hinausgehen **II U6**, 110

  *to **go** over to [ˌgəʊ ˈəʊvə tə] hinübergehen zu; zu jmdm. nach Hause gehen **II U5**, 87

  *to **go** shopping [ˌgəʊ ˈʃɒpɪŋ] einkaufen gehen **I**

*to **go** sightseeing [ˌgəʊ 'saɪtsiːɪŋ] eine Besichtigungstour machen II U3, 52

*to **go** swimming [ˌgəʊ 'swɪmɪŋ] schwimmen gehen I

*to **go** to bed [ˌgəʊ tə 'bed] ins Bett gehen I

*to **go** together [ˌgəʊ tə'geðə] zueinander passen; zueinander gehören I

*to **go** with ['gəʊ wɪð] passen zu; gehören zu I

*to **go** wrong [ˌgəʊ 'rɒŋ] schiefgehen I

*to let **go** (of) [ˌlet 'gəʊ (əv)] loslassen II U4, 72

goal [gəʊl] Tor; Ziel I

god [gɒd] Gott II F3, 96
   for **God's** sake [fə 'gɒdz ˌseɪk] um Gottes willen II U4, 62

gold [gəʊld] Gold II U2, 34

golden ['gəʊldn] golden; Gold- II U3, 46

golf [gɒlf] Golf II AC2, 58

*to be **gone** [bi 'gɒn] verschwunden sein; weg sein II U4, 73

good [gʊd] gut I
   *to be **good** at [bi 'gʊd ˌət] gut sein in I
   *to be in a **good** mood [bi ˌɪn ə ˌgʊd 'muːd] guter Laune sein II U1, 18
   Good morning. [gʊd 'mɔːnɪŋ] Guten Morgen. I

goodbye [gʊd'baɪ] auf Wiedersehen I

I **gotta** (coll) [aɪ 'gɒtə] ich muss II U2, 23

government ['gʌvnmənt] Regierung I

to **grab** [græb] greifen; ergreifen; schnappen II U3, 54

grammar school ['græmə ˌskuːl] Gymnasium II U6, 103

grandad ['grændæd] Opa I

grandchild, **grandchildren** (pl) ['grænʃaɪld; 'grænˌʃɪldrn] Enkel/-in; Enkelkind II U2, 34

grandma ['grænmaː] Oma I

grandpa (AE) ['grænpaː] Opa II U2, 22

grandparents (pl) ['grænˌpeərənts] Großeltern I

granny ['græni] Oma I

great [greɪt] großartig; toll; super I
   the **great** outdoors [ðə ˌgreɪtˌaʊt'dɔːz] die freie Natur II U3, 42
   It's **great** for … [ɪts 'greɪt fə] Es ist super zum/für … I
   … is a **great** sport. [ɪzˌə 'greɪt ˌspɔːt] … ist ein toller Sport. I

green [griːn] grün I

Greenwich Mean Time (= GMT) [ˌgrenɪdʒ 'miːn ˌtaɪm] westeuropäische Zeit I

greeting ['griːtɪŋ] Gruß I

grey [greɪ] grau I

grid [grɪd] Gitter; Tabelle; Raster I

to **grin** [grɪn] grinsen II U3, 44

ground [graʊnd] Boden; Erdboden II U3, 48

group [gruːp] Gruppe; Klasse I
   tutor **group** ['tjuːtə ˌgruːp] Klasse (in einer englischen Schule) I

*to **grow** [grəʊ] anbauen; züchten I; wachsen II U6, 99

*to **grow** up [ˌgrəʊ 'ʌp] aufwachsen; erwachsen werden II U1, 11

to **grunt** [grʌnt] grunzen II U3, 54

to **guess** [ges] raten; erraten; vermuten I

guide dog ['gaɪd ˌdɒg] Blindenhund II AC2, 58

guided tour [ˌgaɪdɪd 'tʊə] geführte Tour; Führung °II U3, 51

guinea pig ['gɪniː ˌpɪg] Meerschweinchen I

guitar [gɪ'taː] Gitarre I

guy [gaɪ] Typ; Kerl; (Pl.) Leute I

H

hair [heə] Haar; Haare II U2, 26
   *to do our **hair** [ˌduː ˌaʊə 'heə] uns frisieren; unsere Haare machen I

half [haːf], **halves** (pl) [haːvz] (of) die Hälfte I

half [haːf] halb I
   half past [ˌhaːf 'paːst] halb (bei Uhrzeitangaben) I
   half-sister ['haːfˌsɪstə] Halbschwester I

hall [hɔːl] Flur; Diele; Korridor II U6, 110

ham [hæm] Schinken I

hammer ['hæmə] Hammer II U5, 87

hamster ['hæmstə] Hamster I

hand [hænd] Hand I
   Clap your **hands**. [ˌklæp jɔː 'hændz] Klatsche/Klatscht in die Hände. I
   On the one **hand** …, (but) on the other **hand** … [ɒn ðəˌwʌn ˌhænd … (bʌt) ɒn ðiˌʌðə ˌhænd …] Einerseits …, (aber) andererseits … II U4, 74

handicap ['hændikæp] Behinderung; Einschränkung °II U3, 51

*to **hang** on [ˌhæŋ'ɒn] (einen Augenblick) warten II U3, 44

*to **hang** out (with) (infml) [ˌhæŋ'aʊt wɪð] rumhängen (mit); sich herumtreiben (mit); sich treffen (mit) II U1, 8

to **happen** ['hæpn] geschehen; passieren I

happy ['hæpi] glücklich; froh; fröhlich I
   Happy Birthday! [ˌhæpi 'bɜːθdeɪ] Alles Gute zum Geburtstag!; Herzlichen Glückwunsch zum Geburtstag! I

harbour ['haːbə] Hafen II U6, 99

hard [haːd] hart; schwer; schwierig II U4, 73

to try **hard** [ˌtraɪ 'haːd] sich anstrengen; sich Mühe geben II U5, 93

hare [heə] Hase II U3, 47

hat [hæt] Hut I

to **hate** [heɪt] hassen; nicht mögen II U1, 18

*to **have** [hæv] haben I
   *to **have** a look (at) [ˌhævˌə 'lʊk ət] anschauen II U4, 65
   *to **have** breakfast [ˌhæv 'brekfəst] frühstücken I
   *to **have** fun [ˌhæv 'fʌn] Spaß haben; sich amüsieren I

*to **have** got [hæv 'gɒt] besitzen; haben I

*to **have** to ['hæv tə] müssen II U1, 10

*to **have** (a sweet) [hæv] (ein Bonbon) nehmen; (ein Bonbon) essen I

he [hiː] er I

head [hed] Kopf I
   With a very big **head**! [wɪðˌə ˌveri big 'hed] Und ein Angeber! II U5, 87

headache (no pl) ['hedeɪk] Kopfschmerzen; Kopfweh II U4, 65

heading ['hedɪŋ] Überschrift; Titel I

headphones (pl) ['hedfəʊnz] Kopfhörer II U5, 84

health [helθ] Gesundheit II U4, 60

healthy ['helθi] gesund I

*to **hear** [hɪə] hören I
   I **hear** … [aɪ 'hɪə] Ich habe gehört, dass … I

hearing ['hɪərɪŋ] Hören II U2, 27
   hearing aid ['hɪərɪŋ ˌeɪd] Hörgerät II AC2, 59

heart [haːt] Herz II U4, 72
   *to learn … by **heart** [ˌlɜːn baɪ 'haːt] auswendig lernen I

heaven ['hevn] Himmel II AC1, 38

heavy ['hevi] schwer II U2, 34

helicopter ['helɪkɒptə] Helikopter; Hubschrauber II U4, 69

hell [hel] Hölle II AC1, 38

Hello [hel'əʊ] Hallo. I
   *to say **hello** (to) [ˌseɪ hel'əʊ tə] grüßen; Grüße ausrichten (an) I

helmet ['helmɪt] Helm II U4, 61

help [help] Hilfe I

to **help** [help] helfen I

helpful ['helpfl] hilfsbereit; hilfreich I

helpless ['helpləs] hilflos I

her [hɜː] ihr/-e; sie I

here [hɪə] hier I
   right **here** [ˌraɪt 'hɪə] genau hier II U4, 62
   Here you are. [ˌhɪə juˌaː] Bitte schön. I
   Here's … [hɪəz] Hier ist … I

hero ['hɪərəʊ], **heroes** ['hɪərəʊz] (pl) Held II AC1, 39

heroine ['herəʊɪn] Heldin II AC1, 39

Hey! [heɪ] Hi.; He!; Hallo. I

Hi. [haɪ] Hi.; Hallo. I

*to **hide** [haɪd] (sich) verstecken II AC3, 114

high [haɪ] hoch; groß I
   high school ['haɪ ˌskuːl] High School (weiterführende Schule in den USA, Oberstufe) II U2, 26

highlight ['haɪlaɪt] Highlight; Höhepunkt II U1, 9

hike [haɪk] Wanderung II U3, 46

to **hike** [haɪk] wandern II U3, 42

hiker ['haɪkə] Wanderer/Wanderin II U3, 48

hiking ['haɪkɪŋ] Wandern I

hill [hɪl] Berg; Hügel II U1, 8

him [hɪm] ihn; ihm I

himself [hɪm'self] er/sich (selbst); selber II U1, 16

historical [hɪˈstɒrɪkl] historisch; geschichtlich **I**

history [ˈhɪstri] Geschichte **II F1**, 20
 living **history** show [ˌlɪvɪŋ ˈhɪstəri ˌʃəʊ] Show, in der historischer Alltag nachgespielt wird **II U6**, 98

*to **hit** [hɪt] schlagen; treffen **I**

hobby, hobbies (pl) [ˈhɒbi] Hobby **I**

hockey [ˈhɒki] Hockey **II U4**, 61

*to **hold** [həʊld] halten; festhalten **I**
 *to **hold** your breath [ˌhəʊld jə ˈbreθ] den Atem anhalten **II U3**, 46

hole [həʊl] Loch **II U2**, 35

holiday [ˈhɒlədeɪ] Urlaub; Feiertag **I**
 holidays (pl) [ˈhɒlədeɪz] Ferien **I**

home [həʊm] Zuhause; Heim **I**; Startseite °**II U3**, 51
 at **home** [ət ˈhəʊm] zu Hause **I**
 home town [ˈhəʊmtaʊn] Heimatstadt **II U1**, 8

home [həʊm] nach Hause **I**

homepage [ˈhəʊmpeɪdʒ] Homepage **II U3**, 51

homework [ˈhəʊmwɜːk] Hausaufgabe(n) **I**

honest [ˈɒnɪst] ehrlich **II AC1**, 39

hope [həʊp] Hoffnung **II U4**, 74

to **hope** [həʊp] hoffen **I**

hopeful [ˈhəʊpfl] hoffnungsvoll **I**

horrible [ˈhɒrəbl] schrecklich; furchtbar **II U2**, 35

horrified [ˈhɒrɪfaɪd] entsetzt **I**

horse [hɔːs] Pferd **I**

hospital [ˈhɒspɪtl] Hospital; Krankenhaus **II U4**, 69

youth **hostel** [ˈjuːθ ˌhɒstl] Jugendherberge **II U3**, 52

hot [hɒt] heiß **I**
 hot dog [hɒt ˈdɒg] Hot Dog (Würstchen im Brötchen) **I**
 hot seat [ˌhɒt ˈsiːt] heißer Stuhl °**II AC1**, 39

hotel [həʊˈtel] Hotel **I**

five-**hour** [ˈfaɪvaʊə] fünfstündig **II U2**, 23

hour [aʊə] Stunde **II F1**, 20

hours [ˈaʊəz] Servicezeiten °**II U3**, 51

house [haʊs] Haus **I**
 to move (**house**) [muːv (haʊs)] umziehen **II U1**, 10

how [haʊ] wie **I**
 How are you? [ˌhaʊ ˈɑː jə] Wie geht es dir?; Wie geht es euch?; Wie geht es Ihnen? **I**
 How many …? [ˌhaʊ ˈmeni] Wie viele …? **I**
 How much (is/are) …? [ˌhaʊ ˈmʌtʃ ɪz/ɑː] Wie viel (kostet/kosten) …? **I**
 How old are you? [haʊ ˈəʊld ə juː] Wie alt bist du?; Wie alt sind Sie? **I**
 How to … [ˈhaʊ tə] Wie man … **I**
 this is **how** you do … [ˈðɪs ɪz haʊ jʊ ˌduː] so machst du … **I**

to **hug** [hʌg] umarmen **I**

huge [hjuːdʒ] riesig; riesengroß; gewaltig **II U1**, 8

humid [ˈhjuːmɪd] feucht **II F1**, 20

hungry [ˈhʌŋgri] hungrig **I**

hunter [ˈhʌntə] Jäger/-in **II AC1**, 39

hunting [ˈhʌntɪŋ] Jagen; Jagd **II U2**, 34

hurricane [ˈhʌrɪkən] Hurrikan; Orkan; Wirbelsturm **II F1**, 20

to **hurry** [ˈhʌri] eilen; sich beeilen **I**

*to **hurt** [hɜːt] verletzen; weh tun **I**
 *to **get hurt** [ˌget ˈhɜːt] verletzt werden **II U4**, 69

hurt [hɜːt] verletzt ⟨**II U1**, 14⟩

husband [ˈhʌzbənd] Ehemann **II AC1**, 39

I

I [aɪ] ich **I**
 I couldn't believe my eyes. [aɪ ˌkʊdnt bɪˌliːv maɪ ˈaɪz] Ich traute meinen Augen nicht. **II U4**, 69
 I don't know! [aɪ ˌdəʊnt ˈnəʊ] Ich weiß (es) nicht! **I**
 I don't like … [aɪ ˈdəʊnt laɪk] Ich mag … nicht.; Ich mache … nicht gern. **I**
 I gotta (infml) [aɪ ˈgɒtə] ich muss **II U2**, 23
 I hear … [aɪ ˈhɪə] Ich habe gehört, dass … **I**
 I like … [aɪ ˈlaɪk] Mir gefällt …; Ich mag … **I**
 I like singing and dancing. [aɪ laɪk ˌsɪŋɪŋ ənd ˈdɑːnsɪŋ] Ich singe und tanze gern. **I**
 I love … [aɪ ˈlʌv] Ich liebe …; Ich mag … total gern. **I**
 I mean [miːn] ich meine **II U1**, 13
 I see. [aɪ ˈsiː] Ich verstehe.; Aha!; Ach so! **II U1**, 13
 I'd like to … (= I would like to) [aɪd ˈlaɪk tə] Ich möchte …; Ich würde gern … **I**
 I'm dog-tired. [aɪm ˌdɒgˈtaɪəd] Ich bin hundemüde. **I**
 I'm English. [aɪmˈɪŋglɪʃ] Ich bin Engländer/-in. **I**
 I'm fine. [aɪm ˈfaɪn] Mir geht's gut. **I**
 I'm from … [aɪm frɒm] Ich bin aus … **I**
 I'm (not) scared of … [aɪm (nɒt) ˈskeəd əv] Ich habe (keine) Angst vor … **I**
 I'm sorry! [aɪm ˈsɒri] Tut mir leid! **I**

ice [aɪs] Eis **I**
 ice cream [aɪs ˈkriːm] Eis; Eiscreme **I**
 ice rink [aɪs ˌrɪŋk] Eisbahn; Schlittschuhbahn **I**

idea [aɪˈdɪə] Idee; Einfall **I**

idiot [ˈɪdiət] Idiot/-in **II U1**, 17

if [ɪf] wenn; falls; ob **I**
 if-clause [ˈɪfˌklɔːz] if-Satz °**II U6**, 104

illegal [ɪˈliːgl] illegal; unrechtmäßig; rechtswidrig **II F1**, 20

to **imagine** [ɪˈmædʒɪn] sich (etwas) vorstellen **I**

immigrant [ˈɪmɪgrənt] Immigrant/-in; Einwanderer/Einwanderin **II U2**, 27

to **immigrate** [ˈɪmɪgreɪt] einwandern **II U2**, 27

important [ɪmˈpɔːtnt] wichtig **I**
 most **important** [ˌməʊst ɪmˈpɔːtnt] wichtigste/-r/-s **I**

impressed [ɪmˈprest] beeindruckt **II U5**, 93

to **improve** [ɪmˈpruːv] sich verbessern; verbessern **I**

in [ɪn] in; im; rein; herein **I**
 in a polite way [ɪnˌə pəˈlaɪt ˌweɪ] auf höfliche Art **II U6**, 103
 in front of [ɪn ˈfrʌnt əv] vor **I**
 in secret [ɪn ˈsiːkrət] heimlich **II U4**, 73
 in the end [ˌɪn ðiˈend] schließlich; zum Schluss **I**
 in the evenings [ɪn ðiˈiːvnɪŋz] abends **I**
 in the middle (of) [ɪn ðə ˈmɪdl] in der Mitte (von); mitten in **I**
 in the mornings [ˌɪn ðə ˈmɔːnɪŋz] morgens; vormittags **I**
 in the photo(s) [ˌɪn ðə ˈfəʊtəʊ(z)] auf dem Foto/den Fotos **I**
 in the street [ˌɪn ðə ˈstriːt] in der Straße; auf der Straße **I**

inch [ɪnʃ] Zoll (Längenmaß, ca. 2,54 cm) **II F1**, 21

to **include** [ɪnˈkluːd] einschließen; beinhalten **II U3**, 47

inclusion [ɪnˈkluːʒn] Inklusion; Einbeziehung **II AC2**, 58

inclusive [ɪnˈkluːsɪv] inklusiv; einschließlich; umfassend **II AC2**, 58

independent [ˌɪndɪˈpendənt] unabhängig **I**

Indian [ˈɪndiən] Inder/-in; indisch **I**

individual [ˌɪndɪˈvɪdʒuəl] individuell; einzeln **II U4**, 61

indoors [ˌɪnˈdɔːz] drinnen; im Haus **II U1**, 8

industrial [ɪnˈdʌstriəl] industriell; Industrie- **II F1**, 21

industry [ˈɪndəstri] Industrie; Branche; Gewerbe **II F1**, 21

information (no pl) [ˌɪnfəˈmeɪʃn] Information; Informationen **I**

ingredient [ɪnˈgriːdiənt] Zutat **II AC3**, 114

injury [ˈɪndʒəri] Verletzung **II U4**, 69

inline skating [ˈɪnlaɪn ˌskeɪtɪŋ] Inlineskatefahren **I**

insect [ˈɪnsekt] Insekt **II U3**, 48

inside [ɪnˈsaɪd] innen; im Innern; hinein; nach drinnen; in; drin **I**

instead [ɪnˈsted] stattdessen **II F3**, 96

instead of [ɪnˈsted əv] statt; anstatt; an Stelle von **I**

instruction [ɪnˈstrʌkʃn] Instruktion; Anweisung **I**

instrument [ˈɪnstrəmənt] Instrument **II U2**, 24

intellectual [ˌɪntlˈektjuəl] intellektuell; geistig **II AC2**, 58

interest [ˈɪntrəst] Interesse **II U5**, 83

to **interest** [ˈɪntrəst] (sich) interessieren °**II U2**, 32

*to be **interested** (in) [bɪ'ɪntrəstɪd ɪn] interessiert sein (an); sich interessieren (für) **II U1**, 13
interesting ['ɪntrəstɪŋ] interessant **I**
international [ˌɪntə'næʃnl] international **I**
internet ['ɪntənet] Internet **I**
interview ['ɪntəvjuː] Interview; Befragung **I**
into ['ɪntə] in; in … hinein **I**
*to be **into** [bɪ'ɪntə] mögen; stehen auf **I**
to **introduce** [ˌɪntrə'djuːs] vorstellen; einführen; einleiten **II F1**, 21
introduction [ˌɪntrə'dʌkʃn] Einführung; Einleitung; Vorstellung **II AC1**, 39
to **invade** [ɪn'veɪd] einmarschieren (in); eindringen (in); überfallen **II F3**, 96
to **invent** [ɪn'vent] erfinden **II AC1**, 39
invented [ɪn'ventɪd] erfunden **II AC1**, 39
invitation [ˌɪnvɪ'teɪʃn] Einladung **I**
to **invite** [ɪn'vaɪt] einladen **I**
Irish ['aɪrɪʃ] irisch; Irisch **II AC1**, 38
irregular [ɪ'regjələ] unregelmäßig **II U2**, 25
island ['aɪlənd] Insel **I**
it [ɪt] es **I**
It took ages. [ɪt tʊk 'eɪdʒɪz] Es dauerte ewig. **II U3**, 44
It's fun. [ɪts 'fʌn] Es macht Spaß. **I**
It's great for … [ɪts 'greɪt fə] Es ist super zum/für … **I**
It's your turn. [ɪts 'jɔː tɜːn] Du bist dran. **I**
It's …/They're … [ɪts/ðeə] Es kostet …/ Sie kosten … **I**
its [ɪts] sein/-e; ihr/-e **I**

J

jacket ['dʒækɪt] Jacke **II U3**, 48
jack-o'-lantern [ˌdʒækə'læntən] Kürbislaterne **II AC1**, 38
jam [dʒæm] Marmelade; Konfitüre **II U6**, 104
traffic **jam** ['træfɪk ˌdʒæm] Stau **II U1**, 11
January ['dʒænjuri] Januar **I**
*to be **jealous** (of) [bɪ 'dʒeləs] eifersüchtig sein (auf); neidisch sein (auf) **I**
jeans [dʒiːnz] Jeans **I**
jelly ['dʒeli] Tortenguss; Götterspeise; Wackelpudding; Gelee **I**
jewellery ['dʒuːəlri] Schmuck **I**
job [dʒɒb] Arbeit; Aufgabe; Job **I**
to **join** [dʒɔɪn] beitreten; sich anschließen; verbinden **II U2**, 24
joke [dʒəʊk] Witz **I**
to **joke** [dʒəʊk] scherzen **II U5**, 92
journey ['dʒɜːni] Reise; Fahrt **II U6**, 101
judge [dʒʌdʒ] Juror/-in; Richter/-in **II U1**, 12
juggling ['dʒʌglɪŋ] Jonglieren **II U2**, 32
juice [dʒuːs] Saft **I**
July [dʒʊ'laɪ] Juli **I**
to **jump** [dʒʌmp] springen **I**
to **jump** the queue [ˌdʒʌmp ðə 'kjuː] sich vordrängeln **I**
June [dʒuːn] Juni **I**
junior ['dʒuːnɪə] Junior- °**II U3**, 51

just [dʒʌst] gerade; nur; einfach **I**

K

*to **keep** [kiːp] halten; behalten; aufbewahren **II U2**, 29
*to **keep** away from [ˌkiːp ə'weɪ frəm] (sich) fernhalten von; meiden **II U2**, 29
*to **keep** up [ˌkiːp 'ʌp] aufrechterhalten °**II U1**, 9
*to **keep** up (with) [ˌkiːp 'ʌp (wɪð)] mithalten (mit); Schritt halten (mit) **II U4**, 72
*to **keep** your fingers crossed [ˌkiːp jɔː ˌfɪŋgəz 'krɒst] die Daumen drücken **I**
key word ['kiː ˌwɜːd] Stichwort; Schlüsselbegriff **I**
key [kiː] besonders wichtig **II U3**, 53
to **kick** [kɪk] schießen; treten **II U4**, 60
kid [kɪd] Jugendliche/-r; Kind **II U3**, 43
to **kill** [kɪl] töten; umbringen **II U2**, 23
kilometre (km) ['kɪləˌmiːtə; kɪ'lɒmɪtə] Kilometer **II U3**, 42
kind [kaɪnd] Art; Sorte **I**
king [kɪŋ] König **I**
kitchen ['kɪtʃɪn] Küche **I**
knight [naɪt] Ritter **II AC3**, 114
knob [nɒb] Griff **II U5**, 87
*to **know** [nəʊ] kennen; wissen **I**
*to get to **know** [ˌget tə 'nəʊ] kennenlernen **II U6**, 104
I don't **know**! [aɪ ˌdəʊnt 'nəʊ] Ich weiß (es) nicht! **I**
Korean [kə'riːən] koreanisch; Koreanisch; Koreaner/-in ⟨**II U4**, 68⟩

L

lake [leɪk] See **I**
boating **lake** ['bəʊtɪŋ ˌleɪk] See zum Rudern **I**
lamb [læm] Lamm; Lämmchen **I**
land [lænd] Land **I**
to **land** [lænd] landen **II U2**, 28
landscape ['lænskeɪp] Landschaft **II AC1**, 39
language ['læŋgwɪdʒ] Sprache **I**
first **language** [ˌfɜːst 'læŋgwɪdʒ] Muttersprache **I**
foreign **language** [ˌfɒrɪn 'læŋgwɪdʒ] Fremdsprache **II U2**, 32
official **language** [əˌfɪʃl 'læŋgwɪdʒ] Amtssprache **I**
lantern ['læntən] Laterne **II AC1**, 38
laptop ['læptɒp] Laptop **II U5**, 89
large [lɑːdʒ] groß **II F1**, 20
largest ['lɑːdʒɪst] größte/-r/-s; am größten **II F1**, 20
lassi ['lʌsi] Lassi **I**
last [lɑːst] letzte/-r/-s **I**
at **last** [ət 'lɑːst] endlich; schließlich **I**
late [leɪt] spät; zu spät **I**
*to be **late** [bɪ 'leɪt] zu spät dran sein; zu spät kommen **I**

later ['leɪtə] später **I**
latest ['leɪtɪst] neueste/-r/-s **II U1**, 10
Latin ['lætɪn] lateinamerikanisch **II U2**, 22
to **laugh** [lɑːf] lachen **I**
leader ['liːdə] Führer/-in; Anführer/-in **II AC1**, 39
*to **learn** [lɜːn] lernen **I**
*to **learn** … by heart [ˌlɜːn baɪ 'hɑːt] auswendig lernen **I**
a lot to **learn** [ə ˌlɒt tə 'lɜːn] viel zu lernen **I**
learner ['lɜːnə] Lernende/-r **II AC2**, 59
at **least** [ət 'liːst] mindestens; wenigstens **I**
*to **leave** [liːv] lassen; verlassen; abfahren; losgehen **II U1**, 16; überlassen **II U5**, 93
*to **leave** a message [ˌliːv ə 'mesɪdʒ] eine Nachricht hinterlassen **I**
*to **leave** it to cool [ˌliːv ɪt tə 'kuːl] kalt stellen **I**
on the **left** [ɒn ðə 'left] auf der linken Seite; links **I**
left [left] übrig **I**
leg [leg] Bein **II U2**, 35
legend ['ledʒənd] Legende; Sage **II AC1**, 39
leisure ['leʒə] Freizeit; Freizeit- **I**
leisure centre ['leʒə ˌsentə] Freizeitzentrum **I**
lemon ['lemən] Zitrone ⟨**II U1**, 14⟩
lemonade [ˌlemə'neɪd] Limonade **I**
less [les] weniger **II U2**, 24
lesson ['lesn] Unterrichtsstunde; Schulstunde; Unterricht **I**
*to **let** [let] lassen **I**
*to **let** go (of) [ˌlet 'gəʊ (əv)] loslassen **II U4**, 72
Let's … [lets] Lass/Lasst uns … **I**
letter ['letə] Buchstabe **I**; Brief **II U5**, 83
library ['laɪbri] Bibliothek; Bücherei **II U5**, 87
*to **lie** [laɪ] liegen **II U2**, 35
*to **lie** down [laɪ 'daʊn] sich hinlegen **II U2**, 35
life [laɪf], lives [laɪvz] (pl) Leben **II U1**, 10
lifeboat ['laɪfbəʊt] Rettungsboot **I**
lifebuoy ['laɪfbɔɪ] Rettungsring **I**
lift [lɪft] Lift; Fahrstuhl **II F2**, 76
to **lift** [lɪft] heben; anheben; sich heben **II U3**, 55
light [laɪt] Licht; Lampe **II AC1**, 38
lightning (no pl) ['laɪtnɪŋ] Blitz **II U5**, 92
likes and dislikes [ˌlaɪks ən'dɪslaɪks] Vorlieben und Abneigungen **II U1**, 8
to **like** [laɪk] mögen; gern haben **I**
would **like** [wʊd 'laɪk] würde-/-st/-n/-t gern; hätte-/-st/-n/-t gern **I**
I don't **like** … [aɪ 'dəʊnt laɪk] Ich mag … nicht.; Ich mache … nicht gern. **I**
I **like** … [aɪ 'laɪk] Mir gefällt …; Ich mag … **I**
I'd **like** to … (= I would like to) [aɪd 'laɪk tə] Ich möchte …; Ich würde gern … **I**

Would you **like** …? [ˌwʊd jʊ 'laɪk]
Möchtest du …?; Möchten Sie …?;
Möchtet ihr …? II **U4**, 62
like [laɪk] wie; als ob I
  like that [laɪk 'ðæt] so I
  like this [laɪk 'ðɪs] so I
line [laɪn] Linie; Zeile I
  finish **line** ['fɪnɪʃ ˌlaɪn] Ziellinie II **U4**, 73
  time **line** ['taɪm ˌlaɪn] Zeitstrahl II **U1**, 10
link [lɪŋk] Link; Verbindung II **U3**, 51
to **link** [lɪŋk] verbinden II **U5**, 94
  linking word ['lɪŋkɪŋ ˌwɜːd] Verbindungswort II **U5**, 84
lion [laɪən] Löwe II **U3**, 47
list [lɪst] Liste I
to **listen** (to) ['lɪsn] zuhören; anhören I
  to **listen** for ['lɪsn fə] horchen auf I
listener ['lɪsənə] Zuhörer/-in II **U4**, 69
listening ['lɪsnɪŋ] Hören I
little ['lɪtl] klein I
a **little** [ə 'lɪtl] ein wenig; etwas I
to **live** [lɪv] wohnen; leben I
live [laɪv] live II **U2**, 24
living room ['lɪvɪŋ rʊm] Wohnzimmer I
living history show [ˌlɪvɪŋ 'hɪstəri ˌʃəʊ] *Show,
in der historischer Alltag nachgespielt
wird* II **U6**, 98
local ['ləʊkl] örtlich; lokal II **U6**, 111
location [ləʊ'keɪʃn] Handlungsort; Lage;
  Standort ⟨II **U3**, 50⟩; °II **U3**, 51
locker ['lɒkə] Schließfach; Spind I
loft [lɒft] Dachboden I
log cabin ['lɒg ˌkæbɪn] Blockhütte II **U3**, 43
LOL (= *laughing out loud*) [lɒl] LOL II **U1**, 8
Londoner ['lʌndənə] Londoner/-in I
lonely ['ləʊnli] einsam I
long [lɒŋ] lang I
  long ago ['lɒŋ əˌgəʊ] vor langer Zeit
  II **AC1**, 38
  (not) any **longer** [nɒtˌeni 'lɒŋgə] (nicht)
  mehr; (nicht) länger II **U6**, 100
look [lʊk] Blick I
  *to have a **look** (at) [ˌhævˌə 'lʊk] anschau-
  en II **U4**, 65
  *to take a **look** at [ˌteɪkˌə 'lʊk ˌæt] einen
  Blick werfen auf II **U2**, 31
to **look** [lʊk] schauen; sehen; aussehen I
  to **look** after [lʊkˌ'ɑːftə] aufpassen auf;
  hüten; sich kümmern um I
  to **look** at ['lʊkˌət] anschauen; ansehen I
  to **look** for ['lʊk fɔː] suchen nach I
  to **look** forward to [lʊk 'fɔːwəd tə] sich
  freuen auf II **U3**, 43
  to **look** out for [ˌlʊk 'aʊt fə] Ausschau
  halten nach; sich in Acht nehmen vor;
  aufpassen auf II **U3**, 43
  to **look** up [lʊkˌ'ʌp] nachschlagen; nachschauen II **U1**, 15
*to **lose** [luːz] verlieren II **U4**, 60
lost [lɒst] verloren II **F3**, 96
  *to get **lost** [get 'lɒst] verloren gehen;
  sich verirren ⟨II **U6**, 107⟩

a **lot** [ə 'lɒt] viel I
a **lot** of [ə 'lɒtˌəv] viel/-e; eine Menge I
lots (of) ['lɒtsˌəv] viel/-e; jede Menge I
loud [laʊd] laut I
  *to read out **loud** [ˌriːdˌaʊt 'laʊd] laut
  vorlesen II **AC2**, 59
love [lʌv] Liebe ⟨II **U6**, 107⟩
Love … [lʌv] Liebe Grüße (*am Briefende*);
  Herzliche Grüße (*am Briefende*) I
to **love** [lʌv] lieben; gern mögen I
  would **love** [wʊd 'lʌv] würde-/st/-n/-t sehr
  gern; hätte-/st-/-n/-t sehr gern I
  I **love** … [aɪ 'lʌv] Ich liebe …; Ich
  mag … total gern. I
luck [lʌk] Glück II **U3**, 42
  bad **luck** [bæd 'lʌk] Pech; Unglück I
lucky … ['lʌki] … der/die Glückliche I
  *to be **lucky** [bi 'lʌki] Glück haben I
  lucky charm [ˌlʌki 'tʃɑːm] Glücksbringer;
  Talisman I
luggage (*no pl*) ['lʌgɪdʒ] Gepäck II **F2**, 76
lunch [lʌnʃ] Mittagessen I
  lunch break ['lʌnʃbreɪk] Mittagspause I
lynx [lɪŋks] Luchs II **U3**, 47

M

machine [mə'ʃiːn] Automat; Maschine;
  Apparat; Gerät I
  answering **machine** ['ɑːnsrɪŋ məˌʃiːn]
  Anrufbeantworter I
  washing **machine** ['wɒʃɪŋ məˌʃiːn] Waschmaschine II **U5**, 87
mad [mæd] verrückt; wütend II **U1**, 12
Dear Sir or **Madam** [dɪə ˌsɜːrˌɔː 'mædəm]
  Sehr geehrte Dame, sehr geehrter Herr
  II **U6**, 103
magazine [ˌmægə'ziːn] Zeitschrift I
magic ['mædʒɪk] Magie; Zauberei II **AC1**, 39
magical ['mædʒɪkl] magisch; Zauber-
  II **AC3**, 114
to **mail** ['iːmeɪl] mailen; per E-Mail schicken
  II **U5**, 89
main [meɪn] Haupt- II **U1**, 18
  main clause ['meɪn ˌklɔːz] Hauptsatz
  °II **U6**, 104
*to **make** [meɪk] machen; tun; bilden; *hier:*
  ergeben I
  *to be **made** up of [bi ˌmeɪdˌ'ʌpˌəv]
  bestehen aus I
  *to **make** a wish [ˌmeɪkˌə 'wɪʃ] sich etwas
  wünschen I
  *to **make** friends [ˌmeɪk 'frendz] Freundschaft schließen I
  *to **make** money [ˌmeɪk 'mʌni] Geld
  verdienen I
  *to **make** notes [ˌmeɪk 'nəʊts] Notizen
  machen I
  *to **make** sb do sth [ˌmeɪk sʌmbədi 'duː
  sʌmθɪŋ] jmdn. veranlassen etw. zu tun
  II **U3**, 55

  *to **make** sure [meɪk 'ʃɔː] sich versichern
  II **U3**, 48
  *to **make** trouble [ˌmeɪk 'trʌbl] Ärger
  machen; in Schwierigkeiten bringen I
mall [mɔːl] Einkaufszentrum II **U1**, 8
man [mæn], **men** (*pl*) [men] Mann I
manga ['mæŋgə] Manga (*japanischer
  Comic*) II **U1**, 16
mango ['mæŋgəʊ] Mango I
many ['meni] viele I
map [mæp] Stadtplan; Landkarte I
  mind **map** ['maɪnd mæp] Wörternetz
  (*eine Art Schaubild*) I
maracas [mə'rækəz] Rumba-Rasseln
  II **U2**, 24
marathon ['mærəθn] Marathon II **U4**, 60
March [mɑːtʃ] März I
to **march** [mɑːtʃ] marschieren °II **U6**, 106
to **mark** [mɑːk] markieren; kennzeichnen
  °II **U6**, 109
market ['mɑːkɪt] Markt I
  flea **market** ['fliː ˌmɑːkɪt] Flohmarkt I
marmot ['mɑːmət] Murmeltier II **U3**, 47
marten ['mɑːtɪn] Marder II **U3**, 47
match [mætʃ] Spiel; Match II **U1**, 13
to **match** [mætʃ] zuordnen; passen zu;
  entsprechen I
mate [meɪt] Schiffsoffizier; Maat I
material [mə'tɪəriəl] Material II **U6**, 103
Math (*AE*) (*infml*) [mæθ] Mathematik;
  Mathe II **U1**, 10
Maths (*infml*) [mæθs] Mathematik; Mathe I
What's the **matter**? [ˌwɒts ðə 'mætə] Was ist
  los?; Was hast du? II **U6**, 110
May [meɪ] Mai I
may [meɪ] (vielleicht) können; dürfen
  II **U5**, 87
maybe ['meɪbi] vielleicht I
me [miː] ich; mich; mir I
  Me too. [ˌmiː 'tuː] Ich auch. I
meal [miːl] Mahlzeit; Essen II **U2**, 35
  ready **meal** [ˌredi 'miːl] Fertiggericht I
*to **mean** [miːn] bedeuten I
  I **mean** [miːn] ich meine II **U1**, 13
meaning ['miːnɪŋ] Bedeutung; Sinn II **U1**, 15
media ['miːdiə] Medien II **U5**, 83
mediation [ˌmiːdi'eɪʃn] Sprachmittlung I
medieval [ˌmedi'iːvl] mittelalterlich II **U6**, 98
*to **meet** [miːt] treffen; sich treffen I
to **melt** [melt] schmelzen II **U2**, 27
member ['membə] Mitglied II **U2**, 24
to **mend** [mend] flicken; reparieren II **U5**, 87
to **mention** ['menʃn] erwähnen II **U2**, 27
message ['mesɪdʒ] Botschaft; Nachricht I
  *to leave a **message** [ˌliːvˌə 'mesɪdʒ] eine
  Nachricht hinterlassen I
  *to take a **message** [ˌteɪkˌə 'mesɪdʒ] eine
  Nachricht entgegennehmen; jmdm. etw.
  ausrichten I
  text (**message**) ['tekst ˌmesɪdʒ] SMS;
  Kurznachricht I
metal ['metl] Metall II **U2**, 34

meter (AE) ['mi:tə] Meter II F1, 21

middle ['mɪdl] Mitte I

  in the **middle** (of) [ɪn ðə 'mɪdl] in der Mitte (von); mitten in I

midnight ['mɪdnaɪt] Mitternacht I

might [maɪt] könnte/n (vielleicht) II U6, 106

mile [maɪl] Meile (brit. und amerikan. Längenmaß) I

milk [mɪlk] Milch I

to **milk** [mɪlk] melken ⟨II U6, 107⟩

million ['mɪljən] Million I

  I've done this a **million** times before. [aɪv dʌn ðɪs ə ˌmɪljən taɪmz bɪ'fɔ:] Ich habe das schon eine Million Mal gemacht. II U5, 87

mind map ['maɪnd mæp] Wörternetz (eine Art Schaubild) I

mine [maɪn] Mine II U6, 110

mine [maɪn] mein/-er/-e/-es II U5, 93

mini [mɪni] Mini- II U4, 62

mining ['maɪnɪŋ] Bergbau II U6, 104

minute ['mɪnɪt] Minute I

to **miss** [mɪs] verpassen; versäumen II U5, 91; vermissen II U6, 100

missing ['mɪsɪŋ] fehlend; verschwunden II U2, 25

mistake [mɪ'steɪk] Fehler I

to **mix** [mɪks] mischen; vermengen °II AC2, 1

  mixed bag [ˌmɪkst 'bæg] buntes Allerlei; bunte Mischung I

mobile ['məʊbaɪl] Handy; Mobiltelefon II U5, 83

modal ['məʊdl] Modalverb °II U5, 83

model ['mɒdl] Modell; Tonmodell; Model I

modern ['mɒdn] modern II U5, 94

moment ['məʊmənt] Moment; Augenblick II U1, 16

  at the **moment** [ət ðə 'məʊmənt] im Moment; gerade I

Monday ['mʌndeɪ] Montag I

  on **Mondays** [ɒn 'mʌndeɪz] montags I

money ['mʌni] Geld I

  *to make **money** [ˌmeɪk 'mʌni] Geld verdienen I

  pocket **money** ['pɒkɪt ˌmʌni] Taschengeld I

  to raise **money** [reɪz 'mʌni] Geld sammeln II U4, 62

monster ['mɒnstə] Monster; Ungeheuer I

month [mʌnθ] Monat I

monument ['mɒnjəmənt] Monument; Denkmal I

mood [mu:d] Stimmung; Laune ⟨II U1, 14⟩

  *to be in a good **mood** [bi ɪn ə ˌgʊd 'mu:d] guter Laune sein II U1, 18

moon [mu:n] Mond I

moose, moose (pl) [mu:s] Elch II U3, 42

more [mɔ:] mehr; weitere I

  not any **more** [ˌnɒt eni 'mɔ:] nicht mehr I

  more … than ['mɔ: ðən] mehr … als I

morning ['mɔ:nɪŋ] Morgen; Vormittag I

in the **mornings** [ɪn ðə 'mɔ:nɪŋz] morgens; vormittags I

Good **morning**. [gʊd 'mɔ:nɪŋ] Guten Morgen. I

(the) **most** [ðə 'məʊst] der/die/das meiste; die meisten I

most important [ˌməʊst ɪm'pɔ:tnt] wichtigste/-r/-s I

mother ['mʌðə] Mutter I

bicycle **motocross** [ˌbaɪsɪkl 'məʊtəʊkrɒs] Fahrradmotocross II U4, 75

mountain ['maʊntɪn] Berg I

  mountain biking ['maʊntɪn ˌbaɪkɪŋ] Mountainbikefahren I

  mountain range [ˌmaʊntɪn 'reɪndʒ] Bergkette II U3, 42

mountainboarding ['maʊntɪnˌbɔ:dɪŋ] Mountainboardfahren II U3, 43

mouse [maʊs], **mice** (pl) [maɪs] Maus, Mäuse I

mouth [maʊθ] Mund I

to **move** [mu:v] (sich) bewegen I

  to **move** (house) [mu:v (haʊs)] umziehen II U1, 10

movie ['mu:vi] Film II U1, 10

  movie theater (AE) [ˌmu:vi 'θɪətə] Kino (amerik.) II U1, 10

Mr ['mɪstə] Herr (Anrede) I

Mrs ['mɪsɪz] Frau (Anrede) I

much [mʌtʃ] viel I

much [mʌtʃ] sehr II U3, 54

  very **much** [ˌveri 'mʌtʃ] sehr I

mud [mʌd] Schlamm II U4, 75

multi-ethnic [ˌmʌlti'eθnɪk] Vielvölker-; international ⟨II U3, 50⟩

mum [mʌm] Mama I

museum [mju:'zi:əm] Museum I

music ['mju:zɪk] Musik I

musical ['mju:zɪkl] Musical II U2, 24

musician [mju:'zɪʃn] Musiker/-in II U2, 23

must [mʌst] müssen I

mustn't ['mʌsnt] nicht dürfen I

my [maɪ] mein/-e I

  My favourite … [maɪ 'feɪvrɪt] Mein/-e Lieblings… I

  My name is … [maɪ 'neɪm ɪz] Ich heiße … I

mysterious [mɪ'stɪəriəs] mysteriös; geheimnisvoll II AC3, 114

N

name [neɪm] Name I

  name day ['neɪm ˌdeɪ] Namenstag I

  My **name** is … [maɪ 'neɪm ɪz] Ich heiße … I

  What's your **name**? [ˌwɒts jə 'neɪm] Wie heißt du?; Wie heißen Sie? I

to **name** [neɪm] nennen; benennen I

  *to be **named** after [bi 'neɪmd ˌɑ:ftə] benannt sein nach I

Can you **name** …? [ˌkæn jə 'neɪm] Kannst du … nennen? I

nap [næp] Nickerchen II U2, 35

nasty ['nɑ:sti] garstig; gemein II U5, 82

national ['næʃnl] national; landesweit I

  national park [ˌnæʃnl 'pɑ:k] Nationalpark; Naturpark I

Native American [ˌneɪtɪv ə'merɪkən] Ureinwohner/-in Amerikas; Indianer/-in; indianisch I

near [nɪə] nahe; in der Nähe von I

nearly ['nɪəli] fast; annähernd II U3, 43

necessary ['nesəsri] nötig; notwendig; erforderlich II U4, 71

need [ni:d] Bedürfnis II AC2, 59

to **need** [ni:d] brauchen; benötigen I

  to **need** (to do) [ni:d] (tun) müssen I

  needn't ['ni:dnt] nicht brauchen; nicht müssen I

negative ['negətɪv] negativ; verneint II U1, 12

neighbour (BE) ['neɪbə] Nachbar/-in I

*to get on people's **nerves** [ˌget ɒn pi:plz 'nɜ:vz] jemandem auf die Nerven gehen I

nervous ['nɜ:vəs] nervös; aufgeregt II U1, 9

nervously ['nɜ:vəsli] nervös; aufgeregt II U5, 93

net [net] Netz II U4, 60

netball ['netbɔ:l] Korbball I

social **network** [ˌsəʊʃl 'netwɜ:k] soziales Netzwerk II U5, 82

never ['nevə] nie; niemals I

new [nju:] neu I

news (sg) [nju:z] Nachrichten; Neuigkeiten II U1, 16

next [nekst] nächste/-r/-s; der/die Nächste(n) I

next [nekst] als Nächstes I

  next to ['nekst tə] neben I

nice [naɪs] nett; schön; lieb I

  Nice to meet you. [ˌnaɪs tə 'mi:t ju:] Nett, dich kennen zu lernen.; Nett, Sie kennenzulernen.; Nett, euch kennenzulernen. II U6, 111

nickname ['nɪkneɪm] Spitzname II U2, 22

night [naɪt] Nacht I

  all **night** [ˌɔ:l 'naɪt] die ganze Nacht I

nil [nɪl] null (beim Sport) II U4, 61

nine [naɪn] neun I

nineteen [ˌnaɪn'ti:n] neunzehn I

ninety ['naɪnti] neunzig I

no [nəʊ] kein/-e I

  no one ['nəʊ wʌn] niemand I

no wonder [nəʊ 'wʌndə] kein Wunder II U3, 55

no [nəʊ] nein I

nobody ['nəʊbədi] niemand I

noise [nɔɪz] Lärm; Geräusch II U3, 44

normal ['nɔ:ml] normal I

north [nɔ:θ] Norden; Nord- I

north [nɔ:θ] nördlich; im Norden I

nose [nəʊz] Nase II F3, 96

not [nɒt] nicht I

not any more [ˌnɒt ˌeni 'mɔː] nicht mehr **I**
not either [nɒt … 'aɪðə; nɒt … 'iːðə] auch nicht **I**
not … any [nɒt ˌeni] kein/-e/-en **I**
not … anything [ˌnɒt ˌeniθɪŋ] nichts **I**
not … until [nɒt ˌənˈtɪl] nicht bevor; erst wenn **II U2, 27**
not … yet [nɒt ˈjet] noch nicht **II U4, 64**
note [nəʊt] Notiz; Anmerkung **I**
*to make **notes** [ˌmeɪk ˈnəʊts] Notizen machen **I**
*to take **notes** [teɪk ˈnəʊts] sich Notizen machen **I**
to **note** [nəʊt] notieren °**II U3, 46**
to **note** down [ˌnəʊt ˈdaʊn] notieren; aufschreiben °**II U2, 31**
nothing [ˈnʌθɪŋ] nichts **I**
There's **nothing** more exciting than … [ðeəz ˌnʌθɪŋ mɔːrˌɪkˈsaɪtɪŋ ðən] Es gibt nichts Spannenderes als … **II U1, 10**
to **notice** [ˈnəʊtɪs] bemerken; wahrnehmen **II U1, 16**
November [nəˈvembə] November **I**
now [naʊ] jetzt; nun **I**
right **now** [ˌraɪt ˈnaʊ] jetzt gleich; sofort; gerade **II U5, 93**
nowhere [ˈnəʊweə] nirgendwo; nirgendwohin **II U6, 100**
number [ˈnʌmbə] Zahl; Nummer **I**
nut [nʌt] Nuss **I**

O

o'clock [əˈklɒk] Uhr *(Zeitangabe bei vollen Stunden)* **I**
object [ˈɒbdʒɪkt] Gegenstand **II U2, 34**
ocean [ˈəʊʃn] Ozean **II U2, 26**
October [ɒkˈtəʊbə] Oktober **I**
Find the **odd** one out! [ˌfaɪnd ðiˌɒd wʌˌnˌ 'aʊt] Finde das Element, das nicht in die Gruppe passt! **II U3, 48**
of [ɒv; əv] von **I**
of course [əv ˈkɔːs] natürlich; selbstverständlich **I**
off to [ˈɒf tə] auf nach **II U3, 42**
*to show **off** [ˌʃəʊ ˈɒf] angeben **II U5, 93**
*to take **off** [teɪk ˈɒf] abheben **II U3, 49**
*to take **off** [teɪk ˈɒf] abnehmen; herunternehmen; ausziehen **II U5, 92**
to turn **off** [tɜːn ˈɒf] abschalten; ausschalten **II U5, 87**
special **offer** [ˌspeʃl ˈɒfə] Sonderangebot **I**
to **offer** [ˈɒfə] anbieten **II U6, 104**
office [ˈɒfɪs] Büro **I**
police **officer** [pəˈliːsˌ ˌɒfɪsə] Polizeibeamter; Polizist/-in ⟨**II U2, 30**⟩
official [əˈfɪʃl] Schiedsrichter/-in **II U4, 73**
official language [əˌfɪʃl ˈlæŋgwɪdʒ] Amtssprache **I**
offline [ˈɒflaɪn] offline **II U5, 89**
often [ˈɒfn] oft; häufig **I**

oh [əʊ] null *(bei Telefonnummern und Uhrzeitangaben)* **I**
Oh! [əʊ] O! **I**
Oh dear! [ˌəʊ ˈdɪə] Oje! **II U6, 110**
oil [ɔɪl] Öl **I**
ointment [ˈɔɪntmənt] Salbe **II U4, 65**
OK [əʊˈkeɪ] o.k.; in Ordnung **I**
old [əʊld] alt **I**
11-year-**old** [ɪˈlevnˌjɪərəʊld] 11-Jährige/-r **II U4, 62**
How **old** are you? [haʊ ˌəʊld ə ˌjuː] Wie alt bist du?; Wie alt sind Sie? **I**
on [ɒn] auf; an; am; in; im **I**
*to be **on** [biˌ ˈɒn] an sein; laufen **II U5, 92**
on Mondays [ɒn ˈmʌndeɪz] montags **I**
on stage [ɒn ˈsteɪdʒ] auf der Bühne **II U2, 24**
on the left [ɒn ðə ˈleft] auf der linken Seite; links **I**
on the right [ɒn ðə ˈraɪt] auf der rechten Seite; rechts **I**
on time [ɒn ˈtaɪm] pünktlich **II U2, 31**
on top [ɒn ˈtɒp] oben; obendrauf **I**
on your own [ɒn jərˌ ˈəʊn] allein; für dich **I**
*to put **on** [pʊtˌ ˈɒn] anziehen; auftragen **II AC1, 38**
Come **on**! [ˌkʌm ˌ ˈɒn] Komm schon!; Komm jetzt! **I**
once [wʌns] einmal; einst **II F1, 21**
one [wʌn] eins **I**
one day [wʌn ˈdeɪ] eines Tages ⟨**II U2, 30**⟩
one hundred [ə ˈhʌndrəd; wʌn ˈhʌndrəd] einhundert; hundert **I**
one way [ˈwʌn weɪ] einfach *(Fahrschein)* **II F2, 76**
twenty-**one** [ˌtwentiˈwʌn] einundzwanzig **I**
one [wʌn], ones [wʌnz] *(pl)* [wʌn] eine/-r/-s **I**
online [ɒnˈlaɪn] online **II U1, 15**
only [ˈəʊnli] einzige/-r/-s **II U5, 93**
only child [ˈəʊnli ˌtʃaɪld] Einzelkind **I**
only [ˈəʊnli] erst; bloß; nur **I**
onto [ˈɒntə] auf **II U3, 44**
Oops! [uːps] Hoppla!; Huch! **I**
to **open** [ˈəʊpn] öffnen; aufmachen **I**
open [ˈəʊpn] offen; geöffnet; aufgeschlagen **I**
opinion [əˈpɪnjən] Meinung **II U5, 84**
opposite [ˈɒpəzɪt] Gegenteil **II U3, 48**
opposite [ˈɒpəzɪt] gegenüber; gegenüberliegend; entgegengesetzt **II F2, 77**
or [ɔː] oder **I**
orange [ˈɒrɪndʒ] Orange **I**
orange [ˈɒrɪndʒ] orange **I**
order [ˈɔːdə] Reihenfolge; Ordnung **I**
organisation [ˌɔːgənaɪˈzeɪʃn] Organisation **II AC2, 59**
to **organise** [ˈɔːgənaɪz] organisieren **I**
*to get **organised** [get ˈɔːgənaɪzd] sich organisieren °**II U6, 108**
to **organize** *(AE)* [ˈɔːgənaɪz] organisieren **II U1, 10**

origin [ˈɒrɪdʒɪn] Ursprung; Herkunft; Abstammung **II U2, 25**
other [ˈʌðə] anders; andere/-r/-s; weitere **I**
each **other** [ˌiːtʃˈʌðə] einander; sich; sich gegenseitig **II U1, 17**
the **others** [ðiˈʌðəz] die anderen **I**
Ouch! [aʊtʃ] Aua! **II U4, 66**
ounce [aʊns] Unze *(Maßeinheit: 28,34952 Gramm)* °**II U2, 35**
our [aʊə; ɑː] unser/-e **I**
out [aʊt] außerhalb; heraus; hinaus; nach draußen **I**
to clear **out** [klɪərˌ ˈaʊt] ausräumen, entrümpeln **I**
*to hang **out** (with) *(infml)* [ˌhæŋ ˈaʊt wɪð] rumhängen (mit); sich herumtreiben (mit); sich treffen (mit) **II U1, 8**
out and about [ˌaʊt ən əˈbaʊt] unterwegs ⟨**II U3, 50**⟩
out of [ˈaʊt əv] aus … heraus **II F1, 20**
outdoor [ˌaʊtˈdɔː] Freiluft-; Outdoor- **II U3, 42**
outdoor activity [ˌaʊtdɔːrˌ ækˈtɪvəti] Freiluftaktivität **II U1, 11**
the great **outdoors** [ðə ˌgreɪtˌaʊtˈdɔːz] die freie Natur **II U3, 42**
outdoors [ˌaʊtˈdɔːz] draußen; im Freien **I**
outfit [ˈaʊtfɪt] Outfit; Kleidung **II U1, 8**
outlaw [ˈaʊtlɔː] Geächtete/-r; Gesetzlose/-r **II AC3, 114**
outline [ˈaʊtlaɪn] Skizze; Umriss °**II U6, 109**
outside [ˌaʊtˈsaɪd] nach draußen; draußen; außerhalb (von) **I**
over [ˈəʊvə] hinüber; über **I**; vorüber; vorbei **II U4, 71**
*to go **over** to [ˌgəʊ ˈəʊvə tə] hinübergehen zu; zu jmdm. nach Hause gehen **II U5, 87**
over there [ˌəʊvə ˈðeə] da drüben; dort drüben **I**
to turn **over** [ˌtɜːnˌ ˈəʊvə] umdrehen; umkippen **II U3, 44**
overnight [ˌəʊvəˈnaɪt] über Nacht **II U2, 23**
to **overreact** [ˌəʊvəriˈækt] überreagieren **II U5, 84**
own [əʊn] eigene/-r/-s **I**
on your **own** [ɒn jərˌ ˈəʊn] allein; für dich **I**

P

p.m. [ˌpiːˈem] nachmittags *(Uhrzeit)*; abends *(Uhrzeit)* **I**
packet [ˈpækɪt] Päckchen; Paket; Packung **I**
pad [pæd] Polster; Schoner **II U4, 61**
to **paddle** [ˈpædl] paddeln **II U3, 52**
page [peɪdʒ] Seite **I**
pain [peɪn] Schmerz **II U4, 64**
to **paint** [peɪnt] anmalen; malen **I**
pair [peə] Paar **I**
palm tree [ˈpɑːm ˌtriː] Palme **II U2, 22**
pancake [ˈpænkeɪk] Pfannkuchen **I**
to **panic** [ˈpænɪk] panisch werden ⟨**II U2, 30**⟩

panther [ˈpænθə] Panther; Puma II U2, 22

pants (pl) (AE) [pænts] Hosen II U3, 48

paper [ˈpeɪpə] Papier II U1, 17

paradise [ˈpærədaɪs] Paradies II U5, 83

paragraph [ˈpærəgrɑːf] Paragraph; Absatz °II U3, 46

parents (pl) [ˈpeərənts] Eltern I

park [pɑːk] Park I

national park [ˌnæʃnl ˈpɑːk] Nationalpark; Naturpark I

theme park [ˈθiːm ˌpɑːk] Vergnügungspark (meist mit einem bestimmten Thema); Themenpark II F1, 20

parking [ˈpɑːkɪŋ] Parken °II U3, 51

part [pɑːt] Teil; Stadtteil I

*to take part (in) [teɪk ˈpɑːt (ɪn)] teilnehmen (an) II U5, 82

partially sighted [ˌpɑːʃli ˈsaɪtɪd] sehbehindert; teilsichtig II AC2, 59

past participle [ˌpɑːst pɑːˈtɪsɪpl] Partizip °II U4, 63

partner [ˈpɑːtnə] Partner/-in I

party [ˈpɑːti] Party; Feier I

pass [pɑːs] Ausweis; Pass II F2, 77

to pass [pɑːs] zupassen; zuspielen II U4, 60

passenger [ˈpæsndʒə] Passagier/-in; Fahrgast II F2, 77

past [pɑːst] Vergangenheit II U3, 57

past participle [ˌpɑːst pɑːˈtɪsɪpl] Partizip °II U4, 63

past [pɑːst] nach (bei Uhrzeitangaben) I; vorbei (an); vorüber (an) II F2, 77

half past [ˌhɑːf ˈpɑːst] halb (bei Uhrzeitangaben) I

quarter past/to [ˈkwɔːtə pɑːst/tə] Viertel nach/vor I

pasta [ˈpæstə] Pasta; Nudeln I

path [pɑːθ] Pfad; Weg II AC1, 39

coastal path [ˌkəʊstl ˈpɑːθ] Küstenweg II U6, 110

pattern [ˈpætn] Muster °II U6, 104

*to pay (for) [peɪ] bezahlen I

PC (= personal computer) [piːˈsiː] PC II U5, 92

PE (Physical Education) [piːˈiː] Sportunterricht I

peace [piːs] Frieden II F3, 96

peak [piːk] Gipfel; Spitze II U3, 42

to peer-edit [ˈpɪərˌedɪt] gegenseitig kontrollieren II U4, 74

pen [pen] Füller I

pencil [ˈpensl] Bleistift; Buntstift I

pencil-case [ˈpensl ˌkeɪs] Federmäppchen; Mäppchen I

penny, pence (pl) Penny (brit. Währungseinheit) I

people (pl) [ˈpiːpl] Leute; Menschen I

per [pɜː; pə] pro II U6, 101

percussion [pəˈkʌʃn] Percussion; Schlaginstrumente II U2, 24

present perfect [ˌpreznt ˈpɜːfɪkt] das Perfekt °II U4, 61

perfect [ˈpɜːfɪkt] perfekt; vollkommen II U2, 23

perfectly [ˈpɜːfɪktli] perfekt II U3, 49

to perform [pəˈfɔːm] aufführen; auftreten; leisten II U2, 24

person [ˈpɜːsn], people (pl) [ˈpiːpl] Person; Mensch I

personal [ˈpɜːsnl] persönlich II U2, 31

pet [pet] Haustier I

phone [fəʊn] Telefon; Handy I

to answer the phone [ˌɑːnsə ðə ˈfəʊn] einen Anruf entgegennehmen I

cell phone (AE) [ˈsel fəʊn] Mobiltelefon; Handy II U3, 43

phone call [ˈfəʊn ˌkɔːl] Anruf; Telefonanruf I

photo [ˈfəʊtəʊ] Foto; Fotografie I

in the photo(s) [ˌɪn ðə ˈfəʊtəʊ(z)] auf dem Foto/den Fotos I

photo story [ˈfəʊtəʊ ˌstɔːri] Fotostory; Bildgeschichte I

*to take photos [ˌteɪk ˈfəʊtəʊz] fotografieren; Fotos machen I

phrase [freɪz] Redewendung; Ausdruck; Satz I

physical [ˈfɪzɪkl] physisch; körperlich II AC2, 58

piano [piˈænəʊ] Klavier; Piano II U2, 24

to pick [pɪk] auswählen; aussuchen °II U6, 99

to pick up [pɪk ˈʌp] aufheben; abholen II U3, 48

picnic [ˈpɪknɪk] Picknick I

picture [ˈpɪktʃə] Bild; Foto I

pie [paɪ] Kuchen; Pastete I

piece [piːs] Stück I

pier [pɪə] Pier; Hafendamm I

pig [pɪg] Schwein I

guinea pig [ˈgɪniː ˌpɪg] Meerschweinchen I

pill [pɪl] Pille; Tablette II U4, 65

pilot [ˈpaɪlət] Pilot/-in ⟨II U2, 30⟩

pink [pɪŋk] pink; rosa I

pipe [paɪp] Rohr; Rohrleitung II U5, 87

pirate [ˈpaɪrət] Pirat; Seeräuber °II U2, 34

pitch [pɪtʃ] Spielfeld; Platz II U4, 60

pizza [ˈpiːtsə] Pizza I

place [pleɪs] Ort; Stelle; Platz I

*to take place [teɪk ˈpleɪs] stattfinden I

to place face down [pʊt ˌfeɪs ˈdaʊn] umgedreht hinlegen °II U6, 109

plan [plæn] Plan; Entwurf II U1, 10

to plan [plæn] planen I

plane [pleɪn] Flugzeug II F2, 77

planet [ˈplænɪt] Planet II U3, 52

planner [ˈplænə] Handbuch; Kalender I

plant [plɑːnt] Pflanze II U2, 37

platform [ˈplætfɔːm] Plattform; Bahnsteig II U3, 44

role play [ˈrəʊl ˌpleɪ] Rollenspiel I

to play [pleɪ] spielen I

to play a trick (on) [ˌpleɪ ə ˈtrɪk ˌɒn] einen Streich spielen I

player [ˈpleɪə] Spieler/-in; Mitspieler/-in II U4, 67

playground [ˈpleɪgraʊnd] Schulhof; Pausenhof; Spielplatz ⟨II U6, 107⟩

Please. [pliːz] Bitte. I

plum [plʌm] Pflaume I

plumber [ˈplʌmə] Installateur/-in; Klempner/-in II U6, 110

plumbing [ˈplʌmɪŋ] Sanitärarbeit II U6, 111

pocket money [ˈpɒkɪt ˌmʌni] Taschengeld I

poem [ˈpəʊɪm] Gedicht I

point [pɔɪnt] Punkt; Komma (bei Zahlenangaben) II U1, 12

point of view [ˌpɔɪnt əv ˈvjuː] Standpunkt; Ansicht; Perspektive II U4, 74

to point [pɔɪnt] zeigen II U1, 11

polar bear [ˈpəʊlə ˌbeə] Eisbär I

police [pəˈliːs] Polizei II U5, 88

police officer [pəˈliːs ˌɒfɪsə] Polizeibeamter; Polizist/-in ⟨II U2, 30⟩

polite [pəˈlaɪt] höflich I

in a polite way [ɪn ˌə pəˈlaɪt ˌweɪ] auf höfliche Art II U6, 103

Be polite. [ˌbi: pəˈlaɪt] Sei/Seid höflich. I

pollution [pəˈluːʃn] Verschmutzung II U1, 11

pony [ˈpəʊni] Pony I

pony trekking [ˈpəʊni ˌtrekɪŋ] Ponyreiten im Gelände II U6, 99

the poor [ðə pʊə] die Armen II AC3, 115

poor [pɔː; pʊə] arm II U1, 12

popular [ˈpɒpjələ] beliebt; populär I

porcupine [ˈpɔːkjəˌpaɪn] Baumstachler II U3, 44

positive [ˈpɒzətɪv] positiv II U1, 12

possibility [ˌpɒsəˈbɪləti] Möglichkeit II U6, 105

possible [ˈpɒsəbl] möglich I

post [pəʊst] Post (Eintrag im Internet) I

to post [pəʊst] online stellen; posten II U5, 82

postcard [ˈpəʊskɑːd] Postkarte I

poster [ˈpəʊstə] Poster I

pound (£) [paʊnd] Pfund (brit. Währungseinheit) I

to pour [pɔː] einschenken; eingießen; schütten I

power [paʊə] Kraft; Macht; Stärke II AC3, 114

power cut [ˈpaʊə ˌkʌt] Stromausfall II U5, 93

Word power [ˈwɜːd ˌpaʊə] die Kraft der Wörter (Wortschatzübung) I

powerful [ˈpaʊəfl] stark; mächtig II F3, 96

practical [ˈpræktɪkl] praktisch II U5, 83

to practise [ˈpræktɪs] üben; trainieren I

practising [ˈpræktɪsɪŋ] Üben I

to pray [preɪ] beten II U2, 35

prediction [prɪˈdɪkʃn] Vorhersage; Voraussage II U6, 101

prehistoric [ˌpriːhɪˈstɒrɪk] vorgeschichtlich; prähistorisch II U6, 104 to **prepare** [prɪ'peə] vorbereiten; zubereiten I

prescription [prɪ'skrɪpʃn] Rezept *(für Arzneimittel)* II U4, 65

present ['preznt] Geschenk I

present perfect [ˌpreznt 'pɜːfɪkt] das Perfekt °II U4, 61

to **present** [prɪ'zent] präsentieren; vorstellen I

presentation [ˌprezn'teɪʃn] Präsentation; Vortrag I

presenter [prɪ'zentə] Moderator/-in II U4, 69

president ['prezɪdnt] Präsident/-in I

to **press** [pres] drücken; pressen II U5, 92

to **pretend** [prɪ'tend] vorgeben; vortäuschen; so tun, als ob … II U3, 54

pretty ['prɪti] ziemlich; ganz schön II U3, 54

price [praɪs] Preis I

print [prɪnt] gedruckt; Druck- II U5, 83

prisoner ['prɪznə] Gefangene/-r II F3, 96

private detective [ˌpraɪvət dɪ'tektɪv] Privatdetektiv/-in II AC3, 114

prize [praɪz] Preis; Gewinn I

pros and cons [ˌprəʊz ən 'kɒnz] Argumente für und gegen etw. II U5, 94

probably ['prɒbəbli] wahrscheinlich II F2, 76

problem ['prɒbləm] Problem; Schwierigkeit I

to **produce** [prə'djuːs] herstellen; produzieren I

profile ['prəʊfaɪl] Profil; Porträt II U5, 82

program *(AE)* ['prəʊgræm] Programm; Sendung II U1, 10

programme ['prəʊgræm] Programm; Sendung II U4, 60

project ['prɒdʒekt] Projekt I

promise ['prɒmɪs] Versprechen II AC1, 38

to **promise** ['prɒmɪs] versprechen II AC1, 38

prompt card ['prɒmpt kɑːd] Stichwortkarte; Rollenkarte °II U2, 29

relative pronoun [ˌrelətɪv 'prəʊnaʊn] Relativpronomen °II U2, 28

pronunciation [prəˌnʌnsi'eɪʃn] Aussprache I

prop [prɒp] Requisite II AC3, 115

to **protect** [prə'tekt] beschützen; schützen II F3, 97

protection [prə'tekʃn] Schutz II U5, 82

proud (of) ['praʊd əv] stolz (auf) II U1, 9

public ['pʌblɪk] öffentlich °II U3, 51

public transport *(no pl)* [ˌpʌblɪk 'trænspɔːt] öffentliche Verkehrsmittel II U1, 11

puck [pʌk] Puck *(Eishockey)* II U4, 61

pudding ['pʊdɪŋ] Pudding; Nachtisch I

to **pull** [pʊl] ziehen I

pullover ['pʊləʊvə] Pullover I

pumpkin ['pʌmpkɪn] Kürbis II AC1, 38

purple ['pɜːpl] violett; lila I

to **push** [pʊʃ] stoßen; schieben; schubsen II U1, 17

*to **put** [pʊt] setzen; stellen; legen I

*to **put** on [ˌpʊt 'ɒn] anziehen; auftragen II AC1, 38

*to **put** through [pʊt 'θruː] verbinden I

*to **put** together [ˌpʊt tə'geðə] zusammensetzen II U5, 87

puzzle ['pʌzl] Rätsel I

Q

quality ['kwɒləti] Qualität I

quarter past/to ['kwɔːtə pɑːst/tə] Viertel nach/vor I

queen [kwiːn] Königin I

question ['kwestʃən] Frage I

question tag ['kwestʃən ˌtæg] Frageanhängsel; Bestätigungsfrage °II U1, 12

queue [kjuː] Schlange; Warteschlange I

to jump the **queue** [ˌdʒʌmp ðə 'kjuː] sich vordrängeln I

quick [kwɪk] schnell I

quickly ['kwɪkli] schnell II U1, 16

quiet ['kwaɪət] still; ruhig; leise I

quiz [kwɪz] Quiz; Rätsel I

R

rabbit ['ræbɪt] Kaninchen I

race [reɪs] Wettlauf; Rennen II U1, 10

camel **racing** ['kæml ˌreɪsɪŋ] Kamelrennen II U4, 60

racquet ['rækɪt] Schläger II U4, 60

radio ['reɪdiəʊ] Radio II U4, 60

raffle ['ræfl] Tombola I

rafting ['rɑːftɪŋ] Schlauchbootfahren I

rain [reɪn] Regen II U3, 48

to **rain** [reɪn] regnen II F1, 20

rainy ['reɪni] regnerisch II U2, 26

to **raise** money ['reɪz 'mʌni] Geld sammeln II U4, 62

mountain **range** [ˌmaʊntɪn 'reɪndʒ] Bergkette II U3, 42

ranger *(AE)* ['reɪndʒə] Ranger °II U3, 51

rap [ræp] Rap I

to **rap** [ræp] rappen I

rat [ræt] Ratte I

raven ['reɪvn] Rabe II U3, 47; °II U6, 108

to **reach** [riːtʃ] erreichen; dran kommen II U5, 87

reaction [ri'ækʃn] Reaktion II U6, 101

*to **read** [riːd] lesen I

*to **read** out loud [ˌriːd aʊt 'laʊd] laut vorlesen II AC2, 59

reader ['riːdə] Leser/-in II U3, 52

reading ['riːdɪŋ] Lesen I

ready ['redi] fertig; bereit II U1, 17

ready meal [ˌredi 'miːl] Fertiggericht I

real [rɪəl] echt; richtig; wirklich II U1, 8

realistic [rɪə'lɪstɪk] realistisch II U3, 56

really ['rɪəli] wirklich I

reason ['riːzn] Grund II U4, 74

to **receive** [rɪ'siːv] empfangen; erhalten; bekommen II U4, 69

to **record** [rɪ'kɔːd] aufnehmen; aufzeichnen II U4, 70

recording [rɪ'kɔːdɪŋ] Aufnahme; Aufzeichnung I

recording studio [rɪ'kɔːdɪŋ ˌstjuːdiəʊ] Aufnahmestudio; Tonstudio I

recycling [ˌriː'saɪklɪŋ] Recycling; Wiederaufbereitung II U1, 16

red [red] rot I

*to **redo** [ˌriː'duː] noch einmal machen II U1, 17

coral **reef** [ˌkɒrəl 'riːf] Korallenriff °II U2, 35

to **reef** the sails [ˌriːf ðə 'seɪlz] die Segel einholen I

region ['riːdʒn] Region; Gegend II F1, 20

regular ['regjələ] regelmäßig; gleichmäßig II U2, 25

rehearsal [rɪ'hɜːsl] Probe II U2, 24

related [rɪ'leɪtɪd] verwandt; bezogen II U1, 18

relationship [rɪ'leɪʃnʃɪp] Beziehung II U4, 74

relative pronoun [ˌrelətɪv 'prəʊnaʊn] Relativpronomen °II U2, 28

to **relax** [rɪ'læks] sich entspannen; sich ausruhen; sich beruhigen ⟨II U2, 30⟩

religious [rɪ'lɪdʒəs] religiös; gläubig I

to **remember** [rɪ'membə] sich erinnern (an); sich merken; denken an I

to **repair** [rɪ'peə] reparieren II U5, 87

to **repeat** [rɪ'piːt] wiederholen II U1, 13

to **replay** [ˌriː'pleɪ] erneut spielen; erneut abspielen II U3, 48

reply [rɪ'plaɪ] Antwort; Erwiderung; Entgegnung I

to **reply** (to) [rɪ'plaɪ] antworten (auf); erwidern; entgegnen I

report [rɪ'pɔːt] Bericht; Meldung II U1, 9

reporter [rɪ'pɔːtə] Reporter/-in II U4, 69

*to **reread** [ˌriː'riːd] noch einmal lesen II U3, 42

rescue ['reskjuː] Rettung II U4, 69

the **rest** [rest] der Rest II U2, 35

restaurant ['restrɒnt] Restaurant; Gaststätte I

restroom *(AE)* ['restrʊm] Toilette °II U3, 51

result [rɪ'zʌlt] Ergebnis; Resultat II U5, 89

*to **retell** [ˌriː'tel] nacherzählen; nochmals erzählen II U1, 18

retired [rɪ'taəd] pensioniert; im Ruhestand II F1, 20

return [rɪ'tɜːn] Hin- und Rückfahrkarte II F2, 76

to **reuse** [ˌriː'juːz] wieder verwenden II U3, 48

*to **rewrite** [ˌriː'raɪt] umschreiben; neu schreiben II U6, 106

rhythm ['rɪðm] Rhythmus I

the **rich** [ðə rɪtʃ] die Reichen II AC3, 115

ride [raɪd] Fahrt; Ritt; Fahrgeschäft II U2, 23

*to **ride** [raɪd] fahren; reiten I

rider ['raɪdə] Reiter/-in II U3, 48

riding ['raɪdɪŋ] Reiten II U4, 75

rigging [ˈrɪgɪŋ] Takelage I

right [raɪt] Recht II AC2, 58

right [raɪt] richtig; korrekt I

*to be **right** [bi ˈraɪt] recht haben I

*to get **right** [get ˈraɪt] richtig beantworten °II U6, 109

on the **right** [ɒn ðə ˈraɪt] auf der rechten Seite; rechts I

right away [raɪt əˈweɪ] sofort; gleich I

right here [raɪt ˈhɪə] genau hier II U4, 62

right now [raɪt ˈnaʊ] jetzt gleich; sofort; gerade II U5, 93

*to **ring** [rɪŋ] klingeln; läuten I

ice **rink** [ˈaɪs ˌrɪŋk] Eisbahn; Schlittschuhbahn I

river [ˈrɪvə] Fluss I

river bank [ˌrɪvə ˈbæŋk] Flussufer II U6, 104

road [rəʊd] Straße II AC1, 39

robber [ˈrɒbə] Räuber/-in II AC3, 114

rock [rɒk] Fels; Stein I

rodeo [rəˈdeɪəʊ; ˈrəʊdiəʊ] Rodeo I

role [rəʊl] Rolle I

role play [ˈrəʊl ˌpleɪ] Rollenspiel I

to swap **roles** [ˌswɒp ˈrəʊlz] Rollen tauschen I

to **roll** [rəʊl] rollen II U2, 35

roller coaster [ˈrəʊlə ˌkəʊstə] Achterbahn II U2, 23

Roman [ˈrəʊmən] Römer/-in; römisch II F3, 96

roof [ruːf] Dach II U6, 110

room [ruːm; rʊm] Zimmer; Raum I

fitting **room** [ˈfɪtɪŋ ˌrʊm] Umkleidekabine II U3, 49

living **room** [ˈlɪvɪŋ rʊm] Wohnzimmer I

roommate [ˈruːmmeɪt] Zimmergenosse/Zimmergenossin I

round [raʊnd] rund II U2, 35

the **Round** Table [ðə ˌraʊnd ˈteɪbl] die Tafelrunde II AC3, 115

to turn **round** [tɜːn ˈraʊnd] (sich) umdrehen; wenden II U1, 17

royal [ˈrɔɪəl] königlich I

rubber [ˈrʌbə] Radiergummi I

rubbish [ˈrʌbɪʃ] Müll; Gerümpel I

rude [ruːd] unhöflich; unverschämt I

rugby [ˈrʌgbi] Rugby II U4, 60

to ruin [ˈruːɪn] ruinieren; zerstören II U4, 73

rule [ruːl] Regel I; Herrschaft II U2, 27

to rule [ruːl] herrschen; regieren II U6, 106

ruler [ˈruːlə] Lineal I

run [rʌn] Rennen; Lauf II U4, 62

*to **run** [rʌn] rennen; laufen I

*to **run** away [rʌn əˈweɪ] wegrennen I

runaway [ˈrʌnəweɪ] Ausreißer/-in; Entlaufene/-r II U2, 27

runner [ˈrʌnə] Läufer/-in II U4, 60

running [ˈrʌnɪŋ] Laufen; Rennen II U4, 62

S

sad [sæd] traurig I

safe [seɪf] sicher; ungefährlich II U3, 48

to reef the **sails** [ˌriːf ðə ˈseɪlz] die Segel einholen I

to **sail** [seɪl] segeln; umsegeln II U2, 34

sailboat [ˈseɪlbəʊt] Segelboot II U6, 112

sailing [ˈseɪlɪŋ] Segel- °II U2, 35

sailor [ˈseɪlə] Seemann; Matrose I

salad [ˈsæləd] Salat I

the same [ðə ˈseɪm] der-/die-/dasselbe; der/die/das gleiche I

the **same** way as [ˌðə seɪm ˈweɪ æz] genauso wie ⟨II U1, 14⟩

sand [sænd] Sand II U2, 35

sandwich [ˈsænwɪdʒ] Sandwich; belegtes Brot I

Saturday [ˈsætədeɪ] Samstag I

to save [seɪv] retten; bergen I; sparen; aufheben II U2, 35

sax [sæks] Saxofon I

saxophone [ˈsæksəfəʊn] Saxofon I

*to say [seɪ] sagen; aufsagen; sprechen I

*to **say** hello (to) [seɪ helˈəʊ tə] grüßen; Grüße ausrichten (an) I

to scan [skæn] scannen; nach Details durchsuchen °II U3, 51

*to be **scared** (of) [bi ˈskeəd əv] Angst haben (vor) I

I'm (not) **scared** of … [ˌaɪm (nɒt) ˈskeəd əv] Ich habe (keine) Angst vor … I

scary [ˈskeəri] unheimlich; gruselig; beängstigend II AC1, 38

scene [siːn] Szene I; Schauplatz II U4, 69

to act a **scene** [ˌækt ə ˈsiːn] eine Theaterszene spielen I

school [skuːl] Schule I

grammar **school** [ˈgræmə ˌskuːl] Gymnasium II U6, 103

high **school** [ˈhaɪ ˌskuːl] High School (weiterführende Schule in den USA, Oberstufe) II U2, 26

schoolbag [ˈskuːlbæg] Schultasche I

schooling [ˈskuːlɪŋ] Schulbildung II AC2, 58

Science [saɪəns] Naturwissenschaften I

science fiction [saɪəns ˈfɪkʃn] Science-Fiction (Zukunftsdichtung) II U3, 52

scissors (pl only) [ˈsɪzəz] Schere II U5, 87

to scoop [skuːp] schöpfen; schaufeln II U2, 35

score [skɔː] Punktestand; Spielstand II U4, 60

to score [skɔː] punkten; ein Tor schießen II U4, 61

Scottish [ˈskɒtɪʃ] schottisch II U6, 99

to screw sth to sth [skruː] etw. anschrauben an etw. II U5, 87

screwdriver [ˈskruːdraɪvə] Schraubenzieher II U5, 87

sea [siː] Meer I

by the **sea** [ˌbaɪ ðə ˈsiː] am Meer II U6, 104

search [sɜːtʃ] Suche; Such- II U1, 15

at the seaside [ət ðə ˈsiːsaɪd] am Meer II U6, 99

season [ˈsiːzn] Saison; Jahreszeit II U2, 34

second [ˈseknd] Sekunde II U1, 12

second [ˈseknd] zweite/-r/-s I

in secret [ɪn ˈsiːkrət] heimlich II U4, 73

secret [ˈsiːkrət] geheim II U2, 35

section [ˈsekʃn] Abschnitt; Paragraf II U3, 52

*to see [siː] sehen I

See you! [siː jə] Bis dann!; Bis … I

I **see.** [aɪ ˈsiː] Ich verstehe.; Aha!; Ach so! II U1, 13

Wait and **see**! [ˌweɪt ənd ˈsiː] Warte ab! I

self-critical [ˈselfˌkrɪtɪkl] selbstkritisch II U5, 84

self-evaluation [ˌselfɪˌvæljuˈeɪʃn] Selbsteinschätzung II U2, 27

selfie [ˈselfi] Selfie II U4, 73

*to sell [sel] verkaufen I

seller [ˈselə] Verkäufer/-in (auf einem Flohmarkt) I

*to send [send] schicken; senden I

*to **send** off [sendˌɒf] abschicken II U6, 103

sense [sens] Sinn II U2, 27

sentence [ˈsentəns] Satz I

conditional **sentence** [kənˌdɪʃnl ˈsentəns] Bedingungssatz °II U6, 99

separate [ˈseprət] separat; getrennt; verschieden I

September [sepˈtembə] September I

serious [ˈsɪəriəs] ernsthaft; ernst I

*to take sth seriously [teɪk ˈsɪəriəsli] ernst nehmen II U4, 72

service [ˈsɜːvɪs] Service; Dienstleistung; Dienst; Verbindung(Zug, Bus) °II U3, 51

set [set] Umgebung; Rahmen II AC3, 115

*to set up [setˌʌp] einrichten; aufbauen I

setting [ˈsetɪŋ] Schauplatz; Rahmen ⟨II U3, 50⟩

to settle [ˈsetl] siedeln; sich niederlassen II U2, 29

settler [ˈsetlə] Siedler/-in II F1, 20

seven [ˈsevn] sieben I

seventeen [ˌsevnˈtiːn] siebzehn I

seventy [ˈsevnti] siebzig I

several [ˈsevrl] einige; mehrere; verschiedene II U2, 31

*to sew [səʊ] nähen II U5, 87

What a shame! [ˌwɒt ə ˈʃeɪm] Wie schade! II U1, 12

shape [ʃeɪp] Form I

to share [ʃeə] teilen II U1, 16

she [ʃiː] sie I

sheep, sheep (pl) [ʃiːp] Schaf I

bighorn **sheep** [ˈbɪghɔːn ˌʃiːp] Dickhornschaf II U3, 42

shhh [ʃ] psst II U3, 46

shield [ʃiːld] Schild II F3, 97

*to shine [ʃaɪn] scheinen; glänzen II U3, 46

ship [ʃɪp] Schiff I

shirt [ʃɜːt] Hemd; Shirt I

shock [ʃɒk] Schock II U3, 44

shocked [ʃɒkt] schockiert; geschockt II U1, 17

shoe [ʃuː] Schuh I

shop [ʃɒp] Geschäft; Laden I
charity shop [ˈtʃærɪti ˌʃɒp] Second-Hand-Laden I

*to go shopping [ˌɡəʊ ˈʃɒpɪŋ] einkaufen gehen I

shore [ʃɔː] Ufer; Küste II U6, 104

short [ʃɔːt] kurz I

shot [ʃɒt] Einstellung; Kameraeinstellung ⟨II U5, 90⟩

should [ʃʊd] sollte; solltest; sollten; solltet II U1, 17

shoulder [ˈʃəʊldə] Schulter II U4, 65

to shout [ʃaʊt] schreien; rufen I

shovel [ˈʃʌvl] Schaufel II U2, 34

show [ʃəʊ] Show; Schau; Aufführung II U4, 67
living history show [ˌlɪvɪŋ ˈhɪstəri ˌʃəʊ] Show, in der historischer Alltag nachgespielt wird II U6, 98
talent show [ˈtælənt ˌʃəʊ] Talentwettbewerb I

*to show [ʃəʊ] zeigen I
*to show off [ˌʃəʊ ˈɒf] angeben II U5, 93

shower [ˈʃaʊə] Dusche I

show-off [ˈʃəʊɒf] Angeber/-in II U1, 8

to shuffle [ˈʃʌfl] mischen II U6, 109

shuttlecock [ˈʃʌtlkɒk] Federball II U4, 61

sick [sɪk] krank; unwohl II U4, 65
*to feel sick [ˌfiːl ˈsɪk] Übelkeit verspüren; sich schlecht fühlen II U4, 65

side [saɪd] Seite II U3, 46

sight [saɪt] Sehenswürdigkeit; Anblick I

sightseeing [ˈsaɪtsiːɪŋ] Sightseeing-; Besichtigungs- ⟨II U3, 50⟩
*to go sightseeing [ˌɡəʊ ˈsaɪtsiːɪŋ] eine Besichtigungstour machen II U3, 52

sign [saɪn] Zeichen; Schild II AC2, 58

to sign [saɪn] unterzeichnen; unterschreiben II AC2, 58

signal [ˈsɪɡnl] Signal; Zeichen II U2, 34

silent [ˈsaɪlənt] still; ruhig; schweigsam; stumm II U2, 35

silly [ˈsɪli] Dummkopf II U4, 72

silly [ˈsɪli] dumm; doof; albern I

silver [ˈsɪlvə] Silber II U2, 34

similar [ˈsɪmɪlə] ähnlich II U2, 36

*to sing [sɪŋ] singen I

singer [ˈsɪŋə] Sänger/-in II U2, 24

single [ˈsɪŋɡl] einfache Fahrkarte II F2, 76

Dear Sir or Madam [dɪə ˌsɜːr ɔː ˈmædəm] Sehr geehrte Dame, sehr geehrter Herr II U6, 103

sister [ˈsɪstə] Schwester I
half-sister [ˈhɑːfˌsɪstə] Halbschwester I

*to sit [sɪt] sitzen I
Sit! [sɪt] Sitz! (Befehl für Hunde) I
*to sit down [ˌsɪt ˈdaʊn] sich hinsetzen; sich setzen I

site [saɪt] Website II U5, 93

situation [ˌsɪtjuˈeɪʃn] Situation I

six [sɪks] sechs I

sixteen [sɪkˈstiːn] sechzehn I

sixty [ˈsɪksti] sechzig I

size [saɪz] Größe; Kleidergröße I

to skate [skeɪt] Inlineskates fahren; Schlittschuh laufen I

skateboard [ˈskeɪtbɔːd] Skateboard I

skateboarding [ˈskeɪtbɔːdɪŋ] Skateboard-fahren I

skates (pl) [skeɪts] Inlineskates; Rollschuhe; Schlittschuhe I

(inline) skating [ˈɪnlaɪn ˌskeɪtɪŋ] Inline-skatefahren I

skiing [ˈskiːɪŋ] Skifahren I

skill [skɪl] Fertigkeit; Geschick I

to skim [skɪm] überfliegen II U3, 51

skirt [skɜːt] Rock II U6, 110

sky [skaɪ] Himmel II U2, 34

skyscraper [ˈskaɪskreɪpə] Wolkenkratzer I

slave [sleɪv] Sklave/Sklavin II F1, 20

slavery [ˈsleɪvri] Sklaverei II F1, 20

*to sleep [sliːp] schlafen I

sleepover [ˈsliːpˌəʊvə] Übernachtung I

sleeve [sliːv] Ärmel II U3, 48

to slice [slaɪs] in Scheiben schneiden I

slide [slaɪd] Rutschbahn I
water slide [ˈwɔːtə ˌslaɪd] Wasserrutsche I

slogan [ˈsləʊɡən] Slogan; Werbespruch II U2, 26

time slot [ˈtaɪm slɒt] Zeitfenster II U2, 32

slow [sləʊ] langsam I

slowly [ˈsləʊli] langsam II U2, 34

small [smɔːl] klein I

smartphone [ˈsmɑːtfəʊn] Smartphone II U4, 71

to smash [smæʃ] schlagen; zerschmettern II U2, 35

*to smell [smel] riechen; duften II U3, 48

smile [smaɪl] Lächeln I

to smile [smaɪl] lächeln I

snack [snæk] Snack; Imbiss I
snack bar [ˈsnæk ˌbɑː] Café; Imbissstube I

to sneak around [ˌsniːk əˈraʊnd] herumschleichen ⟨II U1, 14⟩

to snore [snɔː] schnarchen I

snow [snəʊ] Schnee II F1, 21

to snow [snəʊ] schneien II F1, 21

so [səʊ] so; also I
so (that) [səʊ ˈðət] damit; sodass II U3, 46

soccer (AE) [ˈsɒkə] Fußball I

social [ˈsəʊʃl] sozial; gesellschaftlich II U5, 82
social network [ˌsəʊʃl ˈnetwɜːk] soziales Netzwerk II U5, 82

society [səˈsaɪəti] Verein; Gesellschaft II U6, 111

sock [sɒk] Socke II U3, 49

soda [ˈsəʊdə] Limonade II U2, 35

sofa [ˈsəʊfə] Sofa; Couch I

soldier [ˈsəʊldʒə] Soldat/-in II AC1, 39

solution [səˈluːʃn] Lösung I

to solve [sɒlv] lösen II U6, 110

some [sʌm; səm] einige; ein paar; etwas I

somebody [ˈsʌmbədi] jemand I

someone [ˈsʌmwʌn] jemand I

something [ˈsʌmθɪŋ] etwas I

sometimes [ˈsʌmtaɪmz] manchmal I

somewhere [ˈsʌmweə] irgendwo; irgendwohin II U2, 23

son [sʌn] Sohn II U5, 86

song [sɒŋ] Song; Lied I

soon [suːn] bald II U2, 35
as soon as [əz ˈsuːn əz] sobald II U5, 84

Sorry! [ˈsɒri] Entschuldigung!; Tut mir leid! I
*to be sorry [bi ˈsɒri] leid tun I
I'm sorry! [ˌaɪm ˈsɒri] Tut mir leid! I

soul [səʊl] Seele II AC1, 38

souling [ˈsəʊlɪŋ] Souling (mittelalterlicher Brauch, bei dem man durch Gabe von Broten seine Seele zu retten hoffte) II AC1, 38

sound [saʊnd] Ton; Geräusch; Klang I

to sound [saʊnd] klingen I

source [sɔːs] Quelle II U6, 108

south [saʊθ] Süden; Süd- I

space [speɪs] Raum; Weltraum I

spaceship [ˈspeɪsʃɪp] Raumschiff II U3, 52

Spanish [ˈspænɪʃ] spanisch; Spanisch; Spanier/-in II U2, 25

spanner [ˈspænə] Schraubenschlüssel II U5, 87

*to speak [spiːk] sprechen I

speaker [ˈspiːkə] Redner/-in; Sprecher/-in I

speaking [ˈspiːkɪŋ] Sprechen I

spear [spɪə] Speer II U6, 110

special [ˈspeʃl] besonders; speziell I
special offer [ˌspeʃl ˈɒfə] Sonderangebot I

specialty (AE) [ˈspeʃlti] Spezialität; Besonderheit II U2, 27

speech bubble [ˈspiːtʃ ˌbʌbl] Sprechblase I

*to spell [spel] buchstabieren I

spelling [ˈspelɪŋ] Rechtschreibung I

*to spend [spend] ausgeben (Geld) I; verbringen (Zeit) II U3, 46

spider [ˈspaɪdə] Spinne II AC2, 58

to splash [splæʃ] spritzen; platschen; planschen II U3, 55

spoken [ˈspəʊkn] gesprochen II U4, 74

sponge [spʌndʒ] Rühr-; Biskuit- I

spontaneous [spɒnˈteɪniəs] spontan II U6, 101

sport [spɔːt] Sport; Sportart I
… is a great sport. [ɪz ə ˈɡreɪt ˌspɔːt] … ist ein toller Sport. I

spring [sprɪŋ] Frühling I

squirrel [ˈskwɪrəl] Eichhörnchen I

stadium [ˈsteɪdiəm] Stadion I

stage [steɪdʒ] Bühne II U2, 26
on stage [ɒn ˈsteɪdʒ] auf der Bühne II U2, 24

*to stand [stænd] stehen I
*to stand up [ˌstænd ˈʌp] aufstehen (von einer Sitzgelegenheit) I

star [stɑː] Star; Stern I

to stare [steə] starren; anstarren I

to **start** [stɑːt] anfangen; beginnen; starten I

state [steɪt] Staat; Bundesstaat; Land I

statement ['steɪtmənt] Aussage; Behauptung; Erklärung II AC2, 58

station ['steɪʃn] Haltestelle; Bahnhof; Station I; Sender II U4, 69
bus **station** ['bʌs ˌsteɪʃn] Busbahnhof I

statue ['stætʃuː] Statue; Standbild II U3, 55

stay [steɪ] Aufenthalt II F2, 76

to **stay** [steɪ] bleiben I; übernachten II U6, 100
to **stay** in touch (with) [ˌsteɪ ɪn 'tʌtʃ wɪð] In Kontakt bleiben (mit) II U5, 82
to **stay** up [ˌsteɪ ˈʌp] aufbleiben I

steak [steɪk] Steak I

*to **steal** [stiːl] stehlen II U1, 17

step [step] Stufe; Schritt I
step-by-**step** [ˌstepbaɪˈstep] Schritt-für-Schritt- II U5, 87

stepmum ['stepmʌm] Stiefmutter I

stick [stɪk] Schläger (Hockey) II U4, 61

still [stɪl] Standbild ⟨II U2, 30⟩

still [stɪl] still I

still [stɪl] noch; immer noch I; dennoch II U5, 87

stomach ['stʌmək] Magen; Bauch II U4, 72

stomachache ['stʌməkeɪk] Bauchschmerzen; Bauchweh II U4, 65

stone [stəʊn] Stein II U3, 55

stop [stɒp] Haltestelle; Halt II F2, 76

to **stop** [stɒp] aufhören (mit); anhalten; stoppen I
Stop it! ['stɒp ɪt] Mach/Macht das aus!; Hör/Hört auf! I

storm [stɔːm] Sturm I

stormy ['stɔːmi] stürmisch II U6, 106

story, **stories** (pl) ['stɔːri] Story; Geschichte; Erzählung I
crime **story** ['kraɪm ˌstɔri] Krimi; Kriminalgeschichte II AC3, 115
photo **story** ['fəʊtəʊ ˌstɔːri] Fotostory; Bildgeschichte I

straight [streɪt] gerade; direkt; geradewegs II AC1, 39
straight on [streɪt ˈɒn] geradeaus II F2, 77

strange [streɪndʒ] fremd; seltsam; merkwürdig I

strawberry, **strawberries** (pl) ['strɔːbri] Erdbeere I

street [striːt] Straße (in der Stadt) I
in the **street** [ˌɪn ðə 'striːt] in der Straße; auf der Straße I

strong [strɒŋ] stark II U1, 18

structure ['strʌktʃə] Struktur; Aufbau; Gliederung °II U3, 46

student ['stjuːdnt] Schüler/-in; Student/-in I

recording **studio** [rɪ'kɔːdɪŋ ˌstjuːdiəʊ] Aufnahmestudio; Tonstudio I

stuff [stʌf] Zeug I

stupid ['stjuːpɪd] dumm; blöd II U4, 73

style [staɪl] Stil II U2, 26

subject ['sʌbdʒɪkt] Schulfach; Thema II U2, 25

substitute ['sʌbstɪtjuːt] Ersatz; Ersatz- °II U5, 83

success [sək'ses] Erfolg II AC2, 58

such [sʌtʃ] solch; solche/-r/-s ⟨II U2, 30⟩

suddenly ['sʌdnli] plötzlich; auf einmal I

to **sum** up [ˌsʌm ˈʌp] zusammenfassen °II U1, 18

summer ['sʌmə] Sommer I

sun [sʌn] Sonne II U2, 27

Sunday ['sʌndeɪ] Sonntag I

sunny ['sʌni] sonnig II F1, 20

sunscreen ['sʌnskriːn] Sonnencreme II U3, 48

sunshine ['sʌnʃaɪn] Sonnenschein II U2, 22

superlative [suːˈpɜːlətɪv] Superlativ- °II U2, 25

supermarket ['suːpəˌmɑːkɪt] Supermarkt I

to **supply** [sə'plaɪ] versorgen II U6, 106

sure [ʃʊə; ʃɔː] sicher I
*to make **sure** [ˌmeɪk 'ʃɔː] sich versichern II U3, 48

surfing ['sɜːfɪŋ] Surfen I

surgery ['sɜːdʒri] Arztpraxis; Praxis; Praxisräume I

surprise [sə'praɪz] Überraschung I

to **surprise** [sə'praɪz] überraschen II U4, 73

*to be **surprised** [bi sə'praɪzd] überrascht sein II U1, 16

surprising [sə'praɪzɪŋ] überraschend ⟨II U1, 14⟩

survey ['sɜːveɪ] Umfrage; Studie I

to **survive** [sə'vaɪv] überleben II U2, 35

suspense [sə'spens] Spannung ⟨II U6, 107⟩

to **swap** roles [ˌswɒp 'rəʊlz] Rollen tauschen I

sweet [swiːt] süß I

sweets (pl) [swiːts] Süßigkeiten; Bonbons I

*to **swim** [swɪm] schwimmen I

swimmer ['swɪmə] Schwimmer/-in II U3, 48

swimming ['swɪmɪŋ] Schwimmen I
*to go **swimming** [ˌgəʊ 'swɪmɪŋ] schwimmen gehen I

symbol ['sɪmbl] Symbol I

system ['sɪstəm] System II AC2, 58

T

table ['teɪbl] Tisch I
the Round **Table** [ðə ˌraʊnd 'teɪbl] die Tafelrunde II AC3, 115

tablet ['tæblət] Tablet II U5, 87

question **tag** ['kwestʃən ˌtæg] Frageanhängsel; Bestätigungsfrage °II U1, 12

tail [teɪl] Schwanz; Schweif I

*to **take** [teɪk] nehmen; mitnehmen; wegnehmen; bringen; mitbringen I; dauern; (Zeit) brauchen II F1, 21
*to **take** a look at [ˌteɪk ə 'lʊk æt] einen Blick werfen auf II U2, 31

*to **take** a message [ˌteɪk ə 'mesɪdʒ] eine Nachricht entgegennehmen; jmdm. etw. ausrichten I

*to **take** a test [ˌteɪk ə 'test] einen Test machen °II U5, 89

*to **take** apart [ˌteɪk əˈpɑːt] auseinandernehmen II U5, 87

*to **take** it easy [ˌteɪk ɪt ˈiːzi] immer ruhig bleiben; auf der faulen Haut liegen II U2, 23

*to **take** notes [ˌteɪk 'nəʊts] sich Notizen machen I

*to **take** off [ˌteɪk ˈɒf] abheben II U3, 49

*to **take** off [ˌteɪk ˈɒf] abnehmen; herunternehmen; ausziehen II U5, 92

*to **take** out [ˌteɪk 'aʊt] herausnehmen II U1, 17

*to **take** part (in) [ˌteɪk 'pɑːt (ɪn)] teilnehmen (an) II U5, 82

*to **take** photos [ˌteɪk 'fəʊtəʊz] fotografieren; Fotos machen I

*to **take** place [ˌteɪk 'pleɪs] stattfinden I

*to **take** sth seriously [ˌteɪk 'sɪəriəsli] ernst nehmen II U4, 72

Take turns. [ˌteɪk 'tɜːnz] Wechselt euch ab. I

It **took** ages. [ɪt tʊk 'eɪdʒɪz] Es dauerte ewig. II U3, 44

Take a deep breath. [ˌteɪk ə ˌdiːp 'breθ] Atme(t) tief ein. ⟨II U2, 30⟩

take-off ['teɪk ˌɒf] Start; Abheben II U2, 23

fairy **tale** ['feəri ˌteɪl] Märchen II AC1, 39

talent ['tælənt] Talent I
talent show ['tælənt ˌʃəʊ] Talentwettbewerb I

talk [tɔːk] Vortrag; Rede II U2, 32

to **talk** [tɔːk] sprechen; reden I
to **talk** about ['tɔːk əbaʊt] sprechen über; erzählen von I
to **talk** to ['tɔːk tə] reden mit I

tall [tɔːl] groß; hoch I

to **tap** [tæp] antippen II U5, 92

task [tɑːsk] Aufgabe; Auftrag I

taste [teɪst] Geschmack II U2, 27

tea [tiː] Tee I

*to **teach** [tiːtʃ] unterrichten; lehren; beibringen II U1, 10
*to **teach** somebody a lesson [ˌtiːtʃ ə 'lesn] jmdm. eine Lehre/Lektion erteilen ⟨II U4, 68⟩

teacher ['tiːtʃə] Lehrer/-in I

team [tiːm] Team; Gruppe I

tear [tɪə] Träne II AC1, 39

to **tease** sb [tiːz] jmdn. aufziehen; jmdn. hänseln; jmdn. ärgern II U1, 10

technology [tek'nɒlədʒi] Technologie I

teen [tiːn] Teenager; Jugendliche/-r II U3, 43

teenager ['tiːnˌeɪdʒə] Teenager; Jugendliche/-r I

telephone ['telɪfəʊn] Telefon I

*to **tell** [tel] erzählen; sagen; mitteilen I; erkennen; wissen II U1, 11 *to **tell** sb to do sth [ˌtel sʌmbədi tə ˈduː sʌmˈθɪŋ] jmdm. sagen, was er tun soll **II U3**, 54

Tell me about … [ˈtel mi ˌəˈbaʊt] Erzähle mir von … **I**

temperature [ˈtemprətʃə] Temperatur **II F1**, 21

ten [ten] zehn **I**

tennis [ˈtenɪs] Tennis **I**

tense [tens] Zeit; Zeitform *(grammatisch)* °**II U4**, 63

tent [tent] Zelt **II U3**, 54

terrible [ˈterəbl] schrecklich; schlimm; furchtbar **II U3**, 55

test [test] Test; Klassenarbeit; Prüfung **I**

*to take a **test** [ˌteɪk ə ˈtest] einen Test machen °**II U5**, 89

to **test** [test] testen; prüfen °**II U6**, 109

text [tekst] Text **I**

text (message) [ˈtekst ˌmesɪdʒ] SMS; Kurznachricht **I**

to **text** [tekst] eine SMS schicken **II U5**, 82

than [ðæn] als *(bei Vergleichen)* **II F1**, 21

more … **than** [ˈmɔː ðən] mehr … als **I**

to **thank** [θæŋk] danken **II F3**, 96

Thank you. [ˈθæŋk ju] Danke. **I**

thankful [ˈθæŋkfl] dankbar **I**

Thanks. [θæŋks] Danke. **I**

that [ðæt; ðət] dass **I**

that [ðæt] das; jenes **I**

after **that** [ˌɑːftə ˈðæt] danach **I**

like **that** [laɪk ˈðæt] so **I**

That was close! [ˌðæt wəz ˈkləʊs] Das war knapp! **I**

That's fine with me. [ˌðæts ˌfaɪn wɪð ˈmiː] Das ist in Ordnung für mich. **II U2**, 23

That's what friends are for. [ˌðæts wɒt ˈfrendz ˌɑː ˌfɔː] Dafür sind Freunde da. **I**

that's why [ˌðæts ˈwaɪ] deshalb **II U2**, 35

That's … [ˌðæts] Das macht … **I**

that [ðæt] *Relativpronomen für Personen und Dinge* **II U2**, 27

the [ðə; ði] der; die *(auch Pl.)*; das **I**

the others [ði ˈʌðəz] die anderen **I**

the rest [rest] der Rest **II U2**, 35

the same [ðə ˈseɪm] der-/die-/dasselbe; der/die/das gleiche **I**

the … the … + *comparative form* [ðə … ðə] je … desto … + *Komparativ* **II U4**, 60

movie **theater** *(AE)* [ˌmuːvi ˈθiətə] Kino *(amerik.)* **II U1**, 10

theatre [ˈθiətə] Theater **I**

their [ðeə] ihr/-e *(Pl.)* **I**

them [ðem] sie *(Pl.)*; ihnen **I**

theme [θiːm] Thema; Motto **I**

theme park [ˈθiːm ˌpɑːk] Vergnügungspark *(meist mit einem bestimmten Thema)*; Themenpark **II F1**, 20

then [ðen] dann; danach **I**

there [ðeə] da; dort; dahin; dorthin **I**

over **there** [ˌəʊvə ˈðeə] da drüben; dort drüben **I**

There's nothing more exciting than … [ˌðeəz ˌnʌθɪŋ mɔːr ɪkˈsaɪtɪŋ ðən] Es gibt nichts Spannenderes als … **II U1**, 10

there is/are [ðər ˈɪz/ˈɑː] da ist/sind; es gibt **I**

these [ðiːz] diese (hier) **I**

they [ðeɪ] sie *(Pl.)* **I**

It's …/**They**'re … [ɪts/ðeə] Es kostet …/ Sie kosten … **I**

thing [θɪŋ] Ding; Sache **I**

*to **think** [θɪŋk] denken; nachdenken; glauben **I**

*to **think** of [ˈθɪŋk əv] halten von; denken über **I**

third [θɜːd] dritte/-r/-s **I**

thirteen [ˌθɜːˈtiːn] dreizehn **I**

thirty [ˈθɜːti] dreißig **I**

this [ðɪs] dies; diese/-r/-s **I**

This is how you (do) … [ˈðɪs ɪz haʊ jʊ ˌduː] So machst du … **I**

This is … [ˈðɪs ɪz] Das (hier) ist … **I**

those [ðəʊz] diese dort; jene **I**

thought [θɔːt] Gedanke °**II U4**, 74

thousands of [ˈθaʊzndz əv] Tausende (von) **I**

three [θriː] drei **I**

three and a half times [ˌθriː ˌənd ə ˈhɑːf taɪmz] dreieinhalbmal **II F1**, 21

through [θruː] durch **I**

*to **throw** (at) [θrəʊ] werfen (nach) **I**

*to **throw** away [ˌθrəʊ əˈweɪ] wegwerfen **I**

thunder *(no pl)* [ˈθʌndə] Donner **II U5**, 92

Thursday [ˈθɜːzdeɪ] Donnerstag **I**

ticket [ˈtɪkɪt] Los; Ticket; Eintrittskarte **I**; Fahrschein **II F2**, 76

to **tidy** *(a room)* [ˈtaɪdi] aufräumen; in Ordnung bringen **I**

tidy [ˈtaɪdi] sauber; ordentlich **II U3**, 48

tie [taɪ] Unentschieden **II U4**, 61

to **tie** (to) [ˈtaɪ tə] binden (an); fesseln (an) **II U2**, 35

tiger [ˈtaɪɡə] Tiger **II U3**, 47

till [tɪl] bis **I**

time [taɪm] Zeit **I**; Mal **II U1**, 15

at the same **time** [ət ðə ˌseɪm ˈtaɪm] zur selben Zeit; gleichzeitig **I**

free **time** [ˌfriː ˈtaɪm] Freizeit **I**

on **time** [ɒn ˈtaɪm] pünktlich **II U2**, 31

three and a half **times** [ˌθriː ˌənd ə ˈhɑːf taɪmz] dreieinhalbmal **II F1**, 21

time line [ˈtaɪm ˌlaɪn] Zeitstrahl **II U1**, 10

time slot [ˈtaɪm slɒt] Zeitfenster °**II U2**, 32

Time to get up! [ˌtaɪm tə ˌɡetˈʌp] Es ist Zeit aufzustehen! **I**

What **time**? [ˌwɒt ˈtaɪm] Um wie viel Uhr? **I**

What's the **time**? [ˌwɒts ðə ˈtaɪm] Wie spät ist es?; Wie viel Uhr ist es? **I**

timetable [ˈtaɪmˌteɪbl] Stundenplan; Fahrplan **I**

tin [tɪn] Zinn **II U6**, 110

tinned [tɪnd] Dosen-; aus der Dose **I**

tip [tɪp] Tipp; Ratschlag **I**

to **tiptoe** [ˈtɪptəʊ] auf Zehenspitzen gehen **II U3**, 54

tired [taɪəd] müde **I**

title [ˈtaɪtl] Titel; Überschrift **II U1**, 16

to [tʊ; tə] zu; nach; auf; in; vor *(bei Uhrzeitangaben)* **I**

from … **to** [frəm … tə] von … bis **I**

quarter past/**to** [ˈkwɔːtə pɑːst/tə] Viertel nach/vor **I**

toast [təʊst] Toast **I**

today [təˈdeɪ] heute **I**

together [təˈɡeðə] zusammen; miteinander; gemeinsam **I**

*to put **together** [ˌpʊt təˈɡeðə] zusammensetzen **II U5**, 87

toilet [ˈtɔɪlət] Toilette **I**

tomato, tomatoes *(pl)* [təˈmɑːtəʊ] Tomate **I**

tomorrow [təˈmɒrəʊ] morgen **I**

2nite (= tonight) [təˈnaɪt] heute Abend **I**

too [tuː] auch; zu **I**

Me **too**. [ˌmi ˈtuː] Ich auch. **I**

Too bad! [ˌtuː ˈbæd] Zu dumm!; Schade! **I**

You **too**? [ju ˈtuː] Du auch? **I**

tool [tuːl] Werkzeug; Gerät **II U6**, 111

top [tɒp] Spitze; oberer Teil; oberes Ende **I**

on **top** [ɒn ˈtɒp] oben; obendrauf **I**

topic [ˈtɒpɪk] Thema **II U2**, 31

torch [tɔːtʃ] Fackel; Taschenlampe **II U5**, 93

tornado [tɔːˈneɪdəʊ] Tornado **II U2**, 34

to stay in **touch** (with) [ˌsteɪ ɪn ˈtʌtʃ wɪð] in Kontakt bleiben (mit) **II U5**, 82

to **touch** [tʌtʃ] berühren; antippen **II U3**, 48

tour [tʊə] Tour; Fahrt; Rundgang **II U2**, 22

guided **tour** [ˌɡaɪdɪd ˈtʊə] geführte Tour; Führung °**II U3**, 51

tourism [ˈtʊərɪzm] Tourismus **II U6**, 104

tourist [ˈtʊərɪst] Tourist/-in **I**

tourist board [ˈtʊərɪst ˌbɔːd] Tourismuszentrale; Tourismusbehörde **II U6**, 103

tourist information centre [ˌtʊərɪst ˌɪnfəˈmeɪʃn ˌsentə] Touristeninformation **I**

towards [təˈwɔːds] in Richtung **II U3**, 54

town [taʊn] Stadt **I**

home **town** [ˈhəʊmtaʊn] Heimatstadt **II U1**, 8

toy [tɔɪ] Spielzeug **I**

track [træk] Spur; Fährte; Pfad; Bahn **II U3**, 54; Bahn *(Renn-/Lauf-)* **II U4**, 61

to **trade** [treɪd] Handel treiben **II F3**, 96

tradition [trəˈdɪʃn] Tradition **I**

traditional [trəˈdɪʃnl] traditionell **II U3**, 43

traffic jam [ˈtræfɪk ˌdʒæm] Stau **II U1**, 11

trail [treɪl] Weg; Pfad; Spur **II U3**, 43

train [treɪn] Zug **I**

to **train** [treɪn] trainieren **II U1**, 12

training [ˈtreɪnɪŋ] Training **II U4**, 72

trampoline [ˈtræmpliːn] Trampolin **II U3**, 44

to **translate** [trænzˈleɪt] übersetzen **I**

translation [trænzˈleɪʃn] Übersetzung **I**

transport [ˈtrænspɔːt] Verkehrsmittel; Transport **II U6**, 100 public **transport** (no pl) [ˌpʌblɪk ˈtrænspɔːt] öffentliche Verkehrsmittel **II U1**, 11

trash (AE) [træʃ] Abfall; Müll **II U3**, 48

travel [ˈtrævl] (das) Reisen; Reise **II U3**, 46

travel agent's [ˈtrævl ˌeɪdʒnts] Reisebüro **II U6**, 101

to **travel** [ˈtrævl] fahren; reisen **II U2**, 36

treasure [ˈtreʒə] Schatz **II U2**, 34

treat [triːt] besondere Freude; Belohnung **II AC1**, 38

tree [triː] Baum **I**

family **tree** [ˈfæmli ˌtriː] Stammbaum **I**

palm **tree** [ˈpɑːm ˌtriː] Palme **II U2**, 22

pony **trekking** [ˈpəʊni ˌtrekɪŋ] Ponyreiten im Gelände **II U6**, 99

trial [traɪəl] Qualifikation **II U4**, 62

tribe [traɪb] Stamm; Volksstamm **II F3**, 96

trick [trɪk] Trick; Streich **I**

to play a **trick** (on) [ˌpleɪ ə ˈtrɪk ˌɒn] einen Streich spielen **I**

trick-or-treating [ˌtrɪk ɔː ˈtriːtɪŋ] Süßes oder Saures (Spiel zu Halloween, bei dem Kinder von Tür zu Tür gehen und um Süßigkeiten bitten) **II AC1**, 38

trifle [ˈtraɪfl] Trifle (englischer Nachtisch) **I**

trip [trɪp] Trip; Reise; Ausflug; Fahrt **I**

to **trip** (over) [ˌtrɪp ˈəʊvə] stolpern (über) **I**

trombone [trɒmˈbəʊn] Posaune **II U2**, 24

trouble [ˈtrʌbl] Ärger; Probleme; Schwierigkeiten **II U3**, 52

*to make **trouble** [ˌmeɪk ˈtrʌbl] Ärger machen; in Schwierigkeiten bringen **I**

trousers (pl) [ˈtraʊzəz] Hose **II U6**, 110

true [truː] wahr **II AC1**, 38

trunk (AE) [trʌŋk] Kofferraum (amerik.) °**II U2**, 34

to **try** [traɪ] versuchen; probieren **I**

to **try** hard [ˌtraɪ ˈhɑːd] sich anstrengen; sich Mühe geben **II U5**, 93

to **try** on [ˌtraɪ ˈɒn] anprobieren **II U3**, 49

Try … [traɪ] Versuch es mal mit …; Probier mal … **I**

T-shirt [ˈtiːʃɜːt] T-Shirt **I**

the **Tube** [tjuːb] U-Bahn (in London) **II F2**, 76

Tuesday [ˈtjuːzdeɪ] Dienstag **I**

tunnel [ˈtʌnl] Tunnel **I**

turn [tɜːn] Wendung; Drehung **II U1**, 12

Take **turns.** [ˌteɪk ˈtɜːnz] Wechselt euch ab. **I**

It's your **turn.** [ˌɪts ˈjɔː tɜːn] Du bist dran. **I**

Your **turn.** [ˈjɔː tɜːn] Du bist dran. **I**

to **turn** [tɜːn] drehen; (sich) umdrehen **II U3**, 44

to **turn** (a)round [ˌtɜːn (ə)ˈraʊnd] (sich) umdrehen; wenden **II U1**, 17

to **turn** off [ˌtɜːn ˈɒf] abschalten; ausschalten **II U5**, 87

to **turn** on [ˌtɜːn ˈɒn] einschalten **II U2**, 35

to **turn** over [ˌtɜːn ˈəʊvə] umdrehen; umkippen **II U3**, 44

to **turn** to [ˈtɜːn tə] sich wenden an; sich zuwenden **II U6**, 111

to **turn** up [ˌtɜːn ˈʌp] auftauchen; erscheinen **II U3**, 49

to **turn** [tɜːn] einbiegen; abbiegen **II F2**, 77

tutor [ˈtjuːtə] Klassenlehrer/-in **I**

tutor group [ˈtjuːtə ˌgruːp] Klasse (in einer englischen Schule) **I**

TV (= television) [ˌtiːˈviː (ˈtelɪvɪʒn)] Fernsehen; Fernseher **I**

to watch **TV** [ˌwɒtʃ tiːˈviː] fernsehen **I**

twelve [twelv] zwölf **I**

twenty [ˈtwenti] zwanzig **I**

twenty-one [ˌtwentiˈwʌn] einundzwanzig **I**

twin [twɪn] Zwilling; Zwillings- **II U6**, 111

to **twist** your ankle [ˌtwɪst jɔːr ˈæŋkl] sich den Knöchel verrenken **II U4**, 64

two [tuː] zwei **I**

the **two** of them [ðə ˈtuː əv ðəm] beide **II U5**, 84

two of which [ˈtuː əv wɪtʃ] von denen zwei °**II U6**, 108

typical [ˈtɪpɪkl] typisch **I**

U

u (= you) [juː; jə] du; Sie; ihr **I**

UFO [ˈjuːefˌəʊ] UFO **II U4**, 70

unattended [ˌʌnəˈtendɪd] unbeaufsichtigt **II F2**, 77

uncle [ˈʌŋkl] Onkel **I**

uncool [ʌnˈkuːl] nicht cool **II U3**, 48

to **uncover** [ʌnˈkʌvə] aufdecken; frei legen **II U2**, 34

under [ˈʌndə] unter **I**

Underground [ˈʌndəgraʊnd] U-Bahn **II F2**, 76

*to **understand** [ˌʌndəˈstænd] verstehen **I**

understanding [ˌʌndəˈstændɪŋ] Verständnis **II U5**, 91

unfair [ʌnˈfeə] unfair **II U1**, 17

unfriendly [ʌnˈfrendli] unfreundlich ⟨**II U1**, 14⟩

unhappy [ʌnˈhæpi] unglücklich **II U1**, 16

uniform [ˈjuːnɪfɔːm] Uniform **I**

unit [ˈjuːnɪt] Lektion; Kapitel; Einheit **I**

*to be **unlucky** [bɪ ʌnˈlʌki] Pech haben **I**

to **unscrew** [ʌnˈskruː] losschrauben **II U5**, 87

unsure [ʌnˈʃʊə] unsicher **II U1**, 16

to **untie** [ʌnˈtaɪ] losbinden °**II U2**, 35

until [ʌnˈtɪl] bis **II F1**, 20

not … **until** [ˌnɒt ənˈtɪl] nicht bevor; erst wenn **II U2**, 27

unusual [ʌnˈjuːʒl] ungewöhnlich **II U3**, 48

up [ʌp] hinauf; (nach) oben **II U1**, 13

to end **up** [ˌend ˈʌp] enden; landen **II U1**, 8

*to get **up** [ˌget ˈʌp] aufstehen (aus dem Bett) **I**

*to keep **up** [ˌkiːp ˈʌp] aufrechterhalten °**II U1**, 9

to look **up** [ˌlʊk ˈʌp] nachschlagen; nachschauen **II U1**, 15

up to [ˈʌp tə] bis zu **I**

upset [ʌpˈset] aufgebracht; bestürzt **II U1**, 17

upstairs [ʌpˈsteəz] nach oben; im Obergeschoss; oben **II U5**, 92

us [ʌs] uns **I**

to **use** [juːz] benutzen; verwenden; gebrauchen **I**

useful [ˈjuːsfl] nützlich; hilfreich **I**

usual [ˈjuːʒl] üblich **II U2**, 34

usually [ˈjuːʒli] normalerweise; gewöhnlich; meistens **I**

V

vacation (AE) [vəˈkeɪʃn] Ferien; Urlaub **I**

valuable [ˈvæljuəbl] wertvoll °**II U2**, 34

very [ˈveri] sehr **I**

very much [ˌveri ˈmʌtʃ] sehr **I**

vet [vet] Tierarzt/Tierärztin **I**

video [ˈvɪdiəʊ] Video **II U2**, 24

video chat [ˈvɪdiəʊ ˌtʃæt] Videochat **I**

point of **view** [ˌpɔɪnt əv ˈvjuː] Standpunkt; Ansicht; Perspektive **II U4**, 74

viewer [ˈvjuːə] Zuschauer/-in ⟨**II U3**, 50⟩

viewing [ˈvjuːɪŋ] Hör-/Sehverstehen **I**

village [ˈvɪlɪdʒ] Dorf **I**

villain [ˈvɪlən] Bösewicht **II AC3**, 114

visit [ˈvɪzɪt] Besuch **I**

to **visit** [ˈvɪzɪt] besichtigen; besuchen **I**

visitor [ˈvɪzɪtə] Besucher/-in **I**

vocabulary [vəˈkæbjələri] Vokabular; Wortschatz **I**

voice [vɔɪs] Stimme **I**

volleyball [ˈvɒlibɔːl] Volleyball **I**

voyage [ˈvɔɪɪdʒ] Reise °**II U2**, 34

W

to **wait** (for) [weɪt] warten (auf) **I**

Wait and see! [ˌweɪt ənd ˈsiː] Warte ab! **I**

*to **wake** up [ˌweɪk ˈʌp] aufwachen; aufwecken **II U2**, 35

gallery **walk** [ˈgælri ˌwɔːk] Museumsrundgang; Vernissage °**II U6**, 109

*to go for a **walk** [ˌgəʊ fər ə ˈwɔːk] spazieren gehen **II U3**, 54

to **walk** [wɔːk] gehen; laufen **I**

to **walk** the dog [ˌwɔːk ðə ˈdɒg] den Hund ausführen; mit dem Hund spazieren gehen **I**

wall [wɔːl] Wand; Mauer **I**

to **want** (to) [ˈwɒnt tə] wollen; mögen **I**

to **want** somebody to do something [ˌwɒnt sʌmbədi tə ˈduː sʌmθɪŋ] wollen, dass jemand etwas tut **I**

war [wɔː] Krieg **II F1**, 20

civil **war** [ˌsɪvl ˈwɔː] Bürgerkrieg **II F1**, 20

wardrobe [ˈwɔːdrəʊb] Kleiderschrank **I**

to **warm** up [ˌwɔːm ˈʌp] aufwärmen; sich aufwärmen **I**

warm [wɔːm] warm **II U2**, 37

warrior [ˈwɒriə] Krieger **II F3**, 96

to **wash** [wɒʃ] waschen; sich waschen **I**
washing machine [ˈwɒʃɪŋ məˌʃiːn] Waschmaschine **II U5**, 87
to **waste** [weɪst] verschwenden **II U5**, 87
watch [wɒtʃ] Armbanduhr **II U1**, 13
to **watch** [wɒtʃ] beobachten; (sich) ansehen;
zuschauen **I**
  to **watch** TV [ˌwɒtʃ tiːˈviː] fernsehen **I**
water [ˈwɔːtə] Wasser **I**
  water slide [ˈwɔːtə ˌslaɪd] Wasserrutsche **I**
wave [weɪv] Welle **I**
way [weɪ] Weg; Art und Weise **I**
  *to be in the **way** [biˌɪn ðə ˈweɪ] im Weg
sein/stehen **I**
  by the **way** [ˌbaɪ ðə ˈweɪ] übrigens **II F1**, 21
  *to get in the **way** [ˌget ɪn ðə ˈweɪ] stören;
im Weg stehen **II U4**, 72
  in a polite **way** [ɪnˌə pəˈlaɪt ˌweɪ] auf
höfliche Art **II U6**, 103
  one **way** [ˈwʌn weɪ] einfach *(Fahrschein)*
II F2, 76
  the same **way** as [ˌðə seɪm ˈweɪ æz]
genauso wie ⟨**II U1**, 14⟩
we [wiː; wi] wir **I**
  We're from … [ˈwɪə frəm] Wir sind
aus … **I**
*to **wear** [weə] anhaben; tragen *(Kleidung)* **I**
weather [ˈweðə] Wetter **I**
  weather forecast [ˈweðə ˌfɔːkɑːst] Wettervorhersage **II U6**, 102
webcam [ˈwebkæm] Webcam °**II U3**, 51
website [ˈwebsaɪt] Website; Internetauftritt **I**
wedding [ˈwedɪŋ] Hochzeit **I**
Wednesday [ˈwenzdeɪ] Mittwoch **I**
week [wiːk] Woche **I**
weekend [ˌwiːkˈend] Wochenende **I**
  at the **weekend** [ət ðə ˌwiːkˈend] am
Wochenende **I**
weird [wɪəd] merkwürdig; seltsam; sonderbar **II U5**, 91
Welcome! [ˈwelkəm] Willkommen! **I**
to **welcome** [ˈwelkəm] willkommen heißen
II U2, 26
You're **welcome.** [jɔː ˈwelkəm] Bitte schön.;
Nichts zu danken.; Gern geschehen. **I**
well [wel] gut **II AC2**, 58
  *to get **well** [ˌget ˈwel] gesund werden
II U4, 65
well [wel] tja; nun **I**
Welsh [welʃ] walisisch; Walisisch;
Waliser/-in **II F3**, 97
west [west] Westen; West- **I**
wet [wet] nass **II U3**, 44
what [wɒt] was; welche/-r/-s; was für ein **I**
  what a … [ˈwɒt ə] was für ein/-e …;
welch ein/-e … **II U1**, 9
  What a shame! [wɒt ə ˈʃeɪm] Wie schade!
II U1, 12
  What about … ? [ˈwɒt əˌbaʊt] Was ist
mit …?; Wie wär's mit …? **I**

What colour is …? [ˌwɒt ˈkʌlər ɪz] Welche
Farbe hat …? **I**
  what else [wɒt ˈels] was sonst; was noch **I**
  What is … about? [ˌwɒt ɪz əˈbaʊt] Worum
geht es in/im …? **I**
  What is … like? [ˌwɒt ɪz … ˈlaɪk] Wie
ist …? **U4**, 66
  what it's like [ˌwɒt ɪts ˈlaɪk] wie das ist
I U4, 66
  What on earth …? [ˌwɒt ˌɒnˈɜːθ] Was um
alles in der Welt …? **II U5**, 87
  What time? [wɒt ˈtaɪm] Um wie viel Uhr? **I**
  what to … [ˈwɒt tə] was man … **I**
  What's that? [wɒts ˈðæt] Was ist das? **I**
  What's your favourite …? [ˈwɒts jə ˌfeɪvrɪt]
Was ist dein/-e Lieblings…? **I**
  What's your name? [ˈwɒts jə ˈneɪm] Wie
heißt du?; Wie heißen Sie? **I**
  What's the matter? [ˌwɒts ðə ˈmætə] Was
ist los?; Was hast du? **II U6**, 110
  What's the time? [ˌwɒts ðə ˈtaɪm] Wie spät
ist es?; Wie viel Uhr ist es? **I**
  … **what** to do. [ˈwɒt tə duː] … was ich
tun soll. **II U5**, 84
wheat [wiːt] Weizen **I**
wheel [wiːl] Rad; Steuerrad; Steuer **I**
wheelchair [ˈwiːltʃeə] Rollstuhl **II U1**, 10
when [wen] wenn; wann; als **I**
whenever [wenˈevə] wann immer; jedes
Mal, wenn; so oft **II U5**, 84
where [weə] wo; wohin **I**
  Where … from? [ˌweə … ˈfrɒm] Woher …? **I**
which [wɪtʃ] welche/-r/-s **I**
which [wɪtʃ] *Relativpronomen für Dinge*
II U2, 27
while [waɪl] während **I**
to **whip** [wɪp] *(Sahne)* schlagen **I**
to **whisper** [ˈwɪspə] flüstern **I**
white [waɪt] weiß **I**
who [huː] wer; wem; wen **I**
  Who … for? [ˌhuː ˈfɔː] Für wen …? **I**
  Who's in? [huːzˌɪn] Wer macht mit?; Wer
ist dabei? **II U4**, 62
who [huː] *Relativpronomen für Personen*
II U2, 27
whoa [wəʊ] ho; langsam **II U2**, 27
whole [həʊl] ganz **I**
whoosh [wʊʃ] wusch **I**
whose [huːz] wessen **I**; dessen *(Relativpronomen)*; deren *(Relativpronomen)* **II U2**, 27
why [waɪ] warum **I**
  that's **why** [ˌðæts ˈwaɪ] deshalb **II U2**, 35
wide [waɪd] weit; breit; ausgedehnt **II U3**, 54
wife [waɪf], **wives** [waɪvz] *(pl)* Ehefrau
II U6, 111
wild [waɪld] wild **II U3**, 42
wilderness [ˈwɪldənəs] Wildnis **II U3**, 42
wildlife [ˈwaɪldlaɪf] Tierwelt *(in freier Wild-
bahn)* °**II U3**, 51
*to **win** [wɪn] gewinnen; siegen **I**
wind [wɪnd] Wind **II U2**, 34

window [ˈwɪndəʊ] Fenster **I**
windsurfing [ˈwɪndsɜːfɪŋ] Windsurfen
II U6, 99
windy [ˈwɪndi] windig **II U2**, 34
wine [waɪn] Wein **I**
winner [ˈwɪnə] Gewinner/-in; Sieger/-in
II U3, 48
winter [ˈwɪntə] Winter **I**
wireless [ˈwaɪələs] drahtlos °**II U3**, 51
wish [wɪʃ] Wunsch **I**
  *to make a **wish** [meɪk əˈwɪʃ] sich etwas
wünschen **I**
  Best **wishes** [ˌbest ˈwɪʃɪz] Viele Grüße;
Herzliche Grüße **II U6**, 103
with [wɪð] mit; bei **I**
without [wɪˈðaʊt] ohne **I**
witness [ˈwɪtnəs] Zeuge/Zeugin **II U4**, 69
wizard [ˈwɪzəd] Zauberer **II AC3**, 114
wolf [wʊlf], **wolves** *(pl)* [wʊlvz] [wʊlf] Wolf
II U3, 47
woman [ˈwʊmən], **women** *(pl)* [ˈwɪmɪn]
Frau **I**
no **wonder** [nəʊ ˈwʌndə] kein Wunder
II U3, 55
wonderful [ˈwʌndəfl] wunderbar **II U1**, 16
wooden [ˈwʊdn] hölzern; aus Holz **II U2**, 24
word [wɜːd] Wort **I**
  key **word** [ˈkiː ˌwɜːd] Stichwort; Schlüsselbegriff **I**
  linking **word** [ˈlɪŋkɪŋ ˌwɜːd] Verbindungswort **II U5**, 84
  word cloud [ˈwɜːd ˌklaʊd] Wörterwolke
°**II U4**, 60
  Word power [ˈwɜːd ˌpaʊə] die Kraft der
Wörter *(Wortschatzübung)* **I**
work [wɜːk] Arbeit **I**
to **work** [wɜːk] arbeiten **I**; funktionieren
II U5, 87
workshop [ˈwɜːkʃɒp] Workshop **I**
world [wɜːld] Erde; Welt **I**
worm [wɜːm] Wurm **I**
worried [ˈwʌrid] beunruhigt; besorgt
II U1, 10
to **worry** [ˈwʌri] sich Sorgen machen **II U1**, 10
  Don't **worry**! [ˌdəʊnt ˈwʌri] Keine Sorge! **I**
*to be **worth** [bi ˈwɜːθ] wert sein **I**
would [wʊd] würde/-st/-n/-t **II U2**, 24
  would like [wʊd ˈlaɪk] würde/-st/-n/-t
gern; hätte/-st/-n/-t gern **I**
  would love [wʊd ˈlʌv] würde/-st/-n/-t sehr
gern; hätte/-st-/-n/-t sehr gern **I**
  Would you like …? [wʊd jə ˈlaɪk]
Möchtest du …?; Möchten Sie …?;
Möchtet ihr …? **II U4**, 62
Wow! [waʊ] Wow! **I**
*to **write** [raɪt] schreiben **I**
  *to **write** down [raɪt ˈdaʊn] aufschreiben **I**
writer [ˈraɪtə] Autor/-in; Schriftsteller/-in;
Verfasser/-in **II AC3**, 114
writing [ˈraɪtɪŋ] Schreiben **I**
wrong [rɒŋ] falsch **I**

*to be **wrong** [bi 'rɒŋ] unrecht haben; sich irren **I**
*to go **wrong** [ˌɡəʊ 'rɒŋ] schiefgehen **I**

X

XOXO [ˌhʌɡz̩ ən 'kɪsɪz] Umarmungen und Küsse *(am Ende von E-Mails und SMS)* **I**

Y

yard [jɑːd] Yard *(Längenmaß: ca. 91,44 cm)* **II F1**, 21
yard *(AE)* [jɑːd] Garten **I**
to **yawn** [jɔːn] gähnen **II U3**, 54
yeah *(infml)* [jeə] ja **I**
year [jɪə] Jahr; Schuljahr **I**
  11-**year**-old [ɪˈlevnˌjɪərəʊld] 11-Jährige/-r **II U4**, 62
yearbook [ˈjɪəbʊk] Jahrbuch **II U1**, 8
yellow [ˈjeləʊ] gelb **I**
yes [jes] ja **I**
yesterday [ˈjestədeɪ] gestern **I**
yet [jet] schon; noch **II U4**, 64
  not … **yet** [nɒt 'jet] noch nicht **II U4**, 64
yoghurt [ˈjɒɡət] Joghurt **I**
you [juː; jə] du; ihr; Sie **I**
  You too? [juː 'tuː] Du auch? **I**
  You're welcome. [jɔː 'welkəm] Bitte schön.; Nichts zu danken.; Gern geschehen. **I**
young [jʌŋ] jung **I**
your [jɔː; jə] dein/-e; euer/eure; Ihr/-e **I**
  What's **your** name? [ˌwɒts jə 'neɪm] Wie heißt du?; Wie heißen Sie? **I**
  Your turn. [ˈjɔː tɜːn] Du bist dran. **I**
Yours … [jɔːz] Viele Grüße … *(am Ende von Briefen und Mails)* **II U5**, 91
yourself [jɔːˈself] du/dir/dich/Sie/sich (selbst); selber **I**
yourselves [jɔːˈselvz] selber; ihr/euch/Sie/ sich (selbst) **II U6**, 103
youth [juːθ] Jugend **II U1**, 12
youth hostel [ˈjuːθ ˌhɒstl] Jugendherberge **II U3**, 52
yummy [ˈjʌmi] lecker **I**

Z

zebra [ˈzebrə] Zebra **II U3**, 47; °**II U6**, 108
zero [ˈzɪərəʊ] null **I**
zipline [ˈzɪplaɪn] Seilrutsche **II U3**, 43
to **zipline** [ˈzɪplaɪn] mit der Seilrutsche fahren **II U3**, 45
zoo [zuː] Zoo; Tierpark **I**

Boys' names

Adam [ˈædəm] **II U3**, 44
Algon [ˈælɡɒn] **II AC1**, 39
Antonio [ænˈtəʊniəʊ] **II U2**, 34
Ben [ben] **I**

Bob [bɒb] **I**
Carter [ˈkɑːtə] **II U3**, 44
Dale [deɪl] **II AC1**, 38
Damian [ˈdeɪmiən] **I**
Dave [deɪv] **I**
Desmond [ˈdezmənd] **I**
Drustan [ˈdrʊstən] **II F3**, 96
Frank [fræŋk] **II U5**, 92
Fumio [ˈfjuːmiəʊ] **II U1**, 17
Henry [ˈhenri] **I**
Jack [dʒæk] **I**
Jago [ˈdʒeɪɡəʊ] **II U6**, 111
Jahangir [dʒəˈhʌŋɡɪə] **I**
Jamie [ˈdʒeɪmi] **I**
Jay [dʒeɪ] **I**
Jeff [dʒef] **II U3**, 44
Jim [dʒɪm] **II U3**, 54
Jinsoo [ˈdʒɪnzuː] **II U1**, 14
Jon [dʒɒn] **II U5**, 82
Josh [dʒɒʃ] **II F1**, 21
Juan [hwɑːn] **II U3**, 44
Jude [dʒuːd] **II F1**, 21
Leo [ˈliːəʊ] **II AC2**, 59
Luke [luːk] **I**
Marley [ˈmɑːli] **II U1**, 14
Mike [maɪk] **II U1**, 12
Nathan [ˈneɪθn] ⟨**II U5**, 90⟩
Nick [nɪk] ⟨**II U1**, 14⟩; ⟨**II U3**, 50⟩
Rokuro [rəˈkuːrəʊ] **II U1**, 16
Ryan [raɪən] **I**
Sam [sæm] **II U3**, 44
Satoshi [səˈtɒʃi] **II U1**, 16
Scott [skɒt] **II U3**, 44
Shahid [ʃɑːˈhiːd] **I**
Steve [stiːv] **I**
Todd [tɒd] **II U3**, 44
Tony [ˈtəʊni] **I**
Tyler [ˈtaɪlə] **I**

Girls' names

Alicia [əˈlɪsiə; əˈlɪʃə] **I**
Amber [ˈæmbə] **I**
Amrita [æmˈriːtə] **II U2**, 26
Amy [ˈeɪmi] **II U1**, 10
Anna [ˈænə] **I**
Anne [æn] **I**
Ava [ˈeɪvə] **II U3**, 44
Ayla [ˈeɪlə] **II U4**, 66
Becca [ˈbekə] **II F1**, 21
Bunko [ˈbʌŋkəʊ] **II U1**, 17
Carly [ˈkɑːli] **II U3**, 44
Carol [ˈkærəl] **I**
Claire [ˈkleə] **I**
Emily [ˈemɪli] **I**
Frances [ˈfrɑːnsɪs] **I**
Grace [ɡreɪs] **II U3**, 44
Gwen [ɡwen] **II AC2**, 59
Helen [ˈhelɪn] **II U6**, 111
Holly [ˈhɒli] **I**
Jada [ˈdʒeɪdə] **II U3**, 44
Jenna [ˈdʒenə] **II U3**, 44

Jessie [ˈdʒesi] **II U3**, 44
Judith [ˈdʒuːdɪθ] **II U6**, 106
Julie [ˈdʒuːli] **I**
Laura [ˈlɔːrə] **I**
Lauren [ˈlɔːrən] **II U5**, 84
Lily [ˈlɪli] **I**
Lisa [ˈliːsə] **II AC2**, 59
Lou [luː] **I**
Lucy [ˈluːsi] **I**
Lynn [lɪn] **II F1**, 21
Macy [ˈmeɪsi] **II AC1**, 38
Madison [ˈmædɪsn] **II U1**, 10
Maisie [ˈmeɪzi] ⟨**II U5**, 90⟩
Maya [ˈmeɪə] **II U3**, 44
Megan [ˈmeɡən] **II U6**, 112
Mina [ˈmiːnə] ⟨**II U3**, 50⟩
Olivia [ɒlˈɪviə] **I**
Pia [ˈpiːə] **I**
Polly [ˈpɒli] ⟨**II U2**, 30⟩
Rose [rəʊz] **I**
Ruby [ˈruːbi] **II U5**, 84
Sal [sæl] **II F1**, 21
Sally [ˈsæli] **I**
Scarlet [ˈskɑːlət] **II U1**, 12
Seeta [ˈsiːtə] **I**
Sia [ˈsiːə] **II U3**, 57
Tamara [təˈmɑːrə] **II U6**, 111
Tomoko [təˈmɒkəʊ] **II U1**, 16
Victoria [vɪkˈtɔːriə] **II U3**, 44
Vivien [ˈvɪviən] **II AC3**, 115

Surnames

Andersen [ˈændəsn] **II U1**, 12
Azad [əˈzɑːd] **I**
Barnett [ˈbɑːnet] **II U4**, 65
Bayram [ˈbeɪrəm] **II U4**, 66
Briggs [brɪɡz] **I**
Elliot [ˈeliət] **I**
Fraser [ˈfreɪzə] **I**
Gibson [ˈɡɪbsn] **II U2**, 24
Ness [nes] **II U1**, 12
Nicholls [ˈnɪkəlz] **II U6**, 106
Parker [ˈpɑːkə] **II U4**, 73
Preston [ˈprestən] **I**
Richardson [ˈrɪtʃədsn] **I**
Swindon [ˈswɪndən] **I**
Thompson [ˈtɒmsən] ⟨**II U4**, 68⟩
Walker [ˈwɔːkə] **I**

Place names

Abingdon Street [ˈæbɪŋdən ˌstriːt] **II F2**, 77
Baker Street [ˈbeɪkə ˌstriːt] **II AC3**, 115
Bath [bɑːθ] **II F2**, 76
Battersea [ˈbætəsiː] **II F3**, 97
Begbie Road [ˌbeɡbi ˈrəʊd] **II U5**, 92
Blackheath [ˈblækhiːθ] **II U6**, 102
Bloomsbury [ˈbluːmzbri] **II F2**, 76
the **Bronx** [ðə ˈbrɒnks] **I**
Brook Lane [brʊk ˈleɪn] **I**
Brooklyn [ˈbrʊklɪn] **I**

Caerphilly [keə'fɪli] *walisische Stadt* II U6, 98
Camden Market ['kæmdən ˌmɑːkɪt] ⟨II U3, 50⟩
Carlsbad Caverns National Park [ˌkɑːlzbəd ˌkævnz ˌnæʃnl 'pɑːk] II F1, 20
Cedar Rapids [ˌsiːdə 'ræpɪdz] II U1, 12
Central Park [ˌsentrl 'pɑːk] I
Chicago [ʃɪ'kɑːgəʊ] II F1, 21
Cologne [kə'ləʊn] Köln I
Covent Garden [ˌkɒvnt 'gɑːdn] II F2, 77
Cracow ['krækɒv; 'krɑːkaʊ] Krakau I
Decorah [dɪ'kɔːrə] II U1, 8
Edinburgh ['edɪnbrə] II U6, 99
Everglades National Park [ˌevəgleɪdz ˌnæʃnl 'pɑːk] I
Fort Pierce [ˌfɔːt 'pɪəs] II U2, 34
Greenwich Park [ˌgrenɪdʒ 'pɑːk] I
Greenwich Pier [ˌgrenɪdʒ 'pɪə] I
Havana [hə'vænə] Havanna II U2, 26
Heathrow [ˌhiːθ'rəʊ] *Flughafen in London* II F2, 76
Holborn ['həʊbən] II F2, 76
Hollywood ['hɒliwʊd] I
Isle of Man [ˌaɪl əv 'mæn] II U6, 105
Kidbrooke Gardens [ˌkɪdbrʊk 'gɑːdnz] I
London ['lʌndən] I
Manhattan [mæn'hætn] I
Marble Arch [ˌmɑːbl̩ 'ɑːtʃ] II F2, 77
Miami [maɪ'æmi] II U2, 26
Milwaukee [mɪl'wɔːkiː] II U1, 8
Minneapolis [ˌmɪni'æplɪs] II U1, 8
Munich ['mjuːnɪk] München II F1, 21
New York [ˌnjuː 'jɔːk] I
Nottingham ['nɒtɪŋəm] II AC3, 115
Orlando [ɔː'lændəʊ] II F1, 20
Oxford ['ɒksfəd] II F1, 20
Oxford Circus [ˌɒksfəd 'sɜːkəs] II F2, 76
Paddington ['pædɪŋtən] II F2, 76
Piccadilly [ˌpɪkə'dɪli] II F2, 76
Queens [kwiːnz] I
Rome [rəʊm] Rom °II U6, 106
Russell Square ['rʌsl ˌskweə] II F2, 76
Salt Lake City [ˌsɔːlt leɪk 'sɪti] II F1, 21
South Street ['saʊθ ˌstriːt] I
St Agnes [ˌsənt 'ægnɪs] II U6, 100
St Austell [ˌsənt 'ɒstel] II U6, 104
St. Augustine [ˌseɪnt 'ɔːgəstiːn] II U2, 27
Staten Island [ˌstætn 'aɪlənd] I
Tallahassee [ˌtælə'hæsiː] II U2, 22
Tintagel [tɪn'tædʒl] II AC3, 115
Victoria Park [vɪktɔːriə 'pɑːk] I
Village Way ['vɪlɪdʒ ˌweɪ] I
Washington ['wɒʃɪŋtən] I
Wimbledon ['wɪmbldn] I

Geographical names

Alaska [ə'læskə] I
Alps [ælps] Alpen II U3, 49
America [ə'merɪkə] Amerika I
Arizona [ˌærɪ'zəʊnə] II F1, 20

Atlantic Ocean [ətˌlæntɪk 'əʊʃn] Atlantischer Ozean II U6, 104
Australia [ɒs'treɪliə] Australien I
Austria ['ɒstriə] Österreich II U4, 63
Bakerloo ['beɪkəluː] II F2, 76
Bavaria [bə'veəriə] Bayern I
Bodmin Moor [ˌbɒdmɪn 'mɔː] *Hochmoorlandschaft im nordöstlichen Cornwall* II U6, 104
Britain ['brɪtn] Großbritannien I
British Isles [ˌbrɪtɪʃ 'aɪlz] Britische Inseln II F3, 97
California [ˌkælɪ'fɔːniə] Kalifornien II F1, 21
Canada ['kænədə] Kanada I
China ['tʃaɪnə] China I
Colorado [ˌkɒlər'ɑːdəʊ] II U3, 42
Cornwall ['kɔːnwɔːl] II U6, 98
Cuba ['kjuːbə] Kuba II U2, 25
Death Valley [ˌdeθ 'væli] II F1, 21
England ['ɪŋlənd] England I
Essex ['esɪks] II F1, 20
Europe ['jʊərəp] Europa II U2, 34
Florida ['flɒrɪdə] I
Florida Keys [ˌflɒrɪdə 'kiːz] Florida Keys *(zu Florida gehörige Inseln)* II U2, 37
Germany ['dʒɜːməni] Deutschland I
Grand Canyon [ˌgrænd 'kænjən] I
Gulf of Mexico Golf von Mexiko II AC1, 39
Hawaii [hə'waiiː] I
India ['ɪndiə] Indien I
Iowa ['aɪəʊə] II U1, 8
Isle of Dogs [ˌaɪl əv 'dɒgz] I
Italy ['ɪtəli] Italien II U6, 105
Kent [kent] *Grafschaft im Südosten Englands* ⟨II U4, 68⟩
Lake District ['leɪk ˌdɪstrɪkt] II U4, 69
Lower 48 [ˌləʊə fɔː'tiːeɪt] *Festlandstaaten der USA südlich von Kanada* I
Maine [meɪn] II AC1, 39
Mexico ['meksɪkəʊ] Mexiko II U2, 34
Midwest [ˌmɪd'west] Mittlerer Westen II F1, 20
Minnesota [ˌmɪnɪ'səʊtə] II AC1, 39
Mississippi [ˌmɪsɪ'sɪpi] II AC1, 39
Mount Elbert [ˌmaʊnt 'elbət] II U3, 43
New Hampshire [nju: 'hæmpʃə] II F1, 20
New Mexico [nju: 'meksɪkəʊ] II F1, 20
Northern Ireland [ˌnɔːðn 'aɪələnd] Nordirland I
Pakistan [ˌpɑːkɪ'stɑːn] I
Poland ['pəʊlənd] Polen I
Republic of Ireland [rɪˌpʌblɪk əv 'aɪələnd] Republik Irland I
Riviera [rɪv'jeɪrə] *Küstenlandschaft in Italien oder Südfrankreich* II U6, 99
the Rockies [ðə 'rɒkiz] II U3, 42
Rocky Mountains [ˌrɒki 'maʊntɪnz] II U3, 42
Scafell Pike [ˌskɔːfel 'paɪk] II U4, 69
Scotland ['skɒtlənd] Schottland I
Sherwood Forest [ˌʃɜːwʊd 'fɒrɪst] II AC3, 115
South Africa [ˌsaʊθ 'æfrɪkə] Südafrika I
Spain [speɪn] Spanien II U2, 34

Texas ['teksəs] I
the Thames [ðə 'temz] die Themse I
the United Kingdom (UK) [ði juːˌnaɪtɪd 'kɪŋdəm] das Vereinigte Königreich von Großbritannien und Nordirland I
the US (United States) [ði juːˌes (juːˌnaɪtɪd 'steɪts)] die USA *(die Vereinigten Staaten)* I
the USA (United States of America) [ði juːesˌeɪ (juːˌnaɪtɪd ˌsteɪts əv ə'merɪkə)] die USA *(die Vereinigten Staaten von Amerika)* I
Wales [weɪlz] I
Wyoming [waɪ'əʊmɪŋ] II F1, 21

Other names

Babe [beɪb] II AC1, 39
Big Apple [ˌbɪg 'æpl] I
Big Ben [ˌbɪg 'ben] I
Buckingham Palace [ˌbʌkɪŋəm 'pælɪs] I
the Capitol [ðə 'kæpɪtl] I
chicken tikka masala [ˌtʃɪkɪn ˌtɪkə mə'sɑːlə] *indisches Hühnchengericht* I
Christmas ['krɪsməs] Weihnachten I
Convention on the Rights of Persons with Disabilities [kən'venʃn ɒn ðə ˌraɪts əv ˌpɜːsnz wɪð ˌdɪsə'bɪlətiz] Behindertenrechtskonvention II AC2, 58
Cutty Sark [ˌkʌti 'sɑːk] I
Dinosaur Park [ˌdaɪnəsɔː 'pɑːk] Dinosaurierpark °II U2, 37
Diwali [dɪ'wɑːli] *hinduistisches Lichterfest* I
Docklands Light Railway (DLR) [ˌdɒklændz ˌlaɪt 'reɪlweɪ] *Regionalbahn im Osten Londons* I
Easter ['iːstə] Ostern I
Eden ['iːdn] (der Garten) Eden II U6, 104
Eid [iːd] Opferfest *(islamisches Fest)* I; Fastenbrechen nach dem Fastenmonat Ramadan *(islamisches Fest)* I
Excalibur [ek'skælɪbə] II AC3, 115
Friends of the Earth [ˌfrendz əv ði 'ɜːθ] II U1, 16
Giant's Causeway [ˌdʒaɪənts 'kɔːzweɪ] I
Guy Fawkes Night ['gaɪ fɔːks ˌnaɪt] *Tag zum Gedenken an die Pulververschwörung gegen den englischen König und sein Parlament am 5.11.1605* I
Hadrian's Wall [ˌheɪdriənz 'wɔːl] II F3, 97
Halloween [ˌhæləʊ'iːn] Halloween *Tag vor Allerheiligen* I
Hanukkah ['hʌnʊkə] Chanukka *(jüdisches Lichterfest)* I
Honey ['hʌni] I
Houses of Parliament [ˌhaʊzɪz əv 'pɑːləmənt] II F2, 77
Iceni [aɪ'siːnaɪ] Icener *(keltischer Volksstamm)* II F3, 96
Independence Day [ˌɪndɪ'pendəns ˌdeɪ] Unabhängigkeitstag *(USA)* I

Kennedy Space Center [ˌkenədi ˈspeɪs ˌsentə] II U2, 23

London Eye [ˌlʌndən ˈaɪ] I

Madame Tussauds [ˌmædəm tʊˈsɔːdz] I

Meridian Line [məˌrɪdiən ˈlaɪn] Nullmeridian I

Miami Vice [maɪˈæmi ˌvaɪs] II U2, 28

Minnesota Vikings [ˌmɪnɪˌsəʊtə ˈvaɪkɪŋz] II U1, 13

Mousebook [ˈmaʊsbʊk] II U5, 82

Mr Fluff [ˌmɪstə ˈflʌf] I

Mudchute Farm [ˌmʌdʃuːt ˈfɑːm] I

National Air and Space Museum [ˌnæʃnl̩ eəʳ ənd ˈspeɪs mjuːˌziːəm] I

Natural History Museum [ˌnætʃrl̩ ˈhɪstri mjuːˌziːəm] II U1, 16

New Year's Eve [ˌnjuː ˌjɪəʳ ˈiːv] Silvester I

Notting Hill Carnival [ˌnɒtɪŋ hɪl ˈkɑːnɪvl̩] *Karibischer Karneval in einem Stadtteil Londons* I

the **Olympics** (Olympic Games) [ðiˌ əˈlɪmpɪks; əˌlɪmpɪk ˈgeɪmz] Olympiade II F1, 21

the **Olympics** (Olympic Games) [ðiˌ əˈlɪmpɪks; əˌlɪmpɪk ˈgeɪmz] Olympische Spiele II F1, 21

Overseas Highway [ˌəʊvəsiːz ˈhaɪweɪ] Overseas Highway *(Autobahn übers Meer zu den Keys)* II U2, 37

Pentecost [ˈpentɪkɒst] Pfingsten I

Revolutionary War [ˌrevlˈuːʃnri ˈwɔː] Revolutionskrieg II AC1, 39

Revolutionary War [ˌrevlˈuːʃnri ˈwɔː] Unabhängigkeitskrieg II AC1, 39

Royal Observatory [ˌrɔɪəl əbˈzɜːvətri] I

Rusty [ˈrʌsti] II U1, 12

San Pedro [ˌsæn ˈpeɪdrəʊ] II U2, 34

Sherlock [ˈʃɜːlɒk] I

Shrove Tuesday [ˌʃrəʊv ˈtjuːzdeɪ] Faschingsdienstag I

Sid [sɪd] I

Sky High [skaɪ ˈhaɪ] °II U2, 37

Special Olympics [speʃl̩ əˈlɪmpɪks] II AC2, 59

the **Statue of Liberty** [ˌstætʃuː əv ˈlɪbəti] die Freiheitsstatue I

Sunny [ˈsʌni] I

tae kwon do [ˌteɪkwɒnˈdəʊ] Taekwondo II U2, 32

Thomas Tallis School *(= TTS)* [ˌtɒməs ˈtælɪs ˌskuːl] I

the **Tower of London** [ðə ˌtaʊəʳ əv ˈlʌndən] °II U6, 108

Valentine's Day [ˈvæləntaɪnz ˌdeɪ] Valentinstag I

Water Adventure [ˈwɔːtəʳ ədˌventʃə] Wasserabenteuer °II U2, 37

Westminster Abbey [ˌwestmɪnstəʳ ˈæbi] II F2, 77

the **White House** [ˈwaɪt ˌhaʊs] I

Whitsun [ˈwɪtsn] Pfingsten I

Famous names

Agatha Christie [ˌægəθə ˈkrɪsti] II AC3, 115

Boudicca [ˈbuːdɪkə] II F3, 96

Dr Watson [ˌdɒktə ˈwɒtsən] II AC3, 115

George Washington [ˌdʒɔːdʒ ˈwɒʃɪŋtən] I

Hadrian [ˈheɪdriən] II F3, 97

Juan Esteban de Ubilla [ˌhwaːn eˌsteɪbaːn deˌuˈbiːjə] II U2, 34

Juan Ponce de Leon [ˌhwaːn ˌpɒnθə də ˈleɪɒn] II U2, 28

Julius Caesar [ˌdʒuːliəs ˈsiːzə] II F3, 96

King Arthur [ˌkɪŋ ˈɑːθə] König Artus II AC3, 115

Maid Marian [ˌmeɪd ˈmæriən] II AC3, 115

Miss Marple [mɪs ˈmɑːpl̩] II AC3, 115

Molly Pitcher [ˌmɒli ˈpɪtʃə] II AC1, 39

Paul Bunyan [ˌpɔːl ˈbʌnjən] II AC1, 39

Robin Hood [ˌrɒbɪn ˈhʊd] II AC3, 115

Sherlock Holmes [ˌʃɜːlɒk ˈhəʊmz] II AC3, 114;

German-English dictionary

A

abbiegen to turn II F2, 77

abblocken to block II U5, 85

abbrennen *to burn down II F3, 96

Abend evening I

heute **Abend** 2nite (= tonight) I

Abendessen dinner I

abends in the evenings I

abends *(Uhrzeit)* p.m. I

Abenteuer adventure II U3, 42

aber but I

abfahren to depart II F2, 77

Abfall trash *(AE)* II U3, 48

abfliegen to depart II F2, 77

abhängen von to depend (on) II U6, 101

Abheben take-off II U2, 23

abheben *to take off II U3, 49

abholen to pick up II U3, 48

abnehmen *to take off II U5, 92

Vorlieben und **Abneigungen** likes and dislikes II U1, 8

abschalten to turn off II U5, 87

abschicken *to send off II U6, 103

Abschnitt section II U3, 52

abschreiben to copy I

erneut **abspielen** to replay II U3, 48

Abstammung origin II U2, 25

abstürzen to crash II U5, 93

Ach so! I see II U1, 13

acht eight I

Achterbahn roller coaster II U2, 23

achtzehn eighteen I

achtzig eighty I

Acker field II U1, 8

Ackerland farmland II F1, 21

Action action I

Adler eagle II U1, 8

Adresse address I

Afroamerikaner/-in African-American II F1, 20

afroamerikanisch African-American II F1, 20

AG club I

aggressiv aggressive ⟨II U1, 14⟩

Aha! I see II U1, 13

ähnlich similar II U2, 36

Aktion action I

Aktivität activity I

albern silly I

alle everyone I; everybody II U3, 47

alle/-s all I

wir **alle** all of us II U6, 100

allein alone I

allein on your own I

buntes **Allerlei** mixed bag I

alles everything I

Alligator alligator I

Alphabet alphabet I

als *(bei Vergleichen)* than II F1, 21

als when I

als ob like I

also so I

alt old I

Wie **alt** bist du? How old are you? I

Wie **alt** sind Sie? How old are you? I

Alter age II U3, 44

Alternative alternative II F2, 76

am on I

am besten best I

am liebsten best I

am Meer at the seaside II U6, 99; by the sea II U6, 104

am Wochenende at the weekend I

aus **Amerika** American I

Amerikaner/-in American I

Amerikaner /-in kubanischer Abstammung Cuban-American II U2, 25

amerikanisch American I

Amtssprache official language I

sich **amüsieren** *to have fun I

an on; at I; by II U6, 110

an Bord aboard I

an Bord gehen to board II F2, 77

an Stelle von instead of I

an sein *to be on II U5, 92

anbauen *to grow I

anbieten to offer II U6, 104

Anblick sight I

die anderen the others I

andere/-r/-s other I; else II U3, 45

ein/-e andere/-r/-s another I

Einerseits …, (aber) andererseits … On the one hand …, (but) on the other hand … II U4, 74

(sich) ändern to change II AC1, 39

anders different; other I

Änderung change II U4, 71

Anfahrt drive II U2, 23

Anfang beginning II U1, 18

anfangen to start I; *to begin II F1, 20

anfeuern to cheer II U4, 64

sich anfühlen *to feel II U1, 16

Anführer/-in leader II AC1, 39

angeben *to show off II U5, 93

Angeber/-in show-off II U1, 8

Angeln fishing II U1, 19

von Angesicht zu Angesicht face-to-face II U5, 85

angreifen to attack II U3, 55

Angst fear II U4, 74

Angst haben (vor) *to be scared (of) I; *to be afraid (of) II U2, 35

Ich habe (keine) Angst vor … I'm (not) scared of … I

anhaben *to wear I

anhalten to stop I

den Atem anhalten *to hold your breath II U3, 46

Anhänger/-in fan II F1, 21; II U4, 75

anheben to lift II U3, 55

anhören to listen (to) I

ankommen to arrive II F2, 76

Ankündigung announcement II F2, 77

anmalen to paint I

Anmerkung note I

annähernd nearly II U3, 43

anprobieren to try on II U3, 49

Anruf phone call I

einen Anruf entgegennehmen to answer the phone I

Anrufbeantworter answering machine I

anrufen to call I

Anrufer/-in caller I

anschauen to look at I; *to have a look (at) II U4, 65

sich anschließen to join II U2, 24

etw. anschrauben an etw. to screw sth to sth II U5, 87

ansehen to look at I

(sich) ansehen to watch I

Ansicht point of view II U4, 74

anstarren to stare I

anstatt instead of I

sich anstrengen to try hard II U5, 93

antippen to touch II U3, 48; to tap II U5, 92

Antwort answer; reply I

antworten to answer I

antworten (auf) to reply (to) I

Anweisung instruction I

Anzeige display II U3, 51

anziehen *to put on II AC1, 38

Apfel apple I

App app II U5, 89

Apparat machine I

April April I

Arbeit job; work I

arbeiten to work I

Areal area I

Ärger trouble II U3, 52

Ärger machen *to make trouble I

jmdn. ärgern to tease sb II U1, 10

Argumente für und gegen etw. pros and cons II U5, 94

Arm arm I

arm poor II U1, 12

Armbanduhr watch II U1, 13

die Armen the poor II AC3, 115

Armee army II F3, 96

Ärmel sleeve II U3, 48

Art kind I

Art und Weise way I

auf höfliche Art in a polite way II U6, 103

Artikel article II AC2, 59

Arzt/Ärztin doctor II U4, 64

Arztpraxis surgery I

Assistent/-in assistant II U3, 49

Atem breath II U3, 46

den Atem anhalten *to hold your breath II U3, 46

Atemzug breath II U3, 46

Atlantischer Ozean Atlantic Ocean II U6, 104

atmen to breathe II U4, 72

Atme(t) tief ein. Take a deep breath. ⟨II U2, 30⟩

Atmosphäre atmosphere ⟨II U3, 50⟩; ⟨II U5, 90⟩

Attraktion attraction II U3, 51

attraktiv attractive II U2, 27

Aua! Ouch! II U4, 66

auch too; also I

auch nicht not either I

Du auch? You too? I

Ich auch. Me too. I

audiovisueller Effekt audio-visual effect ⟨II U1, 14⟩; ⟨II U6, 107⟩

auf nach off to II U3, 42

auf on; at; to I; onto II U3, 44

auf dem Foto/den Fotos in the photo(s) I

auf der anderen Seite von across I

auf der linken Seite on the left I

auf der rechten Seite on the right I

auf der Straße in the street I

auf einmal suddenly I

auf Wiedersehen goodbye I

auf Zehenspitzen gehen to tiptoe II U3, 54

aufbauen *to set up I

aufbewahren *to keep II U2, 29

aufbleiben to stay up I

aufdecken to uncover II U2, 34

Aufenthalt stay II F2, 76

aufführen to perform II U2, 24

Aufführung show II U4, 67

Aufgabe task; job; exercise I

aufgebracht upset II U1, 17

aufgeregt excited I; nervous II U1, 9

aufgeregt nervously II U5, 93; excitedly II U6, 110

aufheben to save II U2, 35; to pick up II U3, 48

jmdn. aufheitern to cheer sb up II AC2, 58

aufhören to finish II U3, 53

aufhören (mit) to stop I

aufmachen to open I

Aufmerksamkeit attention II U5, 85

Aufnahme recording I

Aufnahmestudio recording studio I

aufnehmen to record II U4, 70

aufpassen auf to look after I; to look out for II U3, 43

Pass/Passt auf! Be careful! I

aufräumen to tidy (a room) I

aufregend exciting I

aufsagen *to say I

aufschlagen to crash II U2, 35

aufschreiben *to write down I

aufstehen (aus dem Bett) *to get up I

Es ist Zeit aufzustehen! Time to get up! I

aufstehen (von einer Sitzgelegenheit) *to stand up I

auftauchen to turn up II U3, 49

Auftrag task I

auftragen *to put on II AC1, 38

auftreten to perform II U2, 24

Auftritt gig II U2, 24

aufwachen *to wake up II U2, 35

aufwachsen *to grow up II U1, 11

aufwärmen to warm up I

sich aufwärmen to warm up I

aufwecken *to wake up II U2, 35

aufzeichnen to record II U4, 70

Aufzeichnung recording I

jmdn. aufziehen to tease sb II U1, 10

Auge eye II U1, 16

Ich traute meinen Augen nicht. I couldn't believe my eyes. II U4, 69

Augenblick moment II U1, 16

Augenzeuge/Augenzeugin eyewitness II U4, 69

August August I

aus from I

aus Cornwall Cornish II U6, 100

aus … heraus out of II F1, 20

ausblasen *to blow out I

Auschecken Check-out I

Ausdruck phrase I

auseinandernehmen *to take apart II U5, 87

ausflippen *to go crazy II U5, 87

Ausflug trip I

ausfüllen to fill in II U5, 95

den Hund ausführen to walk the dog I

Ausgang gate II F2, 77

ausgeben (Geld) *to spend I

ausgedehnt wide II U3, 54

ausgehen *to go out **II U6**, 110

sich **ausgeschlossen** fühlen *to feel left out **II U5**, 94

(sich) **ausleihen** to borrow **II U5**, 93

auspusten *to blow out **I**

ausräumen to clear out **I**

Ausreißer/-in runaway **II U2**, 27

jmdm. etw. **ausrichten** *to take a message **I**

sich **ausruhen** to relax 〈**II U2**, 30〉

Ausrüstung equipment **II U4**, 61

Aussage statement **II AC2**, 58

ausschalten to turn off **II U5**, 87

Ausschau halten nach to look out for **II U3**, 43

aussehen to look **I**

außerhalb out **I**

außerhalb (von) outside **I**

Außerirdische/-r alien **I**

Aussprache pronunciation **I**

Ausstattung equipment **II U4**, 61

aussteigen *to get out of **II U5**, 92

Ausstellung display **II U3**, 51

austauschen to exchange **II U3**, 47

Auswahl choice 〈**II U3**, 50〉

auswählen *to choose **II U1**, 15

auswandern to emigrate **II U2**, 29

Ausweis pass **II F2**, 77

auswendig lernen *to learn … by heart **I**

Auszeichnung award **II U4**, 66

ausziehen *to take off **II U5**, 92

Auto car **I**

Autofahrt drive **II U2**, 23

Automat machine **I**

Autor/-in writer **II AC3**, 114

Axt axe **II AC1**, 39

B

Baby baby **I**

Bad bath **I**

Badewanne bath **I**

Badezimmer bathroom **I**

Badminton badminton **I**

Bahn track **II U3**, 54

Bahn (Renn-/Lauf-) track **II U4**, 61

Bahnhof station **I**

Bahnsteig platform **II U3**, 44

bald soon **II U2**, 35

Ball ball **I**

Banane banana **I**

Band band **II U2**, 26

Bank bench **II U1**, 11

Bär bear **II U3**, 42

Bargeld cash **II F2**, 76

Baseball baseball **I**

Basketball basketball **I**

Bauch stomach **II U4**, 72

Bauchschmerzen stomachache **II U4**, 65

Bauchweh stomachache **II U4**, 65

bauen *to build **II U2**, 27

Bauernhof farm **I**

Baum tree **I**

Baumstachler porcupine **II U3**, 44

Baumwolle cotton **I**

Beachtung attention **II U5**, 85

beängstigend scary **II AC1**, 38

beantworten *to answer **I**

bedeckt cloudy **II F1**, 21

bedeuten *to mean **I**

Bedeutung meaning **II U1**, 15

Bedürfnis need **II AC2**, 59

sich **beeilen** to hurry **I**

beeindruckend awesome **I**

beeindruckt impressed **II U5**, 93

beenden to end **II F1**, 20; **II U4**, 71; to finish **II U3**, 53

befestigen to fix **II U1**, 12; **II U5**, 87

befolgen to follow **II U3**, 43

Befragung interview **I**

Befürchtung fear **II U4**, 74

Begabung ability **II AC2**, 58

begeistert excited **I**

begeistert excitedly **II U6**, 110

Beginn beginning **II U1**, 18

beginnen to start **I**; *to begin **II F1**, 20

behalten *to keep **II U2**, 29

Behauptung statement **II AC2**, 58

Behindertenrechtskonvention Convention on the Rights of Persons with Disabilities **II AC2**, 58

Behinderung disability **II AC2**, 58

bei with; at **I**; by **II U6**, 110

beibringen *to teach **II U1**, 10

beide both **II U1**, 13; **II U4**, 73

beide the two of them **II U5**, 84

Bein leg **II U2**, 35

beinahe almost **II U1**, 12

beinhalten to include **II U3**, 47

Beispiel example **I**

zum **Beispiel** for example **II U5**, 91

beißen *to bite **II U3**, 48

beitreten to join **II U2**, 24

bekommen *to get **I**; to receive **II U4**, 69

belebt busy **I**

beliebt popular **I**

bellen to bark **I**

Belohnung treat **II AC1**, 38

bemerken to notice **II U1**, 16

benennen to name **I**

benötigen to need **I**

benutzen to use **I**

beobachten to watch **I**

bereit ready **II U1**, 17

bereits already **I**

Berg mountain **I**; hill **II U1**, 8

Bergbau mining **II U6**, 104

bergen to save **I**

Bergkette mountain range **II U3**, 42

Berglöwe cougar **II U3**, 42

Bergsteigen climbing **II U3**, 43

Bericht report **II U1**, 9

Bericht (in einer Zeitschrift, Zeitung) article **II AC2**, 59; **II U5**, 89

berichtigen to correct **II U2**, 27

sich **beruhigen** to calm down **II U1**, 17; to relax 〈**II U2**, 30〉

berühmt famous **I**

berühren to touch **II U3**, 48

beschäftigt busy **I**

beschreiben to describe **I**

Beschreibung description 〈**II U3**, 50〉

beschützen to protect **II F3**, 97

besichtigen to visit **I**

Besichtigungs- sightseeing 〈**II U3**, 50〉

eine **Besichtigungstour** machen *to go sightseeing **II U3**, 52

besiedeln to colonize **II U2**, 27

besitzen *to have got **I**

Besonderheit specialty (AE) **II U2**, 27

besonders special **I**

besondere Freude treat **II AC1**, 38

besonders wichtig key **II U3**, 53

besorgen *to get **I**

besorgt worried **II U1**, 10

besser better **I**

bestehen to exist **II U2**, 27

bestehen aus *to be made up of **I**

besteigen to climb **I**; to board **II F2**, 77

beste/-r/-s best **I**

am **besten** best **I**

bestürzt upset **II U1**, 17

Besuch visit **I**

besuchen to visit **I**

Besucher/-in visitor **I**

beten to pray **II U2**, 35

betreten to enter **II U1**, 16

Bett bed **I**

ins **Bett** gehen *to go to bed **I**

beunruhigt worried **II U1**, 10

bevor before **I**

nicht **bevor** not until **II U2**, 27

(sich) **bewegen** to move **I**

bewölkt cloudy **II F1**, 21

bezahlen *to pay (for) **I**

Beziehung relationship **II U4**, 74

bezogen related **II U1**, 18

Bibliothek library **II U5**, 87

Biene bee **II U1**, 17

Bild picture **I**

bilden *to make **I**

Bildgeschichte photo story **I**

billig cheap **I**

binden (an) to tie (to) **II U2**, 35

Biologie biology **II U2**, 25

bis till **I**

Bis dann! CU (= See you); See you! **I**

von … **bis** from … to **I**

Bis … CU (= See you); See you! **I**

bis zu up to **I**

bis until **II F1**, 20

Biskuit- sponge **I**

ein **bisschen** a bit **II U1**, 10

Bitte. Please. **I**

Bitte schön. Here you are.; You're welcome. **I**

bitten to ask **I**

bitten um to ask for I
blau blue I
bleiben to stay I
Bleistift pencil I
Blick look I
    einen **Blick** werfen auf *to take a look at II U2, 31
Blindenhund guide dog II AC2, 58
Blitz lightning (no pl) II U5, 92
Blizzard blizzard II F1, 20
Blockhütte log cabin II U3, 43
blockieren to block II U5, 85
blöd stupid II U4, 73
bloß only I
Blume flower II U1, 16
Blüte blossom II U2, 22
BMX BMX II U4, 60
Boden bottom I; ground II U3, 48
Bohne bean I
    weiße **Bohnen** in Tomatensoße baked beans (pl) I
Bonbons sweets (pl) I
Boot boat I
an **Bord** aboard I
    an **Bord** gehen to board II F2, 77
böse angry; bad I
Bösewicht villain II AC3, 114
Botschaft message I
Bowlingbahn bowling alley I
Box box I
Branche industry II F1, 21
brauchen to need I
    nicht **brauchen** needn't I
    (Zeit) **brauchen** *to take II F1, 21
braun brown I
brechen *to break I
breit wide II U3, 54
Brief letter II U5, 83
Brille glasses (pl) II AC2, 59
bringen *to bring; *to take; *to get I
    in Schwierigkeiten **bringen** *to make trouble I
britisch British I
Bronzezeit (ca. 2200–800 v. Chr.) Bronze Age II U6, 104
Brot bread I
    belegtes **Brot** sandwich I
Brotkorb breadbasket II F1, 21
Brücke bridge II F1, 21
Bruder brother I
Buch book I
buchen to book II U6, 101
Bücherei library II U5, 87
Büchse can I
Buchstabe letter I
buchstabieren *to spell I
Bühne stage II U2, 26
    auf der **Bühne** on stage II U2, 24
Bundesstaat state I
bunt colourful I
Buntstift pencil I
Burg castle I

Bürgerkrieg civil war II F1, 20
Büro office I
Bus bus I
Busbahnhof bus station I
Butter butter I

C

Cache cache II U6, 110
Café café; snack bar I
Cafeteria cafeteria I
Cajón cajón II U2, 24
Camp camp II F1, 21
Camper/ in camper II U3, 48
Camping camping I
Canyon canyon II U3, 46
Grad **Celsius** degree Celsius (°C) II F1, 21
Cent (Währung) cent I
Center centre I
Charakter character I
chatten (sich online unterhalten) to chat I
Chili chili II U2, 27
christlich Christian I
nach **Christus** AD (= Anno Domini) II F3, 96
vor **Christus** BC (= before Christ) II F3, 96
circa about I
Clown clown II U4, 72
Cola coke I
Comic comic II U4, 74
Comicheft comic II U4, 74
Computer computer I
cool cool I
    nicht **cool** uncool II U3, 48
aus/in **Cornwall** Cornish II U6, 100
Couch sofa I
Cousin/Cousine cousin I
Creme cream I
Cricket cricket II U4, 61
Curry (Gewürz oder Gericht) curry I

D

da there I
    da drüben over there I
    da ist/sind there is/are I
da because I
dabei sein *to be in II U4, 62
Dach roof II U6, 110
Dachboden loft I; attic ⟨II U4, 68⟩
Dachs badger II U3, 47
dahin there I
Sehr geehrte **Dame**, sehr geehrter Herr Dear Sir or Madam II U6, 103
damit so (that) II U3, 46
danach then; after that I
dankbar thankful I
Danke. Thank you.; Thanks. I
danken to thank II F3, 96
    Nichts zu **danken.** You're welcome. I
dann then I
das the I

Das ist in Ordnung für mich. That's fine with me. II U2, 23
das that I
    Das macht … That's … I
    Das war knapp! That was close! I
dass that I
Datum date I
dauern *to take II F1, 21
    es **dauerte** ewig it took ages II U3, 44
die **Daumen** drücken *to keep your fingers crossed I
davonkommen mit *to get away with ⟨II U4, 68⟩
Deck deck I
dein/-e your I
Dekoration decorations (pl) I
dekorieren to decorate I
denken *to think I
    denken an to remember I
    denken über *to think of I
Denkmal monument I
dennoch still II U5, 87
der the I
deren (Relativpronomen) whose II U2, 27
der-/die-/dasselbe the same I
Desaster disaster II U5, 92
deshalb that's why II U2, 35
dessen (Relativpronomen) whose II U2, 27
Detektiv/-in detective II F3, 97
deutlich clear I; clearly II U2, 31
Deutsch German I
deutsch German I
Deutsche/-r German I
aus **Deutschland** German I
Dezember December I
Dialog dialogue I; dialog (AE) II U1, 10
Dickhornschaf bighorn sheep II U3, 42
die (auch Pl.) the I
    die anderen the others I
Diele hall II U6, 110
Dienstag Tuesday I
dies this I
diese/-r/-s this I
diese (hier) these I
    diese dort those I
Ding thing I
direkt straight II AC1, 39; directly II U3, 45
Diskussion discussion II U5, 82
diskutieren to discuss II U2, 27
doch after all I
Dollarnote dollar bill I
Dollarschein dollar bill I
Donner thunder (no pl) II U5, 92
Donnerstag Thursday I
doof silly I
Dorf village I
dort there I
    dort drüben over there I
dorthin there I
Dose can I
    aus der **Dose** tinned I
Dosen- tinned I

Drama drama **II U1**, 18
dramatisch dramatic **II U4**, 69
dran kommen to reach **II U5**, 87
Du bist dran. It's your turn. I
draußen outside I; outdoors **II U1**, 8
nach draußen outside; out I
dreckig dirty **II U1**, 16
drehen to turn **II U3**, 44; to film 〈**II U6**, 107〉
Drehung turn **II U1**, 12
drei three I
dreieinhalbmal three and a half times **II F1**, 21
dreißig thirty I
dreizehn thirteen I
drin inside I
drinnen indoors **II U1**, 8
dritte/-r/-s third I
dröhnen to boom **II U6**, 110
da drüben over there I
dort drüben over there I
Druck- print **II U5**, 83
drücken to press **II U5**, 92
die Daumen drücken *to keep your fingers crossed I
du you I
Du auch? You too? I
Du bist dran. It's your turn. I
du/dir/dich/Sie/sich (selbst) yourself I
duften *to smell **II U3**, 48
dumm silly I; stupid **II U4**, 73
Zu dumm! Too bad! I
Dummkopf silly **II U4**, 72
dunkel dark **II U2**, 35
Dunkelheit darkness 〈**II U6**, 107〉
durch through I; by **II U5**, 87
durchdrehen *to go crazy **II U5**, 87
Durchsage announcement **II F2**, 77
dürfen can I; *to be allowed to (do sth); may **II U5**, 87; nicht dürfen mustn't I
Dusche shower I
DVD DVD I

E

echt real **II U1**, 8
Ecke corner **II U3**, 45
(der Garten) Eden Eden **II U6**, 104
audiovisueller Effekt audio-visual effect 〈**II U1**, 14〉; 〈**II U6**, 107〉
Ehefrau wife, wives *(pl)* **II U6**, 111
Ehemann husband **II AC1**, 39
ehrlich honest **II AC1**, 39
Ei egg I
Eichhörnchen squirrel I
eifersüchtig sein (auf) *to be jealous (of) I
eigene/-r/-s own I
eigentlich actually **II U1**, 10
eilen to hurry I
Eilzug express **II F2**, 76
ein/-e a; an I
ein paar a few; a couple of I
ein wenig a little I

ein/-e andere/-r/-s another I
noch ein/-e another I
einander each other **II U1**, 17
Einbeziehung inclusion **II AC2**, 58
einbiegen to turn **II F2**, 77
Einchecken Check-in I
eindringen (in) to invade **II F3**, 96
eine/-r/-s one, ones *(pl)* **II U2**, 24
Einerseits …, (aber) andererseits … On the one hand …, (but) on the other hand … **II U4**, 74
einfach easy I
einfach *(Fahrschein)* one way **II F2**, 76
einfach just I
einfache Fahrkarte single **II F2**, 76
Einfall idea I
einführen to introduce **II F1**, 21
Einführung introduction **II AC1**, 39
eingießen to pour I
Einheit unit I
die Segel einholen to reef the sails I
einhundert one hundred I
einige some; a few I; several **II U2**, 31
einkaufen gehen *to go shopping I
Einkaufszentrum mall **II U1**, 8
einladen to invite I
Einladung invitation I
einleiten to introduce **II F1**, 21
Einleitung introduction **II AC1**, 39
einmal once **II F1**, 21
einmarschieren (in) to invade **II F3**, 96
einrichten *to set up I
eins one I
einsam lonely I
einschalten to turn on **II U2**, 35
einschenken to pour I
einschlafen *to fall asleep I
einschließen to include **II U3**, 47
einschließlich inclusive **II AC2**, 58
einst once **II F1**, 21
einsteigen *to get into I
Einstellung shot 〈**II U5**, 90〉
eintreten to enter **II U1**, 16
Eintrittskarte ticket I
einundzwanzig twenty-one I
Einwanderer/Einwanderin immigrant **II U2**, 27
einwandern to immigrate **II U2**, 27
Einzelkind only child I
einzeln individual **II U4**, 61
einzige/-r/-s only **II U5**, 93
Eis ice; ice cream I
Eisbahn ice rink I
Eisbär polar bear I
Eiscreme ice cream I
Elch moose, moose *(pl)* **II U3**, 42
Elefant elephant **II U3**, 47
Elektrik electrics **II U6**, 111
Elektriker/-in electrician **II U6**, 111
Elektrizität electricity **II U6**, 110
elektronisch electronic **II U1**, 15
Element element 〈**II U6**, 107〉

elf eleven I
Eltern parents *(pl)* I
E-Mail e-mail I
per E-Mail schicken to mail **II U5**, 89
emigrieren to emigrate **II U2**, 29
empfangen to receive **II U4**, 69
Ende ending; end I
am Ende at the back of I
enden to end up **II U1**, 8; to end **II F1**, 20; to finish **II U3**, 53
endgültig final **II U4**, 71
endlich at last I; finally **II U2**, 28
eng close I
aus England English I
Engländer/-in English I
Englisch English I
englisch English I
englischsprachig English-speaking I
Enkel/-in grandchild, grandchildren *(pl)* **II U2**, 34
Enkelkind grandchild, grandchildren *(pl)* **II U2**, 34
entdecken to discover **II U4**, 75
Entdecker/-in explorer **II U3**, 42
auf Entdeckungsreise gehen to explore I
entgegengesetzt opposite **II F2**, 77
eine Nachricht entgegennehmen *to take a message I
einen Anruf entgegennehmen to answer the phone I
entgegnen to reply (to) I
Entgegnung reply I
entlang down I; along **II U3**, 46
entlanggehen *to go down **II F2**, 77
Entlaufene/-r runaway **II U2**, 27
entrümpeln to clear out I
(sich) entscheiden to decide I
Entschuldigen Sie! Excuse me … I
Entschuldigung! Sorry!; Excuse me … I
entsetzt horrified I
sich entspannen to relax 〈**II U2**, 30〉
entsprechen to match I
enttäuscht disappointed I
er he I
Erdbeere strawberry, strawberries *(pl)* I
Erdboden earth **II AC1**, 39; ground **II U3**, 48
Erde world I; earth **II AC1**, 39
die Erde earth **II AC1**, 39
Erdkunde Geography I; geography **II U6**, 104
Ereignis event I
erfinden to create **II U2**, 36; to invent **II AC1**, 39
Erfolg success **II AC2**, 58
erforderlich necessary **II U4**, 71
erforschen to explore I
erfunden invented **II AC1**, 39
ergänzen to add I
Ergebnis result **II U5**, 89
ergreifen to grab **II U3**, 54
erhalten to receive **II U4**, 69
sich erinnern (an) to remember I
Erkältung cold **II U4**, 65

erkennen *to tell **II U1**, 11
erklären to explain **I**
Erklärung statement **II AC2**, 58
erkunden to explore **I**
ernähren *to feed ⟨**II U6**, 107⟩
erneut abspielen to replay **II U3**, 48
erneut spielen to replay **II U3**, 48
ernst serious **I**
   ernst nehmen *to take sth seriously **II U4**, 72
ernsthaft serious **I**
erobern to conquer **II U2**, 29
erraten to guess **I**
erreichen *to get to **I**; to reach **II U5**, 87
erschaffen to create **II U2**, 36
erscheinen to turn up **II U3**, 49
erst only **I**
   erst wenn not until **II U2**, 27
erstaunlich amazing **II U1**, 17
erste/-r/-s first **I**
   als **Erstes** first **I**
erwachsen werden *to grow up **II U1**, 11
Erwachsene/-r adult **II F2**, 76
erwähnen to mention **II U2**, 27
erwidern to reply (to) **I**
Erwiderung reply **I**
erzählen *to tell **I**
   erzählen von to talk about **I**
   Erzähle mir von … Tell me about … **I**
Erzählung story, stories (pl) **I**
es it **I**
   Es dauerte ewig. It took ages. **II U3**, 44
   Es gibt nichts Spannenderes als … There is nothing more exciting than … **II U1**, 10
   Es ist super zum/für … It's great for … **I**
Essen food **I**; meal **II U2**, 35
essen *to eat **I**
   (ein Bonbon) **essen** *to have (a sweet) **I**
etwa about **I**
etwas some; something; a little **I**
euer/eure your **I**
Euro (Währung) euro **I**
aus Europa European **II F1**, 21
Europa Europe **II U2**, 34
Europäer/-in European **II F1**, 21
europäisch European **II F1**, 21
ewig forever **II U5**, 85
   es dauerte **ewig** it took ages **II U3**, 44
existieren to exist **II U2**, 27
Experte/Expertin expert **II U4**, 71
extra extra **I**

F

Fabel fable **II AC1**, 39
Fackel torch **II U5**, 93
fähig sein zu *to be able to (do sth) **II U5**, 87
Fähigkeit ability **II AC2**, 58
Fahne flag **I**
fahren *to go; *to ride **I**; to travel **II U2**, 36
   fahren mit … *to go by … **I**

Grad **Fahrenheit** degree Fahrenheit (°F) **II F1**, 21
Fahrgast passenger **II F2**, 77
Fahrgeschäft ride **II U2**, 23
einfache **Fahrkarte** single **II F2**, 76
Fahrplan timetable **I**
Fahrrad bike **I**; bicycle **II U4**, 75
Fahrradmotocross bicycle motocross **II U4**, 75
Fahrschein ticket **II F2**, 76
Fahrstuhl lift **II F2**, 76
Fahrt trip **I**; tour **II U2**, 22; drive; ride **II U2**, 23; journey **II U6**, 101
Fährte track **II U3**, 54
fair fair **I**
Fakt fact **I**
fallen *to fall **I**
fällen *to cut **II AC1**, 39
falls if **I**
falsch wrong **I**
fälschen to fake ⟨**II U4**, 68⟩
Familie family **I**
Fan fan **II F1**, 21
fangen *to catch **II U4**, 60
Fantasie fantasy **I**
fantastisch fantastic **II U2**, 31
Fanzeitschrift fanzine **II U2**, 32
Farbe colour **I**
   Welche **Farbe** hat …? What colour is …? **I**
farbenfroh colourful **I**
Farm farm **I**
Farmer/-in farmer **II F1**, 20
Fass barrel **II U1**, 10
fast almost **II U1**, 12; nearly **II U3**, 43
auf der **faulen** Haut liegen *to take it easy **II U2**, 23
Februar February **I**
Feder feather **II AC1**, 39
Federball shuttlecock **II U4**, 61
Federmäppchen pencil-case **I**
Feedback feedback **II U1**, 13
fehlend missing **II U2**, 25
Feier party **I**
feiern to celebrate **I**
Feiertag holiday **I**
sich **fein** machen to dress up **II AC1**, 38
Feld field **II U1**, 8
Fels rock **I**
Fenster window **I**
Ferien holidays (pl); vacation (AE) **I**
fernbleiben von to stay away from **II U5**, 89
(sich) fernhalten von *to keep away from **II U2**, 29
Fernsehen TV (= television) **I**
fernsehen to watch TV **I**
Fernseher TV (= television) **I**
fertig ready; finished **II U1**, 17
Fertiggericht ready meal **I**
Fertigkeit skill **I**
fertigstellen to finish **II U3**, 53
fesseln (an) to tie (to) **II U2**, 35
Fest festival **I**

festhalten *to hold **I**
Festival festival **I**
Festung fort **II F3**, 97
feucht humid **II F1**, 20
Feuer fire **II AC1**, 38
Feuerwerk fireworks (pl) **I**
Fieber fever **II U4**, 65
Figur character **I**
Film film **I**; movie **II U1**, 10
Filmemacher/-in filmmaker ⟨**II U1**, 14⟩
filmen to film ⟨**II U6**, 107⟩
finden *to find **I**
   Finde das Element, das nicht in die Gruppe passt! Find the odd one out! **II U3**, 48
Finger finger **I**
Firma company **II U4**, 75
Fisch fish, fish (pl) **I**
Fischen fishing **II U1**, 19
Fischerei fishing **II U1**, 19
fit werden *to get fit **I**
Fläche area **I**
Flagge flag **I**
Flasche bottle **I**
Fledermaus bat **II F1**, 20
flicken to mend **II U5**, 87
fliegen *to fly **II F1**, 20
Flohmarkt flea market **I**
Flug flight **II F2**, 77
Flughafen airport **II F1**, 21
Flugsteig gate **II F2**, 77
Flugzeug plane **II F2**, 77
Flur hall **II U6**, 110
Fluss river **I**
Flussufer river bank **II U6**, 104
flüstern to whisper **I**
Flyer flyer **I**
folgen to follow **II U3**, 43
Form form; shape **I**
   in **Form** kommen *to get fit **I**
formen to form **II U4**, 71
Formular form **II U6**, 103
Forscher/-in explorer **II U3**, 42
Fort fort **II F3**, 97
Forum forum **II U5**, 83
Foto photo; picture **I**
   auf dem **Foto**/den **Fotos** in the photo(s) **I**
   Fotos machen *to take photos **I**
Fotoapparat camera **II U4**, 67
Fotografie photo **I**
fotografieren *to take photos **I**
Fotostory photo story **I**
Frage question **I**
fragen to ask **I**
   fragen nach to ask for **I**
die **Franzosen** the French (pl) **I**
Französisch French **II F1**, 21
französisch French **II F1**, 21
Frau woman, women (pl) **I**
Frau (Anrede) Mrs **I**
frei free **I**
   frei legen to uncover **II U2**, 34

im **Freien** outdoors **II U1**, 8
Freiheit freedom *(no pl)* **I**
Freiluft- outdoor **II U3**, 42
Freiluftaktivität outdoor activity **II U1**, 11
Freitag Friday **I**
Freizeit leisure; free time **I**
Freizeitzentrum leisure centre **I**
fremd strange **I**
Fremdsprache foreign language **II U2**, 32
fressen *to eat **I**
Freude fun **I**
  besondere **Freude** treat **II AC1**, 38
Freudenfeuer bonfire **I**
sich **freuen auf** to look forward to **II U3**, 43
  sich **freuen an** to enjoy **I**
Freund/-in friend **I**
freundlich friendly **II U2**, 23
Freundschaft schließen *to make friends **I**
Frieden peace **II F3**, 96
friedlich calm **II U3**, 54
frisch fresh **I**
uns **frisieren** *to do our hair **I**
froh happy **I**
fröhlich happy; fun **I**
Frucht fruit **I**
früh early **I**
Frühling spring **I**
Frühstück breakfast **I**
frühstücken *to have breakfast **I**
Frühstückszerealie cereal *(no pl)* **I**
Fuchs fox **II U3**, 47
fühlen *to feel **I**
  sich **fühlen** *to feel **I**
  sich ausgeschlossen **fühlen** *to feel left
  out **II U5**, 94
  sich schlecht **fühlen** *to feel sick **II U4**, 65
Führer/-in leader **II AC1**, 39
Füller pen **I**
fünf five **I**
fünfstündig five-hour **II U2**, 23
fünfzehn fifteen **I**
fünfzig fifty **I**
funktionieren to work **II U5**, 87
für for **I**
  für dich on your own **I**
  Für wen …? Who … for? **I**
Furcht fear **II U4**, 74
furchtbar awful **I**; horrible **II U2**, 35; terrible
  II U3, 55
(sich) **fürchten** *to be afraid (of) **II U2**, 35
Fuß foot, feet *(pl)* **I**
Fußball football; soccer *(AE)* **I**
Fußboden floor **I**
Fußgelenk ankle **II U4**, 64
Fußknöchel ankle **II U4**, 64
füttern *to feed ⟨**II U6**, 107⟩

G

gähnen to yawn **II U3**, 54
Gälisch Gaelic **II F3**, 97
gälisch Gaelic **II F3**, 97

ganz all; full; whole **I**
  die **ganze** Nacht all night **I**
ganz schön pretty **II U3**, 54
Garage garage **I**
garstig nasty **II U5**, 82
Garten garden; yard *(AE)* **I**
Gaststätte restaurant **I**
Gate gate **II F2**, 77
Geächtete/-r outlaw **II AC3**, 114
Gebäude building **I**
geben *to give **I**
  es **gibt** there is/are **I**
Gebiet area **I**
geboren werden *to be born **II U2**, 27
gebrauchen to use **I**
gebräuchlich common **II U2**, 25
gebrochen broken **I**
Geburtstag birthday **I**
  Alles Gute zum **Geburtstag**! Happy
  Birthday! **I**
  Herzlichen Glückwunsch zum **Geburtstag**!
  Happy Birthday! **I**
Gedicht poem **I**
gedruckt print **II U5**, 83
Sehr **geehrte** Dame, sehr **geehrter** Herr
  Dear Sir or Madam **II U6**, 103
gefährlich dangerous **I**
Mir **gefällt** … I like … **I**
Gefangene/-r prisoner **II F3**, 96
Gefühl feeling **II U1**, 9
gegen against **II U3**, 54
Gegend region **II F1**, 20
sich **gegenseitig** each other **II U1**, 17
Gegenstand object **II U2**, 34
Gegenteil opposite **II U3**, 48
gegenüber opposite **II F2**, 77
gegenüberliegend opposite **II F2**, 77
geheim secret **II U2**, 35
geheimnisvoll mysterious **II AC3**, 114
gehen *to go; to walk **I**
  an Bord **gehen** to board **II F2**, 77
  auf Zehenspitzen **gehen** to tiptoe **II U3**, 54
  gehen um *to be about **I**
  ins Bett **gehen** *to go to bed **I**
  nach unten **gehen** *to go down **II F2**, 77
  zu jmdm. nach Hause **gehen** *to go over
  to **II U5**, 87
  Wie **geht** es dir/euch/Ihnen? How are
  you? **I**
gehören (zu) to belong (to) **II U2**, 34
  gehören zu *to go with **I**
  zueinander **gehören** *to go together **I**
gehörlos deaf **II AC2**, 59
Geist ghost **II AC1**, 38
geistig intellectual **II AC2**, 58
gelangweilt bored **I**
gelb yellow **I**
Geld money **I**
  Geld sammeln to raise money **II U4**, 62
  Geld verdienen *to make money **I**
Gelee jelly **I**
gemein nasty **II U5**, 82

Gemeindezentrum community centre **I**
gemeinsam together **I**
genannt werden *to be called **II U2**, 35
genau hier right here **II U4**, 62
genauso wie the same way as ⟨**II U1**, 14⟩
Genie genius **II U5**, 87
genießen to enjoy **I**
genug enough **I**
genügend enough **I**
Geocaching geocaching **II U6**, 110
geöffnet open **I**
Geografie Geography **I**; geography **II U6**, 104
Gepäck luggage *(no pl)* **II F2**, 76
gerade straight **II AC1**, 39
gerade just; at the moment **I**; right now
  II U5, 93
geradeaus straight on **II F2**, 77
geradewegs straight **II AC1**, 39
Gerät machine **I**; tool **II U6**, 111
Geräusch sound **I**; noise **II U3**, 44
gerecht fair **I**
Gern geschehen. You're welcome. **I**
gern haben to like **I**
gern mögen to love **I**
hätte/-st/-n/-t gern would like **I**
hätte/-st-/-n/-t sehr gern would love **I**
Ich mache … nicht **gern**. I don't like … **I**
würde/-st/-n/-t gern would like **I**
würde/-st/-n/-t sehr gern would love **I**
Gerümpel rubbish **I**
Geschäft shop **I**
geschehen to happen **I**; *to go on **II U3**, 44
Geschenk present **I**
Geschichte story, stories *(pl)* **I**; history
  II F1, 20
geschichtlich historical **I**
Geschick skill **I**
Geschmack taste **II U2**, 27
geschockt shocked **II U1**, 17
Gesellschaft company **II U4**, 75; society
  II U6, 111
gesellschaftlich social **II U5**, 82
Gesetzlose/-r outlaw **II AC3**, 114
Gesicht face **I**
Gespräch dialogue; conversation **I**;
  dialog *(AE)* **II U1**, 10
gestern yesterday **I**
gesund healthy **I**
  gesund werden *to get well **II U4**, 65
Gesundheit health **II U4**, 60
Getränk drink **I**
Getreide corn **I**
getrennt separate **I**
gewaltig huge **II U1**, 8
Gewerbe industry **II F1**, 21
Gewinn prize **I**
gewinnen *to win **I**
Gewinner/-in winner **II U3**, 48
gewöhnlich common **II U2**, 25
gewöhnlich usually **I**
Gig gig **II U2**, 24
Gipfel peak **II U3**, 42

Gischt foam **II U2**, 27
Gitarre guitar **I**
Gitter grid **I**
glänzen *to shine **II U3**, 46
Glas glass **I**
glauben *to think; to believe **I**
gläubig religious **I**
der/die/das **gleiche** the same **I**
gleich right away **I**
  jetzt **gleich** right now **II U5**, 93
gleichmäßig regular **II U2**, 25
gleichzeitig at the same time **I**
Glück luck **II U3**, 42
  Glück haben *to be lucky **I**
glücklich happy **I**
Glücksbringer lucky charm **I**
Gold gold **II U2**, 34
Gold- golden **II U3**, 46
golden golden **II U3**, 46
Golf golf **II AC2**, 58
Gott god **II F3**, 96
  um **Gottes** willen for God's sake **II U4**, 62
Götterspeise jelly **I**
graben *to dig **II U2**, 34
Grad Celsius degree Celsius (°C) **II F1**, 21
Grad Fahrenheit degree Fahrenheit (°F)
  II F1, 21
grau grey **I**
grausam cruel **II F3**, 96
greifen to grab **II U3**, 54
Griff knob **II U5**, 87
Grill barbecue **I**
Grillparty barbecue **I**
grinsen to grin **II U3**, 44
groß big; tall; high **I**; large **II F1**, 20
größte/-r/-s largest **II F1**, 20
  am **größten** largest **II F1**, 20
großartig great **I**; fantastic **II U2**, 31
Größe size **I**
Großeltern grandparents (pl) **I**
Großstadt city **I**
grün green **I**
Grund bottom **I**; reason **II U4**, 74
Grund- basic **II U2**, 25
gründen to found **II U2**, 27
grundlegend basic **II U2**, 25
grunzen to grunt **II U3**, 54
Gruppe group; team **I**
gruselig scary **II AC1**, 38
Gruß greeting **I**
  Grüße ausrichten (an) *to say hello (to) **I**
  Herzliche **Grüße** Best wishes **II U6**, 103
  Herzliche **Grüße** (am Briefende) Love … **I**
  Liebe **Grüße** (am Briefende) Love … **I**
  Viele **Grüße** Best wishes **II U6**, 103
  Viele **Grüße** … (am Ende von Briefen und
  Mails) Yours … **II U5**, 91
grüßen *to say hello (to) **I**
gut good; fine **I**
  am **besten** best **I**
  gut sein in *to be good at **I**

guter Laune sein *to be in a good mood
  II U1, 18
  Guten Morgen. Good morning. **I**
  Mir geht's **gut**. I'm fine. **I**
gut well **II AC2**, 58
Gymnasium grammar school **II U6**, 103

H

Haar hair **II U2**, 26
Haare hair **II U2**, 26
  unsere **Haare** machen *to do our hair **I**
haben *to have got; *to have **I**
  hätte/-st/-n/-t gern would like **I**
  hätte/-st-/-n/-t sehr gern would love **I**
Hafen harbour **II U6**, 99
Hafendamm pier **I**
Hähnchen chicken **I**
halb (bei Uhrzeitangaben) half past **I**
halb half **I**
Halbschwester half-sister **I**
die **Hälfte** half, halves (pl) (of) **I**
Hallo. Hello.; Hi.; Hey! **I**
Halt stop **II F2**, 76
halten *to hold **I**; *to keep **II U2**, 29
  halten von *to think of **I**
Haltestelle station **I**; stop **II F2**, 76
Hamburger burger **I**
Hammer hammer **II U5**, 87
Hamster hamster **I**
Hand hand **I**
Handbuch planner **I**
Handel treiben to trade **II F3**, 96
handeln von *to be about **I**
Handlung action **I**
Handlungsort location ⟨**II U3**, 50⟩
Handschuh glove **I**
Handy phone **I**; cell phone (AE) **II U3**, 43;
  mobile **II U5**, 83
jmdn. **hänseln** to tease sb **II U1**, 10
hart hard **II U4**, 73
Hase hare **II U3**, 47
hassen to hate **II U1**, 18
häufig often **I**
  häufig gefragt frequently asked **I**
Haupt- main **II U1**, 18
Hauptstadt capital **I**
Haus house **I**
  im **Haus** indoors **II U1**, 8
  nach **Hause** home **I**
  zu **Hause** at home **I**
  zu jmdm. nach **Hause** gehen *to go over
  to **II U5**, 87
Hausaufgabe(n) homework **I**
Haustier pet **I**
Haustür front door **II U5**, 92
Havanna Havana **II U2**, 26
He! Hey! **I**
Flughafen in London Heathrow **II F2**, 76
heben to lift **II U3**, 55
  sich **heben** to lift **II U3**, 55
Heim home **I**

Heimatstadt home town **II U1**, 8
heimlich in secret **II U4**, 73
heiß hot **I**
heißen *to be called **II U2**, 35
  Ich **heiße** … My name is … **I**
  Wie **heißen** Sie? What's your name? **I**
  Wie **heißt** du? What's your name? **I**
Held hero, heroes (pl) **II AC1**, 39
Heldin heroine **II AC1**, 39
helfen to help **I**
Helikopter helicopter **II U4**, 69
Helm helmet **II U4**, 61
Hemd shirt **I**
heraus out **I**
herausfinden *to find; *to find out **I**
Herausforderung challenge **II U3**, 43
herauskommen aus *to get out of **II U5**, 92
herausnehmen *to take out **II U1**, 17
Herbst autumn **I**; fall (AE) **II F1**, 20
Herd cooker **I**
herein in **I**
hereinkommen *to come in **II U6**, 110
Herkunft origin **II U2**, 25
Herr (Anrede) Mr **I**
  Sehr geehrte Dame, sehr geehrter **Herr**
  Dear Sir or Madam **II U6**, 103
Herrschaft rule **II U2**, 27
herrschen to rule **II U6**, 106
herstellen to produce **I**
um … **herum** around **I**
herumschleichen to sneak around ⟨**II U1**, 14⟩
sich **herumtreiben** (mit) *to hang out (with)
  (infml) **II U1**, 8
herunter down **I**
herunterfallen *to fall off **II U1**, 12
herunterkommen *to come down **I**
herunterladen (aus dem Internet) to
  download **II U5**, 89
herunternehmen *to take off **II U5**, 92
Herz heart **II U4**, 72
Herzliche Grüße Best wishes **II U6**, 103
Herzliche Grüße (am Briefende) Love … **I**
heute today **I**
Hi. Hi.; Hey! **I**
hier here **I**
  genau **hier** right here **II U4**, 62
High School (weiterführende Schule in den
  USA, Oberstufe) high school **II U2**, 26
Highlight highlight **II U1**, 9
Hilfe help **I**
  ohne fremde **Hilfe** alone **I**
hilflos helpless **I**
hilfreich useful; helpful **I**
hilfsbereit helpful **I**
Himmel sky **II U2**, 34; heaven **II AC1**, 38
Hin- und Rückfahrkarte return **II F2**, 76
hinauf up **II U1**, 13
hinaus out **I**
hinausgehen *to go out **II U6**, 110
hinein inside **I**
hineingehen to enter **II U1**, 16
hineingelangen *to get into **I**

hinfallen *to fall over; *to fall I
hinkommen *to get there I
sich hinlegen *to lie down II U2, 35
sich hinsetzen *to sit down I
hinten at the back of I
hinter behind I
Hintergrund background I
hinterhergehen to follow II U3, 43
hinüber over; across I
hinübergehen zu *to go over to II U5, 87
hinunter down I
hinunterfallen *to fall off II U1, 12
hinuntergehen *to go down II F2, 77
Hinweis clue ⟨II U6, 107⟩
hinzufügen to add I
Hirsch deer, deer (pl) II U3, 47
historisch historical I
ho whoa II U2, 27
Hobby hobby, hobbies (pl) I
hoch tall; high I
hochleben lassen *to give the bumps I
Hochzeit wedding I
Hockey hockey II U4, 61
hoffen to hope I
Hoffnung hope II U4, 74
hoffnungsvoll hopeful I
höflich polite I
    auf höfliche Art in a polite way II U6, 103
    Sei/Seid höflich. Be polite. I
Höhepunkt highlight II U1, 9
Höhle cave II F1, 20
holen *to get I
Hölle hell II AC1, 38
aus Holz wooden II U2, 24
hölzern wooden II U2, 24
Homepage homepage II U3, 51
Hoppla! Oops! I
horchen auf to listen for I
Hören listening I; hearing II U2, 27
hören *to hear I
Hörgerät hearing aid II AC2, 59
Hör-/Sehverstehen viewing I
Hose trousers (pl) II U6, 110
Hosen pants (pl) (AE) II U3, 48
Hospital hospital II U4, 69
Hot Dog (Würstchen im Brötchen) hot dog I
Hotel hotel I
hübsch beautiful II U2, 23
Hubschrauber helicopter II U4, 69
Huch! Oops! I
Hügel hill II U1, 8
Huhn chicken I
Hund dog I
    den Hund ausführen to walk the dog I
    mit dem Hund spazieren gehen to walk
    the dog I
Ich bin hundemüde. I'm dog-tired. I
hundert one hundred I
hungrig hungry I
Hurrikan hurricane II F1, 20
Husten cough II U4, 65
Hut hat I

hüten to look after I

I

ich I; me I
    Ich verstehe. I see II U1, 13
    Ich auch. Me too. I
    Ich bin aus … I'm from … I
    Ich heiße … My name is … I
    Ich mache … nicht gern. I don't like … I
    Ich mag … nicht. I don't like … I
    ich meine I mean II U1, 13
    Ich möchte … I'd like to … (= I would
    like to) I
    ich muss I gotta (infml) II U2, 23
    Ich traute meinen Augen nicht. I couldn't
    believe my eyes. II U4, 69
    Ich weiß (es) nicht! I don't know! I
    Ich würde gern … I'd like to … (= I would
    like to) I
Idee idea I
Idiot/-in idiot II U1, 17
ihm him I
ihn him I
ihnen them I
ihr you I
Ihr/-e your I
ihr/-e (Pl.) their I
illegal illegal II F1, 20
im in; on I
    im Innern inside I
    im Moment at the moment I
    im Weg sein/stehen *to be in the way I
Imbiss snack I
Imbissstube snack bar I
immer always I
    für immer forever II U5, 85
    immer noch still I
immerhin after all I
Immigrant/-in immigrant II U2, 27
in in; on; at; to; into; inside I
    im Freien outdoors II U1, 8
    im Haus indoors II U1, 8
    in Cornwall Cornish II U6, 100
    in der Mitte (von) in the middle (of) I
    in der Nähe von near I
    in der Straße in the street I
    in Richtung towards II U3, 54
    in … hinein into I
    in Ordnung OK; fine I
indem as I
Inder/-in Indian I
Indianer/-in Native American I
indianisch Native American I
indisch Indian I
individuell individual II U4, 61
Industrie industry II F1, 21
Industrie- industrial II F1, 21
industriell industrial II F1, 21
Information information (no pl) I
Informationen information (no pl) I
Inklusion inclusion II AC2, 58

inklusiv inclusive II AC2, 58
Inlineskates fahren to skate I
Inlineskatefahren inline skating I
Inlineskates skates (pl) I
innen inside I
Insekt insect II U3, 48
Insel island I
Installateur/-in plumber II U6, 110
Instruktion instruction I
Instrument instrument II U2, 24
intellektuell intellectual II AC2, 58
interessant interesting I
Interesse interest II U5, 83
sich interessieren (für) to care (about)
    II U5, 89
sich interessieren für *to be interested (in)
    II U1, 13
interessiert sein an *to be interested (in)
    II U1, 13
international international I; multi-ethnic
    ⟨II U3, 50⟩
Internet internet I
Internetauftritt website I
Interview interview I
irgendein/-e/-er any I
irgendetwas anything I
irgendjemand anybody; anyone I
irgendwelche any I
irgendwo somewhere II U2, 23; anywhere
    II U5, 91
irgendwohin somewhere II U2, 23
Irisch Irish II AC1, 38
irisch Irish II AC1, 38
sich irren *to be wrong I
Italien Italy II U6, 105

J

ja yes; yeah (infml) I
Jacke jacket II U3, 48
Jagd hunting II U2, 34
Jagen hunting II U2, 34
jagen to chase I
Jäger/-in hunter II AC1, 39
Jahr year I
Jahrbuch yearbook II U1, 8
Jahreszeit season II U2, 34
Jahrhundert century II F1, 20
11-Jährige/-r 11-year-old II U4, 62
Jahrmarkt fair I
Januar January I
je … desto … + Komparativ the … the … +
    comparative form II U4, 60
Jeans jeans I
jeder everyone I; everybody II U3, 47;
    jeder (beliebige) anybody; anyone I
    jede/-r/-s each I
    jede/-r/-s every I
    jede Menge lots (of) I
    jedes Mal lots (of) I
    jedes Mal, wenn whenever II U5, 84
jedenfalls anyway II U4, 72

jemals ever II U4, 62
jemand somebody; someone I
    jemand anderes anyone else II U3, 42
jene those I
jenes that I
jetzt now I
    jetzt gleich right now II U5, 93
Job job I
Joghurt yoghurt I
Jonglieren juggling II U2, 32
jubeln to cheer II U4, 64
Jugend youth II U1, 12
Jugendherberge youth hostel II U3, 52
Jugendliche/ r teenager I; teen; kid II U3, 43
Juli July I
jung young I
Junge boy I
Juni June I
Juror/-in judge II U1, 12

K

Kabine cabin II U2, 35
Kaffee coffee I
Kaiser emperor II F3, 96
Kaiserreich empire II F3, 96
Kajüte cabin II U2, 35
Kaktus cactus, cacti (pl) II AC2, 59
Kalender planner I
Kalifornien California II F1, 21
kalt cold I
    kalt stellen *to leave it to cool I
Kamelrennen camel racing II U4, 60
Kamera camera II U4, 67
Kameraeinstellung shot ⟨II U5, 90⟩
Kamin fire II AC1, 38; chimney II U6, 110
Kampf fight II U1, 17; battle II F3, 96
kämpfen *to fight II AC1, 39
Kaninchen rabbit I
Kanu canoe II U3, 44
Kanufahren canoeing I
Kapitän/-in captain I
Kapitel unit I
kaputt broken I
Karotte carrot I
Karte card I
Kartoffelchip crisp (BE) I
Käse cheese I
Kasten box I
Katastrophe disaster II U5, 92
Katze cat I
kaufen *to buy; *to get I
Käufer/-in buyer I
kein Wunder no wonder II U3, 55
Keine Sorge! Don't worry! I
kein/-e no I
kein/-e/-en not ... any I
Keks biscuit; cookie (AE) I
Kelte/Keltin Celt II F3, 96
keltisch Celtic II F3, 96
kennen *to know I
kennenlernen *to get to know II U6, 104

Nett, dich/euch/Sie **kennenzulernen**. Nice to meet you. II U6, 111
kentern to capsize II U3, 52
Kerl guy I
Kerze candle I
Kerzenlicht candlelight (no pl) II U5, 93
Kilometer kilometre (km) II U3, 42
Kind child, children (pl) I; kid II U3, 43
Kino cinema I
Kino (amerik.) movie theater (AE) II U1, 10
Kirche church I
Kiste box I
Klang sound I
klar clear I; clearly II U2, 31
Klasse group; class I
Klasse (in einer englischen Schule) tutor group I
Klassenarbeit test I
Klassenkamerad/-in classmate I
Klassenlehrer/-in tutor I
Klassenzimmer classroom I
klatschen to clap I
Klavier piano II U2, 24
kleben to glue II U5, 87
Kleid dress I
Kleider clothes (pl) I
Kleidergröße size I
Kleiderschrank wardrobe I
Kleidung clothes (pl) I; outfit II U1, 8
klein small; little I
Klempner/-in plumber II U6, 110
Klettern climbing II U3, 43
klettern to climb I
Klick click II U5, 93
Klicken click II U5, 93
klingeln *to ring I
klingen to sound I
Klub club I
klug clever II U1, 17
knapp close I
    Das war **knapp**! That was close! I
sich den **Knöchel** verrenken to twist your ankle II U4, 64
Koch-AG Cooking Club I
Kochen cooking I
kochen to cook II U2, 28
Kojote coyote II U3, 46
kolonisieren to colonize II U2, 27
Komma (bei Zahlenangaben) point II U1, 12
kommen *to come I
    kommen nach *to get to I
    kommen zu *to get to I
    Komm jetzt! Come on! I
    Komm schon! Come on! I
Kommentar comment II U5, 82
kommentieren to comment (on) II U5, 89
kommunizieren to communicate I
Kompromiss compromise II U5, 85
Konfitüre jam II U6, 104
König king I
Königin queen I
königlich royal I

können can I; *to be able to (do sth) II U5, 87
konnte/-n could II U1, 16
    kann nicht can't I; cannot II U5, 87
    können nicht can't I; cannot II U5, 87
    (vielleicht) **können** may II U5, 87
könnte/-n could II U1, 16
könnte/n (vielleicht) might II U6, 106
Kontakt contact II U2, 31
    in **Kontakt** bleiben (mit) to stay in touch (with) II U5, 82
Kontext context II U2, 36
kontrollieren to check I
    gegenseitig **kontrollieren** to peer-edit II U4, 74
Konversation conversation I
(sich) **konzentrieren** to concentrate II AC2, 59
Konzert concert I
Kopf head I
Kopfhörer headphones (pl) II U5, 84
Kopfschmerzen headache (no pl) II U4, 65
Kopfweh headache (no pl) II U4, 65
kopieren to copy I
Korbball netball I
Koreaner/-in Korean ⟨II U4, 68⟩
Koreanisch Korean ⟨II U4, 68⟩
koreanisch Korean ⟨II U4, 68⟩
Korn corn I
kornisch Cornish II U6, 100
körperlich physical II AC2, 58
korrekt right; correct I
Korridor hall II U6, 110
korrigieren to correct II U2, 27
kosten *to cost I
    Es **kostet** .../Sie **kosten** ... It's .../ They're ... I
    Wie viel **kostet/kosten** ...? How much is/ are ...? I
kostenlos free I
Kostüm costume I; fancy dress II U4, 72
gegen etwas **krachen** to crash II U2, 35
Kraft power II AC3, 114
    die **Kraft** der Wörter (Wortschatzübung) Word power I
Krampf cramp II U4, 66
krank sick II U4, 65
Krankenhaus hospital II U4, 69
kreativ creative II U6, 112
Kreditkarte credit card II F2, 76
Kreis circle II F3, 97
Kreuz cross II U6, 104
kreuzen to cross II F2, 77
Krieg war II F1, 20
Krieger warrior II F3, 96
Krimi crime story II AC3, 115
Kriminalgeschichte crime story II AC3, 115
Kriminalität crime II AC3, 114
Kriminelle/-r criminal II AC3, 114
Kuba Cuba II U2, 25
Kubaner/-in Cuban II U2, 23
kubanisch Cuban II U2, 23

Amerikaner/-in **kubanischer** Abstammung Cuban-American II U2, 25
Küche kitchen I
Kuchen cake; pie I
Küchenschrank cupboard I
Kuh cow I
Kühlschrank fridge I
Kultur culture I
Kummerkastentante agony aunt II U5, 84
sich **kümmern** (um) to care (about) II U5, 89
sich **kümmern** um to look after I
Kunst art II U1, 9
Kunstunterricht Art I
Kürbis pumpkin II AC1, 38
Kürbislaterne jack-o'-lantern II AC1, 38
kurz short I
Kurznachricht text (message) I
Küste coast I; coastline; shore II U6, 104
Küstenverlauf coastline II U6, 104
Küstenweg coastal path II U6, 110

L

Lächeln smile I
lächeln to smile I
lachen to laugh I
Laden shop I
Lage location ⟨II U3, 50⟩
Lager camp II F1, 21
Lagerfeuer bonfire I; campfire II U3, 43
Lamm lamb I
Lämmchen lamb I
Lampe light II AC1, 38
Land country, countries (pl) ; land; state I; countryside II U3, 54
landen to end up II U1, 8; to land II U2, 28
landesweit national I
Landkarte map I
Landschaft landscape II AC1, 39; countryside II U3, 54
Landwirt/-in farmer II F1, 20
lang long I
(nicht) **länger** (not) any longer II U6, 100
vor **langer** Zeit long ago II AC1, 38
langsam slow I
langsam slowly II U2, 34
langsam whoa II U2, 27
langweilig boring I
Laptop laptop II U5, 89
Lärm noise II U3, 44
lassen *to let I
Lass/Lasst uns … Let's … I
Lassi lassi I
lateinamerikanisch Latin II U2, 22
Laterne lantern II AC1, 38
Lauf run II U4, 62
Laufen running II U4, 62
laufen *to run; to walk I; *to be on II U5, 92
Läufer/-in runner II U4, 60
Laune mood ⟨II U1, 14⟩
guter **Laune** sein *to be in a good mood II U1, 18

laut loud I
laut vorlesen *to read out loud II AC2, 59
läuten *to ring I
Leben life, lives (pl) II U1, 10
leben to live I
Lebensmittel food I
lecker yummy I
legen *to put I
frei **legen** to uncover II U2, 34
Legende legend II AC1, 39
jmdm. eine **Lehre/Lektion** erteilen *to teach somebody a lesson ⟨II U4, 68⟩
lehren *to teach II U1, 10
Lehrer/-in teacher I
leicht easy I
Leichtathletik athletics (no pl) II U4, 61
leid tun *to be sorry I
Tut mir **leid**! Sorry!; I'm sorry! I
leise quiet I
leisten to perform II U2, 24
Lektion unit I
jmdm. eine **Lehre/Lektion** erteilen *to teach somebody a lesson ⟨II U4, 68⟩
lernen *to learn I
auswendig **lernen** *to learn … by heart I
viel zu **lernen** a lot to learn I
Lernende/-r learner II AC2, 59
Lesen reading I
lesen *to read I
noch einmal **lesen** *to reread II U3, 48
Leser/-in reader II U3, 52
letzte/-r/-s last I
letztlich finally II U2, 28
leuchtend brilliant II U1, 16
Leute people (pl) I
Licht light II AC1, 38
lieb nice I
am **liebsten** best I
Liebe/-r … (Anrede in Briefen) Dear … I
Liebe Grüße (am Briefende) Love … I
Liebe love ⟨II U6, 107⟩
lieben to love I
Ich **liebe** … I love … I
lieber better I
Lieblings- favourite I
Was ist dein/-e **Lieblings**…? What's your favourite …? I
Lied song I
liegen *to lie II U2, 35
Lift lift II F2, 76
lila purple I
Limonade lemonade I
Lineal ruler I
Linie line I
Link link II U3, 51
links on the left I
auf der **linken** Seite on the left I
Liste list I
live live II U2, 24
Loch hole II U2, 35
lokal local II U6, 111
Londoner/-in Londoner I

Los ticket I
lösen to solve II U6, 110
loslassen *to let go (of) II U4, 72
losschrauben to unscrew II U5, 87
Lösung solution I
Löwe lion II U3, 47
Luchs lynx II U3, 47
Luft air II U1, 10
lustig funny; fun I

M

Maat mate I
machen *to do; *to make I
Fotos **machen** *to take photos I
sich Notizen **machen** *to take notes I
so **machst** du … this is how you (do) … I
Macht power II AC3, 114
mächtig powerful II F3, 96
Mädchen girl I
ein **Mädchen** aus Deutschland a girl from Germany I
Magen stomach II U4, 72
Magie magic II AC1, 39
magisch magical II AC3, 114
Mahlzeit meal II U2, 35
Mai May I
mailen to mail II U5, 89
Mais corn I
Mal time II U1, 15
malen to paint I
Mama mum I
manchmal sometimes I
Manga (japanischer Comic) manga II U1, 16
Mango mango I
Mann man mæn, men (pl) men I
Mannschaftsführer/-in captain I
Mäppchen pencil-case I
Mappe folder I
Marathon marathon II U4, 60
Märchen fairy tale II AC1, 39
Marder marten II U3, 47
Markt market I
Marmelade jam II U6, 104
März March I
Maschine machine I
Match match II U1, 13
Material material II U6, 103
Mathe Maths (infml) I; Math (AE) (infml) II U1, 10
Mathematik Maths (infml) I; Math (AE) (infml) II U1, 10
Matrose sailor I
Mauer wall I
Maus, Mäuse mouse, mice (pl) I
Medien media II U5, 83
Meer sea I
am **Meer** at the seaside II U6, 99; by the sea II U6, 104
Meerschweinchen guinea pig I
mehr more I
(nicht) **mehr** (not) any longer II U6, 100

mehr … als more … than I
mehrere several II U2, 31
meiden *to keep away from II U2, 29; to stay away from II U5, 89
Meile *(brit. und amerikan. Längenmaß)* mile I
mein/-e my I
mein/-er/-e/-es mine II U5, 93
ich **meine** I mean II U1, 13
Meinung opinion II U5, 84
die **meisten** (the) most I
der/die/das **meiste** (the) most I
meistens usually I
Meldung report II U1, 9
melken to milk (II U6, 107)
eine **Menge** a lot of I
jede **Menge** lots (of) I
Mensch person, people *(pl)* I
Menschen people *(pl)* I
Menschenmenge crowd II U4, 67
sich **merken** to remember I
merkwürdig strange I; weird II U5, 91
Messe fair I
Metall metal II U2, 34
Meter meter *(AE)* II F1, 21
Mexiko Mexico II U2, 34
mich me I
Milch milk I
Million million I
Ich habe das schon eine **Million** Mal gemacht. I've done this a million times before. II U5, 87
mindestens at least I
Mine mine II U6, 110
Mini- mini II U4, 62
Minute minute I
mir me I
Mir geht's gut. I'm fine. I
mischen to shuffle II U6, 109
bunte **Mischung** mixed bag I
mit with I
mit *(dem Fahrrad)* by *(bike)* I
mitbringen *to bring; *to take I
miteinander together I
Mitglied member II U2, 24
mithalten (mit) *to keep up (with) II U4, 72
mitmachen to enter II U1, 16
mitmachen *to be in II U4, 62
mitnehmen *to take I
Mitschüler/-in classmate I
Mitspieler/-in player II U4, 67
Mittagessen lunch I
Mittagspause lunch break I
Mitte middle I
in der **Mitte** in the middle (of) I
mitteilen *to tell I
mittelalterlich medieval II U6, 98
mitten in in the middle (of) I
Mitternacht midnight I
Mittwoch Wednesday I
Mobiltelefon cell phone *(AE)* II U3, 43; mobile II U5, 83

Model model I
Modell model I
Moderator/-in presenter II U4, 69
modern modern II U5, 94
mögen to like; to want (to); *to be into I
gern **mögen** to love I
nicht **mögen** to hate II U1, 18
Ich **mag** … I like … I
Ich **mag** … nicht. I don't like … I
Ich **mag** … total gern. I love … I
Ich **möchte** … I'd like to … *(= I would like to)* I
Möchtest du …? Would you like …? II U4, 62
möglich possible I
Möglichkeit possibility II U6, 105
Möhre carrot I
Moment moment II U1, 16
im **Moment** at the moment I
Monat month I
Mond moon I
Monster monster I
Montag Monday I
montags on Mondays I
Monument monument I
Morgen morning I
Guten **Morgen**. Good morning. I
morgen tomorrow I
morgens in the mornings I
Motto theme I
Mountainbikefahren mountain biking I
Mountainboardfahren mountainboarding II U3, 43
müde tired I
sich **Mühe** geben to try hard II U5, 93
Müll rubbish I; trash *(AE)* II U3, 48
Mund mouth I
Münze coin I
Murmeltier marmot II U3, 47
Museum museum I
Musical musical II U2, 24
Musik music I
Musiker/-in musician II U2, 23
Musikgruppe band II U2, 26
müssen must I; *to have to II U1, 10
(tun) **müssen** to need (to do) I
nicht **müssen** needn't I
ich **muss** I gotta *(infml)* II U2, 23
mutig brave I
Mutter mother I
Muttersprache first language I
mysteriös mysterious II AC3, 114

N

nach to I
nach drinnen inside I
nach Hause home I
nach unten downstairs II U5, 92
(**nach**) oben up II U1, 13
nach *(bei Uhrzeitangaben)* past I
nach *(zeitlich)* after I

nach draußen outside; out I
nach oben upstairs II U5, 92
Nachbar/-in neighbour *(BE)* I
nachdem after II U5, 85
nachdenken *to think I
nacherzählen *to retell II U1, 18
nachjagen to chase I
Nachmittag afternoon I
nachmittags *(Uhrzeit)* p.m. I
Nachricht message I
eine **Nachricht** entgegennehmen *to take a message I
eine **Nachricht** hinterlassen *to leave a message I
Nachrichten news *(sg)* II U1, 16
nachschauen to look up II U1, 15
nachschlagen to look up II U1, 15
nächste/-r/-s next I
der/die **Nächste(n)** next I
als **Nächstes** next I
Nacht night I
die ganze **Nacht** all night I
über **Nacht** overnight II U2, 23
Nachtisch pudding I
Nahaufnahme close-up (II U5, 90)
in der **Nähe** von near I
nahe near I; close II U1, 12
nähen *to sew II U5, 87
Name name I
Namenstag name day I
Nase nose II F3, 96
nass wet II U3, 44
national national I
Nationalpark national park I
die freie **Natur** the great outdoors II U3, 42
natürlich of course I
Naturpark national park I
Naturwissenschaften Science I
neben next to I; besides II U6, 104; by II U6, 110
negativ negative II U1, 12
nehmen *to take I
(ein Bonbon) **nehmen** *to have *(a sweet)* I
ernst **nehmen** *to take sth seriously II U4, 72
sich in Acht **nehmen** vor to look out for II U3, 43
neidisch sein (auf) *to be jealous (of) I
nein no I
nennen to call; to name I
benannt sein nach *to be named after I
jemandem auf die **Nerven** gehen *to get on people's nerves I
nervös nervous II U1, 9
nervös nervously II U5, 93
nett nice I; friendly II U2, 23
Nett, dich/euch/Sie kennenzulernen. Nice to meet you. II U6, 111
Netz net II U4, 60
soziales **Netzwerk** social network II U5, 82
neu new I
neu schreiben *to rewrite II U6, 106

neueste/-r/-s latest **II U1**, 10
Neuigkeiten news *(sg)* **II U1**, 16
neun nine **I**
neunzehn nineteen **I**
neunzig ninety **I**
nicht not **I**
    auch nicht not either **I**
    nicht bevor not until **II U2**, 27
    nicht cool uncool **II U3**, 48
    nicht mehr not any more **I**
    nicht mögen to hate **II U1**, 18
    noch **nicht** not … yet **II U4**, 64
nichts nothing; not … anything **I**
    Nichts zu danken. You're welcome. **I**
Nickerchen nap **II U2**, 35
nie never **I**
niederbrennen *to burn down **II F3**, 96
sich niederlassen to settle **II U2**, 29
niedlich cute **I**
niemals never **I**
niemand nobody; no one **I**
nirgendwo nowhere **II U6**, 100
nirgendwohin nowhere **II U6**, 100
noch still **I**; yet **II U4**, 64
    noch ein/-e another **I**
    noch einmal again **I**
    noch einmal machen *to redo **II U1**, 17
    noch mal again **I**
    noch nicht not … yet **II U4**, 64
Nord- north **I**
Norden north **I**
    im **Norden** north **I**
nördlich north **I**
normal normal **I**
normalerweise usually **I**
nötig necessary **II U4**, 71
Notiz note **I**
    Notizen machen *to make notes **I**
    sich **Notizen** machen *to take notes **I**
notwendig necessary **II U4**, 71
November November **I**
Nudeln pasta **I**
null zero **I**
null *(bei Telefonnummern und Uhrzeitangaben)* oh **I**
null *(beim Sport)* nil **II U4**, 61
Nummer number **I**
nun now; well **I**
nur only; just **I**
Nuss nut **I**
nützlich useful **I**

O

O! Oh! **I**
o.k. OK **I**
ob if **I**
oben on top **I**; upstairs **II U5**, 92
    (nach) **oben** up **II U1**, 13; **II U5**, 96
obendrauf on top **I**
oberer Teil top **I**
oberes Ende top **I**

im Obergeschoss upstairs **II U5**, 92
Obst fruit **I**
obwohl although **I**
oder or **I**
Ofen fire **II AC1**, 38
offen open **I**
offline offline **II U5**, 89
öffnen to open **I**
oft often **I**
    so **oft** whenever **II U5**, 84
ohne without **I**
    ohne fremde Hilfe alone **I**
    ohne Umwege directly **II U3**, 45
Oje! Oh dear! **II U6**, 110
Oktober October **I**
Öl oil **I**
Olympiade the Olympics (Olympic Games) **II F1**, 21
Olympische Spiele the Olympics (Olympic Games) **II F1**, 21
Oma grandma; granny **I**; G-ma *(infml)* **II U2**, 22
Onkel uncle **I**
online stellen to post **II U5**, 82
online online **II U1**, 15
Opa grandad **I**; grandpa *(AE)* **II U2**, 22
Orange orange **I**
orange orange **I**
ordentlich tidy **II U3**, 48
Ordner folder **I**
Ordnung order **I**
    in **Ordnung** fine **I**
    in **Ordnung** bringen to tidy *(a room)* **I**
    Das ist in **Ordnung** für mich. That's fine with me. **II U2**, 23
Organisation organisation **II AC2**, 59
organisieren to organise **I**; to organize *(AE)* **II U1**, 10
Orkan hurricane **II F1**, 20
Ort place **I**
örtlich local **II U6**, 111
Ost- east **I**
Osten east **I**
Österreich Austria **II U4**, 63
Outdoor- outdoor **II U3**, 42
Outfit outfit **II U1**, 8
Ozean ocean **II U2**, 26

P

Paar pair **I**
ein paar some; a few; a couple of **I**
Päckchen packet **I**
Packung packet **I**
paddeln to paddle **II U3**, 52
Paket packet **I**
Palme palm tree **II U2**, 22; **II U6**, 99
panisch werden to panic ⟨**II U2**, 30⟩
Panther panther **II U2**, 22
Papa dad **I**
Papier paper **II U1**, 17
Paradies paradise **II U5**, 83

Park park **I**
Partner/-in partner **I**
Party party **I**
Pass pass **II F2**, 77
Passagier/-in passenger **II F2**, 77
passen *to fit **II U3**, 49
    passen zu to match; *to go with **I**
    zueinander **passen** *to go together **I**
    Finde das Element, das nicht in die Gruppe **passt**! Find the odd one out! **II U3**, 48
passieren to happen **I**
Pasta pasta **I**
Pastete pie **I**
Pause break **I**
Pausenhof playground ⟨**II U6**, 107⟩
PC PC *(= personal computer)* **II U5**, 92
Pech bad luck **I**
    Pech haben *to be unlucky **I**
peinlich embarrassing **II U1**, 8
Peng! Bang! **II U5**, 92
Penny *(brit. Währungseinheit)* penny, pence *(pl)* **I**
pensioniert retired **II F1**, 20
Percussion percussion **II U2**, 24
perfekt perfect **II U2**, 23
perfekt perfectly **II U3**, 49
Person person, people *(pl)* **I**
    pro **Person** each **I**
persönlich face-to-face **II U5**, 85
persönlich personal **II U2**, 31
Perspektive point of view **II U4**, 74
Pfad path **II AC1**, 39; trail **II U3**, 43; track **II U3**, 54
Pfannkuchen pancake **I**
Pferd horse **I**
Pflanze plant **II U2**, 37
Pflaume plum **I**
Pfund *(brit. Währungseinheit)* pound (£) **I**
physisch physical **II AC2**, 58
Piano piano **II U2**, 24
Picknick picnic **I**
Pier pier **I**
Pille pill **II U4**, 65
Pilot/-in pilot ⟨**II U2**, 30⟩
pink pink **I**
Pizza pizza **I**
Plan plan **II U1**, 10
planen to plan **I**
Planet planet **II U3**, 52
planschen to splash **II U3**, 55
platschen to splash **II U3**, 55
Plattform platform **II U3**, 44
Platz place **I**; pitch **II U4**, 60
Platz *(Golf)* course **II U4**, 61
plaudern to chat **I**
plötzlich suddenly **I**
Polizei police **II U5**, 88
Polizeibeamter police officer ⟨**II U2**, 30⟩
Polizist/-in police officer ⟨**II U2**, 30⟩
Polster pad **II U4**, 61

Pommes frites chips *(pl) (BE)*;
  fries *(pl) (AE)* **I**
Pony pony **I**
Ponyreiten im Gelände pony trekking
  II U6, 99
populär popular **I**
Porträt profile **II U5**, 82
Posaune trombone **II U2**, 24
positiv positive **II U1**, 12
Post *(Eintrag im Internet)* post **I**
Poster poster **I**
Postkarte postcard **I**
prähistorisch prehistoric **II U6**, 104
praktisch practical **II U5**, 83
Präriewolf coyote **II U3**, 46
Präsentation presentation **I**
präsentieren to present **I**
Präsident/-in president **I**
Praxis surgery **I**
Praxisräume surgery **I**
Preis price; prize **I**; award **II U4**, 66
preiswert cheap **I**
pressen to press **II U5**, 92
prima brilliant **II U1**, 16
Privatdetektiv/-in private detective
  II AC3, 114
pro per **II U6**, 101
  pro Person each **I**
  pro Stück each **I**
Probe rehearsal **II U2**, 24
probieren to try **I**
Problem problem **I**
Probleme trouble **II U3**, 52
produzieren to produce **I**
Profil profile **II U5**, 82
Programm program *(AE)* **II U1**, 10;
  programme **II U4**, 60
Projekt project **I**
prüfen to check **I**
Prüfung test **I**
psst shhh **II U3**, 46
Publikum audience **II U2**, 31
Puck *(Eishockey)* puck **II U4**, 61
Pudding pudding **I**
Pullover pullover **I**
Puma panther **II U2**, 22; cougar **II U3**, 42
Punkt point **II U1**, 12
punkten to score **II U4**, 61
Punktestand score **II U4**, 60
pünktlich on time **II U2**, 31

Q

Qualifikation trial **II U4**, 62
Qualität quality **I**
quer durch across **I**
Quiz quiz **I**

R

Rabe raven **II U3**, 47
Rad wheel **I**

Radfahren cycling **I**
Radiergummi rubber **I**
Radio radio **II U4**, 60
Rahmen setting ⟨**II U3**, 50⟩; set **II AC3**, 115
Rap rap **I**
rappen to rap **I**
Raster grid **I**
Rat advice **II AC2**, 58
raten to guess **I**
Ratschlag tip **I**; advice **II AC2**, 58
Rätsel puzzle; quiz **I**
Ratte rat **I**
Räuber/-in robber **II AC3**, 114
Raum room; space **I**
Raumschiff spaceship **II U3**, 52
Reaktion reaction **II U6**, 101
realistisch realistic **II U3**, 56
Recht right **II AC2**, 58
recht haben *to be right **I**
rechts on the right **I**
  auf der **rechten** Seite on the right **I**
Rechtschreibung spelling **I**
rechtswidrig illegal **II F1**, 20
Recycling recycling **II U1**, 16
Rede talk **II U2**, 32
reden to talk **I**
  reden mit to talk to **I**
Redewendung phrase **I**
Redner/-in speaker **I**
Regel rule **I**
regelmäßig regular **II U2**, 25
Regen rain **II U3**, 48
regieren to rule **II U6**, 106
Regierung government **I**
Region region **II F1**, 20
regnen to rain **II F1**, 20
regnerisch rainy **II U2**, 26
Reich empire **II F3**, 96
die **Reichen** the rich **II AC3**, 115
Reihenfolge order **I**
rein in **I**
reinigen to clean **I**
Reise trip **I**; travel **II U3**, 46; journey **II U6**, 101
Reisebüro travel agent's **II U6**, 101
Reisebus coach **II F2**, 76
(das) **Reisen** travel **II U3**, 46
reisen to travel **II U2**, 36
Reiten riding **II U4**, 75
reiten *to ride **I**
Reiter/-in rider **II U3**, 48
religiös religious **I**
Rennen race **II U1**, 10; running; run **II U4**, 62
rennen *to run **I**
reparieren to fix **II U1**, 12; to mend; to repair
  II U5, 87
Reporter/-in reporter **II U4**, 69
Requisite prop **II AC3**, 115
reservieren to book **II U6**, 101
Restaurant restaurant **I**
Resultat result **II U5**, 89
retten to save **I**
Rettung rescue **II U4**, 69

Rettungsboot lifeboat **I**
Rettungsring lifebuoy **I**
Revolutionskrieg Revolutionary War
  II AC1, 39
Rezept *(für Arzneimittel)* prescription
  II U4, 65
Rhythmus rhythm **I**
Richter/-in judge **II U1**, 12
richtig right; correct **I**; real **II U1**, 8
in **Richtung** towards **II U3**, 54
riechen *to smell **II U3**, 48
riesengroß huge **II U1**, 8
riesig huge **II U1**, 8
Rindvieh cattle *pl only* **II F1**, 20
Ring circle **II F3**, 97
rings umher all around **I**
Ritt ride **II U2**, 23
Ritter knight **II AC3**, 114
Rock skirt **II U6**, 110
Rodeo rodeo **I**
Rohr pipe **II U5**, 87
Rohrleitung pipe **II U5**, 87
Rolle role **I**
  Rollen tauschen to swap roles **I**
rollen to roll **II U2**, 35
Rollenspiel role play **I**
Rollschuhe skates *(pl)* **I**
Rollstuhl wheelchair **II U1**, 10
Rolltreppe escalator **I**
Römer/-in Roman **II F3**, 96
römisch Roman **II F3**, 96
rosa pink **I**
rot red **I**
Rückenschmerzen backache **II U4**, 65
Rückenweh backache **II U4**, 65
Hin- und **Rückfahrkarte** return **II F2**, 76
Rückmeldung feedback **II U1**, 13
Rucksackreisen backpacking **II U3**, 43
rückwärts backwards **II U3**, 55
rufen to shout; to call **I**; to cry **II AC1**, 39
Rugby rugby **II U4**, 60
im **Ruhestand** retired **II F1**, 20
ruhig quiet **I**; calm **II U3**, 54
  immer **ruhig** bleiben *to take it easy
  II U2, 23
ruinieren to ruin **II U4**, 73
Rumba-Rasseln maracas **II U2**, 24
rumhängen (mit) *to hang out (with) *(infml)*
  II U1, 8
rund round **II U2**, 35
Rundgang tour **II U2**, 22
rundherum all around **I**
Rutschbahn slide **I**

S

Sache thing **I**
Saft juice **I**
Sage legend **II AC1**, 39
sagen *to say; *to tell **I**
  jmdm. **sagen**, was er tun soll *to tell sb to
  do sth **II U3**, 54

Sahne cream I
Saison season II U2, 34
Salat salad I
Salbe ointment II U4, 65
sammeln to collect I
  Geld **sammeln** to raise money II U4, 62
Samstag Saturday I
Sand sand II U2, 35
Sandwich sandwich I
Sänger/-in singer II U2, 24
Sanitärarbeit plumbing II U6, 111
Satz sentence; phrase I
sauber tidy II U3, 48
säubern to clean I
Säugling baby I
Süßes oder **Saures** (Spiel zu Halloween, bei
  dem Kinder von Tür zu Tür gehen und
  um Süßigkeiten bitten) trick-or-treating
  II AC1, 38
Saxofon saxophone; sax I
Schachtel box I
Wie schade! What a shame! II U1, 12
Schade! Too bad! I
Schaf sheep, sheep (pl) I
schaffen to create II U2, 36
  Wir haben es **geschafft**! We did it!
  II U4, 73
Schälchen bowl I
Schale bowl I
Schalter desk II F2, 76
Schatz treasure II U2, 34
Schau show II U4, 67
schauen to look I
Schaufel shovel II U2, 34
schaufeln to scoop II U2, 35
Schaukasten display II U3, 51
Schaum foam II U2, 27
Schauplatz setting ⟨II U3, 50⟩; scene II U4, 69
Schauspielen acting ⟨II U6, 107⟩
Schauspieler actor ⟨II U2, 30⟩
in **Scheiben** schneiden to slice I
scheinen *to shine II U3, 46
schenken *to give I
Schere scissors (pl only) II U5, 87
scherzen to joke II U5, 92
schicken *to send I
schieben to push II U1, 17
Schiedsrichter/-in official II U4, 73
schiefgehen *to go wrong I
schießen to kick II U4, 60
Schiff ship I
Schiffsjunge cabin boy I
Schiffsoffizier mate I
Schild sign II AC2, 58; shield II F3, 97
Schinken ham I
Schinkenspeck bacon I
Schlacht battle II F3, 96
schlafen *to sleep I
Schlafzimmer bedroom I
(Sahne) schlagen to whip I
schlagen *to hit I; to smash II U2, 35
Schläger racquet II U4, 60

Schläger (Baseball, Tischtennis) bat II U4, 61
Schläger (Golf) club II U4, 61
Schläger (Hockey) stick II U4, 61
Schlaginstrumente percussion II U2, 24
Schlamm mud II U4, 75
Schlange queue I
schlau clever II U1, 17
Schlauchbootfahren rafting I
schlecht bad I
  sich **schlecht** fühlen *to feel sick II U4, 65
schließen to close I
Schließfach locker I
schließlich at last; in the end; after all
  I; finally II U2, 28
schlimm terrible II U3, 55
schlimm (ugs.) bad I
Schlittschuh laufen to skate I
Schlittschuhbahn ice rink I
Schlittschuhe skates (pl) I
Schloss castle I
Schlucht canyon II U3, 46
Schluss end I
  zum **Schluss** in the end I; finally II U2, 28
Schluss (einer Geschichte) ending I
Schlüsselbegriff key word I
schmelzen to melt II U2, 27
Schmerz pain II U4, 64
Schmuck jewellery; decorations (pl) I
schmücken to decorate I
schmutzig dirty II U1, 16
Schnäppchen bargain I
schnappen to grab II U3, 54
schnarchen to snore I
Schnee snow II F1, 21
Schneesturm blizzard II F1, 20
schneiden *to cut II AC1, 39
  in Scheiben **schneiden** to slice I
schneien to snow II F1, 21
schnell fast; quick I
schnell quickly II U1, 16
Schock shock II U3, 44
schockiert shocked II U1, 17
Schokolade chocolate I
schön nice; fine I; beautiful II U2, 23
schon already I; yet II U4, 64
  schon einmal before II U4, 63
Schoner pad II U4, 61
schöpfen to scoop II U2, 35
Schornstein chimney II U6, 110
schottisch Scottish II U6, 99
Schrank cupboard I
Schraubenschlüssel spanner II U5, 87
Schraubenzieher screwdriver II U5, 87
schrecklich awful I; horrible II U2, 35;
  terrible II U3, 55
Schreiben writing I
schreiben *to write I
schreien to shout I; to cry II AC1, 39
Schritt step I
  Schritt halten (mit) *to keep up (with)
  II U4, 72
  Schritt-für-**Schritt**- step-by-step II U5, 87

schubsen to push II U1, 17
Schuh shoe I
Schulbildung schooling II AC2, 58
Schule school I
Schüler/-in student I
Schulfach subject II U2, 25
Schulhof playground ⟨II U6, 107⟩
Schuljahr year I
Schulklasse class I
Schulstunde lesson I
Schultasche schoolbag I
Schulter shoulder II U4, 65
Schüssel bowl I
schütten to pour I
Schutz protection II U5, 82
schützen to protect II F3, 97
Schwanz tail I
schwarz black I
  schwarz werden *to go black II U5, 92
Schweif tail I
Schwein pig I
schwer heavy II U2, 34; hard II U4, 73
schwerhörig deaf II AC2, 59
Schwester sister I
schwierig difficult II U3, 44; hard II U4, 73
Schwierigkeit problem I
  in **Schwierigkeiten** bringen *to make
  trouble I
Schwierigkeiten trouble II U3, 52
Schwimmen swimming I
schwimmen *to swim I
  schwimmen gehen *to go swimming I
Schwimmer/-in swimmer II U3, 48
Science-Fiction (Zukunftsdichtung) science
  fiction II U3, 52
sechs six I
sechzehn sixteen I
sechzig sixty I
Second-Hand-Laden charity shop I
See lake I
  See zum Rudern boating lake I
Seele soul II AC1, 38
Seemann sailor I
die **Segel** einholen to reef the sails I
Segelboot sailboat II U6, 112
segeln to sail II U2, 34
sehbehindert partially sighted II AC2, 59
sehen *to see; to look I
Sehenswürdigkeit sight I; attraction
  II U3, 51
sehr very; very much I; much II U3, 54
Sehr geehrte Dame, **sehr** geehrter Herr
  Dear Sir or Madam II U6, 103
Hör-/**Sehverstehen** viewing I
Seilrutsche zipline II U3, 43
  mit der **Seilrutsche** fahren to zipline
  II U3, 45
sein *to be I
  Sei/Seid höflich. Be polite. I
Seite page I; side II U3, 46
  auf der anderen **Seite** von across I
  auf der rechten **Seite** on the right I

Sekunde second **II U1**, 12
selber yourself **I**; himself **II U1**, 16; yourselves **II U6**, 103
selbst even **I**
du/dir/dich/Sie/sich (**selbst**) yourself **I**
er/sich (**selbst**) himself **II U1**, 16
ihr/euch/Sie/sich (**selbst**) yourselves **II U6**, 103
selbstbewusst confident **II U1**, 16
Selbsteinschätzung self-evaluation **I**
selbstkritisch self-critical **II U5**, 84
selbstsicher confident **II U1**, 16
selbstverständlich of course **I**
Selfie selfie **II U4**, 73
seltsam strange **I**; weird **II U5**, 91
senden *to send **I**
Sender station **II U4**, 69
Sendung program (AE) **II U1**, 10; programme **II U4**, 60
separat separate **I**
September September **I**
Sessel chair **I**
setzen *to put **I**
sich **setzen** *to sit down **I**
Shirt shirt **I**
Show show **II U4**, 67
sich each other **II U1**, 17
sich fein machen to dress up **II AC1**, 38
sich heben to lift **II U3**, 55
sich verkleiden to dress up **II AC1**, 38
sich in Acht nehmen vor to look out for **II U3**, 43
sicher sure **I**; safe **II U3**, 48
Sie you **I**
sie her; she **I**
sie (Pl.) they; them **I**
sieben seven **I**
siebzehn seventeen **I**
siebzig seventy **I**
siedeln to settle **II U2**, 29
Siedler/-in settler **II F1**, 20
siegen *to win **I**
Sieger/-in winner **II U3**, 48
Sightseeing- sightseeing (**II U3**, 50)
Silber silver **II U2**, 34
singen *to sing **I**
Sinn meaning **II U1**, 15; sense **II U2**, 27
Situation situation **I**
Sitzbank bench **II U1**, 11
Sitz! (Befehl für Hunde) Sit! **I**
sitzen *to sit **I**
Skateboard skateboard **I**
Skateboardfahren skateboarding **I**
Skifahren skiing **I**
Sklave/Sklavin slave **II F1**, 20
Sklaverei slavery **II F1**, 20
Slogan slogan **II U2**, 26
Smartphone smartphone **II U4**, 71
SMS text (message) **I**
eine **SMS** schicken to text **II U5**, 82
Snack snack **I**
so like this; so; like that **I**

so oft whenever **II U5**, 84
so … wie as … as **I**
So machst du … This is how you (do) … **I**
sobald as soon as **II U5**, 84
Socke sock **II U3**, 49
sodass so (that) **II U3**, 46
Sofa sofa **I**
sofort right away **I**; right now **II U5**, 93
sogar even **I**
Sohn son **II U5**, 86
solch such (**II U2**, 30)
solche/-r/-s such (**II U2**, 30)
Soldat/-in soldier **II AC1**, 39
sollte should **II U1**, 17; **II U4**, 66
sollten should **II U1**, 17; **II U4**, 66
solltest should **II U1**, 17; **II U4**, 66
solltet should **II U1**, 17; **II U4**, 66
Sommer summer **I**
Sonderangebot special offer **I**
sonderbar weird **II U5**, 91
Song song **I**
Sonne sun **II U2**, 27
Sonnencreme sunscreen **II U3**, 48
Sonnenschein sunshine **II U2**, 22
sonnig sunny **II F1**, 20
Sonntag Sunday **I**
sonst noch else **II U3**, 45
Sonst noch etwas? Anything else? **I**
Keine **Sorge!** Don't worry! **I**
sich **Sorgen** machen to worry **II U1**, 10
sorgfältig carefully **II U2**, 35
Sorte kind **I**
Souling (mittelalterlicher Brauch, bei dem man durch Gabe von Broten seine Seele zu retten hoffte) souling **II AC1**, 38
sowieso anyway **II U4**, 72
sozial social **II U5**, 82
soziales Netzwerk social network **II U5**, 82
Spanien Spain **II U2**, 34
Spanier/-in Spanish **II U2**, 25
Spanisch Spanish **II U2**, 25
spanisch Spanish **II U2**, 25
spannend exciting **I**
Spannung suspense (**II U6**, 107)
sparen to save **II U2**, 35
Spaß fun **I**
Spaß haben *to have fun **I**
Es macht **Spaß**. It's fun. **I**
spät late **I**
zu **spät** late **I**
zu **spät** dran sein *to be late **I**
zu **spät** kommen *to be late **I**
Wie **spät** ist es? What's the time? **I**
später later **I**
mit dem Hund **spazieren** gehen to walk the dog **I**
spazieren gehen *to go for a walk **II U3**, 54
Speck bacon **I**
Speer spear **II U6**, 110
Spezialität specialty (AE) **II U2**, 27
speziell special **I**
Spiel game **I**; match **II U1**, 13

Olympische **Spiele** the Olympics (Olympic Games) **II F1**, 21
spielen to play **I**
eine Theaterszene **spielen** to act a scene **I**
erneut **spielen** to replay **II U3**, 48
einen Streich **spielen** to play a trick (on) **I**
spielen (Theater) to act **I**
Spieler/-in player **II U4**, 67
Spielfeld court; pitch **II U4**, 60
Spielkarte card **I**
Spielplatz playground (**II U6**, 107)
Spielstand score **II U4**, 60
Spielzeug toy **I**
Spind locker **I**
Spinne spider **II AC2**, 58
Spitze top **I**; peak **II U3**, 42
spitze awesome **I**
Spitzname nickname **II U2**, 22
Sport sport **I**
Sportart sport **I**
Sportunterricht PE (Physical Education) **I**
Sprache language **I**
Sprachmittlung mediation **I**
Sprechblase speech bubble **I**
Sprechen speaking **I**
sprechen *to say; to talk; *to speak **I**
sprechen über to talk about **I**
Sprecher/-in speaker **I**
Sprechgesang chant **II U4**, 64
springen to jump **I**
spritzen to splash **II U3**, 55
Spur trail **II U3**, 43; track **II U3**, 54; clue (**II U6**, 107)
Staat state **I**
Stadion stadium **I**
Stadt city; town **I**
Stadtplan map **I**
Stadtteil part **I**
Stamm tribe **II F3**, 96
Stammbaum family tree **I**
Standbild still (**II U2**, 30); statue **II U3**, 55
ständig always **I**
Standort location (**II U3**, 50)
Standpunkt point of view **II U4**, 74
Star star **I**
stark strong **II U1**, 18; powerful **II F3**, 96
Stärke power **II AC3**, 114
starren to stare **I**
Start take-off **II U2**, 23
starten to start **I**
Station station **I**
statt instead of **I**
stattdessen instead **II F3**, 96
stattfinden *to take place **I**
Statue statue **II U3**, 55
Stau traffic jam **II U1**, 11
Steak steak **I**
stechen *to bite **II U3**, 48
stehen *to stand **I**
stehen auf *to be into **I**
stehlen *to steal **II U1**, 17
steigen to climb **I**

Stein rock I; stone II U3, 55
Stelle place I
  an **Stelle** von instead of I
stellen *to put I
  online **stellen** to post II U5, 82
sterben to die II U2, 35
Stern star I
Steuer wheel I
Steuerrad wheel I
Stichwort key word I
Stiefel boot II U3, 48
Stiefmutter stepmum I
Stil style II U2, 26
still quiet; still I
Stimme voice I
Stimmung mood ⟨II U1, 14⟩; atmosphere
  ⟨II U3, 50⟩; ⟨II U5, 90⟩
stolpern (über) to trip (over) I
stolz (auf) proud (of) II U1, 9
stoppen to stop I
stören *to get in the way II U4, 72
Story story, stories (pl) I
stoßen to push II U1, 17
Strand beach I
Straße road II AC1, 39
  auf der **Straße** in the street I
  in der **Straße** in the street I
Straße (in der Stadt) street I
Streich trick I
  einen **Streich** spielen to play a trick (on) I
Streit fight II U1, 17
(sich) **streiten** *to fight II AC1, 39
Strom electricity II U6, 110
Stromausfall power cut II U5, 93
Strömung current II U3, 52
Stück piece I
  pro **Stück** each I
Student/-in student I
Studie survey I
Stufe step I
Stuhl chair I
Stunde hour II F1, 20
Stundenplan timetable I
Sturm storm I
stürmisch stormy II U6, 106
Such- search II U1, 15
Suche search II U1, 15
suchen nach to look for I
Süd- south I
Süden south I
super great; cool; awesome I
  Es ist **super** zum/für … It's great for … I
Supermarkt supermarket I
Surfen surfing I
süß cute; sweet I
Süßes oder Saures (Spiel zu Halloween,
  bei dem Kinder von Tür zu Tür gehen und
  um Süßigkeiten bitten) trick-or-treating
  II AC1, 38
Süßigkeiten sweets (pl); candy (AE) I
Symbol symbol I
System system II AC2, 58

Szene scene I

T

Tabelle grid I
Tablet tablet II U5, 87
Tablette pill II U4, 65
Taekwondo tae kwon do II U2, 32
Tafel board I
die **Tafelrunde** the Round Table II AC3, 115
Tag day I
  eines **Tages** one day ⟨II U2, 30⟩
Tagebuch diary II U6, 112
Tagebucheintrag diary entry II U6, 112
Takelage rigging I
Talent talent I
Talentwettbewerb talent show I
Talisman lucky charm I
Tante aunt I
tanzen to dance I
Tänzer/-in dancer ⟨II U2, 30⟩
tapfer brave I
Tasche bag I
Taschengeld pocket money I
Taschenlampe flashlight (AE) II U3, 54; torch
  II U5, 93
Tatsache fact I
tatsächlich actually II U1, 10
taub deaf II AC2, 59
Rollen **tauschen** to swap roles I
Tausende (von) thousands of I
Team team I
Technologie technology I
Tee tea I
Teenager teenager I; teen II U3, 43
Teil part I
  im hinteren **Teil** at the back of I
teilen to share II U1, 16
teilnehmen (an) *to take part (in) II U5, 82
teilsichtig partially sighted II AC2, 59
Telefon phone; telephone I
Telefonanruf phone call I
Temperatur temperature II F1, 21
Tennis tennis I
Test test I
teuer expensive I
Teufel devil II AC1, 38
Text text I
Theater theatre I; drama II U1, 18
eine **Theaterszene** spielen to act a scene I
Thema theme I; subject II U2, 25; topic
  II U2, 31
Themenpark theme park II F1, 20
Ticket ticket I
tief deep II U6, 110
Tier animal I
Tierarzt/Tierärztin vet I
Tierpark zoo I
Tiger tiger II U3, 47
Tipp tip I
Tisch table I
Titel heading I; title II U1, 16

tja well I
Toast toast I
Tochter daughter II U1, 10
Toilette toilet I
toll great I; brilliant II U1, 16; amazing
  II U1, 17
Tomate tomato, tomatoes (pl) I
Tombola raffle I
Ton sound I
Tonmodell model I
Tonne barrel II U1, 10
Tonstudio recording studio I
Tor goal I
  ein **Tor** schießen to score II U4, 61
Torte cake I
Tortenguss jelly I
tot dead II AC1, 38
töten to kill II U2, 23
Tour tour II U1, 22
Tourismus tourism II U6, 104
Tourismusbehörde tourist board II U6, 103
Tourismuszentrale tourist board II U6, 103
Tourist/-in tourist I
Touristeninformation tourist information
  centre I
Tradition tradition I
traditionell traditional II U3, 43
tragen to carry II U3, 48
tragen (Kleidung) *to wear I
Trainer/-in coach I
trainieren to practise I; to train II U1, 12
Training training II U4, 72
Trampolin trampoline II U3, 44
Träne tear II AC1, 39
Transport transport II U6, 100
ich **traute** meinen Augen nicht I couldn't
  believe my eyes II U4, 69
Traum dream ⟨II U2, 30⟩
Traum- fantasy I
traurig sad I
treffen *to meet; *to hit I
  sich **treffen** *to meet I
  sich **treffen** (mit) *to hang out (with)
  (infml) II U1, 8
treten to kick II U4, 60
Trick trick I
Trifle (englischer Nachtisch) trifle I
trinken *to drink I
Trip trip I
trocken dry II F1, 20
Trommel drum II U2, 24
trotzdem anyway II U4, 72
Tschüss! Bye! I
T-Shirt T-shirt I
tun *to do; *to make I
  so **tun**, als ob … to pretend II U3, 54
Tunnel tunnel I
Tür door I
Turnier competition II U1, 16
Tüte bag I
Typ guy I
typisch typical I

U

U-Bahn Underground **II F2**, 76
U-Bahn *(in London)* the Tube **II F2**, 76
Übelkeit verspüren **to feel sick **II U4**, 65
Üben practising **I**
üben to practise **I**
über about; over; across **I**
  über Nacht overnight **II U2**, 23
überall everywhere; all around **I**
überall (in) all over **I**
überall *(egal, wo)* anywhere **II U5**, 91
überallhin everywhere **I**
überfallen to invade **II F3**, 96
überhaupt at all **I**
überleben to survive **II U2**, 35
übernachten to stay **II U6**, 100
Übernachtung sleepover **I**
überprüfen to check **I**
überqueren to cross **II F2**, 77
überraschen to surprise **II U4**, 73
überraschend surprising ⟨**II U1**, 14⟩
überrascht sein **to be surprised **II U1**, 16
Überraschung surprise **I**
überreagieren to overreact **II U5**, 84
Überschrift heading **I**
übersetzen to translate **I**
Übersetzung translation **I**
übertrieben exaggerated **II AC1**, 39
üblich common **II U2**, 25; usual **II U2**, 34
übrig left **I**
übrigens by the way **II F1**, 21
Übung exercise **I**
Übungsheft exercise book **I**
Ufer shore **II U6**, 104
UFO UFO **II U4**, 70
Uhr clock **I**
  Um wie viel **Uhr**? What time? **I**
  Wie viel **Uhr** ist es? What's the time? **I**
Uhr *(Zeitangabe bei vollen Stunden)*
  o'clock **I**
um *(bei Uhrzeitangaben)* at **I**
  um Gottes willen for God's sake **II U4**, 62
  um … herum around **I**; round **II U5**, 93
  Um wie viel Uhr? What time? **I**
umarmen to hug **I**
umbringen to kill **II U2**, 23
umdrehen to turn over **II U3**, 44
(sich) umdrehen to turn round **II U1**, 17; to
  turn **II U3**, 44
umfassend inclusive **II AC2**, 58
Umfrage survey **I**
Umgebung environment **II U6**, 104; set
  II AC3, 115
umher around **I**
umkippen to turn over **II U3**, 44
umkippen **to fall over **I**
Umkleidekabine fitting room **II U3**, 49
sich umschauen to explore **I**
umschreiben **to rewrite **II U6**, 106
umsegeln to sail **II U2**, 34
umsteigen to change **II F2**, 76

Umstieg change **II F2**, 76
ohne **Umwege** directly **II U3**, 45
Umwelt environment **II U6**, 104
umziehen to move (house) **II U1**, 10
unabhängig independent **I**
Unabhängigkeit freedom *(no pl)* **I**
Unabhängigkeitskrieg Revolutionary War
  II AC1, 39
unbeaufsichtigt unattended **II F2**, 77
und and **I**
Unentschieden tie **II U4**, 61
Unfähigkeit disability **II AC2**, 58
unfair unfair **II U1**, 17
Unfall accident **II U4**, 61
unfreundlich unfriendly ⟨**II U1**, 14⟩
ungefähr about **I**
ungefährlich safe **II U3**, 48
Ungeheuer monster **I**
ungewöhnlich unusual **II U3**, 48
unglaublich amazing **II U1**, 17
Unglück bad luck **I**; disaster **II U5**, 92
unglücklich unhappy **II U1**, 16
unheimlich scary **II AC1**, 38
unhöflich rude **I**
Uniform uniform **I**
unrecht haben **to be wrong **I**
unrechtmäßig illegal **II F1**, 20
unregelmäßig irregular **II U2**, 25
uns us **I**
unser/-e our **I**
unsicher unsure **II U1**, 16
unten downstairs **II U5**, 92
  nach **unten** gehen **to go down **II F2**, 77
unterer Teil bottom **I**
unten below **I**
unter under **I**
im **Untergeschoss** downstairs **II U5**, 92
unterhalb below **I**
Unterhaltung conversation **I**
Unternehmen company **II U4**, 75
Unterricht lesson **I**; class **II U2**, 28
unterrichten **to teach **II U1**, 10
Unterrichtsstunde lesson **I**
Unterschied difference **I**
unterschiedlich different **I**
unterschreiben to sign **II AC2**, 58
unterwegs out and about ⟨**II U3**, 50⟩
unterzeichnen to sign **II AC2**, 58
unverschämt rude **I**
unwohl sick **II U4**, 65
Ureinwohner/-in Amerikas Native
  American **I**
Urlaub holiday; vacation *(AE)* **I**
  Seid ihr im **Urlaub**? Are you on holiday? **I**
  Sind Sie im **Urlaub**? Are you on holiday? **I**
Ursprung origin **II U2**, 25
usw. *(= und so weiter)* etc. *(= et cetera)*
  II U2, 37

V

Vanillepudding custard **I**

Vanillesoße custard **I**
Vater father **I**
Veränderung change **II U4**, 71
jmdn. **veranlassen** etw. zu tun **to make sb
  do sth **II U3**, 55
Veranstaltung event **I**
verärgert angry **I**
sich **verbessern** to improve **I**
verbessern to improve **I**; to correct **II U2**, 27
verbinden **to put through **I**; to join
  II U2, 24; to link **II U5**, 94
Verbindung link **II U3**, 51
Verbindungswort linking word **II U5**, 84
Verbrechen crime **II AC3**, 114
Verbrecher/-in criminal **II AC3**, 114
(weit) verbreitet common **II U2**, 25
verbringen *(Zeit)* **to spend **II U3**, 46
verdienen to earn **I**; to deserve ⟨**II U4**, 68⟩
  Geld **verdienen** **to make money **I**
Verein club **I**; society **II U6**, 111
Verfasser/-in writer **II AC3**, 114
Vergangenheit past **II U3**, 57
Vergangenheit past **II U3**, 57
vergeben **to forgive **II U4**, 73
vergessen **to forget **I**
vergleichen (mit) to compare (with/to) **I**
Vergnügungspark *(meist mit einem
  bestimmten Thema)* theme park **II F1**, 20
sich **verirren** **to get lost ⟨**II U6**, 107⟩
verkaufen **to sell **I**
Verkäufer/-in assistant **II U3**, 49
Verkäufer/-in *(auf einem Flohmarkt)* seller **I**
Verkehrsmittel transport **II U6**, 100
  öffentliche **Verkehrsmittel** public
  transport *(no pl)* **II U1**, 11
sich **verkleiden** to dress up **II AC1**, 38
Verkleidung fancy dress **II U4**, 72
verlegen embarrassed **II U1**, 9
verletzen **to hurt **I**
verletzt hurt ⟨**II U1**, 14⟩
  verletzt werden **to get hurt **II U4**, 69
Verletzung injury **II U4**, 69
verlieren **to lose **II U4**, 60
verloren lost **II F3**, 96
verloren gehen **to get lost ⟨**II U6**, 107⟩
vermissen to miss **II U6**, 100
vermuten to guess **I**
verneint negative **II U1**, 12
verpassen to miss **II U5**, 91
sich den Knöchel **verrenken** to twist your
  ankle **II U4**, 64
verrückt crazy **I**; mad **II U1**, 12; **II U5**, 89
  verrückt werden **to go crazy **II U5**, 87
versäumen to miss **II U5**, 91
verschieden different; separate **I**
verschiedene several **II U2**, 31
Verschmutzung pollution **II U1**, 11
verschwenden to waste **II U5**, 87
verschwunden missing **II U2**, 25
  verschwunden sein **to be gone **II U4**, 73
sich **versichern** **to make sure **II U3**, 48
versorgen to supply **II U6**, 106

verspätet delayed **II F2**, 77
Versprechen promise **II AC1**, 38
versprechen to promise **II AC1**, 38
sich verständigen to communicate **I**
Verständnis understanding **II U5**, 91
(sich) verstecken *to hide **II AC3**, 114
verstehen *to understand **I**
  Ich verstehe. I see. **II U1**, 13
versuchen to try **I**
verursachen to cause **II U4**, 74
vervollständigen to complete **II U1**, 13
sich verwandeln to change **II AC1**, 39
verwandt related **II U1**, 18
verwenden to use **I**
  wieder verwenden to reuse **II U3**, 48
verzeihen *to forgive **II U4**, 73
verzieren to decorate **I**
verzögert delayed **II F2**, 77
Video video **II U2**, 24
Videochat video chat **I**
Vieh cattle *pl only* **II F1**, 20
viel much; a lot **I**
viel/-e lots (of); a lot of **I**
viele many **I**
  viel zu lernen a lot to learn **I**
  Viele Grüße Best wishes **II U6**, 103
vielleicht maybe **I**
Vielvölker- multi-ethnic 〈**II U3**, 50〉
vier four **I**
Viertel nach/vor quarter past/to **I**
vierzehn fourteen **I**
vierzig forty **I**
violett purple **I**
Vogel bird **II U1**, 10
Vokabular vocabulary **I**
Volksstamm tribe **II F3**, 96
voll full **I**
voll (von) full (of) **I**
Volleyball volleyball **I**
völlig completely **II AC3**, 114
vollkommen perfect **II U2**, 23
von from; about; of **I**; by **II U5**, 87
  von ... bis from … to **I**
vor in front of **I**
  vor langer Zeit long ago **II AC1**, 38
vor (bei Uhrzeitangaben) to **I**
vor (zeitlich) before; ago **I**
Voraussage prediction **II U6**, 101
vorbei over **II U4**, 71
vorbei (an) past **II F2**, 77
vorbereiten to prepare **I**
sich vordrängeln to jump the queue **I**
Vorführung display **II U3**, 51
vorgeben to pretend **II U3**, 54
vorgeschichtlich prehistoric **II U6**, 104
vorhaben *to be up to 〈**II U1**, 14〉
vorher before **II U4**, 63
Vorhersage prediction **II U6**, 101
laut vorlesen *to read out loud **II AC2**, 59
Vorlieben und Abneigungen likes and
  dislikes **II U1**, 8
Vormittag morning **I**

vormittags in the mornings **I**
vormittags (Uhrzeit) a.m. **I**
Vorsicht! Be careful! **I**
vorsichtig carefully **II U2**, 35
sich (etwas) vorstellen to imagine **I**
vorstellen to present **I**; to introduce **II F1**, 21
Vorstellung introduction **II AC1**, 39
vortäuschen to pretend **II U3**, 54; to fake
  〈**II U4**, 68〉
Vortrag presentation **I**; talk **II U2**, 32
vorüber over **II U4**, 71
vorüber (an) past **II F2**, 77

W

wachsen *to grow **II U6**, 99
Wackelpudding jelly **I**
Wahl choice 〈**II U3**, 50〉
wählen *to choose **II U1**, 15
wahr true **II AC1**, 38
während (+ Nomen) during (+ noun) **II U1**, 9
während while; as **I**
wahrnehmen to notice **II U1**, 16
wahrscheinlich probably **II F2**, 76
Wald forest **I**
Waliser/-in Welsh **II F3**, 97
walisisch Welsh **II F3**, 97
walisisch Welsh **II F3**, 97
Wand wall **I**
Wanderer/Wanderin hiker **II U3**, 48
Wandern hiking **I**; backpacking **II U3**, 43
wandern to hike **II U3**, 42
Wanderung hike **II U3**, 46
wann when **I**
  wann immer whenever **II U5**, 84
warm warm **II U2**, 37
(einen Augenblick) warten *to hang on
  II U3, 44
  Warte ab! Wait and see! **I**
warten (auf) to wait (for) **I**
Warteschlange queue **I**
warum why **I**
was what **I**
  was für ein what **I**
  was für ein/-e ... what a … **II U1**, 9
  Was hast du? What's the matter? **II U6**, 110
  Was ist das? What's that? **I**
  Was ist dein/-e Lieblings…? What's your
    favourite …? **I**
  Was ist los? What's the matter? **II U6**, 110
  Was ist mit …? What about …? **I**
  was man … what to … **I**
  was noch what else **I**
  was sonst what else **I**
  Was um alles in der Welt …? What on
    earth …? **II U5**, 87
  … was ich tun soll. … what to do.
    II U5, 84
waschen to wash **I**
  sich waschen to wash **I**
Waschmaschine washing machine **II U5**, 87
Wasser water **I**

Wasserrutsche water slide **I**
Website website **I**; site **II U5**, 93
Wechsel change **II U4**, 71
wechseln to change **II AC1**, 39; **II F2**, 76
Weg way **I**; path **II AC1**, 39; trail **II U3**, 43
  im Weg sein/stehen *to be in the way **I**
  im Weg stehen *to get in the way **II U4**, 72
weg away **I**
  weg sein *to be gone **II U4**, 73
wegen because of **II F1**, 20
wegnehmen *to take **I**
wegrennen *to run away **I**
wegwerfen *to throw away **I**
weh tun *to hurt **I**
Weide field **II U1**, 8
weil because **I**
Wein wine **I**
weinen to cry **II AC1**, 39
weiß white **I**
weit wide **II U3**, 54; far **II U4**, 73
weit weg far away **II U1**, 11
(weit) verbreitet common **II U2**, 25
weitere more; other **I**
weitergehen *to go on **II U3**, 54
Weizen wheat **I**
welch ein/-e … what a … **II U1**, 9
welche/-r/-s what; which **I**
  Welche Farbe hat …? What colour is …? **I**
Welle wave **I**
Welt world **I**
  Was um alles in der Welt …? What on
    earth …? **II U5**, 87
Weltraum space **I**
wem who **I**
wen who **I**
  Für wen …? Who … for? **I**
wenden to turn round **II U1**, 17
  sich wenden an to turn to **II U6**, 111
Wendung turn **II U1**, 12
weniger less **II U2**, 24
  ein wenig a little **I**; a bit **II U1**, 10
wenige a few **I**; few **II U2**, 24
wenigstens at least **I**
wenn when; if **I**
  erst wenn not until **II U2**, 27
wer who **I**
  Wer ist dabei? Who's in? **II U4**, 62
  Wer macht mit? Who's in? **II U4**, 62
Werbespruch slogan **II U2**, 26
werden *to become **I**; *to get **II U1**, 12
würde/-st/-n/-t would **II U2**, 24
  verletzt werden *to get hurt **II U4**, 69
werfen (nach) *to throw (at) **I**
Werkzeug tool **II U6**, 111
wert sein *to be worth **I**
wessen whose **I**
West- west **I**
Westen west **I**
westeuropäische Zeit Greenwich Mean
  Time (= GMT) **I**
Wettbewerb contest **I**; competition **II U1**, 16
wetten *to bet **II U2**, 23

Wetter weather I
Wettervorhersage weather forecast II U6, 102
Wettkampf contest I
Wettlauf race II U1, 10
wichtig important I
  besonders **wichtig** key II U3, 53
  wichtig nehmen to care (about) II U5, 89
wichtigste/-r/-s most important I
wie like; as I
wie how I
  Wie viele …? How many …?; How many …? I
  Wie alt bist du? How old are you? I
  Wie alt sind Sie? How old are you? I
  wie das ist what it's like II U4, 66
  Wie geht es dir? How are you? I
  Wie heißen Sie? What's your name? I
  Wie heißt du? What's your name? I
  Wie ist …? What is … like? U4, 66
  Wie man … How to … I
  Wie schade! What a shame! II U1, 12
  Wie spät ist es? What's the time? I
  Wie viel (kostet/kosten) …? How much is/are …? I
  Wie viel Uhr ist es? What's the time? I
  Wie wär's mit …? What about …? I
wieder again I
  wieder verwenden to reuse II U3, 48
Wiederaufbereitung recycling II U1, 16
wiederholen to repeat II U1, 13
auf **Wiedersehen** goodbye I
Wiese field II U1, 8
wild wild II U3, 42
Wildnis wilderness II U3, 42
Willkommen! Welcome! I
willkommen heißen to welcome II U2, 26
Wind wind II U2, 34
windig windy II U2, 34
Windsurfen windsurfing II U6, 99
Winter winter I
wir we I
  Wir sind aus … We're from … I
Wirbelsturm hurricane II F1, 20
wirklich real II U1, 8
wirklich really I; actually II U1, 10
wissen *to know I; *to tell II U1, 11
  Ich **weiß** (es) nicht! I don't know! I
Witz joke I
witzig funny; fun I
wo where I
Woche week I
Wochenende weekend I
  am **Wochenende** at the weekend I
Woher …? Where … from? I
wohin where I
Wohlfahrt charity I
wohltätige Zwecke charity I
Wohltätigkeitsverein charity I
wohnen to live I

Wohnung flat I
Wohnzimmer living room I
Wolf wolf, wolves *(pl)* II U3, 47
Wolke cloud II U2, 34
Wolkenkratzer skyscraper I
wollen to want (to) I
wollen, dass jemand etwas tut to want somebody to do something I
Workshop workshop I
Wort word I
  die Kraft der **Wörter** *(Wortschatzübung)* Word power I
Wörterbuch dictionary I
Wörternetz *(eine Art Schaubild)* mind map I
Wortschatz vocabulary I
Worum geht es in/im …? What is … about? I
kein **Wunder** no wonder II U3, 55
wunderbar wonderful II U1, 16; beautiful II U2, 23
Wunsch wish I
sich etwas **wünschen** *to make a wish I
würde/-st/-n/-t sehr gern would love I
Ich **würde** gern … I'd like to … *(= I would like to)* I
würde/-st/-n/-t gern would like I
Wurm worm I
Wüste desert II F1, 20
wütend angry I; mad II U1, 12

Y

Yard *(Längenmaß: ca. 91,44 cm)* yard II F1, 21

Z

z. B. *(= zum Beispiel)* e. g. *(= for example)* I
Zahl number I
zählen (auf) to count (on) I
Zauber- magical II AC3, 114
Zauberei magic II AC1, 39
Zauberer wizard II AC3, 114
Zebra zebra II U3, 47
auf **Zehenspitzen** gehen to tiptoe II U3, 54
zehn ten I
Zeichen sign II AC2, 58
zeichnen *to draw I
Zeichnung drawing II U1, 16
zeigen *to show I
Zeile line I
Zeit time I
  (**Zeit**) brauchen *to take II F1, 21
  zur selben **Zeit** at the same time I
  Es ist **Zeit** aufzustehen! Time to get up! I
Zeitalter age II U3, 44
Zeitschrift magazine I
Zeitstrahl time line II U1, 10
Zelt tent II U3, 54
Zelten camping I
zentral central II F2, 76

Zentral- central II F2, 76
Zentrum centre I
zerbrechen *to break I
zerschmettern to smash II U2, 35
zerstören to ruin II U4, 73
Zeug stuff I
Zeuge/**Zeugin** witness II U4, 69
ziehen to pull I
Ziel goal I
Ziellinie finish line II U4, 73
ziemlich pretty II U3, 54
Zimmer room I
Zimmergenosse/**Zimmergenossin** roommate I
Zinn tin II U6, 110
Zitrone lemon ⟨II U1, 14⟩
Zoll *(Längenmaß, ca. 2,54 cm)* inch II F1, 21
Zoo zoo I
zornig angry I
zu too I
  Zu dumm! Too bad! I
zu to I
  zu Hause at home I
zubereiten to prepare I
züchten *to grow I
zuerst first I; at first II U2, 24
Zug train I
Zuhause home I
zuhören to listen (to) I
Zuhörer/-in listener II U4, 69
zujubeln to cheer II U4, 64
zum Beispiel for example II U5, 91
zumachen to close I
zunächst at first II U2, 24
zuordnen to match I
zupassen to pass II U4, 60
zurück back I
zusammen together I
Zusammenhang context II U2, 36
  in **Zusammenhang** stehen *to be connected (to/with) II U2, 31
zusammenhängen *to be connected (to/with) II U2, 31
zusammensetzen *to put together II U5, 87
zusätzlich extra I
zuschauen to watch I
Zuschauer/-in viewer ⟨II U3, 50⟩
zuspielen to pass II U4, 60
Zutat ingredient II AC3, 114
zuvor before II U4, 63
sich **zuwenden** to turn to II U6, 111
zwanzig twenty I
zwei two I
zweite/-r/-s second I
Zwilling twin II U6, 111
Zwillings- twin II U6, 111
zwischen between I
zwölf twelve I;

In the classroom

Die Wörter und Ausdrücke auf diesen Seiten musst du nicht auswendig lernen. Aber in vielen Situationen im Klassenzimmer wirst du sie nützlich finden!

Asking for help and information

Can you help me, please?	Kannst du/Können Sie mir bitte helfen?
How do you do this exercise?	Wie macht man diese Übung?
How do you spell … , please?	Wie schreibt man … , bitte?
Is this right? I'm not sure.	Ist das richtig? Ich bin mir nicht sicher.
Is it OK to …?	Ist es in Ordnung, wenn ich/wir …?
Is it true or false?	Ist das richtig oder falsch?
Sorry, I don't know. Ask …	Tut mir leid, das weiß ich nicht. Frage …
Sorry. Can you say that again, please?	Wie bitte? Können Sie das bitte wiederholen?
What does that mean?	Was bedeutet das?
What's for homework?	Was haben wir als Hausaufgabe auf?
What's that in English/German?	Was heißt das auf Englisch/Deutsch?

Vocabulary for instructions and activities

Act (out) one of the scenes./Act (out) the dialogues.	Spielt eine der Szenen./Spielt die Dialoge.
Add more words/ideas.	Füge weitere Wörter/Ideen hinzu.
Ask questions.	Stelle Fragen.
Answer the questions.	Beantworte die Fragen.
Check each other's work.	Überprüft gegenseitig eure Arbeit.
Collect ideas.	Sammle Ideen.
Compare your answers with your partner.	Vergleiche deine Antworten mit deinem Partner.
Complete the sentences.	Vervollständige die Sätze.
Copy the grid/the mind map.	Schreibe die Tabelle/das Wörternetz ab.
Correct the wrong sentences.	Korrigiere die falschen Sätze.
Describe what happened.	Beschreibe, was passiert ist.
Decide who writes which part.	Entscheidet, wer welchen Teil schreibt.
Discuss different ideas.	Diskutiert verschiedene Ideen.

Draw a picture.	Zeichne ein Bild.
Exchange your flyers/questions.	Tauscht eure Flyer/Fragen untereinander aus.
Explain your answer./Explain why.	Erkläre deine Antwort./Erkläre warum.
Fill in the grid/the form.	Fülle die Tabelle/das Formular aus.
Find the rule/the right order.	Finde die Regel/die richtige Reihenfolge.
Form expert groups.	Bildet Expertengruppen.
Get organised.	Organisiert euch.
Give a two-minute talk.	Halte einen zweiminütigen Vortrag.
Go back to your home group.	Gehe zurück zu deiner ersten Gruppe.
Guess the new words.	Versuche die neuen Wörter zu erschließen.
Imagine you're one of the people in the story.	Stelle dir vor, du bist eine der Personen in der Geschichte.
Improve your text/part of the report.	Verbessere deinen Text/Teil des Berichts.
Learn your text by heart.	Lerne deinen Text auswendig.
Listen to the dialogue.	Höre dir den Dialog an.
Look at the picture/the examples.	Schaue dir das Bild/die Beispiele an.
Look up the words.	Schlage die Wörter nach.
Make sentences.	Bilde Sätze.
Make a poster/a grid/a mind map.	Fertige ein Poster/eine Tabelle/ein Wörternetz an.
Match the sentence parts.	Ordne die Satzteile einander zu.
Note down what is missing.	Notiere, was fehlt.
Peer-edit each other's work.	Kontrolliert eure Arbeiten gegenseitig.
Pick a card.	Nimm dir eine Karte.
Plan the scenes.	Plane die Szenen.
Practise your scenes/the dialogues.	Übe deine Szenen/die Dialoge.
Present your report.	Präsentiere deinen Bericht.
Put in the correct forms/the missing words.	Setze die richtigen Formen/die fehlenden Wörter ein.
Read your text aloud/out loud./ Read (out) the text (to the class).	Lies deinen Text laut vor. / Lies den Text (der Klasse) laut vor.
Record your final report/dialogue.	Nehmt euren fertigen Bericht/Dialog auf.
Repeat the sentences/the dialogues.	Wiederhole die Sätze/die Dialoge.
Say the words/the sounds.	Sage die Wörter/die Laute.
Scan the text for details.	Suche den Text nach Details ab.
Share the information with your partner.	Tausche die Informationen mit deinem Partner/deiner Partnerin aus.
Skim the text for the gist.	Überfliege den Text und finde die wichtigsten Aussagen.
Sum up what happens in each part of the story.	Fasse zusammen, was in jedem Teil der Geschichte passiert.
Swap roles.	Tauscht die Rollen.
Take a (close) look at the map.	Schau die Karte (genau) an.
Take/make notes.	Mache dir Notizen.
Take turns.	Wechselt euch ab.
Talk about yourself.	Sprich über dich selbst.

Talk with your partner.	Sprich mit deinem Partner/deiner Partnerin.
Tell your partner about your plans.	Erzähle deinem Partner/deiner Partnerin von deinen Plänen.
Think of ideas for …	Überlege dir Ideen für …
Translate the words/sentences.	Übersetze die Wörter/Sätze.
Use the ideas/the vocabulary.	Verwende die Ideen/die Vokabeln.
Watch the film.	Schau dir den Film an.
Work with a partner or in a group.	Arbeite mit einem Partner/einer Partnerin oder in einer Gruppe.
Write a short text/a reply.	Schreibe einen kurzen Text/eine Antwort.
Write about the people in the picture.	Schreibe über die Menschen auf dem Bild.
Write down the new words.	Schreibe die neuen Wörter auf.

Useful words

activity	Aktivität		prompt card	Rollenkarte; Stichwortkarte
answer	Antwort		pros and cons	Vor- und Nachteile
(main) character	(Haupt-)Figur		question	Frage
class display	Ausstellung in der Klasse		quiz	Quiz; Rätsel
collocation	Wortverbindung		report	Bericht
description	Beschreibung		revision	Wiederholung
dialogue	Dialog		rhyme	Reim
dictionary	Wörterbuch		role play	Rollenspiel
example	Beispiel		rule	Regel
fact	Tatsache; Fakt		scene	Szene
folder	Ordner; Mappe		signal word	Signalwort
game	Spiel		slogan	Slogan; Werbespruch
grid	Gitter; Tabelle; Raster		sounds and spelling	Aussprache und Rechtschreibung
heading	Überschrift		story	Geschichte; Erzählung
information	Information/-en		(short) talk	(Kurz-)Vortrag
key word	Schlüsselwort; Stichwort		task	Aufgabe
line	Zeile		theme	Thema
list	Liste		title	Titel; Überschrift
mind map	Wörternetz		unit	Lektion; Kapitel
(alphabetical) order	(alphabetische) Reihenfolge		useful phrases	nützliche Ausdrücke
phrase	Ausdruck; Wendung		vocabulary	Vokabular; Wortschatz
point of view	Standpunkt; Ansicht		word cloud	Wörterwolke
presentation	Präsentation; Vortrag		word order	Wortstellung; Satzstellung

Check-out solutions

Unit 1   Page 19

Exercise 1

a) On Saturday, Ryan, Emily and Jack are going to tidy their rooms. All of the cousins are going to do their homework on Saturday. But only Jack and Mike are going to go canoeing too. On Sunday, Ryan and Mike are going to go fishing, and then Ryan, Emily, Jack and Mike are all going to have a barbecue together.

b) Mike isn't going to tidy his room on Saturday. Ryan and Emily aren't going to go canoeing on Saturday, and Emily and Jack aren't going to go fishing on Sunday.

Exercise 2

1. Lou is going to write to somebody.
2. Tony and Lou are going to clean the house.
3. Tony and Lou are going to watch a film.
4. Tony is going to eat a sandwich in bed.

Exercise 3

1. listening to; 2. by; 3. see; 4. show; 5. look at/see; 6. baby; 7. busy; 8. did; 9. did; 10. outdoors; 11. did; 12. go; 13. field(s); 14. can't we; 15. Why (could we be scared); 16. didn't; 17. Well; 18. can you

Unit 2   Page 37

Exercise 1

1. whose; 2. (that/which); 3. (that/which); 4. who; that/which

Exercise 2

Lösungsvorschlag:

Sky High is the newest theme park. It has the most roller coasters and its fastest roller coaster is also the fastest of them all. So it isn't a surprise that Sky High has the most visitors, but it's also the most expensive park. You must pay 52 dollars to go into the park! Water Adventure is older than Sky High, but Dinosaur Park is the oldest theme park. Dinosaur Park has less than a million visitors every year and it has the fewest roller coasters (only three). But its fastest roller coaster is faster than the fastest roller coaster in Water Adventure. Tickets for Dinosaur Park cost as much as tickets for Water Adventure, but they both cost less than Sky High tickets.
Water Adventure has fewer roller coasters than Sky High, but more roller coasters than Dinosaur Park. They have more than a million visitors each year, but not as many as Sky High, of course. I like … best because …

Exercise 3

1. State; 2. name/nickname; 3. ocean/water; 4. beaches; 5. most; 6. waves; 7. take; 8. that/which; 9. (called) the; 10. are; 11. some/lots of; 12. animals; 13. alligators; 14. alligators; 15. very/more; 16. than; 17. who; 18. history; 19. from; 20. came; 21. Americans; 22. slaves; 23. Cuba

Unit 3   Page 57

Exercise 1

2. Sunny jumped up when Emily walked through the door.
3. Sunny waited in the kitchen while the children put their things away./Sunny was waiting in the kitchen while the children were putting their things away.
4. Sunny was standing next to the door when Emily came down to the kitchen.
5. Sunny got excited when Emily took the ball out of the cupboard.
6. Sunny was watching Emily while the family was having dinner.

Exercise 2

Madison's summer camp was perfect for her **because** they had great activities for people in wheelchairs. Madison called Emily **so that** she could tell **her** all about camp. They went riding there every day **although** most people at camp were in wheelchairs. They had special teachers **who** taught them how to ride the horses. Madison liked the last night best **because** they had a party with fireworks.

Exercise 3

1. outdoors; 2. cabin; 3. because; 4. swimmer; 5. wild; 6. moose; 7. leader; 8. tracks; 9. so that; 10. unfair; 11. mountain; 12. because/when; 13. although/but; 14. talent show/song competition/song contest; 15. camp

Unit 4   Page 75

Exercise 1

1. **Luke:** Have you found any interesting information on the internet yet?
   Dave: Yes, I have. I found some (information) yesterday after school.
2. **Luke:** Has Jay drawn any new mangas for his report yet?
   Dave: Yes, he has. He drew some cool new characters at lunch.
3. **Dave:** Have you seen the two new manga comics yet?
   Luke: Yes, I've already finished one of them.

4. **Luke:** Have you seen Olivia today?
   Dave: No, but she sent (me) a text an hour ago./But I sent her a text an hour ago.
5. **Dave:** Has Holly written about guinea pigs?
   Luke: I hope not!/I hope she hasn't! She wrote about guinea pigs last year.

Exercise 2
1. has become; 2. started; 3. used; 4. were; 5. discovered; 6. had; 7. have been; 8. wasn't; 9. I've seen

Exercise 3
1. accident; 2. hurt/twisted; 3. what happened; 4. off; 5. experience; 6. prescription; 7. Is it still bad/Does it still hurt; 8. hurts; 9. on the other hand

Unit 5   Page 95

Exercise 1
1. checks; 2. stay in touch; 3. changes

Exercise 2
1. You should go to the doctor's./Why don't you go to the doctor's?
2. You could watch it on the internet.
3. Maybe you should tell them that you're sorry.

Exercise 3
1. weren't able to; 2. can; 3. aren't allowed to; 4. must; 5. had to; 6. can; 7. were able to; 8. can

Exercise 4
1. posted; 2. social; 3. site/page/profile; 4. share; 5. As soon as; 6. got/received; 7. profile/page; 8. saw/noticed; 9. that/which; 10. on; 11. asked/told; 12. because; 13. want; 14. see; 15. opinion; 16. very much; 17. actually; 18. one/picture; 19. both; 20. right; 21. can/may; 22. on; 23. at last/finally; 24. compromise/solution; 25. cut; 26. that/which; 27. so that; 28. could/was able to

Unit 6   Page 113

Exercise 1
1. will be; 2. will be; 3. won't be, 4. will be; 5. will get; 6. will be; 7. won't rain; 8. will be; 9. will change; 10. will move in; 11. will start

Exercise 2
1. Have; 2. told; 3. want to/'re going to; 4. looking forward; 5. were/went; 6. amazing/brilliant/fantastic/great; 7. If; 8. 'll like/'ll love; 9. 'll; 10. will be; 11. so that; 12. can; 13. time; 14. would; 15. haven't; 16. nowhere/no place; 17. our; 18. wants; 19. different; 20. see; 21. if; 22. idea; 23. can/could/should; 24. travel agent's; 25. can/will; 26. advice/ideas/tips; 27. book; 28. buy/get; 29. should; 30. wants; 31. by; 32. could

Exercise 3
1. When, If; 2. if, when; 3. If, when; 4. when, if

Grammar solutions

Unit 1

G1   Das Futur mit going to
Lösungsvorschlag: Madison is going to go shopping./
Madison is going to go to the mall.
Dave and Luke are going to watch a film/are going to
go to the cinema.
Jack isn't going to ride in the barrel race.
Ryan is going to play the guitar.
Emily and Madison aren't going to go swimming.
Emily isn't going to walk the dog/Emily isn't going to go
for a walk with Sunny.

G2   Bestätigungsfragen
1. didn't he; wasn't it; isn't it;
2. aren't we; do we; don't you

G3   Fragen mit Präpositionen
1. What are you thinking about? – I'm thinking about
    Christmas.
2. What's Madison looking at? – She's looking at a
    magazine.
3. Who are you waiting for? – I'm waiting for my
    cousin.
4. What's Ryan talking about? – He's talking about
    Emily's hat.
5. Who's Emily talking to? – She's talking to her aunt.
6. Who's Emily writing to? – She's writing to Dave.

Unit 2

G4   Steigerung der Adjektive
1. Luke is tall. Holly is taller. But Olivia is the tallest of
    the three.
2. The red car is expensive. The blue car is more
    expensive. But the black car is the most expensive of
    the three.
3. Hook Lane is a busy road. King's Street is busier.
    But London Road is the busiest of the three.
4. Luke has got a good idea. Holly's idea is better. But
    Dave has got the best idea of the three.

G5   Gleich oder verschieden:
Vergleiche mit Adjektiven
Lösungsvorschlag:
The Danube is longer than the Rhine and the Inn.
The Inn is shorter than the Danube and the Rhine.
Nuremberg isn't as big as Cologne.
Munich is bigger than Cologne and Nuremberg.
Munich is the biggest city of the three.
The Zugspitze is the highest mountain. It's higher than
the Großer Arber and the Schneeberg.
The Schneeberg isn't as high as the Großer Arber.
The Saarland is the smallest state. It's smaller than
Saxony and Bavaria.
Bavaria is bigger than Saxony.

G6   Notwendige Relativsätze
a)
1. which/that; which/that; which/that;
2. whose; who; which/that

b)
Do you have any of the Cuban-style music people listen
to in Florida?
I don't like the songs they play on TV.
Oh, that's the photo of St. Augustine I wanted to show
in my presentation.
Those are all projects I don't know.

Unit 3

G7   Die Verlaufsform der Vergangenheit
Lösungsvorschlag:
B: What were Holly and Olivia doing?
A: While Holly was practising/learning new signs, Olivia
    was playing netball.

G8   Adverbialsätze
because; Before/When; so that; When; although;
As soon as/When; while; After; before/when; so that; if

Unit 4

G9   Die einfache Form des Perfekts
A: Have you ever been to London?
B: No, I haven't. What about you/Have you?
A: Yes, I have. It's a great city. Have you and your
    parents already made plans for your next holiday?
B: No, we haven't made any plans yet, but we're going
    to talk about a weekend trip tomorrow.
A: Have you heard the news? Frank has broken his leg.
    He's in hospital now.
B: Really? I hope it's not too bad! I've never broken
    anything in my life and I've never been in hospital.
A: Lucky you! I've been there three times. – I've just had
    an idea: Let's go and visit Frank.

G10   Das Perfekt und die einfache Vergangenheit
Lösungsvorschlag:
a)
1. Have you prepared for Sports Day yet?
2. Have you bought new sports shoes yet?
3. Have you already started eating healthy food?
4. Have you ever hurt your foot while you were playing
    sports?
5. Have you found a name for your team yet?

b)
2. Have you bought new sports shoes yet?
    – No, I haven't. I don't need any new shoes. My old
    ones/shoes are OK.

– Yes, I have. I've just bought some new shoes. Look, they are in this bag.

– Yes, I have. I bought them last week.

3. Have you already started eating healthy food?

– Yes, I have. I've already eaten two apples today.

4. Have you ever hurt your foot while you were playing sports?

– Yes, I have. I've hurt my leg twice/two times. When I was little, I broke my leg at the ice rink. And last year I twisted my ankle while I was playing basketball.

– No, I haven't.

5. Have you found a name for your team yet?

– Yes, I have. But I'm not going to tell you.

– No, I haven't found a nice name yet.

G11 Einfaches Präsens mit futurischer Bedeutung

First, the Hubers are going to go on a trip to London. Their plane departs from Munich at 9.20 a.m. It arrives at London Heathrow at 10.25 a.m. Then on the next day, their train leaves London King's Cross at 3 p.m. and it arrives in Edinburgh at 7.20 p.m.

Unit 5

G12 Adverbialsätze der Zeit, des Grundes, des Zwecks und der Einräumung

Joe: I like your magazine **because** it's always got the interesting news on my favourite stars in it.

Ginny: I buy TeenLife **as soon as/when** I get my pocket money from my parents. I love it!

Lisa: **Whenever/When** I read Ruby's advice, I think she really understands our problems.

Michael: I'm sure Ruby has learned a lot about teenage problems **so that** she can help people with her advice.

Sheila: **Although** I didn't like the make-up which came with the magazine last week, I'm going to buy TeenLife again. I really love the fantastic concert photos.

G13 Modalverben und ihre Ersatzformen

Hi,

Guess what. When I came home from school, there was water everywhere on the kitchen floor. Something was wrong with the washing machine and Dad **had to** fix it before Mum came home. Dad had no idea what he was doing … But I **was allowed to** use his tablet and check for advice in a forum. I **was able to** find a helpful website quickly. All we **had to** do was turn the knob off. So we **were able to** solve the problem in 20 minutes and Mum **was able to** use the washing machine when she came home.

See you at school on Monday – Luke

G14 Die Modalverben should, shouldn't und could

Lösungsvorschlag:

1. You should say sorry (to her)./You could ask if she needs help./You should be more careful when you play netball.

2. You should tell Dave./You could buy him a new book./You could ask how much the book was and give him the money.

3. You shouldn't pull him out from under the bed./You could put some food in front of the bed.

4. You should say sorry (to her)./You could buy her new flowers for her garden./Next time you should ask her first.

Unit 6

G15 Das Futur mit will

1. Olivia: I hope Dave **will love** his new school.

2. Holly: I'm sure the Prestons **will visit** Granny Rose and Aunt Frances in London soon.

3. Luke: I don't think the new home **will be** a problem for Sid. There are lots of fields and he **will be able to** run around. He **will make** new cat friends quickly. He **won't get bored**!

4. Gwen: I hope Dave **won't forget** us.

G16 Verschiedene Möglichkeiten, Zukünftiges auszudrücken

1. Our train **leaves** at 6 o'clock tomorrow. – Don't worry. **I'll be** on time.

2. This bag is heavy! – Wait, **I'll help** you.

3. Look at the sky! **It's going to rain** very soon.

4. I've heard the weather forecast. It **won't rain** this afternoon.

5. Remember to do your homework! – Sure. I **won't forget** it.

6. **I'm going to take part** in a talent show. – I hope the judges **will like** you!

G17 Bedingungssätze Typ 1

Lösungsvorschlag:

If you visit Hamburg, you should see the harbour and try a fish burger. If you go to Cologne, climb to the top of the Dom (the cathedral). If you're interested in cars, you could go to Stuttgart and visit the Porsche Museum/Mercedes Museum. If you go to Eisenach, you should visit the Wartburg and try Thüringer Bratwurst/sausages there. You could also visit the Bachhaus/Lutherhaus.

G18 Die Modalverben can/could, may und might

1. Mum, could/may I go to Gwen's sleepover?

2. My brother is really clever. You could ask him for help.

3. He may/might help you.

4. It could/may/might be true, but I'm not sure/it's hard to believe.

5. Could/May I have another piece of cake, please?

6. Look at the clouds! Take a rain jacket with you, because it could/may/might rain.

Text- und Bildquellenverzeichnis

Textquellen

29.ll. 1–20 © 2016, Fabian Teichmann, web.de; **29.ll. 21–26** © Krone Multimedia GmbH & Co KG 2016; **59** 2016 © Fellbacher Zeitung; **106** From www.poetryarchive.org/poem/romans-britain, © Judith Nicholls; **117** www.muenchen.de, © Landeshauptstadt München, 2017; **127** © 2013 Die Welt; **144–145** From Middle School: How I got lost in London by James Patterson. Published by Random House Children's Publishers. Reprinted by permission Williams & Connolly LLP.; **146–147** Horrid Henry rules the world, Francesca Simon, Orion Children's Books, London, 2008; **148.1** "Halloween Party" © 2005 by Kenn Nesbitt. Reprinted from "When the Teacher Isn't Looking" with the permission of Meadowbrook Press.; **148.2** Haiku Harvest, Matsuo Basho, trans. Harry Behn, Japanese Haiku Series IV, Reprinted with permission of Peter Pauper Press, Inc; **148.3** From "If I don't know" by Wendy Cope, Faber&Faber, London, 2001; **149.1** Heidi Bee Broemer (Heidi B. Roemer); **149.2** © 1998 by J. Patrick Lewis. Veröffentlicht mit Genehmigung Nr. 71271 der Paul & Peter Fritz AG in Zurich.; **150–151** Excerpt from Ratburger by David Walliams, HarperCollins Children's Books, a division of HarperCollins Publishers Ltd, London, 2012 © David Walliams 2012 (adapted); **152–153** Excerpt from "A Harp on the Water" from Welsh Legends and Folktales by Gwyn Jones (ed.), Oxford University Press, 1955 (adapted); **158** Excerpt from Ratburger by David Walliams, HarperCollins Children's Books, a division of HarperCollins Publishers Ltd, London, 2012 © David Walliams 2012 (adapted)

Bildquellen

Cover.1 February Films (Andrew Kemp), London; **Cover.2** shutterstock (ventdusud), New York, NY; **2ff** (Union Jack) shutterstock (suicidecrew), New York, NY; **2ff** (Flagge USA) Thinkstock (Wavebreak Media), München; **2.1** February Films (Andrew Kemp), London; **2.2** Photothek.net Gbr RF (Thomas Köhler), Berlin; **2.3** Thinkstock (altrendo images), München; **3.1** Fotolia.com (Ruth P. Peterkin), New York; **3.2** Photothek.net Gbr RF (Thomas Köhler), Berlin; **3.3** shutterstock (Alex Brylov), New York, NY; **4.1** Alamy stock photo (Golden Pixels LLC), Abingdon, Oxon; **4.2** Klett-Archiv (Thomas Weccard), Stuttgart; **4.3** February Films (Andrew Kemp), London; **5.1** February Films (Andrew Kemp), London; **5.2** Thinkstock (Salah Malkawi), München; **5.3** Fotolia.com (evron.info), New York; **6.1** Fotolia.com (visoook), New York; **6.2** iStockphoto (MattStansfield), Calgary, Alberta; **6.3** February Films (Andrew Kemp), London; **7.1** February Films (Andrew Kemp), London; **7.2** Alamy stock photo (Melissa Gaskell), Abingdon, Oxon; **7.3** Alamy stock photo (Jeff Morgan 06), Abingdon, Oxon; **8.1–3** February Films (Andrew Kemp), London; **9.1** Mauritius Images (RosaIreneBetancourt 9/Alamy), Mittenwald; **9.2** Thinkstock (altrendo images), München; **9.3** Photothek.net Gbr RF (Thomas Köhler), Berlin; **10.1** Photothek.net Gbr RF (Thomas Köhler), Berlin;

11.1 Photothek.net Gbr RF (Thomas Köhler), Berlin; **11.2** Fotolia.com (Gang), New York; **11.3** iStockphoto (LarryLindell), Calgary, Alberta; **14.1** February Films, London; **15.1** February Films (Andrew Kemp), London; **20.1** shutterstock (Songquan Deng), New York, NY; **20.2** shutterstock (Kamira), New York, NY; **20.3** Getty Images (Photolibrary), München; **21.1** shutterstock (Jorg Hackemann), New York, NY; **21.2** Getty Images (Alexander Hassenstein/Bongarts), München; **21.3** shutterstock (Joseph Sohm), New York, NY; **22.1** shutterstock (Peter Titmuss), New York, NY; **22.2** Thinkstock (Ryan McVay), München; **22.3** Getty Images (Joe Raedle), München; **22.4** Photothek.net Gbr RF (Thomas Köhler), Berlin; **22.5** shutterstock (Globe Turner), New York, NY; **23.1** Fotolia.com (Ruth P. Peterkin), New York; **23.2** Getty Images (Joe Raedle), München; **23.3** Getty Images (robertharding), München; **23.4** Fotolia.com (Yael Weiss), New York; **24.1** Photothek.net Gbr RF (Thomas Köhler), Berlin; **25.1** Getty Images (©2009 Derek Latta), München; **26.1** Photothek.net Gbr RF (Thomas Köhler), Berlin; **26.2** Thinkstock (Jodi Matthews), München; **26.3** Fotolia.com (kennykiernan), New York; **27.1** dreamstime.com (Roxana Gonzalez), Brentwood, TN; **29.1** Picture-Alliance (Myakka Pines Golf Club/Handout), Frankfurt; **30.1** February Films, London; **31.1** February Films, London; **37.1** Thinkstock (mlharing), München; **38.1** Thinkstock (Fiantas), München; **38.2** shutterstock (Lisa F. Young), New York, NY; **39.1** shutterstock (Joseph Sohm), New York, NY; **40.1** Alamy stock photo (Richard Wong), Abingdon, Oxon; **40.2** shutterstock, New York, NY; **41.1** dreamstime.com (Szilkov), Brentwood, TN; **41.2** Getty Images (Blend Images), München; **42.1** Getty Images (Photodisc), München; **42.2** shutterstock (Louis W Martin), New York, NY; **42.3** shutterstock (Tom Reichner), New York, NY; **42.4** shutterstock (Chris Rubino), New York, NY; **43.1** shutterstock (Alex Brylov), New York, NY; **43.2** laif (Olivier Renck/Aurora Photos), Köln; **43.3** Getty Images (Design Pics), München; **46.1** Getty Images (Photolibrary), München; **47.1** Thinkstock (Steve Mason), München; **47.2** shutterstock (Lucky Business), New York, NY; **48.1** shutterstock (Izf), New York, NY; **48.2** shutterstock (Mat Hayward), New York, NY; **50.1+2** February Films, London; **51.1** Fotolia.com (Dark Vectorangel), New York; **52.1** Fotolia.com (evron.info), New York; **52.2** ddp images GmbH (Newscom/UPI), Hamburg; **52.3** Fotolia.com (toolklickit), New York; **56.1** Photothek.net Gbr RF (Thomas Köhler), Berlin; **57.1** Fotolia.com (Photo-SD), New York; **57.2** Photothek.net Gbr RF (Thomas Köhler), Berlin; **58.1** Alamy stock photo (BSIP SA), Abingdon, Oxon; **58.2** Alamy stock photo (Golden Pixels LLC), Abingdon, Oxon; **58.3** Conny Wenk; **58.4** Alamy stock photo (Marmaduke St. John), Abingdon, Oxon; **59.1** Stuttgarter Zeitung, Stuttgart; **60.1** Thinkstock (Salah Malkawi), München; **60.2** shutterstock (Bikeworldtravel), New York, NY; **60.3** Klett-Archiv (Thomas Weccard), Stuttgart; **60.4** shutterstock (Eoghan McNally), New York, NY; **61.1** Picture-Alliance (Uli Gasper), Frankfurt; **63.1** Hath, Jessica Alice, Freiburg; **64.1+2** February Films (Andrew Kemp), London; **65.1** Fotolia.com (contrastwerkstatt), New York; **66.1** shutterstock (Glayan),

New York, NY; **67.1** 123rf (sportgraphic), Nidderau; **68.1** February Films, London; **69.1** shutterstock (Georgi Fadejev), New York, NY; **74.1** shutterstock (Michaelpuche), New York, NY; **75.1** dreamstime.com (Mary Katherine Wynn), Brentwood, TN; **76.1** Alamy stock photo, Abingdon, Oxon; **76.2** shutterstock (Jovanovic Dejan), New York, NY; **76.3** shutterstock (Jovanovic Dejan), New York, NY; **79.1** Alamy stock photo (David Robertson), Abingdon, Oxon; **80.1** iStockphoto (iPandastudio), Calgary, Alberta; **81.1** iStockphoto (Salima Senyavskaya), Calgary, Alberta; **81.2** shutterstock (Riekus), New York, NY; **82.1** February Films (Andrew Kemp), London; **83.1** Fotolia.com (vlsoook), New York; **83.2** Getty Images (Photodisc), München; **83.3** Thinkstock (Purestock), München; **83.4** February Films (Andrew Kemp), London; **84.1** iStockphoto (RF/Matt Ramos), Calgary, Alberta; **85.1** shutterstock (Andrey Popov), New York, NY; **85.2** shutterstock (VGstockstudio), New York, NY; **85.3** shutterstock (fizkes), New York, NY; **86.1** 123rf (Alexander Zhiltsov), Nidderau; **86.2** Hesselbarth, Susann (Hasselbarth), Leipzig; **90.1–3** February Films, London; **94.1** www.CartoonStock.com (Cook, Gary), Bath; **95.1** Thinkstock (Elena Elisseeva), München; **97.1** Ullstein Bild GmbH (Archiv Gerstenberg), Berlin; **97.2** shutterstock (PHB.cz (Richard Semik)), New York, NY; **97.3** Dekelver, Christian Illustration, Weinstadt; **98.1** Alamy stock photo (Melissa Gaskell), Abingdon, Oxon; **98.2** Alamy stock photo (Jeff Morgan 06), Abingdon, Oxon; **99.1** Alamy stock photo (Peter Horree), Abingdon, Oxon; **99.2** Thinkstock (versevend), München; **100.1** February Films (Andrew Kemp), London; **103.1** Klett-Archiv (Weccard), Stuttgart; **104.1** iStockphoto (MattStansfield), Calgary, Alberta; **106.1** shutterstock (antb), New York, NY; **107.1** February Films, London; **108.1** iStockphoto (Deejpilot), Calgary, Alberta; **110.1** shutterstock (Helen Hotson), New York, NY; **112.1** Fotolia.com (acceleratorhams), New York; **112.2** Getty Images (Photolibrary), München; **113.1** shutterstock (Atlaspix), New York, NY; **114.1–3** February Films, London; **116.1** shutterstock (Kachalkina Veronika), New York, NY; **117.1** dreamstime.com (Godfer), Brentwood, TN; **117.2** shutterstock (iurii), New York, NY; **117.3** Getty Images, München; **120.1** dreamstime.com (Oleg Shipov), Brentwood, TN; **120.2** February Films (Andrew Kemp), London; **120.3** shutterstock (Happy Stock Photo), New York, NY; **120.4** shutterstock (Zivica Kerkez), New York, NY; **120.5** shutterstock (Air Images), New York, NY; **121.1** Thinkstock (Lynn Bystrom), München; **121.2** shutterstock (YaromirM), New York, NY; **121.3** Interfoto (Danita Delimont/Joe Restuccia III), München; **121.4** Picture-Alliance (newscom/Andre Jenny), Frankfurt; **121.5** Thinkstock (kenowolfpack), München; **122.1** shutterstock (Amy Nichole Harris), New York, NY; **122.2** Thinkstock (MariuszBlach), München; **125.1** Fotolia.com (pdesign), New York; **126.1** shutterstock (pisaphotography), New York, NY; **127.1** iStockphoto (SeanPavonePhoto), Calgary, Alberta; **127.2** Mauritius Images (Mikael Utterström/Alamy), Mittenwald; **129.1** Getty Images (Sonya Hurtado), München; **129.2** Getty Images (Digital Vision), München; **130.1** Thinkstock (SerrNovik), München; **131.1** Thinkstock (Jupiterimages), München; **132.1** Getty Images (Vetta), München; **133.1** Thinkstock (AlbertoChagas), München; **134.1+2** February Films (Andrew Kemp), London; **137.1** Getty Images (E+), München; **137.2** 123rf (Jennifer Barrow), Nidderau; **138.1** iStockphoto (Wavebreakmedia), Calgary, Alberta; **138.2** Rau (vormals Wesner), Katja, Berglen; **140.1** shutterstock (Jovanovic Dejan), New York, NY; **140.2** shutterstock (Jovanovic Dejan), New York, NY; **141.1** Fotolia.com (Kristina Afanasyeva), New York; **141.2** shutterstock (yexelA), New York, NY; **141.3–7** Fotolia.com (Kristina Afanasyeva), New York; **141.8+9** shutterstock (yexelA), New York, NY; **142.1** shutterstock (M R), New York, NY; **148.1** Thinkstock (moodboard), München; **148.2** shutterstock (LilKar), New York, NY; **148.3** shutterstock (kazoka), New York, NY; **149.1** Fotolia.com (chrisbl), New York; **149.2** MEV Verlag GmbH, Augsburg; **149.3** Avenue Images GmbH (Plainpicture RF), Hamburg; **149.4** shutterstock (Vudhikrai), New York, NY; **149.5** Thinkstock (Elena Bessonova), München; **149.6** iStockphoto (Henrik5000), Calgary, Alberta; **156.1+2** PONS GmbH, Stuttgart; **160.1** shutterstock (Ferencz Teglas), New York, NY; **166.1+2** February Films, London; **170.1** Photothek.net Gbr RF (Thomas Köhler), Berlin; **171.1** shutterstock (IVY PHOTOS), New York, NY; **171.2** iStockphoto (Nyul), Calgary, Alberta; **171.3** 123rf (Tracy Fox), Nidderau; **171.4+7** Photothek.net Gbr RF (Thomas Köhler), Berlin; **171.5** 123rf (Varina And Jay Patel), Nidderau; **171.6** Fotolia.com (Markus Mainka), New York; **172.1** Photothek.net Gbr RF (Thomas Köhler), Berlin; **173.1** Photothek.net Gbr RF (Thomas Köhler), Berlin; **176.1** Photothek.net Gbr RF (Thomas Köhler), Berlin; **177.1+3** Photothek.net Gbr RF (Thomas Köhler), Berlin; **177.2+4** Fotolia.com (cjansuebsri), New York; **179.1** Photothek.net Gbr RF (Thomas Köhler), Berlin; **180.1+2** February Films (Elke Bock), London; **180.3** February Films (Andrew Kemp), London; **180.4** February Films (Elke Bock), London; **180.5** Photothek.net Gbr RF (Thomas Köhler), Berlin; **183.1** Photothek.net Gbr RF (Thomas Köhler), Berlin; **184.1** February Films (Andrew Kemp), London; **185.1** Photothek.net Gbr RF (Thomas Köhler), Berlin; **187.1** February Films (Andrew Kemp), London; **190.1** February Films (Andrew Kemp), London; **191.1** Thinkstock (BananaStock), München; **192.1** February Films (Andrew Kemp), London; **196.1** Thinkstock (Hemera), München; **196.2+3** Dream Maker Software (RF), Colorado; **201.1** shutterstock (CREATISTA), New York, NY; **202.1** Klett-Archiv (Christian Günther, Leipzig), Stuttgart; **202.2+3** Dream Maker Software (RF), Colorado; **202.4** Thinkstock (Hemera), München; **203.1** Fotolia.com (micromonkey), New York; **215.1** iStockphoto (craftvision), Calgary, Alberta; **216.1** Wikimedia Deutschland (Eugenia & Julian), Berlin; **223.1** Fotolia.com (forcdan), New York; **238.1** Fotolia.com (Jaroslaw Grudzinski), New York; **286.1** February Films (Elke Bock), London

Sollte es in einem Einzelfall nicht gelungen sein, den korrekten Rechteinhaber ausfindig zu machen, so werden berechtigte Ansprüche selbstverständlich im Rahmen der üblichen Regelungen abgegolten.

Irregular verbs

infinitive	simple past	past participle	German
be [bi:]	was [wɒz]/were [wɜ:]	been [bi:n]	sein
become [bɪˈkʌm]	became [bɪˈkeɪm]	become [bɪˈkʌm]	werden
begin [bɪˈgɪn]	began [bɪˈgæn]	begun [bɪˈgʌn]	beginnen, anfangen
bet [bet]	bet [bet]/betted [ˈbetɪd]	bet [bet]/betted [ˈbetɪd]	wetten
bite [baɪt]	bit [hɪt]	bitten [ˈbɪtn]	beißen
blow [bləʊ]	blew [blu:]	blown [bləʊn]	blasen, pusten
break [breɪk]	broke [brəʊk]	broken [ˈbrəʊkn]	(zer-)brechen, kaputt machen
bring [brɪŋ]	brought [brɔ:t]	brought [brɔ:t]	(mit-)bringen
build [bɪld]	built [bɪlt]	built [bɪlt]	bauen
burn [bɜ:n]	burnt [bɜ:nt]/burned [bɜ:nd]	burnt [bɜ:nt]/burned [bɜ:nd]	brennen
buy [baɪ]	bought [bɔ:t]	bought [bɔ:t]	kaufen
catch [kætʃ]	caught [kɔ:t]	caught [kɔ:t]	fangen
choose [tʃu:z]	chose [tʃəʊz]	chosen [ˈtʃəʊzn]	(aus-)wählen
come [kʌm]	came [keɪm]	come [kʌm]	kommen
cost [kɒst]	cost [kɒst]	cost [kɒst]	kosten
cut [kʌt]	cut [kʌt]	cut [kʌt]	schneiden
dig [dɪg]	dug [dʌg]	dug [dʌg]	graben
do [du:]	did [dɪd]	done [dʌn]	machen, tun
draw [drɔ:]	drew [dru:]	drawn [drɔ:n]	zeichnen, ziehen
drink [drɪŋk]	drank [dræŋk]	drunk [drʌŋk]	trinken
eat [i:t]	ate [et/eɪt]	eaten [ˈi:tn]	essen
fall [fɔ:l]	fell [fel]	fallen [ˈfɔ:lən]	fallen
feed [fi:d]	fed [fed]	fed [fed]	füttern, ernähren
feel [fi:l]	felt [felt]	felt [felt]	fühlen
fight [faɪt]	fought [fɔ:t]	fought [fɔ:t]	kämpfen, (sich) streiten
find [faɪnd]	found [faʊnd]	found [faʊnd]	finden
fit [fɪt]	fit [fɪt]/fitted [ˈfɪtɪd]	fit [fɪt]/fitted [ˈfɪtɪd]	passen
fly [flaɪ]	flew [flu:]	flown [fləʊn]	fliegen
forget [fəˈget]	forgot [fəˈgɒt]	forgotten [fəˈgɒtn]	vergessen
forgive [fəˈgɪv]	forgave [fəˈgeɪv]	forgiven [fəˈgɪvn]	vergeben, verzeihen
freeze [fri:z]	froze [frəʊz]	frozen [ˈfrəʊzn]	gefrieren, erstarren
get [get]	got [gɒt]	got [gɒt]/AE: gotten [ˈgɒtn]	bekommen, erhalten
give [gɪv]	gave [geɪv]	given [ˈgɪvn]	geben
go [gəʊ]	went [went]	gone [gɒn]	gehen, fahren
grow [grəʊ]	grew [gru:]	grown [grəʊn]	wachsen, anbauen, züchten
hang [hæŋ]	hung [hʌŋ]	hung [hʌŋ]	hängen
have [hæv]	had [hæd]	had [hæd]	haben
hear [hɪə]	heard [hɜ:d]	heard [hɜ:d]	hören
hide [haɪd]	hid [hɪd]	hidden [ˈhɪdn]	(sich) verstecken
hit [hɪt]	hit [hɪt]	hit [hɪt]	schlagen, treffen
hold [həʊld]	held [held]	held [held]	halten
hurt [hɜ:t]	hurt [hɜ:t]	hurt [hɜ:t]	verletzen, sich weh tun
keep [ki:p]	kept [kept]	kept [kept]	(auf-)bewahren, behalten

infinitive	simple past	past participle	German
know [nəʊ]	knew [nju:]	known [nəʊn]	kennen, wissen
learn [lɜ:n]	learnt [lɜ:nt]/learned [lɜ:nd]	learnt [lɜ:nt]/learned [lɜ:nd]	lernen
leave [li:v]	left [left]	left [left]	(ver-)lassen
let [let]	let [let]	let [let]	lassen
lie [laɪ]	lay [leɪ]	lain [leɪn]	liegen
lose [lu:z]	lost [lɒst]	lost [lɒst]	verlieren
make [meɪk]	made [meɪd]	made [meɪd]	machen, tun
mean [mi:n]	meant [ment]	meant [ment]	bedeuten, meinen
meet [mi:t]	met [met]	met [met]	treffen
pay [peɪ]	paid [peɪd]	paid [peɪd]	(be-)zahlen
put [pʊt]	put [pʊt]	put [pʊt]	legen, setzen, stellen
read [ri:d]	read [red]	read [red]	lesen
ride [raɪd]	rode [rəʊd]	ridden ['rɪdn]	fahren, reiten
ring [rɪŋ]	rang [ræŋ]	rung [rʌŋ]	klingeln, läuten
run [rʌn]	ran [ræn]	run [rʌn]	laufen, rennen
say [seɪ]	said [sed]	said [sed]	sagen
see [si:]	saw [sɔ:]	seen [si:n]	sehen
sell [sel]	sold [səʊld]	sold [səʊld]	verkaufen
send [send]	sent [sent]	sent [sent]	senden, verschicken
set [set]	set [set]	set [set]	setzen, einrichten
sew [səʊ]	sewed [səʊd]	sewn [səʊn]/sewed [səʊd]	nähen
shine [ʃaɪn]	shone [ʃɒn]	shone [ʃɒn]	scheinen
show [ʃəʊ]	showed [ʃəʊd]	shown [ʃəʊn]	zeigen
sing [sɪŋ]	sang [sæŋ]	sung [sʌŋ]	singen
sit [sɪt]	sat [sæt]	sat [sæt]	sitzen
sleep [sli:p]	slept [slept]	slept [slept]	schlafen
smell [smel]	smelt [smelt]/smelled [smeld]	smelt [smelt]/smelled [smeld]	riechen, duften
speak [spi:k]	spoke [spəʊk]	spoken ['spəʊkn]	sprechen
spell [spel]	spelt [spelt]/spelled [speld]	spelt [spelt]/spelled [speld]	buchstabieren
spend [spend]	spent [spent]	spent [spent]	ausgeben, verbringen
stand [stænd]	stood [stʊd]	stood [stʊd]	stehen
steal [sti:l]	stole [stəʊl]	stolen ['stəʊlən]	stehlen
swim [swɪm]	swam [swæm]	swum [swʌm]	schwimmen
take [teɪk]	took [tʊk]	taken ['teɪkn]	nehmen
teach [ti:tʃ]	taught [tɔ:t]	taught [tɔ:t]	unterrichten, lehren, beibringen
tell [tel]	told [təʊld]	told [təʊld]	erzählen
think [θɪŋk]	thought [θɔ:t]	thought [θɔ:t]	(nach)denken, glauben
throw [θrəʊ]	threw [θru:]	thrown [θrəʊn]	werfen
understand [ˌʌndə'stænd]	understood [ˌʌndə'stʊd]	understood [ˌʌndə'stʊd]	verstehen
wake [weɪk]	woke [wəʊk]	woken ['wəʊkn]	wecken, aufwachen
wear [weə]	wore [wɔ:]	worn [wɔ:n]	anhaben, tragen
win [wɪn]	won [wʌn]	won [wʌn]	gewinnen, siegen
write [raɪt]	wrote [rəʊt]	written ['rɪtn]	schreiben

THE UNITED STATES OF AMERICA

CANADA

WEST
ALASKA
Denali
CANADA

Seattle
WASHINGTON
OREGON
IDAHO
WEST
NEVADA
Salt Lake City
UTAH
CALIFORNIA
San Francisco
HOLLYWOOD
Los Angeles
San Diego

Pacific Ocean

WEST
HAWAII

MONTANA
WYOMING
Rocky Mountain National Park
Denver
COLORADO
Rocky Mountains

NORTH DAKOTA
SOUTH DAKOTA
NEBRASKA
MINNESOTA
IOWA
Minneapolis

MIDWEST

Decorah
Milwaukee
WISCONSIN
Chicago
ILLINOIS
MICHIGAN
Detroit

Great Lakes

KANSAS
OKLAHOMA
NEW MEXICO
El Paso
ARIZONA
SOUTHWEST

TEXAS
Dallas
Houston

MISSOURI
ARKANSAS
Mississippi
LOUISIANA
New Orleans
MISSISSIPPI
ALABAMA

MEXICO

Gulf of Mexico

INDIANA
OHIO
KENTUCKY
TENNESSEE
SOUTH
GEORGIA
Atlanta
St. Augustine
FLORIDA
Tallahassee
Orlando
Miami
Everglades

WEST VIRGINIA
VIRGINIA
NORTH CAROLINA
SOUTH CAROLINA

PENNSYLVANIA
Philadelphia
Washington, D.C.

MAINE
NORTH-EAST
Boston
NEW YORK
New York City

1 VERMONT
2 NEW HAMPSHIRE
3 MASSACHUSETTS
4 CONNECTICUT
5 RHODE ISLAND
6 NEW JERSEY
7 MARYLAND
8 DELAWARE

Atlantic Ocean

CUBA
BAHAMAS
FLORIDA
DOMINICAN REPUBLIC
JAMAICA

1000 km
500 miles
500
0
0

THE BRITISH ISLES

NORTH
WEST — EAST
SOUTH

ORKNEY
ISLANDS

OUTER
HEBRIDES

Inverness

Loch Ness

Aberdeen

▲ Ben Nevis

SCOTLAND

Atlantic Ocean

Glasgow   Edinburgh

North Sea

Giant's
Causeway

Hadrian's Wall   Newcastle
Vindolanda   Tyne

NORTHERN
IRELAND

Belfast

Lake
District

ISLE
OF
MAN

UNITED KINGDOM OF
GREAT BRITAIN AND
NORTHERN IRELAND

York

Hull
Humber

Galway

Irish Sea

Liverpool   Manchester

REPUBLIC
OF IRELAND

Dublin

Chester

Nottingham

Trent

ENGLAND

▲ Snowdon

Birmingham

Cambridge

Cork

WALES

Severn

Big
Ben

Oxford

London

Margate

Cardiff   Bath

Stonehenge

Thames

Dover

Brighton

Devon   Exeter

ISLE OF
WIGHT

Cornwall

Plymouth

English Channel

ISLES
OF SCILLY

0   100   200   300 km

0   100   200 miles